Globalization and Inequalities

Globalization and Inequalities

Complexity and Contested Modernities

Sylvia Walby

SAGE

Los Angeles | London | New Delhi
Singapore | Washington DC

Contents

Acknowledgements	viii
List of Tables and Figures	ix

1 Introduction: progress and modernities — 1

Introduction	1
What is Progress?	3
Multiple Complex Inequalities	18
Modernity? Postmodernity? Not yet Modern? Varieties of Modernity?	24
Globalization	35
Complexity Theory	47
Contents	56

2 Theorizing multiple social systems — 58

Introduction	58
Multiple Inequalities and Intersectionality	60
Regimes and Domains	64
System and its Environment: Over-Lapping, Non-Saturating, Non-Nested Systems	67
Societalization not Societies	69
Emergence and Projects	71
Bodies, Technologies and the Social	75
Path Dependency	79
Coevolution of Complex Adaptive Systems in Changing Fitness Landscapes	90
Waves	95
Conclusions	99

3 Economies — 101

Introduction	101
Redefining the Economy	102

From Premodern to Modern: The Second Great Transformation	109
Global Processes and Economic Inequalities	115
Varieties of Political Economy	132
Conclusions	152

4 Polities — 156

Introduction	156
Reconceptualizing Types of Polities	157
Polities Overlap and do not Politically Saturate a Territory	171
Democracy	178
Conclusions	189

5 Violence — 191

Introduction	191
Developing the Ontology of Violence	193
Modernity and Violence	199
Path Dependency in Trajectories of Violence	208
Global	212
Conclusions	216

6 Civil societies — 218

Introduction	218
Theorizing Civil Society	218
Modernity and Civil Society	221
Civil Society Projects	228
Global Civil Societies and Waves	233
Conclusions	247

7 Regimes of complex inequality — 250

Introduction	250
Beyond Class Regimes	251
Gender Regimes	254
Ethnic Regimes	264
Further Regimes of Complex Inequalities	270
Intersecting Regimes of Complex Inequality	272
Conclusions	275

8 Varieties of modernity — 277

Introduction	277
Neoliberal and Social Democratic Varieties of Modernity	278
Path Dependency at the Economy/Polity Nexus	280
Path Dependency at the Violence Nexus	296
Gender Regime	301
Democracy and Inequality	308

Conclusions	309
Appendix: Data Sources	312

9 Measuring progress — 314

Introduction	314
Economic Development	315
Equality	319
Human Rights	344
Human Development, Well-Being and Capabilities	346
Key Indicator Sets: What Indicators? What Underlying Concepts of Progress?	352
Extending the Frameworks and Indicators of Progress: Where do Environmental Sustainability and Violence Fit?	354
The Achievement of Visions of Progress: Comparing Neoliberalism and Social Democracy	359
Conclusions	365

10 Comparative paths through modernity: neoliberalism and social democracy — 367

Introduction	367
Political Economy	369
Violence	396
Gender Transformations: The Emergence of Employed Women as the New Champions of Social Democracy	409
Dampeners and Catalysts of Economic Growth: War and Gender Regime Transformations	415
Conclusions	417

11 Contested futures — 425

Introduction	425
Financial and Economic Crisis 2007–2009	425
Contesting Hegemons and the Future of the World	433

12 Conclusions — 443

Introduction	443
The Challenge of Complex Inequalities and Globalization to Social Theory	444
Bibliography	456
Index	498

Acknowledgements

I have been helped by many people in the process of writing this book and I have also been engaged, inspired, debated, intrigued, and questioned. This has involved individuals, groups and networks, in the contexts of colleagues, research projects, research students, visits, seminars, and conferences. It could not have been produced outside of an inspirational challenging supportive intellectual environment, in the UK, Ireland, Sweden, the USA, the EU, and beyond. People have introduced me to their networks and shared them with me; as well as looking after me, engaging, and disagreeing. Many have commented on sections of the book, even if they did not know that this was to be the final location of their opinion, and some have read it all. This myriad of intellectual, competing, and cooperative networks and epistemic communities has been the essential environment for producing this book. I have no funders to thank here.

I would, however, like to thank a great many individuals: Joan Acker, Jo Armstrong, Paul Bagguley, Ulla Björnberg, Lisa Brush, Chris Chase-Dunn, Erika Cudworth, Eileen Drew, Susan Durbin, Ruth Emerek, Myra Marx Ferree, Heidi Gottfried, Karin Gottschall, June Greenwell, Elena Haavio-Manila, Gun Hedlund, Bob Jessop, Anna Jónasdóttir, Danielle Juteau, Liz Kelly, Judith Lorber, Joni Lovenduski, Val Moghadam, Makiko Nishikawa, Pat O'Connor, Mari Osawa, Sue Penna, Diane Perrons, Karen Phillips, Andrew Sayer, Karen Shire, Clare Short, Judith Squires, Sofia Strid, Jenny Tomlinson, John Urry, Janet Veitch, Mieke Verloo, and Linda Woodhead.

I would also like to thank my various networks: Lancaster University Sociology Department, Lancaster Complexity Network, GLOW (Gender, Globalisation and Work Transformation Network), QUING (comparing gender equality in the EU), the European Sociological Association, and the International Sociological Association Research Committee on Economy and Society.

Of course I take sole responsibility for the book's contents and any flaws.

List of Tables and Figures

Table 8.1	Political economy indicators	282
Table 8.2	Social expenditure, public expenditure on childcare, childcare use, and strictness of employment protection, OECD	284
Table 8.3	Public social expenditure, income per person, trade unions and women in parliament, OECD	285
Table 8.4	Childcare, public expenditure on childcare, public social expenditure, income per person, and women's presence in employment, parliament, and trade unions, OECD	287
Table 8.5	Strictness of employment protection legislation, trade unions, income per person, public social expenditure, and equality legislation strength, OECD	292
Table 8.6	Equality legislation, trade unions, women in parliament, trade unions, and employment, OECD	293
Table 8.7	Inequality, employment regulation, public social expenditure, childcare public expenditure, OECD	294
Table 8.8	Indicators in the violence nexus	298
Table 8.9	Homicide, gender, and inequality, global	299
Table 8.10	Correlation between aspects of violence, OECD	300
Table 8.11	Indicators of the gender regime	303
Table 8.12	Public and domestic gender regimes, global	304
Table 8.13	Development and public gender regimes, global	305
Table 8.14	Domestic and public gender regimes and inequality, OECD	306
Table 8.15	Varieties of gender regime, OECD	307
Table 8.16	Gendered polity policies and women's political mobilization, OECD	308
Table 8.17	Democracy and polity policies, OECD	309

Table 8.18	Inequality and polity policies, OECD	309
Table 9.1	Income per person in world regions	317
Table 9.2	Economic growth, 1975–2005, world, USA, EU, Ireland, Sweden, the UK	318
Table 9.3	Poverty and inequality, world regions, 1990, 2004	324
Table 9.4	Inequality and poverty in household incomes, OECD: Gini, mid-1980s to 2000; per cent of households with less than 50 per cent and 60 per cent median income	325
Table 9.5	Wealth in world regions, 2000	326
Table 9.6	Wealth shares within countries, 2000	327
Table 9.7	Women as a percentage of employees (non-agricultural wage employment) 1990 and 2005, world regions	332
Table 9.8	Labour force, per cent female, OECD, 1980–2006	333
Table 9.9	Gender wage gap EU, USA, 1996, 2006	334
Table 9.10	Gendered economic inequality: ratio of female to male earned income, 1995, 2005; per cent managers female, OECD, medium developed countries	335
Table 9.11	Gendered economic inequality, USA, EU	336
Table 9.12	Household forms, sexual and reproductive rights, USA, Ireland, Sweden, UK	339
Table 9.13	Depth of Democracy: USA, Ireland, Sweden, UK, EU	343
Table 9.14	Life-expectancy, global regions, USA, EU, Ireland, Sweden, UK	349
Table 9.15	Child and maternal mortality, obesity, world, USA, EU, Ireland, Sweden, UK	350
Table 9.16	Primary education completion rates (%), by sex, 1999, 2005, world, developing, and developed regions	351
Table 9.17	Tertiary education, USA, EU, Ireland, Sweden, UK	351
Table 9.18	Carbon dioxide emissions, world, developing and developed regions	356
Table 9.19	Carbon dioxide emissions, USA, EU, Sweden, UK, Ireland	356
Table 9.20	Violence, USA, EU, Ireland, Sweden, UK, world	359
Table 9.21	Life-expectancy and income over time, world, USA, EU, Ireland, Sweden, UK	363
Table 10.1	Economic inequality: Gini coefficients, mid-1980s to c.2000: USA, Sweden, UK, Ireland	371
Table 10.2	Public social expenditure as per cent of GDP, 1990, 2003: USA, EU, Sweden, UK, Ireland	371

Table 10.3	Comparative trade union density 1970–2003, USA, EU, Sweden, UK, Ireland	371
Table 10.4	Trade union membership patterns, 2004, USA, Sweden, UK, Ireland	371
Table 10.5	Violence: USA, EU, Sweden, UK, Ireland	397
Table 10.6	Female share of employment, trade union membership, and parliamentary seats, 1960–2005	410
Table 10.7	Economic growth, 1840–2005: USA, UK, Sweden, Ireland	417
Table 11.1	Economic recession 2008–2009: USA, EU, Eurozone, Sweden, UK, Ireland	429

Figures

Figure 8.1	Public social expenditure as percentage of GDP, OECD	285
Figure 9.1	GDP per capita around the world, 2008	317
Figure 9.2	Economic income inequality measured by the Gini coefficient around the world	323
Figure 9.3	Increase in democracy and decline of autocracy, 1946–2006	342

1 Introduction: Progress And Modernities

Introduction

The future is contested. What are the implications of the different social models that might come into being? What is progress? Is it being richer, living longer, reduced inequality, or more human rights? What is modernity? Is modernity over, or is the project of modernity not yet completed? Social theory is challenged to take account of complex inequalities beyond class: how can they be included so that they are central, not marginal? Globalization challenges the notion of separate societies: how do global processes change social relations? What difference does the inclusion of complex inequalities and global processes make to the analysis and to social theory? What difference does the inclusion of complex inequalities make to our view as to what constitutes progress? The aim of this book is not only to produce better accounts of social change in a global era, but also to rethink core concepts and theories. A key aid here is the development of complexity theory.

'Progress' is an essentially contested project. There are vigorous disputes over what the proper goals of global policy should be, over the priorities for action by governments and international bodies. The meaning of 'progress' is far from obvious, ranging from economic development to human well-being, equality and human rights. Protagonists vigorously disagree about which is more important, with implications for the goals of global as well as national public policy. How are such contestations conducted? Are they so rooted in values that are so deeply held that to debate is a challenge to fundamental aspects of people and cultures, or are they amenable to rational scientific debate over priorities? In practice, even deeply held values are challenged by appeals to internal inconsistency and empirical evidence about their effects when implemented. This book aims to clarify the alternative framings of the notion of progress and to identify their implications. Does the evidence support or contradict deeply held convictions as to the best way forward? Which project emerges best, when subjected to social scientific Scrutiny?

Modernity has been a key concept in classic Sociology, used to address large-scale social transformation. The transition to modernity preoccupied many of the major social theorists, from Marx and Weber to Durkheim and Simmel. But is modernity still the best way to understand contemporary social relations? Or are we now living in a postmodern era? Challenges to the concept of modernity are aimed at its apparent assumption that there was a single unilinear process of development, and that it was good for everyone. Such a notion is clearly untenable, in view of the horrors of the descent into war and 'ethnic cleansing', the diversity of paths of development, and the uneven position of different social groups in the same country. Are we not yet modern, rather than postmodern, or are there multiple varieties of modernity?

Globalization is a challenge to social theory. It demands a re-thinking of the notion that there are societies constituted as separate bounded entities. It raises questions about the taken-for-granted equation of society and nation-state. Is globalization merely Westernization or Americanization, or does it hybridize all cultures, creating new commonalities? Is it eroding differences between cultures producing convergence? Globalization requires the analysis of new types of global processes, and the re-framing of many ostensibly local or national projects within a global landscape.

Social theory is challenged to address the multiplicity of social inequalities, not only that of class. The significance of diverse inequalities for social life is recognized, but building this insight into the core of social theory rather than remaining in specialist sub-fields has proved more difficult. Traditional social theory addressed class inequality, but had difficulty when trying simultaneously to address gender, ethnicity, age, religion, nation, sexual orientation, and disability, and even greater difficulty in addressing their mutual constitution at points of intersection. Further, these social relations are more complex than class in that they involve not only inequality but also difference, thereby problematizing notions of a single standard against which to judge inequality. The challenge then is to include intersecting complex inequalities within the core of social theory.

In order to insert globalization and complex inequalities into the heart of social theory it is necessary to develop new concepts and to rethink how theories are put together. There is a need both to capture the distinctions, differentiations and nuances of complex inequalities that have been part of what has been driving the postmodern turn, and to simultaneously keep the global horizon in sight. There is also a need to retain the conception of inter-linkages so as to be able to analyse the global level, while not falling into the mistaken simplicities of over-generalization across cultures. Developments in complexity theory offer a new vocabulary on which social theory can usefully draw in developing concepts to meet these new analytic challenges. These offer the opportunity to build a more complex theoretical framework that enables the theorization of both large-scale connections and of sudden ruptures and non-linear processes. Complexity theory enables the re-thinking of the concept of social system to address, without reductionism, multiple systems of social relations.

This chapter addresses first, the contested issue of what progress might be; second, the challenge of theorizing multiple complex inequalities simultaneously; third, the conceptualization of plural forms of modernity; fourth, the challenge of theorizing global processes; and fifth, the usefulness of complexity theory in addressing these challenges in social theory.

What is Progress?

More money or a longer life?

Is it better to have more money or to live longer? People in the United States of America have more money but die sooner than those in the European Union. Americans have over 40 per cent more income than these Europeans, but live on average for two years less (World Bank 2006c).

Is increasing income a measure of progress? Or is living longer a better indicator? There are different ways of thinking about progress, so how should they be evaluated?

What kind of social arrangements produce progress, however it is defined? Is it the greater freedom of the market in the USA as compared with greater state regulation in Europe? Is it the greater inequality in the USA as compared with Europe? Or the more violent nature of the USA than Europe?

The two divergent goals of money and longevity are associated with two quite different conceptions of progress. The first takes the economic, especially money, as an effective summary indicator of progress and of what is good and desirable; it is often used by national and international bodies of financial governance. The second is focused on the outcome for human well-being, of our capacities and capabilities, of which longevity is an indicator. Further, framings of progress include 'equality' and 'human rights'. Indeed many social and political projects have their own distinctive accounts of what constitutes the best social arrangements to produce the 'good life'.

Different social systems have different levels of success in converting economic resources into human well-being. The EU social system is more effective in this than the USA. It is the differences in social systems that are crucial to understanding the implications for individuals. The EU and US social systems link economic resources to human well-being in different ways as a result of differences in how their social systems have developed.

Different cultures prioritize different values. What is meant by progress and what are the preferred goals of public policy? Can there be a single notion of progress in the context of varying values? What kinds of social arrangements achieve progress?

Progress as a contested project

There is no simple answer to the question of what is progress. Rather, it is an essentially contested concept. Indeed, so contested that some will give up all hope that it is a useful project to engage with.

There are three main approaches to the concept and project of progress. First, that modernity is progress. For classical sociologists, analysing the transformation of society that is associated with industrialization and urbanism, modernity was progress, but a development that many saw as double-edged, with a down side as well (as discussed in the next section). A second response is to deny the usefulness of the concept and project of progress: it is too simple, falsely universalistic, and ethnocentric. Rather than a universal 'one size fits all', there are a potentially infinite number of particular ways of thinking about what constitutes the 'good life' and how to get there that are rooted in different cultures. A third position sees progress as a contested project: there are alternative conceptions, but not an infinite number; it exists as a notion that is highly contested; it is argued over in politics and policy, philosophy and theory, data, and analysis.

Within this third approach four key alternative goals of progress can be identified – economic development, equality, human rights, and human well-being – though there are others, including a respect for traditional or fundamental practices. The first is that human welfare is best advanced by economic growth and high levels of economic development. The second prioritizes equality. The third is human rights. The fourth has a focus on human well-being, which is more than just a high standard of living but includes education, health, and longevity.

These goals of progress are embedded in projects that are rooted in civil society. Sometimes these projects will become the foundation of governmental programmes. Finally, they may become embedded in practices in social formations. Today, two major competing projects claim in quite different ways to take forward some of these goals: neoliberalism and social democracy. They claim in varying ways to produce economic development, aspects of equality, human rights, and human well-being.

Economic development

The first framing of progress focuses on economic development and economic growth. Economic development is expected to increase the average income of a person and thereby their standard of living. While this approach appears to treat economic development as an end in itself, it usually rests on the implicit assumption that economic development is a means to the delivery of an improved standard of living and a further additional assumption that this is a popular policy goal. The higher the rate of economic growth, the faster will the standard of living increase. Improved economic performance is assumed to mean a more effective utilization of resources to deliver goods and services. The approach claims to be neutral as to the way in which this income is spent by people and regards this neutrality as positive. Economic growth and development is defended as the best approach to progress, on the basis that this constitutes an indication of the average standard of living of people in a country and that this is what people want because governments are repeatedly democratically elected on a mandate that prioritizes economic growth.

This approach to progress is embodied in many national finance ministries and in some parts of the global institutions of financial governance, such as the International Monetary Fund. It underpins the 'Washington consensus' on economic policy (Stiglitz 2002).

Within social science there is much debate as to the type of social arrangements that best deliver economic growth. A major focus of the discussion has been as to whether countries with the markets that are most 'free', or where markets are carefully regulated and subordinated to other social institutions, actually deliver on this. In particular, this involves analysing the contrasting nature and implications of different types of production, welfare, and regulatory regimes (Barro 1998; Hall and Soskice 2001; Kenworthy 2004). However, there are several challenges to this conceptualization of progress. These include whether untrammelled competition has social costs that need to be set against the benefits of rapid economic growth, and whether it leads to happiness (Oswald 1997; Layard 2005). Is human well-being, equality, or human rights more important?

Equality

An alternative approach to progress is viewed through the lens of justice. This approach prioritizes justice, equality, and human rights rather than material improvements in living conditions and welfare. Various traditions articulate this issue in slightly different ways, including: justice (Sandel 1998; Rawls 1999); equality (Phillips 1995; Holli 1997); rights (Paine 1984; Kymlicka 1991, 1995); human rights (Peters and Wolper 1995; Woodiwiss 1998); citizenship (Marshall 1950); equal opportunities and equity (Acker 1989; Shaw and Perrons 1995); freedom and capabilities (Sen 1999; Nussbaum 2000); democracy, political rights and civil liberties (Gastil 1982); and recognition (Taylor et al. 1994; Honneth 1996; Fraser 1997). While there are many approaches to the notion of progress that have a justice framing, it is possible to group many of them into two categories – equality and rights.

The framing of progress as equality is a key part of the socialist and social democratic tradition (Bobbio 1997). This is a more collective and less individualist framing of justice than the others, according less priority to the individual and more to groups and collectivities. There are variations within this frame including: whether equality is conceptualized as an opportunity or an outcome; which domains and practices are included; whether it is limited to 'excessive' inequality; and how difference is addressed.

Equality may be understood either as an outcome or as an opportunity. Equality of outcomes is the stronger programme; equality of opportunities addresses processes and procedures which may possibly, but not necessarily, lead to greater equality in outcomes. For example, the attempt to increase equality of opportunity by equal treatment laws may reduce discrimination but may also be insufficient to produce an equality of outcome in the absence of structural change (Hoskyns 1996). This equality of outcome usually requires the transformation of both social systems and legal processes.

The principle of equality is often selectively applied. This equality may be regarded as a legitimate outcome in matters of longevity, where class and ethnic differences are often considered unjust. It is more commonly discussed in the economic domain (for example, in the debates over narrowing the gender and ethnic pay gaps) than in civil society where diversity is more often preferred. Further, there are some issues for which equality is considered marginal rather than important (Phillips 1999). Some forms of inequality are regarded as illegitimate because they are 'excessive'. For example, social exclusion and poverty may be regarded as unjust because they are extreme or 'excessive', but not inequality in all its forms; social exclusion is a weaker understanding of inequality (Lister 1998).

Inequalities are often complexly entwined with differences. There is a question as to whether equality requires sameness and the use of a single standard, or equal recognition and the valuation of different contributions, or a larger and more profound transformation (Fraser 1997; Rees 1998). The equal valuation of different contributions is a step away from traditional interpretations of equality that involve a single universal standard. The notion of cosmopolitanism requires mutual respect for different ways of life rather than the adoption of a single universal standard as to what is best (Held 2004; Beck 2006).

Equality is potentially the most radical of the framings of progress. In practice, its application as a principle is often hedged with caveats and limited to specific processes, domains, and practices.

Human rights

In the rights-based approach to justice, every individual is regarded as having inviolable rights, the realization of which constitutes a just society. Each person has an equal entitlement to a specific set of rights. The tradition is predominantly individualist, with the valuation of the rights of individuals positioned as more important than the average welfare of the society as a whole. It ranges from a relatively narrow focus on civil liberties, such as freedom of speech, and political rights, such as free elections (Gastil 1982), to a wider concept of citizenship, which involves socio-economic as well as political and civil rights (Marshall 1950). In its privileging of the individual over society, rights can be interpreted as representing a Western, rather than a universal or global, approach to justice, although this is contested (Woodiwiss 1998).

The notion of rights itself has several variants, including human rights and civil rights (Ferree et al. 2002a), though today human rights predominate in political discourse. There are many theoretical and philosophical interpretations of the longstanding rights-based tradition of justice (Banks 1981; Paine 1984; Wollstonecraft 1992 [1790]). According to Rawls (1999), justice is the overarching framework for all conceptions of progress and the first virtue of social institutions. He considers that each individual has an inviolability that overrides everything else, including the average welfare of the rest of society. Rawls's approach to justice involves a rejection of utilitarian theory in which the justice of a larger number of people can outweigh the injustice and disadvantage of a few individuals. His approach requires that every individual receives the basics as an underpinning of justice. In this way Rawls's 'social contract' approach to justice prioritizes an equal minimum level for all over the welfare of a whole society.

In the current wave of globalization, the human rights interpretation of justice is becoming increasingly important. This draws on a longstanding rights tradition (Banks 1981; Paine 1984; Wollstonecraft 1992 [1790]; Berkovitch 1999) as well as on some components of the equality framework (Peters and Wolper 1995; Woodiwiss 1998). The most important current statement on human rights is that issued by the UN after the end of the Second World War, the Universal Declaration of Human Rights (UN 1948). This claim, endorsed by all governments in the world, states that these rights are in principle universal and not particular. However, this early UN statement on human rights has since been reinterpreted, extending and clarifying its content. The implementation of a rights-based (especially a human rights) approach to justice and progress is often made via a juridical framework. It is through the law, courts and lawyers that human rights are made available to individuals and groups of individuals.

Although there is a component of equality within the human rights approach, not least equality in accessing these rights since they are regarded as universal, this is a limited conception of equality. It is a minimalist and threshold conception – a relatively low threshold is set and must be passed. Beyond that, the framework has nothing to say.

However, the framing of human rights as universal and measured against a single standard is contested by notions of group rights, the equal valuation of different contributions, and by cosmopolitanism. Rights are not always and only linked to individuals: they may also be constituted as group rights, or as the right to a way of life, which intrinsically involves a group or community (Kymlicka 1991, 1995). This implicitly recognizes that there are different standards in relation to which rights can be claimed. The example used by Kymlicka is that of the First Nation, or aboriginal Indians, in Canada, and their collective rights to the use of certain tracts of land that differ from those belonging to the rest of Canada's citizens. A parallel issue is articulated in theories of equal rights in relation to gender, where the concern to respect difference leads to such formulations as the equal valuation of different contributions. However, there is a question as to whether such respect implies an acceptance of practices that might be considered harmful to certain minorities. There is a tension between universalism and particularism in the specification of equality and human rights, even though the traditional interpretation of these has tended to imply a single universal standard.

Human development, well-being and capabilities

A further project, variously named human development, well-being or capabilities, challenges a focus solely on economic development and growth, but is equivocal about equality. This approach to progress replaces a focus on income with a broader conception of human development and well-being. The intellectual inspiration underpinning this approach is the work of Amartya Sen (1999), while broader support comes from practitioners in the international development community and more recently from academics. There is an increasing divergence within this approach between an outcome-oriented project rooted in the international development community and a philosophically-oriented project focused on the concept of capabilities which is separated from that of functionings.

When embedded in the United Nations Development Project (1990), this alternative approach to development promoted an approach to human well-being that required more than just income; outcomes of longevity and education were the preferred form of development. This challenge to the narrowness of the goal of economic growth that had been held up by the institutions of global financial governance such as the International Monetary Fund (IMF) and the World Bank was at least partly successful. The adoption of the UN Millennium Development Goals, which offer a synthesis of human and economic development, by the IMF, the World Bank and OECD among others, represents a modest global political success on the part of this challenge to neoliberal conceptions of economic growth.

Capabilities are the 'substantive freedoms' to 'choose a life one has reason to value', while functionings are 'the various things a person may value doing or being', according to Sen (1999: 74–5). The distinction between capabilities and functioning parallels the distinction between opportunities and outcomes. One of the strengths of the capabilities approach (that it is open to democratic attempts to name and prioritize capabilities) is also a weakness. The flexibility and openness to political pressure in the definition of the list of capabilities mean that a wide range of interpretations of capabilities is possible. The focus on capabilities rather than on functionings deliberately opens the door to choice, but thereby makes possible a choice of inequality as a way to obtain a difference. Opportunities, conceptualized as substantive freedoms and capabilities, are hard to operationalize and to measure. Because the door is deliberately opened to choice, it is thereby opened to the possibility that people may choose inequality through their choice of a form of difference that is linked to inequality. Choice is prioritized over equality. By contrast, the UNDP approach to capabilities problematizes choice: 'Real opportunity is about having real choices – the choices that come with a sufficient income, an education, good health and living in a country that is not governed by tyranny' (UNDP 2006). In this way, certain contexts are taken as key to providing capabilities. The focus shifts to outcomes (rather than opportunities) which are easier to measure against a common standard. The interpretation of this school of thought as developed by the UNDP, with its focus on a wide range of outcomes that are relevant to human development and well-being, is the one preferred here.

Competing projects: neoliberalism and social democracy

The different conceptions of progress – high personal income, human well-being, equality, and human rights – do not necessarily contain accounts of the means to reach these goals. Sometimes they are implied, but in many cases the means to reach these ends are contested. Would prioritizing economic growth raise incomes most effectively, even if at the expense of lesser equality or human rights? Would deepening democracy most effectively promote equality and human well-being, but at the expense of more rapid economic growth? Are there trade-offs between the different goals, or not? How are these combined in different projects in the world?

While there are many projects to reach these goals, neoliberalism and social democracy are the most comprehensive in vision and the most relevant today (Giddens 1998; Held 2004; Harvey 2005). While neoliberalism and social democracy presume modernity, and disagree over the form that modernity should take, other projects promote some aspects of premodernity, as is often the case in religious fundamentalisms. Other projects include human rights. Some have partial rather than comprehensive visions, for example feminism, cosmopolitanism (Beck 2006) and environmentalism (Yearley 1996; Cudworth 2003). Some are hybrid projects – for example, the US Bush Presidency, 2001–2009, combined neoliberalism with Christian fundamentalism – while the 'cosmopolitan universalists' combine social democracy with human rights (Held 2004), and the anti-globalization movement combines anti-neoliberal capitalism, environmentalism and feminism. This book focuses on the contrast between the two major projects, neoliberalism and social democracy.

These projects sometimes become embedded in governmental programmes and sometimes in actual social formations. The extent to which these visions are institutionalized and implemented varies significantly. Projects can be primarily located in civil society, or may become embedded in governmental policy programmes or in actually existing social forms, both large and small. A civil society project usually aims to become the dominant state programme in order to shape actual social relations and institutions, although with varying degrees of success.

Neoliberalism elevates the notion of market effectiveness into a guiding principle for action and attempts to reduce the level of state intervention into the economy, prioritizing the individual over collectivism (Brenner and Theodore 2002; England and Ward 2007). As an intellectual project its current forms draw on the work of Hayek (1960) and Friedman (1962), which argued that freeing the market from state controls was the best way to ensure economic growth, which in turn was believed to deliver human well-being, freedom, democracy, and civil liberties. The project grew in strength during the 1980s, but has a much longer heritage; here the term neoliberal is extended back in time. In the 1980s the neoliberal programme was taken forward by the US and UK governments under Reagan and Thatcher and by global financial institutions, becoming known as the 'Washington consensus', and then spread globally as a result of International Monetary Fund (IMF) conditions on loans to poor countries including 'structural adjustment'. The policies included cutting back state welfare expenditure; the reduction in or deregulation of worker protections and benefit payments for those out of employment; the privatization of publicly owned industries, utilities and services; the expansion of the market into previously non-marketized arenas of the global commons such as the genome; and the substitution of the market as an alternative form of governance to democracy in specific areas, for example welfare provision (Brenner and Theodore 2002; Harvey 2003, 2005; England and Ward 2007). In practice, the record of neoliberalism on economic growth is contested (Stiglitz 2002). The drive to increase incentives to work shifts the balance of power, leading to increased inequalities which then compromise human-well-being (Oswald 1997; Wilkinson 2005).

Social democracy aspires to govern societies democratically, avoiding excessive inequality, promoting human as well as economic development, and enabling minorities as well as majorities to enjoy their human rights. Social democratic projects commit to the provision of education, health and care for those in need, in order to deliver human well-being for all, whether employed or not (Esping-Andersen 1990). There is a commitment to developing policies across a wide spectrum in order to deliver social justice and to reduce inequality. It is considered appropriate for the state to intervene in the running of the economy through regulation not only to prevent market failure, but also to engage in redistribution; the state legitimately taxes and spends in order to deliver its policies.

Social democratic projects vary significantly in the extent to which they promote state or collective ownership as mechanisms to govern the economy, whether they adopt Keynesian macro economic management to reduce the severity of recessions or merely aim for stability. There has been both a retreat (Callaghan 2000) and a transformation (Kitschelt 1994) of social democratic projects into new forms as a response to the reduction in the traditional base of electoral support in male manual workers in manufacturing industries (Przeworski and Sprague 1986), dealignment in class voting practices (Crewe et al. 1977), and changing external circumstances such as globalization (Held 1995). There has also been a slow transition of the social democratic project towards the full inclusion of the concerns of gender and other minorities which is ongoing. Some forms of the project now include full employment for women and an end to discrimination against women and minorities, though a full engagement with ethno-national issues of citizenship and migration is far from complete. Neoliberal critics consider that state intervention compromises economic growth and thereby other goals.

This description of the projects of neoliberalism and social democracy has so far been a summary of ideal types and aspirations. The implications of the projects as they enter governmental programmes and become embedded in diverse social formations can be quite different.

While the self-description of neoliberalism focuses on diminishing governmental interventions into the economy in contrast with social democracy, in practice neoliberalism is associated with the greater expansion of state interventions in other domains than social democracy. In particular, neoliberalism is associated with the greater development and deployment of state violence and associated forms of coercion than is social democracy, for example, in the propensity to go to war, the build up of military capacity, and the use of prisons to contain criminality and maintain social order. So while neoliberalism appears to laud a small state, this is only in relation to the economy; in practice neoliberal governments simultaneously develop a large coercive state to maintain the domestic social order and position in the global state system. In comparing neoliberalism and social democracy, it is important not to confine the analysis to the intersection of the polity with the economy, but also to include other domains including violence.

While there is widespread consensus that the USA is a major example of the neoliberal project and Sweden of the social democratic, the boundary between neoliberalism and social democracy is contested, with some arguing that Britain's New Labour government since 1997 constitutes a new form of social democracy (Giddens 1998) and others arguing that the extent of its use of the market principle means that it is effectively neoliberal (Arestis and Sawyer 2005). The debate concerns a number of issues regarding the state's role in securing social justice. These include the shift away from state ownership of industries and services; away from direct provision of public services by the state to being merely guaranteed by the state but delivered by the market; the development of active labour market policies, such as compulsory counselling and targeted training, to achieve full employment; and away from a goal to reduce inequality to that of reducing social exclusion and the provision of equal opportunities. The move away from state ownership and the provision of goods and services to their regulation by the state (Majone 1996) is not necessarily inconsistent with a social democratic tradition, though the reduction in the role of the state is considered by some to be a move towards neoliberalism. The emphasis on the employment and education of individuals may be interpreted either as a shift to a neoliberal accommodation to global capital (Taylor-Gooby 1997; George 1998; Brine 2006), a shift from a Keynesian welfare state to a Schumpeterian workfare state (Jessop 1999), or in keeping with a social democratic tradition that prioritizes full employment (Giddens 1998, 2001; Crouch 1999), where an appropriate response to globalization is to invest in people's human capital through state initiated training and education (Reich 1993; Quadagno 1999; Esping-Andersen 2002). These changes may well be an accommodation to a changing global environment, but full employment under decent conditions for all without coercion and state ensured access for all to education, health and care and a decent living standard, are among the hallmarks of social democracy. The shift in the conceptualization of the goal of 'equality' to that of 'social inclusion' (Giddens 1998) potentially softens the core principles of the social democratic project (Lister 1998), as does reduced concern with increased inequality caused by the growth in high level earnings and wealth from housing capital, and the evasion of taxation and regulation by private equity forms of capital (Murphy 2007), although the attention to poverty somewhat mitigates this. On this range of concerns, the UK is best considered to be situated on the boundary between social democracy and neoliberalism.

A similar debate addresses whether the EU is best considered neoliberal (Young 2000) or social democratic, which is complicated by the narrower remit of this polity, which excludes welfare payments and the different construction of its democratic processes (Majone 1998). The conclusion of this debate drawn here is that the major division in the world today is one between a more neoliberal USA and a more social democratic EU. The contest between the varieties of modernity of these two global hegemons is crucial for the future of global arrangements.

Contesting conceptions of progress

How is it possible to adjudicate between these contesting conceptions of progress: economic development, human well-being, equality and human rights? Are these issues to be determined by philosophers, or is it a matter of politics, with the strongest forces winning, or a matter of rational argumentation and evidence-based research? Is there a single universal standard, or will there always be particular standards for different cultures and communities? The tension between universalism and particularism runs through all of these framings of progress: between a concept of progress that is universally applicable and one that always varies by social location. Is universalism merely a disguise for new forms of imperialism, colonialism, or Westernization? The postmodern critique of modernity argues that a universally relevant concept of progress is inherently impossible. However, it can also be argued that universal standards are needed, since exceptions can be manipulated by the powerful. How, in an emergent global era, might all voices be involved in determining what global standards should be?

Is there a philosophical grounding of the decision between either a universal or community-based grounding? On the one hand, liberalism and universalism appear to offer a plea to a free-floating form of reason that is universal, drawing on a Kantian heritage (Rawls 2005). There is a claim to universally valid truth, though this usually assumes a coherent individual as the seeker/knower. On the other hand, communitarianism appears to offer grounding in the particular standards of a specific community (Taylor 1994; Sandel 1998). The latter implies that truth is always partial and situated, that we are limited by the communities in which we are located, and that there is always social situatedness and a particularity of values and knowledge (Haraway 1988). In place of the Enlightenment tradition that made universal claims to knowledge, has emerged a postmodern scepticism of the validity and usefulness of the grand 'metanarratives' linking the knowledge and progress that constituted its core components (Lyotard 1984).

Of course, both polar extremes are untenable. Many have sought a resolution or compromise, either by refining the procedures for an assessment of justice claims (Habermas 1989, 1991; Benhabib 1992), or by integrating the concerns of the individual and the community

(Kymlicka 1991, 1995). Habermas (1989, 1991) seeks a resolution by attempting to establish universally valid procedures by which truth may be established, utilizing the dynamics within an assumed desire to communicate to drive the process, and locating it within an idealized situation of equality of contribution. However, by such a location Habermas, despite his intentions, situates rather than universalizes the conditions for truth, since the conditions of free and equal contribution are actually socially specific, not least in their presumption of the implications of democratic involvement. Benhabib's (1992) attempt at overcoming the same dualism by demanding a focus on the other has similar strengths and weaknesses to that of Habermas despite her attempt to move further on (Hutchings 1997). Benhabib seeks to avoid commitment to the communitarian stance, by making an appeal to the ostensibly universally valid criteria of judgement of recognizing the standpoint of the other. But the process of recognizing the standpoint of the other is not natural and automatic, but depends upon socially variable conditions. Thus, Benhabib merely displaces the problem of universalism onto these new procedures for judgement, which are not sufficiently universal to be adequate to the task demanded of them. The act of 'recognition' requires a social process of assessment as to what constitutes the same as or different from oneself. By contrast, Bauman (1991, 1993) simultaneously rejects both poles and with them the search for certain foundations for contemporary ethics and political projects.

But despite the philosophical angst, there are nonetheless many projects that promote alternative conceptions of progress. How should they be understood? Are they best understood as predominantly political? There are protestors who oppose the priorities for globalization as proposed by the world's financial institutions, who are met with organized state and police power, as in the Seattle riots (Klein 1999). There are political struggles within global institutions, for example, coalitions of poor countries preventing the World Trade Organization from adopting certain types of liberalization of world trade that they consider would adversely affect the poor.

Today, many projects engage simultaneously with both knowledge and power, drawing on and deploying scientific research within and alongside political engagement. This can be understood as the development of 'epistemic communities' (Haas 1992) or 'public Sociology' (Burawoy 2005). 'An epistemic community is a network of professionals with recognized expertise and competence ... an authoritative claim to policy-relevant knowledge ... a shared set of normative and principled beliefs ... shared causal beliefs ... derived from their analysis of practices ... shared notions of validity ... and a common policy enterprise' (Haas 1992: 3). Burawoy (2005) refers to the practice of public Sociology, in contrast to professional Sociology, critical Sociology and policy Sociology. This is a Sociology that engages with contemporary issues, researching questions that emerge in civil societal struggles, which draws on the other three Sociologies, not least professional expertise, and is engaged in projects of social transformation, the pursuit of progress. There are many examples of the intermingled nature of politics and science, in which findings from research are central to the struggles over the pursuit of competing projects, including the best way to invest for development (Stiglitz 2002) and the dangerousness of emerging genomic technologies (Winickoff et al. 2005). These draw on the notion that truth is never permanently established even if it temporarily appears to be (Latour and Woolgar 1979), but is instead constantly subject to challenge and to doubt (Habermas 1987 [1981]).

In global arenas there have been several significant and successful challenges to the standards against which global progress is to be measured and in more than one direction. A change from economic growth towards a capabilities understanding of progress has been occurring within global institutions as a consequence of this mix of intellectual and political struggle. In the 1980s the clear goal of the world's financial institutions was economic growth. By 2000, in the UN Millennium Declaration, the World Bank, IMF and OECD additionally supported a capabilities approach. The eight Millennium Development Goals were to: eradicate extreme poverty and hunger; achieve universal primary education; promote gender equality and empower women; reduce child mortality; improve maternal health; combat HIV/AIDS, malaria and other diseases; ensure environmental stability; and develop a global partnership for development (UN 2005). A change in the list of UN-recognized human rights occurred in 1993 as a result of a similar mix of political agitation and research-based evidence (Peters and Wolper 1995). This was to include violence against women as a violation of women's human rights. The potent mix of a global feminist coalition and research on the extent of violence against women was crucial to this change in what were ostensibly 'universal' human rights.

With globalization, the definition of the good life and the policies to promote it are increasingly contested at a global level. Global institutions and the political and civil societal spaces they generate constitute an increasingly important terrain on which these struggles take place. There are appeals to both scientific evidence and to democratically expressed popular priorities as bases for the legitimacy of arguments. Global institutions around the UN have revised their stated goals as a consequence of these processes. There has been a shift in emphasis from a framing of progress as an increase in income to one of capabilities, while the definition of universal human rights now involves explicit reference to women's human rights. At the same time, in a perhaps contrary direction, global financial institutions have promoted economic growth, and military force has been deployed by some polities in pursuit of particularistic goals.

Conclusions

One of the aims of this book is to adjudicate rival claims about progress on the basis of evidence and theory that go beyond philosophy. The concept of progress is not outmoded, as alleged by some postmodern critics. Yet there is no single and universally agreed upon definition of progress, rather there are many competing framings of the project. Thus, a search for a foundational basis for a detailed list of the characteristics of the good life would be in vain. While there is no single foundation for standards of progress, the formulation, encoding and institutionalization of concepts of progress in international conventions and agreements, especially those orchestrated by the UN, proceed apace. This is not the same as a global or universal agreement. Nevertheless, these activities do have consequences. There are active processes of claims-making about what constitutes progress and the proper goals of public policy. In a global era there is renewed interest in claims pitched at the level of the universal. In an era of globalization and increasing valuation and practice of democracy the contestation over the content of the concept of progress is taking new and more global forms. The contested choice of economic growth, or capabilities and well-being, or justice-based considerations of equality or human rights, affects public policy at both global and national levels.

Here, a complex realism is adopted, in which each knowledge claim is underpinned by a set of theoretical and empirical components, each of which is part of a network of knowledge claims. It is a knowledge claim rather than a value claim because of this underpinning. This is not a foundationalist claim, since the theoretical and empirical underpinning is contestable and challengeable. The 'real' can never be known for certain; not even if the best scientific procedures are followed. The concept of complex realism building on critical realism combines the notion that there are procedures by which knowledge claims are contested (subject to refutation) and can be improved with that of uncertainty, in that they can never be known absolutely. In complex realism, the testing of knowledge claims against a network of theories and empirical evidence can lead to a reduction in the errors in knowledge.

Many issues ostensibly posed as ones of value often make implicit claims as to how phenomena are interconnected. Many claims made about the good life, progress, and human well-being are testable to a considerable degree by empirical evidence because they are claims about associations and connections between phenomena. One of the aims of this book is to assess the processes and types of social system that best realize the good life, according to different formulations, addressing its framing as economic growth, human development, equality, and human rights. When do they map onto each other? When do they diverge? What forms of social organization and social development, which varieties of modernity, are associated with each? How general a set of arguments can be made, universal or particular? This book provides evidence of the implications of one dimension of social life inequality for another, thereby reducing the speculative element in some of the debates. Chapter 9 in particular uses comparative data to measure progress in a range of countries according to the different definitions identified here.

Multiple Complex Inequalities

Introduction

Equality matters not only because it is a major contemporary framing of justice and progress, but also because inequalities affect the different forms and speed of economic and human development. Key issues include: how to theorize multiple and intersecting social inequalities in addition to class; how to theorize the relationship between difference and inequality; and the implications of multiple complex inequalities for the analysis of progress and modernity.

Why multiple inequalities? Class is not the only significant inequality. Inequalities are also associated with gender, ethnicity, racialization, nation, religion, able-bodiedness, sexual orientation, age, generation, linguistic community, and more. These inequalities affect the differences between forms of modernity as well as the key dynamics of social change.

Why complex inequalities? Unequal social relations involve difference as well as inequality. Some aspects of the different activities may be positively valued, while others will be regarded as unjust. It is this complicated combination of inequality and difference that the concept of 'complex inequalities' is intended to capture. Complex inequalities are here defined as constituted by the simultaneity of difference and inequality, going beyond the conventional treatment of these as alternatives.

Multiple and intersecting inequalities

While class has traditionally been seen as the main axis of social inequality, this is insufficient. Gender and ethnicity are also important forms of inequality, as can be the case with disability, religion, age and sexual orientation (it is illegal to discriminate on grounds of gender, ethnicity, disability, faith, age, and sexual orientation in the EU: see the European Commission 2007a). While the diversity of social inequalities is widely documented, they are infrequently integrated into macro level social theory. Specialist areas of social science have produced extensive descriptions and analysis of specific inequalities, for example, in the sub-disciplines of gender studies, ethnic and racial studies, and disability studies; however, these have not yet been fully integrated into social theory.

In order to include multiple complex inequalities in addition to class at the centre of social theory, several theoretical developments are needed. The conceptualization of each of the main institutional domains of economy, polity, violence, and civil society needs to be re-thought so as to include and make visible complex inequalities in addition to class. Each of the complex inequalities needs to be theorized as a separate system of social relations, as a regime of inequality spelling out the ontological depth of these regimes. Class is not reducible to economics, nor ethnicity to culture; rather each regime of inequality involves the economy, polity, violence, and civil society. The theorization of multiple regimes of inequality is a further challenge – to go beyond reducing one form of inequality to another, or restricting the account to description.

The concept of the economy, which is often restricted to marketized monetized activities, needs to be widened to include non-marketized non-monetized work if it is to capture gender and ethnic relations. If it is not broadened in this way, then other forms of economic activity, such as unpaid domestic care-work that is an important part of the constitution of gender relations (Oakley 1974; Becker 1981; Delphy 1984) and slavery that was an important part of the constitution of ethnic relations (Walvin 1992), will be omitted from the analysis. If the unit within which inequality is considered is widened from one country to the whole world and inequalities between generations are included, then new forms of inequalities become visible, such as global warming, which has had stronger effects on the poor South rather than the rich North of the world (Roberts and Parks 2007) and on future generations.

The inclusion of non-marketized economic sectors causes problems for some of the most frequently used measures of economic inequality, in particular income inequality. Comparing the income of employed people is relatively straightforward, generating accounts of class, gender and ethnic economic inequality among workers, with measures of the wage spread and the gender and ethnic pay gaps. But how is an unpaid domestic care-worker, often but not always a woman, to be treated in such an approach to economic inequality? Is she to be ignored since she does not have her own earned income? Such an approach is obviously unsatisfactory but is implied in the quite common practice of comparing the income of households rather than individuals, thereby making invisible any gender inequalities within the household (as in most of the studies of economic inequality reported in Chapter 3). Is her domestic care-work left out of focus by centring the analysis on her earned income, asking what proportion of men's earnings are earned by women (a measure used by the UNDP), thereby explicitly treating the lack of income from domestic care-work as a component of gender inequality? Should unpaid domestic care-work be treated as a positively valued activity in its own right? Or is it a key part of gendered economic inequalities?

The conventional concept of the state is too narrow to grasp some key forms of institutionalized politics and governance concerning gender and ethnicity. The broader concept of polity includes a wider range of entities, including transnational polities such as the European Union, and also organized religions, which can be important in the governance of gender and ethnic relations. The conventional operationalization of the concept of democracy focuses on free elections, free political parties, free association, free speech, and the right to bodily integrity such as the right of *habeas corpus* (not to be subject to arbitrary detention). Using these criteria most, though not all, countries can be considered democratic today. However, effective access to power requires a presence in the key arenas of decision making, such as in parliament. If a presence in parliament were to be added to the operationalization of the concept of democracy, then women and minoritized ethnic groups do not have political equality as yet. If the right to bodily integrity were to make visible gender issues, such as women's freedom to control their bodies in sexual and reproductive matters such as abortion and contraception, then there is not yet political equality for women.

Violence needs to be added to the conventional set of institutional domains of economy, polity and civil society, since it is so important in the structuring of gender, ethnic, national, and religious inequalities. Violence is not merely an instrument of power, but can also be constitutive of social relations. The processes of deployment and regulation of violence in both collectively organized and interpersonal forms have important implications. These forms include not only the armies of the state but also domestic violence, sexual assault, harassment, lynching, 'ethnic cleansing', and terrorism. The use of violence by dominant groups against women and minoritized ethnic, sexual, and religious groups is a further indicator of inequality.

Civil society is a domain of social creativity, where there is a development of new ideas and social practices, including various forms of association, non-governmental organizations, social movements, and non-state forms of power struggle (Gramsci 1971) and intimacy. It includes but is not confined to issues of culture, including the media, the arts, sport, and knowledge creation. Whether different participation in these activities constitutes inequality or a valued difference is again an issue in these areas. Nevertheless, the imbalance between social groups in decision-making activities in civil society may often be considered an inequality. Who decides what constitutes news, which leisure activities are to be funded and put on prime-time television, and who makes decisions in trade unions and other associations?

Complex inequalities: difference, inequality and progress

In deciding what counts as inequality there is a troublesome complication: when is something a positively valued difference and when is it inequality? This issue lies at the heart of many disputes about what constitutes progress; what to some is a reduction of a negatively valued inequality, to others might constitute a reduction in a positively valued practice. Rather than forcing a choice, it is better to recognize that most social relations contain both inequality and valued differences. The term 'complex inequality' is used here to signify this simultaneous presence of inequality and positively valued difference.

Complex inequalities potentially constitute a challenge to the concept of progress insofar as there are multiple standards to evaluate what is progress. There are three ways of thinking about equality in this context. First, is to identify a single standard against which inequality is measured. A second position entails equally valuing different contributions. A third approach is that of transformation, whereby the whole system is changed, with all groups and the standards attached to them restructured.

The first position argues that there is or can be a single agreed standard against which to identify inequality. The UN Universal Declaration of Human Rights, which declares that equality in accessing these rights should be universal, exemplifies this position.

A single standard of equality is often implied in monetary economic inequality, where differences in income and wealth are considered to be inequalities. It is implied in the concept of democracy, where the equality of each vote is considered important. Such a conception of equality measured against a single standard is common in the analysis of class relations, where matters of economic and political equality are often at the forefront of the analysis. The feminist vision of de-gendering (Lorber 2000, 2005) implicitly endorses this position, even though a question remains as to its universal application. In practice, the legal dimension of the equality strategy of the EU is based on 'equal treatment' thereby endorsing agreed standards. Indeed some standards, such as equal pay for women and men, may constitute standards that are already held by women as well as by men. While the identification of inequality may appear obvious through the lens of class analysis in relation to inequalities in income and wealth, in the case of complex inequalities other than class, such as ethnicity and gender, where inequality and difference are more obviously present simultaneously, this is not so simple. Some forms of variation are open to alternative interpretations as either difference or equality: for example, a segregated pattern of labour between domestic care-work and waged labour may be a valued difference or an unwelcome inequality or both.

The second position positively values difference (Spellman 1988; Young 1990) and diversity, and assumes the possibility of equally valuing different practices (Taylor et al. 1994). In the desire to move beyond the over-simplifying notion of a single standard against which to measure inequality, there has been a move to recognize and value difference (Young 1990; Taylor 1994; Tronto 1994; Calhoun 1995; Hobson 2000). Young (1990) argues for the recognition of cultural difference – the denial of respect for those who are culturally different and for their ways of life is a problem that needs a political remedy. She argues for the recognition of groups as the bearers of these cultures within the political system, rather than recognizing only the individual of liberalism. This theory of justice ontologically privileges groups over individuals. In contrast to Lorber's (2005) call for de-gendering, Young argues for the deepening of institutions that promote respect for group differences. There are two main problems with this approach. First, in practice, the institutionalization of difference has often entailed inequality in some way. An example here is that of the performance of unpaid domestic care-work by women. This may be a highly valued activity (Tronto 1993), however, it can be inconsistent with the activities necessary to obtain equal pay under certain circumstances (Joshi and Paci 1998). Second, the strategy of 'recognition' has a problematic tendency to lead to the reifying, essentializing (Ferree and Gamson 2003), or ontologizing (Felski 1997) of difference. It can embed differences ever more firmly. The focus on specific identities makes it difficult to engage with change and cross-cutting inequalities. The dilemma becomes how to recognize difference while avoiding the trap of essentialism (Ferree and Gamson 2003).

There have been many attempts to reconcile, merge, hybridize, or otherwise go beyond the dichotomization of sameness and difference approaches to equality (Scott 1988; Kymlicka 1995; Fraser 1997; Holli 1997). One resists a settled focus on identity (Braidotti 1994); a second focuses on sameness in some domains and difference in others (Council of Europe 1998); a third posits a process of transformation of existing standards and their associated institutions (Fraser 1997; Rees 1998). In the first approach, Braidotti (1994) emphasizes the fluidity and changeability of cultural forms by utilizing the metaphor of the 'nomadic' subject to resist settling into established modes of thought and behaviour. She prefers the perspective of difference in order to avoid simply embracing existing identities. However, such a distancing from actually existing social practices runs the risk of rendering the position too abstract to have much practical substantive meaning (Felski 1997; Squires 1999). A second approach allows for equality through sameness in one domain and equality with difference in others (Council of Europe 1998; Verloo 2001). Equality through sameness is specified in the 'equal participation of women and men in political and public life' and 'the individual's economic independence', and education, while equality through equal valuation of different contributions is specified for the family and care-work. However, this is only possible if the links between different domains are loose. If the gender practices in different domains are coupled tightly, it may not be possible to have common standards in one domain and different standards in another.

The third approach to equality requires transformation (Fraser 1997; Rees 1998; Squires 2005). In this perspective, a transition from inequality to equality implies the transformation of the social institutions and standards in which the groups are involved. Transformation entails new standards agreed across diverse social groups that are themselves restructured. As social relations are transformed, then new standards develop. This is an approach that is classically adopted in socialism. There can be no significant practical restructuring of inequalities without the transformation of the social relations that themselves produce the standards against which equalities are measured.

Modernity? Postmodernity? Not yet Modern? Varieties of Modernity?

Introduction

Are we now postmodern, rather than modern, or still premodern in some respects? Are there stages to modernity, so that we are now in high or late modernity (Giddens 1991), reflexive or second modernity (Beck 1992) or liquid modernity (Bauman 2000)? Are there multiple modernities, with quite different principles of modernity (Huntington 1998; Eisenstadt 2002)? Or varieties of modernity, sharing key features but with different paths of development (Hall and Soskice 2001; Schmidt 2006, 2007)?

The answers to these questions depend on the definition of modernity, whether complex inequalities are brought into focus, and whether different types of modernity can be distinguished. The definition of modernity used here draws on the classics, from Marx and Weber to Durkheim and Simmel, inflecting them with contemporary social theory. Bringing complex inequalities, and especially gender, into focus challenges conventional accounts of modernity. Rather than a singular modernity, varieties of modernity are identified.

It is necessary to reconsider the definition of modernity, to rebuild from its classic origins, and to address forms of inequalities that the classics did not fully consider. Five components of modernity are considered: free wage labour; the state monopoly of legitimate violence; rationalization; individuation; democracy and human rights.

Modernity or postmodernity?

Is the concept of postmodernity more appropriate than that of modernity for the twenty-first century (Lyotard 1974; Harvey 1989; Kumar 2005)? Does postmodernity imply that knowledge is so situated and contextualized by particular social groups that no general social theory is possible? Does the inclusion of multiple complex inequalities and cultural diversity mean that the concept of modernity should be rejected as too simplistic and replaced by that of postmodernity? Does recognition of the divergent values and preferences of particular social groups and cultures challenge the vision of a universal conception of modernity (Taylor et al. 1994; Calhoun 1995; Felski 1995; Bhambra 2007; Schmidt 2007)?

Is it appropriate to link modernity with progress, or is the 'Enlightenment' confidence in the possibility of progress misplaced (Lyotard 1984)? Modernity is accused of bringing the Holocaust (Bauman 1989), the destabilization of the environment, high levels of inequality, and the threat of nuclear annihilation. Is it better to reject any link between modernity and progress, and prefer instead an ethical position of distance from such a commitment, articulated as postmodern ambivalence (Bauman 1991)?

However, it was rare that classic social theorists simply equated modernity with progress. They were almost always ambivalent, aware of the negative as well as positive potential of any changes. The double-edged nature of modernity, providing both freedom and also new forms of disciplinary constraint, runs deep in much classic sociological theory (Wagner 1994). For example, Marx saw increased poverty before revolution and socialism, with free wage labour providing both freedom from personal bondage as well as increased discipline, while Weber saw rationality as not only the development of the human capacity for knowledge but also as an iron cage of bureaucracy which narrowed the human range of action. The conceptualization of progress is highly contested and should not be equated with modernity; but classical social theory did not make this mistake.

The recognition of multiple forms of inequalities and differences has been absorbed into postmodernist criticism of modernist analysis. There are potentially many different baselines against which to measure equality. But it does not follow that postmodernism is the best answer to this analytic challenge. The multiplicity of inequalities is not new to a global era, indeed in Simmel's work individuation resulting from diverse webs of affiliations was central to his understanding of modernity. The standards against which inequality and progress are measured are contested, but that is not the same as abandoning such a project as if there were incommensurability.

The challenges posed to social theory and to the simpler forms of modernization theory need to be answered, but there are other ways. One is to re-work the concepts of modernity, moving beyond a false singularity, recognizing the still existing premodern, and theorizing the varieties of modernity. The challenge to the simpler concepts of social system needs to be addressed; the conceptual tools needed to do this can be drawn from complexity theory, as will be shown later.

Late, second or liquid modernity?

Also going beyond modernity is a series of writers who think we have reached not postmodernism, but a late stage in the development of modernity – late or high modernity (Giddens 1991), reflexive or second modernity (Beck 1992, 2002) and liquid modernity (Bauman 2000). These writers have introduced issues of choice and reflexivity, intimacy and family, into the analysis of modernity.

According to Giddens and Beck, we are now more reflexive, more able to knowingly make the decisions that shape our lives. Rather than fixed traditional patterns, there is choice. This analysis is led from an interpretation of the changes in intimacy (Giddens 1992) and the family (Beck 1992, 2002), which are positioned more centrally to social changes than has been common in social theory. Giddens and Beck are right to name intimacy and the family as areas of significant social change, but their analysis of this abandons the approach that they have used for other social relations, neglecting much of the considerable social science work on gender relations that explains these changes in the same way as changes in any other set of social relations. Their move into the language of choice and reflexivity leaves behind much of the heritage of social theory. This is a mistake. Bauman (2000) similarly focuses on change for individuals, but is less focused on the family and intimacy, suggesting that in liquid modernity there is a change from solidly structured social relations to fluidly changing social relations. Bauman goes beyond Giddens and Beck in noting explicitly that the appearance of choice for individuals is not really choice in an unequal society. He is right to point out that choice is better addressed as a personal experience, a superficial appearance, rather than as a reduction in constraints.

All three, Giddens, Beck and Bauman, write as if there were a single modernity. There is no reference to differences between countries. In particular, there is no reference to the differences between the social democratic reorganization of gender and family relations and those in more neoliberal countries. Bauman writes as if all of modernity is becoming neoliberal. But there are differences, with the social democratic version of modernity different from that of neoliberalism. This book explores these differences rather than treating the West as if it were one.

Multiple modernities?

A further response to the challenge of diverse social forms and inequalities to the paradigm of modernity is that there are several forms of modernity, not just one. Much early work on modernization assumed that there was a single form of modernity, in which variations were minor and theoretically insignificant. The presumption of a singular form of modernity can be challenged without abandoning the concept of modernity. There are two ways of conceptualizing the diversity of forms of modernity: multiple modernities (Huntington 1998; Eisenstadt 2000) and varieties of modernity (Schmidt 2006, 2007).

The concept of multiple modernities rejects the notion of a single path of modernity (Huntington 1998; Eisenstadt 2000), rather there are multiple alternative modernities each with its own distinct set of values and practices. Modernity is not the spread of Westernization during processes of globalization, but instead is autonomously developed in different locations around the world. The multiple modernities approach assumes a radical dissimilarity between the forms of modernity. These differences are seen to lie especially in the realms of culture and religion, with an incomparability of value systems between different cultures (Eisenstadt 2000) and different civilizations (Huntington 1998). These approaches aim to overcome a perceived ethnocentric bias in traditional analyses of modernity as emanating and derivative from Western social practices. However, in compensating for Western bias these authors postulate such radical discontinuities that they erode any common basis for the concept of modernity. This position articulates a relatively thin conceptualization of modernity, rooted in cultural values at the expense of economic, political and scientific processes where greater commonalities in trajectories of change might be found (Schmidt 2006). The theorists of multiple modernities rely rather too much on the cultural dimensions of different modernities, neglecting commonalities such as the development of science and market economies (Schmidt 2006). This poses the question of the precise definition of modernity – how should it be characterized and distinguished from premodernity?

Not yet modern?

Some of the social forms that have recently come to be interpreted as variously postmodern or aspects of multiple modernities are instead better conceptualized as not yet modern. This is made clear when complex inequalities are brought into focus.

Many of the classical sociologists, including Marx, Weber, Durkheim and Simmel, constructed dualisms of before and after modernization, the pre-modern and the modern. This dualism was centred on industrialization and its associated transformations in the organization of society. The transition to modernity was located variously with the development of the mode of production (Marx 1954); rationalization (Weber 1948, 1968); differentiation (Durkheim 1984); and the increased complexity of the web of social relations (Simmel 1955). Modernity involves free wage labour (Marx), the monopolization of legitimate violence by the state (Weber), rationalization (education, scientific development and secularization) (Weber), individuation (Simmel), and democracy and human rights (Therborn).

In some important respects we are not yet modern, the project of modernity is not yet complete. This is because in several critical domains, for some sets of social relations other than class, the transition to modernity is not yet complete. When complex inequalities, especially gender, are brought into focus, no country is yet fully modern, but rather a mixture of premodern and modern elements. Where there is not yet free wage labour, as for example where there is domestic labour or forced labour, there is not yet modernity in the economy. When significant numbers of women are dependent housewives, there is not yet modernity. When the state does not have a monopoly of legitimate violence in a given territory, as when there is uncriminalized violence against women and ethnic and other minorities, then the state is not yet modern. No country as yet has free wage labour for all of women's work, the effective criminalization of gender-based and ethnic-based violence, and secularization, though many are in the process of transformations leading in these directions. The argument that modernity has been achieved or surpassed rests upon the false assumption that there is one dominant axis of social inequality. Taking complex inequalities seriously challenges the classic approach to modernity. The simultaneous existence of modern and premodern social forms in the same country challenges conventional forms of social system analysis.

Varieties of modernity

Classic social theory, from Marx to Durkheim to Simmel, was often centred on a single transition to industrialization and modernity. The debate on this issue has continued, both backward looking to these processes historically in the North and forward looking to these processes today in the South (Kerr et al. 1960; Lipset 1960), though with many refinements in the most recent texts (Inglehart 1997; Inglehart and Norris 2003). While the impact of modernization occurs across the whole range of social life (Wilensky 2002), from human development (Sen 1999) to citizenship (Marshall 1950), a key issue has been whether economic development leads to democracy. By contrast, a quite different sociological tradition has considered political events as key to the divergence between different paths of development (Esping-Andersen 1999), although it has not always been theorized using the concept of path dependency (Moore 1966; Skocpol 1979; Korpi 1983; Esping-Andersen 1990). In this perspective, the nature of industrial societies is critically shaped by political processes especially involving states, which lead to different paths of development. Rather than one unfolding process of modernization, there are several paths to and through modernity. Indeed, it has been argued that there is no inevitability that economic development will necessarily lead to democracy, but rather that the form of political governance depends upon the balance of political, especially class-based, forces during industrialization (Moore 1966).

This type of approach is used in the 'varieties of capitalism' approach to differences in the organizational form of market economies (Hall and Soskice 2001; Yamamura and Streeck 2003). It is also implicit in analyses of the implications of different political events in the transition to industrialization, as in the work of Moore (1966) on the different implications of the balance of class forces during industrialization for outcomes of either democracy or dictatorship, and subsequent scholarship on the implications of states and revolutions for the nature of class society (Skocpol 1979), and class alliances at critical moments for the form of welfare state (Korpi 1983; Esping-Andersen 1990). Different routes through industrialization generate different balances of social forces that can lead to divergent outcomes – temporality and sequencing make a difference. These may be the alternatives of dictatorship or democracy (Moore 1966), or different forms of welfare state regime (Esping-Andersen 1990). Rather than one unfolding process of modernization, there is more than one path to and through modernity. In this perspective the nature of industrial societies is seen as critically shaped by non-economic processes, often political ones. The theorization of this range of forms was taken forward by analyses of path dependent rather than unilinear forms of development (Moore 1966; Mahoney 2000; Pierson 2000). The question of the significance of the distinctiveness and nature of the different varieties of modernity can then be addressed more clearly. This question is posed anew in the context of globalization, as to whether the differences between paths of development are eroded by global processes.

There is more than one way of identifying varieties of modernity. Within the varieties of capitalism school, Hall and Soskice (2001) distinguish between liberal market economies and coordinated market economies. Within the welfare state literature, Esping-Andersen (1990, 1999) makes a three-fold distinction between liberal, conservative corporatist, and social democratic forms of welfare state regimes. Within the gendered literature on welfare states, Lewis (1992) makes a distinction based on the extent to which men are the breadwinners and women are the main carers. These typologies are based on different institutional locations: industrial relations, welfare state, gender relations. A more comprehensive typology needs to integrate not only these three, but also violence.

Here, the major varieties of modernity are neoliberalism and social democracy. In addition some social relations are not yet modern, so there is a need to retain the distinction between modern and premodern.

Defining modernity

In order to proceed further in the analysis of modernity, postmodernity, premodernity, multiple modernities, and varieties of modernity it is necessary to more precisely delimit what is meant by modern in each of the main areas of social organization: economy, polity, violence, and civil society.

Free wage labour
The development of free wage labour is a key aspect of modernity. Transforming labour power into a commodity that is sold on the market is a critical part of the development of capitalism (Marx 1954). The commodification of labour power is a key component of the transition from a feudal to a capitalist mode of production. The relations of production between serf and lord in feudalism were more personal in nature, embedded in a web of obligations and power, than those between proletarian and bourgeoisie.

The transformation of labour power into the commodity form involved a double-edged process of both increased discipline and increased freedom (Wagner 1994). It required increased discipline in following the routines of mass labour in the factory, for example longer hours of work increased the relevance of time-keeping (Thompson 1963). It increased and polarized social and economic inequality. Yet it increased some forms of freedom by narrowing the bonds tying the worker to the governing class to those of the sale of their labour power, releasing them from the personal bonds of servitude under feudalism.

The reduction in personal bonds to an employer increases workers' potential for the development of political consciousness and action. Workers have the civil societal and political space to develop alternative ideas and form the associations that underpin the development of various forms of collective action. Marx saw the development of capitalism as progressive, partly in itself and the new forces of production that were unleashed, and partly because of its potential for the next transformation of social relations to socialism and communism. The link between capitalist economic development and political action postulated by Marx is widely supported by contemporary social science (Rueschemeyer et al. 1992). There have been many nuances and subtle theoretical developments as to the nature of the link and the conditions under which it takes different forms (Gramsci 1971; Habermas 1989).

However, Marx restricted this analysis to class relations, leaving out of focus forms of inequality such as slavery and other forms of forced and non-marketised unfree labour together with the implications of the entry of women into free wage labour. Free wage labour is a hallmark of modernity, not only for class relations but also for gender relations and other complex social inequalities. Until labour is free wage labour, we are not yet modern.

State monopoly of legitimate violence
Weber's (1947) definition of the modern state is a body that has a monopoly over legitimate violence in a given territory. The modernization of the state is a process during which the state accrues this form of power to itself, concentrating decisions over its utilization in its increasingly centrally organized body, shifting away from the dispersal of this form of power among feuding barons and roving militias.

This definition of a modern state is widely adopted in contemporary social science (Giddens 1985). Indeed the development of states in Europe over the last thousand years can be described in terms of the de facto concentration of power, especially violence, in the state (Tilly 1990). This analysis runs parallel to Elias's (1994) theory of the civilizing process, in which there is a decreasing use of violence in civil society and a developing state monopoly as the civilizing process proceeds. Foucault (1997) goes further, suggesting that the use of brute force by the state is replaced by disciplining in the modern world.

However, the state does not have a monopoly over legitimate violence or all violence in the contemporary era. When complex inequalities, such as gender and ethnicity, are brought into focus it becomes clear that there are considerable amounts of violence over which the state neither has a monopoly nor seeks to have a monopoly. The existence of a considerable amount of gender-based violence, from domestic violence to rape (Krug et al. 2002), and ethnic-based violence, from racial harassment to ethnic cleansing (Mann 2005), which the state condones by failing to effectively criminalize it, contradicts the notion that contemporary states are modern. While the state does not have a monopoly of legitimate violence by its non-criminalization of significant amounts of gender-based and ethnic-based violence, the state is not yet modern.

Rationalization

Rationalization is key to Weber's (1948, 1968) conception of modernity. Through this process, traditional and charismatic forms of authority give way to rational, legal, and bureaucratic forms. There is a process of disenchantment; a turning away from religion to secularism, an increase in education and in scientific knowledge.

Education is the field in which the process of rationalization has occurred to the greatest extent around the world. The massive increase in educational institutions, the proportion of the population who are educated, and the length of time spent in education have been marked features of the last century. Increased education is a global phenomenon, even though there are significant differences in the content and amount between countries. The narrowing (and in some countries reversing) of the gender gap in education is a major reduction in one kind of complex inequality, though class and ethnic differences remain.

The development of scientific modes of knowledge production might be regarded as the best expression of the process of rationalization in the modern world, as the most quintessentially modern way of thinking, but there are caveats. The constant critique and rejection of previous forms of knowledge are hallmarks of scientific method and this involves challenges to existing scientific claims as well. It is a form of rationalization that takes a near global form (Schmidt 2006) and possesses enormous authority (Haraway 1997). The contemporary public questioning of science has been interpreted as a form of reflexive modernization (Beck 1992); it is not a simple rejection of rationalism, but rather the bringing to bear of a range of forms of knowledge on the output of institutions dedicated to scientific development (Wynne 1996).

The decline in religion associated with secularization has occurred in many developed countries, but not all (Bruce 1996; Norris and Inglehart 2004). While Europe has in general seen a decrease in religiosity, a decline in attendance at churches and an increase in secularism, this is not uniform (Gorski 2000). The USA by contrast, while developing an advanced economy and sophisticated institutions of education and science, has seen little fall in the religiosity of its population (Inglehart 1997). In some places there has been a shift in the content of beliefs away from traditional religions towards New Age spirituality rather than to conventional forms of secularism (Heelas and Woodhead et al. 2004). Further, the rise of various forms of fundamentalism within Christianity (especially in the USA), Islam, Hinduism and Judaism, likewise contradicts any simple rationalization thesis (Marty and Scott 1993). The tenacity of religious belief systems raises serious challenges to the notion that contemporary Western countries are all modern, if secularism is taken as a key feature of modernity. Nevertheless, despite the exceptions, there has been a decline in religiosity in developed countries. The difference between the USA and the EU in their levels of and trends in religiosity constitutes a significant divergence in trajectories within the West.

Individuation

Increasing individuation was seen by Simmel (1955) as the key to modernity. Simmel's understanding of difference and inequality was not restricted to the great social cleavage of class. Rather, he envisaged modern social relations as highly complex and differentiated – instead of one dominant set of social relations there is a multiplicity. This gives rise to a highly individuated social order. However, this does not mean anarchic individualism. Instead there are complex webs of affiliation, with people connected to many others in myriad ways. Social life is conceived as a web of group affiliations.

Simmel differentiates between primitive and advanced thinking and forms of sociality. In the former the circumstances and affiliations due to family and kin are dominant, while in the second 'each individual establishes for himself contacts with persons who stand outside this original group-affiliation, but who are "related" to him by virtue of an actual similarity of talents, inclinations, activities, and so on. The association of persons because of external coexistence is more and more superseded by association in accordance with internal relationships' (Simmel 1955: 128). It becomes a matter of choice as to with whom one is affiliated. It becomes possible for intellectual and educational interests to bring together a new community. He suggests that while before the Renaissance social differentiation was based on either self-interest or emotion, afterwards intellectual and rational interests came to be the more common basis of groups. Higher, more modern, forms of association are those based on rationality rather than simple external characteristics. The modern person belongs to many groups (as compared with earlier times), this being a hallmark of culture. These groups include family, occupation, citizenship, social class, clubs, and many more. The more groups with which a modern person is affiliated, the more individuated this person becomes, because few if any other people are likely to have the same patterns of affiliation. The more groups of which a person is a member, the more attributes they possess. This gives rise to uncertainty rather than to the security of the previous mode. Conflicts between those groups of which an individual is a member encourage that individual both to make adjustments and also to become assertive.

While Simmel sees individuation as a general characteristic of modernity, some have seen this as restricted to Western modernity, while other modernities place the state, community, and family above the individual, though this is perhaps most usually seen as the instrumentalization of culture to defend political authoritarianism (Thompson 2000; Barr 2002).

Simmel (1955, 1984) notes that women are in the process of becoming modern, just reaching the point of experiencing the crossroads of affiliations at which individuality begins. The analysis of individuation is developed in the work of Giddens (1992) and Beck (2002), including the development of reflexive biographies as a consequence of changes in the economy and family, with implications for gender relations. But individuation for women is not yet complete.

Democracy and human rights
Democracy is not included in the classical texts of social theory; as since it was not fully developed at the time that they were writing, it is unsurprising that it was not regarded as a marker of modernity. But in the twenty-first century, when democratic practices are widespread and the aspiration to democracy near-universal, democracy is widely regarded as a hallmark of modernity. A significant part of modernization studies empirically investigated the links between economic development and social and political development, often finding a close association (Kerr et al. 1960; Lipset 1960; Inglehart 1997; Inglehart and Norris 2003; Norris and Inglehart 2004) although sometimes it was seen to be mediated by other factors such as the level of inequality (Bollen and Jackson 1995; Muller 1995a, 1995b) and the direction of the causality from economic to political has been challenged (Ersson and Lane 1996; Leftwich 1996, 2000).

However, the definition of what counts as democracy is highly contested, in particular the relationship between procedural practices and the representational outcome for social inequalities (Held 1995; Phillips 1995; Markoff 1996; Potter et al. 1997; Pitkin 2004). The conventional approach focuses on formal procedures, especially voting, rather than the outcome, such as the proportionate presence of social groups in parliament. Since the presence of women in parliaments makes a difference to the policy outcome (Thomas 1991; Norris 1996a; Wängnerud 2000), the conventional definition of democracy is in need of revision to include their parliamentary (or congressional) presence.

Human rights are likewise not included in the classical texts of social theory as markers of modernity for similar reasons, though they are noted in many texts on political philosophy from the eighteenth century onwards (Paine 1984 [1791]; Wollstonecraft

1992 [1790]). Human rights became a marker of modernity in the period after the Second World War, in the European rejection of the Holocaust and nationalist militarism that had overridden the interests of individuals in the name of the purity of ethnic-nationhood (Therborn 1996). These are encoded in the United Nations Universal Declaration of Human Rights as a fundamental principle of all civilized nations (UN 1948). The interpretation of human rights is highly contested. Are they merely specific to Western countries with their individualistic ethos, or have they become hybridized so as to include Asian and other cultures that are traditionally less individualistic (Woodiwiss 1998)? Is their early formulation gendered, not universal (Nussbaum 2000)? Do they become inclusive of gender inequality insofar as they include sexual and reproductive rights and the right to be free from gender-based violence (Peters and Wolper 1995)? Today, democracy and human rights are markers of modernity, albeit that their meaning remains highly contested.

Globalization

Introduction

What is globalization? Are the distinctiveness of local social arrangements and the capacities of nation-states to act democratically being eroded? Is the world being homogenized into a single US-led modernity? Or are some political institutions resilient to these pressures? How does making multiple complex inequalities visible change the analysis?

The conceptualization of globalization demands an engagement with the changing implications of spatiality and temporality, with space-time compression, an increased rate of flows of people, objects and symbols around the world, and the non-linearity of these processes. It requires re-thinking the concept of society, its boundedness and processes of formation, and the relationships between social systems in the world. Definitions of globalization are diverse and often encompass many different social processes. Globalization has been identified and conflated variously with internationalization, universalization, Westernization, supraterritoriality (Scholte 2000), Americanization, and neoliberalism. In particular, 'globalization' has often been treated as if it were effectively the same as the expansion of capitalist markets (Crouch and Streeck 1997). The conflation of globalization and capitalism is unhelpful because it does not allow for the significance of any social relations other than capitalist ones and, further, precludes analysis of the political actions that might be facilitated by the increased global inter-linkages that might be in opposition to the growth in power of global corporations. It is better to have a definition that is minimalist in the sense that it does not include the causation nor name the processes involved. This is helpful in that it avoids conflating the causation of globalization with its definition and allows for the possibility of more than one wave of globalization with different causes.

Globalization is here defined as a process of increased density and frequency of international social interactions relative to local or national ones. This definition closely follows the definition of Chase-Dunn and colleagues (2000: 78): 'changes in the density of inter-national and global interactions relative to local or national networks'. A more fulsome, though similar, definition of globalization is that used by Held et al. (1999: 16) 'A process (or set of processes) which embodies a transformation in the spatial organization of social relations and transactions – assessed in terms of their extensity, intensity, velocity, and impact – generating transcontinental or interregional flows and networks of activity, interaction, and the exercise of power'. Globalization is a transformative process in which the units within the process change as well as the overall environment. Several dimensions can be distinguished: the extent of networks of relations and connections; the intensity of activities and flows through these networks; a temporal dimension of the speed of the interchanges; and the impact of these phenomena (Held et al. 1999).

While many focus on globalization as a predominantly economic or politico-economic project, it is important to consider violence and civil society as well. Rather than seeing globalization as a single process, it is more appropriate to distinguish between different types of global processes, including the global flows of capital, trade and people, the development of global institutions, networks and hegemons, and global civil societal waves.

One simple difference in approaches to globalization is between those who think that there is such a process and those who do not (Held and McGrew 2002). However, there are further important distinctions. Those who do not think that globalization is a useful framing of analysis include both those who think that there is already a global system and those who think that existing social institutions are effective in resisting such processes. There are four main approaches to globalization. First, that global processes are eroding the differences between societies and exacerbating inequalities. Second, that there are still separate societies that remain resilient in the face of global pressures. Third, that the world is already global, and has been for a long time. Fourth, that global processes restructure social relations and coevolve with trajectories of development. It is the last position that this book adopts and develops.

Globalization as the erosion of distinctive and separate societies

Globalization is frequently viewed as a process that is sweeping away differences between societies, thereby creating similarity or homogeneity. This is often seen as a negative process that corrodes culture and political autonomy and increases inequality (Martin and Schumann 1997), although there are some exceptions that see globalization as a positive force associated with economic growth and development (Ohmae 1990, 1995).

For Castells (1996, 1997, 1998) the development of globalization is associated with the rise of the information society, which he dates as appearing from the 1970s onwards. The origins of globalization lie in increasing global interconnections that are often linked to new information and communication technologies, such as computers and the internet (Castells 1996, 1997, 1998). These new forms of information flows change the nature of the world through their effects on the economy and the way that politics is organized.

Globalization changes the balance of power between capital and labour – capital is more mobile and can go 'regime shopping', potentially moving to whichever country offers the best opportunities, often seen as low taxation and low regulation (Traxler and Woitech 2000). As a consequence, democratic states can lose their power to globally mobile capital, leading to a reduced capacity to set regulatory and welfare regimes in keeping with democratically expressed priorities. In this way, globalization is understood as a corrosive force that erodes and changes the nature of existing social and political entities, such as societies and states, and especially nation-states (Crouch and Streeck 1997). Globalization erodes, undermines, and reduces the capacity for the autonomous action of nation-states, especially over the provision of welfare, and hence their democracy (Cerny 1995, 1996; Held 1995; Martin and Schumann 1997), through the corrosive power of global financial markets (Strange 1996), and the new balance of power between capital and labour. Globalization exacerbates inequalities within and between countries.

Neoliberalism is a global wave of ideas, politics, and policy practices. This project, which promotes free markets and opposes state regulation of the economy in the pursuit of economic growth, has come to dominate the powerful global financial institutions (Stiglitz 2002). It is a doctrine that favours private over public ownership, promoting the privatization of public services and utilities such as water and private ownership of the information about genetics that underlies modern biotechnology, summarized by Harvey (2003, 2005) as 'accumulation through dispossession'.

Globalization undermines some aspects of local and national cultures. Large multinational companies promote their products and associated cultures and undermine the distinctiveness of cultures and the authority of traditional ways of acting. For example, McDonalds spreads its fast food and associated unhealthy practices at the expense of local cuisines (Ritzer 1993). Hollywood shapes our cultural values. Globalization is here understood as a process that impacts on economies, polities, and cultures; although they might resist or be resilient to this process.

While providing a powerful critique of recent changes, there are a number of limitations to this perspective. It tends to overstate the newness of these developments, which have a long history; it also tends to overstate the extent to which all polities are undermined; and it tends to underestimate the significance of political and civil societal responses to these processes.

Resistance to globalization

A contrasting approach suggests that political institutions and cultures can be resilient to global processes and that their paths of development have not always been significantly affected. This thesis has been articulated at the level of whole societies, and also at the level of specific political institutions.

It has been argued that the particularity of societies (Eisenstadt 2002), nation-states (Mann 1997) and civilizations (Huntington 1998) is resistant to erosion by globalization. Modernity does not take merely one form, there are multiple modernities with quite different forms. Neither industrialization nor globalization need lead to the erosion of differences (Eisenstadt 2002). Huntington (1998) argues that cultural and civilizational differences are durable, that rather than a homogenization of the world by economic development and increased communications, we are experiencing a 'clash of civilizations'. There are several distinct civilizations whose basis is cultural and religious, with associated core states: Western, Latin American, African (possibly), Islamic, Sinic, Hindu, Orthodox, Buddhist (barely), and Japanese. Huntington argues that while most civilizations are seeking to modernize, they are not necessarily seeking to

Westernize; that it is possible to have modern technology without social patterns that are perceived as Western, and that cultures deeply rooted in civilizations are robust enough to be able to resist Westernization as they modernize. Controversially, he identifies a fissure between the West and Islam, as a result of differences in core civilizational values. There are empirical weaknesses in his argument related to inconsistency in the application of his principles of the classification of civilizations. For example, he considers that the EU and the USA belong to the same Western civilization, but that Latin America does not because of its political culture even though it shares a Christian religion, compromising his classification system that is based on religion. Further, there are many countries that are economically and politically successful while having several ethnicities and religions, further undermining his argument about the centrality of civilizational divides.

A different approach to resistance to globalization is based on the resilience of some economic and political institutions. There are some forms of services that must be locally provided, so are not subject to pressures to send jobs abroad (Hirst and Thompson 1996). In some countries, the configuration of institutions including the democratic system, nature of group representation, structure of policy making, and structure of welfare provision mean that there is less change under pressure from global forces than in other countries. In the countries that are already more liberal, there have been further changes in that direction with a reduction of regulation and state welfare, while in the more social democratic countries of Europe there has been less change (Swank 2002). Further, in some countries there is an active building of new forms of partnerships, pacts, and coalitions in response to global pressures (Hanké and Rhodes 2001).

Already global

The thesis that the world is newly undergoing globalization is challenged by the view that the world became global a long time ago. This is not a challenge to the idea that we live in a global era, but only to the notion that this is new. This has been argued in different ways using world-systems theory and the world society thesis.

The global expansion of capital was described by Marx (1954; Marx and Engels 1967) in the mid-nineteenth century. The drive by capital for new terrains where commodities can be produced and sold has been a feature of the world capitalist system since its origins. Wallerstein (1974) argues that there has been an expanding world capitalist system since the sixteenth century. Here capitalism is theorized as a world-system, in which states are merely nodes constituted by that system (Wallerstein 1974; Robinson 2001). The analysis centres on the world-system of capitalism as a whole (Wallerstein 1974, 1980, 1989). This system has had a global reach since the sixteenth century, although the process of saturation of all the economic and social relations in the world is still ongoing. States are nodes within this world-system. There can be no concept of autonomous, free-standing societies here, since all social relations are inter-connected through the capitalist world-system, though there are social formations with varying degrees of differentiation from each other. This is both an ontological and empirical claim about globality. This is a theory that privileges the role of capital in explaining social relations and, since capital is global, the analysis of local social formations must also take into account the global formation. This is a theoretical approach that has never lost sight of the need to explain processes of development in the poorer and less industrialized countries of the world, conceptualizing such core-periphery relations as an integral part of the explanation of social relations anywhere.

There are several nuances within world-systems theory, especially in the relationship between the economy and states and the extent to which they are independently causal. World-systems theory started from the position that there was the possibility for a mobility of states up and down the hierarchy of an otherwise stable world-system (Wallerstein 1974). Dependency theory considers that there is no mobility of states within the world system but rather the reproduction of inequalities between the metropolitan and peripheral social formations, that is, the development of underdevelopment (Frank 1975). Robinson (2001) argues that globalization has already produced a developed global capitalist polity beyond specific states, while Chase-Dunn (1998) differentiates global hegemons within the world system. Global commodity chain analysis of the material inequality in a global system focuses on the micro level of the transactions that make up a global capitalist chain. The analysis is of the transfer of value through goods manufactured and distributed through the chain (Gereffi and Korzeniewicz 1993). The concept of a chain can be applied to care-work in the concept of 'global care chains' (Hochschild 2000), where the focus is on mobile caring labour (Yeates 2005), involving the mobility of people as well as the transfer of care.

There are variations in the extent to which different forms of capital are globalized. Finance capital is more globalized than industrial capital, because there is an electronic global marketplace for capital that is different from the relatively more fixed industrial capital. However, even finance capital has a territorial component in the servicing of its workforce, often in global cities (Sassen 2001). Polities are not reducible to a world system; political processes involve pressure from locations in addition to capital; the competition between polities has consequences (Bornschier and Chase-Dunn 1999); globalization comes in historical waves linked to the rise of hegemons (Chase-Dunn et al. 2000).

World society theory also conceives of the world as already global, but, unlike world-systems theory, globalization is here seen to be led by culture. The dating of world society, around the 1930s or immediately post-war, is earlier than Castells' globalization, but later than that of Wallerstein. The focus is on the similarities between societies, even though they are separate and independent. They note the increase in newly independent countries, and that each bears a stunning similarity to other countries in the organizational, governmental, educational, citizenship forms that they take. This includes, for example, the differentiation of government ministries, the form and notions of appropriateness of education, the conducting of a census, and the granting of citizenship to women. These are not driven by endogenous development, but rather by a world-culture which already exists. New independent nation-states replicate the same form as already existing societies. The similarities are too great to have been due to chance, and since the countries are at different levels of economic development this cannot be the cause (Meyer and Hannan 1979; Boli and Thomas 1997; Meyer et al. 1997; Ramirez et al. 1997; Lechner and Boli 2005).

However, while there are some striking similarities between countries there are also major differences (Eisenstadt 2002). Not all countries have the same system of governance: there are non-democratic countries; not all countries allow women access to the vote; human rights are not universally achieved. There tends to be a missing component in the world society thesis – the mechanism by which the transfer of culture is accomplished. This might be a diffusion of ideas, or some form of pressure or coercion to align (Dobbin et al. 2007).

The most important critique of the thesis that the world is already global is that this varies significantly between social institutions. Some are already global, others are not.

Coevolution of global processes with trajectories of development

Here I shall show that globalization is not a single causative process, which might be more or less successfully resisted, nor irrelevant, nor an already completed process. Rather, there are several uneven global processes. There is a mutual adaptation of complex social systems within a changing global fitness landscape. The following components of global processes are proposed:

1. There are uneven global flows of capital, trade, and people, an uneven development of global institutions, networks and hegemons, and global civil societal waves – not a single uniform process of globalization.
2. These flows, institutions, and waves involve the coevolution of economies, polities, violence, and civil societies – there is no simple one-way impact of the economic on the rest that might be successfully or unsuccessfully resisted.
3. There is the restructuring rather than the annihilation of space.
4. There are emergent forms of global civil societal practices as well as glocalization in which cultures are framed by the global – not the homogenization of culture.
5. Globalization has occurred before – it is neither only new nor only old, but it is taking new and deeper forms.
6. While some polities, especially states, are losing power to larger forces, this is not uniform – there are contesting global hegemons, especially the USA and the European Union, as well as the emergence of global institutions.
7. There are global civil societal waves – including neoliberalism, socialism, human rights, feminism, environmentalism, and religious fundamentalisms.
8. Neoliberalism is a powerful global project that has become embedded in some governmental programmes and social formations – it is not the same as globalization, nor is it fully hegemonic.
9. There are competing projects of societalization on a global scale, but none has overwhelmed the others – currently the most important are the contesting projects of modernity associated with the hegemons of the USA and the EU. Global societalization projects cannot be understood without their gender, ethnic, national, and religious components.

There are different kinds of global processes, involving economies, polities, violence, and civil society. There are flows of capital, trade, and technologies (Castells 1996), of free and unfree workers (Cohen 1997), tourists (Urry 2002), students, refugees, and others, often along already established networks. There are global institutions, such as the UN, the World Trade Organization, the International Monetary Fund and the World Bank, as well as more subtle forms of international regimes that depend upon mutual multi-lateral adjustments of states (Keohane 1989; Ruggie 1998; Risse 1999). There are emerging and contesting global hegemons that dominate the rules of the global fitness landscape, such as the USA and EU. There are waves of political and civil societal practices (Berkovitch 1999; Moghadam 2005).

Rather than a simple one-way impact, social entities coevolve in a changing fitness landscape. Globalization involves complex interactive effects between economies, polities, violence, and civil societies. Globalization does not simply erode or undermine, produce resistance or resilience, but is a process of coevolution between a variety of entities. Current changes in the configuration of spatial relations are complex rather than simple and are not well captured by concepts of 'impact', 'erode', or 'resist'. Rather the notion of a 'coevolution' of complex adaptive systems, drawn from complexity theory (Kauffman 1993), better captures the mutual effects of these changes. The concept of coevolution enables us to include the specific phenomena within the wider concept (Krasner 1983; Keohane 1989; Robertson 1992; Ruggie 1996, 1998; Held et al. 1999). Coevolution includes competition and hostility as well as more cooperative forms of relations; there is a competition and contestation to establish the nature of the rules of the global landscape within which all operate.

There is a restructuring of the implications of space for social activities, rather than the annihilation of distance. Globalization involves a decline in the time and resources needed for travelling, transporting, or communicating over distance. There are changes in the spatial scale of social processes. There is an apparent compression of space and thus of the time needed to overcome it, or space–time compression (Harvey 1989). Rather than seeing globalization as annihilating space (Scholte 2000) and equating globalization with a process of de-territorialization, there is a need to consider the irreducible territorial element to human social practices. Most global processes touch down in particular territorial locations for some functions. These processes need to be located somewhere, to have some kind of territorial bases, in which certain sorts of functions can be carried out. Some services, such as key aspects of health, need to be close to where people actually live. Indeed many transnational corporations still have a national base even if they trade globally (Hirst and Thompson 1996). Even the most de-territorialized transnational corporation still needs to have its headquarters somewhere, maybe in specialized 'world cities', and needs to be serviced by both executives and cleaners who have homes somewhere (Sassen 2001). It is important not to equate the phenomenon of transnational corporations with the wider notion of ending all borders. Space is not made irrelevant, but reconfigured by processes of globalization. There are processes for the re-scaling of polities (Jessop 2002).

A simple notion of the homogenization of world culture through globalization is untenable, though the spread of some cultural practices is increasing. Hollywood and McDonalds may have become more important for some peoples in some periods (Ritzer 1993), but not in a consistent way. A variety of conceptualizations attempt to capture the more subtle effects, including transformation (Held et al. 1999), glocalization (Robertson 1992), hybridization, and regime influence (Krasner 1983; Keohane 1989; Ruggie 1996, 1998). In glocalization, the globalization process is not a process of cultural homogenization, but rather one in which cultures may see themselves relative to other cultures in the world, but nonetheless maintaining a discrete, if somewhat reformed, identity (Robertson 1992). Examples include the appeal to the doctrine of universal human rights to protect social practices authorized by religion by some Islamic minorities in the West (Soysal 1994), and the appeal to the Westphalian, now global, doctrine of the sovereignty of nation-states in order to resist external interventions on behalf of oppressed groups. Hybridity captures the two-way exchange that may be taking place, in which some entities are transformed as they merge so that something new emerges rather than merely the subordination of one to another (Gilroy 1993). This is important especially in discussing the extent to which certain political practices, such as the discourse of universal human rights, really are a global hybrid rather than a Western invention imposed on the rest of the world (Woodiwiss 1998).

Globalization has happened before: it is neither only new nor only old. It does not fully exist, rather it is still developing. Chase-Dunn et al. (2000) have identified three waves of globalization, each related to the development of a particular hegemon within a capitalist system, which established the conditions under which trade and travel could flourish. Current globalization is best regarded as a new phase of world integration, with new dynamics, but not as a sudden and completely new phenomenon, and the implications of previous, if less significant, waves of globalization being taken into account.

Although some polities are losing power as a result of global processes, other polities are increasing their capacities. While globalizing processes have often been considered to have a tendency to erode polities (Fukuyama 1992; Cerny 1995, 1996; Ohmae 1995), there is a more diverse range of relationships between globalization and political entities. These include: resistance to globalization (Castells 1997; Huntington 1998), the creation of nation-states by world society (Meyer and Hannan 1979; Meyer et al. 1997), the creation of globalization by hegemons as part of the securing of the conditions for world trade (Bornschier and Chase-Dunn 1999;

Chase-Dunn et al. 2000), as well as a broader global restructuring (Brenner 1999; Held et al. 1999). Some states lose power, with their capacity to act circumscribed by changes in the global environment, as the greater mobility of capital than labour enables capital to go shopping for its preferred regulatory regime, although there are limits to this process due in part to the nature of the polity. However, not all polities lose power because of globalization. The European Union is a hegemon that has increased its powers, using perceived global threats to the small economies of Europe as a powerful legitimation of the development of its remit and regulatory capacity (Bornschier and Zeitlin 1999).

Globalization involves not only economies and states, but also non-state political processes. Global waves of social and political movements are part of the changes that constitute globalization. Some movements may appear to be opposed to globalization, but often they are primarily opposed to the form that globalization is taking. These include environmentalism, anti-neoliberalism, feminism, and human rights. There are also constellations of actors that are pro-globalization, such as those constituting the current neoliberal wave. Social and political movements have arisen to contest particular aspects of globalization (Castells 1997). Their focus may involve the excesses of transnational corporations, the institutions of global financial governance such as meetings of the IMF and G8, as well as specific further targets (Klein 1999). They include global civil societal waves centred on equal rights, feminism, environmentalism, religious fundamentalism, and neoliberalism, which become unevenly embedded in political institutions (Berkovitch 1999; Klein 1999; Johnson 2000; Moghadam 2005).

Neoliberalism is not the same as globalization. Neoliberalism emerged as a civil society project, which was taken up and embedded in political projects, becoming a global wave and then embedded in institutions and the programmes of governmental and global bodies (Brenner and Theodore 2002; England and Ward 2007). While neoliberalism is often rhetorically associated with globalization, it is but one of the projects that competes for hegemonic position. Although neoliberalism can be treated as a contemporary wave, it is continuous with an earlier project and practice of liberalism.

There are competing societalization projects at a global level. Societalization is a process in which a set of principles, or an identity, is generalized throughout a social system, so that the whole system becomes self-reinforcing. This concept, drawn from Weber (1968), is further developed as a sociological variant of the concept of autopoiesis developed in complexity theory to capture the self-organizing nature of systems. In social analysis it is necessary to make it clear that systems are produced and not pre-given, that this takes place in a process that occurs over time and that this is very probably contested by other societalization projects and thus is rarely fully completed. A societalization project may be built around a number of starting points, principles, or identity sources. These have included especially capitalism, various religions, and nation-building projects. Any given instance of the societalization process is usually interrupted by competing principles before it is fully completed. Globalization processes do not have unmediated effects, instead there are complex implications of changes in the overall environment or 'fitness landscape' as a consequence of changes in one or more component systems. The extent to which globalization is a process in which aspects of one societal model come to dominate others is an empirical question explored in the rest of this book.

Hegemons often have global societalization projects. Hegemons shape the global rules, or fitness landscape, so that they suit the characteristics of the dominant hegemon – while these rules are general to all players, the hegemon benefits most. The concept of hegemony is useful because it captures simultaneously notions of asymmetry, power, and yet consent (Gramsci 1971; Anderson 1976/7). It is helpful in grasping the setting of, and implications of, the regulations of many economic aspects of the global system, for example, the rules of international trade as set by the World Trade Organization. The power of the concept of the hegemon is further advanced if it is juxtaposed with the concept of the 'fitness landscape' derived from Kauffman (1993). The US hegemon, by ensuring that its rules are best represented by the WTO, has changed the fitness landscape to its own advantage, contesting the EU in the process. The hegemon not only has power over other countries, but also changes the landscape in which it competes in its own favour.

Rather than treating globalization as a single causative process there are several different global processes, including global flows of capital, trade, and people, the development of global institutions, networks and hegemons, and global civil societal waves. Rather than a process that might be more or less successfully resisted, global processes coevolve with the trajectories of development of specific countries; there is a mutual adaptation of complex social systems in a global fitness landscape.

Implications of globalization for social theory

Global processes make it clear that there are no neatly bounded, hermetically sealed 'societies' (if there ever were), but rather there are inter-connections across national boundaries that must be assumed to be usual rather than exceptional. While globalization is not as new as is sometimes suggested, it is taking on new forms and increased significance.

The concept of society, and its conventional equation with the nation-state in modernity (Giddens 1990), needs to be re-thought in order to be able to address globalization. This book rejects the notion of bounded 'societies' – based on an idealized nation-state – as inadequate to deal with the social linkages in a global era and with the complexity of social divisions originating in many over-lapping polities. It considers the ways in which social formations develop forms of self-organization and how this may be more fruitfully conceptualized in terms of projects of societalization, rather than as a completed process.

The boundaries of different forms of economy, polity and civil society rarely map onto each other in the way such a conflation of society and nation-state demands. In addition, the nature of global political processes goes far beyond the conventional relations between states. Globalization challenges the assumption in some forms of social theory that social processes can usually be analysed within a specific society and that in the modern era these can be effectively equated to nation-states.

Global processes do not simply undermine polities, rather there is coevolution between a variety of entities in a changing global fitness landscape. Globalization is not only associated with a neo-liberal version of capitalism, but is also more complex. Global conflicts cannot be understood without an understanding of the deep social fractures related to ethnicity, nation, religion, and gender, as well as class. Globalization leads variously to new forms of universalism or the maintenance or invention of new particularisms. There is neither simple homogenization nor simple maintenance of differences, but rather the forming and re-forming of social differences and inequalities. The theorization of complex inequalities is key to these processes.

Complexity Theory

Complexity theory comprises a collection of work that addresses fundamental questions on the nature of systems and their changes. While sociology has had something of a hiatus in the development of concepts of systems since the rejection of simple forms of Marxism and functionalism (though with some exceptions such as Luhmann), other disciplines, influenced by complexity theory, have engaged in its revision so as to overcome the oft-mentioned problems of early formulations of the notion of system. Complexity offers a new set of conceptual tools for social theory that are capable of resolving some of the classic dilemmas in social science, in particular the tension between the search for general theory and the desire for contextual and specific understandings (Kiser and Hechter 1991; Griffin 1993; Kiser 1996; Calhoun 1998; Haydu 1998), which lies at the heart of the tension between realist (Archer 1995; Bhaskar 1997; Byrne 1998; Somers 1998; Sayer 2000b) and postmodern (Lyotard 1978; Cilliers 1998; DeLanda 2000) approaches. Complexity theory addresses the postmodern challenge to modernist metanarratives to confront issues of diversity without giving up the quest for explanation. Rather than the conventional sociological focus of developing the concept of system by engaging with the work of Luhmann, the approach here is to synthesize complexity theory with social theory more inspired by the heritage of Marx, Weber, and Simmel, than that of Durkheim and Parsons.

Complexity theory has developed powerful new ways of thinking that may be used to develop social theory. As a trans-disciplinary development (Capra 1997), it is important to carefully specify the nature of the translation of concepts and theories from different disciplines, especially between those based on mathematical abstractions and those complicated by empirical observations. While systems can share common features, they will differ according to their context, for example, whether this is biological, social, or physical, and therefore this needs due consideration. Although there have been some attempts to develop a unified theory of complexity (Holland 1995), the significance of the relationship of a system with its environment, ambiance, or context means that this project is fraught with difficulties (Chu et al. 2003). Sociology has often rejected the application of theoretical developments from the sciences on the grounds that they miss the particularity of what is human (Luhmann 1995). Not only this, but outside of the sub-discipline of social studies of science (Latour 1987; Law 1991; Pickering 1995; Haraway 1997), which, while well developed, is rather segregated from much of social theory, the view as to what constitutes scientific method is often far behind current developments, indeed, even located in a view of science as positivist (Harding 1986). The argument here is that recent developments in science, such as those around complexity theory, have produced concepts that are more sophisticated than most Sociology imagines. There is much to be gained from the examination of the concepts, methods, and epistemology of complexity theory in order to see what insights they can offer for Sociology, after a due process of re-specification to ensure an appropriate application.

Complexity theory offers new concepts for developments within social theory. These include: a renewed rejection of reductionism, drawing on the notion of emergence; a re-worked concept of system, that avoids the problems of stasis, for example using the concept of positive feedback; the system/environment distinction, which enables greater flexibility in thinking about the relations between systems; and concepts for addressing major changes, including the coevolution of complex adaptive systems and path dependency. The notion of system used in much of Sociology, following the Durkheimian tradition, is seriously flawed. It assumes that the social system has a tendency to regain equilibrium and that change is gradual. The traditional concept of system in Sociology developed by Durkheim (1952, 1966, 1984) and Parsons (1949, 1951) presumes self-equilibration, in which the social system returns to balance after pressure to change. Despite refinements, most notably by Merton (1968) and Smelser (1959), to deal with criticisms that this framework dealt insufficiently with conflict, power, a lack of consensus and inequality, this functionalist school is widely regarded as discredited (though see Alexander 1982, 1984, 1998). From the perspective of complexity theory, some of the severe limitations of Durkheimian-influenced theory are a result of utilizing an equilibrium conception of system, which Merton and Smelser did not substantially revise.

A common response to these theoretical pressures on the old concept of system was to abandon the concept of system altogether as part of the postmodern turn, which looked to discourse, deconstruction, and identity as ways out of this perceived theoretical impasse (Lyotard 1978; Barrett and Phillips 1992; Braidotti 1994). This turn was often associated with a prioritization of agency and a rejection of the tendency to ignore human action in many forms of structural or system-led explanations. For example, attempts to meld the analysis of gender with Marxism were sometimes alleged to become 'abstract structuralism' (Pollert 1996). Yet even though the concept of system has often been overtly rejected in Sociology, some nearly equivalent notion is often deployed, though under a different name. There are many concepts in social theory that are similar to and parallel with system and which address both the issue of social inter-connectedness and a social level that is not reducible to individuals. They include the concepts of 'social relations' (Emirbayer 1997; Somers 1998); 'regime' (Connell 1987; Esping-Andersen 1990, 1999); 'network' (Latour 1987; Scott 2000) and 'discourse' (Foucault 1997). Some concept is often found necessary in order to address the conceptualization of social inter-connections. However, the negative connotations attached to the notion of system have been sufficiently great that many prefer to use a term other than system, even while seeking to convey a similar meaning.

New forms of system theory have been developed within complexity theory that challenge old concepts of system in a different way. Within complexity theory the concept of system has been radically transformed so that while retaining a focus on relationships and connections it is able to grasp sudden change as well as the more gradual coevolution of systems. Complexity theory offers a new vocabulary to grasp issues of change, so that simple notions of uni-directional impact are replaced by that of mutual effect, the coevolution of complex adaptive systems in a changing fitness landscape, as well as by concepts to capture sudden non-linear processes of rupture, saltation, and path dependency. This facilitates a more subtle understanding of the diverse processes of social change in an era of globalization. The concept of a social system is necessary in order to be able to theorize complex social inequalities and global processes, but its traditional definition is subject to many challenges, in particular that it is too monolithic, rigid, falsely implies equilibrium, and cannot deal with the plurality of inequalities. It is necessary to revise rather than abandon the concept of system.

Central to the re-thinking of the concept of 'system' is the rejection of old assumptions about equilibrium in favour of analysing of dynamic processes of systems far from equilibrium and re-specifying the relationship of a system to its environment. This enables a more adequate theorization of diverse sets of social relations and the analysis of sudden, non-linear, social change. It thus provides a new framework for enquiries into complex inequalities and social change in a global era.

Complexity theory facilitates a re-revision of those old forms of systems theory that have been rightly faulted for false assumptions of stability, consensus, and rigid nested hierarchies of structures (Capra 1997; Byrne 1998). These problems have been part of the reason that many reject systems thinking along with metanarratives and many large-scale forms of theorizing. However, an understanding of globalization requires concepts that grasp notions of inter-connections on a large scale (Benhabib 1999). There is a new conceptual vocabulary available within complexity theory that enables fresh thinking on the conceptualization of the varied ways in which processes are inter-connected, including that of systems. This involves, for example, notions of the coevolution of complex adaptive systems (Kauffman 1993); of non-linear processes (Prigogine 1997); of emergence (Holland 1995, 2000); of punctuated equilibria (Eldredge 1986); and the re-specification of the system/ environment distinction (Maturana and Varela 1980). These enable much more fluid, complex and subtle ways of addressing old theoretical dilemmas.

The use of these new concepts is beginning to develop within social science including, economics, with work on increasing rather than diminishing returns (David 1985; Arthur 1989); political science, on critical turning points (Pierson 2000) and international relations (Jervis 1997); legal studies, on global law (Teubner 1997); management science, on complex adaptive systems (Mitleton-Kelly 2001) and coevolution (Koza and Lewin 1998); as well as sociology (Luhmann 1995; Byrne 1998; Cilliers 1998; Medd and Haynes 1998; Urry 2003). In this book these developments in complexity theory will be used to develop the analysis, especially in relation to social science concerns with path dependency and critical turning points (Mahoney 2000), and the significance of temporality and sequencing (Abbott 2001).

That systems are self-reproducing is definitional of a system. The work of Maturana and Varela (1980) has inspired much work on the conceptualization of systems as self-organizing (Capra 1997). The process of self-reproduction of a system is self-organizing and self-defining. The system has internal processes that internally connect and reproduce the system. These features are called autopoietic by Maturana and Varela. Autopoiesis is a network of processes in which each element participates in the production or transformation of other elements in the network. In this way the network or system reproduces itself over and over again. The system is produced by its components and in turn produces those components. This includes the creation of a boundary that specifies the limits and content of the system's operations and thereby defines the system as a unit. The system reproduces itself.

The problem of explaining order in the world is shared across many disciplines from the social (Alexander 1982; Lockwood 1992) to the physical and biological sciences. As Bertalanffy (1968) notes, there is a contradiction between, on the one hand, Kelvin's second law of thermodynamics and the tendency to disorder, to the dissipation of energy, and, on the other hand, Darwin's account of the evolution of ever higher order species, where the living world shows a transition not towards disorder and homogeneity but towards a higher order, heterogeneity, and organization. The implication of this contrast is one of the starting points of complexity theory on the nature of systems (Prigogine and Stengers 1984; Kauffman 1993, 1995; Capra 1997). There is a tendency for self-organization to take place where there was previously an absence of such organization. For Kauffman (1995: 23) the extent of the development of order rather than disorder is a sign of the existence of underlying laws of emergence. We as human beings are 'at home in the universe', the consequence of the emergence of self-organizing systems, rather than having developed as the chance result of atomic and molecular interactions. It is this tendency to order that lies at the heart of the notion of the emergence of order and the notion of systems as self-organizing and is key to many of the more empirical-based analytic developments associated with complexity theory from biology (Kauffman 1993, 1995) to political science (Jervis 1997) to legal studies (Teubner 1997).

Complexity is not a single coherent body of thought but is constituted by a range of different traditions and approaches (Thrift 1999). For example, complexity theory has inspired at least two main ways of addressing the issue of change and diversity. The first involves the concept of the coevolution of complex adaptive systems, where the concept of coevolution replaces any simple notion of a single directional impact. The second involves the notion of saltation, of sudden critical turning points, in which small changes, in the context of complex systems, give rise to bifurcations and new paths of development that are self-sustaining. These may be understood either as competing accounts of change reflecting the tensions between the different branches of complexity and chaos theory, the first associated with the Santa Fe school and the second with the Prigogine school, or, ultimately, as reconcilable.

The interpretation of complexity theory by social scientists is varied, not least because the concept of a social system is treated quite differently in different forms of social theory. On the one hand, Cilliers (1998) and DeLanda (2000) emphasize the unknowability of the world, with Cilliers taking complexity theory as a defence of the postmodern as opposed to modern perspective on the social world, and Delanda, full of suggestive metaphors loosely derived from complexity theory, emphasizing the non-linear and a lack of equilibrium in history. On the other hand, Byrne (1998) uses complexity theory as a defence for realism to support the modernist argument about the deterministic nature of the world, arguing that complexity accounts are foundationalist. Much of the criticism of the turn towards complexity theory in social theory has focused on Prigogine-inspired accounts, with an emphasis on the difficulty of interpreting key concepts such as non-linearity (McLennan 2006) and leaving out of focus the more systems-oriented development of complexity theory in social theory.

Perhaps the most developed and widely cited example of the use of complexity notions in social theory, especially in relation to the concept of system, is that of Luhmann (1985, 1990, 1995, 2000). Luhmann (1995) synthesizes functionalism and phenomenology with the insights of early complexity theory (Knodt 1995) and thereby challenges the simpler versions of the critique of functionalism. Luhmann (1990, 1995) attempts to integrate the concepts and insights of complexity theory into Sociology, with modifications to make them suitable for a social rather than a natural system. He especially developed those concepts concerned with systems, such as the system/environment distinction of Bertalanffy, and drew out their epistemological implications. He applied his systems analysis to specific social systems, including those of law (Luhmann 1985) and of art (Luhmann 2000). Key to Luhmann's approach is the simplifying assumption that each system takes all others as its environment. It is this that enables him to move beyond the rigidities of conceptions of systems in terms of parts and wholes. Luhmann is thus one of the first sociologists to draw on and demonstrate the advantages of the new complexity theory for social theory.

However, problems result from Luhmann's integration of insights from complexity theory with both Parsonian functionalism, especially notions of system and of function, and phenomenology, especially the focus on communications (Knodt 1995). The heritage of Marx is relatively absent, as is seen in Luhmann's lack of interest in analysing power, inequality, and the economy. The priority accorded by Luhmann to communication leaves these forms of materiality and power out of focus. Further, the work is highly abstract and, despite attempts at application to specific social systems such as law and art, remains devoid of much content about changing forms of social inequality. Thus Luhmann's work, while a rare and important development of systems thinking in recent Sociology, is limited in its direct relevance to analyses of changes in social inequality. It is unable to adequately integrate, as matters of central rather than marginal concern, issues of conflict, inequality, materiality, and agency. As such, Luhmann is perhaps at best an uninspiring ambassador of complexity theory for much contemporary Sociology, at worst a distraction that slowed the utilization of the larger toolkit of complexity thinking within social theory.

More promising is the range of attempts to take a Marxist (or Weberian) inspired Sociological heritage and either synthesize or inflect with complexity theory (Byrne 1998; Jessop 2002; Urry 2003; Winickoff et al. 2005). In many ways the Marxian heritage is more open to complexity notions because of its interest in theorizing the sudden ruptures of political upheavals and in dynamic systems far from equilibrium (Reed and Harvey 1992; Urry 2003). Although these writers share an interest in social inequality and injustice, they do not however address the issue of the intersection of multiple social inequalities. Marx saw capitalism as a system in a more complex way than Durkheim, theorizing both institutions and social relations, as well as processes of change that included both gradual evolution and processes of sudden transformation (Reed and Harvey 1992; Urry 2003). Unlike the Durkheimian and Parsonian tradition, Marx's (1954) conception of a social system did not involve the assumption of static equilibrium. Marx's (1963; Marx and Engels 1967) theory of change included both long periods of gradualist development and the modernization of the forces of production which are interrupted by revolutionary upheavals led by a self-conscious politically motivated and self-organized class, during which the system abruptly changes into a new form. Marx's conception of a social system is more consistent with complexity theory than that of Durkheim because it does not presume a self-balancing form of equilibrium, but instead allows that the social system may be far from equilibrium, generating a sudden change to the path of development.

Jessop (2002) incorporates some of the insights of complexity theory developed by Luhmann into Marxist theory, as interpreted by Gramsci and Poulantzas. He utilizes these developments in system theory in his own distinctive version of regulation theory, successfully replacing the ideational focus of Luhmann's work with the historical materialism of Marxism. Jessop's theorization of the capitalist state thereby locates it within a capitalist system in a non-reductionist way. He develops the concepts of societalization and ecological dominance, drawing on Gramsci's concept of hegemony. The simple notion of the economic system being determinant in the last instance is replaced by the notion that the economic system has ecological dominance in the capitalist system. The concept of societalization is interpreted as bourgeois societalization, a process in which the bourgeoisie attempts to spread their power and influence in the social formation, against resistance.

Urry (2003, 2005) provides a different melding of complexity theory with Marxism, which avoids the influence of Luhmann, by going directly to the complexity scientists. Here there is a greater focus on non-linearity, of sudden changes, of the unpredictability of changes in systems that are on the edge of criticality and far from equilibrium, though balanced with an analysis of glacial change in systems at other times. One example is the path dependent development of the automobility system, in the context of a wider appreciation of the significance of mobilities in the contemporary era (Urry 2007), in which cars cannot be understood outside of a system that includes assemblages containing roads and the motor industry.

Although the synthesis of social theory and complexity theory offered by Luhmann is the one that is most often adopted, this is a mistake; the better approach is one that draws on a social theory that takes as its central interest issues of power and inequality and finds place for materiality and politics. However, it is also necessary to go beyond the syntheses offered by Jessop and Urry, which leave out-of-focus multiple complex inequalities. The utilization of complexity theory here is not a simple adoption of concepts from other disciplines, but an active process of selecting insights that can be synthesized with social theory, rather than imported or transplanted in their entirety. This hybridization of complexity theory with social theory is positioned within the tradition of social theory inspired by Marx and Weber rather than that of Durkheim and Parsons, the forerunners of Luhmann.

It is time for a paradigm change in sociological theory, in the sense intended by Kuhn (1979) and Lakatos and Murgrave (1970). The old concept of social system has been widely discredited. The attempt to build social theory without (at least implicitly) using the concept of the social system has failed. Complexity theory offers a new toolkit with which a new paradigm in social theory is being built. A new concept of social system is possible that, when linked with a range of associated concepts more adequately constitutes an explanatory framework. The analytic strategy is to break down some of the overly unified and homogenized elements in traditional concepts of the social system in order to address multiple and nuanced forms of inequalities, but to then develop new ways to theorize their linkages so the end product of the deconstruction is not mere fragmentation, but rather more subtle and nuanced ways of addressing their complex inter-linkages.

This involves a fundamental re-thinking of the concept of system, of the ways in which entities are inter-related and of processes of change. These complexities can be better understood if our vocabulary of concepts is extended and developed, including 'coevolution' of 'complex adaptive systems' rather than simple one-way impacts; 'fitness landscapes' to take account of the changing global environment; 'societalization' to capture the process of moving towards the synchronization of economy, polity, violence, and civil society, but rarely reaching a full mapping of these in the same territory; 'path dependency' to capture the multiple rather than single trajectories of development; and 'waves'. The concept of 'wave' is particularly important for grasping some of the new ways in which social processes developed in one space and time are disembedded and re-embedded in a new one, capturing the non-linear spatiality and temporality of such processes. The concept is deployed in order to get a grip on phenomena that simultaneously display temporality, spatiality, sequencing, and non-linearity while lacking a consolidated embedded institutional form. These are often marked by considerable energy yet have relatively few deeply embedded institutions. Waves are very important in the movement of civil societal ideas and practices from one country to another in a global era.

Contents

Following this introductory chapter, Chapter 2 reconfigures social theory in order to be able to address the central significance of multiple complex inequalities and globalization. It draws on the insights of complexity theory to re-work and develop the concepts of social system, path dependency, coevolution, global fitness landscape and wave.

The next set of chapters address in turn each of the main institutional domains of economy, polity, violence, and civil society. In each case the conceptualization of the institutional domain is developed so as to enable a full consideration of multiple complex inequalities and globalization and to identify the main path dependent developments of varieties of modernity. Violence is introduced as a fourth institutional domain alongside the conventional trilogy of economy, polity, and civil society. The last chapter in this group addresses the constitution of the main regimes of inequality, addressing their internal cohesion, their varieties, and the implications of their intersection.

The final set of chapters demonstrates the usefulness of these theoretical reformulations for practical and especially comparative analysis. Chapter 8 searches for and identifies varieties of forms of modernity, especially in employment, welfare, violence, and the gender regime, both globally and among the rich countries of the OECD in the global North. Chapter 9 assesses the 'progress' of these countries according to the different framings of progress identified in this introduction, considering the implications of different ways of approaching these issues, and assessing associations between the different forms of progress and different varieties of modernity. Chapter 10 compares the development of the path dependent trajectories of varieties of modernity of contrasting countries (the USA and three members of the EU: Sweden, the UK, and Ireland). These are selected in order to facilitate a comparison between the routes into neoliberalism and social democracy; the transition from domestic to public gender regimes; between greater and lesser inequality; and more and fewer human rights. Chapters 8 and 9 draw on descriptive statistics from global and OECD datasets in the search for patterns among large numbers of countries, while

Chapter 10 draws on qualitative and historical material that enables a consideration of the significance of the temporality and sequencing of events.

Chapter 11 investigates the potential tipping point of the global system away from neoliberalism towards social democracy, following the financial crisis of 2008. This is centred in the contest between the hegemons of the US and the EU to set the rules for the future global order within which all countries have to operate.

The concluding chapter, 12, draws together the implications of the substantive analysis for the theoretical arguments of the book and shows the importance of complex inequalities and globalization for understanding and theorising the varieties of modernity and the contested project of progress.

2 Theorizing Multiple Social Systems

Introduction

Meeting the challenge of theorizing multiple complex social inequalities in a global era requires fundamental revisions to central concepts in social theory. One response to this challenge to social theory to address the specificity and situatedness of multiple differences has been the postmodern critique. However, while this critique has merit in drawing attention to the myriad of differences and inequalities left out of focus in traditional modernist theory, it goes too far, to the detriment of explanation and the significance of the global. The challenge here is to capture the multiplicity and nuances of social inequalities while retaining the scale and scope needed to grasp the global, to understand difference but not at the expense of the explanation of inequality.

The concept of social system needs to be re-thought, but not abandoned; it is deconstructed and then reconstructed. Systems of both institutional domains and regimes of inequality need to be distinguished. Each set of unequal social relations is conceptualized as a system, as a regime; including (but not only) class, gender, and ethnicity. Each institutional domain is conceptualized as a system: the economy, polity, violence, and civil society. The conventional notion that parts make up a whole system is rejected and replaced by the distinction between a system and its environment, in which each system takes all others as its environment. This distinction between sets of social relations (regimes) and institutional structure (domains) enables the simultaneous theorization of several different sets of social relations within each institutional domain. Each regime of inequality is a system that possesses ontological depth, through the inclusion in each case of the economy, polity, violence, and civil society. These systems are not reducible to each other, although they mutually adapt in a changing global fitness landscape.

Social systems are over-lapping, not saturating any given territory and non-nested. The institutional domains of economy, polity, violence, and civil society may each have a different spatial and temporal reach; likewise, different regimes of inequality may each have a different spatial and temporal reach. These may not map onto each other in time and space. This replaces the conventional notion that typical societies are bounded and that domains of economy, polity, violence, and civil society overlap and are nested.

There are ongoing processes of societalization rather than fully formed societies. The assumption that there are 'societies' in which economy, polity, violence, and civil society are congruent in the same territory is rejected as inconsistent with the globalizing world. This is replaced by analyses of multiple processes of societalization, in which the domains of economy, polity, violence, and civil society, and regimes of inequality have a tendency to move towards alignment, a process often begun but rarely completed before another societalization project intervenes. The concept of emergence is used to characterize the relationship between different levels, including that between agency and structure, so as to avoid reductionism.

Bodies and technology are included within social theory by conceptualizing assemblages of humans and non-humans as actants. The inappropriate marginalization of forms of inequality associated with bodies, such as those linked to violence, reproduction, and sexuality (which are especially relevant to gender inequality), is addressed by re-thinking the conventional distinction between humans and non-humans. This inclusion of non-humans as well as humans also enables a more adequate inclusion in social theory of the significance of new technologies that are associated with globalization.

Rather than a single path of development, as in much modernization theory, there can be several trajectories of development. Social systems do not have to be in equilibrium, but are rather subject to dynamic non-linear forms of change involving positive feed-back loops. The concept of path dependency is developed in order to theorize variations between systems, while not abandoning the project of a general social theory. A series of concepts is introduced to grasp non-linear processes of change, including critical turning points, catalysts and dampeners, and waves. The concept of waves is developed to conceptualize some of the distinctive types of social energy connecting social systems in a global environment, to capture the non-linear non-institutionalized nature of movements of political and civil societal practices that swirl around the globe. Social systems are complex adaptive systems that coevolve as a result of their mutual interactions, instead having a one-way impact. They have unequal power to alter the rules of their global environment or 'fitness landscape'.

Multiple Inequalities and Intersectionality

There are multiple complex inequalities in addition to class. 'Complex inequalities' include: gender, class, ethnicity, race, religion, nation, linguistic community, able-bodiedness, sexual orientation, and age. In each case there is a complex combination of inequality and difference, the balance of which varies according to both the set of social relations under analysis and the interpretation of them. The concept 'complex inequalities' is used to capture the simultaneity of inequality and valued difference.

Are multiple inequalities best conceptualized using a few big categories, or by careful attention to detail and nuance? A theoretical tension exists between the appreciation of detailed differences and the requirements of more general social theory. While the existence of multiple types of social inequalities is well established and empirically documented, their inclusion at the heart of social theory rather than in specialist sub-fields remains a challenge. The task is to theorize the multiple sets of social relations associated with complex inequalities while not losing sight of the macro global horizon. This challenge to macro social theory has been articulated as a general critique of metanarratives (Lyotard 1978), as a series of demands that specific inequalities are taken into account and are not neglected (Stanworth 1984; Calhoun 1995), and as the need to avoid generalizing from the experiences of one group to that of others (Mohanty 1991). Various analytic strategies have developed (Crenshaw 1991; Braidotti 1994; Felski 1997; Young 2000), but there is a tension between essentializing and dispersing categories and between simple powerful models with limited dimensions of complex inequalities and rich thick descriptions of finely differentiated identities (Felski 1997; Sayer 1997, 2000a; Holmwood 2001; Ferree et al. 2002a).

Intersectionality is a term to describe the relationships between multiple forms of social inequality. One of the complications of theorizing multiple inequalities is that at their points of intersection it is insufficient to treat them merely as if they are to be added up because they can also mutually change each other (Crenshaw 1991; Collins 1998; Brah and Phoenix 2004; McCall 2005; Phoenix and Pattynama 2006). This is not a new issue in social theory (Jakobsen 1998) since it lay at the heart of the debates on the intersection of gender and class (Crompton and Mann 1986), especially in dual systems theory (Hartmann 1976; Mies 1986; Walby 1986) as well as other analyses of gender, ethnicity, and class (Westwood 1984; Phizacklea 1990), but it has been given a new inflection under the auspices of the concept of intersectionality, especially as launched by Crenshaw (1991) in relation to the intersection of gender and ethnicity.

There are at least six approaches to the analysis of intersectionality. The starting point is a criticism of false over-generalizations. For example there are divisions within the category of woman by class, by ethnicity, and by whether they are from the North or South of the world (Mohanty 1991). Few would disagree with this point. However, this is sometimes linked to a more general turn in social theory towards the particular and a critique of the so-called meta-narratives (Lyotard 1978; Mirza 1997), which is more open to contestation.

The second approach to multiple inequalities is that of reductionism to a single primary axis of social inequality. One form of reductionism, found especially but not only in Marxist inspired social theory, is to class or capitalism. A range of social inequalities such as gender and ethnicity may be empirically noted, but explained as an outcome of the dynamics of the capitalist system (Seccombe 1974; Pollert 1996; Jessop and Sum 2006).

A third approach is that of micro-reductionism. This position grew from a rejection of the conceptualization of social relations using the concept of system because of the difficulty of theorizing multiple forms of difference and inequality (Barrett and Phillips 1992). In pursuit of the analysis of intersectionality, there is an analytic strategy of identifying and studying neglected intersections (Crenshaw 1991). This is intended to analyse groups at the point of intersection, for example, a group that is simultaneously female and African-American and working class and older. It is often associated with the use of case study, ethnographic and narrative methods of enquiry (e.g. Prins 2006). McCall (2005) in her review of intersectionality refers to this as 'intracategorical intersectionality'. However, there are a number of problems with this approach. It has tended to become a strategy of seeking out ever finer units for analysis, in pursuit of a pure intersecting category. But there are no pure groups, there are always more forms of difference, there will still always be some differences within the group being researched (Jakobsen 1998; McCall 2005). There is also a tendency to cultural reductionism and the use of rather static identity categories, even though a critique of the restrictive use of the concept of 'identity' was one of the starting points for Crenshaw's analysis. Further, with such a micro approach it is hard to address larger questions, such as those involving a global horizon (Benhabib 1999).

The fourth approach rejects the use of categories altogether (anticategorical complexity in McCall's analysis). The limitations of the strategy of identifying groups at specific intersections and in particular identity analysis have led to challenges to the strategy of developing categories at all, as inherently essentializing. A focus on difference is preferred to one on identity. This draws on postmodern and poststructuralist analysis in order to avoid the pitfalls of essentialism (Yuval-Davis and Anthias 1989; Barrett and Phillips 1992; Haraway 1997) and in particular on the Derridian concept of difference and the practice of deconstruction and a Foucaultian derived concept of discourse (Barrett and Phillips 1992). Analytic categories have been seen not only as never adequate representations of the lived world, but also as potentially pernicious in their potential for a false sedimentation of these categories in practice. The destabilization of group categories became the aim of some forms of analysis. Drawing on Deleuze and Guattari (1987), Braidotti (1994) invokes concepts with a metaphorical focus on movement rather than stability in order to achieve this, including the use of the metaphor of 'nomad' to privilege the crossing of borders. However, such a radical deconstruction and destabilization of categories makes substantive analysis, which requires distinctions between categories, rather hard (Felski 1997; Sayer 1997).

A fifth approach, which is centred on the need to avoid essentializing the human agent, deconstructs the notion of the agent, replacing it with a focus on performance (Butler 1990). The performance, rather than the agent behind the performance, becomes the focus. This allows for greater fluidity and sense of possibility, rejecting notions that a person can have a real essence. While this theoretical move is successful in displacing the concept of agency it does so at the expense of a move towards voluntarism and a thin ontology of the social, although in later work Butler (2004) acknowledges the need to avoid flattening the ontology.

Sixth is a segregationary reductionist strategy, in which each set of social inequalities is connected to a single and separate base. Rather than rejecting categories, the analytic strategy is to build up a better analysis of each category. Each set of social relations is considered to have a different and autonomous ontological base. Yuval-Davis (2006: 200–201) puts it thus:

> the ontological basis of each of these divisions is autonomous, and each prioritises different spheres of social relations ... For example, class divisions are grounded in relation to the economic processes of production and consumption; gender should be understood not as a 'real' social difference between men and women, but as a mode of discourse that relates to groups of subjects whose social roles are defined by their sexual/biological difference ... Ethnic and racial divisions relate to discourses of collectivities constructed around exclusionary/inclusionary boundaries.

This approach segregates the bases of each of the categories: class is grounded in the economy; gender is a discourse about sexual and biological differences; ethnicity relates to discourses about exclusion and inclusion. The implication appears to be a relatively simple base-superstructure understanding of each set of social relations.

The segregationary reductionist approach is not new. This analytic strategy was utilized within both Parsonian (Parsons et al. 1955) and Marxist (Althusser 1971; Habermas 1987, 1991) systems theory. In this analytic strategy gender is theorized as if it were accounted for by the institution of the family; the family is treated as the dedicated site of gender relations for the system as a whole. The family as an institution is treated as saturated with gender and patterns of gender relations everywhere are considered to be critically shaped by the family. This approach reduces gender to the family. Such reductionism means there is no analytic capacity to theorize variations in gender relations that are not associated with changes in the family.

Another example of this approach is that of Esping-Andersen (1990, 1999), who tries to include gender as well as class in his analysis of the development of three forms of welfare state regime (liberal, social democratic, conservative corporatist). While empirically noting the importance of gender, Esping-Andersen is unable to theorize its significance adequately. This is not because he thinks that gender is irrelevant to his analysis. This accusation, though often made, does not do justice to his analysis. Esping-Andersen does think women are relevant, indeed in his recent work (1999) he says that he thinks they are very important, but the theoretical tools he uses are too unsubtle, too simple, to achieve an adequate outcome. This is because he does not have an adequate theory of gender relations. He slides between the concepts of family and of gender as if it made no difference which one is used. He treats gender as if it were constituted in the family and that the sole source of change in the family is the welfare state. The concepts he uses to capture changes in gender relations are 'familialism' and 'de-familialism' (Esping-Andersen 1999: 45). He asserts that 'Given women's (or at least mothers') family responsibilities easily restrict their ability to gain full economic independence solely via work, their de-familialization, as many studies have shown, depends uniquely on the welfare state' (Esping-Andersen 1999: 45). As a consequence, he is unable to achieve the analytic payoff that his empirical recognition of the importance of full employment for women within a social democratic regime ought to deliver for his analysis. It does not deliver because he does not theorize the implications of different patterns of gender relations in employment. He ought to theoretically link full employment for women to the other constitutive elements of the pattern of equality and inequality in the welfare regime. But he does not do this because gender is theorized as being constituted within the family, with sources of variation of this restricted to variations in the welfare state. The extent of women's employment is treated as purely dependent on this. Hence, he cannot bring theoretical focus to the significance of different levels of women's employment. He is thus led to the (false) conclusion that there is little difference between a welfare regime in which women have fairly high levels of employment (in particular that of central Europe, such as Germany) and one in which they have fairly low levels of employment (in particular that of southern Europe, such as Italy). Hence, he argues (wrongly) that a focus on gender makes little significant difference to a typology of welfare regimes. He does this because he has no theoretical purchase on the implications of the variation in levels of women's employment. The reason for this is that he can theorize only one set of social relations in each institutional domain: class in the economy and state and gender in the family.

Regimes and Domains

So what is the solution to these theoretical dilemmas? It is necessary to analytically separate the relations of inequality from the institutional domains. This separation is essential in order to be able to theorize multiple inequalities in the same institutional domain and in order to be able to theorize the ontological depth of each set of inequalities. The terms 'regime' and 'domain' are used to distinguish these two forms of system. Each set of social relations of inequality is theorized as a system, as a regime of inequality. Each set of institutions in an area is theorized as a system, as an institutional domain.

This analysis draws on the distinction between institutional and relational conceptions of social structure clarified by López and Scott (2000). Much contemporary social structural analysis takes an institutional approach to social structure, drawing implicitly on or parallel to a Durkheimian tradition. Some, however, use a relational approach (Emirbayer 1997; Somers 1998), drawing implicitly on or parallel to Simmel. The concept of relational structure usually focuses on the struggles and cooperations of distinguishable social groups which benefit or lose from these engagements by which they are constituted. In a few instances both institutional and relational structures are used simultaneously as in some work inspired by

Marx. In the analysis in this book institutional and relational forms are conceived as coexisting and not alternatives. The term 'system' is preferred to 'structure' so as to avoid the connotations of rigidity and to be consistent with complexity theory.

Each set of social relations of inequality is a type of system which is not reducible to other sets of social relations. These are regimes of inequality. They include class, gender, ethnicity, age, and more. These regimes of inequality have relationships with each other, in which they mutually impact on each other, but are not reducible to each other.

Each institutional domain is a different kind of system. The four domains are the economy, polity, violence, and civil society. The relationship between them is not one of simple determination, as in a base-superstructure model. Rather these are complex systems that mutually adapt. By institutional domains is meant an elaborated version of the conventional distinctions between the economy, polity, and civil society. In order to adequately address complex inequalities, the conceptualization of each domain needs to be broadened. Thus the economy includes not only free wage labour, but also domestic labour. The polity includes not only states, but also the European Union, organized religions that govern specific areas of life (such as aspects of intimacy), and some nations (those with developed institutions, such as Scotland) (Walby 2003, 2004a). The Gramscian concept of 'civil society' is used in preference to culture, since it signals the contestations over the constitution of meaning more effectively. A fourth domain of violence is added since inter-personal violence is so important in the constitution of gender and minority ethnic relations and organized military violence is so important in the formation of nations and states.

It is necessary to theorize the full ontological depth of each regime of inequality. Rather than there being merely a single base to each regime of inequality, there is a much deeper ontology, including all four institutional domains of economy, polity, violence, and civil society, and all levels of abstraction, including macro, meso, and micro. The implication of this is that within each institutional domain (economy, polity, violence, civil society), there are multiple coexisting sets of social relations (e.g. gender, class, and ethnicity). All institutionalized domains and all regimes of inequality are conceptualized as systems and not parts of systems; domains are one type of system, regimes another.

Only with this analytic separation between regimes of social relations of inequality and institutional domains is it possible to theorize the complex articulation of different forms of social relations, of class, gender, and ethnicity, within any given institutional domain. Each set of social relations is present in each of the institutional domains of economy, polity, violence, and civil society. The distinction between relational and institutional systems allows for the theoretical possibility of there being more than one set of social relations within any particular social institution or domain. This enables the theorization of social relations of gender, of class, and of ethnicity operating and interacting simultaneously within the institutionalized domain of the economy without conflating or reducing one to another.

Why is this approach not generally seen as an available theoretical solution? This new approach requires the theorization of multiple sets of social relations in the same institutional domain, but pre-complexity systems theory makes this unavailable as a theoretical option. It requires a concept of system that does not insist that it necessarily saturates its territory, but pre-complexity systems theory does not allow that. Instead it requires a concept of system that allows for more than one set of social relations in the economy (and other domains) without insisting on a nested hierarchy, in which all non-class relations were theoretically subordinated to class – but old systems theory does not allow that either. It requires a concept of system that does not insist that gender has an institutionally different base (e.g. culture, family) from that of class (rooted in the economic), but allows both class and gender to have ontological depth, each constituted in all these domains – but the old systems theory does not allow for that either. The attempt to theorize simultaneously multiple inequalities without an necessarily hierarchical and nested relationship between them puts pressure on the old conceptualization of system. It is stretched to breaking point.

In Sociology over the last three decades only a little work has been done developing the concept of system. This is at least partly as a result of the trenchant rejection of both Parsonian structural-functionalism and of Marxism, each of which had contributed systems-based thinking to Sociology. In the avalanche of criticism of 'meta-narratives' (Lyotard 1978), and the turn to a postmodernist frame of reference, there was little enthusiasm in the mainstream of the discipline for development of the concept of system. So the development and refining of the concept, which had been taking place within both functionalism (Smelser 1959; Merton 1968; Alexander 1984) and Marxism (Althusser 1971; Poulantzas 1973), slowed significantly, although there are exceptions (Luhmann 1995; Chase-Dunn 1998; Jessop 2002). In order to address the development of the concept of system it is necessary to draw on the development of the concept of system within complexity theory.

System and its Environment: Over-Lapping, Non-Saturating, Non-Nested Systems

In order to make the analytic separation of regimes and domains needed to theorize the ontological depth of each regime in each domain, and to theorize the mutual adaptation of different regimes within each domain, it is necessary to re-think the concept of social system. It is necessary to move away from the traditional notion of a system as being made up of its parts, and to have a more flexible way of theorizing the relationship between regimes and domains.

The distinction between system and environment is disarmingly simple, but it is key to a series of revisions that enable greater flexibility in the conceptualization of systems. It enables the notion that each system takes all other systems as its environment (Bertalanffy 1968). This makes it possible to go beyond the old notion that the parts of a system make up the whole. It allows for the identification of 'social systems' not only at the level of 'society', but also at lower levels of abstraction and aggregation (Luhmann 1985, 1995, 2000). Each social system (whether the economy, polity, violence, or civil society) takes all other systems as its environment. Likewise each set of social relations (e.g. gender, ethnicity, class) is a system, taking all others as its environment.

This distinction between a system and its environment does not entail a presumption of hierarchy between inter-connected phenomena; rather hierarchy is a special case of differentiated systems. This makes for a more flexible conceptualization, providing the opportunity to avoid rigidities such as that of 'part and whole' (Parsons 1951) and of 'base-superstructure' (Marx and Engels 1967), as well as the ambiguities of 'relative autonomy' (Althusser 1971), which involve some kind of hierarchical relationship between nested sub-parts of a system. The sub-systems in Parsons' (1951) formulation are a particularly rigid example of this. Within Marxist systems theory there were two interpretations of the formulation. The simpler and more popular version was that of a base-superstructure model, in which the economic base determined the political and cultural superstructure. A more complex interpretation was that of Althusser's relative autonomy, that removed the simple hierarchy of these elements making it a relative hierarchy. This in turn raised the question of the degree of autonomy entailed without unduly stretching the notion of the relative hierarchy of the elements. In this new approach, social systems are mutually adaptive, influencing how each develops, though without the loss of their specific identities. The nature of the relationship between the domains of the economy, polity, violence, and civil society is not given a priori in theory, but is to be ascertained in the analysis of actual situations, leaving open, at this theoretical level, the relationship between these domains. These are empirically investigated in later chapters of this book.

Each of the regimes of inequality has a specific temporal and spatial reach. These social systems overlap in some times and places, but are not necessarily congruent. For example, the reach of a specific form of gender regime is not necessarily the same as that of a specific form of capitalism. Each institutional domain has a specific temporal and spatial reach. The specificity of the temporal and spatial reach of each domain and regime is linked to its independence as a system. The differences between the temporal and spatial reach of various regimes and domains are contingent.

The different temporal and spatial reach of a range of cultural 'scapes' – ethnoscapes (persons), mediascapes, technoscapes (technology), finanscapes (global capital), ideoscapes – has already been noted (Lash and Urry 1994; Appadurai 1996). This argument is taken further here, since it is also applied to polities, violence, and economies. The different spatial reach is not the same as deterritorialization, in which space loses its social significance (Brenner 1999; Scholte 2000) since space remains important (Harvey 1989; Sassen 2001); rather it is a different way of thinking of the changing relevance of space.

One set of social relations rarely saturates a given institutional domain or territory. Instead, different regimes of inequality coexist within institutions and within countries. This lack of saturation is a necessary part of the conceptualization of simultaneously existing multiple forms of inequality. Further, a single institution, even a polity, rarely saturates the domain or territory in which it operates. Rather several institutions may coexist, maybe in cooperation, or competition, or both. They may overlap, not sharing the same spatial or temporal boundaries. Social systems institutions should be conceived as non-saturating any given territory; they are porous and web-like (cf. Simmel 1955) rather than dense solids. The lack of saturation of any field by a single set of social relations or a single social institution opens the theoretical agenda that has been prematurely closed by traditional systems thinking. It allows the possibility of an analysis of multiple simultaneous complex inequalities while retaining concepts of social system.

The relationship between these domains is non-nested, since there is no presumption that there is a specific set of determinant inter-connections between them. This position is allowed for by the use of the system/environment distinction. In some circumstances the domains may be nested but not in others. Sociological conceptions of systems have often over-stated the extent to which systems are nested. For example, the notion of a 'society' in the modern era is widely presumed to be a nation-state that contains nested economic, political, and cultural systems (Giddens 1990), but this is theoretically and empirically erroneous.

Rather than looking for and analyzing the function of a part for the reproduction of the whole 'society', here there is the absence of the assumption that systems are nested. Rather the extent of the coherence is a question for empirical research. The institutional domains of economy, polity, violence, and civil society may have a different spatial and temporal reach. The different regimes of inequality may also have a different spatial and temporal reach.

Awareness of globalization has disrupted conventional accounts of neatly bounded, separated, and endogenously determined societies. The simple conception of society as constituted by spatially and temporally congruent structures of the economy, polity, and civil society is rejected on the grounds that such congruency is rarely if ever achieved. This has a series of implications, including the over-lapping nature of systems of social inequality, the non-saturation of a territory by a system, including by a polity, and the non-nested nature of systems. In turn these imply a more nuanced understanding of the relationship between social relations and space: there is neither the complete monopoly of a space by one set of social relations, nor the elimination of the relevance of space.

Societalization not Societies

Fully formed societies in which there is a congruence of the economy, polity, violence, and civil society in a specific territory are very rare. Social systems of gender, class, and ethnicity do not simply map onto each other, are not congruent, in the same territory. They will often have different temporal and spatial reach. There are often competing principles of social organization, and a lack of congruence of the domains. There are many processes that lead towards the creation of a society but they rarely fully achieve this form before they are interrupted.

Societalization is the process of moving towards a 'society'. The term refers to a process of change, rather than to an end state. The concept is fleetingly introduced by Weber to capture the movement towards a coherent and cohesive set of social and political arrangements. 'Bureaucracy is *the* means of carrying "community action" over into rationally ordered "societal action". Therefore, as an instrument of "societalizing" relations of power, bureaucracy has been and is a power instrument of the first order' (Weber 1948: 228). 'Concerning "classes", "status groups", and "parties", it must be said in general that they necessarily presuppose a comprehensive societalization, and especially a political framework within which they operate' (Weber 1948: 195). However, Weber does little to develop the concept further. Jessop (2002) uses the concept of societalization to capture the development of capitalism, based on the principle of accumulation, which he calls 'bourgeois societalization'. He draws variously on the development of the market, imposition of economizing logic in non-economic areas, the ecological dominance of capitalist economy (as opposed perhaps to legality or religion), and economic hegemony, and in each instance faces down opposition and resistance.

Here, the concept of societalization is used to capture the tendency to move towards congruence of the domains of the economy, polity, violence, and civil society, but with no expectation that this movement is ever completed at any specific time. The complete congruence of these domains within a given territory could be described as a 'society'. However, such complete congruence is rarely if ever achieved. There is often a process of 'societalization', that is, a movement, over time, towards the formation of a society, but this is rarely completed because there are often rival bases for the achievement of such congruence.

Most countries will contain more than one societalization project. These may be of several different kinds, for example, a nation that would be a nation-state, an emerging hegemon such as the European Union, 'Westernization', neoliberalism, social democracy, a particular religion. Each project provides a focal point around which other domains can be brought into alignment. For example, a nation may seek to establish a state for itself that would secure the political conditions for the alignment of economic and civil societal systems around the values and practices of that nation. Since there are many more nations than there are states, it is clear that many nations never complete this agenda of societalization.

The process of societalization involves the restructuring of these institutional domains and regimes of complex inequalities, bringing them towards alignment. If there were to be complete congruence of these systems, (both institutional domains and regimes of inequality) in a specific territory this would then be a 'society'. A focus on globalization makes it clearer than previously that the social systems that are institutional domains and regimes of inequality are rarely in sufficient alignment to be appropriately called a society, but the phenomenon of the rarity of fully formed societies is not itself new.

Emergence and Projects

The concepts of 'emergence' and 'project' are used to avoid the pitfalls of reductionism while retaining explanatory power and they are developed drawing on complexity theory. Complexity offers a re-framing of the debate about the importance of a non-reductive analytic strategy, a way of going beyond the unfortunate choice of macro or micro levels of analysis.

Much traditional science, both natural and social, has had a preference for a single level of analysis, a tendency to search for connections that reach back to one fundamental level (Rose 1997). The search for general theory in traditional scientific thought in many disciplines has often involved a process of reducing complex phenomena to simpler ones. This may involve either a reduction downwards to ever smaller units of analysis as in the movement from organisms to cells to genes in modern biology (Rose 1997) or in the methodological individualism of rational choice theory (Coleman 1990; Kiser and Hechter 1991; Goldthorpe 2000), or it may involve a reduction upwards, as in much structuralist thought in the social sciences (Parsons 1951; Althusser 1971). By contrast, other schools of sociology reject these ambitions for a general explanation by means of reduction, sometimes by staying close to the meaning of human actors (Smith 1987) and sometimes by privileging thick rich descriptions over the search for causal explanation. This forced choice between levels of analysis is a significant limitation on explanations. The challenge is to find a way that allows a more effective combination in a richer explanatory account.

This problem has often been expressed in social theory in a tendency to focus on either structure or agency. Traditional social systems theory has been criticized for its inability to theorize agency (Thomson 1963), a longstanding issue in social theory (Marx 1954; Durkheim 1966; Alexander 1984; Archer 1995; Sayer 2000b; Goldthorpe 2000). In classical social theory, both the Durkheimian and Marxist traditions found ways to theorize this relationship between the individual and society without reducing one to the other. In contemporary debates this has come to be seen as more of a challenge. There is a challenge to a macro level analysis to pay adequate attention to the significance of individual and collective agents, as well as a challenge to the analysis of individuals to situate them sufficiently in a structural context. There is a tendency to let either structure (Althusser 1971) or agency (Coleman 1990) take analytic priority. But in the recognition of agency there is a tendency to essentialize the agent. Although Butler's (1990) response to this, in which gender is tenuously constituted through performance and a stylized repetition of actions, involves such an extreme form of destabilization that she is unable to account for the extent of the actually existing stability of gender inequality. Theorists of gender relations have argued for the importance of avoiding the notion that women were victims of oppressive structures and for the significance of attributing them with agency (Hakim 1991; Pollert 1996). There is a tendency to theorize different sets of social relations at different levels of abstraction: a review of introductory sociology textbooks found a tendency for the theorization of class to take place at a macro level (e.g. national economy), ethnicity at a meso level (e.g. group behaviour, segregation) and gender only at micro levels (e.g. socialization) (Ferree and Hall 1996).

In a different approach, Mead (1934) analyses the relationship between the 'I' and the 'me', which provides the basic elements of the system of the individual, which is coupled to other social systems through the accumulation of experience of this in the 'me'. In Mead's account 'I' is never reduced to 'me', a distinction that allows for, indeed requires, reflexivity. Reflexivity is constituted by the dynamic relationship between the 'I' and 'me', in which the moment of performance of 'I' draws on the accumulated memory of the experience of the social in 'me'. It is a mistake to assume that the concept of system leads to the treatment of the individual as a mere cipher. Each individual constitutes a reflexive system constituted by the relation between the I and the me. The interactions between individuals and collectivities involve the active negotiation and struggle over meaning; social systems emerge from these actions but they are not reducible to these. The concept of emergence captures this non-reductionist relationship between individuals and society.

A further disadvantage in the use of the concept of agency is when it is reserved to individuals. This is a mistake. Not only are there collective actors, such as trade unions and activist organizations in civil society, but meaning is also not produced by individuals but is the subject of collective struggle and negotiation. The ability to determine the dominant interpretation, or to create hegemony, is a matter of power and not only ideas (Gramsci 1971). Some of these may be non-cognitive cultural practices, such as music, in the creation of new individual and collective practices (Eyerman and Jamieson 1998), as well as highly cognitive practices of argumentation.

There is a challenge to social theory to combine or balance structure and agency rather than to choose just one as the priority level of analysis (Giddens 1984; Mouzelis 1993). Giddens (1984) attempts to overcome the potential impasse in social theory over structure and agency by arguing that they constitute a duality as merely the opposite sides of the same coin. Giddens (1984: 377) considers 'structures' to be 'rule-resource sets, implicated in the institutional articulation of social systems', and as 'rules and resources, recursively implicated in the reproduction of social systems'. He sought to theorize human reflexivity, although there is a tension in his work as to whether this is an intrinsic characteristic of all human beings (as in his early work; see 1984) or whether it is confined to modernity (his later work; see 1991, 1992). He sought to avoid both upward reductionism to structure and downward reductionism to individual agents. However, his critics find a tendency towards a central conflation of structure and agency (Archer 1995), as indicated by his notion of the 'duality' rather than 'dualism' of structure and agency, and of insufficient analytic separation of the two to enable a grasp of the shorter time scales of agency as compared with structure (Mouzelis 1993, 1995; Archer 1995).

The concept of emergence can be used to address the challenge to theorize the relationship between individuals and society. The concept of emergence links different levels in a system, especially the levels of individual, structure, and system (Sawyer 2005). It enables the thinking of the simultaneous 'existence' of each level. It does not necessarily privilege one over the other, rather they can be recognized as coexisting and linked. Each level has different patterns and can be subject to different kinds of theorization. Patterns at 'higher' levels can emerge in ways that are hard to predict at the 'lower' levels. The challenge long-addressed in Sociology is how such levels are to be linked. This question of the nature of 'emergence' has been framed in a variety of ways including those of 'macro-micro linkage', 'individual and society', the 'problem of order' (Alexander 1982), and 'structure, action, and structuration' (Giddens 1984). There have been many who have sought to integrate a concern with individual social action with a concern with macro level social forms, from Habermas (1987, 1991) and his theory of both communicative action and steering systems and Bourdieu (1984) and his concern with habitus, capital and field to Giddens's (1984) structuration theory. These attempts to deal with the micro-macro relation are involved with the process of 'emergence', of patterning at the macro level despite enormous complexity at the level of individual actors.

The concept of emergence addresses the relationship between different levels, so as to solve the potential problem of reductionism to either the individual or higher level of the system. The emergentist approach constitutes a fundamental rejection of the reductionism found in many types of natural and social science. The tendency to reduce – to seek the key explanation, at ever smaller units, whether individuals constituted as agents in social theory or genes in biological science – is rejected. Also rejected is any tendency to reduce in an upward direction, to a holism that ignores individuals or an ecology that ignores organisms. Rather than treating a system as reducible to its parts, a higher level emerges from the activities of lower levels of systems (Holland 1995), though whether this is better thought of as top down is the subject of debate (Conte and Gilbert 1995; Gilbert 1995; Epstein 1999; Holland 2000). The problematic tendency towards either upward conflation to a high systemic level or conflation or reduction can be addressed using this formulation.

The concept of emergence offers a way of surpassing this polarization by the development of ontological depth that is not at the expense of explanatory power. Emergence refers to the way in which social systems emerge from the multiple actions of individuals, but are not reducible to them. It connects the different levels of abstraction in the analysis without reductionism. The concept of emergence allows for the non-reductive linkage between levels, facilitating the linking of a focus on human reflexivity to social systems. This facilitates the development of some of the concerns of classical social theory, such as combining an understanding of both individual and social structure in a way that does not deny the significance of the self-reflexivity of the human subject while also theorizing changes in the social totality.

In this respect, complexity theory has many parallels with the development of realism in sociological thought (Bhaskar 1979, 1997; Archer 1995; Sayer 2000b; Bunge 2001; Elder-Vaas 2007). Much complexity theory has as a core assumption the importance of ontological depth, of levels that are linked within a system, and that the relationships in one level are not reducible in any simple manner to those in another. This recognizes that each level contains the objects that are present in the other levels, but that they can be analysed differently. It is not so much that the whole is greater than the parts as that it is different from the parts. Examples from biology include that many cells together constitute a living organism; that many individual beasts together constitute a species; that several different species in the same habitat constitute an ecological system (Capra 1997; Rose 1997). Within social science examples include: that individuals living together constitute a household; that individuals working together constitute an organization; that many citizens constitute a nation. The concerns of social science theory thus significantly overlap with those of complexity theory, even as the latter has developed a specialized vocabulary of concepts. The interweaving of the concerns of classic Sociological theory with that of complexity theory has the potential to move both bodies of theory forward. A major strength of most classical Sociology is its ontological depth in that it engages analytically with both individuals and social institutions and often several further ontological levels within a single explanatory framework. Complexity theory facilitates the invoking and developing of these strengths of classical sociology.

The concept of project is an additional concept developed here to capture the collective rather than the individualistic processes in the creation of meaning. Projects are processes within civil society that create new meanings and social goals and are rooted in collective action, meanwhile drawing on a wide range of rhetorical and material resources. Projects involve an orientation to change and this may be achieved in many ways. The concept of project is different from that of social movement, in that it can be more stably based in civil society. A project is not the expression of stable essentialized identities, rather it involves the social reconstitution of subjects through joint activities and discussions. Projects can be transformative processes.

Bodies, Technologies and the Social

While bodies and technologies are important for the analysis of complex inequalities and globalization, they are unevenly incorporated into social theory. In some kinds of social theory, concepts of agency and social structure have developed which scrupulously exclude the body and the machine from the concepts associated with the causation of social processes (Giddens 1984). This 'humanism' has a long tradition, for example, in the work of Durkheim, in which social facts were considered to cause other social facts (Durkheim 1966). The development of Sociology as an academic discipline involved the specification of a field of study of its own. This often involved the rejection of adjacent areas and modes of analysis. In particular it involved the rejection of biology (Benton 1993; Turner 1999), and of psychology (Durkheim 1966). Durkheim's concepts of social fact and social structure excluded the biological and technological. He was so focused on demonstrating that there was a specific terrain of the social on which a system of thought, an intellectual discipline, could be built that issues of bodies and technology were, like the psychological, pushed outside his system of thought. For example, in *Suicide* he argued for the importance of the social in explaining something as apparently as individual as suicide rather than through individual psychologies.

Many forms of social practice involve bodies and technologies. Inter-personal violence has been an important form of dominance in both gender (Mooney 2000) and ethnic relations (Shapiro 1988), involving the deployment of bodies in patterns of coercion. Gender relations involve sexuality, reproduction, and fertility (Stanworth 1987), invoking not only bodies but also the technologies that alter them. The analysis of disability requires an understanding of bodies and the extent to which technology affects the capacity to act (Barnes et al. 1999), as do processes of ageing. The development of new economic forms often involves new technologies and machines, not least in the development of new information and communication technologies associated with globalization (Castells 1996).

Once bodies and technological phenomena are extruded from core sociological conceptions of agency and structure, it is hard to re-integrate them. It has proved difficult to achieve a more adequate integration of the bodily into the social that does not simply assimilate one to the other, so that it is neither under- nor over-socialized. Nevertheless, there are several routes by which this integration of bodies, objects, and technology with the social may proceed.

Not all classic sociologists exclude technology and nature from their core concepts. Marx (1954) achieved some inclusion via his concept of the forces of production that, together with the relations of production, constituted the mode of production. In this way the methods by which nature was appropriated were located within the core explanatory mechanism of his theory. However, with some exceptions (Macnaghten and Urry 1998), this theoretical insight and practice are rarely recognized in contemporary attempts to put nature back into sociology (Benton 1993). A limitation of Marx here is the systematic inclusion of technology only within the economic domain, and not the polity or civil society. Further, his approach to reproduction and gender lacks subtlety, falling back on static naturalistic conceptions of gender relations. While Engels (1940) provided a more dynamic account of the changing relations of production and reproduction and the consequent changes in the balance of power between the sexes, this tends to essentialize gender relations through his utilization of an unduly simple base-superstructure model of causation.

Many radical feminists positioned bodies and technology centrally within their analyses of gender inequality. This included the analysis of reproduction by Firestone (1974), sexuality by MacKinnon (1989), and violence by Daly (1978). For example, Firestone discussed the extent to which new forms of technology might be created and used as a way of overcoming the disadvantages women faced as a result of biological difference in relation to reproduction and associated childcare. However, these accounts were fiercely criticized for reductionism, biologism, essentialism, and technological determinism (Segal 1987; Spellman 1988). In practice, these radical feminist accounts included descriptions of alternative inter-connections of social and biological practices, in particular, the social possibilities that would result if women were to act collectively and politically change the conditions of their existence, so these texts did not constitute simple forms of biological reductionism. Nevertheless, the use of an implicit (Daly 1978) or explicit (Firestone 1974) base-superstructure model of causation did limit the extent to which they were able to theorize the variations in the forms of gender relations. Feminist writers continue to grapple in various ways with the relationship of the body, biology, and gender (Fausto-Sterling 1985; Keller 1985; Martin 1987; Jacobus et al. 1990; Strathern 1992; Moore 1994; Witz 2000).

Foucault's (1979, 1997) writings on the disciplining of sexuality and the body attempted the re-insertion of bodies into sociology through the concept of discourse. Foucault's work inspired many attempts to develop this line of analysis on the significance and regulation of the body, some in a social context (Turner 1987, 1992, 1996; Shilling 1993; Rose 1996), others in a more cultural direction, attempting to read the body as if it were a text (Bordo 1993) and technology as if it were a form of literature or a code (Haraway 1997). A drawback here is the tendency to underestimate the importance of physicality and emotionality (Turner 1987; Williams 1998).

A focus on the social shaping of technology in the economy has provided a series of rich accounts about the relationship between the social and technology (Wajcman 1991; Cockburn and Omrod 1993; Wajcman and MacKenzie 1999). In this approach, technology is seen as shaped by social relations, rather than technology determining social relations. The development of technology is significantly affected by the social context in which this occurs. In this perspective, technology and the social are two mutually exclusive concepts, even though each has an impact on the other. The strength of this work has been the recognition of the impact of the social on the technological.

A further approach to the dilemma as to how to include objects within social theory, developed by Latour (1987, 1988, 1991), together with Law (1991), Callon (1991), and Callon et al. (1986), is to re-think the insistence that only humans can act. Rather than treating objects as necessarily outside the dynamics of social causation, this approach includes both humans and objects in the networks and assemblages that are actants, rejecting the exclusion of the physical. Instead of an exclusive focus on humans as actors, actants are constituted of networks of people and objects. A person rarely acts alone, but a person and object together constitute an actant. For example, a man with a gun is a different actant from a man without a gun. Purity, or the separation of humans and objects, does not exist; we have never been modern, that is, pure (Latour 1993). This does not mean symmetry between humans and objects; there can often be asymmetry in these networks since machines usually have a smaller, narrower range than a human (Suchman 2001).

The strength of Latour's approach is to enable the inclusion of objects and technologies in social theory. Its weakness is the restriction of the analysis to actants and networks and the absence of larger concepts that might position actants within structures and systems. For example, the 'man with gun' only makes sense in relation to a system of violence as in 'crime' or in 'war'. Network can be a rather thin concept to capture the ontological depth involved in the interaction of the various systems in which these actants are embedded.

Haraway's work also challenges the conventional boundary between human and non-human, demonstrating the way in which human bodies have already become cyborgs in the sense that they function only with technology (Haraway 1990). Her focus is on the traffic in metaphor between human and non-human contexts, treating science to the same kind of analysis as a literary text, for example analysing the two-way movements in metaphor between the analysis of human society and primate society (Haraway 1989, 1997). A further example of a system that involves assemblages of both humans and technologies is that of the car system. A car system cannot be understood outside of drivers, roads, and the motor industry (Urry 2004, 2007).

While knowledge has often been considered to be quintessentially human, in modern economies knowledge may in fact be encoded and embedded in organizations and technical systems as well as in human beings. Knowledge may be not only embodied (as in practical skills) and embrained (as when learnt in formal settings), but it may also be encoded (within organizational practices) and embedded (in routines and systems) (Lam 2002). For example, in the call centre industry knowledge is held not only by individual workers, but is also encoded and embedded in the software and technical systems used in order to address the information needs of callers (Durbin 2004, 2007). It may be relevant to speak of the call centre as the actant, or of the call centre worker plus their computer system, since the person answering the phone does not act without a system of machinery. The processes by which knowledge is developed, especially in the move from tacit to explicit forms, are key to the development of contemporary knowledge economies (Nonaka and Takeuchi 1995; Nonaka and Nishiguchi 2001; Nishikawa and Tanaka 2007).

The restricted humanistic conception of agency is rejected here and replaced by a concept of an actant as an assemblage that may include objects, technologies, and bodies. However, actor-network theory is insufficient to grasp the ontological depth of the various systems involved. Technologies are part of the forces of production that are included within the concept of the economy and other domains; they are important for the analysis of globalization. Bodies are included as constitutive parts of actants, and as key to childbearing, as part of the forces of production. Violence is also a form that is not simply reducible to humanist concerns. Both mechanical weapons and bodies as weapons are significant in the understanding of power. These are relevant not only in relation to states, which in modernity seek to monopolize legitimate coercion in their territory, but also in relation to inter-personal violence and forms of group violence that the state does not effectively criminalize. This is important for the analysis of complex inequalities, especially those of gender and ethnicity.

Path Dependency

There is a tension in social theory between a search for explanations with the greatest power and range, and a concern with accuracy and detail about particularities (Haraway 1988; Kiser and Hechter 1991; Sayer 1997, 2000b; Calhoun 1998; Goldthorpe 2000; Walby 2001a, 2001b). This tension is prominent in the debates as to whether there is a single driving logic behind the development of modernity or whether there are divergent varieties of modernity. Do critical turning points into distinct pathways of development contradict the notion of a universal explanatory framework, or can such differences be accommodated, even explained, within it? How significant and resilient are path dependent developments: does globalization mean that the differences between varieties of modernity are being eroded, resulting in convergence? The concept of path dependency is a bridge between a social theory that searches for general explanations and one that seeks to account for particularity.

There are several questions about the nature, theorization, and application of the concept of path dependency (Somers 1998; Mahoney 2000). These include: the nature of path dependency and the extent to which divergent paths are sustained over significant periods of time; the nature of critical turning points and tipping points; the implications of the notion that small causes can have large effects; the development of the concept of feedback loops to include positive as well as negative feedback loops, and the concepts of catalysts and dampeners; the nature of the processes that lock-in a new path; the nature and implications of temporality and sequencing in path dependency. A discussion of these issues is followed by three examples of the use and debate on path dependency in social theory. It concludes with the key questions for path dependency analysis in this book.

There are many potential examples of path dependency, and many more that are disputed. In this book the main substantive issue addressed with the concept of path dependency is that of the development of varieties of modernity, especially neoliberalism and social democracy, and their maintenance in the face of global pressures. Analysis of path dependency has been significantly developed not only within social science (Nee and Cao 1999; Mahoney 2000; Pierson 2000), but also within transdisciplinary debates on complexity theory (Waldrop 1992; Capra 1997). Within the natural sciences the example that is often cited (or imagined) is that of a small disturbance to the atmosphere in one location, perhaps as small as the flapping of a butterfly's wings, tipping the balance of other systems and leading ultimately to a storm on the other side of the globe (Capra 1997). A key example in the economic literature on complexity is that of the development of the QWERTY keyboard rather than the more efficient DVORAK alternative as a consequence of a small but key event in the development of typewriters (David 1985; Arthur 1989). Further examples include the use of VHS rather than Beta for videotapes, and the steel and petroleum car rather than electric cars and other modes of transportation (Waldrop 1992; Urry 2004).

However, there is a debate over the existence, nature, and significance of such turning points and alternative paths of development. On the one hand they may be deviations which are minor, or rare, or temporary, and in which there is an eventual returning to the main path (Liebowitz and Margolis 1995). Or they may be very significant, leading to permanently different trajectories (David 1985; Arthur 1989; Waldrop 1992). For example, whether the changes in post-1989 central and eastern Europe 'transitions' might be understood as these countries returning to the main form of capitalist development or whether they may be considered as undergoing 'transformations' to a new pathway. There is a question as to whether the concept of path dependency is too rigid, with insufficient regard for later changes as a consequence of new circumstances (Crouch 2001). There are

80

implications for the possibility of general theory, in particular whether too many contingent turning points or too complex a set of sequencing destroys this possibility (Kiser and Hechter 1991).

Liebowitz and Margolis (1995) argue that the case for path dependency within economics has been much over-stated. They distinguish between three forms of the argument, which have different implications. First, the path followed may not be sub-optimal and thus not in contradiction of neoclassical assumptions. Second, that it was unknowable whether or not the path was sub-optimal or not at the time that the path was chosen, and thus not in contradiction of neoclassical assumptions. Third, that while the path was sub-optimal, there was no movement to a more optimal path. They suggest that only the third constitutes a serious challenge to neoclassical economics; yet there is often elision between the three models, with a case based on one of the first two being represented falsely as if it were an example of the third. This, they argue, is illustrated by frequent recourse to a very limited number of examples, examples which they think are anyway questionable in that there were reasons by which the preferences could be accounted for within mainstream economic theory. While there may be exceptional circumstances as to why the most effective technology is not implemented at the outset, the institutions of the market will eventually lead to investment in the most effective technology, and an adjustment will occur. This leaves the issue as one that is open to empirical investigation. Do the mechanisms of economic markets eventually, and in the long run, prove dominant over initial choices, and indeed over political institutions?

This question of the extent to which distinct paths of development are sustainable in the long run and not just the short run is a key issue in many debates about the nature of globalization (Held et al. 1999). Complexity theory re-frames these debates about globalization in terms of the sustainability of path dependent forms over the long run. A central question is whether economic pressures that are increasingly constituted at a global level will transform local political formations, or whether locally specific paths of development are and can be self-sustaining (Castells 1996, 1997, 1998; Crouch and Streeck 1997; Pierson 2001). On the one hand it is argued that global economic forms will dominate, that is, universalist processes will overcome path dependent forms of nation-state economic and political regulations (Ohmae 1990, 1995; Crouch and Streeck 1997; Martin and Schumann 1997). On the other hand, the continued existence of varieties of capitalism (Hall and Soskice 2001) and distinct welfare state regimes (Esping-Andersen 1990) depends upon the resilience of path dependent processes. Pierson (2001) argues that mature welfare states have self-reinforcing processes over extended periods of time, not least as a result of shifting the framework within which actors construct and understand their own interests. Swank (2002) demonstrates that some types of polity are better able to sustain welfare expenditures than others; in particular those of a more social democratic form sustain state provision to a greater extent than polities of a more liberal form. The implication here is that some forms of lock-in of paths of development are more robust than others and that path dependent forms of development can themselves be revised. The extent of path dependency is thus at least partly a question for empirical investigation, so Chapter 8 is an empirical identification of the varieties of modernity.

A critical turning point is a key moment when there is a sudden change in a system, taking it onto a new path of development. This occurs when the system has become unstable and far from equilibrium. A specific sub-type of a critical turning point is a 'tipping point', in which a slow build up leaves the system vulnerable to sudden change if the next small event were to occur (Gladwell 2000). This may be because the threshold for a 'critical mass' has been reached (Ball 2004). In each instance small events lead to the formation of distinct new paths of development.

There is a debate as to whether the critical turning point should be conceptualized as 'contingent' since it is not usually explicable within the larger theoretical framework. While the contingency of the event that starts a particular path of development is assumed or asserted by many writers on path dependency (Arthur 1989; Mahoney 2000; Pierson 2000), this is both an unnecessary and a problematic feature of the current dominant conceptualization of this process. Mahoney (2000: 507), for example, goes as far as to make this contingency a key part of this definition of path dependence, as 'those historical sequences in which contingent events set into motion institutional patterns or event chains that have deterministic properties'. He understands contingency to mean 'the inability of theory to predict or explain, either deterministically or probabilistically, the occurrence of a specific outcome' (Mahoney 2000: 513). The limitation of this approach is its deliberate incompleteness. This approach rejects what might be considered to be one of the strengths of those interpretations of complexity thinking that locates such critical events as emergent bifurcations of an unstable system far from equilibrium. Mahoney (2000) leaves the wider system dynamics out of analytic focus and hence severely under-utilizes the explanatory potential of the concept of path dependency within complexity theory. The sociological theory on revolutions and political crises (Moore 1966; Skocpol 1979; Korpi 1983; Esping-Andersen 1990) does not have such self-limiting ordinances. Rather, in the work of these writers, 'critical junctures' 'emerge' from their analysis of social 'systems'. It is by deploying a strong sense of 'system' that these writers are able to explain why certain events become 'critical'.

These events may be apparently small occurrences, but it is by locating them within an explanatory account of social and political pressures within a social system that these writers are able to explain their 'criticality'. In short, the level of 'system' is an essential component of a full and satisfactory explanation of 'path dependency'. Without a concept of system the critical junctures become merely 'contingent', resulting in the ensuing explanation remaining merely partial. This sociological literature of revolutions and political turning points encompasses a theorization not only of 'normal' development, but also of the build-up of various pressures into the critical political juncture, and of the explanation as to which pathway from a series of possibilities is taken. This typically involves explanations at different levels of abstraction, including not only individuals but also institutions, structures, process, and the level of the system as a whole. This concern with the different levels and their interconnections is re-framed by the concept of emergence.

A further conceptual addition is proposed to the concept of a critical turning point: 'catalysts and dampeners'. Two social systems each on trajectories of transformation may change at different rates. There may be factors that speed or 'catalyse' the rate of change while others slow or 'dampen' the rate. They may not independently change the nature of the system, other than its rate of change. Certain forms of polity speed or catalyse economic development, while others slow or dampen economic development. The concepts of catalysts and dampeners draw on the conception of positive feedback within a system as part of this. This distinction between those institutions that catalyse and those than dampen development goes beyond the rather static conception of lock-in and path dependency that has developed. An example of a catalyst is a wave of new practices from another place, although this may not always function to catalyse change. An example of a dampener might be the religious regulation of women's domestic role, though again this may not always function in this way. The different rates of change may have implications for the relationship of systems to other systems, perhaps altering the balance of power in determining the fitness landscape. This may change the way that systems coevolve. For example, a higher rate of economic growth in one country as compared to another may alter the resources they have available to bargain as to the nature of global regulations.

Crucial to the notion of a 'critical turning point' is that the event that precipitates one path of development rather than another is small in relation to the events that unfold as a consequence. Small changes at critical moments can have large effects on unstable systems far from equilibrium. These changes may be sudden, akin to processes of saltation, as a moment of crystallization of a new structure and form. The smallness of the event that precipitates these large-scale changes is disproportionate, and hence inconsistent with some conventional accounts of causality which assume proportionality between cause and effect. It is outside simple forms of mathematical modelling based on linearity, being instead non-linear (Kauffman 1993, 1995; Gladwell 2000). Critical turning points between paths of development thus challenge certain assumptions about the linearity of causal connections (Capra 1997; Mahoney 2000; Pierson 2000). The lack of a directly proportionate linear relationship between cause and effect is troublesome for conventional science and its associated mathematics (Abbot 2001; Byrne 2002). Complexity theory emphasizes the importance of non-linear changes, that small events can lead to large-scale changes in systems thereby precipitating new paths of development.

The notion of the lack of proportionality between the scale of an event and its consequences is a challenge to old conceptions of causation. Newtonian notions of general laws, which can be discovered by science, enable the identification of the cause of a specific event. This Newtonian conception of cause in which one phenomenon impacts on another in a one-way direction involves the notion of directly proportionate impact. Complexity theory has challenged the easy assumption that direct proportionality – linearity – is normal (Prigogine and Stengers 1984; Prigogine 1997). In statistical and graphical terms, a critical turning point means that that there is no simple linear relationship between phenomena, but rather one that is non-linear (Nicolis and Prigogine 1989; Byrne 2002). Conventional statistical analysis in particular is problematized by this challenge to the prevalence of linear relationships. In practice, many social analyses using modern statistics have utilized rather simple equations, assuming a direct proportionality, a linear relationship, between the changes in the size of the phenomena under investigation (Abbot 2001; Byrne 2002). This lack of direct proportionality is seen by Prigogine as a fundamental epistemological challenge to conventional conceptions of science (Prigogine and Stengers 1984; Nicolis and Prigogine 1989). However, while complexity theory challenges Newtonian conceptions of causation, this does not necessarily mean that analyses of causal pathways cannot ultimately be developed in many instances (Byrne 1998), but rather that they are much more difficult than previously thought. Since relations between phenomena are not simple their statistical modelling demands equations of enormous, non-linear, complexity. This is especially the case in relation to attempts to model positive rather than negative feedback loops in systems far from equilibrium (Arthur 1989). In some cases the complexity of the equations means that they cannot be solved using the traditional analytic method, and only the power of modern computers can lead to their solution. In others, the equations are too complicated to be soluble by existing resources. This means that while the phenomena may still be considered to be determined, equations modelling them are unspecifiable using contemporary techniques.

Old types of systems theory involved a presumption of a tendency to return to a single equilibrium point achieved through negative feedback loops. Later conceptions of systems based on complexity thinking include, indeed focus on, positive as well as negative feedback, and an interest in systems that are far from equilibrium and hence much more subject to rapid and radical change. Much sociological conceptualization of systems has been based on the early version of system theory that used the notion of negative feedback, which acted to stabilize a system and return it to equilibrium. For example, Giddens (1994) has a limited conception of feedback, which is primarily homeostatic, that is restoring a system to a state of equilibrium, while Parsons (1951) utilizes only negative, self-balancing, feedback loops, giving rise to excessive stability in the account of the system and difficulty in conceptualizing change. However, there have always been alternative views, including some interpretations of Marx.

The concept of feedback is central to the idea of a system (Bertalanffy 1968). A feedback loop is: 'a circular arrangement of causally connected elements, so that each element has an effect on the next, until the last "feeds back" the effect into the first element of the cycle' (Capra 1997: 56). A negative feedback loop entails a mechanism in which a change in one aspect of the system leads to a change in that mechanism which in turn leads to a change that restores the system to its original condition. A thermostat is an example of such a mechanism, responding to small changes in temperature so as to maintain the system at a near constant temperature. The concept of a negative feedback loop is associated with the notion of a system as tending towards equilibrium. Any change or perturbance to the system is met with a response internal to the system that restores it to the original state, that is, maintains equilibrium. A positive feedback loop, by contrast, is a mechanism that drives small changes in a system onwards, escalating change. Thus, rather than restoring a system to equilibrium positive feedback loops drive a system further away from equilibrium. The account of these positive feedback loops in economic systems (David 1985; Arthur 1989) profoundly challenged conventional economic analysis (Waldrop 1992), which had been predicated upon the assumptions of tendency to equilibrium and a declining return to investments.

Arthur (1989, 1994) demonstrated the significance of disequilibrium in explaining the dynamism of certain economies. He develops the understanding of the importance of positive, not just negative, feedback loops, in which increasing rather than decreasing returns to scale drive the system forward rather than returning it to equilibrium. Rather than the traditional notion that returns to an investment tail off, Arthur (1989) found that there could be increasing returns under specific circumstances. This is a radical challenge to the neoclassical paradigm since it posits the notion that there can be multiple rather than a singular equilibrium point; that it is possible for systems to be in equilibrium in more than one position. This concept of increasing returns to scale implies a positive rather than a negative feedback loop within the system. He argues further that the events that precipitate a shift in the system may occur as if by chance, and that the earlier they occur in a series of events the more important they may be. These developments in systems theory challenge not only conventional economic analysis, but also those sociological conceptions of system that assume a tendency to return to equilibrium. The notion of positive feedback underpins radically different conceptions of change as compared with that of negative feedback.

It is necessary to explain why, once a new path of development has begun, it is continued rather than returning to the previous form of development. Institutions lock-in the different paths of development through a series of feedback processes. Within economic theory this is a significant departure from conventional theory, with the development of the analysis of the significance of institutions in economic life and not just individual rational actors. Institutions are important because of the significance of transaction costs and imperfect information and because institutions prioritize the interests of those with the power to set the rules on which they run (North 1990).

The process of this 'lock-in' to the new path of development is addressed through the concept of positive feedback and by recognition of the importance of institutions. In Arthur's (1994) account, lock-in was due to four main reasons: large set-up or fixed costs; learning effects; and coordination effects; and adaptive expectations (Arthur 1994) which could lock-in an initial small advantage. Under these circumstances profits and growth could escalate rather than diminish over time; a small economic advantage could turn into a large one in a non-linear fashion.

There are varying conceptions of the nature and means by which institutions lock-in the different paths of development. In the economic literature the focus has been on the significance of set-up costs, learning effects, coordination effects and adaptive expectations (Arthur 1994), reformulated as investments in learning, related technologies, standard setting and compatibility requirements by Rycroft and Kash (1999), while North (1990) focuses on issues of power and interests. Pierson (2000) argues that four features of political life make path dependency more likely than in economic life: the central role of collective action; the high density of institutions; political power; and intrinsic opacity and complexity. Mahoney (2000) distinguishes four approaches to the mechanisms of institutional reproduction: rational cost-benefit analysis of individual actors; functions for the overall system; elite power; and moral legitimation. These varied analyses point up the significance and yet the under-developed nature of the social scientific analysis of the institutions that lock-in paths of development.

The concept of path dependency requires and facilitates the inclusion of temporality and sequencing within social theory. Path dependency means that events that occur at one moment in time have consequences at later times and that the order in which events and developments occur has consequences. Path dependent processes can involve embedding the outcome of social events at one moment in time in an institution that endures over time, thus carrying the effect of the past into the present and future. A specific aspect of temporality in path dependency is that the factors present early on in a trajectory are likely to be more important than those that are present later. There is a presumption that the sequencing of events within a trajectory matters (Goldstone 1998; Haydu 1998).

There are many examples of path dependency processes. In addition to the examples discussed so far, the concept is useful in the analysis of the post-1989 developments in eastern and central Europe (Illner 1999; Nee and Cao 1999; Stompka 1999), the relationship between economic development and democracy, and the development of welfare regimes (Esping-Andersen 1999).

The question as to whether the post-1989 developments in eastern and central Europe should be considered a 'transition' (i.e. a return to the normal path of modernization) or a 'transformation' (i.e. something new) can be illuminated by framing it within the debates on path dependency (Illner 1999; Nee and Cao 1999; Stompka 1999; Szalai 1999; Ferree 2000). The issue is whether, with the introduction of economic markets and political democracy, these countries are making a transition to a societal model common in the West, or whether (and if so, how) the institutions of the communist era are leaving a permanent as opposed to a temporary mark on these social formations (Hauser et al. 1995; Illner 1999; Stompka 1999). Is the power of economic markets such that eventually the social patterns established by the socialist era will be eroded to the point of insignificance, or will the political and cultural institutions leave an enduring legacy (Szalai 1999; Ferree 2000)? In particular, are the new elites drawn from the same social strata as the elites in the earlier era, suggesting a continuity with the old, or are they drawn from new ones, indicating a more substantial rupture? The conceptualizing of the process as one of 'transition' is dependent upon a more universalist, more general social theory, in which economic markets drive towards common social forms. Its conceptualization as one of 'transformation' is associated with the notion of path dependency, in which the rupture in 1945 and the experience of nearly half a century of communist institutions leave traces on East European social formations so that they will not converge with Western capitalist democratic development. The former is more generalist while the latter more particularistic approach is that of path dependency.

A similar re-framing of the debates about the relationship between economic development and political democracy can be performed. This is the debate as to whether or to what extent there is a logic to industrialism and capitalism, of economic development and modernization, or whether politics and culture make a significant difference to the outcome (Lipset 1960; Moore 1966), for instance, to welfare regimes (Esping-Andersen 1990). In the first, the development of democracy is part of the logical process of modernization (Lipset 1960; Inglehart 1997). In the second, the clash and historical compromise of class-based political forces are regarded as capable of producing a critical turning point in the path of development, which is locked-in via political institutions which constrain the path of development thereafter (Korpi 1983; Pierson 2000). Modernization theorists have argued that there is a process of development that involves social and political development proceeding along with economic growth, increases in per capita income, an increase of the proportion of the workforce employed outside of agriculture, and an increase in education for all. This approach takes a variety of forms since it was originated by Kerr et al. (1960) and Lipset (1960) and has been refined and developed since then (Inglehart 1997; Inglehart and Norris 2003), but they share the search for a powerful general explanation. By contrast, other sociological schools, especially those influenced by a Marxist tradition, have theorized politics and, in particular, the nature and balance of forces during class struggle, either democratically (Korpi 1983) or in political crises and revolutions (Moore 1966; Skocpol 1979), as being critical to the shaping of the ensuing social formation. In this latter perspective, the nature of industrial societies is critically shaped by key moments of political struggle that have consequences after becoming locked-in via the particular state and welfare institutions (Esping-Andersen 1990, 1999).

Again, this is a debate between, on the one hand, those seeking general theory, in this case the institutional logic of industrialization or modernization, and, on the other hand, those prioritizing particularity due to political struggle. Moore (1966), Korpi (1983), Skocpol (1979) and Esping-Andersen (1990) may all be re-interpreted as theorists of path dependency, because of their focus on the significance of critical turning points that transform the social formation and set it out on one of a number of different possible paths of further development. The mechanism that acts to 'lock-in' the new pathway in these accounts is that of the state and its associated institutions. Rather than one unfolding process of capitalist development, there are several different varieties of modernity, including bifurcations into democracy or dictatorship (Moore 1966), or social democracy or liberal democracy (Korpi 1983), or a three-fold split into social democracy, liberal democracy, or conservative corporatism (Esping-Andersen 1990). The re-framing of this sociological debate within the complexity theory debate on path dependency facilitates the development of the concept of path dependency.

The nature of path dependency is addressed both substantively and theoretically in this book. The first implication of path dependency is that there is no single unified world system or world society, there are different paths of development and different varieties of modernity. This book investigates the extent to which different paths are significant rather than ephemeral, in particular whether globalization is eroding differences between varieties of modernity. Second, divergent paths of development start with critical turning points or tipping points. The nature and origin of these is investigated, in particular considering the implications of political processes involving complex inequalities in addition to class. Third, feedback in social systems can be positive and driving change forward, as well as negative and returning to balance. The concept of positive feedback is developed here with the concepts of catalysing and dampening change. Fourth, temporality and sequencing are important for social theory; the order of events does matter. In this instance this is taken to include not only issues of economies and politics, but also violence.

Coevolution of Complex Adaptive Systems in Changing Fitness Landscapes

Complexity theory provides new ways of theorizing change. Some early accounts of change use a simple notion of a force impacting on another entity. Within complexity theory, the concept of coevolution replaces this notion of one entity having a simple impact on another entity. Since every system takes all other systems as its environment, systems coevolve as they complexly adapt to their environment (Kauffman 1993, 1995). These are 'complex adaptive systems', sometimes termed 'complex evolutionary systems' (McKenzie 2000). The concept of autopoiesis is important for understanding the way that systems coevolve and adapt to each other, rather than one simply impacting on another (Maturana and Varela 1980). Since each system has an internal system, any initial impact will have complex effects upon the internal relations of the other system.

Systems interact with each other. They may do so in such a way (called coupling by Maturana and Varela) that they assist in the reproduction of each other. In this case the mutual modifications of the systems as they interact do not lead to the loss of the identity of each system. Of course some interactions with other systems may lead to the loss of identity of one or both systems, but this is not coupling. Coupling may lead to the generation of a new unity in a different domain from that in which the coupled entities maintain their identities. This new unity may itself be autopoietic, in the sense of self-reproducing. Thus, there may be a network of autopoietic systems dependent upon each other for the maintenance of their identities. 'An autopoietic system whose autopoiesis entails the autopoiesis of the coupled autopoietic unities which realize it, is an autopoietic system of a higher order' (Maturana and Varela 1980: 109).

In order to respond to its environment a system changes internally. Since its environment is composed of other systems, these other systems also change internally. Systems impact on each other in ways other than those of a simple hierarchy or of a simple impact on a stable environment. Rather, systems are coevolving; they are complex adaptive systems (Kauffman 1993, 1995; Holland 1995, 2000). This notion that a system changes as well as the systems with which it is interacting goes beyond the old conception that an entity simply acts on another entity. Rather, there is mutual impact. They both change as a result of this interaction; they coevolve.

Kauffman (1993, 1995) addresses the complex nature of this coevolution among and between multiple systems via the concept of 'fitness landscapes'. This concept is initially derived from analyses of the evolution of species, but is potentially relevant for other types of systems. As one system evolves, it changes the landscape for others, changing their opportunities, and thereby their potential for success or weakness. The landscape can be adapted or deformed by systems as they coevolve. This alters the opportunities faced by other systems, with complex consequences for their development.

The process of interaction between a system and its environment involves selection and temporality (Luhmann 1995). It involves selection in that the system has to recognize which phenomena, out of a range, are to be responded to. It involves temporality, since a process of change takes time. Coevolution is not instantaneous, but a process that takes place over time. Internal processes have to adjust to external changes. The temporal lag in the changes within systems as a result of their interaction is not merely inevitable, but is key to understanding the nature of social change.

The implications of the concept of the coevolution of complex adaptive systems for empirical research include the imperative to look at the interaction between entities and not to presume a one-way direction of causality. Further, it is likely that both (or several) of these entities will change during their interaction thus requiring a complex appreciation of the objects under study.

The relationship between systems may not involve their mutual benefit even though it involves their mutual interaction. The concept of coevolution might appear to carry connotations of consensual harmonious change, but this is far from what is intended. A change in one system may well be to the disadvantage of the other system. Changes may entail changes in the environment within which the other systems operate. Kauffman (1993, 1995) develops the 'changing fitness landscapes' to capture the uneven implications of changes in the environment for systems. The features of a landscape may be such as to advantage or privilege one type of system over another. There may be strife over the nature of this fitness landscape or environment, because of its implications for the functioning of different systems. An example is the contestation over the setting of the global rules for trade by the WTO: some countries have a disproportionate influence over the setting of rules that affect most of the world. The concept of a fitness landscape enables the incorporation of the relations between systems in a way that takes account not only of their mutual influence on each other, but also the way that a system can change the environment in which it and other systems operate to the advantage or disadvantage of those other systems.

Eldredge (1985, 1986) developed a concept of 'punctuated equilibria' in order to grasp the way in which some periods are marked by relative stability and others by sudden change. He challenged the traditional interpretation of evolution as a process of steady development based on the gradual selection of genetically better adapted individual organisms. Instead he demonstrated that the process of selection could be better understood if the level of the species became the focus rather than that of the organism. This is because evolution does not take place gradually, with individual organisms slowly changing as a result of natural selection between organisms of the same species, but instead is a process of 'punctuated equilibria' in which there are long periods of stability followed by periods of change in which many species become extinct and many new ones are generated. Species, rather than genes, are the key level of analysis. A reduction to the level of the organism, or indeed of genes, is less helpful to an explanation than the focus on the emergent level of species. The concept of punctuated equilibria is relevant to conceptualizing uneven patterns of change.

There are several advantages and wide-ranging implications of the conceptualization of change using concepts of coevolution of complex adaptive systems, a changing fitness landscape, and punctuated equilibria when newly applied to social systems.

The first is that they capture the way that social change takes place not only as a result of the internal development of a social system, but also as a result of the interaction between social systems. In the context of globalization it is especially important that concepts of change are able to capture the dynamic relations between systems, and to not only focus on internal development.

The second is that the concept of 'impact' is replaced by that of 'coevolution of complex adaptive systems'. The concept of 'impact' usually implies a singular direction of impact and of causality. This is at odds with the nature of the social world, where such a singular direction is unusual and mutual impact is more common. Many social forces are affected by the social phenomena with which they interact and are changed during the process of interaction; the social force or system complexly adapts during the process of interaction and both systems are changed, not just one. Hence, the 'coevolution of complex adaptive systems' provides a better conceptualization of many social interactions than does that of impact.

Third, any unduly restrictive notion of a limited number of paths is eliminated. Since a system takes all other systems as its environment, there are many potential patterns of development. As the environment of a system or its fitness landscape changes, the system will coevolve. The notion of a limited number of paths is replaced by a need to analyse any clustering that occurs in the nature of social forms.

Fourth, the concept of a 'changing fitness landscape' is useful in capturing the changing nature of the environment in which any system operates. These changes in the fitness landscape may enable a system to function more or less well, to grow and expand or diminish in range. A system may be able to alter or deform the landscape in such a way that this is to its advantage, thereby altering the positioning of other systems. Changes in the fitness landscape cannot be understood without a concept of power. The ability to alter an environment so as to advantage one system over another is a vital form of power. In this way the notion of power is embedded in the analysis.

These concepts are especially useful in developing analyses of global processes in which there are changing relationships between polities and other social systems, and the development of the European Union where there have been changes in both the nature and composition of the EU and in the character of its Member States. The competition to change rules and conventions at a global level has major implications for the capacity of one polity to grow at the expense of others. Changes in the global environment concerning issues such as the terms of trade and discourses of political legitimation have significant implications for the relative positioning of polities and social groups.

Conventional accounts have often described globalization as a process that impacts on nation-states, reducing their capacity for autonomous action especially in relation to the welfare of their citizens (e.g. Crouch and Streeck 1997; Martin and Schumann 1997). But the notion of 'impact' leaves out of focus the process of dynamic adjustment of polities to each other in the context of globalization. In the context of the response of European countries to globalization, such an approach has particular difficulty in grasping the changing nature of the European Union during this process. The use of the concepts of coevolution of complex adaptive systems in a fitness landscape re-frames this process and enables a more adequate account. Rather than asking about the impact of globalization on European states, it is more appropriate to ask about the coevolution of globalization, the European Union (which has grown in powers), and Member States (who despite giving up their powers to the EU are better able to complete their domestic agendas having done so) (Walby 1999a). These Member States have transferred powers to regulate the economy from the domestic, country specific, arena to the European Union. But to treat this as a zero-sum game would be inadequate. Rather the domestic agendas of the governments of these relatively small European countries are better achieved by such a transfer of powers (Milward 1992).

The concept of coevolution captures this process better than that of impact. Further, globalization does not simply act on the European Union, but this polity is itself part of a process of creating globalization, for instance in its role in re-negotiating international trade regulations at the World Trade Organization. The process of coevolution involves the complex adaptation of the systems of European countries, the European Union, and global institutions. This coevolution has resulted in a changed fitness landscape within which the Member States and European Union operate, with different implications for the powers of these entities. Within a changing global landscape, the European Union has increased its powers over the regulation of the economy while the Member States have reduced theirs. 'Impact' is far too blunt a concept to capture these complex processes. Rather the concepts of 'coevolution', 'complex adaptive systems' and 'fitness landscapes' facilitate an improved understanding of these processes, with the proviso that power relations are understood as embedded in these processes.

If there is close coupling of the economy, polity, violence, and civil society, then there is a tendency for changes in each domain to be closely associated. Under these circumstances changes in the economy are likely to affect the polity, violence, and civil society. Perhaps more importantly there are mutual effects from the interaction of these complex adaptive systems. If there is close coupling then economic development is more likely to lead to changes in the polity. However, while traditionally, social theory has suggested that it is reasonable to assume such close coupling, there are reasons to doubt that this is actually the case, except in unusual circumstances. This is because there are often divergent temporal and spatial reaches to domains of economy, polity, violence, and civil society. A polity may be spatially smaller or larger than the associated economy. For example, the emerging European Union changes the spatial scale at which political decisions are taken, but the economy and civil society are not changing the spatial scale at the same rate. Further, the Catholic Church is a transnational entity, straddling states and economies, but having significant effects on the regulation of sexuality and marriage.

There is a tendency, over time, for loosely coupled systems to self-organize into more closely coupled systems. This is societalization, in which there is a slow process of bringing into alignment the practices of the different systems that constitute a potential society. However, this process, while often started, is frequently interrupted by challenges to societalize around a different set of practices. While there is a potential infinity of forms of social systems, in practice there are clusters of forms, sharing common characteristics. There thus appear to be limits to the infinite possibility of social forms.

Waves

The existing conceptual vocabulary for social change is insufficient to grasp some of the non-linear forms of change in a global era. The concept of wave is used in order to capture some specific aspects of the simultaneous temporal and spatial dimensions of social change in a global era associated with the interaction between systems. The increase in global processes puts a premium on developing concepts that capture the nature of how an event and patterns of social relations at one point in time and space have implications for an event or social relations at another point in time and space. The concept of wave is developed here to capture the way that an event in one social system can have repercussions on social systems elsewhere in time and space. A wave starts in one temporal and spatial location, builds rapidly through endogenous processes, and then spreads out though space and time to affect social relations in other locations. These events are connected, but not in a simple deterministic manner, passing through networks and social institutions.

The concept of 'wave' captures the sudden transfer of social practices from one social system to another, especially those associated with social movements. These are increasingly important forms of social linkages across national boundaries. They are more than simply networks (such as transnational advocacy networks: see Keck and Sikkink 1998; Zippel 2004), and more than new forms of community (such as epistemic communities: see Haas 1992), although they do include features of network and community, since these concepts do not capture the rapid temporal escalation of the phenomena in question. The concept of wave deployed here draws on at least five different sources for its intellectual heritage.

First, the concept of wave draws on the concept of rounds of restructuring, which has been used to capture the effects of a widespread change in the economic environment upon a spatially varied pre-existing institutional structure (Massey and Meegan 1982; Bagguley et al. 1990). The concept was used to theorize aspects of spatial unevenness in social processes. The outcome of any given round of economic restructuring varied between different localities because of pre-existing differences in the social, economic, and political institutions of different places. The interaction of the round of restructuring with these varied institutions produced different outcomes, rather than simply producing conformity around a new principle of social and economic organization. It was intended to embed historical and spatial dimensions into the analysis of political and economic change (Bagguley et al. 1990). The concept of wave captures the notion that a common factor may have different local implications as a result of variations in the pre-existing institutional structure.

Second, a wave captures a different kind of social process from those centred on institutions; it is not an institution or a system. Instead it is a form of social energy, a process. It may pass through institutions and systems, thereby disturbing them, but is not itself organized as an institution or system. In this way the concept of wave draws upon our already existing understanding of the distinction between wave and particle. Light is energy that is without mass and takes the form of a wave, while particles have mass and organization. The concept of wave is likewise concerned with the transmission of energy – this time social energy – in a form and process that are not heavy with institutions.

Third, the concept of wave draws on the heritage of social movement theory (Freeman and Johnson 1999). As in social movements, the focus of an analysis of waves is on the process of a development of new (or re-worked, revived) civil societal projects. Social movement theory has built a sophisticated range of a concepts and explanatory practices to capture the rise, impact, and fall of social movements. They typically rise out of civil society and seek to impact on and change established institutions, being themselves changed in the process. The concept of wave draws on this, but goes beyond it with the added dimension of spatiality.

Fourth, the concept of wave draws on that used in the analysis of the history of feminist movements. Its primary use there has been to capture the temporal, rather than spatial, dimension of feminist movements. There was a powerful feminist movement in the latter part of the nineteenth and early twentieth centuries, which succeeded in winning the vote for women as well as reforming the laws on marriage and practices in employment and education (Banks 1981; Spender 1983; Berkovitch 1999). There was also a further powerful feminist movement starting in the late 1960s in the USA, in the 1970s in the UK, and then spreading around the world. In between these two movements there was not a total cessation of feminist activity, but it was less public, less confrontationist, less visible, and less powerful. The concept of wave is used in order to capture the notion that while feminism did not go away completely, neither was it sustained at the same level of visibility and activity. Like an ocean, feminism is with us always as long as there is gender inequality, but there are waves of publicly visible activism only some of the time.

Fifth, the concept of wave captures a social process marked by an absence of linearity in the relationship between events and in the temporality of the process itself. An initial event may build suddenly to large proportions, or it may fade away with little impact. The classic, metaphorical, example of the former is the flapping of the butterfly's wings that disturbs the air in a way that indirectly leads to a storm elsewhere in the world. This is the terrain of chaos theory (Gleick 1988). It draws on the way that many social and 'natural' systems are not in stable equilibrium so that a small event can create a positive feedback mechanism which builds into a large event. This is an account of the world in which the simple abstractions of linear analysis, in which an event has a direct and proportionate response, do not apply (Capra 1997). The non-linear dimension of time and impact are elements pertinent to the understanding of some social phenomena. Biggs (2001) demonstrates that the dynamics of social movements, such as strikes, especially in their very rapid, non-linear, rate of development, have parallels in nature with phenomena such as forest fires. They share a form of endogenous development with a positive feedback loop speeding the process of 'contagion'. These events are governed by a power law whatever the scale, that is, they take a power fractal form (Mandelbrot 1982). This is because any one agent can affect a set ratio of other agents, provoking them to either action or combustion. My concept of wave draws on these arguments. A wave transforming social action can have significant endogeneity. It is the endogeneity and the positive feedback loops that are crucial to the explanation of the suddenness of waves of civil societal movements and of the rapidity of the generation of their intensity and power.

The concept of wave developed here integrates these notions of the spatial, temporal, non-linearity, and transformative social energy. A wave of political activity is initiated at one point in time and space and travels to other places, reaching them at slightly later times. It has somewhat different impacts, depending on the prior institutional structure at those locations. Its starting point depends on the particular contradictions in social relations and institutions, the resources available to participants, the availability of a potential network, and the available frames. The rate of increase in the intensity of the wave depends not only on the resources available to participants but on the nature of the endogenous feedback processes within the movement and between the movement and potential participants. The extent of the spread of the wave depends on external circumstances, the connectedness of its networks, resources available to participants, and the energy generated by endogenous processes. In the contemporary world such waves can become global, while a century ago the horizon of activity might have been more restricted. The level of impact depends on the conjuncture of circumstances, which affects whether it is a mere ripple or a tidal wave of tremendous proportions. The effect of the wave is significantly affected by the nature of the local circumstances with which it interacts. The impact may be one of simple change in the direction of the flow, or it may be one in which it is absorbed via a complex process of hybridization with prior local practices, or it may result in a fierce resistance which can have a backwash effect towards the point of origin. The notion of wave bears some resemblances to the concept of network, in that it is an attempt to conceptualize linkages which are not simple, direct, and linear, and in which there are loose connections between individuals. But it is more specific in the nature of these linkages, with its specification of a beginning, of its stimulation of a concatenation of events, intensification through endogenous processes, and of the primary direction of its momentum.

Waves today can be global although, historically, regional waves were more common. Indeed the phenomena of waves becomes more important in the context of an unevenly spatialized set of social relations that are only loosely connected. While many, especially of the better documented, waves may be constituted as pro-modernist, seeking to speed the modernization of social relations with a justice and egalitarian oriented perspective, there have also been a series of anti-modernist waves.

Waves are forms of connections between social systems. They can promote relatively small, specific projects, or large projects of societalization. The former may be more easily absorbed or hybridized, the latter are more likely to provoke resistance or backlash. The former may merely speed a process of development already begun by some social forces, and its ideas championed within that social formation. Alternatively waves may challenge the foundations of the social order, bearing projects that imply societalization around different principles. The potential implications of the project contained by the wave for key elite groups in the host country are likely to be of particular importance in determining the nature of the response.

Global waves cross-cut paths of national development. For example, as would-be nation-states try to societalize around selected principles and practices, they are subject to waves of influence of different kinds from other lands. In the interaction of the wave and the nation-state project there are several options. The wave may be absorbed readily, perhaps by a key group that uses it as a support for its own agenda, perhaps by pushing forward a modernist or anti-modernist agenda. Or it may be rejected, involving hostility against the source of the wave and those who propound its values. Or it may be hybridized into something new. Waves are considered further in Chapter 6 on civil societies and in Chapter 10 comparing country trajectories.

Conclusions

Theorizing multiple complex inequalities is a challenge. The analysis must include the ontological depth of multiple regimes of inequality in the institutional domains of the economy, polity, violence, and civil society rather than flatten this to a single dimension of culture or economics. But the old concept of social system did not allow for more than one major axis of inequality in each institutional domain. This led many who prioritized the significance of multiple inequalities in social theory to reject the concept of social system. However, in so doing they lost the capacity to simultaneously theorize their ontological depth. In order to theorize the ontological depth of each of these multiple inequalities it is necessary to revisit and revise the concept of social system.

The selective integration of complexity notions enables the revision of the concept of social system. The complexity notion of the system/environment distinction enables a more nimble conceptualization of systems and their interactions. This allows the rejection of the notion that a system must saturate its territory, enabling multiple systems of inequalities in the same space or institutional domain. It enables the rejection of the notion that parts must be nested within a whole, and thus a rejection of the reduction of one set of social relations of inequality to another. Complexity theory provides the theoretical flexibility to allow a systematic analysis of social interconnections without the reductionism that so marred the old. The re-working of these core concepts of social theory is necessary in order to adequately theorize the ontological depth of intersecting multiple systems of social inequality. This includes re-thinking the excessive humanism that excludes bodies and technology from explanations, and the inclusion of individuals as systems in themselves.

Drawing on complexity theory as well as classic and contemporary social theory enables new ways of theorizing non-linear social change. It is important to develop new concepts to address the tension between the goal of general social theory and understandings of particular development. These include: path dependency, varieties of development, critical turning points, tipping points, the coevolution of complex adaptive systems in changing fitness landscapes, the catalysing and dampening of the rate of change, and waves.

The concept of wave is developed to capture for a global era processes that link social systems speedily yet without solid institutions. A wave is a distinct set of social processes with a particular kind of temporal and spatial characteristics that can suddenly transfer social practices from one location to another; it can build suddenly, interact with a social system, and either produce change or decay, or hybridize. It is especially important in relation to understanding the implications of emergent civil societal projects on established social formations.

These developments build on and develop the re-thinking of time and space in social theory prompted by the increasing development of global processes. The significance of space is not reduced, rather it has changed. Social processes still take time. But social relations in one part of the world can be brought more rapidly into other social environments than before. This is not just a process of 'speeding up' or 'acceleration', but can also take a more complex 'wave' form which combines a non-linear escalation of a phenomenon and an incorporation or backlash.

The concept of system is revitalized by the insights of complexity theory, especially: the simplifying distinction between a system and its environment; the non-nested coupling of systems; the coevolution of complex adaptive systems; that systems do not necessarily tend to equilibrium; non-linear patterns of change; path dependency and critical turning points. The distinction between social relations and social institutions allows for the possibility of more than one set of unequal social relations within any institutional complex, and thus the theorization of complex inequalities that are not reduced to a single dimension. The analysis of the complex interconnections between social systems during globalization is facilitated by the notion that social systems are open and not closed, and by the development of the concept of wave.

3 Economies

Introduction

This chapter reconceptualizes the economy so as to more adequately address complex inequalities and global processes; reconsiders what is meant by economic inequality in this new context; and differentiates between alternative forms of the economy in a way that takes into account gender and other complex inequalities. This chapter also establishes the revised economic concepts needed for the comparative analysis in chapters 8, 9 and 10.

The conventional understanding of the economy as limited to marketized and monetized activities is challenged by the significance of domestic labour and state welfare. Economic inequalities look different when complex inequalities such as gender are included. Inequalities are complex: entwined with positively valued differences as well as inequalities.

Taking gender relations in the economy seriously means recognizing that not all social relations in the economy are yet modern; domestic labour is outside the market and performed under premodern social relations. The transition to modernity in the economy takes place at different times for class, gender, and ethnic relations. There is a second 'great transformation' still ongoing in the shift from household to market production. This transformation of the gender regime has implications for changes in class and other relations, through its implications for labour and for political constituencies.

Globalization is not a unified phenomenon, but is constituted by several different kinds of processes: global flows of capital trade and people; global institutions, networks, and hegemons; and global waves of civil societal projects. These global processes have complex interactions with national ones. Rather than eroding difference between economies, these are restructured. Inequalities are constituted not only within a country, but also between countries. Global economic inequality requires taking both kinds of inequality into account.

There are alternative ways in which modern economies can be organized. Neoliberalism is not an inevitability; in the global North there are also social democratic forms, as well as a variety of further forms in the global South. The conventional typologies of varieties of economies are challenged to include complex inequalities in addition to class relations.

Redefining the Economy

The conventional definition of the economy is developed in this section so as to include complex inequalities in addition to class. This enables a rethinking of what is meant by economic inequalities.

The economy is the system of relations, institutions, and processes concerned with the production, consumption, distribution, and circulation of goods and services to support human life. It is an institutional domain containing multiple regimes of inequality. In order to take account of complex inequalities and global processes, a series of conceptual developments are needed to redefine the concept of the economy. The concept of the economy needs to be widened so as to include not only marketized activities, but also domestic labour and state welfare.

It is important to distinguish between tasks, social relations, and the site of production. The criteria used to distinguish the economy from the non-economy is that of its tasks – not the social relations, which can vary between market, state, and domestic forms, nor the site of production, which can be anywhere including in the home. The redefinition of the economy has implications for the conceptualization of its inequalities. The inclusion of domestic labour raises the question as to how to address the concentration of women in domestic labour: is it intrinsically an inequality that leads to inequalities in other aspects of gender relations, or is it a valued difference? Perhaps it is best understood as both an inequality and a valued difference simultaneously.

Taking global processes into account challenges the traditional analysis of inequality within countries: whether or not economic inequality is seen to be increasing or decreasing depends upon whether the whole world rather than individual countries is the unit within which inequality is measured. Global processes affect processes within countries, as well as the world as a whole.

Domestic labour as labour

Is the economy just the market economy, the economy where money is used in transactions? This is the convention in mainstream economics, where the size of an economy is measured in terms of its monetary value. But this leaves labour that is not involved in money out of account and out of focus: housework and care-work in the home would be left out; and likewise forced labour, such as slavery, and those who are trafficked (forms of labour that are key to gender and ethnic relations). Care-work in the home is often not considered as work at all; housewives are considered 'economically inactive'. While these forms of labour are not performed as free wage labour, nonetheless they are labour and should be included within the concept of the economy. The economy is more than just the market economy.

Domestic labour or domestic care-work has variously been defined in relation to the nature of the tasks and outcomes of the work, the gendered social relations usually involved, and the domestic site of the labour. The definition here is centred on the tasks and the outcomes of the work. The implications for the partially overlapping concerns of social relations and site of the work are addressed later.

Domestic labour, or household production, is a set of activities that produces accommodation, meals, clean clothes, and the care of children and adults, via a series of intermediary inputs including cleaning and shopping (Ironmonger 2001). It is the care-work of looking after children and other household members, such as the sick, frail elderly, and disabled (Gardiner 1997) as well as cooking and food preparation, cleaning both the home and clothes, and the maintenance of that home and its equipment (Bose 1979). Oakley (1974) argued that housework was indeed work by demonstrating that the activities involved were similar to other forms of work by means of a painstaking empirical examination. It is work like other work; there are empirical similarities between the tasks and outcomes of domestic labour and paid work (Reid 1934; Oakley 1974; Delphy 1984).

The tasks accomplished by domestic care-work could be accomplished as either welfare provided by the state, or as goods and services purchased on the market (inside or outside the home). These activities are part of the economy and should be considered to be production (Reid 1934; Delphy 1984). It is the conceptualization of domestic care-work as a set of tasks that is most challenging to economic and social theory.

The conceptualization of unpaid domestic care-work as part of the economy is a challenge to the narrow definition of the economy as activities that have monetary value. This is a challenge to the measurement of the size of the economy in monetary terms of the

Gross Domestic Product (GDP) and to the standard of living as the GDP per person (per capita) (HM Treasury 2006). It is a challenge to the conceptualization of unpaid domestic workers as 'economically inactive'. It challenges the 'strategic silence' on gender in the economy (Bakker 1998).

This revised conceptualization of domestic care-work as part of the economy is a challenge to those forms of social theory that conceptualize these activities as primarily cultural. Women's activities in the home have been seen as ideological, where the family is an ideological state apparatus (Althusser 1971), or the lifeworld where meaning is created outside of the steering system of the economy (Habermas 1989, 1991), and as socialization (Parsons 1955). This is not to say that there are not civil societal aspects to these activities; there are. But they are economic.

The conceptualization of domestic care-work as part of the economy draws on feminist traditions in social theory that cross-cut conventional divisions. Engels (1940) conceptualized domestic labour as reproduction, and as part of the economy alongside production and thereby as part of the material basis of social relations. A century ago, feminists such as Schreiner (1911) and Gilman (1966) conceptualized women's household work as labour and as part of the economy, and addressed its relations with class and imperialism. The relationship of domestic labour with capitalism was the subject of the 'domestic labour debate' (Seccombe 1974; Malos 1980). The forms it takes have been documented and analysed (Oakley 1974), including its use of technology (Silva 2000), its implications for the use of time (Gershuny 2000), and the tension between time spent on care-work and paid work (Hochschild 1997; Gatrell 2004). Domestic production can be conceptualized as a scarce resource in marginalist economics through a focus on time as the resource that might be put to alternative uses (Becker 1965, 1981); there is a choice between the use of time in production in the household and its use in the market (Mincer 1962; Mincer and Polachek 1974), which requires the understanding of the implications of choices at one point in time for options at a later time drawing on game theory and theories of bargaining to enable the understanding of household inequalities (Humphries 1998). Not all those making such decisions experience them as economically rational, being situated within complex moral economies where the priority is understood to be to do the right thing in relation to care (Duncan and Edwards 1999), but that does not make them any less decisions about the economy.

What are the implications of treating care-work as part of the economy for the analysis of economic inequalities? Is the division between domestic care-work and paid employment best thought of as a positively valued difference or as inequality? In some locations a positive value is attached to care-work because of the long-term and important emotional work that is involved (Hochschild 2000; Himmelweit 2002). Indeed, some consider that this is the case for care-work whether it is paid or unpaid (Himmelweit 1999); although the uniqueness of the emotional involvement in care-work is overstated since many paid workers become committed to their work and to the quality of its output. However, even when there is a positive valuation of domestic care-work, it simultaneously contributes to gender inequality since domestic care-work is not paid and employment is paid. In addition, the gendered division of labour contributes towards other forms of gender inequality: it has a tendency to reduce women's access to formal political power (see Chapter 4), and to increase their vulnerability to domestic violence (see Chapter 5).

When care-work is the basis of a person's livelihood it is associated with economic inequality, even though it may be highly valued. This paradox of the simultaneity of inequality and valued difference lies at the heart of the 'complex inequality' that is gender. Most analyses of economic inequality treat care-work as if it is of no value, because the dominant frame of reference considers only monetary value. This is problematic, but so also is the treatment of care-work and free wage labour as if they had equal consequences for gender inequality. A livelihood based on care-work is much less likely than one based on free wage labour to deliver access to economic resources, political influence, freedom from violence, and personal independence. The resolution to this dilemma is to treat gender as a complex inequality, in which difference and inequality are entwined. Care-work can be simultaneously highly valued and also a source of inequality across the breadth of the gender regime.

State welfare as part of the economy

The economy is constituted not only by the private market and the domestic sphere, but also by some of the activities of the state. Some of the welfare aspects of the polity are also part of the economy, while other aspects of the polity are part of the governance of the economy. The welfare state, which involves the provision of public services such as education, health, and care and the redistribution of income through taxation and social benefits, is considered here. The governance of the economy through the regulation of labour and macroeconomic policy is considered later.

The concept of welfare is complicated because it straddles activities carried out in different sites and organized through different social relations. The concept and practice of welfare are wider than the subset of activities that constitute the welfare state. These activities, especially education, health, and care, can be performed not only by the welfare state but also by the market and by unpaid domestic carework, and, in some instances, institutions associated with organized religions. In different varieties of modernity the balance between these three sites and sets of social relations under which this welfare is carried out varies considerably.

While it is possible to analytically separate the redistributive aspects of the welfare state from the provision of public services, the dominant historical account of the welfare state is that redistribution and the provision of public services are inextricably bound up with each other (Beveridge 1942; Marshall 1950). Redistribution takes place not only in the tax-benefit and pensions systems, but also through the provision of services of education, health, care, and sometimes housing to all or most of the population, but paid for disproportionately by the better off. Redistribution can be understood in two ways. The first concerns a distribution from the rich to the poor, as a contribution to the reduction in economic inequality generated by capitalism. The second focuses on the risks of modern life, such as illness, old age, and unemployment, where there is a need to provide assistance through services and income support (Beck 1992). Redistribution is not always from rich to poor, it can also be used to support complex inequalities such as gender (Lister 1997) and ethnicity (Quadagno 1994; Williams 1995).

The interpretation of the activities of the welfare state as primarily redistributive can sometimes obscure the understanding of the simultaneously economically productive aspects of public services. The production of human capital through education is a major contribution to the development of the economy, especially the knowledge-based forms of the economy. While access to education is significant in shaping life chances and thus not irrelevant to issues of inequality and redistribution, nevertheless education is also a major investment in the productive capacity of the economy. Similarly, while the provision of quality childcare by the state is an act of gender redistribution since this work would otherwise usually be mostly performed by women and is paid for by taxes typically contributed more by men than women, it is also a major investment in the productive capacity of women as workers, who are thereby enabled to have more continuous employment histories. Welfare state activities are not only redistributive, they are also investments in the productive capacity of the economy (Reich 1993; Quadagno 1999; Pierson 2001; Esping-Andersen 2002; Walby 2007b).

The welfare parts of the economy provided by (some) states thus include health, education, and care. In addition there are forms of regulation of the economy that have important welfare effects, especially for full employment, including macroeconomic policy, active labour market programmes, and the structure of the tax-benefit system. The state provision of welfare has implications not only for class, but also for gender, ethnic and other minoritized groups. It can be important in enabling access to employment, especially since the state provision of care facilitates higher levels of employment by women.

What are economic inequalities? What is progress in the economy?

What are economic inequalities? The conceptualization and operationalization of economic inequality has major implications for whether particular inequalities are made visible or invisible.

The inequalities can be considered by individuals or households; within countries and between countries; between generations; and in the world as a whole. They can be differentiated using an implied class analysis, or differentiated by gender, ethnicity, and other minoritized status. The choice of unit has implications; for example, if the household is chosen as the unit, as is common in cross-national studies of income inequality, then gender inequalities within the household are made invisible. The inequalities can be restricted to monetized forms, or include non-monetized exchanges; be limited to income, or extended to wealth. Inequalities include: inequalities in the income paid to workers (the wage distribution, the gender pay gap); gaps in employment and unemployment rates between different groups; occupational segregation and lower proportions of women and minoritized groups in top jobs; income inequalities between households (as well as individuals); and inequalities in wealth (housing, savings, and other capital) between individuals or between households. They include inequalities between individuals and families within countries, inequalities between countries, and inequalities at a global level.

Not all labour is performed under market conditions as free wage labour. Sometimes it may be under voluntary non-market social relations, as in many households. It may also be coerced or forced, under menace and involuntary, as a result of indentured labour, as in slavery, or as a result of trafficking or threats (ILO 2005). The performance of labour under coercion should be considered a form of inequality in itself.

Equality is a key framing of progress in the domain of economics, but not the only one. Alongside it is economic growth and development, where the goal is increased income. These are often positioned as contesting priorities in debates on economic development (Rankin 2001), but need not be (Lorgelly and Owen 1999; Forsythe et al. 2000; Kenworthy 2004). A further frame is that of capabilities, where the focus on human development, such as longevity, health, and education, is often used to contest or modify the focus on economic growth. An additional frame is that of human rights, less often deployed, but used especially in contesting forced labour (ILO 2005). A comparison of these is provided in Chapter 1 and Chapter 9.

Environmental sustainability is an issue of inequality with implications for inequality between generations (present and future) and between the rich and poor of the world (for example, the poor are more likely to die in floods than are the rich) (Roberts and Parks 2007) and complex inequalities such as gender (Cudworth 2005). The form of energy used in the current phase of economic development is creating global warming, which is leading to extreme weather events and major changes in the world's climate that will cause flooding in areas of high population density, create drought in other regions that will make agriculture impossible, and generally lead to a severe diminution in the quality of life for those who survive (IPCC 2007; Stern 2007). This is an issue of inequality and potential solidarity between generations; actions today have implications for future generations associated with a significant global project to achieve the changes in social activities needed to avoid global catastrophe. There is a further range of environmental issues, including pollution, contestation over the use of land and resources (Macnaghten and Urry 1998) and risky new technologies such as genetically modified foodstuffs and nuclear energy (Beck 1992; Wynne 1996). There are major differences between countries in their prioritization of action on this issue: the USA is reluctant to change its form of economic development despite the risks, the EU is more concerned to exercise caution, with contests fought out in emerging global institutions such as the World Trade Organization (Winnicott et al. 2005). The UN is a major site of contestation over these issues in the search for global protocols to move countries to action (Kyoto Protocol 1997; UN 2007b). The environmental system includes humans as one of its constituent parts. The inclusion of non-human objects within the concept of the social system is important in the analysis of the implications of human-environmental changes for economic sustainability. The rapid burning of fossil fuels and the consequent changes to the planet's climate are undermining the possibilities for life in potentially unstoppable ways (Mol and Sonnefield 2000; Mol 2001; UN 2007b).

From Premodern to Modern: The Second Great Transformation

Not all of the relations under which labour is performed by women are yet modern, even in the most developed countries. Only free wage labour is 'modern' labour. This classic insight from Marx resonates widely in many different theorizations of modernity, from Weber to Simmel. Economic relations are not yet modern while there is not universal free wage labour. Domestic labour is performed outside of the market. The continued existence of domestic labour, even in advanced economies, means that not all labour takes a free and waged form. No country's economy is yet completely modernized.

The transition to free wage labour for most women takes place later than for men, as the shift away from domestic labour takes place after the initial development of commercial manufacturing and services. This constitutes a second 'great transformation', with radical implications not only for the household sector but also for the rest of the economy. In some cases the transition to free wage labour for minority ethnic groups takes place later than the majority ethnic group, for example in the USA, with slavery.

There is not just one economic transition to modernity but several, each linked to the modernization of the economy in different regimes of inequality. Industrialization and the development of capitalism represent merely the first of the transitions in the movement of the economy towards modernity. There is a second 'great transformation' in the transition away from household production to market production, associated, albeit unevenly, with the wider modernization of the gender regime. The transition to modernity did not happen in one stage, rather there was a series of partial transitions, affecting gender as well as other sets of social relations. There are different key moments during the modernization of the economy affecting different sets of social relations within the economy at different times.

The hallmark of the first great economic transformation that was the development of capitalism and industrialization was free wage labour (Marx 1954). Labour was simultaneously freed and constrained in new ways, which were implicated in the transformation of all other social relations. Free wage labour made possible new forms of political combination and practice, generating both new forms of independence and new forms of collectively experienced subordination. But, with a few contested exceptions, these were the experiences of men only. Most women remained outside these new economic relations, experiencing them only indirectly, and vicariously, through their husbands and fathers. Bringing into focus sets of social relations in addition to those of class, such as gender and ethnicity, makes it easier to see that the transition to modernity may take place in steps rather than all at once, each step being associated with a particular form of social relations. The modernization of gender relations in the economy is constituted by the transition from domestic to market labour for women and a decline in the domestic sector as the basis of women's livelihood.

The increase in women's employment and the decline in domestic labour is not a simple uni-linear development associated with industrialization. Instead, the early stages of industrialization are often marked by a decline in women's employment. Rather than a linear relationship between industrialization and women's paid employment, there is a non-linear U-shaped relationship in which women's employment initially declines with industrialization, rising again only later (Boserup 1970). This has been found in both quantitative (Pampel and Tanaka 1986; Çagatay and Özler 1995) and qualitative (Boserup 1970; Walby 1986; Bourke 1993) studies. There are a number of reasons for this complexity. During the initial stages of industrialization women's traditional industries decline and are not immediately replaced; women do not have access to the independent legal persona necessary for independent credit; women face competition and discrimination in the new industrial sector of the economy; and women are not organized to protect their interests in same way as men (Boserup 1970; Walby 1986). The changed political structure leaves women disadvantaged since their primary location within the domestic sphere creates difficulties for women's effective political organization and the representation of their interests in the state, especially if they do not have the vote. This lack of political power has serious consequences. Further, the shift in the balance of productivity in the two sectors of the economy is very complex. In the very early stages of economic development there is an advantage in terms of the overall standard of living of households if women work at home, which is only later followed by a reversal to the more usual situation of an advantage to women's working in the market sector (Bourke 1991). In the early stages of industrialization, men often possess and utilize organizational resources to exclude women from some of the better areas of developing employment (Hartmann 1976; Walby 1986). As women gain political citizenship they are able to more effectively contest this exclusion from the public. This gendered struggle, in combination with a developing capitalist economy, is leading towards the transformation of the gender regime from a domestic to a public form (Walby 1990).

Once women's employment has started to grow and the domestic sector to decline a new era begins. The productivity in the market sector of the economy usually grows as a result of economic development. This is associated with increased capital, the development and use of new and improved technology in machines, as well as the increase in human capital and skills. These developing forces of production are entwined with emerging forms of relations of production which enable the greater inclusion of women. This tilts the balance of productivity between labour in the household and market sectors in favour of the latter. The output in goods and services per hour worked increases in the market sector relative to the household sector. The shifting balance of productivity is demonstrated in the changing rewards to the use of women's time and the rise in women's wages in the market sector compared with the value of the goods and services that they can produce with the same amount of labour in the home. Women's wages go up as they increase their human capital through more education and spend more time in employment (Joshi and Paci 1998; Budig and England 2001; Walby and Olsen 2002; Olsen and Walby 2004). This process is described within a variety of theoretical frameworks from Marxism (Braverman 1974) to neoclassical economics (Mincer 1962; Becker 1965, 1981; Mincer and Polachek 1974), to feminist economics (Bergmann 1986; Gardiner 1997; Humphries 1998).

Changes in the economy lead to the substitution of publicly produced goods and services for household production. These goods and services are sometimes obtained from the market and sometimes provided by the state or polity. The purchase of these commodities is often associated with an increase in women's earnings as there is more money in the household to buy these goods and services from outside the household for use within it. There has been a reduction in household production as a result of the purchase of substitute goods and services from the national and global marketplace. This takes several forms. There is an increase in domestic production goods, such as heating systems, fridges, washer-dryers and dishwashers, which reduces the amount of labour time (Gershuny 2000; Silva 2000), although some of this potentially 'freed up' time is used to increase the quality of provision rather than reduce labour time (Bose 1979). There is an increase in the purchase of services and goods from outside the home, such as ready-made clothes, pre-processed food, meals from restaurants and take-ways, and care services for children and elderly relatives, such as nannies and cleaners. There is a decline in time spent in household production (Gershuny 2000). There is a global component here: goods and labourers from the South enter households in the North. Domestic appliances may be wholly or partially manufactured in countries where labour is cheaper than in those where the appliances are used. Global care-chains involving migrant labour from the South provide care-work in households in the North enabling Northern women to be employed, though this is more common in the USA than in Europe (Hochschild 2000; Yeates 2005). In this way homes in the North derive benefit ultimately from the labour in the South. Second, the carers in the North may be migrants from the South, seeking wages that may then be remitted to the South (Parreñas 2001).

These changes coevolve with changes in the household form and structure, and in the number of children that a household raises. Within two-parent households, there has been a very slight change in the distribution of domestic labour within the household, with women doing slightly less and men very slightly more than before, especially concerning the care of children (Gershuny 2000), with significant differences between countries (Aliaga 2006). There has been an increase in the number of one-parent households, largely lone mother households, in which mothers do almost all of the domestic labour including care-work (Hobson 1994). There is a reduction in the amount of household labour associated with the decline in fertility (Hobcraft 1987), since there are fewer children to look after. The decline in fertility associated with the transition in the form of the gender regime is significant, although it varies especially with the level of state support (Castles 2003).

There are two major ways in which the state or polity can promote the transition to the free wage labour for women: the provision of services, especially care-work, which would otherwise have to be purchased on the market, and the regulation of employment and education so as to remove discriminatory barriers to women's employment and to facilitate the combination of care-work and employment for both women and men. These are not uniform changes, but vary significantly between countries. Further, the direction of change is not simply uni-directional and linear. These issues are addressed through an examination of childcare provision, the gendered regulation of employment, and early industrialization. Increases in both childcare provision and in the gender equality regulation of employment are common across many countries, but the extent of their provision is highly varied.

The care of children is a central focus of policies to increase the provision of care outside the home, though elder care policies are increasingly important. This may take place either through the direct establishment of places for childcare, or through the provision of funds to facilitate this occurring. There are further forms of care for the elderly and disabled that are similarly organized and have similar implications. The provision of this care plays a significant role in facilitating the employment of mothers who may otherwise have chosen to look after children in a domestic setting. The greater the extent of state childcare, the higher and more rapidly the rate of female employment rises. However, high levels of female employment do also occur without state support, when households can afford to purchase services on the market, as is the case in the USA. There are a variety of forms of state intervention and a complexity of effects. State supported childcare is most developed in social democratic Nordic countries. However, the increase in state support for childcare is occurring not only in the Nordic countries, but in others as well, including those that have been labelled neoliberal and conservative corporatist, as well as in countries undergoing recession (OECD 2007). It is increasing in countries conventionally considered neoliberal, including the UK, which has seen substantial increases in state support for childcare since 1997 (Sainsbury 1994, 1996; Fraser 1997; Mahon 1997, 2002; O'Connor et al. 1999; Hobson 2000; Wincott 2006; Nishikawa and Tanaka 2007). It is also increasing in countries considered by some to be 'conservative corporatist', since even the German government is increasing funding for childcare from 2005 (Pearse 2005). In Sweden, despite a severe recession in the early 1990s during which the state curtailed the level and access to many social benefits, there was an increase in the proportion of children utilizing state childcare (Palme et al. 2002).

The second major form of polity intervention that promotes women's employment is the removal of patriarchal barriers in the labour market and their replacement by legislation to regulate the workplace so as to limit discrimination and also make it easier to combine care-work and employment (Zabalza and Tzannatos 1985; Pyle 1990; Pillinger 1992; Hoskyns 1996; Joshi and Paci 1998; Walby 1999b, 2004a; European Commission 2007a). The promotion of education for girls and women is associated with economic growth (Klasen 2002).

The form of the polity affects both the speed and the nature of the transition. In some countries polities speed or catalyse the transition, in others they slow or dampen the transition. In some countries there are competing polities that push in opposite directions, for example, a religious polity committed to a domestic gender regime, a democratic state committed to a public gender regime, and the EU that promotes a public gender regime.

The political processes involved in these changes are not always centred in the country where the changes are taking place. Global feminist waves, with new civil societal and political projects, at repeated intervals have been associated with these changes. These waves have included conceptions of human rights and equal rights (Berkovitch 1999) as well as specifically feminist ideas. Sometimes the outcome is a change in the direction of the wave, sometimes it is a reaction against it. Sometimes there are opportunities for alliances with socialist class forces, leading to a renewed social democratic project; sometimes there are not.

During the transition from domestic labour to free wage labour, women are changing their political preferences along with their material position. This parallels the earlier process during industrialization when working men emerged not only as an economic class but also as a political force, though with varying impact depending on alliances with other social forces. These changes in the gender composition of employment are generating a new political constituency that favours the development of public services of education, health, and care. Employed women are becoming the new champions of social democracy (see Chapters 4 and 10). The increased representation of women in civil society organizations including trade unions as well as in parliaments has contributed to the development of a political project to regulate employment for gender equality and to develop childcare and other public services. The implications of this project depend on alliances between supporting groups and the historical legacy of political and industrial institutions. This has effects on the governance of the economy, which are only just beginning to be seen. Employed women are the force behind the defence of public services and the expansion of childcare services; they are also the force behind the regulation of employment to promote gender equality and the combination of care-work with employment. There is a positive feedback loop connecting the increased employment of women with the changes in the regulation of employment and the provision of welfare, which in turn increase the employment of women. This change also has implications for the defence of the project of social democracy. The new constituency of employed women is likely to ally themselves with projects seeking public services.

The emergent public gender regime can take either a neoliberal or a social democratic form. The outcome depends at least partly on the institutional legacy and on the political resources of potential allies during the period of transition. This moment is a critical turning point for the form of the gender regime.

This gender transition has implications for the rate of economic growth of the overall economy. The income of households rises due to women's increased employment, thereby increasing their purchases and further driving the economy forward. The timing and rate of the transition to free wage labour and the rate of economic growth are sometimes connected with positive feedback loops, with economic growth spurts appearing at such moments. In these cases the rate of economic growth cannot be explained without reference to the transformation of these complex inequalities. The rapid growth of the Swedish economy in the 1970s and the Irish economy during the 1990s has been associated with a substantial increase in women's employment (see Chapter 10).

The economy is not yet modern anywhere. Until the second great transformation is complete and women and minorities are free wage labourers, then we are not yet modern. There is more than one moment during the transition to economic modernity and these differ for different regimes of inequality. The transition for women is later than that for men – it is not yet complete, its consequences are still happening.

Gender relations in the economy are not reducible to class relations. In some aspects of economic inequality, employment regulation, and welfare provision, gender inequalities are moving in a different direction from class inequalities. One of the major reasons for this is that the transformation of women's labour from domestic to free wage labour is still ongoing; gender labour relations are not yet fully modern.

The transformation of the gender regime from the domestic to public form is an important driver of changes in the contemporary global economy. Not only does it in itself constitute a major restructuring of economic and other inequalities between women and men, but it also changes aspects of the rest of the economy partly through its restructuring of employment and welfare relations and partly because it gives rise to a new political constituency with a tendency to support social democracy.

Global Processes and Economic Inequalities

Are global processes increasing economic inequality, or not? Is economic inequality increasing (or decreasing) for reasons within countries rather than the global level? Are changes due to some interaction between these global and local processes? When looking at inequality, it has been usual to consider it within a country, so the comparisons are with other people living in the same country.

In a global era, might it be more appropriate to compare everyone in the world and not merely in the same country? What are the implications for conclusions about the shape and level of inequality of taking the country, regional, or the global level as the focus? Inequalities between countries do not necessarily change in the same direction and speed as inequalities within countries. What are the implications of taking account of complex inequalities other than class, such as gender, in this analysis?

Globalization is not new. Rather, it is a general feature of capitalist expansion (Marx 1954). There have been waves of globalization before this current one, associated with the expansion of different European empires, including those of the Dutch and British (Arrighi 1994; Chase-Dunn et al. 2000). Global economic inequality concerns not only money and class, but also inequalities associated with gender, ethnicity, and nation. The British Empire created a distinctive form of slavery, using force supported by the military to remove people from Africa and transport them to colonies in the Caribbean and the USA where they would grow the raw materials, such as cotton and sugar, that were needed to support British industry. British cotton manufacturers depended on the production of cotton, and their industrial working class ate sugar that for them was cheap, all at the expense of the African slaves (Walvin 1992). The inclusion of an account of these coercive transnational trades is necessary to understand the rapid development of the British and US economies. While that form of slavery no longer exists, it still leaves its mark in the racialization and economic and social position of minority ethnic groups within the USA, the UK, and elsewhere (Rex 1973), and is an important contributor to the weak development of the welfare state in the USA (Quadagno 1994; Manza 2000).

Economies have never been fully nationally bounded, but the current wave of globalization further reduces the significance of national states in regulating economies. The conventional view that an economy maps neatly onto a polity and a civil society in a given territory thereby constituting a society and a nation-state (e.g. Giddens 1990) is rejected here. Rather the economy, polity, violence, and civil society are each seen to have a different spatial and temporal reach. They overlap, but not completely so; nor are they nested in a simple hierarchical manner.

Capital takes several forms, some of which have a wider spatial reach than others. The conventional focus was once on fixed or industrial capital in machinery and buildings but finance capital is of increasing importance, with implications for globalization since it can speed further and faster around the world than the relatively fixed industrial capital (Strange 1986; Young 2000). The development of new financial instruments using synthetic securities increase rather than reduce the level of risk in economies world-wide (Tavakoli 2003), producing 'bubbles' and crises in financial markets in the USA that began to spread around the world in 2007–2008 (Soros 2008).

During early industrialization there is often an increase in economic inequality within countries which is followed by a plateau and then a decline: this is known as the 'Kuznets curve' (Kuznets 1955). Have recent global processes ended the slow decline in inequality associated with the demise of low wage agriculture? Are global processes eroding differences between countries, levelling down to the lowest level (Crouch and Streeck 1997; Standing 1999)? Or do differences between countries remain? In 1950, Latin America was the most unequal region in the world, followed by continental Europe, East Asia, South Asia, the Nordic countries, and the Anglo countries (based on measurements of the mean Gini index by macro-region: see Mann and Riley 2006). Have these regional differences been maintained or restructured in the recent period of globalization?

In the period from industrialization to the mid-1970s the evidence is unequivocal: the rich countries got richer more rapidly than the poor, increasing the economic inequalities between countries. While in the early nineteenth century the average incomes in the richest countries were around four times greater than those in the poorest, by the end of the twentieth century their incomes were 30 times greater (Firebaugh 1999). Inequalities between countries are composed of two elements: the extent of the exploitation of one country by another, and the differences in the rate of economic growth. In a global system the terms of trade tend to favour the stronger richer countries, which are then able to influence global regulations in order to suit their own interests; they are able to change the 'fitness landscape' in which all countries operate so as to advantage themselves. Between-country inequalities are also affected by the rate of economic growth. If rich countries grow more quickly than poor ones, then the inequalities between countries increase: if rich countries grow more slowly than poor ones, then the inequalities between countries decrease.

What global processes?

Globalization involves several different types of processes including: global flows of capital, trade and people; global financial institutions; global hegemons; and global waves. It is important to differentiate between the forms of these global processes and the content that they carry rather than conflate these into a single process of globalization. Neoliberalism is not an inevitable consequence of globalization, but instead a key project carried by and implicated in some global processes; and always contested.

Global capital flows

Increased flows of financial and industrial capital are a key feature of the current wave of globalization. The movement of capital out of the North in search of cheaper labour in the South is implicated in the increase in inequalities in countries in the North; of course, such flows of capital may also be associated with economic growth in the South. The strongest case for globalization increasing economic inequality focuses on the increased amount and speed of flows of capital associated with new information and communication technologies, transport, and political restructuring. Increased global flows of capital are seen to lead to a shift in the balance of power between capital and labour and a reduction in the capacity of states to support good conditions of work and the welfare of workers and citizens. Global capital flows have been linked to processes of deregulation and the degradation of the conditions of working life as a result of the increased global interconnections consequent on new ICTs, which tilts the balance of power between capital and labour towards capital partly because it is more mobile than labour (Castells 1996, 1997, 1998; Crouch and Streeck 1997; Standing 1999; Sassen 2001), although there are debates as to the extent to which capital goes 'regime shopping' (Traxler and Woitech 2000). The reduction in (or the threat of a reduction in) employment reduces the bargaining capacity of labour as compared with capital (Alderson and Nielson 2002). This engages a process through which states reduce social protection and increase the flexibility of their workforces in order to follow prevailing views about the best way to compete in a global marketplace (Cerny 1996). Martin and Schumann (1997) see global capital undermining the conditions of working life; Crouch and Streeck (1997) see capital undermining national welfare states; Sennett (1998) argues that these changes are leading to a corrosion of character since people need the stability of the old ways of working. These divisions are re-configured spatially, reducing the extent to which these are primarily intra-national inequalities and increasing the extent to which they are inequalities between countries as a result of the position of different countries within a global market, though some significant development of local elites continues. The positioning of countries depends on whether they are a core or peripheral country within a global system, their relationship with global hegemons and regional networks, as well as on local developments such as in education (Reich 1993), form of governance structures (Evans 1995), and telecommunications (Huws et al. 1999).

During the 1990s and the start of the twenty-first century, there was an increase in 'private equity' as compared with equity invested in companies that are quoted on the stock market and subject to public scrutiny and reporting requirements. Similarly avoiding such controls is the development of 'off-shore' tax havens to avoid scrutiny and taxation. These developments of even more mobility by capital reduce democratic control over capital and its taxation.

Finance capital has different global dynamics from that of industrial or fixed capital. With globalization there is a stock market open somewhere around the world almost all the time; exchanges can take place electronically and near-instantaneously. The increased size and speed of the flows of finance around the world contribute to the significance of the speculatory gambles that can lead to financial crises. Financial bubbles are a routine feature of global financial markets, in which financial speculation or gambling inflates values before a crash. Usually, the richer speculators will be able to make profits during the up-swing while the crash will disproportionately affect smaller investors (Strange 1986; Perez 2002). Such bubbles are common in financial markets because of the lack of direct information that can be used to stabilize a valuation; instead, a reflexive process among traders will tend to exaggerate both the up-swings and down-swings. Financial markets are often far from equilibrium rather than being self-equilibrating (Soros 2008).

The volatility of global financial markets has increased since 1999 with the invention of credit derivatives – including synthetic securitizations or collateralized debt obligations and credit default swaps – to manipulate financial risk. Since the 1990s until the crash of 2008 there had been a rapid increase in the scale of this market. The original intent was to use securitization to move mortgage-backed securities and other loans off the bank's balance sheet risk, reducing its exposure to risk. However, the practice has developed in such a way that banks have increased their exposure to risk. This was compounded by poor assessment of the risk by the ostensibly specialized risk rating agencies. More important, however, was that the general dismantling of the regulation of the financial markets that had been introduced after the Great Depression of the 1930s (Krugman 2008; Soros 2008) as part of the neoliberal project. Although there were significant variations in the extent to which national states deregulated their financial markets, the USA and the UK being among the most extreme, the consequences have been global (even though uneven) such is the extent of the global interconnectivity and flows of finance. During 2007 and 2008 a series of escalating financial crises started in the USA and spread around most of the rest of the world (see Chapter 11). Global capital flowed towards the core countries from the semi-periphery as part of the process of this recapitalization of banks in the core but to the detriment of the economies outside the core. In this way the global financial crisis, though started in the USA, has had disproportionate effects upon poorer countries.

Global trade flows

Global trade concerns movements in goods and services rather than capital and some definitions of globalization focus on these elements. Does the current increase in global trade increase or decrease economic inequality? This question can be answered with either a focus on the economic inequalities within countries or the economic inequalities between countries.

First, there are implications for inequalities within countries where the argument is parallel to the arguments about the flow of capital. The increased flow of goods and services brings workers in the North into closer competition with less well paid workers in the South, particularly the less skilled workers in the North. There are fewer workers in the South who can match highly skilled workers with high levels of education and human capital. This reduces the demand for less skilled workers more than would be so with skilled and highly educated workers, thus driving up wage inequalities in the North (Wood 1994).

Second, there are implications for economic inequalities between countries which depend on the relative rate of growth of different economies. There are two radically divergent arguments here. On the one hand the world systems, especially dependency, theorists argue that the terms of trade are so organized by global hegemons in their own interests that trade is an instrument in which the rich North exploits the poor South, or rather, the core countries exploit those in the periphery of the world system (Wallerstein 1974; Frank 1975). The rules of world trade are set not by a democratically elected world council but by the world's richest countries in their own interests, with tariffs in place to protect their goods (for example, US steel and EU agricultural production) that are combined with demands to remove tariffs for the rest of the world. On the other hand, the World Trade Organization and others (Dollar and Kray 2001) have argued that globalization, understood as increased world trade, encourages economic growth and thereby reduces poverty and inequality. It encourages economic growth because free trade allows countries to better specialize in their comparative advantages and adds pressure for the removal of the protection of special interests. Here the data as well as the arguments are fiercely contested (Wade 2004). For example, the concepts of 'poverty' and 'inequality' need to be distinguished. Economic growth does have a tendency to lift people above a given threshold of poverty – for example, defined as living on less than $1 dollar or $2 dollars a day (UN Millennium Development Goals 2007a) – but this is not the same as reducing inequality, understood either as the gap between the top and the bottom of a country's population or as the gap between rich or poor countries.

Global flows of people
The restructuring of patterns of inequality is associated with flows of people and the consequent reconstitution of national and ethnic relations within countries (Urry 2007). Migration is not new (Therborn 1995), but takes new forms in a global era (Cohen 1997). Migrants may not have access to full citizenship entitlements, leaving them especially vulnerable to economic exploitation since they might be reluctant to seek help from the authorities. In 'global care chains' (Hochschild 2000), caring labour is mobile from the South to the North (Yeates 2005); unequal social relations are embedded in these global chains, constituted by class, gender, ethnicity, nationality, and position in the North or South. While some movements of people are voluntary, and indeed eagerly embarked upon, others are coerced, with a consequent extreme vulnerability to continuing inequalities and violence. Human trafficking is one of the more pernicious forms of inequality associated with increased global mobility (Raymond et al. 2002; Huda 2006).

Global institutions
Global institutions that affect economies include those that are focused on finance as well as those more concerned with security and with justice. Global financial institutions are implicated in increasing economic inequalities not only because they are becoming more important in the regulation of economies around the world but also insofar as they carry a neoliberal project. They include formal multi-lateral institutions, especially the International Monetary Fund, the World Bank, and the World Trade Organization; international regimes with agreed rules of conduct, such as the Bretton Woods 1944–1971 monetary agreement; and more informal gatherings of leaders of the world's largest economies such as the G8 and G20 (Keohane 1989; Ruggie 1996, 1998; Held et al. 1999). The International Monetary Fund lends money to governments in financial crisis but attaches stringent conditions to the loans, sometimes demanding the significant restructuring of the government's budget and the way a country's economy is governed. It also monitors economic and financial developments and provides expertise (International Monetary Fund 2007). The World Bank lends

money to developing countries in a way that is supposed to be intended to assist their economic development (World Bank 2007a). The World Trade Organization oversees the rules and import tariffs used in world trade; it has a long-standing ambition to reduce tariffs and to promote free trade, engaging in negotiations over many years to take forward this project (World Trade Organization 2007). While such international institutions are more important than ever before, they are not entirely new; the nineteenth century also had an international monetary system (Hirst and Thompson 1996). The neoliberal 'Washington Consensus' promoted by such institutions is contested in various formal and informal ways. For example, within the UN the 'Group of 77' – established in 1964 and with 130 members and a permanent institutional structure by 2007 – represents developing states in global trade negotiations, although it is not as powerful as the US-led institutions (Group of 77 2007). Further, the International Labour Organization (ILO), founded in 1919, has long promoted worker rights (Thomas 1996; ILO 2005).

It is not only the existence and powers of global financial institutions that are important, but also the kinds of projects, policies, and programmes that they run. Since the 1970s these institutions have largely operated within a neoliberal understanding of economics and their actions have had a tendency to increase economic inequality. A wave of financial deregulation, with the demise of the Bretton Woods agreement in 1971, entailed the removal of controls on the movement of capital, thereby enabling the development of rapid movements of capital around the world. The conditions attached to loans by the IMF and World Bank often require the structural adjustment of economies away from public services and towards greater privatization (Sparr 1994; Stiglitz 2002). At moments of financial crisis governments and governing elites are often divided and in a weak position to resist the neoliberal policies of the global financial institutions, despite their uneven record in assisting economic recovery (Stiglitz 2002; Klein 2007). This neoliberal content is linked to increased gender inequality (Elson 1991, 1995; Sparr 1994; Peterson and Runyan 1999; Grown et al. 2000; Rankin 2001; Dennis and Zuckerman 2006), although there have long been attempts at taking gender more seriously in global financial institutions (Murphy 1995; Haxton and Olsson 1999).

However, the neoliberal content of the programmes of these governmental institutions is contested. Countries from the South refused to sign up to the Doha round of trade negotiations that had been organized by the WTO and were aimed at removing trade protections. Protesters at meetings of these entities, most famously of the WTO in Seattle in 1999, have ensured that an alternative view is seen and heard. Intellectuals and activists have challenged the indicators that are used to measure progress (Bardhan and Klasen 1999; UNDP 2006), fighting both outside and inside the global financial institutions (Wade 2002). For example, the rate of economic growth is no longer the sole indicator of progress for the IMF and World Bank, which have adopted the broader UN Millennium Development Goals that include human capabilities such as education and health in addition to economic growth (UN 2007a).

The global financial crisis of 2008 led to calls for a new 'Bretton Woods' to restructure the global financial architecture to ensure that such a crisis could not be repeated. Such restructuring would involve a greater regulation of finance – a further challenge to the neoliberal project.

Financial institutions are not the only international institutions to be relevant to the shape of economic development. Decisions over the legitimacy and conduct of war and economic sanctions, made by the UN Security Council, are also important for economic inequalities.

Global hegemons

Global hegemons are important in setting the rules of the global financial system and the global security system, even when these decisions are ostensibly taken by international bodies. Since the middle of the twentieth century this has been the USA. Previously, the global hegemon was the UK.

The USA is not uncontested as a global hegemon as the EU is an increasingly powerful entity on the global stage. The EU regularly disagrees with the USA in global financial institutions such as the World Trade Organization, over matters such as the regulation of world trade and the use of the precautionary principle in the assessment of risk in environmental matters (Winickoff et al. 2005). With the rapid economic development of China, at some point in the future there is likely to be a further re-balancing of global power over economic policy (Hutton 2003).

Global waves

Global political and civil societal waves are a further form of global process. Neoliberalism is a powerful global wave. Neoliberalism started as a project in civil society that became a governmental programme in the world's most powerful hegemon during the Reagan presidency of 1981–1989 and is now rooted in the USA's social formation and in many global financial institutions. It has become the preferred political project of US capital. It is important not to conflate the form of global processes with the content that they carry.

The neoliberal project gained support in the context of fears about global economic pressures, which were used to support arguments about the inevitability of welfare retrenchment in order to maintain economic competitiveness (Schwartz 2001). Crisis situations may be used as opportunities to restructure (Klein 2007). Indeed the reversal of the prioritization of low inflation and low unemployment towards low inflation often involves an apparent crisis, which provides an opportunity for neoliberal restructuring (Korpi 2003). The political project of neoliberalism centrally involves a deregulation of the market and a reduction in the provision of welfare by the state; it also includes de-unionization and pressure to keep the minimum wage low. The political pressure to deregulate the workplace has led in some countries to the removal of protections for workers, as well as a downward pressure on the extent and quality of welfare provision (Cerny 1995, 1996; Held 1995; Martin and Schumann 1997; Standing 1999).

There are other global waves of political and civil societal practices that carry quite different projects. Among those that concern the economy are: the anti-neoliberal/global justice project; rights (including both equal rights and human rights), and feminism. These global waves spread suddenly around the world in non-linear ways and interact with quite different sets of social relations in diverse countries. Global waves carry not only neoliberalism but also other contesting civil societal projects. For example, the protest against the neoliberal globalization project at the meeting of the WTO in Seattle in 1999 was a key moment in the generation of a global anti-neoliberal-capitalism wave. In 2008, the aftermath of the global financial crisis is providing a new context for social democratic challenges to the 'market fundamentalism' (Soros 2008) of neoliberalism.

Country processes

Global processes are not the only forces restructuring economies and their inequalities. Processes at the country level not only interact with global processes and neoliberal projects, but can also generate pressures towards the increase or decrease of economic inequality. Some of these processes apply to all countries though at different times; some of them apply unevenly to countries.

Changing balance of economic sectors within a country
The changing balance of economic sectors has implications for the shape and extent of inequality in a country because some sectors, usually the newly developing ones, will pay higher wages than others. When only a few people work in a new sector these higher wages have only a marginal effect on the overall wage distribution,

but as these numbers grow they stretch the overall wage gap thereby increasing the overall economic inequality which reaches its maximum when the two sectors are equal in size. As the high wage sector continues to expand and the low wage sector reduces, the numbers on low wages decline thereby reducing the overall economic inequality.

The Kuznets (1955) curve, concerning the increase and then decrease in economic inequality in countries undergoing industrialization, is accounted for by the changing balance between the low wage agricultural and higher wage industrial sectors. As the latter grows relative to the former inequality rises until the sectors are of equal size thereafter declining. When all of the workforce are in the industrial sector, there is no 'Kuznets' effect based on the decline of the low wage agricultural to continue to decrease inequality.

While Kuznets looked only at the relationship between the agricultural and industrial/service sectors, a parallel analysis could be applied to the changing relationship of other economic sectors, in particular the knowledge economy and the domestic economy. The knowledge economy is a new type of economic sector with average higher wages than the older non-knowledge sector. As the higher paying knowledge grows relative to the older sectors, then inequality increases until they are of equal size thereafter declining. The domestic sector is an old economic sector that creates no monetary income for those who work in it; its coexistence with the monetized economy contributes to overall economic inequality. As the domestic sector declines in size, so its contribution to economic inequality in the economy as a whole declines. This is in addition to its effects on gender inequality, between men (disproportionately in the new monetized sector) and women (disproportionately in the domestic sector), which should decline as the domestic sector declines. This could be described as 'gendering the Kuznets curve'.

The knowledge economy
In the latest phase of economic development knowledge itself has become a factor of production, in human skills and in the development of new information and communication technologies, and in their many interconnected assemblages (Castells 1996, 1997, 1998). There is a new form of capital in addition to financial and industrial capital – human capital, made up of skills and experience. The scale and significance of the knowledge economy have been much disputed: sceptics suggest that much is merely over-blown hype (Thrift 1999) while others consider that it is transforming the totality of employment (Handy 1994). The knowledge economy has been associated

with ostensibly divergent accounts of its implications for social inequalities. For some, the development of a knowledge-based economy provides higher skilled jobs with greater autonomy, flatter hierarchies, more flexible working time schedules, and an improved quality of working life (Flores and Gray 2000). The belief that a knowledge-based economy can provide high quality as well as more jobs underlies EU economy policy as expressed in the 2000 Lisbon European Council's adoption of the goal that the European Union should become "the most competitive and dynamic knowledge-based economy in the world capable of sustainable economic growth with more and better jobs and greater social cohesion" (Rodrigues 2003; European Commission 2007f). For others, the development of a knowledge economy stretches the gap between wages, thereby increasing inequality by producing larger numbers of workers in the higher skilled occupations (Glyn 2001; Smeeding 2002).

One of the reasons for the different accounts is that different definitions are being used that produce quite different profiles and scales of the knowledge economy. Is it high technology and science, embedded or encoded in machines? Or is it knowledge, embrained in highly educated and trained people? Or is it the jobs associated with new ways of processing information by using computers? Three different kinds of knowledge economy can be distinguished. First is high technology manufacturing, including aerospace, computers, electronics-communications, pharmaceuticals, biotechnology, and scientific instruments. Second are the knowledge intensive services, including water and air transport, post and telecommunications, financial intermediation, real estate, computer services, research and development services, education, health and social work, recreational, cultural, and sporting activities. A third kind lies in between and is associated with information, including publishing, printing and the reproduction of recorded media, post and telecommunications, computing-related activities including software, and recreational, cultural, and sporting activities (European Commission 2001; Eurostat 2005a, 2005b; OECD 2005; UN Statistics Division 2005a, 2005b; Shire 2007; Walby 2007).

The first sector – the high technology manufacturing – fits the image of the new economy as based on science and technology. It is a machine-based conception of innovation. The second – knowledge intensive services – is quite different, being based on people possessing knowledge not machines. This knowledge or human capital is developed in education (Becker 1993; Reich 1993) as well as within workplaces in the dynamic relationship between the tacit and explicit knowledge of workers and managers (Nonaka and Takeuchi 1995; Nonaka and Nishiguchi 2001; Nishikawa and Tanaka 2007). A considerable proportion of workers in knowledge intensive services work in health and education (Walby 2007b). The third type of sector, focused on information, best fits the image of the workers that are more autonomous, more flexible, in better quality jobs, coordinated through flatter hierarchies and networks because the nature of the work requires cooperation and communication rather than coordination through simple hierarchies. They have greater flexibility in the use of labour time and a reduction in certain types of spatial constraints on where work is carried out, facilitating the development of new forms of careers and attachments to the providers of work (Reich 1991; Drucker 1993; Handy 1994; Nonaka and Takeuchi 1995; Castells 1996, 1997, 1998; Seltzer and Bentley 1999; Flores and Gray 2000; Nonaka and Nishiguchi 2001; Lam 2002; Rodrigues 2003).

The high technology sector is a very small proportion of the workforce as is the information sector; by contrast the knowledge intensive sector is substantial. In the UK, high technology manufacturing is 2 per cent, information 4 per cent, and knowledge intensive services 42 per cent of the workforce (Walby 2006). While the information sector is most frequently taken as emblematic of the knowledge economy, it is tiny; knowledge intensive services are more representative. The most distinctive feature of the knowledge economy is not the development of more sophisticated machines, but the development of new types of knowledge held by human beings. It is the ownership of this knowledge, this human capital, by workers themselves that has the potential to change the nature of social and economic hierarchies.

Has there been a larger increase in higher or lower level jobs? Even when technology is cutting edge there is no necessary reason why the associated occupations should be disproportionately high skill (Fleming et al. 2004). However, the evidence here is of a disproportionate increase in the higher level jobs associated with the knowledge economy: within the European Union between 1995 and 2000 over 60 per cent of new jobs were created in the high-skilled non-manual occupations (European Commission 2001).

While most of the early concerns over the implications of globalization concerned the pay and conditions of those at the bottom of the job market in advanced economies, part of the growth in inequality is associated with an increase in incomes and wealth at the top as well as the bottom end of the economy. These processes concern not only class, but also gender relations (Walby et al. 2007). Are women winners in a new economy that places a high value on human capital derived from the high levels of education increasingly obtained by women, or are they the losers in a segregated workforce confined to the non-technological parts of the economy (Brine 2006; Mósesdóttir et al. 2006)? Serrano-Pascual and Mósesdóttir (2003) doubt that women benefit as much as men from the high skill components of these developments for two main reasons: first because of the role of occupational segregation by sex, which remains in all labour markets (Anker 1998), and second because women's formal educational qualifications may translate less well into employment assets than those of men.

If the knowledge economy is understood as the high end technology present in manufacturing and bioscience, then it is a small proportion of the economy and overwhelmingly male. If the knowledge economy is understood as highly expert people, then it is present in services such as health and education and slightly more populated by women than men (Shire 2007; Walby 2007b; Walby et al. 2007). The shift in the economy towards a knowledge-based economy places a higher premium on human capital. This advantages those people who have acquired the relevant type and level of education. Increasingly this is women, or rather women are increasingly among those who are educated at the levels that facilitate their participation in the knowledge economy. However, there is a need for caution since the sex segregation of both education and employment means that there is no easy translation between education and employment position (Mósesdóttir, Pascual and Remery 2006).

The development of the knowledge economy does tend to increase the proportion of more highly skilled and better paid jobs. Simultaneously, this tends to increase economic inequalities because it stretches the wage spread (Glyn 2001; Smeeding 2002). The extent to which this is a major rather than a minor contribution to economic inequality needs to be treated with caution however, given the scale of the other processes occurring at the same time (Card and DiNardo 2002).

The decline of the domestic economy
The decline of the domestic sector of the economy and the concomitant shift from domestic labour to free wage labour by women, typically decreases the overall economic inequality as well as specifically gendered economic inequality. This shrinking of an economic sector that provides no monetary income while simultaneously increasing the proportion of adults who have some, rather than no, monetary income is the reason for this. Thus, the upward trend in the proportion of women in employment and the proportion of the workforce that is female are both indicative of a decline in overall economic inequality. The size of the gender pay gap is another indicator of gendered economic inequality.

However, if economic inequality is measured by the inequality between household units rather than individuals then any decline in the domestic economy is rendered irrelevant, since this effect is hidden inside the household that is treated as the unit. This means that measurements of inequality that use the household as the unit are inadvisable.

Decline in economically-based constituencies for social democracy or not?
The level of priority given to economic equality by a polity depends at least in part on the strength of the social forces that support such a project. Traditionally, economic equality has been part of the social democratic project that has been disproportionately supported by male manual workers in manufacturing industries. With a decrease in the size of this economic sector and the growth of the service sector, there has been a decline in the size of the traditional class support for social democracy (Przeworski and Sprague 1986). The decline of the traditional base in electoral support in the male manual manufacturing industry has been seen to at least partially explain this retreat (Callaghan 2000) and transformation (Kitschelt 1994) of social democracy, and thus the opening of the political space for neoliberalism. In addition there has been a tendency for the dealignment of class and voting practices (Crewe et al. 1977).

However, when gender and other complex inequalities are brought into focus these arguments about the declining socio-economic base for a social democratic project are brought into question. Employed women tend to support the public provision of services and hence to support those political parties and projects that are socially and democratically inclined. This has occurred most obviously in those countries where there is a near-full employment of women – Sweden and the USA (Manza and Brooks 1998) – but is also emerging in many advanced economies (Huber and Stephens 2001).

When gender as well as class forces are taken into account the thesis that there is a decline in the socio-economic base for social democratic projects is challenged.

Fiscal crisis of the welfare state?
One of the challenges to the thesis that global pressures are forcing a retrenchment of the welfare state and hence its amelioration of economic inequality is that there are long term domestic reasons for this. The shift from an industrial to a post-industrial economy in the context of the maturing of the welfare state produces fiscal pressures on the welfare state that might account for its austerity (Pierson 2001). The recent tendency towards austerity can be linked to the rise of the service sector, which has little potential for increases in productivity, the ageing of the population with consequent increases in expenditure on pension and care needs (Pierson 2001), and changes in the size and position of groups fighting over distribution (Iversen 2001).

However, bringing gender into focus challenges some of these arguments. The increase in women's employment increases the proportion of the population paying income tax while not in itself increasing the numbers of those claiming benefits. The transformation of the gender regime thus potentially reduces the fiscal pressure on the state. Therefore structural changes within a country could have implications for the fiscal viability of welfare provision in either direction and not only towards austerity.

Despite the global pressures, there has been little change in public spending on social expenditure in OECD countries in the period 1990 to 2003 (OECD 2007b: 193). Public social expenditure very slightly increased over this period, with many countries growing during the period towards the peak in 1993 with a slight decline since then. There are variations within this, such as a slight rise for the UK since 1999 (associated with the change in government to the Labour Party). However, since these figures include unemployment benefits they are affected by an increased expenditure associated with high levels of unemployment (e.g. Sweden in 1993) (Korpi 2003).

Political institutions and coalitions

Political actors and institutions at a country and regional level have significant effects on the balance between neoliberalism and social democracy, with implications for the regulation of finance and of employment and the state provision of welfare. Insofar as they experience global economic pressures, they interpret and mediate them so that global processes may lead to new sources of difference rather than homogeneity. These national processes have been thought of as a form of resilience or resistance to these global processes (Swank 2002), but this may be better thought of as interaction or coevolution of these processes since the country and regional practices can have implications for the global level. The political institutions of advanced capitalist countries have different kinds of capacities to respond to the challenges of global processes as a consequence of forms of electoral system, the nature of interest group representation, the relative centralization or decentralization of policy-making authority and the structuring of welfare programme provision, and only in those countries that have a more liberal political structure do global pressures lead to reductions in the welfare state while in the large welfare states of northern Europe there has been little impact (Swank 2002). To the extent that such institutions mediate the response to global pressures, there can be no simple assertion that globalization leads to a general undermining of the conditions of employment.

An important set of such institutions is the trade unions, with their density, influence, and resilience varying considerably between countries (Ebbinghaus and Visser 1999). The neoliberal attack on trade unions, the minimum wage, and other institutions that promote economic equality has been stronger in some countries (such as the US and UK) than in others. The significance of declines in unionization and the minimum wage has featured strongly in several accounts of increasing economic inequality in the USA (DiNardo et al. 1996; Lee 1999; Card and DiNardo 2002). Card and DiNardo (2002) assess the thesis that rising income inequality is due to the skills-biased technical change associated with the development of the knowledge economy. They show that while in the USA wage inequality rose in the 1980s and stabilized in the 1990s there were continuing advances in new computer technologies in the later as well as the earlier period. They conclude by suggesting that a decline in the minimum wage is the likely cause of the increase in wage inequality. DiNardo et al. (1996) found that deunionization and the drop in real value of the minimum wage were important factors in the rise of wage inequality from 1979 to 1988. Lee (1999) finds that a decline in the real value of the federal minimum wage was also important in explaining the rise in wage inequality in the USA during the 1980s.

A different aspect of resilience and resistance is that of the building of new political coalitions and projects in which political actors forge new projects, alliances, and institutions; new forms of partnership, social pacts, and corporatism (Hanké and Rhodes 2001); and move from 'social' to 'competitive corporatism' (Rhodes 1998, 2001). The European Union itself is one example of the development of a new political project and coalition that proactively engages with global processes (Walby 1999b). These new political projects and coalitions involve not only class forces but also forces that are gendered and engage with religion and nation.

Summary

Globalization is made up of many different processes. These include global flows of capital, trade and people; global institutions; hegemons; networks; and waves. These global processes need to be separately identified and not merged into a single process of globalization. Economies are shaped by the mutual adaptation of systems at a country level and these global processes, which involve not only economies but also polities, violence, and civil societies. These restructure inequalities in complex ways, as is investigated empirically in Chapter 9 on 'measuring progress'.

Varieties of Political Economy

One important division is that between modern and premodern forms of economy, while other distinctions can be made between modern forms. Within the modern economy path dependent processes can be identified in employment relations, welfare provision, and the nature and regulation of finance. A key distinction is between neoliberal and social democratic forms. In the neoliberal variety there is little democratic intervention or regulation of employment and finance as compared with the social democratic form; there is much less state welfare provision than in the social democratic form; and there is more economic inequality than in the social democratic form.

Complex inequalities challenge the traditional categories and analyses of varieties of employment relations and welfare provision. Rather than treating all social relations within the economy as if they were the consequence of class relations there are significant differences between regimes of inequality, in particular, between those of class, gender, and ethnicity. Whether or not regimes of inequality map onto each other should be treated as an empirical question rather than as a presumption. There is a further question as to whether all aspects of political economy are tightly coupled or whether there is divergence between the varieties of employment regulation and welfare provision.

As well as identifying the different varieties of political economy it is important to ask about their causes. This involves a consideration of critical turning points and the different pathways and the institutions that lock them in. These can occur at different times for different regimes of inequality and involve different polities and social forces. One question here is whether global processes are eroding and ending the distinct pathways and varieties of economies.

The focus in this chapter and in the subsequent empirical analysis is on employment regulation and welfare provision. However, it is important to note that other aspects of the economy could be subject to parallel analyses. In particular, there is considerable variation between countries in the regulation of finance capital. This is despite the extent of the globalization of finance capital, often regarded as more globalized than other forms of capital. In the USA and the UK there are few regulations of finance; new financial instruments have been invented that lie outside of those banking regulations introduced after previous crises in the banking and finance sector. However, in some EU Member States such new forms of financial capital have not been encouraged – and speculation and financial bubbles are less common and less severe as a consequence. This may be seen as a further aspect of the differentiation of more neoliberal and more social democratic forms of economies.

Varieties of employment relations

Early distinctions in forms of capitalism focused on changes over time. These are indeed significant, but are not the main concern of this section. One example of a temporal approach to differences in the form of capitalism is that from Fordism to post-Fordism, where Fordism is the social organization that was associated with mass production and mass consumption, while post-Fordism or flexible specialization is the social organization associated with craft specialization and niche consumerism (Piore and Sabel 1984; Boyer and Durand 1997). Another approach addresses the shift from a Keynesian welfare state to a Schumpeterian workfare state (Jessop 2002).

Here interest lies in the varieties of employment relations across different countries at the same point in time. The existing analysis tends to focus on those institutions associated with market-based production, especially the nature of the relations between employers, labour, and governmental institutions, sometimes in wider social contexts (Olson 1982; Piore and Sabel 1984; Lash and Urry 1987, 1994; Streeck 1992; Crouch 1993; Hirst and Zeitlin 1997; Hollingsworth 1997; Hollingsworth and Boyer 1997; Kitschelt et al. 1999; Whitley 2000; Hall and Soskice 2001; Streeck and Yamamura 2002; Swenson 2002; Yamamura and Streeck 2003). These distinctions have often been typified as a dichotomy into which different groups of countries can be clustered, though with varying conceptualization and with an emphasis on different institutions. These include the distinction between corporatism and liberalism (Crouch 1993), liberal market or coordinated market economies (Hall and Soskice 2001), institutionally thin and thick societies (Streeck 1992), and liberal and non-liberal (Streeck and Yamamura 2002); social democracy is often conflated with coordinated or corporatist forms. These writers differ on a series of dimensions. The main forces are differently conceptualized: capital, firms (Hall and Soskice 2001), employers, employers' organizations (Swenson 2002), or service class (Lash and Urry 1987); workers, trade unions, trade union density or coverage, collective bargaining, centralization or coordination (Gallie 1998; Ebbinghaus and Visser 1999), worker representation in parties and government (Huber and Stephens 2001); the welfare state. They vary in the extent to which social institutions, arenas and forces beyond capital and labour are included: welfare state (Esping-Andersen 1990; Pierson 2001), education and skills regime (Estevez et al. 2001), macroeconomic policy

(Young 2000; Iversen 2001; Korpi 2003), civil society, culture and organized religion (Lash and Urry 1994), political representation and access to governance (Huber and Stephens 2001). There are differences in the extent to which the analysis is realist or constructionist, focused on actors or structures (Herrigel 2005), and the extent to which there is full integration of actors and institutions into a single system or not, with implications for the extent of path dependency (Morgan and Kubo 2005).

A slightly different approach from employment relations and capitalist production regimes is that of 'corporatism'. The key distinction is between liberal and corporatist, where the liberal form was primarily coordinated through the market and the corporatist is coordinated through institutions including employers, workers, and the state (Schmitter 1974). The focus is on the extent to which the inherently conflictual relationship between capital and labour is institutionalized and mediated by the state. Corporatism is a form of economic governance that involves organizations of employers, trade unions, and government making bargains and compromises in order to secure their common interests in economic development. It is usually centralized at a national level, with meetings at periodic intervals to make binding agreements (Olson 1982; Crouch 1993). Corporatism involves compromises over the round of pay rises with usually the government giving something to enhance worker incomes in some other way, normally though not always in the form of a social wage or social benefits. It is sometimes assumed that the leading form of corporatism is its social democratic form, in the Nordic countries of Sweden, Norway, Denmark, and Finland. However, this is far from always the case. It has taken a more regressive form in relation to complex inequalities other than class, as in the conservative corporatist forms found in some parts of central Europe, such as Germany and Austria.

More recently, new forms of corporatism and corporatist analysis have developed with a more nuanced analysis than that of a dichotomy between liberal and corporatist, with different kinds of corporatist arrangements or social pacts (Rhodes 1998, 2001; Boucher and Collins 2003; Baccaro and Simoni 2007), social partnerships (Roche 2007), or 'concertation' (Ebbinghaus and Hassel 2000) being analysed. This includes 'competitive corporatism' in countries such as the Netherlands and Ireland, which involves new forms of distributional and productivity coalitions consolidated in social pacts that prioritize economic growth and lowering unemployment, with agreements on incomes policies, a reduction in the social protection of elite groups, and a prioritization of education and training (Rhodes 1998, 2001). In such types of corporatism, it is necessary to distinguish between the form – in the sense of the partners to the agreement – and the content – which can include not only social democratic but also neoliberal policies.

Amid this myriad of slightly differing distinctions, the distinction between liberal and coordinated market economies has emerged as the leading typology (Hall and Soskice 2001). Hall and Soskice (2001: 8) distinguish between 'liberal market economies' (LMEs) in which 'firms coordinate their activities primarily via hierarchies and competitive market relations' and 'coordinated market economies' (CMEs) in which 'firms depend more heavily on non-market relationships to coordinate endeavours with other actors and to construct their core competencies'. In LMEs the demand and supply of a market are important, in CMEs the strategic interactions between firms and other actors are important. The firm is placed as the central actor in this analysis, rather than the relations between organizations of capital and labour and the differential organizational strength of labour. Nevertheless, the range of institutions considered relevant still includes the traditional range of employer associations, trade unions, share-holding networks, and legal systems. In addition, the institutional structures for the acquisition of skill and other forms of human capital are included. In liberal economies the individual acquisition of skills and education in schools and colleges are more important than employer-based systems, while in coordinated economies skill acquisition is centred in employer-based systems that are supported by the long-tenure of jobs so that both worker and employer can benefit from such an investment.

The operationalization of the forms of employment regulation that lie at the heart of the distinction between liberal and coordinated varieties of capitalism is centred on the strictness of employment protection (Estevez-Abe et al. 2001). This is based on OECD (1994, 1997a) measures of the difficulty of employers dismissing workers, calculated through the nature of the rules governing the hiring and firing of individuals and collective dismissals (redundancy). Estevez-Abe and colleagues have added to this their own measure of company-based protection, although (with the exception of Japan) this correlates so highly with the state legislation-based measure that this makes little difference to the relative position of the countries.

The approach by Hall and Soskice and others to the varieties of capitalism entails a dichotomy in which social democracy is made invisible, being subsumed within the category of 'coordinated' market economies. The empirical analysis tends to use Germany as the emblematic example of coordination, rather than the social democratic form of Sweden, in comparison with the USA as the example of liberal economies. This obscuring of the socialist and social democratic tradition of organizing advanced economies does not bring clarity to an analysis of the origin of this path-dependent form. Few have attempted to build the project of coordination, yet many have and still do attempt a social democratic project. Germany is not the leading example of social democracy: rather somewhere to its right, positioned in between a liberal and social democratic form. A dichotomy based on liberal versus coordinated capitalism is less helpful than one based on liberal versus social democratic.

Employment protection legislation has developed over many years. In countries with the greatest strictness of protection, this was developed and consolidated in the post-war years, from the 1950s to the 1970s, during a period of social democratic ascendancy and trade union growth in several Western and Northern European countries. However, the development of neoliberalism has led to a reduction in these protections in some countries, though not all. This was often associated with a drive to reduce the power and significance of trade unions. For example, during the 1980s the UK saw a reduction in these traditional forms of legal employment protection (Crouch 1993; Dex and McCulloch 1997; Korpi 2002, 2003).

Employment protection was usually only provided for 'standard' forms of employment. In practice this meant for those people who worked for a single employer, with regular hours (such as 9 to 5, Monday to Friday) and expectations of continuous employment. The erosion of the significance of employment protection took place not only through a direct challenge to this legislation, but also by the growth of employment that was outside of the 'standard' forms that had this protection. These forms of non-standard employment concern the 'new temporalities, new contractualities and new spatialities' of employment today (Walby 2007b). They include the growth of part-time and temporary employment in those countries where full-time working provided access to protections, thereby undermining the proportion of the workforce covered by such regulations. Such newly expanding non-standard forms of employment are often disproportionately filled by women and minoritized ethnic groups, thereby exacerbating divisions and inequalities in the workforce (Gottfried 2003; Durbin 2007; Gottschall and Kroos 2007; Perrons 2007; Shire 2007; Walby et al. 2007). In such a context, workers in standard forms of employment (disproportionately male) enjoy protections, while workers in non-standard forms of employment (disproportionately female and minority) are more exposed to the market. However, in some countries the development of equality legislation has eroded this differential exposure of women and minorities.

Employment relations and complex inequalities

These distinctions between varieties of capitalism and employment regulations tend to neglect social divisions other than class. References to gender, ethnicity, and other complex inequalities are rarely more than brief empirical notes with few perceived theoretical implications; the substantial literature on gender and employment and ethnicity and employment is rarely integrated into these analyses. What would it mean to include complex inequalities in addition to class within an analysis of the varieties of employment relations?

There are additional types of regulation and institutional practices that need to be included in order that complex inequalities are included in the conceptualization of varieties of employment relations – those that support inequality as well as those that are intended to erode inequality. Some legal regulations overtly restrict women's employment, such as the marriage bar under which women were obliged to give up their jobs when they marry, from pre-EU Ireland (Curtin 1989) to Japan (Horton 1996). Other legal regulations indirectly support inequality by providing benefits for dominant gender and ethnic groups, leaving women and minoritized groups exposed outside these protections, such as the use of criteria for access to benefits that women and minorities are less likely to meet. Examples include the number of hours worked (excluding part-timers who are disproportionately women), or contractual status, excluding temporary and agency workers (who are more likely to be minorities). These exclusions may appear to be of minor importance when introduced, but become more significant as employers disproportionately expand employment in the unprotected niches. Workers in non-standard conditions are least likely to have employment protections, and are also least likely to be from the dominant gender and ethnic groups (Shire 2007; Walby et al. 2007). Employment 'protection' legislation, such as that which protects workers against redundancy, may reduce inequalities when analysed using a class lens (comparing the interests of employers and workers), but increase inequality when analysed using a gender and ethnic lens (comparing workers from the dominant and subordinate gender and ethnicities).

In addition to these legal regulations there are institutional practices that support or entrench complex inequalities, the most important of which is segregation. Segregation is of women and minorities into specific occupations, industries, and non-standard forms of employment defined by their temporality (e.g. part-time hours, shift working, night work) and contractual status (e.g. temporary or agency worker). Segregation is associated with lower pay and worse employment conditions for women and minorities.

The reproduction of segregation draws on direct and indirect forms of discrimination, and differences in the acquisition of general and specific skills that are rooted in institutions of education and training (Walby 1986; England et al. 1988; Kilbourne et al. 1994; Jacobs 1995; Cotter et al. 1997; Tam 1997; Anker 1998; Blackwell 2001; Tomaskovic-Devey and Skaggs 2002).

In contrast to the regulations that entrench inequalities are regulations that erode inequalities (Pillinger 1992; Hoskyns 1996; Wahl 2005). Regulations eroding inequalities have increased over time, especially since 1970, and they also have a path dependent element. These most frequently concern gender and ethnic inequality, but they have been extended, in some countries, to sexual orientation, religion, age, and disability. These regulations are stronger or weaker in three ways. First, at the lowest level they engage with direct discrimination; at higher levels they engage with indirect discrimination in the workplace; at the highest levels they engage with the wider structural origins of the inequality. Second, the form of implementation ranges from individual legal complaint through collective legal engagement to making promotion of equality a duty on employers and public bodies. Third, a wide range of inequalities beyond gender and ethnicity are named as legally unacceptable.

The most basic level is seen in regulations that address equal treatment in employment, such as laws covering equal pay for equal work. This type of equality law can have a limited impact because the better paid work is often segregated from the worse paid work, making it hard to compare the value of the work: inequality is often hidden behind the 'difference' produced by segregation. One way forward has been the development of job evaluation schemes that compare the value of jobs by using points for each component of the work (Acker 1989), thereby addressing the issue that men and women rarely work in the same occupation. A second development was to apply equal treatment laws not only to groups of visible men and women or visible ethnicities, but also to the employment categories in which women and minorities were more often to be found. In particular, the EU has a law that requires the equal treatment of part-time employment, which is disproportionately performed by women in segregated employment niches, with full-time work. A similar principle underlies the extension of the right to equal treatment to temporary work, so that the pay and conditions are the same even if the length of the contract is different. This is relevant to women and also to minority ethnic groups, especially recent migrants, who may be disproportionately found in such employment niches.

The most developed types of regulations are those that address the underlying structural generation of the inequalities. These differ significantly for different forms of inequality, since each regime of inequality is constituted differently. In relation to gender, there are employment regulations that address the relationship between care and employment, in the context where women disproportionately provide care in a way that is to their detriment in employment. The regulation of working time is designed to structurally rebalance these gendered domains in order to generate equality; including work/life balance policies such as maternal, paternal and parental leaves, and those restricting the ability of employers to demand excessively long working hours. In relation to disability, some countries place a duty on employers to make a reasonable accommodation of the working environment in order to facilitate the employment of disabled people. The EU has a full set of such employment legislation (European Commission 2007a, 2007d).

There are variations in the mode of implementation of these regulations, from individual complaints to more collective forms, including affirmative action, class actions, support from equality bodies or trade unions, and collective bargaining; placing duties on employers to establish a workplace free from harassment and to monitor equality; placing duties on public bodies to promote equality; and the mainstreaming of equality, especially gender equality, policies. The more collective forms tend to produce more change than the individual forms. The USA once had the most developed forms with the early development of affirmative action and class actions in the courts (Willborn 1989), but since the implementation of the 1999 Treaty of Amsterdam the EU is now more advanced, with policies on gender mainstreaming and duties on public bodies to promote gender and ethnic equality (European Commission 2007a, 2007b).

The early development of these legal regulations tended to focus on one inequality, only later spreading into other axes of inequality. In the USA early developments were on 'race' and were then followed by gender, and to a lesser extent age and disability. In the EU, early developments were on gender, but between 1999 and 2006 were extended to cover ethnicity, disability, religion/belief, age, and sexual orientation (European Commission 2007d), thus becoming more inclusive than the USA.

The strength of equality laws in employment can be summarized and operationalized for empirical research using these three sets of differences: beyond direct to indirect discrimination; collective rather than individual routes to the implementation of laws; and the range of inequalities covered by such laws. There is both a developmental component and beyond this path dependent varieties. These fit along a neoliberal to social democratic continuum – less state intervention the more neoliberal, more state intervention the more social democratic.

This is a distinction between different kinds of employment regulations. Not only are there employment protections (which form the almost exclusive empirical focus in the operationalization of these), there are also regulations that promote equality. The nature of the employment regulations matters because if protections are applied not to all groups but only to elite groups (often demarcated either directly or indirectly by gender and ethnicity) then they can be regressive in effect.

How should these be integrated with the distinction between employment relations that are not regulated and those that are? If there is to be a single category for regulations, then it is inappropriate for this to be driven solely by protections that can feed inequalities. One solution is to make an explicit distinction between protection and equality regulations and to produce both operationalizations for analysis. This option produces clarity, but at the expense of a loss of simplicity. An alternative solution is to include equality regulations when operationalizing the concept of regulated labour markets. This latter option is consistent with a single continuum from neoliberal to social democratic.

Why should the non-liberal category be social democracy rather than coordinated, including complex inequalities beyond class?
If there is to be a single dichotomy between unregulated and regulated labour markets, the best way of distinguishing varieties of employment regulations is that between neoliberal and social democratic forms. The comparison of the liberal with coordinated instead of social democratic is less helpful as it obscures the more significant differences.

It is important to be able to name forms of coordination that include a universalistic approach to equality as part of the project, that is, social democracy. It misdescribes the world if the project concerned with social inclusion, equality, and justice is left out of focus. If complex inequalities are to be included, and the distinctions between employment practices relevant to them are also to be included, then the distinction between neoliberal and social democratic better captures contemporary divisions than does that between neoliberal and coordinated.

The type of labour markets previously called 'conservative coordinated' are declining in number and also an unstable category. They are declining because the proportion of women in the workforce in those countries once considered conservative coordinated is rapidly increasing towards social democratic levels. They are also declining because the practices that enabled a section of the workforce, in particular white men, to be privileged are being eroded by new legislation that makes discrimination in employment illegal. They are unstable since the articulation of conservative class interests is increasingly taking place via neoliberal discourse and practice rather than conservative corporatism. For example Germany, often the leading example of non-social democratic coordination, has rising rates of female employment that have nearly reached social democratic levels and is subject to EU equality laws. The privileged positions of class fractions and dominant gender and ethnicities in employment are being eroded. The distinctive form of conservatism that Germany once had is in decline. The clustering of varieties of employment regulation into either neoliberal or social democratic forms is increasing as the category of non-social democratic coordination is in decline. There is both a reduction in the traditional forms of employment protection as a result of the neoliberal wave and an increase in equality regulations as a result of the emergence of feminist social democracy. The directions of change of class and gender are different, indeed opposite, as gender and the class dynamics of employment regulation are not to be conflated.

The theoretically most important form of labour market regulations in advanced economies concerns equalities. These regulations are relatively new and are growing in importance. Old forms of protective legislation that are not fully inclusive are in decline. The most important theoretical, political, and policy contrast with neoliberalism is social democracy, not coordination.

A measure of the strictness of employment protection legislation may work well for the comparison of liberal versus coordinated varieties of employment regulation, with a lens on class as employer versus worker. However, it obscures the treatment of groups within the workers. For this it is necessary to use an additional indicator – the strength of equality regulation.

Whether the strength of equality regulation maps onto the strength of employment protection regulation is contingent. The development of these forms of regulation drew on different social forces and different forms of polities. Employment protection legislation developed first, and drew on the organization of workers in trade unions and their political parties at a time when women and minorities were poorly represented in both trade unions and parliaments. The development of equality legislation is more recent, drawing on the increasing representation of women in trade unions and parliaments. In addition, much employment protection was developed by countries before the EU came to have the effective powers necessary to regulate the employment relations of its member states, so the legislation originates in different types of polities.

Conclusions

The most important division in varieties of employment regulation is that between little regulated neoliberal employment relations and social democratic employment relations in which there are both employment protections and equality regulations. In order to take complex inequalities other than class into account it is necessary to include equality regulations, since employment protections can lead to the protection of the workforce elite alone. The 'other' to neoliberal practices is best conceptualized as social democratic rather than coordinated, since the concept of coordinated hides the important distinction of whether or not regulations are intended to erode complex inequalities beyond class.

Rather than treating the economy as a unity, the distinction between employment regulations and welfare provision is made here. Whether or not they map onto each other is a question for analysis and not given a priori.

Varieties of welfare provision

Welfare is a set of tasks that are part of the economy. Welfare is performed in three ways: state welfare, both as free wage labour in the provision of public services of education, health, and care, and in a redistribution of income through the tax-benefit system; as free wage labour in the market; and in the home as unpaid domestic care-work performed largely by women. The balance of activities between state, market, and domestic is key to the varieties of forms of advanced welfare systems. Class has often been seen as central to the development of different forms of welfare but this is insufficient as gender and ethnic relations are also important.

State welfare includes the provision of goods, services, and income to provide for the welfare of the population. The distributional aspects of state welfare mean that a greater provision of services is likely to entail some redistribution to poorer social classes. These services include health, education, and care. Some aspects of state welfare, such as childcare, are especially important for gender relations, for the transition from a domestic to a public gender regime.

The extent of state welfare provision is partly linked to economic development, especially in less developed economies. Among more developed economies, a further increase in the level of economic development is often thought to make little difference to the amount of state expenditure. After this, a major part of the variation in the extent of state welfare is often considered to be a result of divergent paths of development (Flora and Alber 1981; Korpi 1983; Esping-Andersen

1990, 1999; Wilensky 2002). Do global pressures erode these differences or are they maintained (Montanari 2001; Pierson 2001; Swank 2002)?

In advanced welfare economies, is there little further development of state welfare? Or when gender, and not only class, is brought into focus, is there a continuing development of state welfare provision? The implications of the modernization of the gender regime are a challenge to both class-led and gender-led theories of welfare.

Neoliberal and social democratic varieties of welfare provision
There are various ways to distinguish between welfare state regimes. The most important distinction is that between neoliberal and social democratic welfare states. This follows the same principles as that used in the analysis of varieties of employment relations, though it takes on different forms and practices in this different area. In this typology the state tends to provide welfare (social democratic) or does not (neoliberal).

There have been many attempts to develop further categories. In the work of Esping-Andersen (1990) there is a third category that is additional to liberal and social democratic: conservative corporatism. In this variety of welfare regime, collective entities other than the state are involved in welfare structures, leading to unequally stratified welfare outcomes which reflect market inequalities. Countries are clustered into three forms: Anglos tend to be liberal, Nordics are social democratic, while continental West Europeans tend to be conservative corporatist. The theoretical principle behind the distinctions made by Esping-Andersen concerns whether there is a tendency to 'de-commodification' in the provision of welfare, or whether individuals are exposed to the workings of the capitalist market.

Esping-Andersen's three-fold typology generated many responses suggesting further nuances and additional categories (Arts and Gelissen 2002). Further suggested forms include a residual form, found especially in the Mediterranean countries where state welfare was little developed especially for women (Leibfried 1993; Ferreira 1996); and a wage earner form, found especially in Australia, where wage earner funds rather than the state provided relatively generous welfare benefits (Castles and Mitchell 1993). Esping-Andersen (1997) himself later suggested that Japan should be considered a hybrid form of conservative corporatist and liberal, but rejected the suggestion that there was a distinctive Asian form of welfare regime. There were many suggestions as to how gender might be better included (Lewis 1992, 1993, 2002; Orloff 1993; Jenson 1997; O'Connor et al. 1999; Daly and Rake 2003).

Most of those in dialogue with Esping-Andersen have suggested additional categories; by contrast, Hicks and Kenworthy (2003) argue that on the basis of statistical analysis of 18 rich countries over the 1980s and 1990s there is only one principle dimension from liberal to social democratic, reducing the conservative component to a secondary dimension. In their analysis the difference between liberal and social democratic is one of degree, forming a continuum or gradient, and is best thought of as a dimension in the analysis, rather than thinking of discrete clusters of countries. This finding is accepted by Esping-Andersen (2003). However, Hicks and Kenworthy's suggestion that the main dimension be re-described as one concerning 'progressive liberalism' rather than social democracy or socialism is robustly rejected by Esping-Andersen (2003) as an inappropriate erasure of the socialist tradition that brought about most of the policies under discussion.

However, the secondary dimension of conservatism is yet again misspecified, with insufficient analytic attention given to the centrality of the different forms of gender inequality involved. This is an a-theoretic eclectic category, which is declining in empirical, political and analytic significance and compounded by an insufficient conceptualization of its gender components. The most important issue here is that of domestic welfare – when this is addressed (see below), a major reason for the existence of the category of 'conservative corporatist' falls away.

A key distinction in types of welfare state in advanced economies is between neoliberal and social democratic forms, where provision is predominantly from the market or the state. The distinction between liberal and social democratic welfare systems is sometimes associated with a similar division in a range of other institutions including employment regulation. However, the extent to which these map onto each other is a question to be empirically investigated rather than presumed.

Including gender: premodern forms of welfare as domestic labour
Welfare is provided not only by the state and the market, but also by (largely) women's unpaid domestic care-work. This does not fit into either of the categories of market or state welfare and hence potentially disrupts the distinction between neoliberal (market) and social democratic (state) welfare. The market and state forms of welfare provision, and the typology associated with them, refer only to those forms of welfare that are performed in the monetized economy, that is, in the modern economy. The welfare provided under non-monetized domestic relations is an additional issue that must also be addressed. The need to include this gendered form of

welfare has been a major challenge to class-led accounts which has produced various responses.

In Esping-Andersen's work the significance of women's work is addressed in two ways. In his early writing (Esping-Andersen 1990), those countries where there was significant provision of welfare by women's domestic labour were located within the category of 'conservative corporatist' alongside the special treatment of class fractions such as civil servants, as if it were a path-dependent variety of welfare capitalism. The three-fold typology generated critical responses from those who sought to add additional nuanced categories and from feminists who argued for a greater focus on the theorization of this gendered form of welfare provision (Orloff 1993; Sainsbury 1994, 1996; O'Connor et al. 1999; Hobson 2000; Daly and Rake 2004).

The significance of gender relations challenges the theorization of welfare states led by Esping-Andersen, in which de-commodification was seen as progressive because it reduced the hold of capital over people's lives. This is a challenge because gender relations have a different relationship to de-commodification than do class relations; not only is domestic labour not yet commodified, so that de-commodification is not an option, but commodification might also be progressive rather than regressive for women in these circumstances. The implications of the commodification of women's labour (from domestic to wage labour) for their welfare are underestimated within a theoretical framework that asserts that de-commodification (from dependence on the wage to support from the state) is the most effective basis of equity (Orloff 1993). Rather the commodification of women's labour in its move from the domestic to the public sphere is progressive. This is acknowledged by Esping-Andersen (1990, 1999) in his account of women's full employment in the social democratic model and the process of defamilialization as progressive, but is not fully integrated into his theoretical model, which reduces gender to the family thereby excluding gendered employment from the theoretical model (see Chapter 2 for a more detailed account of this theoretical problem).

In contrast to Esping-Andersen's class-first analysis of welfare state regimes, with a focus on the balance of state and market provision of welfare, is a gender-first analysis that focuses on the balance of domestic and state provision of welfare. Lewis (1992) with Ostner (Ostner and Lewis, 1995) developed a typology that centres on the extent to which there is a 'male breadwinner–female housewife' model. This ranges from 'strong male breadwinner', 'modified male breadwinner' to 'weak male breadwinner' (sometimes referred to as 'dual earner'). Ireland is taken as most typical of the strong male breadwinner model (Lewis 1992), with Britain sometimes being included (Lewis 1992) while at others being seen, like Germany, as modified male breadwinner (Lewis 1993). France is seen to follow a 'modified' (Lewis 1992) male breadwinner model, while Sweden is seen to follow a 'weak' male breadwinner model (Lewis 1992), sometimes, dual-earner.

While important in addressing gender, this model and its analysis suffer from a series of problems. First, the typology does not address the situation of households where there is no man at all. Hence the rather odd situation of Ireland being described as a strong breadwinner model, while a rather large proportion of Irish households have no male breadwinner at all; Ireland is thus not well described as having a strong breadwinner model when so many households do not have a male breadwinner. Second, there is a series of nuances in the way that the welfare state addresses care-work which are underestimated in the model. Women may be treated within the welfare system as wives or mothers or workers (Sainsbury 1996). The mode of resourcing care may be as a service, money to purchase services, or as money for time at home. With a focus on care (Jenson 1997), rather than unpaid work, distinctions can be made between who cares, who pays, and how is care provided. A further distinction is in the outcome of the system for women's income and wellbeing (Hobson 1994), for instance, whether the gender welfare regime provides 'the capacity for a woman to form and maintain an autonomous household' (Orloff 1993: 319). Others have usefully broadened the range of issues considered (Haintrais 1995; O'Connor et al. 1999) and have distinguished different forms of defamilialization (Leitner 2003). There is in addition a third option: the performance of care tasks on the market. The possibility of the purchase of a wide range of goods and services, from meals to childcare, means that it is not sufficient to only differentiate between domestic and state relations: it is important to include a further category of the market, rather than domestic or state, provision of care-work.

The way forward is first to separate the concepts of gender and family, but not reducing one to the other. The family is merely one part of the construction of gender relations: gender is also constituted by social relations in employment, the polity, violence, and civil society. Second, the movement of work outside the household ('defamilialization' for Esping-Andersen) is not only the consequence of the development of state welfare, but can also be the consequence of the increase in women's paid employment. There are two forms of public gender regime: one is associated with state welfare and the second with the expansion of the market, providing both welfare; also employment for women.

The transition from a domestic to a public gender regime is a developmental change. The domestic provision of welfare is not a stable, path dependent form, but one that is reducing in scale and significance. Insofar as domestic welfare is considered to be a key part of conservative corporatism, then conservative corporatism is in decline and not a stable path dependent form of welfare regime. Insofar as domestic welfare is considered to be central to the notion of a strong male breadwinner regime, then strong male breadwinner regimes are in decline and are not a stable path dependent form. The analysis by both Esping-Andersen and his feminist critics assumes too much stability in domestic labour. It is in decline and thus so are the associated social forms. This is a more generic developmental, rather than path dependent, phenomenon.

The change from a domestic to a public gender regime can lead to different forms of public gender regime. These may involve either state or market welfare. There are major ongoing reductions in the provision of domestic welfare; these coevolve with the transformation of the gender regime from a domestic to a public form. These reductions in domestic welfare are associated with an increase in either market welfare or state welfare. The extent to which the market or the state takes over these activities is path dependent.

At the centre of the investigation of different forms of welfare, in particular the relationship between domestic welfare and public welfare (both state and market forms), lies the provision of childcare, and to a lesser but increasing extent other forms of care such as that of frail elderly and disabled people. The extent to which (and the way in which) childcare is performed is central to these debates. However, many of the leading accounts of welfare provision select substantive examples that at best marginalize childcare services and at worst omit childcare altogether. See, for example, Esping-Andersen's classic (1990) work which focuses on pensions.

Welfare is social democratic welfare when the state takes a leading role in the provision of welfare. Neoliberal is when it is performed on the market. Premodern is when it is performed in the home.

Do varieties of employment regulation and welfare map onto each other?
Do varieties of class regime map onto gender and other complex inequalities?
Do neoliberal and social democratic varieties of economies map onto each other? Are they aligned across domains? Are they aligned across regimes of inequality, such as class and gender? The analysis of varieties of political economy has engaged two main institutional foci – employment relations and welfare provision – and two main sets of social relations – class and gender. Do varieties of institutions and social relations map onto each other, or do they diverge? Here this is explored on the basis of theory and existing research, while in chapters 8 and 10 it is addressed empirically.

The distinctions between forms of employment regulation might appear to have similarities with the distinctions between forms of welfare provision. Both the employment-focused (Hall and Soskice 2001) and the welfare-focused (Esping-Andersen 1990) varieties of capitalism have argued that there is just one typology that applies across both the employment and welfare aspects of the economy, although in practice they each lead the analysis from one substantive area or the other. This assumption of a single typology relevant to both employment and welfare is found in a range of writers (Lash and Urry 1994; Hollingsworth 1997; Huber and Stephens 2000, 2001; Jessop 2002).

Yet the practical integration of the typologies developed for each field has proven challenging (Ebbinghaus and Manow 2001). Why might this be? The allocation of cases to typologies would diverge if the political forces and/or the institutions centrally involved in the construction of employment regulation were to differ from those involved in the construction of state welfare. There are two main reasons for thinking that this might be the case. One is that the social forces are different, or differently positioned, in relation to these fields, in particular gender and ethnic forces and various relations with class forces. A second is that there are different polities involved, in particular that in the European Union while employment is predominantly regulated by the European Union level, welfare is almost entirely provided by the Member State level of governance.

First, the main social forces are not only a variety of class forces; there are also different gender forces; some seeking to privilege men while others seek gender equality; and also diverse ethnic forces, some seeking to privilege white people while others seek equality. While both employment regulation and state welfare involve the state, class forces and gender forces, there have been varied prioritizations and mobilizations in the different areas (Walby 1986; Huber and Stephens 2001; Mósesdóttir 2001). In particular, the later transition of women than men into free wage labour typically means that the political mobilization of women and their engagement in formal political institutions occur later than for men (Inter-Parliamentary Union 1997). Employed women typically support projects for public services associated with social democracy (Manza and Brooks 1998). However, whether this has had significant effects may depend on the availability of effective allies in organized working men (Huber and Stephens 2001).

Second, the different policy fields of employment and welfare may or may not be directly connected even at a national level (Ebbinghaus and Hassel 2000). In the context of the European Union, there is even greater separation of decision-making processes in the fields of employment and welfare. In the EU, the regulation of employment is primarily decided on at a European level, while state welfare is primarily decided on at Member State level. Different historical legacies are embedded in these institutions of governance at state and EU level; it should be anticipated that these might give rise to discrepant forms of intervention. The gender project of the EU is more oriented to a public gender regime than many of its Member States, with implications for its gendered regulation of employment (Pillinger 1992; Hoskyns 1996, Walby 1999b, 2004a).

Do variations in the class and gender aspects of the political economy of welfare and employment map onto each other; or can there be polity intervention to reduce gender economic inequality but not class-led inequality? It is often argued that varieties of class inequalities and varieties of gender inequalities map onto each other. In work on welfare states, Esping-Andersen argued this case not only in his early work (1990) but also in his response to his feminist critics (1999), while Estevez-Abe (2005) similarly put forward that patterns of gender relations in employment are led by the distinction between varieties of capitalism. Korpi (2000: 142), however, cautions that state institutions might promote different levels of class inequality from levels of gender inequality. The evidence is that there can be contrary directions of change in gender-led and class-led inequalities in both employment regulation and in state welfare provision (Walby 2007b). Class and gender do not necessarily map onto each other. Further evidence on this disjuncture is shown in Chapter 8 on varieties of modernity.

Critical turning points into varieties of political economy

The identification of the varieties of path dependency is not the same as an explanation of them (Rothstein 1992). This requires in addition an account of the critical turning points into new paths and the mechanisms that lock-in the path. The neoliberal and social democratic varieties of political economy (employment relations and welfare provision) are path-dependent trajectories of development, differentiated at critical turning points and locked-in by specific institutions.

At the critical turning points the combination of power resources and institutional capacity can produce new paths of development. While there has been important analysis of the role of class struggle in these turning points (Moore 1966; Korpi 1983; Lash and Urry 1987; Esping-Andersen 1990; Nee and Cao 1999), there has been little that considers the significant role of other complex inequalities such as gender and ethnicity as contributing to the power resources involved. Similarly, in the approach that focuses on institutional legacies, there is little that considers the sedimentation of gender and ethnic forces in addition to class. The approach to path dependency that focuses on the mobilization of political forces has usually focused on class forces, varying in the extent to which capital and labour are articulated in a few or several class fractions and whether agricultural workers and owners are included (Moore 1966; Korpi 1983; Lash and Urry 1987; Esping-Andersen 1990). Rarely have gendered political forces been included, yet these are clearly relevant to the development of employment regulations that promote either gender inequality or equality (Hartmann 1976; Walby 1986; Mósesdóttir 2001). In parallel, ethnic forces both promoting exclusion and inclusion are relevant to the forms of regulation that develop (Miles 1989). Not only is the presence of these forces important to the outcome, but also the extent to which there are solidaristic forms of cooperation or the building of joint projects drawing on progressive class, gender, and ethnic interests.

An approach that considers the historical legacy of institutions overlaps with that on the mobilization of political forces, differing in the focus on the sedimentation of the outcomes of these political contests in institutions, especially state institutions. Again, however, the gender and ethnic components of these legacies are less frequently considered (exceptions include Skocpol 1992; Walvin 1992; Quadagno 1994; Manza 2000), even though they are important to the outcome. Further, the development of democracy (Moore 1966) and its deeper forms (Fung and Wright 2001) has implications not only for class but also for women and minoritized groups, providing institutionalized routes to the effective expression of their political projects. The winning of democracy is a critical turning point in the development of employment regulations and welfare provision not only for men and class relations but also for women (Walby 1990) and minority ethnic groups. Sequencing matters: for example, the institutionalization of medical occupations as professions at a time before women had the vote had negative implications for the position of women's occupations (Witz 1992). The temporality of paths of development is considered in Chapter 10.

Crises are often important contexts for critical turning points. The phenomenon of financial crises is often an opportunity for capital to restructure to its advantage. Military defeat and victory can lead to the reconstruction of states, as in the creation of the European Union and the demilitarization of Germany and Japan. The surge in unemployment following the 1974 shock of significantly increased oil prices, further sustained by neoliberal projects, brought to an end the era of social democratic advance in Western Europe (Korpi 2002, 2003). The financial crises in Southeast Asia and Latin America provided the opportunity for a restructuring of value: at times of financial crisis the IMF makes loans conditional on a move towards neoliberal policies (Stiglitz 2002; Harvey 2003, 2005). Military coups in Chile and 'natural' disasters such as Hurricane Katrina also provide new opportunities for a neoliberal turn (Klein 2007). The financial crisis of 2008 that started in the USA and extended to most of the rest of the world is a further potential critical turning point, a new context for the contestation of neoliberal and social democratic projects in the economy (see Chapter 11).

The locking-in of social democratic pathways in political economy depends upon a series of institutional developments, including trade union membership and organizational form, social democratic parties in government, industrial relations systems, and welfare state development (Western 1999; Huber and Stephens 2001). A series of associated institutions lock-in early differences in trade union membership and organizational effectivity, including the Ghent system in which trade unions (in the Nordic countries and Belgium) act as the agents for unemployment insurance, legislation to facilitate trade union membership, and action such as the legality of the closed shop, strikes, and picketing (Ebbinghaus and Visser 1999). A further set of associated institutional lock-ins occurs with the development of political parties aligned with trade unions, promoting social democracy and the establishment of the welfare state (Bartolini 2000; Huber and Stephens 2001). The establishment of state welfare can further lock-in these developments, due to the formation of interest groups of recipients and workers (Pierson 2001) and the entrenched policy preferences of citizens (Brooks and Manza 2006).

The most important varieties of political economy in modern advanced economies are neoliberal and social democratic, which can be separately identified in employment relations and in welfare provision. In addition most countries with advanced economies do not yet have fully modern economies, in that there is still some work performed for a livelihood as domestic labour that is outside the monetized economy. A domestic livelihood sector may be compatible with the concept of a neoliberal modern sector of an economy but not with a social democratic economy, since full employment is a defining characteristic of a social democratic economy.

The use of a category of coordinated market economy in employment relations or conservative corporatist in welfare provision is overtaken by this typology. These categories often contained a hidden gender component; in this proposed formulation gender is made visible and explicit and allows for its adequate integration into theories of gender relations and the integration of gender into mainstream socio-economic theory.

In contrast to the attempt to squeeze the analysis of employment relations and welfare provision into the same conceptual category, this analysis explicitly allows for potential divergence as well as potential alignment. Divergence might be expected where different polities are involved in employment regulation and welfare provision, as is the case in the Member States of the EU where employment is regulated at the European level and welfare is provided at Member State level, and where different coalitions of class, gender, and ethnic political forces are involved in the various aspects of political economy. Alignment might be expected where there is a strong political coalition leading to pacts that can address both institutional arenas and all social groups.

In contrast to the attempts to reduce the analysis of the economy to a class-led account of capital and labour, this analysis explicitly allows for a potential divergence as well as a potential alignment. Divergence might be expected as a consequence of the different moments at which democratic access was gained by men, women, and minoritized ethnic groups, with consequent effects on an ability to argue for protective or an equality legislation and welfare provision. Alignment might be expected where there is a strong political coalition that forges a project that addresses all such social groups.

Conclusions

The concept of the economy has been broadened here in order to address complex inequalities: domestic labour and state welfare need to be included. This extends the definition of the economy beyond the conventional restriction to monetized and marketized activities. Only when the concept is extended in this way is it possible to make sense of the changes associated with the transformation of the gender regime and the implications of the shift of women from unwaged to waged work.

Globalization is often linked to increasing economic inequalities within countries. The increased flows of capital, trade, and people increase the tendency towards economic inequalities by both reducing the bargaining position of less skilled workers who are exposed to global competition while the development of the knowledge sectors of the economy is associated with increases in the wages paid to increasingly skilled workers in these sectors. At least as important as these economically-led global processes is a neoliberal global political wave that exacerbates economic inequalities with its practices of de-regulation and de-unionization. The capture of global financial institutions and the US hegemon by this neoliberal discourse extends its effectivity from civil societal institutions to the level of global governance. However, these tendencies are far from universal in their practice and effects. At a country level, the uneven historical legacy of particular forms of political institutions and the emergence of new coalitions of political forces ensure uneven effects. These may be either the continuation of path dependent practices of particular forms and levels of economic inequality, or their restructuring or coevolution into new trajectories of development. Global processes have not produced convergence.

While class-led forms of economic inequalities have increased during this recent period of globalization, those associated with gender have decreased. The dynamics of gender relations do not simply map onto the dynamics of class relations. The decrease in gendered economic inequalities is linked to the transformation of the gender regime and the movement of women from unpaid domestic labour to waged labour, thereby narrowing the gap in monetized economic rewards between women and men. This increasingly large constituency of employed women tends to support the provision of state welfare and the political projects associated with this policy, especially social democracy. Through this emergence of new champions for democratic projects, the transformation of the gender regime has implications for the overall level of economic inequality.

There is no single trajectory of economic development, instead there are different path-dependent forms. The most important current distinction in the modern sector of the economy is that between neoliberal and social democratic trajectories of development. This distinction can be separately identified in the different forms of regulation of employment, of finance and in the provision of welfare: they do not necessarily align because different polities and social forces are involved in their production. This distinction can be separately identified in different regimes of inequality as class has a different dynamic from gender, even though there is a tendency to coevolution of these regimes. In addition to these differences in the modern sector of the economy, there are differences between countries in the extent to which the premodern domestic sector of the economy still exists as a form of livelihood for women.

Globalization of the economy has implications for the conventional presumed units of analysis of nation-state and society. The boundaries of different economic forms do not map onto a single polity or civil society or violence nexus in a global era. The emergent institutions of global financial governance do not fully regulate the economy, nor do states fully regulate the economy in their own territory. The EU is more important in regulating the economy in its territory than are its Member States, even though matters of taxation and welfare are still determined by the latter. The economy, polity, violence, and civil society neither map onto each other nor are they nested.

Global processes make a difference to economic development. The movement of capital as well as goods, services, and labour around the world has tended to increase competition thereby leading to pressure to reduce pay and conditions of employment. However, whether this pressure leads to significant changes varies according to the nature of country specific political institutions and coalitions. There are global political and civil society processes as well as economic ones. Global political waves of human rights, equal rights and feminism have resulted in greater gender equality in access to education and employment rights at earlier stages of economic development in the contemporary world than in the older industrialized economies. The development of institutions of global governance such as the International Monetary Fund and the World Bank has implications for the economic policy of those countries that need to call on them. The regulation of world trade in the World Trade Organization is the result of contestation at a global level between the USA, the EU, and groups of developing countries in the South. The competition between the EU and the USA is currently critical in the determination of trade rules for the world and for the economic processes that underlie them.

Neoliberalism is often conflated with globalization. This is a mistake. Neoliberalism and global processes are analytically separate. Neoliberalism is one global project carried initially as a civil societal wave that is then embedded in governmental programmes and in social formations. There are other projects carried by global waves including projects centred on rights, social democracy, and environmentalism. Neoliberalism attempts a global hegemonic status but it remains contested. It interacts with ongoing changes in the social relations in specific countries, creating a diversity of effects on economic inequality. Some processes that have sometimes been attributed to globalization, as if there were inevitable outcomes to global economic processes, are better attributed to a specific political project of neoliberalism.

Transitions to modern forms of the economy are affected not only by the forms of the economy but also by polities and civil societies. While there are linkages between these systems that may drive forward the process of transition to modern forms of the economy, the conception of a singular universal form of transition omits many important aspects of these transitions. The different forms of polity and civil society can entail different pathways of transition and thereby path-dependent forms of economic development. The mutual interaction between different sets of social relations associated with these economic developments may produce yet further differentiations in the processes of transformation and their outcomes.

Polities may speed or catalyse these economic changes, or may slow or dampen them. They can catalyse by promoting the transition to the free wage labour for women – the provision of services, especially care-work, which would otherwise have to be purchased on the market and the regulation of employment and education so as to remove discriminatory barriers to women's employment. Polities may dampen the transition by legislating or allowing discriminatory barriers to women's employment and by promoting a domestic gender regime.

Bringing those complex inequalities that are additional to class into focus has a series of implications for an analysis of the economy. The intersection of these multiple sets of complex inequalities has mutual effects on each other and on economic development. Most importantly, there is more than one critical moment in the transition to a modern economy. In particular, the transformation of gender relations associated with the shift from household to free wage labour often takes place at a later time than the transition associated with class relations.

So does globalization mean the erosion of a divergent path-dependent development and convergence? Not in any simple way. While there is an increased importance of the global level in economic governance, globalization is not a simple process of Westernization or Americanization: it involves contesting forces, not least those between the hegemons of the USA and the EU.

4 Polities

Introduction

Polities constitute an institutionalized domain, a sedimentation of political forces in a system of centralized institutions that govern the economy, violence, and civil society. The nature of political institutions is the outcome of past political struggles that continue to have implications into the future as a consequence of their embeddedness in institutions. States and polities need to be reconceptualized in order to fully take into account complex inequalities and global processes. Four themes are addressed in this chapter: the reconceptualization of types of polities; the non-saturation of a territory by any one polity, and the implications of their overlaps; rethinking the conceptualization of democracy; the development of democracy.

First, the concept of state is too narrow to capture the range of political institutions that are made visible when complex inequalities are brought into focus. The broader concept of polity is needed so as to encompass not only states but also nations, organized religions, hegemons, and emerging global institutions. Further, the assumption that nation-states were ever common is challenged, not only in a global era. Understanding a globalizing era requires new concepts for polities.

Second, polities overlap and rarely politically saturate any given territory, especially in a global era. This is a challenge to conventional analyses of the state, which assume that a single polity has a monopoly over political authority. In particular it is a challenge to the concept of the nation-state: nations and states rarely completely map onto each other. There is often more than one significant polity in a country, and they compete as well as cooperate.

Third, a modern polity is a democratic polity. The conventional definition of democracy, however, insufficiently captures the varying depth of democracy that is so important for women and minoritized groups. It is important to identify separately the depth of democracy separately for different regimes of inequality, since these often do not coincide. A ten-point scale is introduced, and distinctions between suffrage-democracy, presence-democracy, and the breadth of democracy.

Fourth, while economic development has traditionally been seen as the most important force behind men's suffrage-democracy, a wider range of forces appear relevant for the suffrage-democracy associated with complex inequalities. In a global era a wider range of forces is potentially relevant, from global waves of democratization to the interventions of global hegemons.

Reconceptualizing Types of Polities

Introduction

The concept of state needs to be rethought to address complex inequalities and global processes. As indicated in Chapter 1, while globalizing processes have often been considered to have a tendency to reduce the powers of states (Fukuyama 1992; Cerny 1995, 1996; Ohmae 1995; Castells 1997; Habermas 2001), there is a more diverse range of relationships between globalization and political entities including: resistance to globalization (Castells 1997; Swank 2002); the creation of nation-states by a world society (Meyer and Hannan 1979; Meyer et al. 1997); the constitution of states within a world-system of capitalism (Wallerstein 1974, 1980; Robinson 2001); the development of hegemons (Chase-Dunn et al. 2000); as well as broader global restructuring (Brenner 1999; Held et al. 1999); and the development of multi-level (Ruggie 1998), transnational (Haas 1958, 1964; Habermas 2001), and global (Held 1995; Robinson 2001) forms of governance of the system as a whole. Understanding globalization also necessitates understanding the changing nature of the global landscape in which polities are embedded, as to whether this is becoming de-territorialized (Scholte 2000) or not (Sassen 2001, 2008), more or less regionalized (Hettne et al. 1999), or increasingly regulated by global bodies (Held 1995).

Much analysis of the state, democracy, and globalization has focused on social processes primarily connected with changes in capitalism and associated class relations. However, this is unduly restrictive, as it excludes other complex inequalities stemming from ethnicity, 'race' (Wilson 1987), nation (Smith 1986; Calhoun 1995; Brubaker 1996), religion (Beyer 1994), and gender (Kenworthy and Malami 1999). When these complex inequalities in addition to class are made visible, then a wider set of polities comes into focus. In particular, religions are prime carriers of ethnic, national, and gender projects into global and regional conflicts. Such conflicts (for instance, that between fundamentalism and 'the West') are hard to understand without the inclusion of interests of gender and ethnicity alongside those of class and economics. It is important to consider the full range of polities and not only the sub-set constituted by states if the politics associated with complex inequalities are to be included in the analysis.

A minimal definition of a polity is an entity which has authority over a specific social group or territory or set of institutions, which in turn has some degree of internal coherence, some degree of centralized control, some rules, the ability to typically enforce sanctions against those members who break its rules, the ability to command deference from other polities in specific arenas over which it claims jurisdiction, and which in turn has authority over a broad and significant range of social institutions and domains. The forms of authority and power, and the means to enforce sanctions, are varied. There are different kinds of power of polities, including coercion, economic, legal, and symbolic power. These can be coordinated in different ways and have varied spatial and temporal reach. The notion of membership is needed to ascertain who is within and who is without a polity, and most have complex rules regarding entry and exit (for example, membership if the parent was a member or if birth was within its territory), with complex processes or rituals mediated by bureaucrats or priests. This definition of polity is wider than that traditionally used, however, it is not intended to capture all forms of governance structures within this definition. There are some forms of governance that do not have the temporal and spatial scale or the institutional range necessary to constitute a polity. Small-scale specialized institutions of governance, such as business firms, labour unions, hospitals and universities, are not within the concept. Not all sets of political institutions constitute polities. There are a number of borderline cases, for instance, national projects that have strong institutions within civil society. If a political collectivity is not able to enforce deference to its rules from its members and from established polities then it falls outside the definition of polity. Only very well developed national projects will meet these criteria, and many embryonic projects will not. Similarly, communities based on criteria of ethnicity or racialization or linguistic commonality may or may not establish sufficiently developed institutions for them to constitute a polity.

Polities include, in addition to states, nations (if they have well-developed sets of civil society institutions), regional polities (such as the European Union), some organized religions (such as Catholicism and Islam), empires and hegemons. 'Nation' should not be conflated with 'state' (as in 'nation-state') if the greater number of states than nations and conflicts between nations and states are to be explained. Empires should not be conflated with nation-states, because of the political significance of multiple nations subject to a common state. Organized religions should not be excluded from the category of polity, if the ethnic, national, and gender political projects that they carry onto a global stage are to be understood. The European Union is a significant polity, with consequences for gender, ethnicity, and nation, as well as class, but defeats categorization as either a state or a committee of states. Both the USA and the EU are hegemons. In addition there are emergent global political institutions.

States

States today are usually polities. This is a pared-down concept of state, from which the notion of nation has been stripped out, which does not make the presumption of a congruent civil society and economy. Most contemporary states have sufficient power and authority to command internal governance and external deference, to warrant being conceptualized as polities. However, there are occasional exceptions, such as when a state's institutions of internal governance have suffered serious collapse due to a civil or foreign war, for example, as was the case in Somalia at the turn of the twenty-first century. States are distinguished from most other forms of polities by their use of force to obtain and maintain consent, among other forms of governance. States have relations with other states in an inter-state system.

Nations

Nations can be a type of polity under certain circumstances. A nation is a social and political group which is perceived to have a common history and destiny (Anderson 1983; Hobsbawm and Ranger 1983), sometimes a common ethnic origin (Smith 1986), although this may not necessarily be so (Gellner 1983), and a set of governing institutions that root such beliefs in the social and political practices. It can be a polity when its institutions are well developed and it is able to demand some external deference. It can be distinguished from a state

(Guibernau 2004) because it does not have a full range of centralized political institutions, such as those that control the majority of the use of force. One example is the Irish nation in the period just before the establishment of the Irish state (Miller 1973; Larkin 1975) while another is contemporary Scotland (McCrone 1992). Nations can be important in carrying ethnic, religious, and gendered projects.

Nation-states?

Nation-states exist more in myth, as aspirations, than as empirical entities. It is inappropriate to treat nation-states as the main type of contemporary polity for several reasons: there are many more nations than states; several key examples of supposed nation-states were actually empires; and there are diverse and significant polities in addition to states, including the European Union and some organized religions.

There are far more nations than states (Guibernau 1999; Keating 2002; Minahan 2002). It is rare for a territory to have one nation and the whole of that nation, and one state, and the whole of that state. Most nations and national projects do not have a state of their own, instead they often share a state with other nations and national projects. This pattern of cross-cutting nations and states can be a result of migration (forced or voluntary), or of war or conquest. This is not to argue that there are not states, but rather that there are not often stable *nation*-states. For instance, within Britain or the United Kingdom in the post-empire period there are nations of English, Scottish, and Welsh, as well as part of the Irish nation (Nairn 1977; McCrone 1992; Bryant 2006). The struggle over the location of the border between the UK and Ireland is an example of the militarized conflict and terrorism that can be generated when there is a contestation rather than the neat mapping of state and nation. Within Spain and France there is the Basque nation that seeks separation and a state of its own. The break up of the Soviet empire has precipitated many nations and would-be nations into seeking states of their own, with several of these having not achieved their objective despite the multiplicity of new states that have been created. The state of Canada contains not only Canadians but also the French speaking, state-seeking nation of Quebecois. The nation of Germany had two states for half the twentieth century. The boundaries of states can change rapidly, as, for instance, in the case of Germany, established as a state only in the nineteenth century, which has seen the repeated movement of pieces of territory between itself and France, enlargement and contraction during the middle of the twentieth century, partition into two quite different states in the second half of the twentieth century, followed by a short recent period of reunification of East and West. Europe is riddled with cross-cutting nations, aspiring nations, and states (Therborn 1995; Brubaker 1996; Boje et al. 1999). Minahan (2002) finds 300 developed or emerging national groups. Cohen (1997) estimates that there are around 2000 'nation-peoples', that is, around ten times as many as the states recognized by the United Nations. Nation-states with the whole of one nation and no other and one state and no other polity, which are stable in time and space, are hard to find in Europe and indeed anywhere elsewhere in the world. At most, nation-states exist for short moments in history before being reconstructed yet again.

Many key examples of nation-states were actually empires. Nation-states are often considered to become a common political and social form after the Treaty of Westphalia in 1648. The hey-day, the height, of this form is usually considered to be from the eighteenth or nineteenth centuries until the mid-twentieth century, and its most frequently found location is usually assumed to be Europe (Tilly 1990; Mann 1993a). For instance, Mann, despite his interest in early, pre-1760 empires (Mann 1986), leaves this conceptualization behind in his analysis of the post-1760 period, where he treats Britain and France as if they were nation-states (Mann 1993a). Yet several of the key examples of nation-states (for example, Britain, France, Spain and Portugal) were actually empires during the nineteenth century and not nation-states. It does not make sense to consider people who were subject to such empires to be either members of European nation-states or members of their own local nation-states. At the time of these empires most people were not within an entity that could reasonably be called a nation-state, since those colonized would hardly recognize themselves as part of the colonizing 'nation'. To consider the British and other empires to be nation-states rather than empires is to erase from history the experiences of those many people who were subject to these states. It is also to neglect the use of political and military domination to restructure economies in the interest of the imperial power. It is not appropriate to ignore these empires in accounts of the rise of nation-states, as if those under the rule of empires were of little significance, as if Europe and North America constituted the whole of the world. Empires have states, not nation-states. The nineteenth century was the hey-day of empires, not nation-states.

Nation-states are largely mythical entities, frequently aspired to, but rarely realized in practice. Disaggregating nation and state can be more helpful than conflating them in a spurious unity of nation-state. The tensions that can exist as a result of the usually incomplete and partial mapping of nation onto state are a major cause of contemporary militarized conflicts and terrorism. The conflation of important distinctions between nation, state, and nation-state thus leaves out-of-focus points of disjuncture between these entities that are important in generating social and political struggle and change. Such disjunctures have important consequences for social and political strife. Different polities often carry different gender and ethnic projects, so the outcome of these conflicts has implications for the form and degree of complex inequalities.

To argue that nation-states are largely mythical does not mean that beliefs about them are unimportant (contra Bruce and Voas 2004). Myths are powerful. Ideas move people to action. Invented traditions have effects (Hobsbawn and Ranger 1983). A myth is a narrative story that is considered to represent a tradition and to provide information about core values and the conduct necessary to achieve them. The myth of the nation-state is that a nation will find full and true expression of its values and will secure its economic well-being only if it has a state of its own in a territory of its own; and that it is possible to achieve this, with the evidence being that there are believed to be many examples of successful nation-states. It is predicated on the assumption that it is possible and desirable to bring into alignment in one place culture, economy, and political representation through a state.

The myth of the nation-state is a very powerful force. It does not depend upon there being any actually existing nation-states, only a belief that there are. Many national movements believe that it is possible as well as desirable to achieve a nation-state. The myth of the nation-state has launched many political movements and militarized conflicts. The nation-state is a powerful myth about purity. It is about a nation having a state of its own so that it can self-regulate its environment in conformity with its values. The nation-state myth is about the close fit of a nation and its own state, with its own politics, economy, and culture mapping onto one another in the same territory.

The desire of a nation, or would-be nation, for a state of its own has been a tremendous force in human history. On the one hand it can be understood in terms of a discourse of self-determination, of community, of democracy, of the realization of a society in conformity with the values of the nation, free from the impositions of invasive, colonialist, exploitative, foreign powers. On the other hand it can also be a terrible force. It can unleash militarism and armed struggle, by regular armies, guerrillas, and terrorists, as nations seek to establish a state of their own in a territory of their own. It can be a force that seeks purity where there is none, driving genocide, ethnic cleansing, communal murders, and pogroms. The nation-state is a powerful and resilient myth. The aspiration of nations for states of their own is a powerful driving force in contemporary politics. However, nationalists seldom achieve a state just for themselves and usually have to settle for some sort of messy compromise with other nations and polities.

Organized religions

Organized religions constitute polities in those instances where they have significant powers of governance over significant aspects of people's lives. Religions frequently have authority over the regulation of intimacy, and sometimes economic matters, such as whether it is acceptable to pay interest on loans (usury), though there may be contestation or negotiation with a state for authority over these matters (Inglis 1987; Farrell 1988; Kandiyoti 1991). This can include the regulation of marriage, divorce, non-marital sexuality, clothing, and diet. Organized religions have three main routes to authority: moral authority articulated through religious belief; political pressure on states and other polities; and the power to sanction members of the religious community if they break the rules of a religion. It might be thought that, in the modern world, the powers of organized religion have been reduced to the first two and that only the state has the right to sanction citizens for breaking community rules. However, this is mistaken. This power is still potent in some locations, especially in the regulation of intimacy (that is, in areas of sexuality and family relations such as marriage, divorce, contraception, abortion, and homosexuality). Sanctions can include a religion's refusal to carry out rituals which are considered essential (e.g. communion for those ex-communicated; divorce; church re-marriage for those divorced by the state); exclusion from a religious community with implications for a way of life, condemnation to some kind of hell in a believed-in afterlife, that is, the threat of eternal damnation (e.g. for abortion); a refusal to recognize unions and legitimate offspring with implications for property entitlements as well as moral standing, and various forms of penitence (Smyth 1992; Hardacre 1993; Moghadam 1993; Helie-Lucas 1994).

Religion is sometimes considered as no longer relevant to analyses of modernity (Thompson 1995), largely because of a presumption that modernization produced secularization. While the process of secularization is an important process (Bruce 2002) its extent can be exaggerated, while the significance of its restructuring in relation to secular polities can be under-estimated (Gorski 2000). There are important variations in the secularization process in different countries, with the process much more advanced in Europe than in the USA (Inglehart 1997; Norris and Inglehart 2004).

Organized religions typically have a different range of power resources from those of states. Nevertheless, in certain contexts they may effectively govern important social institutions such as intimacy (sexuality, reproduction, marriage, and divorce). Not all religions take the form of a polity. The concept is restricted to those religions that have regularized structures of governance and a hierarchy of organizational practices. Only salvational religions are likely to develop such governance structures.

Organized religions are important on the global political stage. For example, in international politics Islam constitutes a significant polity that has various effects on the policies of other bodies. Islam can be an actor on the global stage, despite very important internal differences and multiple centres of power. It can constitute a frame of reference within which Islamic individuals perceive themselves to be acting. Jihadists are prepared to die in the pursuit of goals that they perceive as part of Islam. A further example of the presence of both Catholicism and Islam as polities on the global stage was that of the alliance between Islam and Catholicism in opposition to the EU at the fourth UN world conference on women in 1995, on the nature of women's human rights in relation to fertility and sexuality. Catholicism was represented by the Pope's representatives since the Vatican is treated by the UN as if it were a state. The religious coalition sought to restrict the extension of rights to individual women to make their own choices on matters of intimacy, especially abortion, contraception, and sexuality. The EU, by contrast, was a significant advocate of a woman's individual right to choose (Moghadam 1996). The argument here is that the major salvational religions of Catholicism and Islam constitute polities. They govern significant aspects of life, especially intimacy, among significant numbers of people.

Empires

Empires are an important form of polity in history (Mann 1986), with lasting effects. There have also been various attempts to broaden the usage of the concept to some modern polities (Van Alstyne 1974; Hardt and Negri 2000, 2006).

An empire is a specific form of polity in which a single main state rules over many other countries using formal political hierarchies supported by military force. Military force is usually necessary to establish the political hierarchies through which routine rule is maintained. Routine rule may be further supported by religious and other ideological forms for cultural domination. The British state ruled many countries around the world, from Ireland to Africa, from

Canada to Australia, as part of the British Empire. Most of Africa was subject to colonial rule from Britain, France, and Portugal. Most of South America was subject to colonial rule from Spain and Portugal until almost the end of the nineteenth century. De-colonization of Africa from the British Empire was not complete until the 1970s (Banks and Muller 1998). Several countries in central Europe did not achieve independence from empires, such as the Hapsburg and Ottoman, until 1918 (Therborn 1995). During the nineteenth and most of the twentieth centuries the Russian empire grew to stretch from East Asia to the middle of Europe, including by the middle of the twentieth century countries in Eastern and Central Europe. Russian de-colonization did not take place until after 1989. A ruling group of people, while clearly distinct from the subordinated people, may deny their separateness (Kumar 2000).

The expansion in military power of the USA, for example in its invasions of Vietnam and Iraq, has led some to consider that it takes the form of an empire (Van Alstyne 1960; Johnson 2000; Mann 2003). However, while significant military power was used, the formal political hierarchies that are a defining feature of empires were never successfully established by the USA. This was partly because public adherence to the notion of respect for national sovereignty meant that such political hierarchies had to be covert rather than overt in order for this public rhetoric to be sustainable, and partly because of a practical assumption that dominance could be maintained without such political mechanisms, resting on military force and economic pressure alone. As Mann (2003) noted, this stance led to incoherence and a lack of sustainability for this US project.

Hardt and Negri (2000) have addressed the new forms of power that are consequent on globalization. They consider that there is now one empire, one sovereign power, which governs the whole world as a consequence of the globalization of economic and cultural exchanges. It does not have a geographical centre, nor territorialized instruments of rule; its nationalities are merged and blended. Hardt and Negri (2006) assert that we are now in a state of global war. This is not an argument that capitalist power is absolute, but one in which there are also a wide-ranging set of oppositions. The multitude is better placed than before to effect a transformation. Hardt and Negri are right to argue that there are new forms of political interconnections in this global era; power is more fluid (cf. Bauman) and interconnected; political configurations take new spatialized forms; boundaries between countries are treated more lightly in some respects. However, their picture of a globalized polity over-states the extent to which deterritorialization of political forms has occurred. Corporate capital still needs concentrated territorial locations for some of its functions (Sassen

2001), while geographical distance is implicated in many forms of capitalist appropriation (Harvey 2003). Powers are still concentrated in specific states and other polities which are in opposition to each other rather than merged into a unity. While they are right to integrate an analysis of the importance of violence into political economy they over-generalize – the USA may be leading a war but not all countries have joined in. The concentrations of power and its alternative configurations are important for understanding the potential for alternative futures. Hardt and Negri (2000) have invented a novel use for the term empire, which traditionally has been used to denote a geographically located dominant state that has power over many peoples outside its home territory through the use of formal political structures supported by military power. While new concepts are needed to grasp the particularities of global organization, it is not useful to use a term that has a clearly established meaning. We need new terms to denote new concepts to capture new forms of global hierarchy.

Hegemon

Hegemon is a term that more usefully captures the concept of a dominating state that is able to deploy a range of forms of power over many other countries in the contemporary era (Chase-Dunn 1998; Bornschier and Chase-Dunn 1999; Chase-Dunn et al. 2000). Dominance is created through a range of technologies of power, including military, political, economic, and civil societal means. Each of these forms of power is a contingent rather than an essential part of the powers of the hegemon. Following Gramsci, hegemony is achieved through a mix of coercion and manufactured consent; the mix varies over time and place so that at some times coercion is dominant while at others consent is achieved without visible coercion. The concept of hegemony is useful in invoking notions of asymmetry, power, and coercion simultaneously with consent (Gramsci 1971; Anderson 1976/7).

The concept of hegemon captures the new modalities of power in a global era better than the more traditional concepts of empire and militarism. The concept of hegemon, drawing on Gramsci's concept of hegemony, better captures the dynamic mix of coercion and consent. It allows for the various combinations of these forms of power, signalled in Gramsci's notions of wars of position as well as wars of manoeuvre. The concept avoids the notion of overt formal political hierarchy, which is a time-specific form of global power from a previous era. It enables a consideration of the nature of power that avoids some of the simplicities of a 'zero-sum' approach.

This includes a range of issues, including that countries may perceive benefits from acquiescence rather than contestation, that there can be mutual benefits in the avoidance of hostile contestations, and also that in some instances there can be meaningful co-development. Polities are complex adaptive systems that coevolve. The concept of hegemon signals the range of forms of power, as well as their shaping by the economic, political, military, and civil societal environments. Hegemons have societalization projects, which are directed externally as well as internally. These are never complete but always in process, as rival hegemons and other entities compete to set the rules by which all must live. Within the territory of a hegemon there may well be competing projects, for example of organized religions.

Hegemons set the global rules in order that they suit the characteristics of the dominant hegemon, so that while these rules are general to all players nonetheless the hegemon benefits most. The concept is helpful in grasping the setting and implications of the regulations of many economic aspects of the global system, for example, the rules of international trade as set by the World Trade Organization. The power of the concept of hegemon is further advanced if it is juxtaposed to the concept of 'fitness landscape' derived from Kauffman (1993). The US hegemon, by ensuring that its rules are best represented by the WTO, has changed the fitness landscape to its own advantage. It is not just that the hegemon has power over other countries, but also that it has changed the landscape in which they all compete in its own favour. The environment, or fitness landscape (Kaufmann 1995), within which these polities operate is changing as a result of increased global linkages. These increased links are partly the result of new technologies that speed communications both physically and electronically and partly consequent on new political institutions and practices developing at regional and global levels. Changes in the fitness landscape have implications for the construction of political preferences and for an ability to carry these through. Some political actors thrive under one set of conditions but wilt in others. Their capacities for action are the result of their interaction with their environment and not only their intrinsic capacities.

Both the European Union and the United States of America are currently hegemons. Both have economic, cultural, and political powers, though these are differently constituted and deployed. But they do differ critically in relation to military force. The EU does not have significant armed forces of its own (though its Member States do), while the USA hegemon depends on its armed forces.

While the EU meets the definition of a polity, there have been extensive arguments over whether or not the EU meets the conventional definition of a state. These focus in particular on its lack of armed forces and the question of its degree of autonomy from Member States. Conventional definitions of states (following Weber) include a monopoly of legitimate force in a territory. The EU does not have its own standing army, militia, or police. Early attempts to create a military arm – the European Defence Community in the 1950s – failed (Kapteyn 1996). However, since 2004 there has been the capacity for the EU to engage in a temporary military deployment through the European Union Force (EUFOR) by drawing temporarily on the armed forces of Member States, as it did in Bosnia in 2004, Congo in 2006, and Chad in 2007 (Council of the European Union 2007b). This lack of a standing army either means that the EU is not a state or that the conventional definition of a state needs to be revised so as to encompass such bodies as the EU.

The second reason offered as to why the European Union might not be a state is that it is merely an inter-governmental body, used as a tool by Member States to complete their own domestic agendas (Milward 1992; Moravcsik 1993). This position is based on giving primacy to the consent of Member States through their signature on treaties rather than to the actions of the EU machinery of governance, and considering the Council of Ministers as more important in the internal governance of the EU than the European Commission, the European Parliament, or the European Court of Justice. However, these arguments that the EU is merely an inter-governmental body are not convincing. This is because the EU, through the European Court of Justice and European Commission, has powers not only to coerce recalcitrant Member States to obey its rulings, but also allows EU citizens direct access to EU legal rulings on those matters within its remit (Wallace 1994; Leibfried and Pierson 1995; Kurzer 1997). The EU has sufficient internal coherence, rules of actions, ability to enforce its rules through sanctions, and institutional depth and breadth to constitute a polity even though it is not a conventional state. Its prominence as an actor at a global level means that it is a hegemon and not only a polity. In particular, the EU conducts a distinctive foreign and security policy with global implications despite differences between Member States. It also conducts trade and economic policy for all Member States, including negotiations with the WTO (Smith 2003; Smith 2004).

The USA is a state, polity, and hegemon: it is also close to being a nation and a nation-state. The USA is a hegemon in a different way from the EU. It does not have a queue of countries wanting to join voluntarily. While it is joined by Mexico and Canada in a free trade area (NAFTA), these countries did not change their regulations in order to do so. The USA is more assertive in setting the parameters of global economic policy than the EU and enforcing its policy preferences. The USA is much more assertive in foreign affairs as a result of its use and threat of use of military force. The USA is currently a more powerful hegemon than the EU.

There are further potential or would-be hegemons. Japan has sometimes been considered a third hegemon alongside the USA and the EU, because of its influence over economic development, especially in South East Asia (Hettne et al. 1999). However, a lack of economic growth since the 1990s as well as political and financial difficulties have reduced its capacity for action and influence. Islamic radicals have their own project to counter Western military aggression and secure universal respect for their religious ideals. However, this project does not involve the whole of Islam even if it is done in its name. Despite Huntington's (1998) assertions of the clash of civilizations, Islam is not best currently understood as a singularity, but instead enjoys considerable variations (Kandiyoti 1991) and internal contestations over changes. However, some within the radical Islamic movement do conceive of their project as potentially hegemonic, indeed they proclaim a *jihad* or holy war in order to achieve this. China is likely to become a future hegemon. This is due to its current rapid economic growth which means that in the foreseeable future it will become the world's largest single economy, its relative internal cohesion and an increasing tendency towards involvement in global bodies such as the WTO, influencing diplomacy in international crises, and hosting global events such as the UN conference on women and the 2008 Olympics. However, the speed of this trajectory is not clear and neither is the extent to which China will seek influence outside its borders (Hutton 2003).

The contemporary contestation between two hegemons, the EU and the USA, is key to the emergence of the new economic world order. For example, their battles within the World Trade Organization determine the level of risk allowed in food production through the use of new technologies such as the genetic modification of organisms and the use of antibiotics on farm animals; deciding the tariffs on goods and services that encourage or discourage trade and particular types of economic development. The WTO's rules establish the fitness landscape under which some economies thrive and others suffer. More frequently the USA wins these contests with the EU, as in the case of the WTO adjudication of the riskiness of genetically modified foods (Winickoff et al. 2005), though there are exceptions, such as in the case of data privacy standards where EU regulations do have an effect on the USA, with the WTO protecting the EU from threats of retaliation from the USA (Shaffer 2000). This contestation between the

EU and US hegemons and their varieties of modernity is discussed further in Chapter 11.

Global political institutions

A series of political institutions have been established at a global level that assist in the governance of global finance, militarism, and human rights. These are best regarded as emergent polities rather than as fully formed.

They include the global financial institutions discussed in Chapter 3 on Economies, including the International Monetary Fund (IMF), the World Bank, and the World Trade Organization (WTO) that lend money to governments in times of financial crisis and act as regulators of the global economic environment through a series of conventions, groups, and meetings (for example the G20). They are not entirely new – even the nineteenth century had a global financial system, while the Bretton Woods monetary agreement lasted from 1944 to 1971 – but they are increasingly important (Keohane 1989; Hirst and Thompson 1996; Ruggie 1996, 1998; Held et al. 1999).

There has also been the development of international 'security' structures, such as the UN Security Council and regional military pacts such as NATO (Held 1995; Ruggie 1996, 1998); and the emergence of global institutions with the ability to compromise the power of states especially over issues of human rights. There are near-global legal institutions, especially in relation to human rights and crimes against humanity, including the United Nations (with its power to declare wars legal and legitimate), and the International War Crimes Tribunal. There have been developments in international law covering legal rights for individuals that are over and above the legitimate powers of states, concerning the implementation of the UN Declaration of Universal Human Rights (Haas 1964; Held 1995; Ruggie 1996, 1998).

The state is only one of several types of polity. Rather than focusing only on the concept of the state, it is important to consider a wider range of polities, including not only the state but also the nation, organized religion, empire, and hegemon. This increase in the range of polities beyond states is needed in order to include the significance of complex inequalities in addition to class for centralized political institutions. Nations and organized religions often carry gender and ethnic projects, as well as class ones. Including these entities within the analysis of polities is important in order to analyse and theorize the significance of complex inequalities in addition to class.

The nation-state is a very powerful myth; its institutional existence is very rare. The recognition of the normal lack of congruency of nations and states (and also ethnicity and religion) and the strenuous efforts to achieve this elusive alignment are crucial to explaining the extent and nature of group and state violence, which so often takes place along these fractures. Attempts to bring nations and states into alignment are part of the process of societalization, and their frequent failure to complete the process to produce a society that has a full alignment of economy, polity, violence, and civil society is usual.

The concept of hegemon is needed to theorize global processes, since their emergence and relative significance are central to understanding the emerging form of globalization and societalization. The globalizing world is not made up of similar types of polities, of nation-states, but rather a much richer variety of entities. Globalization has not resulted in a single polity or empire, but rather of a contestation between hegemons and the emergence of would-be hegemons.

Polities Overlap and do not Politically Saturate a Territory

In a global era, it becomes especially clear that it is rare for one polity to politically saturate any given territory. In any given territory it is rare that any one polity controls all possible political niches and domains. The concept 'saturate' is introduced in order to address this issue. Polities variously cooperate, compete, fight, and accommodate each other – and they can overlap in the same territory. Different kinds of polities often govern different areas of social life. While some polities that coexist in a given territory may reach an accommodation as to their respective remits, others may continually contest this. Sometimes polities will agree overtly, or accommodate de facto, to their division of jurisdiction over different institutions. Such a division means that two different polities can coexist in a given territory, since they will govern different institutions. The notion of a monopoly of political control must give way. The exceptions to the conventional notion of political monopoly constitute the norm, not the exception. It is in the tension between different overlapping polities within the same territory that many important issues are shaped.

For instance, a church and a state that coexist in the same territory may divide between themselves those institutions over which they can claim authority and jurisdiction. The variable boundary between religion and state is an example of these processes. There are significant variations in the institutions over which church and state can claim jurisdiction. Many institutions have been effectively claimed to be within the remit of the church in some times and places and in others by the state. In most of Europe, various churches have, over recent centuries, been slowly if unevenly ceding to the state (often after a struggle) the authority to regulate many aspects of intimacy or 'personal' life, such as contraception, abortion, marriage, divorce, homosexuality, and sexual practices (Smyth 1992; Snyder 1992; Nelson and Chowdhury 1994). These have often been constructed as 'moral' issues when they have been under religious jurisdiction, but have become more 'political' the more they come under the jurisdiction of a state. This change is related to processes of modernization and to a change in the nature of the gender regime (Walby 1990, 1997). This transfer of remit of this arena is not complete in Europe, but is openly contested in Ireland (Smyth 1992) while it is more settled in the Nordic countries. The location of the boundary between religion and the state in the regulation of intimacy is an important focus in many fundamentalist movements, both Christian and Islamic, from Asia to the USA, which seek to reverse this transfer of authority (Marty and Appleby 1993).

Islam has complex relations with the states with which it coexists. In many though not all Moslem countries, Islamic religious or Sharia law directly governs intimacy while in other matters Islamic principles merely guide the state. In practice, there is a vast variety of relations between Islam and various states, ranging from the formal separation of religion and the state in Turkey and the application of 'personal' religious laws to Muslims only as in Malaysia, to the integration of religion and state in a theocratic state under the Ayatollah in post-1979 Iran (Ibrahim 1980; Kandiyoti 1991; Moghadam 1993; Shamsul 1996; Afshar 1998). The contestation of the remit of the state and Islam has been particularly acute in the area of 'personal laws' regulating marriage, divorce, women's clothing, and whether wife beating is within the remit of secular or religious law. There have been quite different outcomes to this contestation among such Muslim countries as Malaysia, Iran, and Turkey (Sisters in Islam 1991; Hardacre 1993; Moghadam 1993, 1994; Helie-Lucas 1994). There are significant variations in its form, at least partly due to the interactions between Islam and the state, and with the economy of the country as well as the ethnic identity of its location (Moghadam 1993; Shamsul 1996; Afshar 1998). The detailed implications of the Koran for conduct are interpreted by local as well as regional and global Islamic leaders and can vary according to the social and economic environment. For instance, interpretations of the rules surrounding interest on savings and related banking transactions are more conducive to modernization in Malaysia than in Pakistan or Saudi Arabia. In Malaysia there has been a process, albeit contested and uneven, of a reformation of Islam so that it has become more conducive to economic development than is the case in contemporary Pakistan (Said 1996; *The Economist* 2000). The ethnic composition of the population is a further source of variance, since the form of Islam more typically practised by Arabs can differ from that of other ethnic groups, such as the Malays in Malaysia (Said 1996; Shamsul 1996). Further, the political economy of Islamic countries varies according to whether they possess oil or not.

Polities cut across each other. Nations rarely coincide with states, and still less with ethos and religion, as any analysis of Europe demonstrates (Brubaker 1996; Boje et al. 1999). Many states contain more than one nation, while nations may straddle more than one state. Diaspora may or may not have national aspirations, and always straddle state boundaries (Cohen 1997). Some religions have a global reach (Beyer 1994) and follow rules that are in contest with those of the host state.

The EU is not in a monopoly position in the area that it covers, nor does it not saturate all the political arenas within its territory. Rather there are other polities with which it overlaps on the same territory. Not only are there Member States, there are also other polities including the Catholic Church and nations without states. Most of the time there is a clear division as to which institutions are governed by the EU, which are by Member States, and which are by other polities, though this is occasionally contested. Initially the remit of the EU was restricted to a specific range of economic matters that focused on the creation of a single, fair, and competitive market for products, services, and labour. However, its remit has grown in recent years especially following the Treaty of Amsterdam, although many policy matters are currently still outside its remit and belong to Member States.

Power relations are not always zero-sum. While the relations between polities may be one of contestation, there may also be relations of cooperation where each helps the other to fulfil their goals. For example, while the EU is legally superior to Member States on those areas within its remit, this superiority is not best conceptualized as always being a zero-sum game between these polities. Instead, sometimes, the EU enables Member States to carry out domestic agendas more successfully than if they were not part of the EU (Milward 1992; Moravcsik 1993). In particular, the development of the Single European Market has made it more possible for some Member States to have successful domestic economies in a global era. For some Member States the EU has increased their discretion in policy making, though this may not be the case for all. In another example, the Church in Ireland had complex relations with the developing national project and establishing state. Sometimes they were in conflict over their spheres of action, as over the development of state welfare provision (Whyte 1971), and at other times they provided mutual support (Larkin 1975; Inglis 1987). Polities coexisting in the same space may sometimes be rivals and sometimes not.

Polities do not usually exist in nested hierarchies, although these do exist within a federal polity. For example, there are nested hierarchies within federal polities of the USA and Germany, where clearly demarcated powers are devolved to more local levels. However, most of the relations between the polities under discussion here are not nested. Political relations within the USA are not an appropriate template for understanding the relations between polities elsewhere. Rather, there is a range of types of relations between polities, including cooperation, symbiosis, conflict, and accommodation.

Instead of a nested hierarchy, the relations between polities are conceptualized, as noted in Chapters 1 and 2, as the mutual adaptation of complex systems operating in a changing fitness landscape. The mutual adaptation involves changes to interacting polities rather than simple impacts. These mutual adaptations change the environment for other political systems. The changing political environment in which these interactions between polities take place affects the nature of the polities and their interactions. For example, the increase in global linkages changes the environment for polities, while the development of the European Union changes the environment for states in Europe.

Polities do not have exclusive authority over a given territory, nor are their powers limited to a specific territory. This is not a new phenomenon, as is sometimes suggested in accounts of the ostensibly restricted power of the nation-state in the era of globalization (Brenner 1999). Several religions, including Islam and Catholicism, have always straddled state boundaries and have often been accommodated by a state, dividing authority over different areas of social life (Kandiyoti 1991). Polities such as the EU share legitimate authority with their Member States within negotiated and agreed arenas (Leibfried and Pierson 1995; Walby 1999a, 1999b). Even states have rarely exercised the monopoly of legitimate violence in a given territory, given the extent to which they have condoned, and thus accepted as legitimate, the use of violence by husbands against wives within the home (Dobash and Dobash 1980; Walby 1990). Further, the power of some states extends way beyond their borders as a result of their exercise of military or economic power. There are overlapping polities with differing remits over differing areas of social life; the boundaries between these different remits themselves variously contested and accommodated.

The extent to which polities are constituted in and through space is variable. Mid-twentieth century states were more intensely territorialized than many other entities. Early empires did not have the technologies of power necessary to have such an intense hold on their territories, such as bureaucracies with sophisticated means of surveillance (Mann 1986). Religions are less intensely territorialized, in the sense that members of religious groups often retain their affiliations whether or not they are in the heartland of their religion, although they are stronger when they have at least the amount of proximity needed for groups to meet in churches and temples. Ethnic groups likewise usually retain their sense of belonging whether they like it or not, even when they are a minority. The retention of such ethnic and religious identities constitutes the basis of the phenomenon of diaspora (Cohen 1997); religions and ethnic groups may strongly maintain group boundaries without a dependence on territorial boundaries.

By contrast, the dominant conception of the contemporary state usually includes a territorial element, locating this entity in a spatialized location. This lies behind the conception of a 'Westphalian' state that has sovereignty over its territory within its physical borders. This concept is used widely in social science and not only in international relations (Waltz 1979). Weber (1948) defined the modern state as that body that had a monopoly of legitimate coercion in a given territory. However, this spatialized conception of a state serves us badly when we come to try to understand globalization. This is because there are many exceptions to a state having that monopoly of legitimate coercion in a given territory, and indeed to many other forms of monopoly authority (Krasner 1995). The temptation is then to declare these exceptions to the idealized notion of the Westphalian state as new and indeed as a consequence of globalization. However, deterritorialization is not entirely new. The extent to which polities and other social entities have been constituted in and through space has always been variable and constantly subject to change. This is despite accounts of globalization in which enhanced mobility and communications are seen newly to undermine societies. There have rarely if ever been states that politically or otherwise saturated their territories. There have always been overlapping powers, other entities that claimed authority over specific domains, even the authority to use coercion. The conventional notion of space and authority is one in which space has traditionally been conceptualized as a solid that could be under one authority or another. This needs to be replaced with a notion of space that is more of a porous sponge than a solid, as a location where many fluid entities can overlap and coexist as well as sometimes competing.

Polities can be fluid and polities are created: over 100 new states have emerged since the formation of the United Nations in 1945

(Inter-Parliamentary Union 1995). Polities can also disappear, subsumed involuntarily within other states or empires (McNeill 1963; Mann 1986); and polities can change, voluntarily forming alliances such as that of the European Union which entail the loss of sovereignty (Leibfried and Pierson 1995); their borders can change, losing and gaining territory, such as Russia/Soviet Union and Germany (West, East, and now united). Stability is unusual, even though more social theory is written about polities that have a long history than those which do not (Moore 1966; Skocpol 1979).

In any one country there is likely to be more than one polity often, but not always, governing different aspects of social relations according to different practices with a different spatial and temporal reach. Each is likely to constitute a focus for a project of societalization in which other domains are brought into alignment with its priorities and principles of social organization. As the relations between the polities change with the changing fitness landscape, then their implications for different sets of complex inequalities will also change.

It is necessary here to have an understanding of the global political system. This wider framework has been variously understood to be a determining system (Wallerstein 1974), an influential regime (Krasner 1983), or merely a background global arena. There are epistemological and ontological issues here as to whether individuals, polities, or the system in which they are embedded are seen as the prime mover in the analysis (Cerny 1990; Ruggie 1998). There are ontological debates as to whether the focus should be on the polity or system, as well as substantive debates as to whether time-space compression alters the relationship between the polity and the global. This analysis has ranged from realist international relations theory in which states are understood to be the prime movers (Waltz 1979) to Marxist accounts which see the world system as the prime mover and in which states are merely nodes (Wallerstein 1974).

The conventional understanding of the relations between states suggests that they follow their own interests in international settings. However, states can adjust to, shape, or otherwise co-evolve with the global fitness landscape. However, there is a question as to how these perceptions of their own interests are formed and indeed the content of these interests (Ruggie 1998). Rather than treating the interests of states as self-evident, as in the realist international relations tradition, it is important to see these as socially constructed (Ruggie 1998). This is not a denial of the notion of state self-interest, but rather that the pursuit of this self-interest may take several different routes, and that these cannot be simply read off from the balance of power (Ruggie 1996). Such strategizing will involve both the particular and the contingent in the interaction of regime and polity. Ruggie (1996, 1998) develops the notion of multi-lateralism, which sits in between the notion of a polity-led or a system-led analysis. Rather, it is states that jointly construct new sets of expectations and understandings and build these into new institutions. This implies a notion of an international regime that significantly conditions the actions of other states (Krasner 1983).

The argument here is that at least both the levels of polities and global system are needed for the analysis and that it is inappropriate to consider only one to be inherently primary. Some levels of the system are emergent from others, and it is important to develop a multi-level analysis of interacting complex systems in a changing fitness landscape. The changing global fitness landscape facilitates the emergence of new polities as well as the restructuring of their powers and capacities.

While military and economic power are pre-eminent in the global fitness landscape, there is also some power in argumentation. Risse (1999), inspired by Habermas, locks onto the space between knowledge and power where knowledge and power do not quite equate to the other, arguing that argumentation is an important part of the political process in relation to the application of international norms, especially those concerning human rights which are diffusing, via a process of the socialization of states. 'Human rights are embedded in a whole variety of international regimes and organizations and thus form part of the normative setting of international society. They increasingly define what constitutes a "civilized state" as a member of the international community in "good standing"' (Risse 1999: 529–30). Risse suggests there are three types of process: the forced imposition of norms, strategic bargaining, and instrumental adaptation; processes of institutionalization and habitualization; and processes of moral consciousness raising, argumentation, dialogue, and persuasion.

There are coalitions of countries in global fora which can be significant for outcomes of global negotiations although they do not constitute a polity. The 'Group of 77' at the United Nations, established in 1964 and with 130 members in 2007, is the largest inter-governmental organization of developing states at the UN (Group of 77 2007). This group is important in global trade negotiations, and has sometimes thwarted the ambitions of countries of the North in negotiations over trade liberalization in the WTO.

There is usually more than one polity in any geographical area as any one polity does not saturate any given territory. Polities coevolve, unevenly, in a changing global fitness landscape. They overlap. They contest and cooperate in the same territory, sometimes in different spheres of governance. Some are more dominant than others: the most powerful are global hegemons, with a disproportionate influence on the rules through which the globe is governed on matters from trade to human rights. A key difference between polities is the extent to which they are governed democratically.

Democracy

Democracy is treated here as a key indicator of both modernity and 'progress', despite dissenting voices. Democratic governance is a key component of good governance, which also involves the rule of law, the protection of minorities, human rights, and those institutions sufficiently developed to deliver democratic intent. The conventional definition of democracy is too narrow: in order to address complex inequalities it needs to be broadened to include, in addition to suffrage and elections, the presence of women and minorities within the institutions of governance. Here a ten-point scale is proposed to capture three levels of the depth of democracy: suffrage-democracy, presence democracy, and broad democracy. Conceptualizing democracy in a global era is also a challenge. The depth of democracy is linked to the development of neoliberalism or social democracy. The analysis of the development of democracy is challenged when complex inequalities are included since it arrives in stages and not all at once. Further global as well as country-specific processes are involved.

Democracy and modernity

Democracy today is a major hallmark of modernity while polities that are not democratic are premodern. Democracy is often framed as progress, as a universal value. It is valued in North and South, USA and EU, and enshrined in many UN statements. However, there are exceptions to this framing of democracy as progress and modernity, in particular from the perspective of multiple modernities.

In the discourse of 'Asian values' democracy is not seen as part of modernity or progress because of the priority given to the collectivity over the individual, of a combination of consensus and hierarchy (Thompson 2000; Barr 2002), but this view is widely contested as being merely self-serving for elites in some Asian countries (Sen 1997). Another challenge to the valuation of democracy is the communist prioritization of socialist economic development over individual rights, as in the former Soviet Union and in China today (Woodiwiss 1998). Similar issues concerning individuation are discussed in Chapter 6 on civil societies.

The absence of democracy is here understood as a lack of completion of the project of modernity. The comprehensiveness of access to political power through democratic procedures and the depth of that democratic power are here taken as indicators of modernity and progress.

Redefining democracy

The conventional definition of democracy is too narrow. In order to include procedures that are necessary for effective access to political power for women and minoritized ethnic groups, it is necessary to reconsider this definition of democracy. Polities that allow access to political power for some groups but not others are not fully democratic. Democracy can vary in its depth (Fung and Wright 2001; Beetham et al. 2002). While the oft-stated goal of democracy is to provide equal access to political decision making for all citizens and to ensure the accountability of government, in practice the conventional definition is primarily procedural, involving universal suffrage and free, fair, and competitive elections that elect representatives of the population to parliament in the context of freedom of speech and association (Dahl 1971; Held 1995; Potter et al. 1997; Freedom House 2008). These are indeed important, but not sufficient to capture the depth of democracy.

The focus here is on the full range of procedures that are needed to achieve democracy. The timing of democracy is often different for different social groups, with implications for the depth of the democracy of the polity as a whole. Ten indicators of the depth of democracy in a country are:

1. no hereditary or unelected positions, including a monarch and members in either chamber of parliament;
2. no colonies (i.e. no governance of territories that do not also meet these criteria);
3. no powers of governance held by an additional non-democratic polity (e.g. organized religion);
4. universal suffrage, de facto as well as de jure;
5. elections, especially those that are free, fair, and competitive, in a context of free speech and free association and developed civil society associations;
6. a low cost for electioneering, either by law or by custom;
7. an electoral system with proportional representation;
8. an electoral system with quotas for under-represented groups such as women;

9. a proportionate presence in parliament of women and minorities;
10. a range of institutions (e.g. welfare services) that are governed by the democratic polity.

These ten points are grouped into three forms of democracy each of a different depth. The shallowest is that of 'suffrage-democracy' (involving points 1–5) which concerns the absence of hereditary, military, and religious governance together with universal suffrage and free, fair, and competitive elections in the context of a free civil society. A deeper form of democracy is that of 'presence democracy' (additionally including points 6–9) and the presence of all groups in the governing institutions. The deepest form is 'broad democracy' (which includes point 10), concerning the application of democratic principles of governance across a broad rather than a narrow range of institutions.

First, the absence of a hereditary principle is a basic precondition for democracy. Surprisingly it is often passed over as if it is of no account that hereditary monarchs still exist (e.g. in the UK and Sweden), and that in some (e.g. the UK) they still have constitutional duties, even if these are severely circumscribed – indeed the UK in 2009 still had 92 hereditary peers in the upper chamber of its parliament. Democracy entails elections to all governing institutions. Once again there are some curious exceptions here, such as appointments to the upper house (the majority method of selection in 15 out of the 58 countries with a second chamber), including those by the government in both Ireland (11 out of 60 members) (Russell 1999) and the UK (in the second chamber most are appointed for life; short-term appointments include top judges and religious leaders; no one is elected).

Second, there is an absence of colonies. Colonies in an Empire are not democratically governed. Hence any country that is an empire is directly responsible for the absence of democracy in those territories that it colonizes. Several European empires, such as the British, French, and Portuguese empires, did not break up until the last half of the twentieth century. Former colonies typically had universal suffrage on their day of independence but not before. There are perhaps a surprising number of 'territories' that continue to be ruled by some countries which are not geographically contiguous and have attained only partial integration into the full set of democratic processes of the main state. The USA has several of these, including Guantanamo Bay.

Third, is an absence of governance by non-elected religious bodies. A key set of polities that are not democratic are organized religions. While these do not govern all aspects of social life, in some cases they are important in the governance of intimacy, including marriage, divorce, contraception, abortion, and sexual practices. Organized religions have significantly different modes of governance than states, confining access to decision making to small groups of anointed rather than democratically elected leaders which usually excludes women. The more important organized religion is in the governance of personal life, the less democratically governed that area of life will be. Countries in which an organized religion governs intimacy compromise democracy.

Fourth, is universal suffrage. Universal suffrage might seem an obvious essential for democracy but some analysts have settled for male suffrage or even majority male suffrage as the indicator of democracy, for example, Rueschemeyer et al. (1992) take suffrage for 60 per cent of men as their indicator of democracy. This is a mistake, as the omission of women and minority ethnic groups from the franchise precludes the designation of a country as democratic. Women and ethnic minorities have often gained the right to vote later than men in the dominant ethnic group. When fully universal suffrage without exceptions for women and ethnic minorities is taken as an essential benchmark for democracy, the timing of the democratic transition traditionally used by scholars is put back by several decades for most countries in the North (Therborn 1977; Paxton 2000; Paxton et al. 2003), though less frequently for those in the South where universal suffrage will often have been won at independence. Suffrage requires the de facto right to vote, not only its de jure existence. In the USA, the disenfranchisement of African-American slaves in the southern states by 'Jim Crow' laws until the civil rights movement appeared, means that the claim that the USA became democratic before the late 1960s is compromised.

Fifth, free, fair, and competitive elections in the context of free speech and free association are an important part of democratic procedure. This is well recognized and captured, for example, in the Freedom House (2008) indicators of political rights and civil liberties, which rank all countries of the world on a 1–7 scale for each of these: most Western countries were awarded full marks.

Sixth, is access to the democratic process through the low cost of electioneering. Several detailed procedural matters have a significant impact on the differential access of less and more advantaged citizens to political power. Levels of expenditure can have a significant effect on the outcome of an election, especially for challengers (rather than incumbents) (Jacobson 1978). Some countries, such as the UK and Ireland, have implemented a cap that limits the amount of money that can be spent on elections in an attempt to ensure that those without rich supporters can still effectively stand for election (Walecki 2007). In the USA candidates can spend very large sums of money contesting elections: for example, the cost of running for election for the President of the USA in 2004 was $367m for the winner (Bush), and $328m for the loser (Kerry) (Rooney 2007), while the amount for the 2008 election contest between Obama and McCain rose to around $1 billion.

Seventh, there are electoral systems with proportional representation; eighth, there are electoral systems with quotas for underrepresented groups such as women; and ninth, the proportionate presence in parliament and governing institutions of women and minoritized groups. Suffrage, free elections, and free association are not sufficient to deliver democracy if the concept is interpreted as the procedures necessary to facilitate the equal involvement of all social groups in political decision making – a presence in parliament is also required. The presence or absence of women in parliament makes a difference to political priorities and policy outcomes; there is evidence of this from a range of countries including the UK (Norris 1996a), the USA (Thomas 1991), and Sweden (Wängnerud 2000).

On average, elected women are more likely to support policies that directly or indirectly support gender equality. In Sweden, Wängnerud (2000) finds that the presence of women in the Swedish parliament (*Riksdag*) makes a difference in that women in the *Riksdag* are more likely than men to hold to the notion that gender equality is a good thing. In the UK, Norris (1996a) finds that the increase in women politicians in Westminster makes a difference to support for gender equality issues and other social democratic matters. Women MPs and candidates to be MPs are more likely than men to support women's rights on abortion, criminalizing rape in marriage and domestic violence, and promoting equal opportunities, as well as on some other important issues including, nationalization/privatization, trade union power, equal opportunities for ethnic minorities, use of the death penalty, nuclear weapons, and defence spending. In a comparison of states within the USA, Thomas (1991) finds that women do make a difference. Women in states with the highest percentages of female representatives introduce and pass more priority bills dealing with issues about women, children, and families than men in the same states and more than female representatives in legislatures where they are low in number. She also suggests that women can diffuse their policy priorities in two ways: through high percentages of women in office, or through the presence of a formal women's legislative caucus.

Drawing on Kanter (1977), she argues that relative numbers are critical in shaping interaction dynamics: a critical mass of women makes a difference as well as women's caucuses in the legislature. In a 'skewed' group that has 15 per cent or less of the total its members are seen as token, continuously responding to their status. In 'tilted' groupings minority members form 15–40 per cent. Where there is 'balance' – a 60/40 split – members of the minority are less often perceived as aberrant. This is highly relevant in a context where few countries can match Sweden's 47 per cent of women in parliament in 2007. Indeed the USA has only 16 per cent of women in its legislature and Ireland 13 per cent (Inter-Parliamentary Union 2007), the proportion where they may only be seen as not much more than token. However, even in the USA, the increase in women in parliament is associated with significant changes in gender policy since 1945, with a movement away from separate spheres gender policies towards equal opportunities in areas of violence, employment, maternity leave, and childcare (Burstein et al. 1995).

The significance of women in parliament for policies requires a rethinking of the conventional operationalization of the notion of 'representation' and the relationship between 'descriptive representation', where representation reflects the identified groups, and 'substantive representation' where the presumption is the representation of the interests of the group (Pitkin 1967, 2004; Norris and Lovenduski 1995; Phillips 1995; Squires 1999). The relative lack of presence of women and minority ethnic groups in parliament has been shown to reduce their prospect of influencing governmental decision making; while they are formally represented via the electoral system, the representation of their views is less established. Presence matters. A proportionate presence in parliament should be included in the operationalization of the concept of democracy. However, while the presence of women is necessary for the representation of women's interests it is still not sufficient (Jones and Jónasdóttir 1988; Jónasdóttir 1991).

A series of procedures exist that are more likely to lead to the less unequal presence of women. These include: voting systems that involve proportional representation rather than 'first past the post'; multi- rather than single-member constituencies (Norris 1985; Kenworthy and Malami 1999); and the use of quotas (Dahlerup 1998). Proportional representation makes a difference in the representation of minoritized ethnic groups as well as of women. In the UK in 2007 using 'first past the post', 2 per cent of elected MPs were from minority ethnic groups as compared with 6 per cent of UK representatives to the European Parliament who were elected using proportional representation (*Economist* 2007).

Tenth, there is the application of the democratic principle to a broad range of institutions. This is revealed in 'democratic audits' that consider a wider range of institutions (Beetham et al. 2002) and a concern for the depth of democratic practice, particularly the deliberative or empowered participatory governance involving citizens more directly in decision making (Fung and Wright 2001). Three types of institutions in particular vary in the extent to which they are governed by democratic practices: welfare institutions, employment, and the military. First, education, care, and health services, and the criminal justice system are under democratic control and directly provided by the state in some countries, while in others (to varying degrees) they are organized through the market. This tends to align with the difference between social democratic and neoliberal forms of governance. The move towards neoliberalism is often accompanied by the privatization of previously public services (Hedlund 1998; Harvey 2005). This shift is facilitated by the (much disputed) WTO directive on the liberalization of public services. Privatization of public services is an example of the shrinking of the remit of the democratic polity. This is often represented as if it were a reduction in the state and bureaucratic control of services, but if the state is democratic then it is also a reduction in democratic control. Second, the governance of the workplace and employment may be at the discretion of employers or can be subject to regulation by the polity and sometimes by the participation of worker representatives, usually unions. Third, is the extent to which military institutions are controlled by a democratic polity or have significant autonomy (Geneva Centre for the Democratic Control of Armed Forces 2008). This varies as a result of different forms of state reconstruction through war – the extent to which organized economic interests are entwined with the military in a military-industrial complex, including the privatization of security operations (Mills 1956; Harris 2005). All three types of institutions (welfare, employment, and military) are subject to greater democratic control in social democratic as compared with neoliberal forms of development.

Bringing into focus gender and other complex inequalities thus requires revisions to the conventional definition of democracy. The depth of democracy does matter: it is necessary to distinguish between suffrage-democracy that is limited to suffrage and free elections, presence-democracy that includes the procedures to ensure the presence of women and minorities in governing institutions, and broad democracy in which democratic practices are extended to a wide rather than narrow range of institutions. When these distinctions are drawn, inequalities in access to democratic power between social groups are made more visible. This increased visibility enables the differentiation of the time at which different levels of democracy are accessed by different groups, typically later for women and minority ethnic groups than for men of the dominant ethnicity. The depth of democracy is linked to the extent to which a country is neoliberal or social democratic.

The development of democracy

Does economic development drive the creation of democracy, as is conventionally argued, or are processes in civil society and violence also important? Are processes within countries the most important, or are global processes also significant? Democracy does not arrive all at once for all people, instead it occurs at varying levels and times for different regimes of inequality. Do the same processes in the development of democracy apply to gender and ethnic regimes of inequality as that of class, or do they differ? To what extent do political processes create negative or positive feedback loops in the development of democracy and modernity?

There is a robust correlation between democracy and economic development when it is limited to male suffrage-democracy (Lipset 1959; Diamond 1992; Muller 1995a). There are several ways in which economic development facilitates the development of suffrage-democracy. One is through the growth of a larger middle class and the development of education, which reduces the grounds for extremist politics and promotes tolerance and the legitimacy of democratic values (Lipset 1959). However, higher levels of inequality tend to reduce the prospects for, and stability of, democracy such as in Latin America during the 1980s (Muller 1995a), probably because it increases the resistance of the powerful to sharing power (Rueschemeyer et al. 1992; Muller 1995b). The second way in which economic development feeds the development of democracy is by increasing the resources available for the struggles of the disadvantaged. Economic development is associated with an increased independence of free wage labour and the resources to build organizations for a robust civil society and political struggle. This increases the efficacy of the struggle of the working class by facilitating growth in the economic and organizational resources that the under-represented groups need in order to struggle effectively for access to political power, thereby translating economic power into political power (Rueschemeyer et al. 1992). But it is not reducible to economic development, opening up the possibility of divergent paths of development to democracy (Moore 1966).

Presence-democracy for working-class men and parties representing their interests in parliament was not simultaneous with male suffrage but came later. It depended on the development of civil society organizations, especially trade unions, to form the organizational strength to have both a presence in parliament and to introduce a labour agenda within parliament. This occurred most readily in those countries where there developed strong trade unions with high rates of membership and a centralization of activities as well as the development of a labourist or socialist party. This trade union and party pattern became common in Nordic countries such as Sweden, moderately so in the UK, but was much less developed in the USA and Ireland. The development of social democracy was strongest in those countries with the strongest development of trade unions (Kitschelt 1994; Callaghan 2000).

The development of democracy is not only the outcome of processes at the country-level, but is also affected by global and regional processes of various forms. Military intervention in the aftermath of the Second World War led to the reconstruction of authoritarian states as democratic ones in Germany and Japan. The 1920s and 30s in Europe saw divergent waves of fascism in the south and social democracy in the north, with the former attacking embryonic forms of democracy and the latter enhancing them. During the mid- and late-twentieth century a wave of decolonization was associated with democratization as nationalist movements world wide adopted a democratic agenda.

What difference does taking complex inequalities in addition to class into consideration make to this analysis? Does the correlation between economic development and democracy apply to complex inequalities other than class? And does it apply equally to suffrage, parliamentary presence, and a range of potentially democratically governed institutions?

Access to democracy often occurs at different times for different social groups. Women have often achieved suffrage later than men in the North, though more often at the same time during decolonization in the South. Minoritized ethnic groups are sometimes excluded from access to suffrage and other democratic procedures. There may be de facto exclusions, such as those of the 'Jim Crow' practices in the southern states of the USA, which excluded African-Americans, the former slaves, from voting (Potter et al. 1997), including acts of violence (Shapiro 1988). African-Americans in the south of the USA only obtained the vote after the efforts of a strong civil rights movement (Tilly 1978; McAdam 1999). There may also be formal legal barriers to political citizenship, as in the case of in-migrants who may work and live in a country without political entitlements. In some countries a second generation acquires political citizenship at birth (e.g. the UK); in others citizenship can only be inherited from parents. In cases where the in-migration was not legally approved, political citizenship cannot be acquired. Increased global migration for economic reasons can thus sometimes entail political disenfranchisement.

Unlike the case for men, the winning of female suffrage does not correlate with either economic development (Therborn 1977) or women's employment. In North-West Europe and North America, most countries granted women the vote around 1918–1920, with a second wave in southern and eastern Europe around 1945. This challenges a simple link of economic development and democracy for women. Rather there was a global, or perhaps better, a regional wave of female suffrage. While Ramirez et al. (1997) link women's suffrage to the development of world society, in which each country adopts similar practices concerning citizenship as a result of a global diffusion of cultural and political practices rather than economic development, this misses the specificity of female suffrage and the intense and highly contested feminist struggles for the vote in the period up to 1918, which is not best captured by the rather gentle notion of a process of diffusion. In the UK the process involved women from all classes, from those organized in unions in the cotton textile mills of northern England to middle-class ladies, with their actions ranging from mass property damage (e.g. smashing windows in fashionable shopping streets, setting fire to post boxes, and burning 'votes for women' into golf courses) with consequent imprisonment, hunger strikes, and force feeding, to petitions, lobbying, and mass demonstrations (Evans 1977; Liddington and Norris 1978; Purvis and Joannou 1998). Suffrage-democracy for women is not as driven by economic development as for men, but instead is more associated with global and regional civil societal waves.

Presence-democracy for women, in which women are elected as representatives in parliament and are present in executives and other governing bodies, does however correlate with economic development (Matland 1998), more especially women's free wage labour (Rule 1981, 1987; Matland 1998; Paxton and Kunovitch 2003), the presence of women in higher level jobs (Kenworthy and Malami 1999; Knutsen 2001), and women's education (Rule 1981, 1987). Thus, while economic development is not clearly linked to suffrage-democracy for women, it is linked to presence-democracy. This is in addition to its association with the use of proportional representation rather than majoritarian voting systems, multi-member rather than single-member constituencies (Rule 1981, 1987, 1994; Norris 1985; Darcy et al. 1994; Kenworthy and Malami 1999). Thus, a combination of economic development, which includes women's free wage labour and education, and specific electoral forms drives the development of presence-democracy for women.

A further global aspect of presence-democracy for women has been the development of quotas to address the shortage of women in parliament (Dahlerup 1998; Karam 1998). In 1995 only three countries (Bangladesh, Eritrea, and Tanzania) had statutory quotas, but by 2003 there were 40 countries which had a constitutional or statutory quota and 62 had a political party quota, so that overall 83 countries had some form of quota system (some had more than one kind) (Inter-Parliamentary Union 1995; IDEA 2005). While in some cases the process of the introduction of quotas may have a predominantly national focus, in others development is as a result of local activists drawing on a near global feminist movement and learning from ideas and practices in other countries to push for change in their own (Dahlerup and Freidenvall 2005).

Presence-democracy also deepens as a result of the increasing organization of women in civil society organizations. While the highly visible aspects of women's movements have declined somewhat (Taylor 1989; Bagguley 2002), there has been substantial growth in the organization of women in civil society, including trade unions, professional associations, and many NGOs. Contrary to Fraser (1997), much of this is associated not with cultural issues but rather with economic and political issues. In many countries the proportion of women who are members of trade unions has been growing strongly and in several (including Sweden and the UK) it is now around 50 per cent of trade union membership (Hicks and Palmer 2004). Alongside this change, the proportion of women in leadership positions in trade unions has grown (Ledwith and Colgan 2000), there is a developing equalities agenda within trade union bargaining strategies (Ellis and Ferns 2000), and there is a new representation of women's interests in workplace bargaining as a result of these changes in trade unions together with women's increased presence in the labour market (Gagnon and Ledwith 2000).

Most Western countries now have established national feminist organizations that coordinate activity across a variety of fronts. The European Union actively encourages this development through its funding of the European Women's Lobby, with representatives coming from each Member State's 'peak' feminist organization (European Women's Lobby). At a global level feminist coalitions seek and find international spaces, especially in the interstices of the United Nations, to develop shared platforms for action, as for example in Beijing in 1995 (UN 1995). These have implications for the development of positions put forward at a national level, from suggestions for the reform of democratic procedures, such as quotas (Dahlerup 1998), and the development of state institutional machinery to take forward gender equality issues at a national level (Mazur 2002), to shared feminist programmes.

The development of democracy, the modernization of the polity, is not simply driven by economic development, but a consequence of the complex interaction of economy, polity, violence, and civil society. Democracy for women and minoritized ethnic groups is often but not always later than for men of the dominant ethnicity. It is important to note the varying depth of democracy and to go beyond the traditionally narrow focus on suffrage-democracy, to include presence-democracy and broad democracy.

Conclusions

Making visible complex inequalities and global processes requires the deconstruction and rebuilding of the conceptualization and theorization of polities and democracy. It also requires the use of the broader concept of polity rather than the narrower one of state, the rejection of the misleading concept of nation-state, and the understanding that polities overlap and do not saturate their territory. It demands differentiation of the depth of democracy so as to capture variations in the access to political power of different groups at different times.

The concept of state is too narrow and should be replaced by the broader concept of polity, which encompasses a variety of forms including states, nations, organized religions, empires, and hegemons in order to facilitate the visualization of conflicts between political projects involving complex inequalities such as ethnicity and gender more fully. Any one polity rarely saturates its territory. Instead nations, states, religions, and hegemons overlap, contesting and accommodating in the same geographical space. Different polities carry differently gendered, classed, and ethnicized projects, so the contestation between these polities has implications for the nature of gender and ethnic relations as well as that of class. The concept of the nation-state with its purported settlement of one nation and one state misleads since this is rarely fully achieved. It is preferable to disaggregate the different polities to be able to examine the implications of their lack of mapping onto each other, such as the militarized conflict associated with nation-state projects when a nation, state, and religion do not map onto each other. The myth of purity associated with the nation-state project is a terrible driving force in history when combined with the low likelihood of its achievement. Global processes will create new fitness landscapes within which competing polities variously thrive or decline. Emerging and contesting global hegemons are key to setting up the rules of such global landscapes.

The concept and operationalization of democracy are revised so as to include issues related to complex inequalities. Ten indicators of the depth of democracy are identified: no hereditary or unelected positions, including a monarch and members in either chamber of parliament; no colonies, that is, no governance of territories that do not also meet these criteria; no powers of governance held by additional non-democratic polity, for example organized religion; universal suffrage, de facto as well as de jure; elections, especially those that are free, fair, and competitive; a context of free speech and free association and developed civil society associations; a low cost for electioneering, either by law or by custom; an electoral system with proportional representation; an electoral system with quotas for under-represented groups such as women; a proportionate presence in parliament for women and minorities; a range of institutions (e.g. welfare services) governed by the democratic polity. Democracy may be shallow or deep: suffrage-democracy though conventionally equated with democracy is its most shallow variant; presence-democracy in which women and minorities are present in governing institutions is a deeper form; the deepest of all is broad-democracy, where a broad range of institutions (welfare, employment, military) is governed by democratic practices. Neoliberalism typically has no more than suffrage-democracy, while social democracy has both presence-democracy and broad-democracy.

The development of democracy rarely happens all at one point in time for all social groups, despite the convention of dating democracy from the year of men's suffrage. Even suffrage-democracy was usually at different times for men and women in the North, though more often simultaneous during the decolonization of the South. Presence-democracy is still rather uncommon, found in few countries other than the Nordic ones. Broad-democracy is confined to social democratic countries. While suffrage-democracy for men is often linked to economic development, suffrage-democracy for women is not, although presence-democracy is.

5 Violence

Introduction

The importance of violence for people's well-being, for regimes of inequality, and for other institutional domains, is much underestimated in social theory; indeed it is frequently rendered invisible. Yet the regulation and deployment of violence is part of the constitution of the social order, complex inequalities, and globalization. The conceptualization of violence should be neither simply naturalistic, nor solely discursive. Violence is not a significant part of the classical sociological tradition of Marx, Durkheim, and Simmel, nor of contemporary social theory; rather it is examined within rather specialized social science traditions associated with international relations and criminology and not integrated into mainstream social theory. Four challenges are made to social theory in order to theorize violence.

First, the development of an ontology of violence. Violence is a social phenomenon, not reducible to psychological traits, hormones, emotions, or individualized pathology. Violence constitutes a social system, an institutional domain, that is parallel to those of economy, polity, and civil society. When complex inequalities are brought into focus, the range of phenomena visible as violence is extended beyond the traditional focus on war and criminal violence to include non-criminalized forms of inter-personal and group violence. The inclusion of group violence and war between states alongside interpersonal violence in the same theoretical frame of reference challenges the academic division between international relations and criminology. The institutions of violence are concerned with its deployment and regulation; they are interconnected. Violence is a distinct institutional domain; it is not reducible to the polity nor dispersed in civil society.

Second, the traditional view of the relationships between violence and modernity, and between violence and inequality (drawn from Weber, Merton, and Foucault) is transformed when complex inequalities are brought into focus. The Weberian conceptualization of the contemporary state as modern, on the assumption that it has the monopoly of legitimate violence in its territory, is challenged by making visible the existence of widespread uncriminalized violence against women and minoritized ethnic and national groups that is de facto condoned by the state. In a challenge to conventional criminological theory, from Merton to neo-Marxist, since making gender- and ethnic-based violence visible reverses the assumption of who are the disadvantaged and who are the victims. Until violence against women and minorities is subject to criminalized regulation the state is not yet modern. Democracy increases the regulation of violence and decreases its deployment: the deepening of democracy to include women and minorities is associated with the criminalization of violence against them; mature democratic states are less likely to launch wars against each other. The Foucauldian conceptualization of changes in the modern form of governance from punishment to discipline is challenged by making visible gender- and ethnic-based violence. Rather than a shift from punishment to discipline, this violence is newly subjected to punishment as crime. While the Foucauldian distinction between forms of social order based on the deployment of overt brutal violence by the state and on the disciplining of the self is useful in pointing up the importance of processes in civil society as well as the state for building social order, the direction and universality of such a temporal shift are challenged by the inclusion of complex inequalities other than class.

Third, there are path dependent trajectories of the regulation and deployment of violence in modernity; not a single path of development. There are higher levels of violence in neoliberal countries than in social democratic ones. Higher levels of violence are associated with both inequality and lower levels of democracy. A neoliberal state is not a small state: instead it has expanded institutions of violence, criminal justice, and the military. In social democracy there is less violence and smaller state institutions to deploy or regulate it. Militarized institutions once established are hard to diminish, unless there are exceptional circumstances restructuring polities.

Fourth, the increasing significance of global processes restructures the deployment and regulation of violence. The different understandings of globality and violence affect the scale and nature of the deployment of military violence in different polities. The increased political salience of terrorism at a global level changes the prioritization of civil liberties in some locations. Global waves of human rights and feminism change political priorities in regulating and criminalizing different forms of violence, thereby affecting its deployment. The development of universal human rights and embedding these in national and international institutions changes the regulation of violence.

Developing the Ontology of Violence

The ontology of violence is not obvious. Violence is neither simply naturalistic, nor solely discursive. The deployment and regulation of violence are socially constituted. Too often violence has been individualized as if it were the product of personal psychology and isolated failures of socialization; but it is not reducible to these. That many violent practices have been rendered socially, politically, and theoretically invisible does not mean that they are not significant. The calling of violence into view and its naming are key parts of the process of analysis. The construction of the object of enquiry is riddled with theoretical implications. The claim here is that these violences are interrelated social practices – they involve its deployment and regulation, they are embedded in and constituted by social institutions, and they are significant for the making and reproduction of regimes of inequality. Violence is not merely an instrument or tool of already constituted power; it is itself constitutive of power. The varied forms it takes in its deployment and regulation contribute to the constitution of power and inequality; they are not merely a reflection of them. Violence is an institutional domain, a social system in its own right and not reducible to any other. The possibility of the use of violence and its potential implications varies according to its environment or fitness landscape, including the form of the state and its criminal justice system and military, the depth of democracy, the extent of economic autonomy, and the nature of the global environment.

Violence is deployed and regulated by states, individuals, and groups. Violence has been most visible in social theory when it involves the state as war-maker against other states: it is most frequently studied as part of inter-national relations, but it also depends on domestic social relations and institutions. Inter-personal violence has been most visible when it has been criminalized by the state. It is most frequently studied as part of criminology yet there are also important non-criminalized forms. Group violence is rarely studied (with some exceptions for terrorists and ethnic cleansers) but has a long history.

The development and use of military force is a significant aspect of the deployment of violence. The military are a very significant form of power and not reducible to the state, having their own set of institutions (Mann 1986). Military force is a significant element in the conduct of state, national, ethnic, religious, and hegemonic projects. It varies significantly in the form that it takes and the effects that it has (McNeil 1963; Tilly 1990, 2003; Rummel 1997; Bornschier and Chase-Dunn 1999; Shaw 2005; Kaldor 2006).

States have a set of coercive institutions in addition to the military. This includes in particular the criminal justice system. Criminal justice systems vary in the extent to which brutal violence or other forms of disciplining are used. At one extreme is the use of the death penalty and there are also prisons, the police, and other coercive institutions. The extent to which states spend their resources on the military and criminal justice systems varies significantly.

There is also 'irregular' state violence. Not all the violence used by the state against its citizens and foreigners is within its own laws of conduct. States and religions have used violence in subduing resistance and opposition at home and abroad. There is documented use of torture and other coercive methods to extract information and to subdue prisoners. People are held in custody and camps outside of the rule of law (Gregory 2004). Periods of heightened militarization are conducive to the erosion of civil liberties and to the use of coercive methods against perceived opponents and enemies.

Some of the more severe interpersonal violence is criminalized – murder, assault, and robbery (theft with violence). This is well studied in its own sub-discipline of criminology (McLaughlin et al. 2003). This violence varies widely over time and between countries.

But not all interpersonal violence is criminalized. When forms of inequality beyond class are brought into focus, important further forms of violence become visible. Gender-based violence is only partly or recently criminalized: domestic violence, rape, sexual assault, stalking and harassment. Interpersonal violence oriented towards other minoritized groups (for example, the harassment of gays and lesbians, and ethnic and religious minorities) is also only slowly becoming criminalized. Group violence oriented towards ethnicity, religion, and nation is unevenly criminalized: lynching, pogroms, ethnic cleansing, genocide, terrorism, and harassment.

The wider range of regimes of inequality involved in violence challenges traditional approaches to interpersonal violence that have often viewed it through a class lens. The dominant criminological approach to interpersonal violence attributes it to the frustrations of the economically disadvantaged, a position found within a broad range of theoretical perspectives from functionalism (Merton 1968) to neo-Marxism (Lea and Young 1984; Garland 2001). The socio-economically disadvantaged are seen to commit most crime, from theft to violence, because while they endorse the dominant values, they are unable to attain these goals as a result of economic disadvantage. In response they break the rules in order to achieve these goals. The underlying cause is the tension between the dominant social value of achievement and the social institutional framework that precludes the disadvantaged from obtaining this. Only if the rules are broken, can the socio-economically disadvantaged reach these goals. Criminals are seen as being drawn predominantly from disadvantaged groups whose aspirations for the established markers of success are thwarted as a result of their restricted resources due to their social backgrounds: they break the rules in order to reach these goals.

This approach has been developed through an analysis of subcultures which help to sustain the deviant minority (Wolfgang and Ferracuti 1967). The account receives evidential support if the focus is on a single dimension of inequality associated with class; those who commit crimes then appear disproportionately to be poor men. However, this account is only sustainable if gender and other forms of inequality beyond class are ignored. It is not poor *people* who commit most crimes against property and persons, but poor *men* and not poor women. If gender is brought into focus (Lenton 1995), then it is not the most disadvantaged who commit crimes since men are not disadvantaged as compared with women. Violence is often deployed as a form of instrumental power by dominant groups, though its implications depend on its regulation and the resources and resilience of the potential victims. There are significant amounts of inter-personal violence that are not effectively criminalized. When complex inequalities beyond class are brought into focus, these additional forms of violence come into view as significant. The predominant theorization of inter-personal violence as a consequence of a disadvantaged class position is challenged by its use by dominant groups to maintain gender and ethnic/racialized/national/sexual hierarchies.

The proportion of women who have experienced gender-based violence at some point during their lives ranges from one quarter to one half, according to the World Health Organization and many national surveys (Krug et al. 2002). A national US survey found that 22 per cent of women had suffered domestic violence at some point in their lifetime, 18 per cent had been subject to completed or attempted rape, and 8 per cent had been stalked (Tjaden and Thoennes 2000a, 2000b). A UK national survey found that over their adult life-times, 21 per cent of women had been subject to domestic violence, 5 per cent had been raped, and 19 per cent had been stalked, with 45 per cent being subject to one or more of these forms (Walby and Allen

2004). Victims of domestic violence may have been subject to a series of incidents constituting a coercive pattern of conduct; though these patterns vary, ranging from 'patriarchal terrorism' to 'situational couple violence' (Johnson 1995; Johnson and Leone 2005). In the UK, female victims of domestic violence experienced an average of 20 incidents per year (Walby and Allen 2004).

Inter-personal violence significantly affects the quality of life. Many women suffer severe harms to their physical and mental health (Krug et al. 2002). In addition to physical injuries many women who are subject to domestic violence will suffer depression and post-traumatic stress disorder, especially if they are raped, from which they can take years to recover (Breslau et al. 1998; Golding 1999). The repercussions of domestic violence can reverberate widely, limiting women's productive employment as a result of injuries, anxieties, threats from partners, and the need to move house (Lloyd 1997; Raphael and Toman 1997), as well as restricting their mobility through fears about certain types of public locations (Stanko 1990; Johnson 1996). These effects then reverberate through a wide range of social practices, including the welfare state, the economy, and family break-up, as well as on children (Walby 2004b).

Racialized, or ethnically, nationally, or religiously inspired violence, takes both individual and group forms, including actions by individuals, by ephemeral groups (such as lynch mobs) and by organized groups. They may involve networks and loose organizations, as well as more individualized actions involving a shared value system that legitimates this conduct. Non-state violence is a key and not a marginal feature of periods of contestation between ethnic, national, and religious groups. Harassment is repeated abusive or intrusive conduct towards another person. It may be verbal, but it can include assault. This can occur across racialized differences and inequalities. Harassment of racialized minorities overtly seeking equal rights is common. This was widely noted during the civil rights campaign in the American South during the 1960s (Shapiro 1988; Griffin 1993). It continues today, now sometimes known as 'hate crime' (Perry 2003). Inter-ethnic violence can take a gendered form, when the violence of men from one ethnic group is directed towards women from an opposing ethnic group, as in acts of mass rape in wartime (Brownmiller 1976; Jacobs et al. 2000).

Ethnic cleansing and pogroms represent the practice of attacks by a dominant group on a minority social group, involving variously the destruction of property, being driven from their homes, physical threats, the coerced denial of an economic livelihood, and physical assault and killing. Pogroms in European history especially took place against Jews. There are also instances of pogroms in Asia, for instance, against the Chinese minority in the post-war period in South-East Asia. Ethnic cleansing is a similar process; this term was especially used in the complex Balkan conflict between ethno-national groups in the 1990s to refer to systematic attempts to drive out minorities in order to create a more ethnically homogeneous 'homeland' (Bertilsson 1999; Mann 2005). Europe before the First World War was composed largely of multi-ethnic empires, but following the violent pursuit of the chimera of a pure nation-state it had by 1950 reached an unprecedented level of ethnic homogeneity (Therborn 1995; Stamatov 2000). Genocide is the deliberate destruction of an entire people, identified by their ethnicity, racialization, religion, or nation.

Lynching performed by members of a dominant group on members of weaker social groups accused of a crime by-passes the criminal justice system, with its procedures for trial and due process. Lynching was prevalent in US history in the period after the end of slavery, when whites lynched African Americans in the formerly slave owning South (Shapiro 1988; Griffin 1993). Harassment and physical and sexual assaults against slaves were routine and widely carried out during the era when slavery was legal in the USA (Davis 1981), further suggesting that extremes of dominance are conducive to high rates of violence.

While many of these examples of group violence concern complex inequalities other than class, there are also instances of this form in class conflicts. In particular, at times of heightened industrial conflict and strikes violence has been used. In late nineteenth-century America, there were violent attempts at breaking strikes and unions by employers using their own forces which were then ignored by the criminal justice system (Smith 2003).

Terrorism is the deliberate use of violence against a civilian population in order to create terror that will in turn achieve political change. Terror has been especially used by some nations and would-be nations that are seeking to establish a state of their own and to remove all those they regard as outsiders. There are several examples in Europe's present and recent history, including those seeking the unification of Ireland and the Basques seeking a separate state (Anderson 1995). The nationalist contestation of the boundary between Britain and Ireland has involved waves of irregular military and terrorist interventions since Eire's independence from the United Kingdom left the six northern counties in Ireland under British sovereignty in 1922. There are also terrorist attacks such as 9/11 which claim their inspiration from radical or fundamentalist interpretations of Islam, thus condemning the perceived imperialism and corruption of the West especially as exemplified by the USA and the thwarting of efforts to build a Palestinian state. However, far from all contemporary terrorism – even suicide bomber terrorism – should be regarded as part of a fundamentalist Islamic *jihad* (Pape 2003).

Violence straddles the traditional distinction between human action and objects. Violent action involves differently abled bodies and technologies as well as human subjects and institutions. Its conceptualization and theorization thus demand rethinking traditional humanist conceptions of agency. The ability to exercise violence against another person usually depends upon the possession of a capable body that has been informally or formally trained which can then be deployed as a weapon. It is necessary to go beyond the tendency to push anything biological, such as bodies, outside the frame within which analysis can be conducted (Benton 1993). The recognition of the differential ability to use the body as an instrument of power need not be a return to biological essentialism. However, it requires the rejection of the humanist-inspired narrowing of the conception of agency to activities of the mind only, and the development of a concept of agency that can include the body. The inclusion of bodies within the analysis of violence is not merely the inclusion of a biologically-based power, since it depends upon their positioning within a mesh of institutions that may variously sanction the violence or protect potential victims. In order to fully locate the significance of bodies as weapons it is necessary to consider the wider sets of social systems that constitute the environment within which it may or may not be possible to deploy a body as an instrument of power effectively. The theorization of violence requires a rejection of the traditional humanist narrowing of concepts of agency and structure in order to include violence, which is partly constitutive of complex inequalities, within social theory.

Violence is a form of power that is used to dominate others, to create fear and to shape their course of conduct. It is deployed and regulated by individuals, groups, and states. It is used by members of dominant groups against members of weaker social groups, as well as in response. This contradicts the conventional account that most interpersonal violence in civil society is predominantly used by the disadvantaged against the powerful. When the notion of inequality is confined to class, these inequalities associated with the use of interpersonal violence as power remain out of focus. When the conception of social inequality is broadened beyond a single dimension associated with class, so as to include gender and other complex inequalities, then this new picture emerges. It is deployed and regulated by groups (especially ethnically, religiously, and nationally defined groups) against others. It is deployed and regulated by states through their military and criminal justice systems against and for other states, groups, and individuals. These forms of violence are interconnected, constituting a social system, an institutional domain of violence.

Modernity and Violence

Modernity is linked to variations in the deployment and regulation of violence in several ways. Weber linked modernity with the concentration of legitimate violence in the state. Foucault linked modernity to a shift from the use of overt violence by the state to technologies of discipline. While these have been important contributions, they miss some of the key links between modernity and violence that exist because of the development and deepening of democracy. Violence tends to decline with the development of the economy and democracy (Rummel 1995, 1997; Eisner 2001, Tilly 2003), though there are dissenting voices (Bauman 1989). The development of democracy is important in reducing violence for at least two reasons. First, the development and deepening of democracy tends to lead to greater regulation through the criminalization of violence against women and ethnic, racialized, and national minorities. Second, mature democracies tend not to initiate the deployment of military power through going to war, especially against each other.

Following Weber (1947), it has been conventionally assumed that the modern state has a monopoly on the use of legitimate violence in a given territory (Giddens 1985; Elias 1994). The state is considered to accumulate power and particularly the monopoly of legitimate violence during a long process of development associated with the modernization of the social system. There is a shift from feuding barons, roving militias, and armed tribes towards the centralization and concentration of coercive power in the state. This centralization and concentration of coercive power includes the development of the rule of law and its associated institutions. This covers the criminal justice system and the civil legal system – police, courts, lawyers, judges, prisons, reform programmes, and the death penalty (Tilly 1990).

However, while there is indeed a tendency for the use and regulation of legitimate violence to be concentrated during the processes of state formation and modernization this process is not yet complete, especially for that violence which occurs along gender or ethnic, religious or national divisions. There is a significant amount of inter-personal violence that is not criminalized by the state, hence the state does not have a monopoly on legitimate violence. If gender-based violence were effectively criminalized and its perpetrators were hunted down and punished, then the state would have a monopoly over legitimate violence in a given territory even if it did not catch all of the offenders. In the absence of such actions the state effectively condones this violence. The existence of significant amounts of non-state violence which is in practice condoned by the state requires a re-theorization of both violence and the modern state. The state is not yet modern while there is extensive violence against women and minorities that effectively goes uncriminalized and unregulated by the state.

The existence of inter-personal violence does not by itself constitute a contradiction to the notion that the modern state has a monopoly on legitimate coercion in a given territory. It is when such violence is not de-legitimated by a process of effective criminalization that the state loses its monopoly on legitimate coercion. There is much inter-personal violence that is so criminalized. In particular, violence inflicted by lower-class men on strangers in public places is routinely regarded as criminal. It is the absence of criminalization of inter-personal violence between particular categories of people that is the issue here.

An important aspect of lynching, harassment, ethnic cleansing, and genocide – and of domestic violence and sexual assault – is that the state does not effectively intervene to either prevent this violence or to criminally punish the perpetrators (Shapiro 1988; Griffin 1993; Harris and Grace 1999; Hoyle and Sanders 2000). These acts of violence are against statute law but this is not sufficient to accord the state a monopoly on legitimate violence. The law, and still less the state, is not merely a set of statutes but is also a social institution which includes the police, sheriffs, lawyers, judges, legal procedures, juries, prisons, and a hierarchy of courts. While statute law is subject to modification by state institutions such as parliaments and legislatures, its implementation depends on the local practices of sheriffs and juries and, in some jurisdictions, case law. If the local police will not arrest, or juries will not convict, or if a higher court finds someone not guilty, then the perpetrator of an act of violence is treated as if they were innocent. By non-enforcement of statute law the state condones the acts of violence and treats these as if they were either legitimate actions or outside its remit. Thus it can be said that the state does not have a monopoly over legitimate violence in a given territory. The state, of course, is not a monolithic body, and different agencies and institutions of the state may follow slightly different courses of action. Nevertheless, there are forms of coherence, hierarchies of command, and a presumption of political responsibility in modern states that would describe themselves as democratic. In the context of conflicting priorities, an outcome of non-action constitutes a course of action. Only when inter-personal violence against women and minorities is effectively criminalized can it be said that the state does not condone it.

In the case of gender relations, power through violence can be possessed by the male head of a household, a husband, partner, or father. Historically, the state did not challenge the 'monopoly of legitimate violence' as exercised in 'his' home by the male 'head' of a household. Rather, it considered the 'private' sphere of the home as outside of its remit of action. Although in the same geographical territory, there was a division of legitimate authority to use violence between male heads of households and the state. The state did not have a monopoly of legitimate violence in its own territory, instead this was shared with the patriarchal heads of households. And in some cases the regulation of a 'family' and intimacy is shared, further, with organized religion.

One example is that of rape in marriage. This was rarely illegal in any country until a few countries started to criminalize the practice of sex without consent from the 1990s. Until then, husbands were entirely within the law if they raped 'their' wives (Russell 1990). In practice, convictions of a man for rape are extremely rare if the woman has ever consented to sex with him; husbands did (and are usually still able to) rape 'their' wives with legal impunity (Kelly et al. 2005). It is also still the case that rape, even outside of marriage, is rarely effectively criminalized (Lees 1996; Martin 2005). Over 90 per cent of cases in which a woman reports rape to the police do not lead to a criminal conviction. In the UK, only 5.6 per cent of reported rapes led to a criminal conviction in 2002 (Kelly et al. 2005). Domestic violence until recently was a further obvious example. In nineteenth-century England a man could beat 'his' wife so long as the stick was no thicker than a man's thumb with legal impunity (Dobash and Dobash 1980). Only since the 1970s has the legal impunity for a man to beat 'his' wife or partner begun to be challenged (Hague and Malos 1993; Hearn 1998). While there have been important recent developments (Hanmer et al. 1989; Hanmer and Griffiths 1998; Home Office 2005; UNDP 2005), the effective criminalization of this practice is still not complete (Kelly et al. 1999, 2005; Lewis 2004). Indeed, the relative invisibility of domestic violence in the criminal justice system is illustrated by the absence of such a category in most official or criminal statistics.

In the USA, in the post-slavery era, an absence of police intervention was a contributory cause in the lynching of African-American men. However, in some instances the police did intervene and a potential lynching was averted (Raper 1933). It is this historical counterfactual which provides such strong support to the argument that the criminal justice system should be treated as a variable in the explanation of lynching (Griffin 1993). African-Americans were especially vulnerable to white violence while they were politically disenfranchized and economically weak (Shapiro 1988). During the slave era, up until the late nineteenth century, white owners could routinely use violence on black slaves with no sanctions from the criminal justice system, except very occasionally in the case of killing (Davis 1981). In the post-slave era, African-Americans were subjected to extensive and varied forms of white violence which were condoned by the state to which they were denied democratic access by Jim Crow laws and other racist practices. The economic weakness produced by the post-slavery agricultural system of sharecropping compounded this vulnerability.

This vulnerability to white violence was reduced by the effects of the civil rights movement in the 1950s and 1960s which won effective political citizenship, such as the practical right to vote from the Voting Rights Act 1965 and its enforcement, by migration to the northern cities of the USA where economic freedom and the absence of Jim Crow laws facilitated the growth of a black electorate which could impact on federal politics, and by the new availability of television and other media to communicate the evils of the system facilitated by the new tactics and strategies of emerging political leaders such as Dr Martin Luther King (Maidment 1997). The complex inter-connection of political citizenship and economic independence led to the de-legitimation of white violence against African-Americans in the late twentieth century. After the political enfranchisement of African-Americans with the removal of the Jim Crow laws which had prevented them voting and the ending of legal segregation, as a consequence of the civil rights movement of the 1950s and 1960s, the USA saw the beginning of some enforcement of laws against violence against African-Americans (Shapiro 1988).

The criminalization of violence to ethnic and racialized minorities is not complete in the contemporary UK either, as the failed investigation into the murder of the black teenager Steven Lawrence in Britain in the 1990s (Macpherson 1999) demonstrated. Indeed the police have also been seen as part of the problem in their disproportionate use of 'stop and search' methods on black people in the UK (Bland et al. 2000). There are other minorities who also have a heightened vulnerability to violence as a consequence of their limited ability to gain the protection of state institutions. These include groups defined by their sexuality, such as lesbian and gay people, who can be subject to homophobic violence and again with minimal police intervention (Mason and Tomsen 1997). The conceptualization of the contemporary Western state as modern, as in the Weberian tradition, is mistaken. While there is so much violence against women and ethnic and other minorities that is de facto condoned by the state, the state is not yet modern.

The inclusion of women and minorities within democratic processes has been necessary before there is a use of state power to regulate and reduce violence by dominant groups. The development of the effective criminalization of inter-personal violence against women and minorities is part of the process of the modernization of the state. Key to this process is the deepening of democracy, the effective political representation of the interests of women and minorities. Political pressure from these non-dominant groups and their allies is key to the criminalization of inter-personal and group violence from dominant men. Only when this violence is effectively criminalized does the state have the monopoly over legitimate coercion in its territory. The completion of the project of modernity requires deep democratization.

The analysis of governmentality and violence engages with long-standing questions in social theory about the nature of social order, social control, and social cohesion (Alexander 1984; Giddens 1984; Lockwood 1992; Archer 1995). It addresses the issue of social integration and the relationship of the individual to the social, at both micro and macro levels.

Elias (1994) sees the civilizing process as one in which self-control over emotions and violence develops with the advent of modernity, thus reducing the extent of violence over time. In Elias's theory of 'the civilizing process', state formation is associated with processes of increased self-control, the inhibition of spontaneous emotions, and the ability to refrain from open displays of aggression. In this way changes in the social structure have implications for the form of personalities and their likelihood of violent behaviour. Insofar as violence is seen as a result of little development in social control and uninhibited emotions, then it is likely to diminish with the development of the civilizing process; macro-level changes in societal development have implications for the level of violence.

These questions are posed in different ways by Foucault's (1991, 1997) approach to modernity which involves a shift from governance based on punishment through brutal state power to one based on discipline and the development of self-regulation. Foucault's choice of image for a traditional sovereign power is that of public execution. This is highly visible and brutal, a form of power that is tightly focused on the state or sovereign. The threat of the use of this terrible power is considered crucial to the maintenance of social order and it is a notion of justice based on retribution. It is public and overt, indeed it is constituted as spectacle. With modernity and democracy there is a change in the form of governance to one that is achieved through the development of institutions that can secure the internalization of the norms needed for social life. Foucault's (1997) choice of image for discipline includes that of a prison that seeks to reform its prisoners within a regime of surveillance so that they will choose to make different choices when they are released. More broadly, he identifies a multiplicity of technologies of power throughout social life by which a person comes to choose courses of action that are consistent with the maintenance of social order. This is captured by the notion of 'governing the soul' (Rose 2000).

The shift from a regime of punishment to one of discipline was linked to the development of democracy – which undercut old forms of authority – requiring new forms of practice to ensure social cohesion (Foucault 1997). These practices that ensure the normalization of the population are widely diffused. Modernity requires these new forms of governance in response to democratization. Normalization is the process that ensures the maintenance of a social order under democracy. Overt power is replaced by a disguised disciplinary grid. Thus Foucault's thesis concerning modernity is the displacement of the brutal power of the sovereign or state by a multiplicity of technologies of power in civil society that will ensure the alignment of the individual with the social order.

While this dichotomous distinction between sovereign power and discipline remains the dominant reading of Foucault's work, a distinction within the category of discipline can be identified in some of his later writings. Here, Foucault distinguished a third category, that of governmentality (1991), which concerns the securitization of the whole population and uses a range of technologies of power including the economic. The focus in this case is not on a few potential deviants, but on the level of risk among the population as a whole. In this regulatory regime such focus is no longer on the disposition of the individual, but rather on decreasing the risk to the population as a whole of experiencing crime. It is the population that are subject to this form of governance, in order to improve their security. In securitization, the entire population is cajoled into developing their own protection from risk.

> First of all, the state of justice, born in the feudal type of territorial regime which corresponds to a society of laws – either customs or written laws – involving reciprocal play of obligation and litigation; second, the administrative state, born in the territoriality of national boundaries in the fifteenth and sixteenth centuries and corresponding to a society of regulation and discipline; and finally a governmental

> state, essentially defined no longer in terms of its territoriality, of its surface area, but in terms of the mass of its population with its volume and density, and indeed also with the territory over which it is distributed, although this figures here only as one among its component elements. This state of government which bears essentially on population and both refers itself to and makes use of the instrumentation of economic savoir could be seen as corresponding to a type of society controlled by apparatuses of security. (Foucault 1991: 104)

Foucault thus positions individuals as targets of governance in the first two forms only, while in the third this becomes the population as a whole. Foucault's work straddles and re-works the conceptual division between civil society and state (Cohen and Arato 1992). In developing a new vocabulary of concepts to address these technologies of power, Foucault's work acts as an inspiration for a wide range of domains.

However, there is an ambiguity in Foucault's (1991) writing as to whether the three forms are temporally sequential or coexisting (Merry 2001), though some would remain convinced that they can coexist (Rose 1999). The above quotation – which refers to the period covering the feudal regime followed by the administrative territorial state of the fifteenth and sixteenth century and then followed by a non-territorially defined governmental state – appears to support the interpretation that these are sequential stages of development. However, the quotation below from the same article suggests simultaneity.

> Accordingly, we need to see things not in terms of the replacement of a society of sovereignty by a disciplinary society by a society of government; in reality one has a triangle, sovereignty-discipline-government, which has as its primary target the population and as its essential mechanism the apparatuses of security. (Foucault 1991: 102)

Foucault's initial dichotomous distinction is clearly a temporal shift in the form of governance associated with the onset of modernity. However, it is less clear whether his three-fold classification is intended as a shift from one form of governance to another or whether the new form is that of coexistence (Merry 2001).

There is a challenge to Foucault's analysis in that the development of state and societal responses to gender- and ethnic-based violence does not follow the temporality he proposed. The state is not the first stage in the regulation of this violence. Rather, women and minorities had to look to their own resources first, to secure their own protection, and only after democratization were they able to access state support in addition. That is, democracy is not associated with a move from a state to a civil society regulation of this violence, but rather with the development of an effective state response. Bringing complex inequalities into focus challenges the temporality of Foucault's account.

While the discussion of the regulation and deployment of violence so far has centred on the changing relationship of the state and civil society during the development of modernity, it is also important to consider the significance of economic development. The question here concerns the nature of the relationship between the different forms of regulation and the deployment of violence associated with the level of economic development. Economic development in the long term has been linked to changes in the level of violence in a variety of ways. An increase in economic development and in the income per person has been associated over the long term with a reduction in homicide. Economic development specifically associated with women and minorities can increase resilience through the increased resources needed for autonomy and for flight. The level of homicide is the best indicator for comparing violent crime between countries: it is almost always reported to the authorities and so is a robust measure, and in addition the extent of other crimes such as non-lethal violence strongly correlates with the level of homicide (Barclay and Tavares 2002).

There is some historical evidence to support the thesis that during the last centuries of economic development in Europe there has been a decline in the rate of homicide in Europe (Gurr 1981; Eisner 2001). Further, the rate of homicide is lower in richer as compared with poorer countries in the contemporary world, being inversely correlated with GDP per capita (Van Wilsem 2004). The modernization of economic relations associated with the transition to free wage labour provides greater economic autonomy that can facilitate a resilience to violence. The acquisition of independent economic resources supports the practices needed to escape risks and threats of violence. The ability to escape, to flee, to not be dependent on the person or group who constitutes the threat often depends on the possession of economic resources. For example, women who are employed and thus have independent access to economic resources are less vulnerable to domestic violence than those who are not (Walby and Allen 2004).

Does modernity reduce the likelihood of war? There is a well-supported thesis that mature democracies do not initiate wars with each other, nonetheless among democracies some countries spend considerably more of their income on their military than others and have different propensities to go to war.

Democracy provides important limits to war. Democracy is linked to the extent of use of military force; military power is used less in a mature democracy than in other regimes; mature democracies rarely if ever initiate wars against each other (Rummel 1995). This may be because of the nature of political culture in a democracy (Weart 1998). Further, democracies can provide routes by which those whose lives are put at risk by military engagement can find a political voice and effective resistance. These processes can link domestic and external politics. An increase in the proportion of regimes that are democratic should thus be associated with a decrease in violent warfare.

Militarization and war are associated with the absence of an effective democracy. The death of young men in war is, in a democracy, subject to the popular will. Usually this sacrifice is considered appropriate only if there is a real and present external threat. If this threat is weak, then young men and their associates are likely to be able to resist by using democratic means. If there is no effective democracy, then these objections do not have a route for effective expression and action. So democracy is likely to limit the capacity of a state to initiate war.

While there are general processes that can link democracy to the containment of militarism, this does not mean that democratization always reduces militarism. The relationship is mediated by both levels of inequality and also by path-dependent processes for the development of military institutions. For example, while it has suffrage-democracy the USA not only spends a higher proportion of its budget on the military (World Bank 2006c) but also engages more readily in wars than many other democratic countries. Here it is necessary to add some qualifications (Walt 1999), especially to the concept of democracy. First, is the qualification 'mature' to democracy, since newly emerging democracies are as likely to go to war as non-democratic regimes, possibly because of the allure of nationalism in the process of forging statehood in the context of as yet unstable political institutions (Mansfield and Snyder 1995).

A second qualification is to consider the depth of the democracy and the extent to which social inequality reduces the capacity for resistance to war. Some countries that are formally democratic may still lack the processes for an effective representation of all political views. Further, processes of democracy depend upon a free civil society and the adequate circulation of accurate information. The effective use of the myth of the weapons of mass destruction by the US and UK governments in the decision-making process of going to war in Iraq may be considered as one example of where the potential of democratic processes was less than fully realized (Gregory 2004). The effectiveness of democratic limits on war mongering depends at least partly on whether the voices of poor men – drawn especially from minority ethnic groups who make up most of the armed forces – and their associates (e.g. family who care about them) are significant in the democratic process. High levels of social inequality make it less likely that the voices of poor ethnic minorities are significant in the political process. There is also the gendering of democracy. Women are more likely than men to oppose war (Woolf 1938), although not exclusively so and they are not altogether absent from military support systems (Enloe 1983). This includes women's views as expressed in opinion polls and elections and in their presence in anti-war social movements (Wiltshire 1985; Oldfield 1989). So where women have more access to democratic political power there may be a lower probability of the development of militarization and war.

The development and deepening of democracy in modernity is associated with reduced violence in at least two ways. Democratization is linked to a reduction in the likelihood of war, since mature democracies rarely initiate war on each other and women are less likely to promote militarism. Deep forms of democratization entailing the political presence of women and minorities facilitate the criminal regulation of and reduction in violence against them.

Path Dependency in Trajectories of Violence

Changes in the regulation and deployment of violence are not only linked to the development of modernity, but also with its path-dependent forms that are associated with the depth of democracy, the extent of economic inequality, and the history of militarism. The depth of democracy and the extent of economic inequality are linked to the path dependent development of neoliberalism and social democracy: there is more violence in countries that are neoliberal than in those that are social democratic. Militarism has a specific set of legacies and once entrenched it takes very unusual circumstances to reduce it.

The depth of democracy is not only linked to the development of modernity, but also to path dependent forms of modernity – democracy tends to be deeper in social democratic countries. With such deeper democracy in more social democratic countries, there is a tendency towards a fuller criminalization of violence against women and minorities and the lesser deployment of harsh penalties in the criminal justice system such as the death penalty. There is also the more effective articulation of the voices of women's political projects in deeper forms of democracy, which tends to mean more opposition to militarism.

There is an association between inequality and the deployment and regulation of violence. Countries with higher degrees of economic inequality have higher crime rates (Halpern 2001). The association between economic inequality and higher rates of violence can be found in at least three areas: higher rates of homicide in countries with higher rates of economic inequality; higher rates of domestic violence in homes where there is greater inequality between partners; and more punitive criminal justice procedures in countries and times where there is greater economic inequality. The rate of homicide is higher where there is greater economic inequality (Van Wilsem 2004). Several studies have found that countries with higher degrees of economic inequality have higher crime rates (Fajnzylber et al. 1998; Halpern 2001).

There is a link between greater gendered economic inequality and higher rates of domestic violence. Women with fewer economic resources are more vulnerable to domestic violence. Studies from the USA (Tjaden and Thoennes 2000a, 2000b, 2000c), the UK (Walby and Allen 2004), and Sweden (Lundgren et al. 2001) found higher rates of domestic violence in poor households and in particular where women have lower wages (Farmer and Tiefenthaler 1997) and where women find it impossible to raise small sums of money at short notice (Walby and Allen 2004). When conflict occurs, egalitarian households are the most resilient to the possibility of violence and asymmetrical households are more likely to succumb to violence when conflicted than symmetrical ones (Coleman and Strauss 1986). Women's dependency in marriage is correlated with violence: among women with high marital dependency – operationalized as to whether the woman was employed, whether she had children aged 5 or younger at home, and whether her husband earned 75 per cent or more of the couple's income – the rate of severe violence was much higher (Kalmuss and Straus 1982). Greater gendered economic inequality is thus linked to greater gender-based violence.

The turn in some countries towards neoliberalism is linked to an increase in the harshness of the criminal justice system. There has been a 'punitive turn' in the criminal justice systems of some countries, in particular in the USA and UK, with the development of harsher and more brutal punishment and a move away from 'penal welfare' (Garland 2001). This involves an increased use of imprisonment in both the UK and the USA and a reintroduction of the death penalty in the latter. Rather than a continuing shift away from overt force and towards discipline, as is suggested by Foucault, there has been a reversal of this process in the field of criminal justice in these countries since the 1980s. However, this is not a uniform trend. There have been varied increases in the rate of imprisonment since 1990: between 1991 and 2001, imprisonment rates rose by 61 per cent in the USA as compared with 26 per cent in the EU. There is one particular exception here, the social democratic Nordic region: in Denmark and Finland the rate of imprisonment declined by 9 per cent, while in Norway there was little change with an increase of 3 per cent, although in Sweden there was an increase of 17 per cent (Barclay and Tavares 2002, 2003). The exceptionalism of this social democratic region suggests that there is no inevitability about the process of an increasingly punitive criminal justice system, but rather that the variety of modernity makes a significant difference to this process. Where there is a turn towards neoliberalism there is a punitive turn in the criminal justice system, but not in those countries that continue to be social democratic.

Violent crime is more common in neoliberal forms of governance than social democratic and is more likely to be met with a punitive (high rates of imprisonment and use of the death penalty) rather than a penal welfare approach than in social democratic countries. This is at least partly due to the association of the more frequent deployment of violence with inequality, which is greater in neoliberal than social democratic countries. High rates of inter-personal violence and punitive criminal justice systems are associated with greater militarization of the state. Neoliberal governments often extol the virtues of low taxation, but the violence nexus that is associated with neoliberalism is associated with high state expenditure on law and order and the military, thereby requiring taxation. Neoliberal states are not quite such low expenditure states when the level of violence that is associated with this type of governance is brought into focus. The regulation and deployment of violence is part of the difference between neoliberal and social democratic projects, programmes, and social formations. Neoliberalism and social democracy are not only concerned with political economy. Despite the ostensible conflict with the discourse on the desirability of a small state that is rhetorically associated with neoliberalism, in practice neoliberalism requires a big state in order to create the social order that would otherwise be provided by a range of institutions in the civil society and welfare state in a social democracy.

Militarism and warfare are important forms of violence in the contemporary world (Shaw 2005; Kaldor 2006). There are three ways in which variations in militarism and warfare can be understood as path dependent developments: there are links between militarism and neoliberalism; militarisms have their own set of institutions with an historical legacy of their own; there are differences in the entrenchment of the myth of the nation-state.

There are several links between militarism and neoliberalism: there is a coevolution of militarization, the depth of democracy, and economic inequality. Not only does democracy reduce militarism,

militarism can also reduce the civil liberties that are an essential component of democracy. Although ostensibly a separate institution that is externally oriented, in practice, military activities have implications for the internal securitization of a homeland. This involves increased surveillance that entails a loss of privacy, an increased entitlement to survey, to question, and to hold persons for interrogation. This tips the balance between the state and civil society, leading to an increased penetration of civil society by the state. The external threat makes this change more likely to be internally acceptable. The erosion of civil liberties may make the political resistance to war more difficult to articulate and organize. An erosion of civil liberties is more likely where there is more social inequality. Militarization is thus associated with a reduction in civil liberties, which in turn is associated with a decreased political opposition to war.

Militarized institutions can become embedded in the economic institutions of a country in a path dependent way. The development of a military-industrial complex, a mutually supporting growth and development of both the military and the arms industry, embeds the military into economic welfare for workers as well as capital. Companies that make their profits from wars have interests in continuing militarization. A close linkage between military institutions and those industries making armaments may lead to increased political support for militarization (Mills 1956; Harris 2005).

A history of military engagement can create a military legacy that is hard to put aside. A colonial or imperial heritage is associated with the development of military institutions which are hard to lay down: the rise and maintenance of an empire leads to the entrenchment of militarized institutions. Even though decolonization entails the end of a requirement for a high level of militarization, military institutions can be difficult to reduce or end because of entrenched interests.

Conflicts over borders between those nations in pursuit of a state of their own can similarly entrench militarized institutions. The history of Europe in the eighteenth, nineteenth and twentieth centuries was continually marked by such disputes. The development of the European Union was a deliberate and highly successful attempt to erode the nationalist basis of militarism (Haas 1958; Hallstein 1973), with no wars between the Member States of the European Union for half a century. While this has not precluded terrorism around nationalist issues in the north of Ireland and in the Basque country, there have been no wars between Member States of the European Union. Peace in the EU is not kept via the threat of superior military power, since the EU does not have an armed force of its own for use in the EU (Kapteyn 1996).

Kaldor (2006) argues that in the current global era there are new forms of warfare. By comparison with the 'old' wars, 'new' wars are more decentralized, more likely to use tactics of terror to destabilize, to more often attack civilian rather than military targets, and to be based on identity politics. In some of the examples that Kaldor examines, especially Bosnia-Herzegovina, these are indeed features that contrast with both World Wars. However, she overstates the prevalence of the new and underestimates some continuities with the old as a consequence, in particular of a tendency to neglect the activities of the USA. 'Identity' politics is not so much new as a re-combination of three forms of organized violence that have been traditional in Europe which have not infrequently taken a decentralized form: the practice of nations using military means to seek states of their own (much nationalism has taken this form) (Smith 1986); the driving out of religious or national minorities (for example, European pogroms against Jews occurred regularly in European history) (Therborn 1995); and Medieval Europe had decentralized warring lords and princes before the concentration of military might in states (Tilly 1990). There is a contrast to be made with WW1 and WW2, but perhaps the degree of centralization and the regulation of the forms of combat in these wars might be regarded as exceptional rather than the rule from which new wars deviate. In particular, Kaldor has curiously little to say about America as a centralized military hegemon with an intentionally global reach, which has engaged in a series of 'old-style' wars, even though referring to the US military intervention in Iraq. Do the wars in which the USA is involved really fit the notion of new wars as involving 'the fragmentation and decentralization of the state' (Kaldor 2006: 95)? In her enthusiasm for detailing some specific forms of contemporary war (correctly) she mistakenly over-generalizes to include all current wars. The USA has a centralized state with coherent military powers.

So these forms of decentralized warfare with a special focus on nations seeking to 'purify' a territory and create a state of their own are premodern, taking place where often there is not yet modern economic development. Once economies are developed there are two major forms of security strategy – unilateralist and militarist, most often found in neoliberalism (for example, the USA) and multilateral broad-based less militarist, most often found in social democracy (for example, the EU).

Global

Global processes have variously been implicated in increases and decreases in the deployment and regulation of violence. The global is invoked by the development of nuclear weapons with the potential to destroy life on the planet as a whole, generating global attempts to restrict their proliferation. At a global level, a core remit of the UN is to attempt to reduce violent conflict. The development of the USA into a global hegemon has increased the scale of its warring; in contrast the development of the EU has led to the cessation of its history of internal European wars in pursuit of the impossible goal of the pure nation-state. Increased global flows of capital, trade, and people can intensify the competition for scarce resources. Increased global communications have speeded up the opportunities for knowledge about conflicts and wars, the development of global terrorism, increased vulnerabilities, and the development of an opposition to war and violence (Boswell and Chase-Dunn 2000; Harvey 2003; Harris 2005; Shaw 2005; Kirby 2006).

There is a globalization of the effects of war with the development of weapons of mass destruction and global mass communications. Nuclear weapons, first deployed by the USA against Japan in 1945, have the potential to annihilate all human life on the planet. Possessed by the hegemons and a limited number of other powers, they create a state of potential global catastrophe. The response has been directed through the UN, especially through its Security Council and related agencies, with efforts to defuse crises and to establish and monitor non-proliferation treaties. The globalization of the media has the implication of internationalizing knowledge about conflicts and wars, albeit unevenly. Wars can no longer be so easily hidden from view. Publics back home can become aware of the implications of military actions done in their name, with consequences for the mobilization of opposition as well as support for wars, although governmental control over the media may limit this process.

Global hegemons have divergent strategies in relation to violence, as a consequence of domestic as well as international contestations. These strategies rest in part on theories about the relationship of violence to power: does violence by itself provide access to power or is it more effective if meshed with softer forms of influence? They also rest on theories about the global order: whether military power can be effectively exercised unilaterally or if it is more effective when exercised with stakeholders and allies around the world. Does unilateral narrow military violence deliver power, or does the embedding of military force in a nest of multilateral alliances and softer forms of pressure and diplomacy deliver more effective power?

The US under the Bush administration, 2002–2008, adopted the former strategy, while the EU took the latter. The USA's aim is to win wars, by unilateral action if necessary and without expending additional resources on nation building. Its strategists assume that violence is sufficient to overcome the enemy if there was enough of it to 'shock and awe' the opposition. Raw violence is seen as power with a wider policy engagement viewed as unnecessary (Harris 2002).

By contrast, the European Security Strategy seeks to address global challenges by creating an 'international order based on effective multilateralism' and developing good policies on trade and development, as well as the development of the European Union's armed forces (Council of the European Union 2003). As the European Union has emerged as a global actor it has developed a distinctive security strategy in which violence is deliberately embedded in softer forms of power in order to be effective (Smith 2003; Smith 2004; Bretherton and Vogler 2006).

There are further divisions between the USA and the EU in their approach to the global divisions that underpin these security strategies. The world may be understood to be divided in different ways: first, into distinct hegemons or regions, each with their own interests and priorities; second, into one of three categories of stable market economies with democracies, stable peripheral market economies with near-democracy, and a terrorist-generating set of countries that are economically developed without democracy and sometimes collapsed states; or third, into inter-dependent states and regions.

Within the United States military academies there is lively debate between the first two positions (Harris 2002; National Defense University 2008). The first position appears supported by a state centric or clash of civilizations (Huntington 1998) view, translating into an approach in which the US is treated as a hegemon. The second position is more aligned with the neoliberal view that economic development delivers democracy and all good things. In practical terms the alternatives are whether the US sees the main threat as coming from a regional power (once Russia, now potentially China), or whether this is terrorism from non-state as well as state actors in the economically poor, politically unstable and undemocratic parts of the world (Harris 2002; Institute for National Strategic Studies 2008).

By contrast the EU adopts the third position, seeing the world as inter-dependent and understanding its own interests as best realized by cooperation alongside a view that it is 'inevitably a global player' because of the size of its population and economy and possesses a concept of 'European interest' (European Council 2003). A failure by the USA to acknowledge the multipolarity of world power is a source of its current weakness (Zakaria 2008).

The use of different theories regarding the relationship of violence to power and the nature of globality by the USA and EU is associated with quite different strategic approaches to the use of violence by polities.

Processes of globalization affect the regulation of violence through the development of the discourse of universal human rights. The development of the discourse of universal human rights and its institutionalization in law, tribunals, and courts has reframed and increased the regulation of several forms of violence. It has been key to the development of tools of intervention using new forms of international law, regulation, and argumentation. The longstanding, initially Western, tradition of equal rights has been articulated and institutionalized in various stages and forms (Meyer et al. 1997; Berkovitch 1999), the most important of which was the Declaration of Universal Human Rights by the newly formed United Nations in 1948 (UN 1948).

In practice, there have been two main substantive foci in these developments to hold governments to account for their breaches of human rights' codes. One concerns their use of torture and other inhuman practices on those who are imprisoned or those who have been captured in war, as well as concern for war crimes such as genocide. This includes global mobilization to abolish the death penalty in state criminal justice systems. A second concerns the use of human rights' rhetoric and institutions to change policies on violence against women and minorities. Both involve using the UN as a resource.

Campaigns on human rights focused on examples of their violation through the use of extreme violence by states against which it was appropriate for international agencies to intervene. The institutional power available to implement human rights has been increased by the establishment of the international war crimes tribunal in the Hague, which has been especially active in the use of violence against minority ethnic and religious groups, and the incorporation of the European Convention of Human Rights into European Union law and hence the EU and the domestic legal systems of EU member states (Held 1995; Peters and Wolper 1995; Therborn 1995, 1999; Kelly 1997). These developments give legitimacy to a set of practices protecting individuals from the arbitrary, cruel, inhumane, and excessive exercise of force by states. The UN-sponsored International Criminal Court, established by UN Treaty in 1998, was established in the Hague in 2002 after 60 countries signed up in order to try individuals for war crimes, genocide, and crimes against humanity (UN 2002; McMorran 2003). The death penalty is now considered by the Council of Europe, the European Convention on Human Rights adopted by the EU, and the UN General Assembly, to be contrary to human rights. The Council of Europe called on states to reject the death penalty on human rights grounds in 1983; the UN Commission on Human Rights did likewise in 1997. The UN General Assembly adopted resolutions stating that it was desirable for states to abolish the death penalty in 1971 and 1977. In December 2007 the UN General Assembly called for a global moratorium on executions (UN General Assembly 2007).

A second use of human rights interventions in violence has been that to underpin justice for women and minorities. In the context of gender, this has particularly meant the framing of violence against women as a human rights violation. Despite its ostensible universality, the operationalization of the concept of human rights is varied in time and place. The concept was broadened when, in 1993, a UN conference accepted that women's rights were human rights and that violence against women constituted a violation of their human rights (Bunch 1995; UNIFEM 2000b). The conference stated that violence against women was a violation of human rights and therefore national governments must strengthen the response of their criminal justice systems in support of women. This was done as if it was an already existing universal human right, even as it was known that it had been recently constructed through struggle (Davies 1993; Peters and Wolper 1995; Heise 1996).

The increased regulation of inter-personal violence is facilitated by the development of the discourse of universal human rights and its embedding in transnational institutions. It provides a significant form of legitimacy and rhetorical power to those seeking to persuade states to effectively criminalize and thus regulate non-state violence against women and minority ethnic and religious groups. Activists can draw down on this resource in many countries, whatever the level of economic development.

These developments have produced a re-framing of gender-based violence as a human rights violation, although this is not universally the case. There has been a shift in the political understanding of violence against women away from the view that this was a brutal oppression of women by men (Brownmiller 1976; Daly 1978; Mackinnon 1989), towards a view that it is a violation of women's human rights (Peters and Wolper 1995; Keck and Sikkink 1998; Kelly et al. 2005), while not losing sight of its role in constituting gender equality.

Conclusions

The deployment and regulation of violence are social processes. Violence is a distinctive institutional domain. It should not be reduced or collapsed into the state, conceptualized merely as its instrument, nor should it be dispersed into individuals behaving in non-social and emotional ways. It involves bodies and weapons as the means of violence, not only humanistic agency. Violence is socially patterned, embedded in institutions and regimes of inequalities. The different institutions involved in the deployment and regulation of violence are interconnected. The more unequal a country is, the higher the rate of violence. There is a link between the amount of violent crime and the harshness of the state's responses: the higher the rate of homicide the higher the rate of imprisonment and use of the death penalty. The greater the militarization of a country and its propensity to go to war, the more group and inter-personal violence is found.

Making complex inequalities in addition to class visible changes the understanding of the relationship between inter-personal violence and inequality. Violence is more usually from the dominant to less powerful groups than the other way around when gender, ethnicity, and sexual orientation are brought into focus, challenging the assumptions of much contemporary criminology. Most states are not yet fully modern in that they do not fully criminalize and delegitimize violence against women and minorities. Since democracy is being deepened by the increasing access of women and minorities to democratic political power, the criminal regulation of inter-personal violence is increasing. States are slowly moving towards modernity.

While there is some reduction of violence in modernity, linked to the deepening of democracy, there is no simple one-way trajectory of change. There are path-dependent developments, there are reversals, and there are changes at different times for different social groups. Those countries that are more unequal and less democratic, the more neoliberal countries, have higher rates of violence of all forms – from interpersonal to the criminal justice system to the military – than do those countries that are less unequal, more fully democratic, and more likely to be social democratic. The US hegemon is more violent than the EU. The myth of the nation-state, the myth of the purity of an ethnic group, of a religion, of a nation, and its 'right' to solely inhabit and run a particular territory, is a terrible force underlying many temptations to the use of violence at individual, group, and state levels.

The global environment and global processes shape the deployment and regulation of violence by polities, groups, and individuals. Strategies of military violence used by hegemons and other states diverge according to their interpretation of globality and the relationship between violence and power. The perceived increase in the threat of global terrorism changes the deployment of state violence against other states and their own citizens. Global waves of feminism and human rights bring civil societal pressure to bear on the regulation and deployment of violence. The embedding of conceptions of universal human rights in international institutions changes the regulation and deployment of violence.

6 Civil Societies

Introduction

Civil society is a key institutional domain for the transformation of meanings, the creation and hybridization of projects, the practice of individual and collective agency, and the contested production of frames and discourses. Approaches vary considerably in the extent to which meaning is seen as a source of contestation or consensus, and the nature of the link between civil society and other institutional domains.

The notion of what constitutes modernity in forms of civil society is particularly contested: are there multiple modernities; a distinction between premodern and modern, postmodernity; or varieties of modernity? When complex inequalities, especially gender, are brought into focus these issues are particularly acute.

The inclusion of global processes challenges the tendency to understand civil society as constituted primarily and more authentically at a local or national level. Global civil societal waves have important effects on social relations around the world, whether as conformity or backlash.

Theorizing Civil Society

Quite different approaches to the theorization of civil society are offered by Habermas, Foucault, Bourdieu, and Gramsci. While all avoid both the reduction of civil society to the economy and its representation as a free-floating domain, they each offer different accounts as to its links with other institutional domains, the extent of contestation or consensus, heterogeneity or homogeneity, and its relationship to power (Cohen and Arato 1992; Thompson 1995; Alexander

2006). While providing a rich set of theoretical and conceptual tools, however, these writers are limited in their engagement with complex inequalities and global processes, though others have sought to make appropriate revisions (Fraser 1989; Ramazanoglu 1993; Adkins and Skeggs 2004).

Habermas offers two concepts of civil society and its relationship to capital and the state: 'the public sphere' (1989) and the 'lifeworld' (1987). The public sphere of free and rational debate depends on both the publicness and equality of social relations in this space. For a short moment in eighteenth-century London these conditions were met for a few men, but evaporated with the interventionism of the state and the commercialization of the press. Habermas's concept of the public sphere is used in contemporary discussions of the conditions under which rational debate and authentic values can be developed (Emirbayer and Sheller 1998; Crossley and Roberts 2004), including the international community of states (Risse 1999), and epistemic communities that blend shared values and scientific knowledge (Haas 1992). However, Habermas's own analysis is largely insensitive to inequalities beyond class in access to these conditions, in particular the gendered nature of the division of public and private that so often restricts the public to men (Landes 1998). In later work, Habermas (1987, 1991) locates the realm of authentic communication within the 'lifeworld', a private haven protected from the steering systems of capital and state power. However, this tends to romanticize the personal and domestic as a source of authentic meaning, neglecting the gendered power relations in family household relations (Hernes 1987; Fraser 1989).

In Foucault's (1979, 1991, 1997) analyses of civil society, power is everywhere, operating in 'capillary' types of action rather than centred within the state or capital. Technologies of power are used to discipline the population, using diverse instruments, procedures, modalities, and levels of application. However, while power is seen always to meet with resistance, this is not connected to identifiable groups of people. Subjectivity is merely an effect. Foucault's analysis tends to treat capital and democracy as the presumed background rather than the foreground for analysis. While the concept of discourse has been used fruitfully in research (du Gay 1996; Rose 1996), the lack of connectedness to structural inequalities remains a weakness (Ramazanoglu 1993; Adkins and Lury 1999).

Bourdieu (1984) conceptualizes culture as a form of capital within a field, where the habitus or taken-for-granted practices of individuals reproduce social hierarchies. Cultural capital enables individuals to make distinctions that can provide them with further privileges. Class privilege is reproduced in the field of culture through non-cognitive, or not consciously reflexive, action of habitus. This extends the concept of capital from the economic to culture, but retains that part of its meaning that connotes the resources that can be used to deploy power. The relationship between the different fields in which various kinds of capital operate is not clearly specified. However, the concepts, especially that of habitus, are not nimble enough to be useful in the analysis of political struggle and social change, being too rooted in learning from prior events and insufficiently focused on the processes of change in meanings and practice.

Gramsci (1971) develops the concept of a civil society level in his explanation of the shape of the social formation, rejecting economic reductionism and with a focus on struggles over politics and ideas. He avoids the trap of economic reductionism while still providing a theorized account of the relationship between civil society, the state, and the economy, and has been widely influential in building non-economically reductionist analyses of class relations (Laclau and Mouffe 1985). Civil society is a site of struggle between social classes involving the contestation of meaning, in which the ability to achieve hegemony over ideas is an important part of power. Civil society is seen as a key domain in which the existing social order is already grounded and in which a new one could be founded. While brute force is an important form of power it is potentially destabilizing, so the achievement of ideological supremacy, the ability to define a situation through a set of concepts that can interpret the world favourably to the dominant class grouping, is a significant form of power. There are different levels of consciousness, one closer to everyday life in which bourgeois ideas are treated as common sense, with another the subjective constitution of the class as an actor in its own interests, while the highest form of consciousness is seen as that which would transcend immediate class interests to take account of all social groups and be truly transformatory. The struggle for hegemony over culture so that socialist ideas might replace the values of the bourgeoisie is key to the modern form of class struggle for Gramsci. The working-class counter-struggle for hegemony draws not only on worker organization but the ideas developed by organic intellectuals to provide leadership of a movement so that it could become more than merely economistic. Gramsci distinguished between a war of position – in which there is a solid process of reformation of ideas backed by organizational strength – and a war of manoeuvre in which state power might be seized for a moment but would remain fragile and fail (Gramsci 1971; Cox 1999; Danieli 2006).

The strengths of Gramsci's concept of civil society include its inclusion of practices as well as ideas, the foregrounding of the processes of contestation over ideas rather than implied consensus, the concept of hegemony which invokes contested power in the terrain of ideas, the overt linking of macro and micro levels in the relationship of civil society to economy, polity, and violence, and the differentiation of different types of strategies of struggle (Laclau and Mouffe 1985; Cox 1999). There are some weaknesses and some inconsistencies in the conceptualization – sometimes the concept is based on a simple dichotomy of state versus a civil society that included the economy, sometimes making a distinction between a civil society and the economy. It does not adequately recognize the significance of the multiplicity of complex inequalities, instead focusing only on class.

Key aspects of the concept of civil society used in this book are derived from Gramsci's concept: the presumption of contestation as well as accommodation over a plurality of ideas and practices, and the significance of these struggles for the institutions and system of power. However, there is a need to extend the conceptualization of social forces and systems of power to include those that are relevant to complex inequalities such as gender and ethnicity as well as class.

Modernity and Civil Society

The meaning of modernity is much contested. In classical social theory, modernity in civil society was associated with rationalization, secularization (Weber 1947), individuation (Simmel 1955), and the development of political consciousness and action (Marx 1963). In contemporary debates these themes have been expanded to include democracy, human rights, and the emancipation of women. Bringing into focus complex inequalities has challenged the simplicities of the conventional analysis of modernity (Taylor et al. 1994; Felski 1995). The re-interpretation of the contemporary era as postmodern has been a major response to this challenge (Lyotard 1978; Barrett and Phillips 1992; Kumar 2005), but this approach has a tendency to over-state the fragmentation of the social world (Walby 1992). Differences between forms of civil society have alternatively been interpreted as distinctions between premodern and modern (Inglehart and Norris 2003), between multiple modernities (Eisenstadt 2002), and between different stages (Giddens 1991; Beck et al. 1994; Bauman 2000) or varieties (Schmidt 2006) of modernity (see the discussion in Chapter 1). A key issue in the discussion of multiple modernities is where to draw the boundary between modernity and premodernity. Does the absence of individuation, especially in intimacy, indicate a different form of modernity or rather premodernity? The resolution of these questions requires a specification of the definition of modernity in civil society. Key topics concern individuation and intimacy, sexuality and reproduction – issues where gender relations are central. The challenge is to define modernity in civil society in a way that is sensitive to complex inequalities, such as gender, and to different social formations, especially in the area of intimacy.

Is modernity in civil society universal or does it take particular forms? Are some cultural forms instances of different modernities, demonstrating the existence of multiple modernities (Huntington 1998; Eisenstadt 2002), or are they better understood as premodern? Is individuation merely a Western form of modernity, rather than common to all modernities (Eisenstadt 2002)? In some non-Western cultures, such as those involving Asian or Confucian values, the priority between individualism and social solidarity appears to be tilted towards the latter. The individualism associated with human rights, democracy, and free speech is considered less important than family, community, and consensus. This can be considered a distinctively non-Western form of modernity, as has been argued by Asian leaders in Singapore and Malaysia especially during the 1990s. However, this position is highly contested. Alternatively, these practices may be understood as projects by authoritarian political leaders to instrumentalize culture in order to maintain their political supremacy, which would be eroded with the development of democracy (Sen 1997; Thompson 2000; Barr 2002). The lack of individuation is then better understood as premodern rather than as a different form of modernity.

The extent of individuation in civil society varies not only between countries but also with regimes of inequality. This is especially clear in the areas of human rights and of intimacy. The concept and practice of human rights is a form of individuation that varies not only between countries but between genders, despite the claims that have been made for their universality (UN 1948; Gastil 1982; Therborn 1995; Woodiwiss 1998; Rawls 1999). Bringing complex inequalities into focus makes visible the varied nature and practice of human rights, for example some 'human' rights have gender implications (Bunch 1995; Berkovitch 1999). Whether sexual and reproductive autonomy are considered to be human rights or not is contested, not least by the USA, the Catholic Church, and Islam (Moghadam 1996; Ferree et al. 2002b; Human Rights Watch 2006). Further, the designation of violence against women as a violation of women's human rights was added to the UN list of human rights only in 1993 (Bunch 1995; Peters and Wolper 1995).

Increased individuation has been linked to progress via the positive values of freedom and independence, civil liberties, and human rights (Gastil 1982; Donelly 2003), and by contrast is lamented if it is seen as leading to social isolation and a loss of social capital

(Coleman 1990; Putnam 2000), with implications for domestic social relations (Beck 1992; Irwin 2005), the development of the neoliberal entrepreneurial self (Rose 1996), and the erosion of the life-world (Habermas 1987). Underlying the debates about intimacy are varying views as to whether individuation delivers social justice and progress to women and others. On one side individuation is seen as leading to the loss of social engagement (Putnam 2000): there is concern here that the erosion of traditional domestic forms of intimacy undermines social bonds that are important for human well-being (Habermas 1987; Beck 2002). Habermas laments the erosion of the 'life-world', which he considers the main site of authenticity, by capital and the media. Beck (1992: 94) fears the 'contradiction' between women's entry into the labour market and 'social bonds' which lead to divorce and insecurity. On the other side, this transformation can lead to an increase in the range and form of social bonds and also their range; individuation may involve an increase in an individual's choice and self-determination (Giddens 1992). It can be celebrated as freedom, independence, and equality for women as well as promoting well-being for all.

The same gendered changes lamented by Habermas as eroding the life-world and by Beck as eroding social bonds are hailed by Bergmann (1986) as the erosion of the confinement of women to the home thereby facilitating the development of wider social bonds – the economic emergence of women with its associated freedoms. Giddens (1992) sees the transformation of intimacy as a process of democratization and decreasing gender inequality, while Berkovitch (1999) and Moghadam (2005) point out increases in women's rights worldwide. This latter interpretation of modernity is consistent with that of Simmel (1955), for whom individuation in modernity led to a 'web' of 'social affiliations', a myriad of choices as to social connections. Individuation for women often takes place later than for men. It is associated with the transition from a domestic to a public gender regime – from domestic work to free wage labour, access to education, and the formal political sphere, as well as independence in decision making in relation to sexuality and fertility and bodily integrity. Changes in gendered forms of intimacy are linked to changes in the form of the gender regime.

One reason for the divergent interpretations of individuation within modern civil society as progressive or not lies in the differences between the forms of individuation. The more neoliberal forms are associated with isolation and lesser social engagement, the more social democratic forms with an increased range and diversity of social engagement. The neoliberal form is indicated in the commercialization and objectification of sexuality in prostitution and pornography, as compared with the proliferation and acceptance of diverse forms of sexuality as mutual exchange. This analysis rests on approaching sexuality and intimacy as socially constituted.

Sexual practices have been and still are socially constituted. While they involve bodies and emotions, they are not reducible to biological or even psychological processes (Foucault 1979; Richardson 2000). The inclusion of sexuality within the realm of the social requires social theory to incorporate bodies and technologies. While early attempts by radical feminists to address the social construction of sexuality as a form of gendered power (Mackinnon 1989) have been dismissed as biologically essentialist (Segal 1987; Butler 1990), they have nevertheless put analysis of the social aspects of sexual relationships on the agenda. The discursive construction of sexuality in the work of Foucault (1979) consolidated the inclusion of sexuality within the realm of the social even while it softened the focus on inequality as a consequence of its conceptualization of power as dispersed (Ramazanoglu 1993). Addressing sexual and gendered practices as performance rather than as identities further shifts the focus of the analysis away from macro-level social structures (Butler 1990). Rethinking sexuality through the lens of citizenship refocuses analysis on the social institutions that construct the different forms of sexuality (Jackson 1999; Richardson 2000).

Sexuality can constitute a complex inequality in its own right, especially as a result of the negative sanctions often applied to same sex relationships (Weeks 1995, 2007). It is also partially constitutive of complex gender inequalities. This is partly through the institution of heterosexuality, the more negative sanctioning of women's non-marital sexuality than that of men, the existence of sexual violence and practices such as female genital mutilation, and because of the gendered regulation of related practices such as reproduction, marriage, and divorce (MacKinnon 1989; Jackson 1999; Richardson 2000). Indeed most contemporary gender identities are partially constituted on the presumption of heterosexuality, so any erosion of the polarization between heterosexuality and gay/lesbian identities would constitute a change in the nature of gender itself (Butler 1990; Seidman 1996). However, sexuality is only one among several of the constituents of gender relations and not definitive of its totality.

There are considerable variations in the regulation and practice of intimacy, some associated with the distinction between premodern and modern forms, but other variations within modernity according to the path dependent forms of neoliberalism and social democracy. There is a pluralization of forms of intimacy in modernity: while some traditional forms remain (Jamieson 1998), there are new forms of sexual relationship, cohabitation, and friendship (Weeks 1995, 2007).

There are very considerable differences in the practices of sexuality (Haavio-Manilla 1985) and attitudes towards sexual conduct (Scott 1998). A comparative survey of many countries finds that there are significant variations in attitudes towards pre-marital and same sex sexuality between countries, degrees of religiosity, ages, and over time. While over time there is a tendency towards greater liberalism, religiosity was the variable most consistently associated with disapproval of non-marital forms of sexuality (Scott 1998). The extent of religiosity is in turn associated both with secularization and with the balance between religion and state in the governance of intimacy. Variations in the forms of polity are associated with the path-dependent development of the regulation and practice of intimacy and other forms of individuation.

Not all forms of non-domestic sexuality are associated with equality and independence, however. An example of this can be found in the newspaper reporting of sex crimes. Before the 1970s this was quite rare and such articles were short and cryptic. From the 1970s onwards there was increasing coverage, moving the issue into the public sphere. Potentially this was a positive move, increasing the possibility of a serious public debate on issues that had previously been kept hidden. However, the newspaper reporting was not only sensationalist but highly sexualized so the presentation was sometimes almost another form of pornography (Soothill and Walby 1991). Protesting feminist voices were excluded from this forum. It was not an example of an ideal speech situation or public sphere of the kind to which Habermas aspires, rather it is a new terrain for struggle over the representation of sexuality, gender, and power.

The public gender regime is associated with high rates of repartnering (often associated with low rates of marriage), as well as divorce, cohabitation, and children born outside of marriage. This contrasts with the domestic gender regime where partnering was usually for life. Within the public gender regime there are neoliberal and social democratic forms of the organization of intimacy. In social democratic forms the cost and care of children are much more often borne collectively by state services and payments than in the neoliberal forms. The privatization of childcare costs in the neoliberal forms creates a greater disincentive for men to repartner women with children from a previous relationship than in the social democratic forms where these costs are shared with the state. The implication of this is that often in social democratic forms there are lower rates of lone parenthood than in neoliberal forms (see Chapter 9).

There are significant variations in the regulation of practices that affect the experience of sexual autonomy, including legal and practical access to contraception, abortion, divorce, and separation

(Richardson 2000; Human Rights Watch 2006). The presence or absence of polity regulation confining sexuality to marriage is not the only consideration. A removal of the pressures that confine sexuality to the married domestic arena may merely change the form of sexual exploitation rather than reduce it, as in, for example, the increased circulation of pornography and a rise in prostitution. An increase in the practice of non-marital sexuality may be associated with gender equality and an increase in sexual autonomy for women, but this depends on a range of other circumstances. In their absence, a reduction in regulation may merely lead to greater commercialized instead of domestic sexual exploitation of women. As individuation is increasingly the experience and practice of women, intimacy and the domestic are transformed. While this is not a simple liberation for women, neither is it best understood as the erosion of social bonds. Individuation involves the transformation of these activities; modernity is both freeing and disciplining for women as well as for men.

There is a struggle among global hegemons and world religions over the standards set for civil society at the global level of the United Nations which has important outcomes in some locations around the world. There is serious contestation between the EU – which supports a more social democratic public gender regime – and the USA, Catholicism, and Islam – which support more domestic forms of gender regimes – in matters concerning intimacy and sexual and reproductive rights (Peters and Wolper 1995; Moghadam 1996). In 1995 the UN Beijing conference on women set the standards for a more public and more equal gender regime than existed in many of the world's countries in its Platform for Action (UN 1995). The reluctance of the USA post-Reagan to endorse reproductive freedoms for women, such as rights of access to abortion, has slowed but not stopped the endorsement of gender equality by the UN in other areas.

Secularization and the decline of religion have traditionally been regarded as key components of modernity. Modernity was expected by classical social theory to lead away from religion towards secularism and science. Contemporary support for this thesis is found at a near global level in the association of economic development with secularization in the World Values Survey (Norris and Inglehart 2004). In much of Europe, from the UK to Ireland, there has been a significant decline in Christian religious practices such as attending church and believing in God (Bruce 1996, 2002; Norris and Inglehart 2004), although there is some growth in 'New Age' spiritual practices (Heelas and Woodhead et al. 2004). Secularization is gendered, with women giving up organized Christianity to a greater extent than men (Woodhead 2007), and linked to the declining salience of Christian beliefs which endorse a domestic form of gender regime that has been in long-term decline, at least in Europe. The decline of organized religion is also a decline in a non-democratic polity and hence an increase in the depth of democracy. The religiosity of the USA and the rise of various religious fundamentalisms have been used to challenge the thesis that modernity is associated with secularization (Finke 1992). In the USA there are strong mainstream religious groups with political salience (Manza and Brooks 1999), as well as fundamentalist Protestant sects which are opposed to Darwinian theories of evolution and the practice of abortion (Ferree et al. 2002b). Numerous fundamentalisms have developed as minority approaches within many world religions (Marty and Scott 1993) with ethnic and national dimensions as well as gendered ones (Hardacre 1993). However, the religiosity of the USA is more the exception than the rule among developed economies. One source of the differences between the United States and Europe may be levels of inequality, since more unequal countries with perhaps less experience of personal security have lower rates of secularization (Norris and Inglehart 2004). This greater religiosity of the USA as compared with the EU has consequences for the divergence in the forms of gender regime promoted by these hegemons at a global level.

The development of scientific forms of knowledge is conventionally linked with modernity and the development of certain forms of science is linked with economic development and good health through medicine. However, any overly simplistic association of science with progress can be contested, since professions may be as controlling as enabling (Foucault 1979) while modern techniques may be used to kill people more easily (Bauman 1989). The implications of scientific development often depend on the nature of the project with which it is associated. There are divergent patterns of scientific development in neoliberal and social democratic contexts. In a neoliberal context where capital is dominant, knowledge may be expropriated from its original producers and sold on for profit. 'Accumulation by dispossession' is part of the neoliberal expansion of global capital (Harvey 2003, 2005), sometimes involving in particular the appropriation of knowledge produced in the South and by women (Mies and Shiva 1993).

The regulation of the risk associated with new forms of science and technology varies according to the positioning of capital and democratic forces in neoliberalism and social democracy. The EU holds to a precautionary principle – namely, that it is more cautious until it is more certain that something is safe – rather than stopping only when harm has become clear. The US position supports greater risk-taking in the development and exploitation of scientific advances. The EU position might be understood as more social democratic in that it prioritizes the potential victims of mistakes; the USA as more neoliberal in prioritizing capital. This contrast in approaches underpins global contestations as to the acceptable level of risk in relation to environmental issues, such as climate change and genetically modified foods. The EU and the USA contest these issues in the global forum of the World Trade Organization (Winickoff et al. 2005) and the UN. The development of science is not simply associated with modernity and progress, but also depends on the extent of democratic input into its regulation at increasingly global levels and its intersection with changing complex inequalities.

Bringing complex inequalities such as gender into focus has implications for the debates on modernity and civil society. The development of individuation, especially in intimacy, is seen more clearly as a change from the premodern to modern; its absence is premodern, not another form of modernity. The form of civil society, from intimacy to science, varies as to the neoliberal or social democratic environment. Commercialized forms of sexuality and science are found with neoliberalism, greater regulation by democratic forces in social democracy.

Civil Society Projects

The concept of 'project' is developed in this book in order to take forward the analysis of civil society. Civil society contains many projects. A project contains a set of goals and ideas about how the world works and how it could be improved, and is taken forward by its constituencies using particular methods and technologies of change and particular forms of organization and resources. A project is not reducible to the socio-economic location of its participants nor an unfolding of pre-given interests, but neither is it simply free-floating outside of structured economic inequalities. A project is not only ideational, not only a framing, but also has ontological depth in its methods, resources, and constituencies. Projects contest and change using a range of ideational, political, and other resources.

New forms of governance and social formations can start within governments or be led by economic change. But changes in forms of governance are very likely to be influenced by innovations in civil society projects, where innovative new social forms are both argued and struggled over. Civil society is the space where new ideas, practices, programmes, and visions of alternative social formations are developed. They respond to changes in resources, power, and material positioning, reworking the frames and discourses that provide meaning. States and their programmes are a prize, key fulcrums of power but rarely the starting point. This is not to argue that power is principally bottom-up, for it is not. Civil societal projects are situated in the interstices of multiple forms of power; power that can take the form of capital, systematic violence, and political domination. Projects can be from the right as well as the left; authoritarian as well as libertarian; anti-modernist as well as modernist. But, especially in countries with even minimal levels of democracy, civil society is a critical terrain of struggle over new social forms. It may sometimes appear that a civil society project that once took the form of a social movement has gone into abeyance when it has lost its visibility to the media (Taylor 1989; Bagguley 2002). However, it may be that it has become institutionalized and that its repertoire of actions has changed towards those that are less visible and more internal to governance systems, such as lobbying rather than street protest, or the establishment of specialized branches of government such as women's units (McBride and Mazur 1995; Mazur 2002).

Often, class-based projects are analysed very differently from projects that invoke gender or ethnicity. The analysis of class-oriented projects tends to focus on the economic and organizational resources available and on the implications of changes in structured economic inequalities, with relatively little attention paid to the more ideational processes of the framing of demands. An example is in the development and deployment of the concept of 'power resources' (Korpi 1983). The analysis of gender and ethnic politics and projects tends to focus on the more ideational processes and less on the economic and organizational resources that might be mobilized. One example here is the discussion of the balance between the concepts of difference and equality in feminist projects (Holli 1997). There is often a split between the types of analysis of class politics and of social movements, as if they were very different. This specialization of explanatory approaches is unnecessary and mistaken. Both ideational and resource issues are important in the explanation of projects and there is a need for synthesis.

The theorization of civil societal projects requires analysis of the economic, organizational, and other resources available (McCarthy and Zald 1977; Chafetz and Dworkin 1986); the framing of its ideas (Snow et al. 1986; Diani 1996; Ferree et al. 2002; Verloo 2005); and its relationship with allies and enemies in adjacent or competing projects (Jakobsen 1998; Vargas and Wieringa 1998; Della Porta and Diani 1999; Woodward 2004). It is important not only to identify the issues, but also to understand the sources of variations in these projects over time and between countries (Nelson and Chowdhury 1994; Keck and Sikkink 1998). This analysis starts with the traditional issues of class analysis and then genders them before turning to the issues of ethnic and gender analysis and including class.

Socio-economic structural changes can affect the size of the constituency promoting a particular project. Male manual workers in the manufacturing industry have traditionally been the workers most likely to support labourist and social democratic projects through their trade unions and political parties. Hence the decline in manufacturing in most countries in the North, associated with both globalization and with technical change, has been linked to a decline in trade union membership and support for social democratic parties (Przeworski and Sprague 1986). However, this analysis depends upon a gendered gaze. When gender is brought into focus the size of the working class must be reconsidered. There has been a major transformation in the relations of production for many women – changing from domestic relations to free wage labour – during recent decades. This entails the restructuring rather than decline of the working class.

One of the most important organizational resources of labourism and social democracy is trade unionism. While a key part of this is the extent or density of membership, the nature of the organization is also important: coverage, centralization, and coordination. The coverage of the workforce by trade union agreements is, in some countries such as Germany, considerably higher than the extent of trade union membership. The degree of centralization of trade union organization, in particular the extent to which a national level body is given the authority to coordinate action, is a further dimension of strength. A final dimension is that of coordination; the centralization of trade union governance is not the only way of securing national coordination (OECD 1997a; Visser 2006).

The density, coverage, centralization, and coordination of trade unionism vary very significantly between countries, in particular higher in countries that are more social democratic than those that are neoliberal. The strength of trade unionism depends partly on a number of institutional features that can embed it more or less deeply in the economic, legal, and social fabric. In those countries where social insurance for unemployment is organized by trade unions (the Ghent system as used in Belgium and the Nordic countries), the density of trade union membership is higher. There is a relationship between the strength of trade unionism and the extent to which trade unions are protected by law and embedded into industrial relations systems (Ebbinghaus and Visser 1999).

There has been a general decline in membership of trade unions in the global North. This has sometimes been associated with the restructuring of the working class, in particular with the decline in the manufacturing industry where trade unionism was traditionally strongest (Przeworski and Sprague 1986). However, it has occurred very unevenly between countries. One explanation for this variation is that it has occurred most in those countries where trade unions are least embedded – namely, not using the Ghent system of social insurance, having least protection in law, and implementing fewest corporatist arrangements (Ebbinghaus and Visser 1999).

However, when gender is brought into focus a different picture emerges. Women's membership of trade unions has in general not been falling but rising. In many countries women now make up nearly half the membership of trade unions and in some they are in the majority (EIRO 2004). Accounts of trade union strength that do not recognize the contrary direction of change between women and men miss a very important dimension of the changes in trade unionism. The changing gender composition of trade unions is associated with a change in the trade union bargaining agenda towards equalities issues that concern women (Briskin and Eliasson 1999; Gagnon and Ledwith 2000). Trade unions are becoming the largest mass organizations of women supporting social democratic projects (see Chapter 10).

Traditional analysis of feminist organizations has investigated small organizations within the context of a feminist movement, with the focus on the movement rather than the organizations. Through the lens of social movement analysis, there has been a tendency to see a decline in women's political activity associated with a decline in visible protests and street demonstrations (Taylor 1989; Bagguley 2002). When the focus is shifted to the extent, nature, and power of feminist organizations a different picture emerges. There has been a steady growth and development of feminist organizations. These are increasingly coordinated through coalitions at national and international levels. There has been a shift in the form of feminist activity away from separatist autonomous groups towards groups and coalitions oriented to lobbying states for changes in legislation and resources. The European Union funds its own Women's Lobby. There are network-type organizations active in the international spaces created by the UN. The coalition and network form of much feminist organization is often a response to the need to address the intersection of gender with other complex inequalities, especially ethnicity. The content of these politics includes the entire range of feminist issues, but with greatest emphasis placed on gender-based violence and economic issues. Contra Fraser (1997), contemporary feminism is not primarily culturalist (Briskin and Eliasson 1999; Gagnon and Ledwith 2000).

Violence is an oft-neglected dimension in analyses of civil societal projects which more usually focus on economic and organizational issues (Tilly 2003). It is perhaps most brought into view in the context of contestations that involve ethno-national-religious projects seeking 'purity' and a state of their own (Mann 2005). Since 'purity' can never be realized and not all such projects can have a state of their own, these are projects often faced with failure. Such projects may use group violence, perhaps developing militias, in order to pursue their goals. Once violence has been used it is hard to go back; its use throws into relief categories of ethnic/national/religious or other identifications that might have lain dormant, provoking them into a more active existence. This insight underpins the strategy used by terrorists. Suicide bombing is a current form of such political violence. Violence is of course used in class and gender conflicts too, often at moments of crisis and potential turning points in the history of these projects. Violence is also used to break strikes and to quell demonstrations.

Political opportunities and state capacity structure the environment in which projects operate (Kitschelt 1986). The extent of access to state power powerfully shapes what is possible for many civil societal projects. Projects that develop their own political parties have potential access to considerable power to embed their project in governmental programmes and then into social formations. The depth of democracy differentially affects projects of the disadvantaged and the strong. Projects that have become governmental programmes may change the nature of the state and its capacities, including deepening democracy, protecting or discouraging trade unions, building welfare capacity, and creating specialized units of the state such as women's units.

Ideas are a key aspect of projects; but not the only one. In democracies contestation between ideas is a necessary and significant part of the contest between projects, even though resources are often key to whether different positions are heard clearly or misrepresented. Projects may be framed in terms that are oppositional to the mainstream or close to it, anti-system or reformist, building a new political vocabulary or revising the old one (Della Porta and Diani 1999). While frame analysis has most often been applied to social movements concerned with gender (Ferree et al. 2002; Mazur 2002; Verloo 2005), regionalism and nationalism (Diani 1996), and ethnicity, it can be applied to class-oriented projects as well, as in the analysis of the rapid rise of neoliberalism in Eastern Europe after 1989 (Bockman and Eyal 2002). Argumentation and not only framing is important: epistemic communities draw not only on shared values but also on scientific work (Haas 1992) and they are especially important in environmental projects, and increasingly so in feminist projects. Holding states to account in matters of human rights has been facilitated by the requirement of consistency in their arguments (Risse 1999).

Projects are affected by their allies and enemies. Feminist projects do best where there are three types of gender allies: grassroots or NGO feminists; women parliamentarians; and gender equality units of civil servants, (though analyses vary as to exactly which allies: see Vargas and Wieringa 1998; Woodward 2004). Feminism and labourism may be allies in co-building social democracy or antagonists, promoting different sections of the workforce. The point of intersection of complex inequalities may be the site of coalitions or competitor projects.

The concept of the project develops the theorization of civil society. It is focused, yet can also encompass a wide repertoire of collective actions; it indicates a level of cohesion, but is not confined to a specific organization; it contains ideas, but is not confined to the ideational level.

Global Civil Societies and Waves

While some have claimed that a global civil society has already been achieved (Hardt and Negri 2000, 2006; Keane 2003; Lechner and Boli 2005), the evidence does not support this. But neither is civil society confined to a national or country specific level; there are transnational forms. In addition there are global waves, increasingly global forms of civil society, and several specific global civil societies, but all this does not currently form a single global civil society. The concept of a global wave is an important addition in order to grasp the global processes present in civil society.

While there have been some near global aspects of civil society since the rise of capitalism and the British Empire, including the spread of both Christian and socialist projects, the current round of globalization pushes further and faster the reach of civil societal projects. Some projects that started as local resistance to particular global projects have become global themselves, for example 'anti-globalization' projects that became global anti-neoliberal projects (Klein 1999).

Projects can be global in respect of either or both of their active members and their framing. Some involve both activists around the world and the use of global frames, as in the case of opposition to violence against women as a violation of women's human rights and environmentalism. Some use a global framing of their projects but only aspire to, rather than achieve, a global network of practitioners, with elites colonizing key nodes in global networks and institutions. Others may share a global project of ideas and goals, but nevertheless focus any implementation at the level of the national state, where the key levers of power are understood to be located (Peters and Wolper 1995; Keck and Sikkink 1998; Benhabib 1999; Tarrow 2005; Chesters and Welsh 2006).

There is not just one global civil society but several, competing and contesting. Most started as global waves of social energy before becoming institutionalized in civil society. The state level is still important and not all social movements do become global: some will stay local, national, or regional. But increasingly they are becoming global. New concepts are needed to grasp the specifically global dynamics of civil society and to go beyond concepts developed to capture phenomena that were predominantly local or national. Wave is one of these concepts.

The concept of wave captures the simultaneous temporal and spatial dimensions of social change in a global era in which there are new possibilities of forms of contact between social systems. The concept of wave catches the way that a critical event in one social system can have repercussions on social systems elsewhere in time and space. A wave starts in one temporal and spatial location, builds rapidly through endogenous processes, and then spreads out through time and space to affect social relations in other locations. The concept of wave captures the sudden transfer of social practices from one social system to another, passing as a form of social energy through networks rather than more institutionalized forms of social organization. The implications of a wave may be backwash and resistance as well as transformation in the direction of the wave as well as hybridization (this is laid out in more detail in Chapter 2.) Waves are not permanent, they are intrinsically non-linear and unstable forms of social energy. They may become institutionalized. This institutionalization may be within civil society, the establishment of associations and organizations outside the state. However, many civil society projects aspire to change the nature of governance and the nature of society itself. They may become institutionalized in governance programmes. If they are very successful they become embedded in new social forms, new social systems, but not necessarily in the way they initially intended. The implications of waves depend on the context in which they land. In particular, outcomes are different if there are pre-existing networks, groups, or constituencies that welcome, absorb, translate, and sympathetically amplify the content of the wave. Heterogeneity, divisions, and plural networks should be expected, although their positioning in an institutional context needs explanation. This institutional context varies; some are more open to the project of the wave than others.

Waves are a specific form of civil society project that go beyond the local and the national to regional and global levels. A series of changes has increased the spatial reach of civil society projects in several ways: rise in economic, organizational, and knowledge-based resources to facilitate global civil societal activities; growth in global political opportunities; growth in discursive resources at a global level.

First, increased global communications, media, and mobilities shrink the distance in time and space between events, so that live news footage of a conflict can be beamed to millions around the world. This increases awareness within quite general publics about incidents beyond their own country. These facilitate interconnections between political activists, especially cheaper air travel, faster trains, and the development of cheaper and more reliable phone, fax, and email. These facilitate the exchange of ideas and practices between people located in different countries and regions of the world (Thompson 1995; Castells 1997; Anderson and O'Dowd 1999b; Timms 2005; Urry 2007). These new forms of mobilities are resources enabling global waves and global civil societal projects, by ensuring that distance is no longer an obstacle to action. This is a new form of developing of the resources that have long been seen as necessary for political mobilization (McCarthy and Zald 1977).

Second, the development of global events and conferences has increased the number of spaces where international interactions, dialogues, and networking between activists can take place (Moghadam 2005). These especially include those belonging to the UN, which has encouraged the growth of events for non-governmental organizations alongside official governmental meetings (Annan 1999). The development of the World Social Forum and its regional offshoots provides dedicated locations for the development of global forms of civil society (World Social Forum 2007). This is a different kind of resource, but one that is important for the development of networks on which a global wave thrives. These events develop global co-optable communications networks that facilitate social movements (Freeman and Johnson 1999) to take the form of global waves.

Third, there is an increase in the knowledge, education, and expertise to support challenges to the status quo with the global development of higher education. The university-based knowledge system globalized early with the development of world journals, translation, and the global sale of books, internet and email, and regional and global conferences. This has supported the development of global epistemic communities (Haas 1992), in which networks of professionals with a recognized expertise and authoritative claims to policy-relevant knowledge share beliefs and values as to what constitutes progress in their field.

Fourth, there has been the development of new organization forms that can facilitate global organizing. In order to achieve a global form civil society projects must address issues of difference. In practice there are many issues that might potentially lead to divisions that could prevent the emergence of a common project. A global civil society is intrinsically diverse in its ethnicity, gender, standard of living, and lifestyle, so the building of some form of consensus cannot be on the basis of a simple homogeneity. Further, traditional forms of organization based on democratic centralization or consensus building require forms of stability of community and levels of resourcing that are inconsistent with a global civil society. The development of global civil societies has invoked forms of coordination that involve networks, coalitions, and alliance, rather than democratic centralism or consensus. These are able to absorb and constructively address the differences within and between the constituencies of a global civil society. They are loose, fluid, flexible, and changeable in the light of changing circumstances, shifting interests, and foci of attention, able to hybridize different projects and options (Gilroy 1993; Ferree and Hess 1995; Jakobsen 1998; Keck and Sikkink 1998; Keane 2003). This is not identity politics, rather the continual building and modification of projects.

Fifth, there has been the development of political opportunity structures that are global (Tarrow 2005). This is associated with the development of global institutions, including the World Bank, the International Monetary Fund, the World Trade Organization, the UN, and its various agencies and projects such as the Millennium Development Goals (Keane 2003; Anheier et al. 2005; UN 2007a), as well as events involving the global elite, such as the meeting of G8 leaders or gathering at Davos (Klein 1999; Chesters and Welsh 2006). These provide opportunities for engagement, as well as acting as a focus for global justice and anti-neoliberal capital protests. In addition, there are within the global inter-state system increased opportunities for influencing state conduct by argumentation and shaming. Human rights have become embedded in a variety of international regimes and organizations and are increasingly defining what constitutes a 'civilized state' as a member of the international community in 'good standing'. The process of argumentation potentially unsettles fixed identities and perceived interests which become subject to discursive challenges, potentially leading to argumentative 'self-entrapment' and change (Risse 1999).

Sixth, there is the development of global framings. Waves of civil societal projects can only become global if they are framed in a way that is globally relevant. The resources that are needed for global waves are symbolic as well as economic, organizational, and informational. Symbolic resources to challenge the existing social order are important (Eyerman and Jamieson 1991); the ideas held by a movement are important to participants and not merely instrumental (Melucci 1989). The kinds of framings of issues that organize experiences and events, thus making them meaningful, matter (Snow et al. 1986; Diani 1996; Della Porta and Diani 1999). Examples of global framings include universal human rights and global climate change. The development of UN Conventions that further articulate the principles behind the Universal Declaration of Human Rights (UN 1948) has assisted this process by providing legitimatation to globally framed projects. The major international human rights instruments are: the International Convention on the Prevention and Punishment of Genocide (1948); the International Convention on the Elimination of all Forms of Racial Discrimination (1965); the International Covenant on Civil and Political Rights (1966); the International Covenant on Economic, Social and Cultural Rights (1966); the Convention for the Elimination of Discrimination Against Women (1979); the Convention against Torture and other Cruel, Inhuman or Degrading Treatment or Punishment; and the Convention on the Rights of the Child (1989) (UNDP 2007a). In addition, the UN world conference on human rights in Vienna in 1993 declared that women's rights were human rights and that violence against women constituted a violation of women's human rights (UN 1993). Further, there are several UN Conventions on Fundamental Labour Rights, including: freedom of association and collective bargaining (87, 98); the elimination of forced and compulsory labour (29, 105); the elimination of discrimination in respect of employment and occupation (100, 111); and the abolition of child labour (138, 182) (UNDP 2007).

Claims about what constitutes 'the good' are increasingly made at a global level and draw on a framing in terms of the universal. The arguments about the importance of context and situation are being restructured as a result of globalization. There are no longer any self- contained, homogeneous communities; all know of others who are both similar in some respects and different in others. This is re-framing the way in which claims about the goals, values, and means to achieve these are presented. The appeal to the global level is often presented as if it were an appeal to a timeless universal. Yet the global is not the same as the abstract universal. Instead the global is a practical, special, and time-specific realm, even as it can be purported to encompass the totality of contemporary human life. The global and the universal have an uneasy and ambiguous relationship in many contemporary analyses. This is because many political projects today make claims to justice on the basis of an ambiguously defined conception of the global/universal.

This appeal to a global level is especially occurring in the case of the appeal to 'universal' human rights. A successful elision between the global and the universal is an important move in contemporary politics. The ability to claim access to a universal standard of justice has been used by an increasing number of political projects as a powerful form of legitimation. The nature of this global framing is especially important given the ease with which an elision between the global and the universal can be made. The global is no more than a specific social construction situated in a specific time. In this way it is quite different from the universal, which is usually understood as timeless and lacking spatial specificity.

The elision of the 'universal' with the 'global' lies at the heart of this development. It is implied that if the entire world agrees to something through open debating in forums of persons selected in a representative manner from each country then the Habermas-type conditions of procedure have been met, which in turn will mean that truth can be approached as closely as is humanly possible. Simultaneously there is an appeal to the liberal principle of universal individual human rights, as if this is above time-bound and space-bound calculations of interest. In these developing global fora political activists devise and change those principles of justice that are understood as human rights. They successfully treat the global as if it is the same as the universal, all the better to claim authority for their actions.

The re-framing of contemporary politics by globalization has given rise, not only to the politics opposed to this change, but also to the creative and innovative adaptation and expansion of the notion of universal human rights. This new framing elides the distinction between the global and the universal as part of its legitimation strategy. The attempted reference group for these politics is that of a common humanity. This opens up a new round of political struggles in the construction of such rights, even as they are held up as timeless and universal.

Examples of waves

Some civil society projects have a moment when there is a burst of energy, becoming regional or global waves. Before this energy subsides some become institutionalized, some in civil society and others deeper than that in governmental programmes or even social formations. Increasingly waves are becoming global, for the reasons discussed above.

The following list contains several of the more important waves, though it does not claim to be comprehensive. The discussion on each describes their content, the circumstances of their development into waves, their varied implications regionally and globally, and the extent of their subsequent institutionalization. They include: the Reformation; socialism; first wave feminism; nationalism and decolonization; fascism; the alternative movement of the 1960s; second wave feminism; environmentalism; neoliberalism; global justice; fundamentalisms; and human rights. Civil society projects are not all conventionally progressive and the list contains some violent, sectional, and authoritarian projects. The earlier waves were regional, focused on Europe or the North Atlantic rim, while the later waves are increasingly global in range.

The Reformation
The Reformation of the Christian Church in Europe was a regional wave that was precipitated in 1517 by Martin Luther nailing his critique of the Catholic Church to the door of a church in what is now Germany and came to an end in 1648 with the peace of Westphalia. The Reformation swept through north-west Europe, producing new forms of Christian doctrine and restructuring the relations between church and state. It had a particularly strong effect in Scandinavia in its Calvinist variant, but also extended southwards from Britain to Switzerland. The unified form of the Catholic Church straddling state boundaries in Europe and the development of education along with the utilization of the use of the relatively new practice of printing helped to spread the Reformation (Cameron 1991). The resulting boundary with Catholicism opened up a fracture across Europe that had repercussions in later centuries, from religious persecution to intensifying disputes across national boundaries, such as that between Britain and Ireland.

Socialism
In the late nineteenth century a wave of socialism spread out from Europe. At its centre were the struggles of organized workers and their allies in the industrializing core, growing from labourism to demands for democracy and radical societal transformations. In much of Western Europe this socialist wave became institutionalized in trade unions and parties of the left, varying from small communist parties to the more common social democracy (Kitschelt 1994; Bartolini 2000). While initially European, the socialist wave spread around the world. There was very limited institutionalization at a global level in the International Labour Organization in 1919, linked to the League of Nations, which survives to the present day modestly supporting trade unions around the world and building campaigns and setting global standards (Valticos 1969: ILO 2005). More important were the

revolutions in Russia in 1917 and China in 1949. The social democratic regimes can be seen as platforms to the next step by Korpi (1983) and as one part of a spiralling of forms of socialism and capitalism (Boswell and Chase-Dunn 2000), though it is more common to see social democracy as in retreat (Callaghan 2000).

First wave feminism
The first feminist wave started in the middle of the nineteenth century in Europe and especially Britain, and in North America, especially the USA, spreading out during the early twentieth century beyond Europe to Australasia and creating ripples in the emerging oppositions in the European colonies. This feminist movement addressed a wide range of issues, from access to employment and education to regulating prostitution and male violence, but is known especially for its struggles for suffrage (Gilman 1966; Evans 1977; Jayawardena 1986). The timing of the development of the women's suffrage movement in each country, unlike that for men, was not associated with the level of economic development (Therborn 1977); rather the movement was part of a regional and then a global civil societal wave. Women won the vote at the same time in many countries of Northwest Europe and North America: between 1913 and 1920 in Norway, Iceland, Denmark, Sweden, the USA, Canada, the USSR, Luxembourg, Austria, Czechoslovakia, Germany, the Netherlands, Poland, Ireland, and the UK (Inter-Parliamentary Union 1997). Although Ramirez et al. (1997) have argued that the suffrage struggle was national rather than global, they in fact show that 'Western status' is the most important explanatory factor – namely, that it was a predominantly regional phenomenon.

Suffrage for women was later than suffrage for men in those countries that granted suffrage to men before 1920, that is, the industrially developed West. A second round of suffrage victories for women at the end of the Second World War spread across most of southern and eastern Europe. Thereafter, few if any countries granted suffrage for men without simultaneously granting it to women: in practice, decolonization meant universal suffrage, not only suffrage for men (Inter-Parliamentary Union 1997). In some locations feminists fighting for suffrage found allies among socialists and among nationalists fighting for decolonization, but not everywhere at all times.

What happened to first wave feminism? It changed the nature of government and government programmes towards gender, at least insofar as women became recognized as political citizens. Its impact on social formations is probably not what it intended, contributing to the transition from domestic to public gender regimes rather than ending gender inequality. Its own civil society organizations faded, divided internally by the militarist nationalism of many countries in the First World War and also divided by contrasting visions of progress for women, as to whether women should be protected from the worst of the public domain and excesses of employment by promoting a better form of domesticity or fighting for further forms of formal equality. Nonetheless, it continues in less visible civil society organizations such as, in the UK, the Fawcett Society.

Fascism
Fascism was a European fundamentalist project, centred in Germany and Italy but also important in Austria, Hungary, Romania, and Spain, marked by a search for racial purity, anti-Semitism leading to concentration camps and the genocide of millions of Jews, the violent and sometimes lethal treatment of gays and the disabled, disapproval and domesticity for women who were removed from employment and public positions, and an aggressive nationalist militarism. It has similarities with other fundamentalisms in its project of ethnic purity and the domestication of women, but is distinguished by its lack of a religious component. It was a powerful wave, though of rather limited duration (the 1930s and 1940s) and limited geographical range, being restricted to central and southern Europe though expanded by militarism to a wider part of Europe and over by 1945. There were ripples and collaborators across Europe, for example Oswald Moseley and his followers in Britain, and there were outliers in countries associated with Europe, such as the development of apartheid in South Africa in this period. The project seized state power in Germany in the 1930s and was in the process of transforming the social formation when it was defeated by the military power of threatened states, especially Russia but including a broad Western alliance, and eliminated by the victorious state forces. Attempts to revive it in civil society have largely met with effective opposition in civil society and states (Koonz 1988; Bauman 1989; Mann 2004).

Nationalism and decolonization
Nationalism and decolonization are important movements with major effects on state formation, but the timing of the major wave is highly contested. The earliest dating is Smith's (1986) location of the origins of nations in ethnic groups, though this is not quite the same as the rise of nationalism. Several have associated the rise of nationalism with the early development of capitalism and especially early technologies for mass communication such as the invention of printing (Anderson 1983; Hobsbawm and Ranger 1983). Others have focused on what is assumed to be the development of nation-states in Europe, with the creation of Germany and Italy during the nineteenth century (Mann

1993b). But while these might be precursors of some of the ideas that are involved in nationalism, these were not yet the major nationalist wave. In the middle of the nineteenth century most European countries were or aspired to be empires and not nation-states. A better dating of the most powerful wave of nationalism is in the mid-twentieth century, when in opposition to colonial rule nationalism was utilized as a powerful legitimating discourse, drawing on its earlier intellectual heritage. The modern conception of a nation depends on a notion of would-be self-government that is inextricably bound up with modern notions of democracy; by the mid-twentieth century nationalist conceptions of citizenship involved universal suffrage. Before then democracy was absent and nationalism was little more than a romanticism used by ruling elites to provide legitimacy for their state-building projects. The founding of the UN from the ashes of the League of Nations provided global legitimation to these nation-state building projects, supported by the emerging global hegemon of the USA at a time that saw the decline of the former global hegemon, Britain, whose Empire was thereby delegitimated (Walby 2003; Kelly and Kaplan 2007). A wave of decolonization between 1947 and the late 1960s saw the end of the British, French, and Portuguese Empires. This decolonization, supported by nationalist rhetoric, was truly a global wave.

The 1960s Movement

This movement was linked to a broader libertarian wave that developed during the 1960s, especially in the USA, spread to Europe, and encompassed a range of issues including feminism and opposition to the US war in Vietnam. 1968 was a key year, with simultaneous events in Paris, the United States, and many other Western cities. This movement was key to stopping the war in Vietnam, but did not restructure the militarization of the US state. There was a student movement for democracy in the universities which frequently changed their governance structure. The associated feminist movement, discussed below, sought to change civil societal practices of gender relations as well as state programmes. Together these movements created a radical cultural wave from the USA that was echoed in Europe and spread around the world. Its institutionalization into the US state however was less marked (Tarrow 1998; Freeman and Johnson 1999).

One important component of this movement in the USA, but not in many other countries, was an anti-racist civil rights movement. In the USA, the foundations of this movement were laid down in the 1930s–1950s. It reached its peak in the USA in the 1960s, and had some effects elsewhere. This movement won effective rights to vote, some desegregation of schools and other public places, and equal opportunities legislation in employment (Shapiro 1988;

McAdam 1999): the consequences of political citizenship are still developing. While there were some ripples of the wave elsewhere, such as in South Africa in opposition to their apartheid system, and the adoption of equal opportunities legislation in the UK, its global effects were limited, not least because of the specificity of the US ethnic situation as it derived from the history of slavery.

Feminism

Feminism was a leading part of the radical wave of the late 1960s in the USA where it took both radical libertarian and liberal forms. Together these encompassed a wide range of issues from promoting equality in employment to reconstructing sexual behaviour, confronting men's violence to women and rethinking the meaning of the political. In the 1960s and early 1970s the United States led the world in the development of equal opportunity legislation and abortion was legalized. But overall the US state was slow to respond, with relatively low levels of incorporation into political institutions, and the movement continued to build up its energy.

Feminism spread around the world as a global wave, with movements not only in Europe but also in other continents and in global fora. The movement took different forms in different countries. In countries with a socialist or social democratic tradition feminism hybridized into socialist feminism and thus saw the development of women's committees in trade unions and a challenge to incorporate women's issues, such as public childcare, into social democratic programmes. Sweden in the mid-1970s saw the development of public childcare. There was a wave of equal opportunities legislation in Europe in the early 1970s including the EU Equal Treatment Directive in 1975, in Britain in 1970 and 1975, and in Ireland in 1973. There was a wave of establishing refuges and phone help lines for women who had suffered male violence, appearing in Europe from the mid-1970s (with the first refuge in Britain opening in 1973) and spreading around the world. Incorporation into global institutions involved UN conferences on women starting in 1975, which peaked in the 1995 Beijing conference and its Platform for Action but with continuing effects in other UN bodies including the World Bank (Hague and Malos 1993; Moser 1993; Nelson and Chowdhury 1994; Murphy 1995; Hoskyns 1996; Keck and Sikkink 1998; Peterson and Runyan 1999).

A further development has been the hybridization of feminism with the universal human rights tradition (see below). The claim to universal human rights has had a long history in feminism (Banks 1981; Wollstonecraft 1992 [1790]; Berkovitch 1999) and is now undergoing a resurgence. It was a legitimating principle during suffrage struggles. It was present in claims to equal worth, equal pay, and equal treatment at work in the European Union from the mid-1970s (Pillinger 1992; European Parliament 1994; European Commission 1999), in Japan (Yoko et al. 1994), and elsewhere around the world (Nelson and Chowdhury 1994). This claim to universalism is often knowing or strategic, by which is meant that the protagonists know that the 'universal' is but a contingent social construct (Bunch 1995). Indeed, there has been significant feminist activity devoted to redefining and reconstructing what constitutes 'universal' human rights (Peters and Wolper 1995; UNIFEM 2000a). This occurs in UN conferences, which attract a massive attendance of feminist activists from around the world, both North and South, and supplements and influences the official delegations (UNIFEM 2000b). In 1993 in a UN conference in Vienna, violence against women was constructed for the first time as a violation of women's human rights and thus of human rights. This was presented as if it was an always and already existing universal human right, even as it was known that it was being socially constructed as a result of negotiation and struggle (Davies 1993; Bunch 1995; Peters and Wolper 1995; UNIFEM 2000b; Kelly 2005). A universalist framing was used to promote the significance and generality of the issue of stopping violence against women as a human right, whilst knowing it to be contingent and constructed and not absolute.

Feminism has become institutionalized in civil society, in governmental programmes at national and international levels, and in some social formations. In becoming institutionalized, many issues can no longer gain the high media profile associated with a conventional social movement. This has led some to suggest that feminism is in abeyance (Taylor 1989; Bagguley 2002), or that it is predominantly interested in recognition rather than redistribution (Fraser 1997), (though see Hobson 2003). Rather, feminism is becoming institutionalized.

Environmentalism
Environmentalism is a project with a long history that has recently built into a global wave. It now has a number of targets, from reducing pollution to slowing down the rate and harmful effects of human-caused climate change. These invoke a global solidarity since pollution crosses borders and affects countries and people other than those that caused the pollution. Global climate change invokes not only global solidarity but also inter-generational solidarity, since the energy systems of the present will affect future generations more than the present. It has an intrinsic global institutional focus, even though it states that have to act. One early global event was the UN conference in Rio in 1992; another was the Kyoto agreement; more recently was Bali in 2007. It has involved the development of

an epistemic community acting alongside the civil society project. Most recently it has become embedded in some government programmes, at least partly because of the global movement leading to international agreements (Beck 1992; Lash et al. 1995; Grove 1996; Yearley 1996; Macnaghten and Urry 1998; Mol and Sonnefield 2000; Mol 2001; Cudworth 2003, 2005).

Fundamentalisms
Major world religions have always been global in aspiration, even when accommodating others in practice (Bruce 1996). However, there have also been radical movements associated with these religions that have not been so deeply institutionally embedded and which take a more civil societal form. These include radical and fundamentalist religious movements seen especially in Islam and Christianity, but also in Hinduism and Judaism (Marty and Scott 1993). This is not a clash of civilizations (contra Huntington 1998), but rather of their radical outriders, better described as Jihadists. Radical Islamism first made its impact via the Iranian revolution of 1979, subsided a little, and then grew in strength and global reach following on from the US invasion of Iraq (Gregory 2004) and amid repeated failures to resolve the Palestinian issue, currently taking up new forms of armed struggle in Al Qaeda and suicide bombing. Fundamentalist Christianity became established in the USA in the 1980s, especially contesting issues of gender and intimacy such as legal abortion and gay marriage, and supporting right-wing presidencies.

Neoliberalism
Neoliberalism arose as a right-wing project opposing socialism and social democracy during the 1980s in the USA and UK. It urged the importance of freeing markets from regulatory controls and rolling back the state, asserting that this would create economic growth and freedom for individuals. It built on older forms of conservative and liberal projects, and sought to break the post-war settlements that had embedded some levels of welfare and state regulation of the economy. It had a base in right wing think tanks and among a minority of university economists, including Hayek (1960) and Friedman (1962), and was then taken up to revitalize the agendas of conservative US and UK governments under Reagan and Thatcher in the 1980s, entering the global financial institutions and their associated knowledge creation institutions and becoming hegemonic in the USA. It dominated the economic agenda of the World Bank, the International Monetary Fund, and the World Trade Organization. The expansion of global capitalism during and since the 1980s was associated with the neoliberal project, which sought the development of market

capitalism in ever newer locations, from public services to the exploitation of the human genome (Brenner and Theodore 2002; Harvey 2003, 2005; Saad-Filho and Johnston 2005; England and Ward 2007).

The suddenness of the arrival of neoliberalism in the former communist countries of east and central Europe around 1989–1990 surprised many commentators. It was too sudden to be explained via the diffusion of ideas. There were however already outposts of neoliberalism within intellectual elites in the countries of eastern and central Europe, albeit expressed in coded terms (Bockman and Eyal 2002; Fourcade-Gourinchas and Babb 2002). But more important is the understanding of the processes within a crisis, and the positioning of US neoliberals backed by the US state to take advantage of social and political disorganization. Intervention at the point of disaster was a long-standing practice of US neoliberalism (Klein 2007).

Global justice movement/anti-neoliberal capitalism
The global justice movement arose in the 1990s to challenge neoliberal globalization and mutated into an anti-neoliberal capitalist movement as the movement itself became global. It came to world attention in Seattle, with confrontations over a summit of world economic leaders, which inspired many similar events around the world. Although led by its anti-neoliberal capital agenda it gains its inspiration from many sources and takes on board issues relating to the environment, anti-racism, indigenous people's rights, and feminism. It was a global wave from its inception, although not comprehensive in its remit and reach. It has made some impact on some governmental programmes, especially at a global level, and is partly institutionalized in the meetings of the World Social Forum (Klein 1999; Rowbotham and Linkogle 2000; George 2004; Kiely 2005; Timms 2005; Chesters and Welsh 2006; Hardt and Negri 2006; World Social Forum 2007).

The contestation by the global justice movement wave of the attempted hegemony of neoliberalism met with some partial success, for example, policy revisions by the World Bank (World Bank 1992; Kiely 2005) and the adoption of the Millennium Development Goals that prioritized human as well as economic development (UN 2007a).

Universal Human Rights
There has been a global wave seeking universal human rights. A long-standing, initially Western, project for equal rights (Paine 1984 [1791]), which has been articulated and institutionalized in various stages (Meyer et al. 1997; Berkovitch 1999), has been reinvigorated and transformed by global processes and the development of global institutions. The appeal to universal human rights depends not only upon a philosophy and commonly accepted rhetoric, but also upon a set of institutional practices which give it a practical expression

which is increasing with globalization. There was a critical turning point in the embedding of the principle of universal rights in international institutions formed in the aftermath of the Second World War as part of the rejection of the Holocaust and extreme nationalist and militarist projects, especially in Europe, the most affected continent, but also in newly formed global institutions. Human rights were key to the United Nations Charter signed in 1945 (United Nations 1945), initially and powerfully codified in the Universal Declaration of Human Rights (United Nations 1948), and included and broadened in several UN Covenants since, such as the International Covenant on Civil and Political Rights, the International Covenant on Economic, Social and Cultural Rights, and the International Bill of Human Rights (Buergenthal et al. 2002). The increasing range of the covenants and the hybridization of these notions with local traditions may be understood as a broadening of the notion of human rights beyond their Western origins and also beyond narrower concerns with civil liberties, coming to address wider economic as well as social democratic concerns (Woodiwiss 1998). Human rights have become an integral part of the European conception of modernity since 1945 (Therborn 1995). The Council of Europe, founded in 1949, adopted a Convention for the Protection of Human Rights and Fundamental Freedoms in 1950, and established a legal authority, the European Court of Human Rights, in 1963 in The Hague to implement this for member countries (Council of Europe 2006). This has now been incorporated into the law of the European Union and is legally binding on all Member States.

These developments give legitimacy to a set of practices protecting individuals from the arbitrary and excessive exercise of power. The human rights discourse is undergoing significant further developments, both broadening its field of application and increasing the institutional power available to implement it. The increasing significance of the global discourse of universal human rights, and their embedding in international law, tribunals and courts, means that these are no longer matters on which individual countries can remain autonomous.

Conclusions

Civil society is the institutional domain in which many competing projects develop. The process of the transformations of meaning and the emergence of new political projects is not reducible to either the economic, as has so often happened with class, or the cultural, as has so often happened with gender and ethnicity. To include multiple complex inequalities beyond class it is important to address the ontological depth of each. Civil society is a terrain of change, struggle, and innovation in meaning.

The deployment of the concept of civil society by Gramsci (1971) forged an alternative way of balancing and integrating change at the level of both social structure and system and the meanings held by individuals and groups. It avoids the tendency to voluntarism inherent in the concept of agency (Giddens 1992), and the tendency to stasis inherent in the concept of habitus (Bourdieu 1984). The concept of civil society allows for an approach to meaning and social change that is more dynamic and more open to the complexities of multiple social inequalities than that of identity (Hall 1996). It leaves open the issue of the relationship between material position and social action, avoiding either conflation to the economic (as in some reductionist readings of Marx) or conflation to culture (as in some uses of the concept of identity), to remember the important distinction between a class in itself (or other social entity) and an entity for itself. Much previous use of the concept of civil society, including by Gramsci, neglects the significance of complex inequalities. The analysis here widens the range of regimes of inequalities and the social relations included.

Modernity in civil society is associated with individuation, secularization, the development of science and technology, and the transformation of intimacy. Individuation has been linked to both freedom and diversity with multiple webs of affiliation and with social isolation and the erosion of human capital and social solidarity. These processes have implications for gender relations, partly because secular polities are more open to democratic governance of intimacy than religious ones, and partly because the transformation of domestic forms of intimacy has such significant implications for gender relations. However, there is no simple set of implications for equality since the nature of these changes depends on the context within which they occur. The outcome depends on the form of modernity, in particular as to whether it takes a more neoliberal or a more social democratic form. The development of secularization with modernity is likewise varied, with its slower development in countries with higher levels of inequality. The transformation of intimacy is bound up with changes in the gender regime, and is implicated in changes in the practice and sanctioning of same sex relationships. High rates of permeability of households with divorce and cohabitation do not have to mean high rates of lone-parenting: it might simply be re-partnering. Attempts to block these transitions by some forms of polity, such as the Catholic Church, and civil societal projects such as fundamentalism, can dampen the speed of the transition. Variations exist in the form of modernity in civil society.

Modernity in civil society does not happen all at once, it emerges for different social groups at different times. In particular it often happens later for women than for men, with contested implications for intimacy, sexuality, and the domestic sphere. Rationalization and the development of science and technology have implications for global processes, speeding and deepening them, but doing so unevenly.

There is no single global civil society, nor is there a world society. Instead there are global waves carrying a diverse range of civil societal projects around the world. There is a global component to civil society which takes a dynamic and diverse form. Civil societal projects are becoming increasingly global with the development of global communications and events providing new resources facilitating engagement at a global level, a shift in forms of organizing to coalitions and networks to better address the differences that inevitably arise in global discussions, the increase in political opportunities at a global level with the development of global institutions, and the development of global framings that can interpret issues within a global horizon. While civil society projects that reach beyond national boundaries are not new, they are increasing qualitatively in their depth, range, and significance. The contestation between neoliberalism and its opponents is taking place at a global level. The discourse of universal human rights is bound up with a global framing of justice, as is that of the notion that the environment of the planet itself is in danger.

Global waves are an increasingly important form of civil societal project. Some, but not all, become institutionalized in civil society institutions, governmental programmes, and social formations. This is a contested process involving alliances and contestations among a variety of forces, each drawing strength from their positioning in the domains of economy, polity, and violence. Waves are not new to the twenty-first century, but early instances were more likely to be regional than global. Waves are increasingly global as communications and mobilities become faster and more far reaching – as global events facilitate networking, as education and expertise become more available, as coalitions and networking replace more formal types of organizational form facilitating working across difference, with the development of global political opportunities with the emergence of global institutions as well as the development of global framings. These waves may become institutionalized in civil society, governmental programmes, and social formations, though some may fade away instead. Their effects will depend upon the nature of social relations and the institutions that they encounter. Sometimes they may catalyse changes in social situations that were already unstable and ripe for change, while in others they may be resisted with little outcome or will cause only small changes; they may hybridize to form something new; they may provoke a backlash, which itself may have diverse effects according to circumstances.

7 Regimes of Complex Inequality

Introduction

There are several regimes of complex inequality, including those of class, gender, and ethnicity. These are complex inequalities, combining inequality and difference simultaneously. They are analytically distinguishable; different forms of complex inequality are not reducible to each other within one social system, although they intersect and mutually adapt. Each regime of inequality involves all institutional domains of economy, polity, violence, and civil society, as well as macro, meso, and micro levels. Multiple regimes of inequalities, including those of gender, class, and ethnic relations, coexist within the institutional domains of economy, polity, violence, and civil society, which establish the ontological depth of the regime. Each regime of inequality has ontological depth because of its constitution in this range of institutional domains and levels of abstraction. The traditional concept of society overstates the degree of cohesion and the alignment of complex inequalities in a country. Rather than an a priori theoretical assumption of the close coupling of these regimes and institutions, there is an empirical question to investigate as to the internal cohesion of each regime of inequality and their intersection. The analytic strategy here is to disentangle systems that were previously overly integrated or even reduced to each other, to analyse them separately from each other, and then to investigate the extent of their alignment and which conditions produce this. These potential alignments include the level of modernization of the social relations in the regime and the variety of modernity, from neoliberal to social democratic.

This chapter discusses the main types of regimes of inequality, including those of gender, class, and ethnicity, addressing five major issues. First, the balance between difference and inequality in the complex inequality that constitutes the regime of inequality. Second, the ontological depth and cohesion of each regime: the four domains of economy, polity, violence, and civil society; the micro, meso, and macro levels; and the nature and extent of the cohesion between domains and levels especially during processes of change. Third, the spatial and temporal dispersion and boundaries of regimes – neither nation-state nor global but somewhere in between. Fourth, the nature of the path dependent varieties of neoliberalism and social democracy in each regime, after the transition from premodern to modern; and the significance of temporal discrepancy and the sequencing of these developments between regimes. Fifth, the intersection with other regimes of inequality and how they mutually affect each other although this is done asymmetrically.

Beyond Class Regimes

The analysis of systems of inequality has not often distinguished between different types of inequalities. It is usually led by class, either implicitly or explicitly, with an assumption that other types of inequality will tend to follow (Marx 1954, 1963, 1967; Gramsci 1971; Bourdieu 1984; Habermas 1989). The conflation of different forms of inequality into a single regime is a mistake, since they can have quite different dynamics. Nevertheless, this is an important literature and has been extensively drawn on in the chapters on the four domains of economy, polity, violence, and civil society. The outline of the analysis will be briefly recapitulated in order to provide the context for the discussion that identifies the differences between regimes of inequality.

Class can be a complex inequality, although it is often seen as a simple one. Class is often seen as a simple inequality in which the defining feature is one of economic exploitation, a presumption of a common standard of access to income and wealth against which to measure inequality. However, it can also be a complex inequality in that some aspects of difference are also present, for example the positive valuing of forms of solidaristic activity within the working class, which is linked to the commonality of economic and social position, is a feature of some historical periods (Thompson 1963).

A class regime is constituted not only in the economy, but also in the polity, violence, and civil society. Some simpler analyses have focused on the economic, however, more nuanced accounts have also included other domains. While accounting for class relations through a simple base-superstructure model in which the economy determines the political and ideological superstructure has long been rejected, there remains a question as to the relative significance of the different institutional domains and their degree of cohesion. Many approaches in rejecting the base-superstructure model have attempted to theorize the greater significance of economic power without falling into simple reductionism. The notion of 'relative autonomy' was developed by Althusser (1971) to capture both the ultimate cohesiveness of the system (since the economy determinant in the last instance) and the absence of simple determinism, since the political and ideological levels were important in shaping any given social formation. This rejected the simple notion of economic determinism, but did not answer questions concerning the degree and manner of the operation of this relative autonomy. Subsequent theorizing of the relationship between the state and capitalism further developed a non-reductionist account by Poulantzas (1973) that nevertheless notes the overriding influence or 'ecological dominance' of the economic (Jessop 2002). Nevertheless, there remains a tendency for some aspect of the old base-superstructure model to sneak in through the back door occasionally. The development of interest in culture (Bourdieu 1984), the public sphere, the life-world (Habermas 1989), and civil society (Gramsci 1971; Laclau and Mouffe 1985; Cohen and Arato 1992) offers a theorization of class relation that is still further removed from economic determinism. Other work challenges the reduction of violence to the state (Mann 1986). However, the focus on the global level has refocused attention on the power of capital through the restructuring of economies, raising questions as to whether it is sweeping away distinct political and civil societal formations. In some formulations of globalization, the economy resurfaces as the major institutional domain that restructures all other forms of social relations. The major theoretical challenge to this increasing pre-eminence of the economic has come from the development of theories of path dependency, in which political institutions are particularly important as sites of both critical turning points and the locking in of new paths of development (Moore 1966; Korpi 1983; Esping-Andersen 1990; North 1990; Pierson 2001). Aspects of the cultural turn in social theory are challenged by globalization, in which economic and political processes are not reducible to the cultural.

The analysis of global processes has refocused attention on the power of capital to restructure political and cultural institutions (Crouch and Streeck 1997; Held et al. 1999). The analysis of path dependency challenges any simple return to economic determinism in the analysis of globalization. The expansion of global capital does not have the same effects on all countries; path dependent trajectories of development rooted in political institutions have proven resilient to global capital in some countries. Debates on the significance of path dependency are simultaneously debates on the relative significance of economy and politics. Further, politics are important in the critical turning points into different trajectories of development; revolutions and historic class compromises are not reducible to economics (Moore 1966; Korpi 1983; Skocpol 1979; Esping-Andersen 1990). Within class theory, organized violence is often seen as a merely instrumental power deployed by the capitalist state and hence reduced to it. Such an approach leaves violence out of focus in much theory of political economy and class, even when it is noted empirically. When violence is visible it is seen as a rare occurrence confined to crises, such as moments of revolution (Moore 1966, Skocpol 1979) or a contestation between hegemons (Bornschier and Chase-Dunn 1999). There are a few exceptions, such as the analysis of the process of the formation of modern states alongside the development and concentration of capital (Tilly 1990), and those who see the military as an important form of power that is non-reducible to states (McNeill 1963; Mann 1986).

The spatial and temporal boundary of the class regime is much disputed: for some it is already global (Wallerstein 1974; Robinson 2001) while for others there are still significant differences between social systems in separate societies or nation-states (Jessop 2002). Some aspects of different spatial and temporal reach are linked to different aspects of capital: finance capital has become the nearest to the global (Strange 1986, 1996), though not quite (Sassen 2001, 2008); industrial capital is more subject to regulation by polities and states, especially in its employment aspects (Crouch and Streeck 1997); employment and welfare provision can be regulated by different polities, especially in the EU where employment is primarily regulated by the EU and welfare by the Member States.

There are divergent paths of development of class regimes, of which the two main forms in modernity are neoliberal and social democratic. The key distinguishing features concern the extent of democracy and inequality in each of the four domains of economy, polity, violence, and civil society. In the economy, neoliberalism entails high levels of inequality and little democratic regulation. In the polity it entails shallow rather than deep democracy. While the nature of neoliberalism and social democracy has been investigated in the economy and polity (Held 2004; Harvey 2005), it has been less well specified in relation to violence and civil society. Too often the self-proclaimed rhetoric of neoliberalism, that it entails a small state, is uncritically accepted: rather, in the domain of violence, neoliberalism means a large state apparatus engaged in the deployment of violence, both in the military and the criminal justice system, alongside high rates of interpersonal violence. Neoliberal civil societies are thinner and more commercialized (Putnam 2000) than the denser, more mutualist forms in social democracy.

The nature of class regimes is affected by their mutual adaptation with other regimes of inequality, as well as by the level of economic development. At these intersections, class regimes have often been thought to be dominant, however it is better to consider this to be a contingent matter, as is shown later.

Gender Regimes

Gender is not an absolute, but exists only as a social relationship (Hawkesworth 1997; Lorber 2005; Oakley 2005). It is a relationship that reproduces itself, whether or not the individuals involved are aware of it, hence it has the key characteristics of a system, a gender regime. Gender relations are a complex inequality, involving both inequality and difference, and the extent to which inequality or difference is prioritized varies (Felski 1997; Fraser 1997).

There is a challenge to theorize gender relations without either oversimplifying in a reductionist manner or providing so much detail that it becomes only descriptive. There is a range of approaches from, at one pole, a base that determines the remaining aspects of gender, to the other, with the dispersal of gender relations so there is no cohesive concept of gender let alone woman. In between these extremes there have been attempts to identify a limited number of key components, with variations in these being used to explain variations in the form of gender relations. Throughout this debate lies a question as to the level of cohesion between different aspects of gender inequality, as to whether the connections between the different elements are close or loose.

There are four main approaches to the theorization of the degree of cohesion between the institutional domains that contribute to the constitution of gender relations. Some theories seek out a single base to explain gender inequality, reducing other aspects of gender to this. Early versions of this thesis have been widely rejected as reductionist and essentialist. In response to these difficulties some writers have rejected notions of gender as a system altogether, either by a second approach that focuses on the micro level of identities at the point of intersection with other social divisions or by using a third approach that disperses the category of gender and prioritizes difference. Rather than these extreme poles, a fourth approach is to build models of gender relations made up of several elements – neither a single base, nor an infinite number of components.

The first type of approach identifies one key element as the cause of gender inequality and the changes in it. In early feminist theory this approach was common although the selection of key element varied widely, including women's confinement to the domestic (Rosaldo 1974), heterosexuality (MacKinnon 1989), sexual violence (Brownmiller 1976), reproduction (Firestone 1974), a domestic mode of production (Delphy 1984), and the sexual division of labour (Bergmann 1986). However, all such models have intrinsic problems in that with only one causal element they are unable to theorize variations and changes in gender relations. There has been criticism of such simple models as being reductionist, even essentialist (Segal 1987; Spellman 1988). These approaches to gender often have difficulty theorizing the differences between women and the intersection of gender with other inequalities (Mohanty 1991; Mirza 1997). There have also been criticisms of the level of abstraction of this type of approach, its use of the concept of social structure and system which were assumed to neglect agency (Barrett and Phillips 1992; Pollert 1996). For some writers even the concept of agency was considered too essentializing, leading to further fragmentation in the focus on performance (Butler 1990).

Despite these criticisms, the practice of identifying a single major base to explain gender inequality re-emerges in the work of many contemporary mainline social theorists. Some of these approaches combine an approach that has a single base explaining gender relations with a different base explaining class relations and further bases for other forms of social relations (Esping-Andersen 1990, 1999; Yuval-Davis 2006). For example, Yuval-Davis in her (2006) work on intersectionality argues that each strand of unequal social relations has a different but single ontological base: 'the ontological basis of each of these divisions is autonomous, and each prioritizes different spheres of social relations' (2006: 200). This approach segregates the bases of each of the categories: class is grounded in the economy; gender is a discourse about sexual and biological differences; ethnicity relates to discourses about exclusion and inclusion. The consequence is a relatively simple base-superstructure understanding of each set of social relations, with all of the problems that were identified in earlier versions of this style of explanatory approach.

A similar re-emergence of a base-superstructure model is found in modernization theory as applied to gender relations (Giddens 1992; Beck and Beck-Gernseim 1994; Castells 1997; Inglehart and Norris 2003; Therborn 2004). In this approach economic development is seen to increase women's employment which in turn erodes the traditional family form and then all other forms of gender inequality. There is a holistic conceptualization of a social system in which gender is an integral part – changes in one part lead to changes in the others. The process is seen as common to all advanced industrialized or post-industrial societies, with little recognition of variations in the forms of gender relations.

In rejection of this approach, others prioritized the analysis of the differences in gender relations, in particular, by seeking to identify and analyse neglected groups at the intersection of multiple inequalities (Crenshaw 1991; Anthias and Yuval-Davis 1992; Bhopal 1997; Mirza 1997; Medaglia 2000; Lykke 2004). One route to achieve this is to focus on a more micro level in order to capture agency, performance, subjectification, and the specificity of the experiences of women from different classes and ethnicities. The differences under scrutiny became especially those of the intersection of gender with ethnicity, racialization, and nation, though there were exceptions such as Skeggs (1997) with an interest in gender and class, and McClintock (1995) who examined the intersection of sexuality, ethnicity, and gender. This focus on specific groups at the point of intersection has often, but not always, been associated with the use of case studies and ethnographic and narrative methods of enquiry (Prins 2006). There has been a tendency, but not an inevitability, to prioritize subjectivity and lived experience (Skeggs 1997; Acker 2000).

A number of limitations to this body of work can be identified. One of the tendencies of these studies of specific groups of women in minoritized ethnic and racialized groups was to focus on the concept of identity. This focus on the 'identity' of specific groups has a tendency to over-stabilize the category (Fuss 1989; Felski 1997; Squires 1999). There has been a tendency to seek out ever smaller finer units for analysis, in pursuit of a pure intersecting category that does not contain further differences (McCall 2005). However, this is of course impossible, since all groups will always be mixed already (Jakobsen 1998). With such a micro approach it is hard to address larger questions such as those involving a global horizon (Benhabib 1999) or large-scale institutions such as states and other policy making entities such as the EU, while the prioritization of subjectivity and lived experience has tended to be at the expense of social structure (Risman 2004). In addition there is a tendency to cultural reductionism alongside a reductionism to a micro level, leaving out the economic and political constitution of identities and practices and the use of rather static and essentializing identity categories. The doxa of difference overwhelms the analysis of commonalities (Felski 1997). While the micro is relevant it is but one of the levels: reductionism to just one level to the exclusion of the meso (e.g. segregation) and the macro is to be avoided (Ferree and Hall 1996). Despite these difficulties, these studies provide rich thick descriptions of the variety of women's lives and experiences though not explanations.

The third approach uses a more abstract concept of difference, rejecting the strategy of developing categories, rejecting any conceptions of gender relations as systems, and rejecting large-scale theorization, generalizations, modernism, and metanarratives (Butler 1990; Barrett and Phillips 1992; Braidotti 1994). This approach draws on poststructuralism (Foucault 1997), deconstructionism (Derrida 1976), and postmodernism (Deleuze and Guattari 1987). The theoretical project is to radically destabilize all analytic categories on the grounds (Staunæs 2003) that they are not only never adequate representations of the world, but are indeed also potentially pernicious in their potential to sediment these categories in practice. One example of this approach was the development of the metaphor of 'nomad' to privilege the crossing of borders rather than staying within them (Braidotti 1994). However, such a radical deconstruction and destabilization of categories makes substantive analysis, which requires distinctions between categories, rather hard (Felski 1997). Categories need some stabilization, in a strategic way, in order to be useable for analysis (Sayer 1997; McCall 2005). This approach makes its contribution as a critique of some aspects of other approaches, but itself is not a sufficient basis for social science investigations.

The way forward is a middle way between a single base and the dispersal of gender relations. This means developing a model that includes a limited number of key elements. This approach rejects the reduction of gender relations to a single base or to a micro level of identity, as well as the dispersal and fragmentation of the analysis of gender. Earlier attempts to build such a model include the gendered welfare state regime literature, and Connell (1987, 2002) as well as Walby (1990, 1994b, 1997, 2004a).

Debates on the gendered welfare state regime involved a model of gender relations that in some ways went beyond one element. A key focus was on the duality of the family-welfare state relationship to produce distinctive varieties of male breadwinner regimes. The extent of welfare provision, especially for care, was seen as central to the form of the family since state care enabled women's employment. This was supported by a dominant ideology that was aligned with the different forms. In Lewis (1992) there are differences in the extent to which there is a 'male breadwinner-female housewife' model, ranging from 'strong male breadwinner' and 'modified male breadwinner' to 'weak male breadwinner' (sometimes referred to as 'dual earner'). Ireland is taken as most typical of the strong male breadwinner model (Lewis 1992), with Britain sometimes being included (Lewis 1992), while others, such as Germany, are seen as modified male breadwinner (Lewis 1993). Sweden is seen to follow a weak male breadwinner model (Lewis 1992) and sometimes dual earner.

Despite the ostensible inclusion of more elements, so potentially enabling an escape from the problems of 'base superstructure' models, in practice the model assumed alignment between the nature of the family and state welfare provision, which along with an accompanying ideology jointly shaped the remainder of gender relations. Hence there was in practice a single driver of difference – the extent of state welfare provision.

There have been multiple revisions to the model, several of which made further nuanced distinctions within the form of the family/welfare-state nexus. One was to distinguish between women's family role as wives or as mothers, leading to three types of welfare state support to women: as wives, mothers, or workers (Sainsbury 1996). Related to this are distinctions between the state resourcing of care as a service, as money to purchase services, or as money for time at home; and distinctions between care and unpaid work since care-work may be paid, thus leading to three distinctions – Who cares? Who pays? How much is provided (Jenson 1997)? A further addition was to include the regulation of the labour market, the significance of feminist movements, and state actions in relation to contraception, abortion, and sexual expression (O'Connor et al. 1999). Another approach to the issue included an assessment of the outcome for women (Hobson 1994), for example, as to whether the gender welfare regime provides 'the capacity for a woman to form and maintain an autonomous household' (Orloff 1993: 319).

One of the simultaneous strengths and weaknesses of this literature on gendered welfare state regimes is its relatively narrow focus. On the one hand the tightness of the focus has assisted the development of the field, by providing conditions that will facilitate the cumulation rather than the dissipation of knowledge. On the other hand there are many aspects of gender relations that are not included, or are included in only marginal ways (Adams and Padamsee 2001), not least because of a tendency to focus on issues of primary concern to working mothers (Brush 2002). Some of the most important omissions are labour market regulations (Walby 1997, 1999a, 1999b), democracy, and gender-based violence. A further problem with the gendered welfare state regime approach has been a tendency to reify, even essentialize, the differences between countries with different gendered welfare state regimes, and to underestimate the theoretical significance of more general processes that may affect them, especially those of economic development and globalization.

An alternative approach to the analysis of systems of gender relations is to start by engaging with all the key dimensions of gender, not only those focused on the welfare state. In parallel and independently, both Walby (1986, 1990, 1997, 2004a) and Connell (1987, 1990,

1995, 2002) developed such models. In both cases it is the plurality of such key elements that provides the potential to theorize variations in the forms taken by the gender system. Connell's (2002) 'gender order' 'of a society' contains four structures: production relations, power, emotional relations especially sexuality, and symbolic relations. For Connell, each social institution contains a specific gender regime. In work on masculinity, Connell (1995) differentiates between different forms of masculinity, in particular the splitting and then replacement of the old form of hegemonic masculinity of the gentry by a new hegemonic form and the emergence of a series of subordinated and marginalized masculinities. However, this richly detailed account of these diverse forms makes little analytic use of the four structures and instead deploys a different conceptual repertoire. The result is that the account is more descriptive than explanatory, as Connell (1995: 186) notes, 'only a sketch of a vastly complex history'. The strengths of Connell's analysis lie in including a wider range of elements than are found in the gendered welfare state debate; however, these are not systematically used to develop an explanation of variations in the form of the gender order.

In the model developed here, there are four levels or modes of abstraction. The most abstract level is that of gender regime, by which is meant a system of gender relations which is analytically separate from other regimes of inequality.

At the second level, distinctions are made between different forms and different varieties of gender regime. Gender regimes take both domestic and public forms, distributed along a continuum between these two poles. In the domestic form of gender regime, women are more confined to the domestic arena than in the public form. Within the public form of gender regime, there is a further distinction between neoliberalism and social democratic varieties, distributed along a continuum (there may be further varieties, but these are not discussed here). The neoliberal variety of gender regime is more unequal and less democratic than the social democratic one.

Third, distinctions are made between the gender relations in each of the major institutional domains: economic (divided, in industrial countries, into market and household); polity (including states, transnational bodies such as the EU, and organized religions); violence (including gender-based violence, militias, and armies); and civil society (including social movements, sexuality, and knowledge-institutions). These institutional domains are not exclusive to the gender regime, rather multiple sets of social relations are to be found in each domain. Different forms of gender relations may be found in each of the institutional domains. The change from a domestic to a public form may take place at different rates and times in the different domains. Such uneven development is to be expected, despite the tendency for these domains to coevolve towards alignment, since this tendency is likely to be interrupted before it is completed. Gender relations are constituted in each of these four major domains; there is no single privileged domain. This is part of what is meant by the ontological depth of the gender regime.

Fourth, distinctions are made between gender relations at meso and micro levels in more finely grained social practices, ranging from occupational segregation to the production of the self. At this more empirical level, the intersection with other sets of social relations is important in constituting particular empirically identifiable practices. Gender relations are constituted in all levels of abstraction and in all domains.

A gender regime is constituted in all institutional domains (economy, polity, violence, and civil society) and is not reducible to just one base. It is constituted at all levels of abstraction: micro, meso, and macro. This is what is meant by the ontological depth of the gender regime. The relationship between levels is best understood as one of emergent effects. As the form of gender relations changes at any or all of these levels, so do the conceptions as to what constitutes women and men and the perceptions of what might constitute their cultural, political, and economic preferences and projects. There are significant variations in the form of gender regimes due to development over time, path dependent development, intersection with other systems, and international influences. A gender regime is best regarded as a multilevel macro level concept, for example different countries may have different gender regimes.

There is an important distinction between the domestic and public form, the premodern and modern, forms of gender regime. In the domestic form of gender regime women are relatively confined to the domestic sphere of the household; in the public form women are not so confined but can enter the public sphere of employment, education, and polity. In the domestic gender regime the technologies of power are predominantly exclusionary, excluding women from locations and relations of influence; in the public gender regime they are segregationary, allowing women into the public sphere but limiting their operations there. These forms of social relations apply both to the regime as a whole and to gender relations in each of the specific institutional domains. In the economy of the domestic gender regime women's labour is not free wage labour, but is organized instead under tied non-market relations in the household; in the public gender regime women's labour is organized as free wage labour. During the transition both forms occur. In the polity of the domestic gender regime women are only rarely present in the formal institutions of political power, such as parliaments, cabinets, and the governing bodies of organized religions; in the public gender regime women are present in these institutions. Within the domain of violence in the gender regime there are few fully modern examples, in that many states do not yet have a complete monopoly of legitimate violence in a given territory since violence against women is rarely fully criminalized. Insofar as there has been a movement from a domestic to a public form of gender regime in the domain of violence, it is possible to identify more neoliberal forms in which there is little polity or civil societal intervention against violence against women, and more social democratic forms in which there is much greater polity and civil societal intervention. The actual level of violence is affected by the articulation of the gender regime with other regimes of inequality and the institutional legacy in the violence domain. In the civil society of the domestic gender regime women's sexuality is confined to marriage and women are excluded from influential positions in cultural institutions; in the public gender regime sexuality is not confined to marriage and women are engaged in cultural institutions.

In most of the developed world there is a tendency towards a transformation of the gender regime from a domestic to a public form. In most countries the transition to the public form of the gender regime from the domestic form is not yet fully complete. This means, for example, that the premodern form in which domestic labour was the basis of a person's livelihood is still present to a limited extent and that the state does not yet have a complete monopoly of legitimate violence in its territory. It is possible for this to go into reverse, with movement from a public towards a domestic gender regime, but this is uncommon. While there is some unevenness in the transition to the public form of gender regime across the domains nevertheless there is an important clustering of forms, indicative of the coevolution of these domains.

This clustering of the public forms of institutional domains can be seen empirically across a range of domains. In a public gender regime women are more likely to be in free wage labour, to be in parliament, to be in education, and to be able to access legal abortion than in a domestic gender regime. Using a data set of around a hundred countries, a statistically significant correlation is found between all of women's free wage labour, women's presence in parliament, women's educational enrolment, and the legality of abortion. This means that where one of these practices is found, the others are likely to be present as well. These aspects of public gender regime cluster together. (Table 8.12 in the next chapter shows this correlation.)

A second distinction is that between forms of public or modern gender regimes. There is more than one way of addressing the varieties of modern gender regimes. In the gendered welfare state regime literature discussed above there is an underlying assumption that differences in the form of the family (breadwinner or dual earner) are predominantly influenced by differences in the extent to which the state provides welfare, which enables women to enter employment. However, this account can be challenged in at least two main ways. First, there are countries where women have high rates of employment without state welfare, such as the USA. Second, there are significant changes over time within countries. In order to meet these challenges it is necessary to differentiate more fully between the different components of the gender regime, as in the model of the gender regime argued for here.

While the gender modernization school (Beck 1992; Giddens 1992; Inglehart 1997; Inglehart and Norris 2003) theorizes differences in gender relations as stemming almost entirely from differences in the level of development, the gendered welfare state regime school theorizes differences in gender relations as stemming almost entirely from deeply sedimented institutional differences between countries.

Here it is not a case of one or the other, but rather both: the level of development and differences in the paths of development matter, including the intersection and coevolution of the gender regime with other regimes of inequality and systems of social relations. These divergent paths of development are often established at critical turning points or tipping points and the subsequent coevolution of different social systems. Such critical turning points arise as a consequence of the struggles between social forces, especially those that involve and have consequences for the state or polity. These social forces include not a single set of interests, but an intersection of class, gender, and ethnic forces. They may be domestic in scope or involve regional or global influences, stemming from global flows, waves, networks, or polities, and involving regimes of inequality from elsewhere. The gender regime intersects and coevolves with other regimes of inequality, other social systems. These regimes of inequality form the environment within which the gender regimes develop. This relationship with other regimes may take various forms. The different regimes may be tightly or loosely coupled (this may vary by institutional domain), they may be co-equal in significance or asymmetrical (this may vary by institutional domain). The form of the gender regime varies not only between countries but between different ethnic, racial, and national groups within a country (Walby 1990; Bhopal 1997; Medaglia 2000).

Different routes during the transformation of the gender regime from a domestic to a public form may lead to different varieties of public gender regime. There is no single simple form of public gender regime, but a continuum from the neoliberal to the social democratic. The neoliberal and social democratic distinction is not confined to class analysis but is relevant to other regimes of inequality as well, including that of gender. The location on the neoliberal-social democratic continuum may vary between the different domains of economy, polity, violence, and civil society, and while there is a tendency to move towards alignment this may be far from complete.

Within the economic domain in the gender regime the most important distinction is that between neoliberal and social democratic forms of employment relations and state welfare provision. Employment relations may be democratically regulated to promote gender equality or may not. The state may provide welfare or it may not. It is possible to identify examples of countries at different ends of the neoliberal-social democratic continuum in the domain of the economy. The USA is an example of the neoliberal form where the provision of the services necessary to support women in employment takes place through market mechanisms, with childcare and other services purchased on the market. The high rates of female employment there cannot be attributed to high levels of state social provision, contrary to the assumptions of the male breadwinner model. By contrast, at the social democratic end of the continuum is Sweden together with the other Nordic countries (Norway, Finland, and Denmark) in which the development of public services especially but not only to provide childcare gave women the capacity to increase their paid employment. There are also many countries in between. For example, the UK has levels of state welfare that are on the neoliberal side of average, while as a member of the EU it has high levels of social democratic equality regulations in employment.

The polity is particularly important in entrenching different paths of development. This is because the form and institutions of the state can be deeply sedimented and have effects long after the moment at which the form of institutions was forged. A key part of this is whether democracy is deep or shallow for gender relations. This is not often at the same depth as for other regimes of inequality. In particular presence democracy varies significantly by regime, often being achieved much later for gender than for class.

Some institutional domains in the gender regime move towards the public form more quickly than others. The extent to which this is the case varies between countries. In several cases the economy is the first domain to shift towards a more public form, with an increase in women's employment before any changes in other domains. In other cases, changes take place in different domains at the same time (the reasons for this and the implications involved are investigated in the chapters comparing the transitions in four countries). In particular, the significance of the gender democratization of the polity is of key importance.

Gender regimes are also shaped by their intersection with regimes of inequality in other countries. There are international and regional influences on the development of the gender regime in any one country. These influences can take many forms – from the effects of regional and global hegemons such as the EU and USA, to global civil societal and political waves. There are important international influences associated with globalization that can affect the form of the gender regime in different countries. These include emergent global institutions, global hegemons, networks, and waves. Global civil society and political waves have been important in the movement of ideas and political practices from one part of the world to others.

The gender regime has ontological depth: it should be neither reduced to a single base, nor dispersed in a rejection of categories, and it has different levels of abstraction that are linked through emergence. Gender is constituted in four major institutional domains: economy, polity, violence, and civil society. While there is some cohesion and movement towards alignment, this is rarely if ever complete. There are significant variations in the form of gender regime, not only a distinction between domestic and public forms but also between different forms of public gender regime, including neoliberal and social democratic forms.

Ethnic Regimes

Ethnicity is not an absolute; it is only meaningful as a social relation between ethnic groups. Ethnic groups usually perceive themselves as sharing a common descent and heritage (Smith 1986) in contrast to other types of groups. Ethnic relations are complex inequalities involving both difference and inequality, often in contested proportions (Taylor et al. 1994). There is usually a positive valuation of the culture of each ethnic group, even when this is associated with inequality and exploitation by another ethnic group. Residential segregation is an example of this, in that it often involves both a positive valuation of living together as a community with their own practices even if it also means a lower standard of living and is partially the result of discrimination by other ethnic groups (Wilson 1987; Wieviorka 1995). The minoritization of some ethnic groups is an active process and not pregiven (Omi and Winant 1994), and involves the economy, polity, violence, and civil society, even though dominant ethnic groups will often treat themselves as the norm without an ethnicity (Kumar 2000). There can be many ethnic divisions in a country and not just one regime of ethnic inequality. This multiplicity of ethnic regimes is unlike class and gender regimes where there is a primary or singular division.

As in the analysis of other regimes of inequality there is a tendency in the analysis of ethnicity to flatten the ontology, which should be resisted in favour of investigating its full depth in economy, polity, violence, and civil society. One important attempt to theorize ethnic inequality uses the concept of identity (Taylor 1989; Hall 1996) which has been extended to other inequalities and especially gender (Young 2000). The concept of identity has a broad intellectual heritage. It was introduced and developed within symbolic interactionism, where the focus is on the negotiation of meaning in social interaction (Goffman 1969). It has been interpreted and developed using Foucauldian notions of discourse and the Derridian concept of difference (Hall 1996). The concept often rests implicitly or explicitly on the notion of a community as the social that supports the identity (Kymlicka 1991, 1995). Substantively the concept has been developed in analyses of a wide range of non-class phenomena, including ethnicity and post-colonialism (Hall 1996), nation and gender. This concept of identity can include the notion of a social constituency coming to see itself as an identifiable group and developing a perception of a set of common interests (Grossberg 1996). However, sometimes the analysis of this process is truncated, with an assumption that the interests on which any identified constituency would act are obvious. In some ways this is parallel to the Marxist analysis of a class in itself becoming a class for itself, in which some writers address each step in the process while others use merely a shorthand summary. Such truncated analyses miss important parts of the process which may have a variety of alterative outcomes, since it is not in fact obvious how a particular social constituency should identify let alone advance its interests. If each step is performed in the analysis then a full ontology will be utilized, but a shortcut is likely to lead to a flattened ontology disproportionately emphasizing culture.

A strength of the concept of identity for the analysis of complex inequalities is its flexibility to engage with any social constituency that produces an identity, especially one that might produce a basis for social action. However, this flexibility is a weakness since it entails a vague and perhaps elusive and amorphous concept (Brubaker and Cooper 2000). It also has a weakness in that it contains an implicit or explicit assumption of homogeneity within the identified group – this is always mistaken. It is also hard to analyse cross-cutting inequalities using the concept of identity even though there is a need to address intersectionality which may be either additive (e.g. a double disadvantage in employment) or mutually constitutive (e.g. gender and ethnicity produce very different outcomes). It is hard to address such a plurality using the concept of identity since it implicitly or explicitly (Castells 1997) accords priority to a single dimension. It is ironic that a concept that has been important in ensuring the significance of non-class forms of social relations in social theory has itself a problem when it comes to engaging with the plural and cross-cutting nature of these relations. The use of the concept of identity tends to lead to a cultural reductionism, to flatten the ontology. It is a mirror image of the problem facing Marxist analysis. It may well be that sophisticated users of the concept (e.g. Grossberg 1996) do make distinctions between the identification of the category, the process of developing shared values, and the practice of a shared political project, but others do not. They conflate these processes assuming that politics can be read off from identity. The deployment of the concept of identity may lack or leave unspecified any link to wider macro concerns and thus any macro theoretical framework within which identities are to be analysed. A theory of social changes, of the linkages between domains, is a necessary ambition.

In conclusion, the concept of identity has been a productive way of bringing the range of complex inequalities beyond class into mainstream social theory. Its weakness can lie in its shallow culturalist ontology and a lack of ambition as to its relationship with macro social change, although specific applications overcome these potential weaknesses. Ethnic regimes of inequality have ontological depth, just as class and gender regimes do. The tendency to prioritize the cultural level in contemporary social theory of ethnic relations, using the concept of 'identity' (Hall 1996) and a focus on music, food, and clothing, among other cultural symbols (Gilroy 1993) at the expense of economy, polity, and violence, should be resisted as is argued below.

The economy is involved in the constitution of ethnic relations in many ways. Slavery cannot be understood without an analysis of its economic dimension, nor the development of English and US capitalism without an analysis of slavery. The economic exploitation of African slaves was a key part of the early accumulation of capital that underpinned the Industrial Revolution in England, providing cheap cotton for mill owners and cheap sugary food for workers (Walvin 1992). Free wage labour for minoritized ethnic groups can develop later than for dominant ethnic groups, as in the case of slavery in the USA. Different ethnicities then make the transition to modernity at different times. Ethnic relations in employment often involve the disadvantaging of minority ethnic groups to the advantage of the majority ethnic group (Wilson 1987; Phizacklea 1990). Industrial and occupational segregation by ethnicity is part of the process by which ethnic inequality is produced in the economy and beyond (McCall 2001). Migration for employment opportunities restructures ethnic relations in the host country (Hochschild 2000); post-colonialism as well as colonialism has an economic as well as a cultural dimension.

The polity is important in structuring ethnic relations. Empires usually have an ethnic dimension in their structures of subordination. In the current world, the polity allows or sanctions discrimination and abuse or does not, and this includes policing. States are also a target for ethnic projects, especially when these are aligned with national projects seeking a state of their own (Smith 1986). Ethnic relations affect the extent to which the state is used to provide welfare or not and the forms this takes (Quadagno 1994, 2006), underpinning national and nation-state projects (Smith 1986). The passions associated with ethnicity are major drivers of political movements and processes, especially when they overlap with other social divisions such as religion, nation, or class. State and polity formation involve not only class but also gender and ethnicity. Ethnicity is a key component of many national projects and therefore of state formation. The European Union was formed as a reaction to the excesses of nationalism and ethnic cleansing of the fascist era. Organized religions are key polities. War often has an ethnic, national, and religious component, not only class; terrorism even more so. Political upheavals will usually, rather than rarely, include passions related to ethnicity, nation, and religion that can alter the course of these events. Struggles for national independence focus on nation and restructure class relations. Major cleavages in current world politics focus on Islamic/Western tensions with hot spots along Palestinian/Israeli boundaries. Today conflicts over relations between the UK and the EU bitterly divide political parties in the UK. Politics in a global era are not reducible to class, but involve nation, ethnicity, and religion at the very least.

Ethnic relations may be partially constituted through the deployment and regulation of violence (Wieviorka 1995). Violence was an essential part of the institution of slavery (Walvin 1992), genocide (Bauman 1989), ethnic cleansing (Mann 2005), and lynching (Shapiro 1988), and everyday harassment may be included here. Violence is not only a consequence of ethnic divisions, but may also exacerbate such divisions where they have been in abeyance, as for example in the Balkans region.

Ethnic relations are constituted at the macro, meso, and micro levels, however the analysis of ethnic relations has tended to prioritize the meso level, such as segregation (Ferree and Hall 1996). It is better to include all levels, indeed without a macro level colonialism could be left out of focus. The analysis needs both agency and structure: there is a need to find a balance between a tendency to over-stabilize the categories and to de-stabilize, thus making a comparative empirical analysis very difficult. The conceptualization of processes of minoritization and racialization (Omi and Winant 1994) adds a temporal dimension to the analysis.

Regimes of ethnic inequality have always been shaped by global processes, including empires, colonialism, and de-colonization, as well as in the current global era (Rex 1973; Walvin 1992; Therborn 1995). These processes leave a legacy of enduring effects on the shape of migration and ethnic inequality in the former colonial powers as well as the rest of the world (Castles and Miller 2003). Global flows of people, in voluntary and forced migration, have long been important in the restructuring of ethnic relations not least as diaspora (Cohen 1997). The forced migration of peoples from Africa to slavery in the Americas was a key part of this process which left its mark in the ethnic inequalities in the USA and beyond. The current development of globalization is not unique in this respect, though it increases the speed and scale of these movements. The phenomenon of temporary migration for education, refuge, and employment, for example global care chains (Hochschild 2000), and short periods of travel for tourism and leisure, provide the occasion for the further complex mobilities that restructure ethnic relations (Urry 2007). Post-colonial social relations invoke ethnicity and the global. Regimes of ethnic inequality intrinsically involve global processes, either as part of their legacy or in their current restructuring.

Regimes of ethnic inequality vary in the extent to which they are neoliberal or social democratic. This shares similar features with class and gender regimes as well as with some that are either specific to or more important for ethnicity. In the economy there is greater employment regulation for equality and greater state welfare in social democracy as compared with neoliberalism. In the polity there is a greater depth of democracy, including the presence of minoritized ethnicities in governing institutions in social democracy. In social democracy violence against minoritized ethnic groups is more criminalized and less common, while they are not subject to disproportionately harsh sanctions from the criminal justice system. In social democracy civil society is more plural, less dominated by a single ethnic value system, and less segregated by ethnicity.

The intersection between different regimes of ethnic inequality takes different forms, including assimilation, cosmopolitanism, and hybridity. The Chicago School found that there was a shift over time among migrant groups towards assimilation into the practices of the dominant ethnic group in Chicago (Park and Burgess 1925).

However, this is not a universal pattern. An intersection of ethnicities may mean a mutual adaptation of these complex adaptive systems rather than one way. The concept of hybridity is used to invoke the new forms that arise from the conjoining of two or more old forms, where there is either symmetry between the two forms or at least the incomplete dominance of the more powerful form. Hybridity is used by Gilroy (1993) to capture the contribution of African and American cultures, especially in relation to music, in his notion of the Black Atlantic. White culture is changed, not only the minority Black culture. Hybridity can be more than the sum of already existing parts being something new, formed not just from the addition of existing elements but also by their transformation during the process of fusion. The concept of hybridity works because it can evoke the notion of previously existing boundaries as well as change; without boundaries as predecessors there is no point to the concept of hybridity (Nederveen Pieterse 2001). A further model is that of cosmopolitanism (Held 1995). In other instances ethnic boundaries are not eroded but rather are maintained or even enhanced, especially if aligned with other group signifiers such as religion and language and when in association with the development of nations and nationalism in conflictual and contested social settings (Anderson 1983; Hobsbawm and Ranger 1983; Smith 1986).

Ethnic relations are not reducible to other inequalities, although they are significantly shaped by an intersection and coevolution with other regimes of inequality. Ethnicity sometimes intersects and overlaps variously with 'race', nationality, and religion. As a consequence of different histories, in Europe the mutual constitution of ethnicity and nation is marked, while in the USA the focus is more often on ethnicity and 'race'. An alignment of ethnicity with nation, state, and religion has often been sought not least within the project of the nation-state. The political and sometimes violent and militarized struggles around such projects of alignment can constitute important critical turning points as a consequence of the sedimentation of the outcome of these struggles in new state institutions. Regimes of ethnic inequality coevolve with class and gender regimes of inequality – they mutually adapt, albeit in asymmetrical ways. The intersection of ethnic relations with class (Rex 1973; Miles 1989), gender (Crenshaw 1991; Collins 1998), and other sets of social relations including sexuality (McClintock 1995) is important. Some analyses of intersections with class relations will prioritize an economic dimension (Wilson 1987), but not always (Walvin 1992; Omi and Winant 1994). Contestations at their points of intersection are crucial in understanding the critical turning points to different paths of development.

Further Regimes of Complex Inequalities

There are many different forms of complex inequalities. These can be specified in a number of different ways. In the EU gender and ethnicity, disability, belief/religion, age, and sexual orientation are all deemed sufficiently important inequalities to be subject to legal (EU) regulation. The EU Charter of Fundamental Rights (2000) lists seven additional grounds – social origin, genetic features, language, political or other opinion, membership of a national minority, property, and birth – though these have not been currently activated in EU legislation.

Each of these regimes of inequality has ontological depth in the sense that it is constituted in the institutional domains of economy, polity, violence, and civil society, and at macro, meso, and micro levels. Each regime takes all other regimes as its environment and adapts to this. This is not, however, an argument that they are symmetrical in their mutual impacts.

In this section just two examples out of the many further regimes of inequality are described to illustrate such analyses: disability and sexual orientation.

Disability

Disability is sometimes primarily considered as a medical matter concerning impaired bodies and as having little to do with society. However, the implications of a physical impairment for social relations depend on the social environment: this is not best understood as individualized in a person's body. The environment may be enabling or disabling. An impaired body is only disabled if the environment is disabling. For example, with contact lenses a person with poor eyesight is not visually disabled and with appropriate modifications to buildings and working environments many people with impairments are not disabled. Whether or not an environment is disabling is key to the question as to the extent of social inequality associated with physical (or mental) impairment (Barnes et al. 1999; Swain et al. 2004).

Disability is an inequality, though it may be considered a difference in some contexts. A reduction in inequality is often associated with the development of specific targeted policies rather than the convention of equal treatment.

Disability is constituted in all four institutional domains. There is an economic dimension: a disabling environment may mean that people with impairments have difficulty earning a good income while economic resources are needed to ensure that an environment is not disabling. Disability has a political dimension: access to political power affects whether the economic resources required are made available to produce a less disabling environment. Disability has a violence component: disabled people have an increased vulnerability to violence from others. Disability has a civil society dimension: the meaning of disability is highly contested and the development of a social movement by and for the disabled has challenged old meanings and generated new ones, not least in shifting the concern from the individual medicalized body to the disabling social environment with consequences for politics and the distribution of resources (Swain et al. 2004).

Environments are highly varied as to whether they are disabling or enabling. In some cases more resources and technologies are made available at higher levels of economic development, but this is not a simple relationship. A neoliberal regime is associated with greater differentiation of provision of a less disabling environment linked to the possession of economic resources than is the case in a social democratic regime.

Sexual orientation

Sexual orientation is a location of both difference and inequality. It can be a positively valued difference as well as a location of discrimination and stigmatization. The balance between difference and inequality varies significantly over time and between social locations.

Sexual orientation is a regime of inequality that is analysed here as socially constituted, though it has sometimes been analysed more as a matter of biology. There is a tendency to reduce the construction of sexual preference to the civil societal or cultural level. However, it is better analysed as a regime of complex inequality with ontological depth. The civil societal level is important as there are negotiated and highly contested meanings: social movements have been important in creating changes to the meaning and implications of being gay, lesbian, or bisexual. However, the institutional domains of economy, polity, and violence are also significant in structuring sexual preferences and opportunities. The economic domain partly structures sexuality: there can be discrimination in employment and in access to resources. There can be difficulties in making partnership arrangements to set up a common household, to share and pass on entitlements to housing tenure and survivors' rights in pensions. There are increased risks of interpersonal violence and harassment against gay and lesbian people, an increased, though varying, risk of being the target of violence from those who are homophobic. The polity is important in the regulation of discrimination in the economy, in the legal standing of partnerships, and homophobic violence. There are variations in the extent to which gay and lesbian sexuality can be openly practised, free from harassment (Plummer 1975; Richardson 2000; Weeks et al. 2001).

Intersections with other complex inequalities can have mutual effects. There are significant aspects to the mutual adaptation of sexuality and gender. The existence of lesbian and gay sexuality challenges some traditional assumptions about gender relations, especially those regarding the 'naturalness' of heterosexuality. This is most strongly argued in queer theory (Seidman 1996). However, a mutual adaptation of practices of gender and sexuality is only ever partial and never reaches full co-constitution.

Sexual orientation and disability are two examples of several forms of regimes of complex inequalities. They are best analysed as having ontological depth rather than as reduced or ontologically flattened to a single base. There are variations in the forms of these regimes, associated not only with the level of economic development but also with different paths or trajectories of development.

Intersecting Regimes of Complex Inequality

Regimes of complex inequality while having different temporal and spatial reach do intersect at points in the same temporal and spatial location. The regimes coexist, do not saturate the space, and are usually non-nested. At these points of intersection regimes of complex inequality adapt to each other. This adaptation of regimes is often asymmetric; there can be imbalances of power and effectivity and some regimes will have less developed institutional domains than others. Intersecting regimes may be at different levels of development to and through modernity, even though they inhabit the same territory at the same time. This analysis goes beyond the traditional approaches to intersectionality outlined in Chapter 2, beyond reductionism to a single master system such as capitalism or to a cultural micro level as in much identity theory, beyond the rejection of categories and beyond segregationary reductionism (Esping-Andersen 1990; Crenshaw 1991; Taylor et al. 1994; McCall 2005; Yuval-Davis 2006).

Regimes of complex inequality coexist in the same territory – they do not saturate a space but rather overlap, often in a non-nested form. The forms of dispersion are varied: women are dispersed across households; ethnic groups are often residentially clustered in relatively segregated areas, but may be dispersed as diaspora across countries; capital is expanding and deepening with globalization.

Regimes of complex inequality have different temporal and spatial reach. The domestic gender regime has had a very long temporal duration and a very wide, near global, spatial reach. By comparison capitalism is more recent and has had a shorter duration. It is expanding, but not yet fully global. Regimes of ethnic relations are very varied in their duration and spatial reach: many contemporary forms developed during the period of empires and have continued, restructured, in post-colonial locations. The spatial and temporal boundaries between types of regimes can take varied forms. They may sometimes be sharp (for example, state frontiers or critical turning points) and at other times they may be more gradual or uneven.

Regimes of complex inequality can intersect and mutually adapt during their coevolution in a changing global environment. Each regime takes all other regimes and social systems as its environment. As regimes of inequality coevolve in a changing global fitness landscape they will have mutual effects on each other. The complexity approach provides a conceptual vocabulary that better enables the analysis of the intersection of multiple regimes of inequality. It does not a priori make claims as to the nature of this intersection, instead it leaves open the question as to the nature of the intersection for empirical enquiry.

In this intersection regimes of complex inequality are rarely coequal. Often one regime may be more significant than another, though this is rarely overwhelming. Rather there are complex asymmetrical intersections between regimes as each regime takes all others as its environment. This asymmetry has at least two aspects, the influence of each regime and the extent to which institutional domains in a regime are thinly or extensively populated by practices.

The way in which regimes may have different levels of influence can be illustrated by an example of the accommodation and tension between capitalism and the gender regime. While this has sometimes been assumed to be one of continuous harmonious accommodation (Hartmann 1976), it is better understood as sometimes being one of tension and conflict. There can be conflict between capital and husbands over the deployment of women's labour, either in the home or in the factory (Walby 1986). There is a tendency for an expanding capitalist regime to catalyse a shift from a domestic towards a more public form as a consequence of the demand by employers for labour, including that of women. A further example is that of the relative significance of the dynamics of class and ethnic regimes of

273

complex inequality. There is also an issue as to the extent to which capitalism is the dominant system (Rex 1973; Wilson 1978) and the extent to which there are mutual effects, especially through the implications of slavery and the colonial relationship on the development of Western capitalism up until the present day (Walvin 1992).

A slightly different approach to this question of the relationship between regimes of inequality is that regarding the extent of the development of practices in the institutional domains associated with each regime. In some intersecting regimes there is a dense development of practices in some institutional domains, while in others this may be thinner. An example is Gottfried's (2000) analysis of the intersection in terms of a gender contract that is embedded in a capitalist system: gender contracts are seen as embedded in capitalism and women are political actors who are shaped, but not entirely subsumed, by capital labour relations. In this analysis the relative importance of capitalism and gender is tilted towards capitalism and perhaps too far. Another example of a treatment of the asymmetrical relationship between regimes of inequality is that of Medaglia's (2000) analysis of the intersection of ethno-national forms of patriarchy in London. Medaglia finds that both English and Italian forms coexist and interact, but that while the English patriarchal system utilizes the full range of social domains, the Italian form involves some institutions from the English system, especially that of education. This means that there is an asymmetric relation between the two systems which contributes to changes in the forms of patriarchy experienced by those younger women who unlike their mothers experience an English rather than Italian education.

The nature of the asymmetric relationship between regimes of inequality is not given a priori in theory; it must be investigated on each occasion.

Regimes of complex inequality that co-habit in the same space do not necessarily have the same level of modernity, or the same trajectory of development. They can be modernized to different extents, and to the extent that they are modern have different positions on the neoliberal-social democratic continuum. While there is some tendency towards alignment as they coevolve this is often interrupted by contesting projects. The extent to which there is an alignment of paths of development through modernity is empirically investigated in Chapter 8 on varieties of modernity.

Much development and modernization theory assumes that the level of development in a country is shared by class, gender, and other social relations, that economic development drives changes in all sets of social relations at the same time (Inglehart and Norris 1997, 2003). This is a mistake. Regimes of complex inequality in the same country rarely share the same level of development of modernity. In particular the modernization of the gender regime is usually much later than that of class or ethnicity. In most countries free wage labour becomes the majority form of labour relations for men long before this is the case for women; men also often gain access to parliamentary representation before women. The temporal gap in the modernization of class and gender relations varies significantly between countries. In some, women entered free wage labour only a few decades after men; in others, it took many decades. In some, winning the right to vote occurred simultaneously for women and men (especially in newly independent countries in recent decades), while in others (especially North America and Europe), there is a gap measuring decades. The temporal gap and sequencing of aspects of modernization between regimes of inequality vary. This has potentially important implications for all the intersecting regimes of inequality as they coevolve in a country. The significance of this different sequencing is explored in the comparative case studies outlined in Chapter 10.

Conclusions

Regimes of complex inequality can be separately identified, even though they affect each other as they intersect. Each regime has ontological depth, being constituted in the institutional domains of the economy, polity, violence, and civil society, and at the macro, meso, and micro levels. Regimes of inequality intersect within each institutional domain and there are usually multiple regimes within each such domain. Within each regime of inequality each institutional domain takes all other systems, including other domains, as its environment, mutually adapting and coevolving. Each regime of inequality takes as its environment all other systems, including all other regimes of inequality. Each intersects and coevolves with the other regimes.

Each complex inequality involves difference and inequality simultaneously. However, the balance between these can vary. In many contemporary Western countries, it is common to see class more as an inequality than a positively valued difference since there is broad consensus that disparities in income and wealth are forms of inequality, than is the case for ethnicity and gender, where the disparities can be positively valued even as they also constitute inequalities.

Each regime of complex inequality is constituted in the institutional domains of civil society, economy, polity, and violence. When addressing class inequalities the most frequent focus has been on the economy, with only a secondary interest in culture and civil society. By contrast, when addressing gender and ethnicity there has been a tendency to theorize culture as the primary location rather than the economy or polity. The argument here is that both are mistaken because these analytic strategies flatten the ontology. Rather all inequalities are partly constituted in each of the economy, polity, violence, and civil society. However, the relationship between the domains can vary somewhat between different regimes.

There is a tendency towards an increased coherence of the institutional domains of economy, polity, violence, and civil society within each regime of inequality. However, this process is rarely completed before it is interrupted. Similarly there is a tendency for regimes of inequality within any given territory to move towards coherence, but this process is also rarely completed before it is interrupted. These moves towards a coherence of institutional domains and regimes of inequality constitute the wider process of societalization. This is a movement towards a coherent society with the alignment of institutional domains and regimes of inequality, but it is rarely completed before being interrupted by another principle of societalization.

There are significant differences between class regimes and between gender regimes, as well as between other regimes of inequality. The sources of difference include not only the extent of modernity, but also path dependent varieties of development and intersections with other regimes of inequality in a changing global fitness landscape. The extent to which regimes of inequality are aligned within a given territory or country varies. Each regime of inequality has a distinct pattern of development which to some extent takes path dependent forms, generating different varieties of these regimes. Each of the domains within a regime may develop at different speeds and to varying forms. These are predominantly along a continuum from neoliberal to social democratic. Different regimes of inequality may have different temporal and spatial reach. Regimes of inequality (for example, class, gender, ethnicity) do not necessarily directly map onto each other in any given territory or country. Whether or not they are aligned with each other is a question rather than something that can be answered a priori.

8 Varieties of Modernity

Introduction

Differences between countries are due not only to the level of development but also to different path dependent trajectories leading to varieties of regimes of inequality.

A challenge to existing accounts of path dependency is to take adequate account of complex inequalities in addition to class. Do varieties of class and gender regimes map onto each other or not?

Most analyses of path dependency have focused on the nexus of political economy conflating employment and welfare. Are varieties of employment regulation and welfare provision the same, or are there distinctions between them? Even more challenging is whether violence constitutes a third type of path dependency which does not map onto that of political economy.

The concept of nexus is used to specify a set of institutions that have been found to be inter-related in order to draw attention to the intersection of a range of institutions that are not conventionally regarded as being clustered in the same domain.

Each of the key concepts is operationalized using indicators that are supported by quantitative data that are available for cross-national comparisons. An indicator is not a direct and full representation of the concept, but merely the best that can be found in the current state of knowledge. It is a sign or representation of the concept being investigated. An indicator may be constituted from several items of information. The data and definitions of several of the indicators in the political economy section have been developed by the OECD (1997a, 2006). However, in the case of most of the gendered distinctions, and the nexus of violence, the indicators are specifically developed here. The definitions of indicators are provided in tables 8.1, 8.13, and 8.17. The locations of the data sources are provided in the Appendix to this chapter while the data are available on Sylvia Walby's web-site.

The unit of comparison is 'country'. This is chosen on pragmatic grounds and is constrained by the available data sources. 'Country' is an empirical category, identified in data sources. It is not the same as the theoretical concept of society. No assumption is made here as to the closeness of the empirical category of country to the theoretical category of society. This is addressed in the more historical and qualitative analysis in Chapter 10.

Comparative data on countries at both a global scale and also a sub-set of the 30 rich countries in the OECD are used to identify and investigate the clusters of countries following specific path dependent trajectories, as well as to discover the extent of more general processes of development. The near global data set is used where possible, but some of the comparative data needed to support some distinctions are only available from the OECD. Using data at a country level unavoidably leaves out of focus certain processes, especially global ones. Chapter 10 compares the trajectories of development in a limited number of countries, bringing into focus political struggles, critical turning points, and positioning in relation to global processes, to explore the temporal development of these phenomena.

This chapter investigates the extent to which there are clusters of countries with the same varieties of modernity by examining correlations. The search for statistically significant correlations is consistent with complexity thinking on coevolution, in that it seeks to identify associations without the presumption of a one-way causal direction that is so often implied by multiple regression analysis. For example, the analysis of correlations allows for the coevolution of polity and economy and not merely the one-way impact of one upon the other. Possible causal pathways are reviewed in the earlier chapters on institutional domains and also in Chapter 10 on comparative trajectories of development. In this chapter, the focus is trained more narrowly on establishing the extent of associations between different types of institutionalized practices in order to identify the extent and nature of clusters in paths of development.

Neoliberal and Social Democratic Varieties of Modernity

Drawing on the theoretical reviews in the chapters on the economy, polity, violence, and civil society, a distinction has been established between neoliberal and social democratic forms of modernity and detailed in each of the four institutional domains. Central to the distinction between neoliberalism and social democracy is the depth of democracy and the degree of inequality.

In the economy the distinction between neoliberal and social democratic forms is made separately for welfare provision and for employment regulation, each of which is further separated for class-oriented and gender-oriented practices. Class-oriented state welfare provision is indicated by the extent of general public social expenditure, gender-oriented welfare provision by the extent of public expenditure on childcare. Class-oriented employment regulation is indicated by the strictness of employment protection, gender-oriented regulation by employment regulation for equality. Further there is a distinction related to inequality – indicated in particular for class by the Gini index of economic inequality between households – and for gender by the proportion of top jobs held by women and the female share of earned income.

In the polity the distinction between neoliberal and social democratic forms lies in the depth of democracy, a continuum of ten dimensions. The depth of democracy is indicated by its ten dimensions grouped into three levels: suffrage democracy, presence democracy, and broad democracy. The achievement of suffrage democracy is operationalized by the use of the Freedom House indicators of political rights and civil liberties, the achievement of presence democracy by the proportion of parliamentary seats held by women.

In violence the distinction between neoliberal and social democratic forms lies in the extent of the deployment and regulation of violence. The neoliberal form has a greater deployment of violence by individuals, groups, and the state, and the narrower regulation of violence: the social democratic form has less violence and greater, criminalization of violence against women and minorities. Indicators of the extent of violence are the rates of homicide, imprisonment, use of the death penalty, state spending on law and order, and state spending on the military.

In civil society the distinction between neoliberal and social democratic forms lies in the extent of personal freedoms, including sexual and reproductive rights, and whether interpersonal engagements are marked by commercialization and inequality or by mutuality and equality. Indicators include the Freedom House list of civil liberties and the availability of contraception and abortion.

While the four institutional domains have been separately identified in the operationalization of the concepts of neoliberalism and social democracy, there are additional levels of aggregation and abstraction that are important. In particular, this chapter will examine the extent of path dependency at the economy/polity nexus, at the violence nexus, and in the gender regime.

Path Dependency at the Economy/Polity Nexus

Accounts of path dependency in the social sciences have predominantly focused on issues of political economy. The analysis of path dependency has been a challenge to the notion that processes of social transformation are predominantly driven by economic changes with uniformity in the nature of development being a consequence. Instead, social and political institutions are seen to lock-in social transformations leading to the divergence of paths or trajectories of development. This is a central issue about the nature of political economy, of the greater importance of markets or political institutions (David 1985; Esping-Andersen 1990; North 1990; Arthur 1994; Hall and Soskice 2001). The conclusion of these studies is that both economic development and path dependency are relevant to the explanation of forms of political economy.

Other aspects of this debate are not so clearly settled. In particular, the relationship between employment regulation and welfare provision and the relationship between class and the gender dimensions of path dependencies. To address these questions two dimensions are separated here in order to avoid conflations that have obscured the underlying processes.

First, a distinction is made between employment regulation and welfare provision in order to investigate whether or not this distinction makes a difference to the analysis of path dependency. Some writers have suggested that the same dynamics affect both employment regulation in capitalist production and the extent of state welfare provision (Hall and Soskice 2001). For example, Huber and Stephens (2001: 315) argue that 'there has been an overall correspondence between these production relations and the welfare state regimes' because 'welfare state regimes with generous replacement rates are embedded in production regimes supporting high-skill-high-wage production and having highly regulated labour markets'. Others have argued that the integration of the typologies of regulation in capitalist production and the form of the welfare state regime is more challenging (Ebbinghaus and Manow 2001). The analysis below investigates whether or not there is path dependency separately for employment regulation and state welfare provision, and then asks if the typologies map onto each other.

Second, the analysis of class relations is separated from that of gender relations in order to investigate whether this makes a difference to the analysis of path dependency. Do different paths of development in political economy for class and for gender relations map onto each other? Some writers have suggested that there is no difference in the typology used for class from that for gender in either the analysis of state welfare (Esping-Andersen 1999) or employment and production relations (Estevez-Abe 2005). Others have argued that there may be different dynamics for class and for gender; states may support different levels of gender inequality or class inequality in welfare provision (Korpi 2000: 142) and in employment regulation (Walby 2007b). The analysis below investigates whether class and gender map onto each other. In order to take the first dimension into account, the analysis is conducted separately for employment regulation and for state welfare provision. Data limitations preclude extending this analysis to ethnicity.

The analysis below addresses not only whether there is path dependency in the development of the political economy nexus, but also addresses this in a more nuanced way by separately analysing employment regulation from state welfare provision and by separately analysing class and gender practices.

The indicators used in the analysis of political economy are listed in Table 8.1. Correlations on specific issues are provided in subsequent tables. Any correlation marked with * or ** is statistically significant; the larger the number (Pearson coefficient), the closer the association. Any number not marked * or ** is not statistically significant. Sources are provided in the Appendix to this Chapter.

Welfare provision

Introduction
The main debate over differences in the forms of welfare provision has contrasted state and market forms of provision (together with some intermediary forms). The debate addresses whether the differences stem from levels of economic development or from path dependent varieties originating in class-based struggles. There is a question here as to the potential significance of gender as well as class forces.

There is a question about the relationship of the class and the gender dimensions of welfare provision. While education and health have gender as well as class components, the state funding of childcare has a more sharply gendered focus. Does gendered state welfare spending map onto class-focused state welfare spending, or is there a separate gender dynamic?

The restriction of welfare provision to state and market forms is challenged by the addition of a third category in which the provision of welfare takes place in the home by the unpaid labour or carework of women. Is this the result of deeply sedimented institutional

Table 8.1 Political economy indicators

Income per person
Income per person is measured as Gross National Income per capita. This is often used to indicate the level of economic development.

Women in the workforce
Women in the workforce is the percentage of the non-agricultural workforce that is female. It can indicate the level of gendered economic development.

Public social expenditure
Public social expenditure as a percentage of GDP is used as an indicator of state welfare provision. The OECD (2006: 180) definition used here, includes 'cash benefits, direct "in-kind" provision of goods and services, and tax breaks with social purposes'. Such benefits may be 'targeted at low-income households, the elderly, disabled, sick, unemployed or young persons', while such programmes involve 'redistribution of resources across households, or compulsory participation'.

Childcare public expenditure
Public expenditure on childcare as a percentage of GDP is an indicator of the gendering of state welfare.

Childcare use
Childcare used by those under three years of age can be provided by either the state or the market; it is confined to childcare in a non-domestic setting.

Trade union organization
There are five measures of trade union organization: trade union density (the extent to which workers are individually members of trade unions); trade union bargaining coverage (even if not all workers are members of trade unions, sometimes unions have the right to bargain on their behalf); centralization of collective bargaining (dispersed bargaining is usually seen as weaker than when it is centralized); coordination of collective bargaining (more coordinated bargaining is usually seen as stronger); and women in trade unions: the percentage of trade unionists that are women (a measure of the gendering of the trade union movement, though only at the level of individual membership, not governance of the union).

Women in parliament
Women in parliament indicates the percentage of parliamentary (lower house only if two chambers) representatives that are female.

Employment protection strictness
The strictness of employment protection legislation is measured by the OECD indicator summarizing 18 items concerning 'employment protection of regular workers against individual dismissal e.g. months of notice, severance pay', 'regulation of temporary forms of employment e.g. number of successive fixed term contracts that are allowed' and 'specific requirements for collective dismissals e.g. delays before notice can start' (OECD 2004: 102). It indicates the regulation of employment with a focus on class relations.

Equality legislation
The strength of equality legislation is indicated by the breadth and depth of equal treatment regulation, the range of inequalities addressed (in the EU: gender, ethnicity, disability, religion/faith, age, and sexual orientation), the use of enforcement mechanisms beyond individual complaints, and the extension to indirect routes to inequality including working time. This is estimated from the literature: the Nordic countries have the highest ranking 3, the rest of the European Union 2, USA and Canada 1.5, other countries 1. (See Chapter 4 on economies for details.)

Gini inequality
Economic inequality between households is indicated by the Gini coefficient; the lower the number the less the inequality. This has a class focus because of the use of the household rather than the individual as the unit of analysis.

OECD
The information on political economy is provided for countries in the OECD only; there are up to 30 countries.

differences between countries or is there any association with economic development in addition to path dependency?

State welfare
While several previous investigations of state welfare have focused on very specific aspects (e.g. pensions in Esping-Andersen 1990) the focus here is broader, encompassing a wider range of welfare spending and provision. The indicator is that of social expenditure by the state as a percentage of GDP. The OECD (2006: 180) definition of social expenditure used here includes 'cash benefits, direct "in-kind" provision of goods and services, and tax breaks with social purposes'; such benefits may be 'targeted at low-income households, the elderly, disabled, sick, unemployed or young persons', while such programmes involve the 'redistribution of resources across households, or compulsory participation'.

The extent of state welfare provision is partly driven by the level of economic development and partly dependent on the pathway (Esping-Andersen 1990; Wilensky 2002). In the OECD there has been an increase in state social expenditure from 17.9 per cent of GDP in 1990 to 20.7 per cent in 2003, which is associated with economic growth (OECD 2007b: 193). However, differences in the level of economic development are not significant in distinguishing between those countries with higher or lower levels of state expenditure on welfare: there is no significant correlation between a higher income per person (Gross National Income per person, Purchasing Power Parity) and higher proportions of national income devoted by governments to social expenditure in OECD countries in 2003, as shown in Table 8.2 and Table 8.3.

Nevertheless there are significant differences in the extent to which states spend on welfare provision (see Figure 8.1). In the OECD the average percentage of GDP used for state social expenditure is 20.7 per cent in 2003. Countries that spend more than this are counted as 'high', while those that spend less than this are counted as 'low' (see Table 8.2).

Differences between countries with high and low levels of social expenditure are associated with the classic institutional markers of working-class organization, the strength of trade union organization. There is higher state spending on welfare where there is a high coverage, centralization, and the coordination of collective bargaining. This is consistent with the varieties of capitalism and welfare state literature.

However, there is not only an association here with working-class mobilization. There is also an association with women's mobilization via their representation in parliament. State expenditure on welfare

Table 8.2 Social expenditure, public expenditure on childcare, childcare use, and strictness of employment protection, OECD

Country	High public social expenditure	Low public social expenditure	High public expenditure on childcare	Low public expenditure on childcare	High childcare use	Low childcare use	More strict employment protection	Less strict employment protection
Australia		17.9		.2	29.1			1.5
Austria	26.1			.2		4.1	2.2	2.2
Belgium	26.5			.2	38.5		2.5	
Canada		17.3	.			19.0		1.1
Czech Rep	21.1			.1		3.0		1.9
Denmark	27.6		1.0		61.7			1.8
Finland	22.5		1.0		35.0			2.1
France	28.7		.5		26.0		2.9	
Germany	27.6			.0		9.0	2.5	
Greece	21.3			.2		7.0	2.9	
Hungary	22.7			.1		6.9		1.7
Iceland		18.7	1.2		58.7		.	.
Ireland		15.9		.1		15.0		1.3
Italy	24.2			.1		6.3	2.4	
Japan		17.7		.2		15.2		1.8
Korea, Rep		5.7		.1		19.9		2.0
Luxembourg	22.2		.4			14.0	.	.
Mexico		6.8		.0		3.0	3.2	
Netherlands	20.7			.2	29.5		2.3	
New Zealand		18.0		.2	32.1			1.3
Norway	25.1		.7		43.7		2.6	
Poland	22.9			.0		2.0		2.1
Portugal	23.5		.4		23.5		3.5	
Slovak Rep		17.3		.1		17.7	3.1	
Spain		20.3		.1		20.7	2.6	
Sweden	31.3		.8		39.5		3.5	
Switzerland		20.5		.1				1.6
Turkey		13.2			.			
UK		20.1		.2	25.8			1.1
United States		16.2	.3		29.5			.7
OECD average	20.7	20.7	.3	.3	22.7	22.7	2.2	2.2

Table 8.3 Public social expenditure, income per person, trade unions and women in parliament, OECD

	Public social expenditure	Income per person	Trade union coverage	Centralization of collective bargaining	Coordination of collective bargaining	Women in parliament
Public social expenditure						
Income per person	.323					
Trade union coverage	.751**	−.119				
Centralization of collective bargaining	.756**	−.017	.865**			
Coordination of collective bargaining	.512*	−.020	.488*	.528*		
Women in parliament	.524**	.372*	.531*	.492*	.132	

Figure 8.1 Public social expenditure as percentage of GDP, OECD OECD, 2003.
Source: OECD (2007: 193) Statlink: http://dx.doi.org/10.1787/030338861358

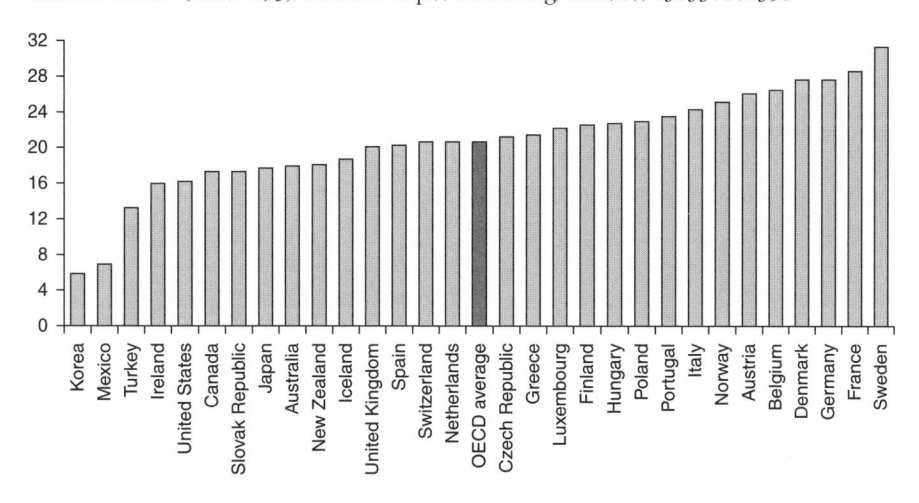

is path dependent and associated with particular types of political institutions and mobilization, not only class but also with gender forces.

Increased state spending on welfare is associated with economic development and path dependent varieties of political economy.

Gendered state social expenditure

State welfare expenditure, such as education and health, has implications for both class and gender relations. However, some aspects of social expenditure are more focused on gender relations than others.

In particular, state expenditure on childcare provision is very important for the nature of gender relations, not least because such expenditure supports the transition from a domestic to a public gender regime. Data on public childcare expenditure are newly available in a robust comparable form from the OECD (2007a).

The issue here is whether gender aspects of the welfare state are aligned with, or map onto, the generic or class-oriented aspects of the welfare state. One approach suggests that they would be in alignment because of a theoretical claim that class and gender are aligned more generally (Esping-Andersen 1990, 1999). A different approach is to reject class and gender alignment on the grounds that these are conceptually distinct systems and that any alignment is merely contingent (Korpi 2000). The gendered welfare state debate has suggested that there are very deeply sedimented differences between countries in relation to their patterns of gender welfare (Lewis 1992; O'Connor et al. 1999). However, there is a question as to whether there is a general developmental logic to the increase in state provision of childcare as well as a path dependent one.

First, does the extent of state social expenditure correlate with the extent of state expenditure on childcare? The answer here is no. There is no statistically significant correlation between state social expenditure and state spending on childcare (see Table 8.2 and Table 8.4).

In Table 8.2 it is possible to discern the traditional Nordic cluster (Sweden, Denmark, Finland, Norway) joined by France, Luxembourg, and Portugal, which has both high social expenditure and high state expenditure on childcare. In this cluster of countries there is an alignment of class- and gender-oriented aspects of state welfare. There is also a cluster of countries that have both low social expenditure and low state expenditure on childcare: Australia, Ireland, Japan, Korea, Mexico, New Zealand, the Slovak Republic, Spain, Switzerland, and the UK (although the UK is close to average on both). However, there are countries that represent important exceptions to these two clusters: one in which low social expenditure is combined with high or average state spending on childcare (Iceland, the USA), and another in which high social expenditure is combined with low state spending on childcare (Austria, Belgium, the Czech Republic, Germany, Greece, Hungary, Italy, the Netherlands, and Poland). The United States is notable in having low state public spending yet also the OECD average state expenditure on childcare.

Class-oriented and gender-oriented expenditure on state welfare are not aligned; they do not systematically map onto each other.

Are the variations in state spending on childcare associated with a developmental process or one that is path dependent?

Table 8.4 Childcare, public expenditure on childcare, public social expenditure, income per person, and women's presence in employment, parliament, and trade unions, OECD

	Children <3 in childcare	Childcare public expenditure	Public social expenditure	Income per person	Women in workforce	Women in parliament	Women in trade unions
Children <3 in childcare							
Childcare public expenditure	.810**						
Public social expenditure	.232	.348					
Income per person	.417*	.377*	.385*				
Women in workforce	.453*	.387*	.388*	.367*			
Women in parliament	.593**	.504**	.558**	.372*	.487**		
Women in trade unions	.468	.725**	.189	−.020	.683**	−.002	

Gender aspects of welfare states have a development component as well as a path dependent component. There is a correlation between higher levels of state expenditure on childcare and higher levels of economic development (GNIpc), as well as with higher levels of women's political representation in parliament and of women's membership of trade unions. While social expenditure correlates with trade union bargaining coverage, centralization, and coordination, state childcare expenditure does not.

Both generic and gender-oriented state expenditures correlate with an increased female presence in parliament. Thus while social expenditure is associated with both class and gender forces, childcare is predominantly associated with gendered forces.

Insofar as women's political mobilization in parliaments and trade unions is a path dependent form of development of the gender regime, then state-funded childcare has a gendered path dependent component (see Table 8.4).

Gender and public or domestic welfare
Bringing gender into focus widens the range of forms of welfare provision that are made visible. Not only can welfare be provided in the state and market, but it can also be provided in the home by the unpaid labour of women. The domestic relations under which such care-work is performed are not only an important part of the gender regime, but are also an important part of the understanding of the welfare system as a whole. The assumption behind the

conventional debates is that welfare is provided either by the state or market. Most of the debate concerns nuances about welfare provision by collective bodies that are somewhere between state and market, such as worker/trade union/professional bodies as in the conservative corporatist (Esping-Andersen 1990) and wage-earner forms (Castles and Mitchell 1993). But there is a large additional and very different form of provision – that of domestic provision in the home with the unpaid labour of women.

There are three major forms of welfare provision: state, market, and domestic (as well as a myriad of intermediate forms). This has the implication of splitting the category of 'liberal' in the conventional distinction between liberal and coordinated/social democratic forms of welfare provision. The category 'liberal' has often hidden the important distinction between the provision of welfare by the market and its provision by domestic labour. There are two alternatives to state provision, both domestic labour and market provision.

The indicator of the domestic provision of childcare is the absence of public childcare (state or market). It is important to note that childcare can be obtained through the market; state funds are not the only way in which public childcare is provided. The average percentage of children aged under 3 using childcare in the OECD is 22.7 per cent. Countries with more than this are counted as 'high' and countries with less than this are counted as 'low'. As before, countries in which the state uses more than the average 20.7 per cent of GDP on social expenditure are counted as 'high', while those that use less are counted as 'low'.

Do countries cluster? Is there an association between high social expenditure and non-domestic childcare? Are the countries that are traditionally considered social democratic those that have high levels of non-domestic (state or market) childcare? There is no correlation – the high social expenditure countries are evenly divided as to whether or not they have high or low levels of domestic childcare. Those that have class-oriented 'high' social expenditure on welfare and combine this with high levels of non-domestic childcare include the classic Nordic cluster (Denmark, Finland, Norway, and Sweden) as well as Belgium, France, and Portugal. But there are other countries that are combining a high class-oriented social expenditure on welfare with high levels of domestic childcare (Austria, the Czech Republic, Germany, Greece, Hungary, Italy, and Luxembourg).

Countries that are traditionally considered liberal are also divided as to whether or not there are high or low levels of domestic childcare. One set of countries that are conventionally considered liberal, with low levels of social expenditure, combines this with domestic childcare (Canada, Ireland, Japan, Korea, Mexico, and the Slovak Republic).

However, another set of countries that are conventionally considered liberal, with low social expenditure, combines this with non-domestic welfare and high rates of childcare outside the home (Australia, Iceland, New Zealand, the UK, and the USA; see Table 8.2).

There is no correlation between class-oriented distinctions between high and low state spenders on welfare and the gender-oriented distinction between high and low levels of non-domestic childcare. Instead of two clusters, there is a roughly even distribution between the four possibilities. Even Esping-Andersen's conservative corporatist cluster is broken up, with Belgium and France having high social expenditure and high childcare and with Austria, Germany, and Italy having high social expenditure and low childcare.

The overall conclusion here is that the domestic provision of welfare can be present in the same country as either liberal or democratic social expenditure patterns. This means that class and gender relations do not map onto each other in this area.

Is the distinction between domestic and non-domestic welfare associated with children a developmental or a path-dependent clustering?

It is both. Higher rates of non-domestic (state or market) childcare as compared with the domestic provision of this form of welfare are associated with higher levels of economic development, especially gendered economic development. It correlates with high GNIpc, high rates of women in employment, a high percentage of women in parliament, a high proportion of women in tertiary education. There is a developmental component to the increased use of non-domestic childcare, associated not only with generic economic development as measured by income per person, but also with gendered economic development as measured by the proportion of women in the workforce. This means that it is associated not only with the level of economic development, but also with the transition of the gender regime from a domestic to a public form.

Are there any indications of path dependency in addition to these developmental components? It has already been shown that it does not map onto class-oriented path dependent varieties of welfare. Does it represent gender-oriented varieties of welfare?

A correlation can be seen between the use of childcare for children under 3 years of age and the public expenditure on childcare (see Table 8.4). This suggests that state expenditure is an important part of this provision. In several countries there are high or moderate rates of both use of childcare for under 3s and high levels of state expenditure on childcare (high Nordic countries – Iceland, Denmark, Sweden, Norway, Finland; see Table 8.2). There is a further association between high rates of non-domestic childcare with women's political mobilization in parliament. This is consistent with a state-supported path dependent form of the public gender regime that is different from a market-supported pathway.

Conclusions on welfare

There are three forms of delivery of welfare: domestic, market, and state. Using a gender lens makes visible the domestic as a form of delivery of welfare additional to the traditional interest in state and market forms. Whether welfare takes a domestic market or state form depends on gender as well as class forces.

When class-oriented welfare is the focus, in relation to the distinction between state and market forms, the differences cannot be accounted for by the level of economic development, with the implication that differences are associated with divergent paths of development. These divergent paths in state social expenditure are associated not only with the working class forces associated with trade union organization, but also with gender mobilization in both trade unions and in parliament.

The class and gender dimension of welfare are not aligned. Patterns of state social expenditure do not map onto patterns of state expenditure on childcare. There is both developmental and path dependency in gender aspects of welfare. Thus unlike class-oriented social expenditure, gender-oriented expenditure increases with the level of economic development across the OECD. Gendered trajectories do not routinely align with class trajectories, though there are some contingent points of overlap.

Domestic welfare, as indicated by the domestic or public (state or market) forms of childcare, decreases as the level of economic development and women's employment increase. In addition to this developmental component there is a path dependent component. The path dependent component is associated with the increased representation of women in parliament.

The amount of welfare provision has both developmental and path dependent components. Class and gender paths of development are not aligned, except contingently.

Employment regulation

Employment regulation is a second part of political economy, which is here investigated separately from welfare rather than conflated with it. The regulation of employment concerns the intervention of the state or polity into the workings of labour markets and the conditions of employment, affecting the relations between employers and workers. There are three issues. First, are differences in the strictness of employment protection legislation associated with the level of economic development, or are they path dependent? Second, is there a separate gender dimension to employment regulation and if so does this map onto the class dimension? Are class and gender patterns aligned? Third, are variations in the strictness of employment protection legislation associated with variations in the varieties of state welfare or not? Is there a close link between varieties of capitalist production and varieties of capitalist welfare or not?

The indicator of employment regulation used here is that produced by the OECD and focuses on the strictness of employment protection legislation. It summarizes 18 items concerning the 'employment protection of regular workers against individual dismissal e.g. months of notice, severance pay', 'regulation of temporary forms of employment e.g. number of successive fixed term contracts that are allowed', and 'specific requirements for collective dismissals e.g. delays before notice can start' (OECD 2004: 102).

Path dependency?
There is stricter employment protection legislation among the less economically developed countries of the OECD. However, the strongest correlations are with trade union organization – trade union coverage, centralization, and the coordination of collective bargaining (see Table 8.5). This is consistent with variations due to both economic development and path dependency.

Regulating employment: the gender focus
The OECD indicator of employment protection concerns the regulation of individual and collective dismissal and temporary work, thereby focusing on the class relations between employers and workers. There are in addition to these other regulations of employment that concern gender relations in employment, some of which have been extended to the protection of other minoritized groups. There are two types of these regulations of complex inequalities beyond class. First are regulations concerning equal treatment or equal opportunities in employment. These make illegal the treatment of a minoritized group that is worse than the majority group in employment practices concerning recruitment, promotion, dismissal, and payment. They include gender and complex inequalities. In the EU they extend to gender, ethnicity, disability, religion/faith, age, and sexual orientation, while in the USA they principally cover ethnicity and gender, with some extensions to age and disability but

Table 8.5 Strictness of employment protection legislation, trade unions, income per person, public social expenditure, and equality legislation strength, OECD

	Employment protection strictness	Trade union coverage	Centralization of collective bargaining	Coordination of collective bargaining	Income per person	Public social expenditure	Equality legislation strength
Employment protection strictness							
Trade union coverage	.700**						
Centralization of collective bargaining	.750**	.865**					
Coordination of collective bargaining	.581**	.488*	.528*				
Income per person	−.408*	−.119	−.017	−.020			
Public social expenditure	.142	.751*	.756**	.512*	.385*		
Equality legislation strength	.095	.677**	.640**	.175	.294	.717*	

not to religion/faith or sexual orientation. In the EU, but less frequently in the USA, they extend to practices that might indirectly treat one group worse than another, e.g. the requirement to treat as equal part-time workers with full-time workers in the EU but not in the USA. A second type of gender equality regulation concerns the regulation of working time so as to enable the combination of employment and care-work, with particular benefits to working parents. This type of regulation includes the legal entitlement to (paid and unpaid) maternity, paternity, and parental leave across the EU, but only unpaid leave for some workers in the USA, and the right of parents of young children to reduce their working hours (the EU and not the USA). The ranking for OECD countries presented below combines both types of complex equality regulations and is estimated here on the basis of a reading of the laws themselves as well as the literature. The Nordic countries have the highest ranking of 4; the rest of the European Union is 3; the USA, Canada, Australia, and New Zealand are 2; the rest are at 1. The phrase '(gender) equality' is used to denote the centrality of gender to these forms of regulation, which in some instances are extended to non-class inequalities in addition to gender, especially but not only ethnicity.

A series of questions can be raised here. First, does the pattern of (gender) equality regulation change with the level of economic development, or is it path dependent? Second, do variations in these non-class regulations map onto variations in class regulations?

Table 8.6 Equality legislation, trade unions, women in parliament, trade unions, and employment, OECD

	Equality legislation	Trade union coverage	Centralization of collective bargaining	Women in parliament	Women in trade unions	Women in workforce
Equality legislation						
Trade union coverage	.677**					
Centralization of collective bargaining	.640**	.865**				
Women in parliament	.600**	.531*	.492*			
Women in trade unions	.719**	−.066	.010	−.002		
Women in workforce	.498*	−.114	−.194	.487**	.683**	

While there is no statistically significant correlation between (gender) equality regulations and the level of economic development between countries today, there has been a substantial increase in these regulations over time. There is no statistically significant correlation between (gender) equality regulations and class-oriented strictness of employment protection legislation (see Table 8.5). Variations in class and gender forms of employment regulation do not map onto each other. Gender cannot be reduced to class.

The extent of (gender) equality regulations does correlate with the extent of women's political mobilization, as indicated by the percentage of parliamentary seats held by women and the percentage of trade union members who are women, as well as with trade union organization (see Table 8.6). The most important part of this is women's mobilization: a regression equation with (gender) equality regulations as the dependent variable and the percentage of parliamentary seats held by women and the percentage of trade union members who are female accounts for 90 per cent of the variance and is significant at 000 level, with an F score of 59. This suggests that there is path dependency in the development of these regulations and that this is gendered as well as being associated with working-class mobilization.

Employment and welfare
The extent of the strictness of employment protection does not map onto the extent of state welfare spending (see Table 8.5). There is no significant correlation between the two. This is a challenge to the version of the varieties of capitalism thesis that attempts to integrate both employment regulation and state welfare into the same system.

Table 8.7 Inequality, employment regulation, public social expenditure, childcare public expenditure, OECD

	Gini inequality	Equality legislation	Employment protection strictness	Public social expenditure	Childcare public expenditure
Gini inequality					
Equality legislation	−.540**				
Employment protection strictness	.212	.095			
Public social expenditure	−.537**	.717**	.142		
Childcare public expenditure	−.408*	.617**	.050	.348	

While there are examples of the traditional view of a clustering between a high state social expenditure and a high state regulation of employment, there are too many exceptions for this to be statistically significant in the OECD. There is high state social expenditure and more strict employment protection in Belgium, France, Germany, Greece, Italy, the Netherlands, Norway, Portugal, and Sweden (see Table 8.2). There is low state social expenditure and less strict employment protection in Australia, Canada, Ireland, Japan, Korea, New Zealand, the Slovak Republic, Switzerland, the UK, and the USA. But there is high state social expenditure and less strict employment protection in the Czech Republic, Denmark, Finland, Hungary, and Poland. There is low state social expenditure and more strict employment protection in Mexico, Spain, and Turkey. The countries that are the exceptions to the traditional view of the clustering of high levels of state expenditure and employment protection particularly include either newcomers to the EU (joining in 2004) and OECD that were previously communist (the Czech Republic, Hungary, and Poland) or relatively poor (Mexico and Turkey). A focus on a narrow range of countries enables the specific path dependency thesis linking social expenditure and employment regulation to be sustained while widening the range of countries disrupts this thesis. The post-communist European countries, perhaps not surprisingly given the history of restructuring of their states, have a distinctive pattern that is different from the countries of the west and north of Europe, which combines low levels of regulation of employment with higher levels of state expenditure.

With a focus on gender, there is a significant correlation between the amount of social expenditure, the amount of childcare expenditure, and the strength of (gender) equality employment regulation (see Table 8.7). With a gender-lens, the practices of high social expenditure, high gendered social expenditure on childcare, and (gender) equality employment regulation do map onto each other. There is cohesion in these parts of the gender regime.

Inequality

A lower level of inequality between households, as indicated by the lower size of the Gini coefficient, is associated with higher levels of social and childcare expenditure and with stronger equal opportunities legislation, but has no statistically significant relationship with stricter employment protection legislation (see Table 8.7).

Conclusions on political economy

Four different dimensions of the polity/economy nexus have been identified: the regulation of employment in terms of the strictness of employment protection; the regulation of employment for (gender) equality; state welfare as indicated by state social expenditure; gendered state welfare as indicated by state spending on childcare.

While economic development is associated with some differences, the dominant picture among the OECD countries is one of path dependency. In the class-focused part of the analysis employment regulation and state welfare were sometimes divergent, only mapping onto each other in a limited number of countries (predominantly those in EU15 and North America) but not in the newer members of the EU and OECD. High levels of spending and regulation were associated with trade union organization. In the gender-focused part of the analysis there was a significant overlap between the employment and welfare aspects of political economy; these were associated with women's political mobilization in parliaments and trade unions. Lower levels of economic inequality between households were associated with higher levels of state expenditure (gendered and ungendered) and with higher levels of equal opportunity legislation, but not with class-oriented employment protection legislation.

There is considerable divergence between class and gender dimensions of varieties of political economy. This is especially the case in employment regulation. The one location of alignment was in state welfare expenditure.

This confirms the case for path dependency, but not to the exclusion of all aspects of change associated with economic and human development. It shows the necessity of analytically separating the class and gender dimensions of these developments, especially in relation to employment regulation, where the class and gender forces produce different outcomes.

Path Dependency at the Violence Nexus

Modernity and path dependency

There is a further path dependent nexus which is associated with violence. The deployment and regulation of violence varies partly as a result of modernity and partly as a result of different path dependent trajectories. There are four major ways in which a link between the rise of modernity and a reduction in violence has been argued. One is that violence, especially legitimate violence, becomes concentrated in the state rather than being more widely dispersed (Weber). This is linked to a specific argument that violence against women and ethnic, religious, national, and sexual minorities might be reduced if it were to become effectively criminalized. The second is that the use of violence by the state as a form of social control (e.g. via the death penalty) gives way to a wide variety of disciplining techniques based in civil society (Foucault). This is linked to a third theme, that in a civilized society violence in civil society as a form of expression is suppressed in the emerging modern forms of personality (Elias). A fourth is that mature democracies, a form of governance that develops with modernity, do not launch wars on each other.

However, there are some voices of hesitation about the thesis of a decline in violence in modernity – that modernity may simply organize violence more efficiently, as in the Holocaust orchestrated by the Nazis (Bauman), and that there has been a recent turn away from penal welfare towards a more punitive criminal justice regime, at least in the USA and the UK, associated with changes in the balance of class forces (Garland 2001).

An alternative thesis is that the deployment and regulation of violence takes a path dependent form of development. This can be argued in two ways. First, that there is a clustering of the different forms of violence as one form feeds off another through a series of interconnections in social institutions especially that of the state. Second, that higher levels of violence are associated with higher levels of economic inequality. The latter has been previously and effectively argued in the link between social inequality and violent crime. But the argument here is that the nexus of violence is broader than that of violent crime and inequality and encompasses a wider range of forms of violence, including the tendency to resort to violence in settling matters between states which is witnessed through the build up of the military. Path dependent trajectories of the deployment and regulation of violence include forms that are not only inter-personal, but also those between the state and the individual, and those between states.

So does the rate of violence decline with economic and democratic development? Are there different paths of development, associated, for example, with inequality? In order to investigate this comparatively, it is necessary to have some measures of the violence deployed in civil society and the state, as well as those of economic development and inequality.

Indicators

Five aspects of violence can be measured in a way that is sufficiently robust for comparable analysis. First is homicide, as the rate per 100,000 population. This is indicative of the rate of violence in civil society, since it correlates well with other forms of violent crime. This is the most reliable of the official measures of violent crime, since homicide is one of the few under-reported crimes and this measure is reasonably robust for comparisons across countries. Second is the number of prisoners per 100,000 population. This is a measure of the degree of coerciveness in the state criminal justice system. Third is use of the death penalty. Fourth is state spending on law and order, measured as a percentage of GDP. This is indicative of the priority use of the resources by the state in its pursuit of law and order. Fifth is state spending on the military as a percentage of GDP, which is indicative of the extent of militarization of the state. Sixth is a summary indicator of government expenditure on law and order and the military as a percentage of GDP. Seventh are gendered homicide rates. While there are not yet reliable comparative statistics on the full extent of violence against women and minorities, it is possible to differentiate between the rates of homicide of women and men. Since around half of female homicide victims are killed by their partners or former partners, the rate of female homicide may be taken as an approximate proxy of domestic homicide and domestic violence. By contrast most homicides of men are by other men.

An indicator measure of economic development is Gross National Income per person. An indicator of economic inequality is the Gini statistic, which rises with income inequality between households. An indicator of women's political mobilization is that of the proportion of women in parliamentary seats. (The indicators are shown in Table 8.8). These data are available for most OECD countries; a sub-set is available at a global level.

In the analysis several questions are posed. To what extent is there an association between levels of development (economic and

Table 8.8 Indicators in the violence nexus

Homicide
Homicide, as the rate per 100,000 population. There are two sources for this: one for developed OECD countries, a second for a more global data set provided by the World Health Organization.

Prisoners
The number of prisoners per 100,000 population.

Death penalty
Use of the death penalty.

State spending on law and order
State spending on law and order, measured as a percentage of GDP.

State spending on the military
State spending on the military, as a percentage of GDP.

Military spending, as a percentage of government expenditure

Gendered homicide rates
Homicides of men as the rate per 100,000 population.
Homicides of women as the rate per 100,000 population.

Economic development
A measure of economic development, Gross National Income per person.

Economic inequality between households
A measure of economic inequality is the Gini statistic, which rises with income inequality between households.

Women's political mobilization
An indicator of women's political mobilization is that of the proportion of women in parliamentary seats.

These data are available for most OECD countries. A sub-set of these data is available at a global level.

---

human) and the extent of violence? To what extent is there path dependency in the extent of violence? Does gender make a difference to the answers to the questions about development and path dependency? Is there a relationship between the violence nexus and economic inequality?

Development, inequality, and violence

At a global level, there is a statistically significant negative correlation between homicide and the level of economic development, as measured by GNI per capita (−.416**). This means that the homicide rate is higher in poorer, less developed countries than in richer countries. With increasing levels of economic development there is a lower level of homicide. This is consistent with the thesis that modernity reduces the level of inter-personal violence.

There is a positive correlation between homicide and the level of economic inequality as measured by Gini (see Table 8.9). There is

Table 8.9 Homicide, gender, and inequality, global

	Homicide of men	Homicide of women	Gini inequality	Women in parliament
Homicide of men				
Homicide of women	.727**			
Gini inequality	.513**	.239		
Women in parliament	−.247	−.294*	−.190*	

a higher rate of homicide in countries that are more economically unequal.

Gendered violence

Are there any differences between the homicide of men and the homicide of women? The homicide of men correlates with inequality, as indicated by Gini, which measures income inequality between households, while the homicide of women does not (see Table 8.9). The Gini measure of economic inequality used here in taking a household as the unit tends to capture the inequality between men rather than that between women and men. So the homicide of men correlates with economic inequality between men, while the homicide of women does not.

The homicide of women inversely correlates with the percentage of women in parliament. The homicide of women is lower when women are better represented in parliament, indicative of an association between forms of female empowerment and reduced violence against women.

Path dependency of the violence nexus in OECD countries

The pattern of violence is slightly different among the small group of richer countries in the OECD than that at a global level. These countries have reached a relatively high level of economic development, and differences associated with income do not emerge in this group. Among this group of rich countries, there is no correlation between homicide and the indicator of economic (GNIpc) development. Among countries at this higher level of economic development, there is no longer a significant correlation between violence and further economic development: this is associated with a narrower range of variance of the violence indicators of the richer countries.

Table 8.10 Correlation between aspects of violence, OECD

	Homicide	Prisoners	Death penalty	Military spend as per cent govt expenditure	Military spend as per cent of GDP	Law spend as per cent GDP
Homicide						
Prisoners	.851**					
Death penalty	.454**	.589**				
Military spend as per cent govt expenditure	.681**	.629**	.787**			
Military spend as per cent of GDP	.658**	.614**	.332	.786**		
Law spend as per cent GDP	.671**	.660**	.037	.121	.551*	

Among the richer OECD countries other divergences emerge associated with path dependency. There is a striking set of correlations between the various aspects of violence (see Table 8.10). If there is a higher homicide rate, then there is also more likely to be a higher rate of imprisonment, use of the death penalty, and a higher expenditure on law and order (as a percentage of GDP) and on the military (both as a percentage of GDP and as a percentage of government expenditure). There is a cluster of phenomena of violence: homicide, prisoners, death penalty, expenditure on law and order and expenditure on the military. If any one of these is higher in a country, then it is likely that the others will be also. Among rich countries there is a clearly identifiable violence nexus, in which some countries are more violent (along a series of dimensions) than others. This violence nexus is not associated with the level of economic development.

Among the richer countries of the OECD, this nexus of violence does not change with economic development. There is no statistically significant correlation between any of the measures of violence and the level of income per person among these countries. So are there other phenomena to which it is related?

Violence, economic inequality, and the polity/economy nexus

Violence and economic inequality are related along some dimensions but not all. There are correlations between economic inequality, as measured by Gini, and some, but not all, aspects of violence. The higher the level of economic inequality, the more likely a country is to have higher rates of imprisonment and higher levels of military expenditure as a percentage of GDP. The correlation between the Gini measure of economic inequality and the level of military expenditure is .454*. There is no correlation with the level of regulation of employment.

The homicide rate is negatively correlated with social expenditure: the more a country is spending on social matters, the lower the homicide rate will be on average. The Pearson correlation here is .447* (significant at the 0.05 level).

Conclusions on violence

At a global level, amongst a wide and economically diverse set of countries, there is an association between economic development and lower levels of violence. In addition, there is a specific correlation between the homicide of women and women's level of representation in parliament. This is consistent with the thesis that violence reduces with modernity and that there are different trajectories for different sets of complex inequalities.

Within the smaller group of richer, more developed countries within the OECD a path dependency can be seen to emerge, rather than an association with further increases in the level of economic development. This can be drawn from the correlation of indicators of different dimensions of violence: homicide, use of the death penalty, imprisonment, government spending on law and order, government spending on the military.

Among the richer countries of the OECD there is considerable path dependency in the deployment and regulation of violence. In these countries there is not the association of violence with economic development as is seen at the global level. Instead there is a strong clustering of countries in the extent to which they are violent in a series of inter-related aspects.

Gender Regime

A gender regime is a set of inter-related gendered social relations and gendered institutions that constitutes a system. There are different forms of gender regime. Gender regimes may have more or less unequal gender relations. One distinction in the forms of gender regime is that between a domestic and a public gender regime; during the transition to gendered modernity there is a transformation of a domestic to a public form of gender regime. There are further distinctions between the forms of public gender regime: neoliberal and social democratic forms. Different trajectories through the transition from domestic to public gender regime and coevolution with other regimes of inequality lead to different forms of public gender regime.

The gender regime theory developed here is different from other models of gender relations in several ways. First, there is a greater range of domains and institutions. For example, unlike the 'male/dual breadwinner' typology found in much of the gendered welfare state debates it includes gendered participation in parliament, education, civil society, and violence. Second, there is not only a continuum from the domestic to the public, parallel to male to dual breadwinner form, but also a set of distinctions among the forms of public gender regime.

There is more than one possible route for the transition from a domestic to a public gender regime. The difference between the routes affects the form of the public gender regime. The provision of publicly-funded childcare is only one route among three. There are three possible routes to a public form of gender regime: first, market led; second, polity provisioning led; third, polity regulatory led. The extent to which these different routes can be identified empirically is the first focus of this section. This approach challenges the assumption in much gendered welfare state literature that publicly-funded childcare is the main route by which gender relations as a system are transformed. There are other routes including, in particular, that of the market.

Degrees of inequality are potentially important in the differentiation of different types of gender regime. Is the public form more or less unequal than the domestic form? Do the different forms of public gender regimes have different levels of gender inequality?

This analysis analytically separates gender regimes from class regimes. However, this does not imply that class relations are irrelevant for the development of different forms of gender regime. The question of whether different forms of gender regimes and class regimes map onto each other is treated here as an issue for empirical investigation. There is also a further issue of the dynamic coevolution of the different regimes of inequality, which is addressed in Chapter 10.

The analysis builds on the theoretical and conceptual work in earlier chapters on theorizing multiple social systems, economies, polities, violence, and civil societies. The task here is to see first if it is possible to empirically identify sets of inter-related gendered institutions associated with either a domestic or a public gender regime, and then to distinguish between different forms of public gender regimes. From there it falls to investigate the extent to which these different forms of gender regime are associated with

Table 8.11 Indicators of the gender regime

Women in the workforce
Women in the workforce is the percentage of the non-agricultural workforce that is female. It can indicate the level of gendered economic development. A high level indicates a public gender regime.

Gendered inequality in employment
Gender pay gap.
Female share of earned income.
Managers, legislators, and senior officials, percentage women.
Professional and technical workers, percentage women.
Gender employment gap.

Equality legislation
The strength of equality legislation is indicated by the breadth and depth of equal treatment regulation, the range of inequalities addressed (in the EU: gender, ethnicity, disability, religion/faith, age and sexual orientation), the use of enforcement mechanisms beyond individual complaints, and the extension to indirect routes to inequality including working time. This is estimated from the literature: the Nordic countries have the highest ranking 3, the rest of the European Union 2, USA and Canada 1.5, other countries 1. (See Chapter 4 on economies for details.)

Childcare use
Childcare used by those under three years of age can be provided by either the state or the market; it is confined to childcare in a non-domestic setting. A public gender regime is indicated by high use of childcare for children under three.

Childcare public expenditure
Public expenditure on childcare as a percentage of GDP is an indicator of the gendering of state welfare.
High level indicates social democratic form of public gender regime.

Gendered education
Educational enrolment of women, percentage of the possible.
Tertiary education of women, percentage of the possible.
High level indicates public gender regime.

Women in parliament
Women in parliament indicates the percentage of parliamentary (lower house only if two chambers) representatives that are female.
High level indicates public gender regime.
High level indicates social democratic form of public gender regime.

Women in trade unions
The percentage of trade unionists that are women (a measure of the gendering of the trade union movement, though only at the level of individual membership and not governance of the union).

Gendered civil liberties
Whether abortion is legal or not.
Legality indicates public gender regime.
Legality indicates social democratic form of public gender regime.

inequality and to then investigate the extent to which different forms of gender regime map onto different forms of class regime.

The investigation of these issues using a cross-sectional quantitative methodology requires indicators that distinguish these different forms of gender regime. Chapter 10 addresses the issues over time and with a global perspective that is necessarily excluded from this chapter by the nature of the data used. (Indicators of the gender regime are shown in Table 8.11.)

Public and domestic gender regimes

The distinction between domestic and public forms of gender regime can be found in each of the institutional domains of economy, polity, violence, and civil society, as well as at the level of the gender regime as a whole. Within the economy, the public form is that women are free wage labourers rather than domestic labourers. This is indicated by the extent to which women are in non-agricultural employment (excluding agriculture, where employment may not take the form of free wage labour but instead may be under domestic relations) and the extent to which childcare is public rather than domestic. Within the polity the public form is indicated by the extent to which women are present in parliament and not merely by whether they have the formal right to be, and is measured by the proportion of parliamentary seats that are held by women. Within the domain of violence, the public form would be indicated by the extent to which violence against women, especially domestic violence, is effectively criminalized; however, there is no comparable robust indicator available to measure this across countries, so it is not included here. Within civil society, the public form is indicated by the extent to which women are fully engaged in education and have the full range of civil rights, including bodily integrity, such as the right to avail of abortion and contraception. It is here measured by the extent to which young women are enrolled in education at all levels as a percentage of what is possible and by whether abortion is legal.

One question is whether the public form of gender relations in each of the institutional domains of economy, polity, violence, and civil society is aligned. Features of the public gender regime can be found to be associated in the near-global data set. High levels of women's (non-agricultural) employment are associated with greater female representation in parliament, higher levels of educational enrolment at all levels, and a greater likelihood of abortion being legal (see Table 8.12). The implication of this finding is that it is possible to distinguish between the domestic and public forms of gender regime, that there is coherence to the public form across diverse institutional domains.

Table 8.12 Public and domestic gender regimes, global

	Women in workforce	Women in parliament	Women in education	Abortion legal
Women in workforce				
Women in parliament	.397**			
Women in education	.566**	.403**		
Abortion legal	.409**	.257**	.486**	

Table 8.13 Development and public gender regimes, global

	Women in workforce	Women in parliament	Women in education	Abortion legal	Income per person	Life expectancy
Women in workforce						
Women in parliament	.397**					
Women in education	.566**	.403**				
Abortion legal	.409**	.257**	.486**			
Income per person	.284**	.460**	.640**	.378**		
Life expectancy	.347**	.215*	.746**	.421**	.563**	

Development and the public gender regime

A more public gender regime is partly associated with economic development. A higher level of income per person is associated with the public gender regime. In the near global data set higher levels of women's employment, the educational enrolment of women, the presence of women in parliaments, and the legality of abortion, are all correlated with both economic development and human development.

In countries with higher levels of economic development there is more likely to be a public form of gender regime than among countries with lower levels of economic development (see Table 8.13).

Domestic and public gender regimes and gender inequality

Is the public form of gender regime less gender unequal than a domestic gender form? The conceptualization of the distinction between the domestic and public forms of gender regime used here does not necessarily imply that the public form of the regime is less unequal than the domestic one. This is deliberately left open for empirical investigation.

Investigating whether or not there is an association between the form and the degree of inequality requires the separation of indicators of the public form of gendered institutions from indicators of gender inequality. This process is complicated by some degree of

Table 8.14 Domestic and public gender regimes and inequality, OECD

	Women as managers	Women as professionals	Women in tertiary education	Women in the workforce	Women in education	Women in parliament	Gini inequality
Women as managers							
Women as professionals	.747**						
Women in tertiary education	.426*	.382**					
Women in the workforce	.721**	.789**	.571**				
Women in education	.449*	.282	.761**	.610**			
Women in parliament	.390*	.265	.474*	.487**	.574**		
Gini inequality	−.007	−.446*	−.255	−.451*	−.218	−.381*	

overlap between indicators that might be used and by conceptual debates as to whether some forms of difference are also forms of inequality.

Some indicators of gender inequality overlap with indicators of the public gender regime. These include higher levels of women in employment (non-agricultural), parliaments, and education. In these instances the increased presence of women is simultaneously a matter of the form of the social relations and also an indicator of gender inequality. The inclusion of women in employment as an indicator of gender inequality, though sometimes considered controversial, was established earlier. Indicators that more unequivocally indicate gender inequality include the proportion of women in top jobs (professions and management) and the ratio of women to men in education.

A public gender regime is less gender unequal than a domestic gender regime. Indicators of gender equality (higher proportions of women in management and professions and in tertiary education) correlate with the greater presence of women in employment, education, and parliaments.

Does gender inequality map onto class inequality? Gini is a measure of income inequality between households rather than a measure of gender inequality. The level of inequality of the gender regime overlaps with the level of class inequality in some areas but not others. It overlaps in relation to the proportion of women in professional jobs, the proportion of women in the workforce, and the proportion of women in parliaments, but not in relation to the proportion of women in managerial jobs nor the level and proportion of women's presence in education (see Table 8.14).

Varieties of public gender regimes

Differences do exist between the forms of public gender regime. There are two main forms: neoliberal and social democratic. The transition to a public gender regime may involve the substitution of the domestic economy by the market or the provisioning state, or by the removal of discriminatory barriers to women's employment, or by some mix of the three. In addition it involves transformations within the polity, violence, and civil society.

While the extent of social expenditure by the polity is consistent with the distinction between the neoliberal and social democratic substitutions for the domestic economy, more important, and with a tighter focus on gender issues, is the extent to which childcare for the under-3s is provided by the polity or bought privately. The main indicator of the distinction between neoliberal and social democratic forms of public gender regime is that of the extent to which formal childcare is provided by the polity rather than privately on the market and is measured as the percentage of GDP spent on public childcare for the under-3s. A newly emerging third potential route is the removal of barriers to employment by the gendered regulation of employment by the polity, as indicated by the strength of equal opportunities laws.

The data set used here is restricted to the more developed countries of the OECD, since the information is not available for the wider data set. Contrary to frequent assumptions, the public expenditure route to formal childcare is not the only one – childcare that is privately purchased on the market is important in contributing to the total amount of childcare and in some countries this is the main route. Among those countries that have above average levels of use of childcare, half fall into the traditional state provisioning route (Denmark, Iceland, Finland, Norway, Sweden, and France), while the other half have a low state expenditure on childcare (Australia, Belgium, Netherlands, New Zealand, and the UK). The USA, with a high level of childcare, has an average state expenditure on childcare (see Table 8.15).

Table 8.15 Varieties of gender regime, OECD

	Women in workforce	Childcare (any)	Public childcare expenditure
Women in workforce			
Childcare (any)	.453*		
Public childcare expenditure	.387*	.810**	

Both the use of childcare and its public provision correlate with high rates of female employment. But what difference does the provision of childcare by polity or private means make? The difference

Table 8.16 Gendered polity policies and women's political mobilization, OECD

	Childcare public expenditure	Equality legislation	Women in parliament	Women in trade unions	Gini inequality
Childcare public expenditure					
Equality legislation	.617**				
Women in parliament	.504**	.600**			
Women in trade unions	.725**	.719**	−.002		
Gini inequality	−.408*	−.540**	−.381*	−.511	

here should not be exaggerated. However, there is a nexus of correlations between polity expenditure on childcare for the under-3s, the strength of equal opportunities legislation, women's presence in parliaments, women's organization in trade unions, and a lower level of income inequality between households. This is consistent with the thesis that the political mobilization of employed women is associated with policies that facilitate their employment, including greater public social expenditure, especially on childcare, as well as supportive employment regulations (see Table 8.16).

There are two forms of state-led policy for gender equality: childcare provisioning and the regulation of employment for equality.

Democracy and Inequality

There are three indicators of the depth of democracy: political rights, civil liberties, and the presence of women in parliaments. These three correlate among themselves, especially political rights and civil liberties.

There are four indicators of policies towards equality, two gender-focused and two class-focused: polity childcare expenditure; general public social expenditure; equal treatment laws; and employment protection legislation.

The greater the depth of democracy, the more likely a country is to have class- and gender-focused public expenditure and strong equal treatment laws (see Table 8.17).

Three indicators of inequality are used: the class-focused Gini index of economic inequality between households; the gender-focused percentage of managers who are women; and the gender-focused female share of earned income. Four indicators of polity policy towards equality are used, of which two are gender-focused – childcare expenditure and equal treatment laws – and two are class-focused – general public social expenditure and employment protection legislation.

Table 8.17 Democracy and polity policies, OECD

	Political rights	Civil liberties	Women in parliament	Childcare public expenditure	Public social expenditure	Equality legislation	Employment protection strictness
Political rights							
Civil liberties	.922**						
Women in parliament	.630**	.621**					
Childcare public expenditure	.503**	.543**	.504**				
Public social expenditure	.630**	.508**	.558**	.348			
Equality legislation	.598**	.440*	.600**	.617**	.717**		
Employment protection strictness	−.315	−.398*	.021	.050	.142	.095	

While the two indicators of gender inequality are correlated, there is no statistically significant correlation between the class-focused and gender-focused indicators of inequality (see Table 8.18). The lesser the Gini measured economic inequality between households, the more likely there is to be public social expenditure, public childcare expenditure, and strong equal treatment laws. There is a positive association between equal treatment laws and women as managers, and between women having a higher share of earned income and state childcare expenditure.

Table 8.18 Inequality and polity policies, OECD

	Gini inequality	Women in management	Women's share of income	Childcare public expenditure	Public social expenditure	Equality legislation	Employment protection strictness
Gini inequality							
Women in management	−.007						
Women's share of income	−.358	.399*					
Childcare public expenditure	−.408*	.026*	.448*				
Public social expenditure	−.537**	.367	.296	.348			
Equality legislation	−.540**	.401*	.200	.617**	.717**		
Employment protection strictness	.212	−.396	−.397*	.050	.142	.095	

Conclusions

Much of the conventional class-based analysis in both the employment regime and welfare state regime literature discussed above has assumed or claimed that class is the dominant social relation and that gender does not significantly alter the basic categories of analysis (e.g. Esping-Andersen 1999). But do differences in gender regimes actually map onto differences in class-based regimes or not? Do the distinctions made here produce a different answer to this question as to the relationship between class and gender?

The distinction between domestic and public gender regime is partly associated with the level of economic development, while the distinctions between varieties of class regime (welfare or employment) are not. The transition from a domestic to a public gender regime is the transformation of gender relations from premodern to modern. It has similarities with the transition to capitalism for class relations. It is thus to be expected that there is a relationship with economic development for these forms of gender relations as there was for class relations.

A more appropriate question is whether the varieties of public gender regime map onto the varieties of class relations. Overall there is no simple mapping of the varieties of gender regime onto varieties of class relations. However, at a more detailed level, where state welfare is differentiated from the regulation of employment, a more nuanced answer about interconnections appears. When the focus is on the regulation of employment there is little association: polity intervention to regulate employment protection in relation to temporary work and individual and collective dismissals has quite a different pattern among countries than that found for polity intervention to promote gender equality in employment. When the focus is on state welfare there is a more complex picture. In some cases there is an overlap between generic state welfare expenditure and gendered state welfare expenditure on childcare, but it is far from a complete mapping. While for class relations there is a disjuncture between employment regulation and welfare spending, for gender relations employment regulation and state spending are aligned.

This chapter has identified forms of path dependency in the greater or lesser regulation of employment, the greater or lesser provisions of state welfare, and the extent of violence. These differences map onto the distinction between neoliberalism and social democracy. Unregulated employment is neoliberal, regulated employment is social democratic; little state welfare is neoliberal, much state welfare is social democratic; a lot of violence is neoliberal, a little violence is social democratic.

The link between neoliberalism and scant employment regulation and state provision of welfare is well established. The neoliberal project seeks to limit the extent of democratic state involvement in the economy, including employment and welfare.

A distinction is made between the class and gender components of social democracy. The provision of state welfare may be class oriented or may include gender-oriented aspects, especially the state provision of childcare; the employment regulation may be class-oriented protections or may include gender equality components. The gender components are essential for the welfare and regulations to be categorized as fully social democratic. Narrow class- or labourist-oriented welfare and regulations are not sufficient for social democracy though they may be a step towards this, perhaps even proto-social democracy.

The link between neoliberalism, social democracy, and violence is newly made here. One link is through equality and democracy. Countries that are less equal and less democratic have higher rates of violence; these are characteristics of neoliberal rather than social democratic countries. However, the violence nexus is not fully reducible to the political economy nexus – there is a further path dependency here.

There are path-dependent varieties of modernity. Modernity takes different forms as a result not only of economic development but also of its path dependent trajectory. A path dependent nexus has been identified in the extent of employment regulation, state welfare provision, and violence. These map onto the distinction between neoliberalism and social democracy, though with some important variations.

The inclusion of complex inequalities other than class makes a significant difference to the analysis of the varieties of modernity. Varieties of gender regime do not simply map onto varieties of class regime, though there are some specific points of alignment in some countries.

Gender regimes and class regimes intersect and mutually adapt. They intersect in all institutional domains. The conventional focus on care-work as the primary locus of this intersection is too limited.

There is more than one institutional nexus that leads to path dependency. The analysis of path dependency in political economy needs to differentiate between those forms that centre on employment regulation and those that centre on state welfare expenditure. While these are aligned for gender relations, they are not aligned for class relations. A further basis for path dependency is found in violence: political economy is not the only set of institutions that provide the 'lock-in' needed for path-dependent trajectories of development. Some countries have a more violent trajectory of development than others.

Variations in regimes of inequality are the consequence of both economic development and path dependent development. In particular, the gender regime is still in transition from a domestic (premodern) to a public (modern) form; the public form may be more neoliberal or more social democratic.

Democracy and inequality are associated with some aspects of the violence nexus in that less democratic countries tend to spend more on the military and more unequal countries tend to have higher rates of homicide. They are associated with some aspects of the polity/economy nexus in that more democratic countries tend to spend more money on social matters and are more likely to have equal opportunities legislation.

The polity is important to these path dependent varieties of modernity, especially in its different depth of democracy and its openness to political pressure from the working class and employed women. A more democratic polity is associated with a more social democratic variety of modernity.

Appendix: Data Sources

The data set used in the analysis in this chapter and others is available on Sylvia Walby's web-site: http://www.lancs.ac.uk/fass/sociology/profiles/34/

The data may be used for further analyses with appropriate citation of this data set and the original providers of the data, who retain the title and ownership of the data. Any citation should include details of this book (author, title, publisher, date of publication), together with the original title and details of the data.

One part of the data set is confined to the OECD; other parts are near-global. The analysis is centred on 2003, since this was the latest date for which key parts of the OECD data were available in 2008.

Childcare expenditure: public expenditure on childcare (for under 3s) as a percentage of GDP, 2003. OECD (2008) *OECD Family Database* http://www.oecd.org/document/4/0,3343,en_2649_34819_37836996_1_1_1_1,00.html PF10 Public spending on childcare and early education. Table PF10.1. Public expenditure on childcare and early education services, per cent of GDP, 2003. Updated 30/03/08.

Social expenditure: public social expenditure as a percentage of GDP, 2003: OECD (2007) *OECD Factbook 2007*. (Paris: OECD). Page 193. http://miranda.sourceoecd.org/vl=1880195/cl=21/nw=1/rpsv/factbook/index.htm

Strictness of employment protection legislation, 2003: Summary indicator including regulation of regular employment, temporary employment and collective dismissals. OECD (2004) *Employment Outlook*. (Paris: OECD). Table 2.A2.4. page 117. http://www.oecd.org/dataoecd/8/4/34846856.pdf

Trade union density, bargaining coverage, centralization of collective bargaining and the coordination of collective bargaining (1994): OECD (1997) *Employment Outlook*. (Paris: OECD.)

Trade union membership of women, 2003: European Industrial Relations Observatory On-Line (2004) *Trade Union Membership 1999–2003*. EIRO. Accessed on 27 September 2006 at http://www.eiro.eurofound.eu.int/2004/03/update/tn0403105u.html

Equality legislation strength: Estimated from laws and literature: Nordic 3; other EU 2; US, Canada 1.5; the rest 1.

Women as a percentage of professional and managerial employment: UNDP (2005) *Human Development Report 2005*. (New York: Oxford University Press.)

Life expectancy (2004), Women as a percentage of non-agricultural workforce (2003), Gini (most recent year), Gross Domestic Product, Gross Domestic Product per person, PPP, World Bank (2006b) *World Development Indicators*. (Washington DC: The World Bank.) Accessed via ESDS International, (MIMAS) University of Manchester.

Divorce rate per 1,000 population, 2003: United Nations Statistics Division (2006). *Divorces and Crude Divorce Rates*. Available at http://unstats.un.org/unsd/demographic/products/dyb/DYB2003/table25.xls

Women as percentage of parliamentary representatives (2003) (lower house if there are two houses): Inter-Parliamentary Union (2006) *Statistical Archive: Women in National Parliaments*. Available at http://www.ipu.org/wmn-e/world-arc.htm

Law, order and defence expenditure as percentage of GDP, 2003: OECD (2006) *OECD Factbook 2006*. (Paris: OECD.)

Rates of homicide per 100,000 population, and homicide of women (global): Krug et al. (2002) *World Report on Violence and Health*. (Geneva: World Health Organization.)

OECD homicide and prisoners: Rates of homicide per 100,000 population recorded by the police (OECD), average of 1999–2001; Prisoners as percentage of 100,000 in 2001; Barclay, Gordon and Tavares, Cynthia (2003) 'International comparisons of criminal justice statistics 2001'. Accessed on 13 May 2006 at http://www.homeoffice.gov.uk/rds/pdfs2/hosb1203.pdf

Death penalty, whether legal, 2006: Amnesty International (2006) *The Death Penalty*. Available at http://web.amnesty.org/pages/deathpenalty countries-eng. Accessed on 02/10/2006.

Abortion, whether legal, around 1998: Kenworthy, Lane and Malami, Melissa (1999) 'Gender inequality in political representation: A worldwide comparative analysis', *Social Forces*, 78, 1, 235–269. Data set available at http://www.u.arizona.edu/~lkenwor/sf99-gender.htm

9 Measuring Progress

Introduction

The meaning of progress is contested. As described in the introductory chapter, there are four major types of approach to progress in the contemporary global era: economic development; equality; human rights; and capabilities. The goal of economic development is often the pre-eminent goal of governments and the global institutions of financial governance. This has long been seriously contested by the projects of equality and of human rights. More recently it has been challenged by the capabilities project. All of these have very significant variations.

What are the implications of using one rather than another of these contested framings of progress? When different definitions are used, how do countries fare? The assessment of these diverse framings of progress is investigated here using robust comparable data. In order to simplify this process complex data are transformed into simpler indicators. The process of operationalizing concepts of progress into indicators is itself highly contested; there is always a distinction between the concept and a quantitative measure that is intended to represent the concept. There is no simple mapping, only closer or more distant approximations to be argued over and improved.

There is a long history of the development of indicators in an increasing range of domains of social life that are cross-nationally comparative (Berger-Schmitt and Jankowitsch 1999; Noll 2002). There are now diverse indicators operationalizing different approaches to progress, including: the UNDP Human Development Index; the UNDP Gender-related Development Index; the UNDP Gender Empowerment Measure; the UN Millennium Development Goals; the EU Laeken Indicators of Social Exclusion; the EU Indicators of Equality between Women and Men; and the FreedomHouse index of Political Rights and Civil Liberties. While each set contains a mix of underpinning theoretical framings, they are generally built around a primary framing.

There are four major challenges in the development of indicators of progress. First, how can they encompass complex inequalities? The conventional indicators of progress within each of the major framings rarely include aspects that are central to complex inequalities other than class; frequently, they will require revision in order to achieve their stated aim. The second challenge is to include the whole range of domains – economy, polity, violence, and civil society. While all frames aspire to be relevant for outcomes in most domains, some are focused relatively narrowly. Third, do different framings of progress overlap or map onto each other, or are they alternatives with trade offs? Fourth, how do countries and social groups compare when different indicators of progress are used? What are the implications of different indicators when answering the question as to whether globalization has led to progress or not?

In this chapter there is a focus on five geographic levels – the world; the regions of the world, the OECD, the USA, and the EU; and the USA, UK, Ireland, and Sweden. Countries are pragmatically used here as convenient empirical categories of territorial units; they do not signify societies, nor that there is congruency of economy, polity, violence, and civil society in that territory.

Economic Development

The concept of economic development is centred on the level of productive resources used for the standard of living. It is widely invoked as an indicator of progress, especially by national governments and international bodies. Its use as such rests on the assumption that increases in economic development are linked to increases in other aspects of the good life. The main challenges to the use of these indicators of economic development as measures of progress are that using the average across a country hides the inequalities in accessing these living standards between different people, and that there are other matters that are more important including human rights and a broader notion of human and not just economic development. There is also a further challenge to the assumed link between economic development and progress in non-economic domains.

There are several small but significant differences between the indicators of economic development. First, is the difference between the achieved level of economic development and the rate of economic growth. Both are pertinent, but it is important not to conflate them. For example, current high levels of economic development may be due to growth spurts in the past rather than to current high growth rates. Second, indicators may concern a country or an individual, per capita (pc). A focus on the individual is more appropriate when the interest is in the standard of living. Third, the measure may be the Gross Domestic Product (GDP) or the Gross National Income (GNI). The difference between them is rarely great, but the latter is preferable since it takes into account transfers of money across national boundaries. For example, the repatriation of profits will reduce the GNI relative to the GDP which is significant in the case of Ireland where significant profits are transferred to the USA. However, it is technically harder to get the information needed for the GNI than for the GDP, so while the GNI is available for the OECD data used here it is not similarly available for the global data sets. Fourth, is the use of Purchasing Power Parity (PPP) or not. This adjustment is included in order to take account of the differences in what the same amount of money can buy in different countries. PPP is important in global data sets where such differences can be large, while the differences between most OECD countries are relatively small so the adjustment need not be made here.

Which regions and countries have the highest income per person? Global inequalities in income per person (GDPpc) are shown in Figure 9.1 and Table 9.1. People in the countries in the OECD have the highest incomes, those in Sub-Saharan Africa the lowest. A comparison of incomes in the USA, the EU, Sweden, the UK, and Ireland, as shown in Table 9.2, finds that people in the USA have significantly larger incomes (GDPpc) than those in the EU, but that there is considerable variation between the three countries of the EU under comparison with people in Ireland having more income than people in the UK and Sweden.

Where has income increased most rapidly? Comparisons will look different depending on the unit of measurement used – country or individual (see Table 9.2). The World Bank measures the rate of economic growth as the rate of increase in GDP of a country per year. On this measure the US economy outperforms that of the EU over the period 1975–2005: the USA sustained an increase of 260 per cent over this period as compared with 199 per cent for the EU. However, when the rate of increase in GDP per capita is compared, then the USA and the EU have very similar rates of growth over the periods 1975–2005 and 1990–2005. The GDP per capita in the EU rose to 181 per cent of its 1975 level in the 30 years to 2005, as compared with a rise of 189 per cent in the USA. During 15 years, 1990–2005, the US GDP per capita PPP grew at 2.1 per cent a year, as compared with 2.1 per cent in Sweden, 2.5 per cent in the UK, and 6.2 per cent in Ireland.

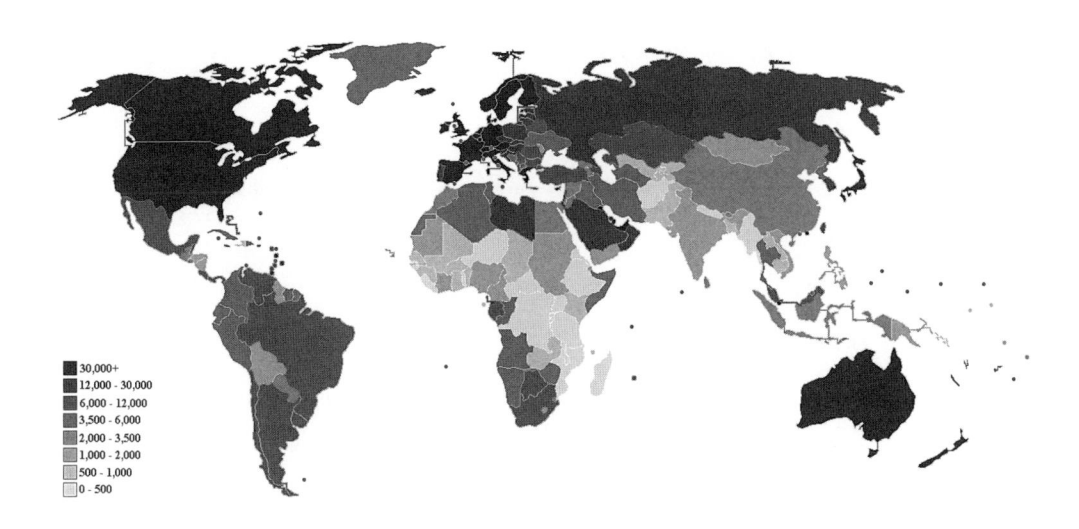

Figure 9.1 GDP per capita around the world, 2008
Source: Sbw01f (2008a).

Legend:
- 30,000+
- 12,000 - 30,000
- 6,000 - 12,000
- 3,500 - 6,000
- 2,000 - 3,500
- 1,000 - 2,000
- 500 - 1,000
- 0 - 500

Table 9.1 Income per person in world regions

	World	High income OECD	East Asia & Pacific	Europe & Central Asia	Latin America & Caribbean	Middle East & North Africa	South Asia	Sub-Saharan Africa
Income per person $ 1975 (1)	4834	15750	806		5581	3980	1101	1945
Income per person $ 2005 (2)	8476	29997	5284	8398	7575	5506	2825	1849
2005 GDPpc as per cent of 1975 (3)	175	190	856		136	138	257	95
GDPpc annual growth rate 1975–2005 (4)	1.4	2.1	6.1	1.4	0.7	0.7	2.6	−0.5

1. Gross Domestic Product per capita, Purchasing Power Parity based on constant 2000 international dollars. *Source*: World Bank (2006c).
2. GDP per capita, PPP, constant 2000 international dollars. *Source*: World Bank (2006c).
3. Calculated from data in table.
4. *Source*: UNDP (2007a).

Which is the better indicator – country or per person? If the point of the comparison is to understand the changes in the living standards of people then the best indicator is income per person

Table 9.2 Economic growth, 1975–2005, world, USA, EU, Ireland, Sweden, the UK

	World	USA	EU	Ireland	Sweden	UK
GDP per capita $, 1975 (1)	4834	19830	14359	8544	16993	15506
GDP per capita $, 2005 (2)	8476	37437	26038	36621	27784	28628
Increase in GDP per capita $: 2005 as per cent of 1975 (3)	175	189	181	429	164	185
GDP per capita annual growth rate, 1990–2005 (4)	1.5	2.1		6.2	2.1	2.5
GDP 1975 PPP$ billion (5)	14592	4277	3299	27	148	798
GDP 2005 PPP$ billion (6) (7)	36411	11141	6562	122	266	1607
Increase in GDP PPP$: 2005 as per cent of 1975 (8)	250	260	199	452	180	201
Population 1975 million (9)	4061399	215973	279739	3177	8193	56226
Population 2005 million (10)	6437784	296497	310597	4151	9024	60203
Population 2005 as per cent of 1975 (11)	159	137	110	131	110	107

(1) GDP per capita, PPP, constant 2000 international dollars, 1975. *Source*: World Bank (2006c).
(2) GDP per capita, PPP, constant 2000 international dollars, in 2005. *Source*: World Bank (2006c).
(3) Calculated as the percentage increase in GDP per capita (PPP constant 2000 international $) using data in this table. EU is European Monetary Union.
(4) GDP per capita annual growth rate, 1990–2005. *Source*: UNDP (2007a) Table 14.
(5) GDP per capita, PPP, constant 2000 international dollars. EU is EMU. *Source*: World Bank (2006c).
(6) GDP per capita, PPP, constant 2000 international dollars. EU is EMU. *Source*: World Bank (2006c).
(7) The GDP for EU27 is larger than for EMU, at $12,886,810. Calculated from World Bank (2007b).
(8) Calculated from data in this table.
(9) *Source*: World Bank (2006c).
(10) *Source*: World Bank (2006c).
(11) Calculated from data in this table.

(GDP per capita), but if the point of the comparison is to compare the power of countries on the world stage then the GDP of the country is the best indicator. It is only when countries are considered as wholes that the US economy seems to be getting bigger than the EU economy. When the focus is on the implications for individuals' standard of living, then there is very little difference between the EU and the USA. When the focus is on people, the best measure of economic growth is the rate of increase in GDP per capita per year. This is the headline indicator of economic growth used by the European Commission (European Commission 2004: 29 final/2 Graph 16).

The reason for the difference between the two measures is that increases in the total GDP in a country are driven not only by increases in GDP per person, but also by increases in the number of people living in that country. In the case of the USA, there has been a substantial increase in its population size during the period 1975–2005, such that in 2005 its population was 137 per cent of its 1995 size. By contrast, the increase in population of the EU over this same period was smaller, growing to 110 per cent of its 1975 population size. Most of these increases are due to immigration, since the fertility rate has not been above the replacement rate for either the USA or the EU during this period (World Bank 2006c). Hence, the difference between the EU and the USA in rates of growth of the overall GDP is associated with the higher rate of immigration into the USA than the EU during this period.

There is a widespread impression that the US is not just richer, but that it has a more successful economy; this is mistaken. The US economy is getting bigger, but it is not delivering increases in income to its citizens at a faster rate than the EU. There is very little difference between the rate of growth in GDP per capita between the USA and the EU.

As discussed more fully in Chapter 10, the higher income per person in the USA is a consequence not of its current economic performance, but of spurts of economic growth in the past. It is not uncommon that countries experience economic growth spurts at certain points of their history that then subside (Maddison 2003). Ireland experienced such an economic growth spurt during the 1990s and early 2000s (see Table 9.2), as is also the case for China (8.4 per cent GDPpc a year during 1975–2005) (UNDP 2007a: Table 14). Sometimes there is a coincidence between these growth spurts and changes in social relations other than class, for example, the increased employment of women or migrants. War and regime change both tend to reduce the rate of economic growth.

Equality

Equality is the main challenge to the conceptualization of progress as economic development. Economic growth can be of little benefit to the most disadvantaged if the rewards of economic development are confined to those who already have the most, while inequality can be inherently damaging to health, happiness, and other aspects of human well-being. It is the leading concept among a series of justice-oriented framings of progress. Equality is a relational concept in that it always implies the relative standing of two or more groups.

There are many challenges in the interpretation and operationalization of this concept. First, how is the difference component of complex inequalities to be addressed within the equality frame? Second, is equality better understood as an outcome or a process, such as equal opportunities? Third, what is the appropriate range of domains and practices to which the principle of equality should be applied? Fourth, in a globalizing world is the country or the world as a whole the more appropriate unit within which to analyse inequality? Fifth, in the context of the transformation of the gender regime, is the traditional use of the household rather than the individual as the unit for the analysis of economic inequality any longer appropriate?

Complex inequalities constitute a difficulty for the equality approach to progress because they contain positively valued differences as well as negatively valued inequalities. How are positively valued differences that produce or are entwined with inequality to be dealt with? The vast field of responses to this dilemma, from philosophy to practice, was described in the introduction to this book. One response is to argue for the equal valuation of different contributions, which means finding a common standard against which to measure things that only superficially appear different. Another is that equality can only be achieved when there is a transformation in which differences are eradicated or reduced. When operationalizing equality, however, this requires a single standard for each issue otherwise it is impossible to measure.

The strongest approach to equality addresses it as an outcome, while more modest approaches address it as a process, as equal opportunities or equal treatment. Many policies that are framed by equality in practice address it as a process, with equality of outcome a rather shadowy presence. For example, equality legislation in the EU and USA often focuses on the equal treatment of different people in employment.

The range of domains and practices for which equality is considered a legitimate goal varies widely, with equality often regarded as justified in some but not in others. The application of the principle of equality to issues in civil society and political process is widespread, especially in the West. For example, the concept of equality is invoked within the concept of universal human rights as one of an equal entitlement to access to these rights. An application of the principle of equality to the economy is less common, and here it is more often applied as a principle for process than one for outcome – equal opportunities but not equal ownership.

Sometimes a category of 'excessive' inequality is distinguished whereby while some levels of inequality are regarded as acceptable but higher levels are not. This lies behind the use of the concept of poverty, which is treated as if it were an unacceptably high level of economic inequality and distinguished from inequality in general.

The unit within which equality is measured makes an important difference to its significance and scale. Global processes are changing the balance between the significance of the country or the world as the unit of analysis; while changing gender inequalities are changing the balance of the significance of the household or individual as the unit of analysis.

Global processes challenge the conventional practice of using a country as the unit within which inequalities are analysed. If the world is globalized, should not the unit within which inequalities are analysed be the whole world instead? The choice of either country or world as the unit within which inequality is measured makes a profound difference to the answer to the question of whether inequality is increasing or decreasing. Of course the world is neither fully compartmentalized into countries, nor fully globalized into one unit, but rather is something in between. Insofar as globalization increases, then the relevance of the global rather than the country as the unit for analysis of inequality also increases.

Changes in gender relations challenge the conventional practice of using the household as the unit between which inequalities are analysed. Changes in gender inequalities in employment and the gendered structure of households mean that gender processes as well as class processes will shape inequalities between households. The more public the gender regime becomes, the more appropriate it is to use individuals rather than households as the unit of analysis.

Economic inequality

The size and direction of the change in economic inequalities varies with the measures that are used. Economic inequality can be measured not only as income but also as wealth; income can be restricted to wages or can include taxes and benefits; it can be counted for individuals or averaged across households; it can be analysed separately for different types of inequality or not; it may involve comparisons between people within the same country or around the whole world. Taking complex inequalities, especially gender, into account challenges the conventional use of the household as the unit of analysis, while a global perspective challenges the conventional focus on inequalities within countries.

Measuring income inequality between households using the Gini coefficient is common among academics, but relatively rare in global indicator sets. This measure takes the range as 0 to 100, where the larger the number is the higher is the inequality; it takes into account inequality across the whole spectrum. The Gini index measures the difference between a Lorenz curve – which plots the cumulative percentages of income against recipients – and a hypothetical line of perfect equality. A Gini index of 0 would be perfect equality, while 100 is perfect inequality. The data on income and size of household to support the index are derived from surveys of households, hence the coefficient will vary depending on the survey used. Usually all of the income is included, though this can vary as to whether this includes benefits or not. Usually the household is the unit and this is equivalized for household size (the EU uses the modified OECD scale: 1st adult = 1; additional household members 14 years+ = 0.5; additional household members <14 years = 0.3) (Deininger and Squire 1996; Alderson and Nielson 2002; Goodman and Shephard 2002; Brewer et al. 2006; World Bank 2008).

There are other measures of income inequality, including the ratio of incomes of richest 10 per cent to poorest 10 per cent (UNDP) and the share of the poorest 20 per cent in the national income (MDG Goal 1, Indicator 3).

Poverty is a concept related to economic inequality. However, it is a threshold concept rather than one centred on the social relationship of inequality between groups. In practice it usually means extreme or 'excessive' economic inequality and is often used in a context where some inequality is regarded as legitimate to demarcate it from that which is not. Poverty is an important concept in the UN Millennium Development Goals and the EU indicators of social inclusion. Poverty can be understood as absolute or as relative. The first MDG indicator concerns absolute poverty, measured as the proportion of the population living on less than a dollar a day. In developed economies it is more usual to use a relative measure: the EU indicators of social inclusion use 60 per cent of the median income.

Economic inequality within countries and regions around the world
Economic inequality between households as measured by the Gini coefficient (a low number means less inequality than a high number) varies considerably between different countries around the world, as is shown in Figure 9.2. As can be seen from this map, in some countries inequality is much higher than in others. Further there is some clustering of patterns of inequality into global regions with some global regions more unequal than others. Latin America and southern Africa have some of the highest rates of inequality.

Figure 9.2 Economic income inequality measured by the Gini coefficient around the world

Source: Sbw01f (2008b)

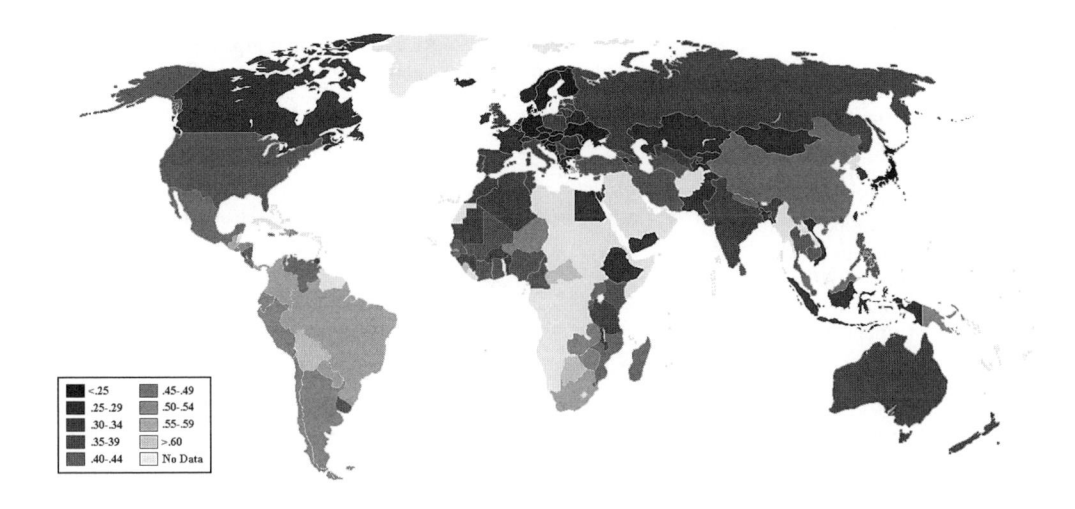

A target of the Millennium Development Goal 1 was to eradicate extreme poverty, between 1990 and 2015 halving the proportion of people living on less than a dollar a day. In 1990 nearly half (47 per cent) of people in Sub-Saharan Africa lived in such poverty, as did 41 per cent of those in Southern Asia, and a third (33 per cent) of those in South-Eastern Asia. During the period 1990 to 2004 there has been a significant reduction in the proportion of people in such extreme poverty living in developing regions, dropping from 32 per cent to 19 per cent. However, this drop in extreme poverty has not been paralleled by a similar drop in inequality. During the same period there has been a slight fall from 5 per cent to 4 per cent of the share of the poorest quintile (fifth) of the population in developing regions in national consumption (if there were equality this fifth would consume 20 per cent of the national total, MDG 1.3: see Table 9.3).

This pattern of regionally clustered inequality varies over time. Covering the period 1950–1999, and using Gini data from WIID, Mann and Riley (2006) have described the changing degrees of economic inequality between households across world regions. Latin America is consistently the most unequal region; South Asia is of middle-high inequality; East Asia has middling levels of inequality which decrease then increase over the period; the Anglo-Saxons are middling, but there has been a significant move from relatively low to relatively high inequality; in Continental Europe there has been a significant movement from relatively high inequality to

Table 9.3 Poverty and inequality, world regions, 1990, 2004

	Per cent population living on <$1 a day 1990	Per cent population living on <$1 a day 2004	Share of poorest fifth in national consumption 1990	Share of poorest fifth in national consumption 2004
Sub-Saharan Africa	47	41	3	3
Southern Asia	41	30	7	7
Eastern Asia	33	10	7	5
South-Eastern Asia	21	7	6	6
Latin America and the Caribbean	10	9	3	3
Northern Africa	3	1	6	6
Western Asia	2	4	6	5
Commonwealth of Independent States	1	1	8	6
Transition countries of South-Eastern Europe	0	1	8	8
Developing regions	32	19	5	4

Source: UN (2007a: 6–8).

relatively low inequality; the Nordics are least unequal and with decreasing inequality over this period.

Within the OECD, a group of 30 of the richest countries of the North, there is considerable variation in the degree of inequality in (see Table 9.4). There is a gradient from the most unequal neoliberal (Anglo-Saxon: 30.5, 30.1, 30.4, 33.7, 32.6, 35.7) to the less unequal social democratic (Nordic: 22.5, 26.1, 26.1, 24.3), with continental Europe (25.2, 27.3, 27.7, 34.7, 26.1, 25.1) in between but closer to the social democratic Nordics than the liberal Anglo-Saxon. The neoliberal USA (Gini 35.7) is the most unequal of the developed countries in the OECD (only Mexico and Turkey are more unequal); social democratic Sweden is the second least unequal (24.3: only Denmark is less unequal); and the UK (32.6) and Ireland (30.4) are in between and close to the OECD average of 31.0.

Within the OECD countries, there has been an average increase in inequality since 1980 at the same time as the recent wave of globalization. As measured by the Gini coefficient, the level of inequality rose from 29.3 to 31.0 between the mid-1980s and 2000 (OECD 2006a), as shown in Table 9.4. While the overall pattern is of a slight increase in economic inequality, the changes vary between countries. There is an increase in the more neoliberal Anglo economies, including the UK and the USA, in the UK rising from 29 to 33, and in the USA from 34 to 36. There is also an increase in inequality in some social democratic countries, especially the Nordic countries; for example, Sweden rose from 20 to 24 although even at the end of this period the Nordics are less unequal than the

Table 9.4 Inequality and poverty in household incomes, OECD: Gini, mid-1980s to 2000; per cent of households with less than 50 per cent and 60 per cent median income

	Mid-1980s	Mid-1990s	2000	Per cent households with less than 50 per cent of median income 2000–2004	Per cent households with less than 60 per cent of median income 2006
Australia	31.2	30.5	30.5	12.2	
Austria	23.6	23.8	25.2	7.7	13
Belgium				8.0	15
Canada	28.7	28.3	30.1	11.4	
Czech Rep		25.7	26.0	4.9	10
Denmark	22.8	21.3	22.5	5.6	12
Finland	20.7	22.8	26.1	5.4	13
France	27.6	27.8	27.3	7.3	13
Germany		28.3	27.7	8.4	13
Greece	33.6	33.6	34.5	14.3	21
Hungary		29.4	29.3	6.7	16
Ireland	33.1	32.4	30.4	16.2	18
Italy	30.6	34.8	34.7	12.7	20
Japan	27.8	29.5	31.4	11.8	
Luxembourg	24.7	25.9	26.1	6.0	14
Mexico	45.1	52.0	48.0		
Netherlands	23.4	25.5	25.1	7.3	10
New Zealand	27.0	33.1	33.7		
Norway	23.4	25.6	26.1	6.4	11
Poland		38.9	36.7	8.6	19
Portugal		35.9	35.6		18
Slovakia				7.0	12
Spain	36.7	33.9	32.9	14.2	20
Sweden	19.9	21.1	24.3	6.5	12
Switzerland			26.7	7.6	
Turkey	43.5	49.1	43.9		26
UK	28.6	31.2	32.6	12.5	19
USA	33.8	36.1	35.7	17.0	
OECD average	29.3	30.9	31.0		
EU 25					16

Sources:
Gini: OECD (2006: 219).
50 per cent median income: (UNDP 2007a).
60 per cent median income: Eurostat (2008) *At-risk-of poverty rate*.

average OECD country – this is a break from the pattern identified by Mann and Riley (2006). The continental European countries show a mix of stability and increased inequality (a break from the pattern of declining inequality found by Mann and Riley). There are exceptions to these clusters, for example, Ireland (often identified as an Anglo neoliberal economy) has seen a decline in inequality, with a fall in the Gini coefficient from 33 to 30.

There are wide variations in the proportion of the population living in poverty, defined here using the UNDP standard of less than 50 per cent of median income and an EU standard of less than 60 per cent of median income. Among OECD countries, using the UNDP threshold of 50 per cent of median income, the USA has the most people living in poverty.

Wealth inequalities within countries

Income inequality is not the only form of economic inequality, there are also differences in the extent to which households (and individuals) own wealth, such as houses, shares, and savings. These tend to show greater inequalities than income (Davies et al. 2008), including along ethnic divisions (Oliver and Shapiro 1997). The median Gini value of wealth inequality within countries around the world is 0.7 (Davies et al. 2008: 21).

There are significant variations in the extent of wealth in different world regions (see Table 9.5).

Table 9.5 **Wealth in world regions, 2000**

World region	Wealth per adult (US$)	Population share per cent	Wealth share per cent
North America	190653	6	34
Latin America and Caribbean	17892	8	4
Europe	67315	15	30
Africa	3415	10	1
China	3885	23	3
India	1989	15	1
Rich Asia-Pacific	165008	5	24
Other Asia-Pacific	5889	18	3
World	33875	100	100

Source: Davies et al. (2008: 8).

There are also significant variations in the inequality of wealth distribution in different countries (see Table 9.6). In the USA, 33 per cent of the wealth is owned by 1 per cent of the population and 70 per cent by the top 10 per cent (Gini 0.801); in the UK, 23 per cent of the wealth is owned by the top 1 per cent and 56 per cent by the top 10 per cent (Gini 0.697); in Ireland, 10 per cent is held by the top 1 per cent and 42 per cent by the top 10 per cent; in Sweden 59 per cent is held by the top 10 per cent (Davies et al. 2008: 4, 9).

Global economic inequality

One new way to think about economic inequalities in the world is to treat the whole world as the unit within which the analysis is

Table 9.6 Wealth shares within countries, 2000

Country	Share of top 10 per cent	Share of top 1 per cent	Gini
Australia	45		0.622
Brazil			0.784
Canada	53		0.688
China	41		0.550
Denmark	76	29	
Finland	42		
France	61	21	0.730
Germany	44		0.667
India	53	16	0.669
Indonesia	65	29	0.764
Ireland	42	10	
Italy	49	17	0.609
Japan	39		0.547
Korea, South	43	14	0.579
Mexico			0.749
New Zealand	52		
Norway	51		
Spain	42	18	0.570
Sweden	59		
Switzerland	71	35	0.803
Turkey			0.718
UK	56	23	0.697
USA	70	33	0.801

Source: Davies et al. 2008: 4, 9.

made. This is different from the more traditional way of thinking about global inequality as the summation of the inequalities within each country. In a globalizing era is it better to think of inequalities on a truly global scale, or are our horizons and reference groups still effectively limited by the countries in which people live? The answer is that both are relevant: for many people the country in which they live is the most relevant unit for analysing socio-economic inequalities, but as globalization proceeds then there is an increasing number of people and processes for which the whole world is the more relevant unit.

If global economic inequalities are the summation of changes in national inequalities, then this would mean that there is a global increase in class economic inequality, since many countries have had an increase in these inequalities though not an increase in gender economic inequality.

If the world as a whole is taken as the unit of analysis for global economic inequality, then global economic inequality is made up of two elements – not only inequality within countries, but also inequality between countries. The best way to place individuals in the global economy hierarchy then is to combine both inequality within their own country and also the position of their country in a global hierarchy (Milanovic 2005). The larger component is that of inequality between countries, accounting for between 67 per cent and 90 per cent of overall global inequality (Korzeniewicz and Moran 1997; Firebaugh and Goesling 2004). Hence analyses of changes in global inequality that take the whole world as the unit focus on inequality between countries rather than within countries. When the whole world is taken as the unit of analysis for inequality, then the popular assumption that there is increasing global economic inequality (Mazur 2000) is engaged by rival theories and empirical evidence (Wade 2004; Milanovic 2005) as to whether this is the case (Korzeniewicz and Moran 1997) or not (Dollar and Kraay 2001; Firebaugh and Goesling 2004).

Increasing global economic inequality is predicted by the thesis that the rich core countries of the global economic system shape the rules of the global system in matters such as trade and finance so that they advantage themselves. Unequal terms of trade and investment mean the rich countries in the core of the world system grow more rapidly at the expense of development in the periphery (Wallerstein 1974; Chase-Dunn 1998). Decreasing global economic inequality is predicted by the thesis that the neoliberal wave of deregulation of global trade and finance allows the economies of poorer developing countries to thrive and catch up with the older industrialized countries, as they are able to specialize in economic niches no longer blocked by protectionist tariffs (Ohmae 1990; Dollar and Kraay 2001).

During previous waves of globalization, global economic inequalities between countries have grown substantially. Average incomes in the richest countries were four times more than those in the poorest countries; this had risen to around 30 times more by the end of the twentieth century (Firebaugh 1999).

But has this increase in global economic inequality stopped, and if so has it stopped for reasons associated with the recent wave of globalization? The case for a continued increase in world income inequality since 1965, especially during the 1980s, is made by Korzeniewicz and Moran (1997). They use data for 46 countries from the World Bank – accounting for 68 per cent of the world's population – comparing the changes in the Gross National Product per capita (GNPpc) using exchange rate data from 1965 to 1992. Using the Gini coefficient, they find that there is a considerable increase in the gap in GNPpc between countries in this period, rising from .682 in 1965 to .738 in 1992, a growth in inequality of 8.2 per cent.

But the detailed assumptions on which they base their statistical analysis have been challenged. There are two major contested assumptions. First, how is income to be compared when the same amount of money can buy different amounts of goods and services in different countries? The same amount of money, measured in official exchange rates, will typically buy more things in a poor country than in a rich one (as most global tourists are well aware). There is a technical device to address this – introducing a ratio so as to bring the effective purchasing power into alignment, called 'Purchasing Power Parity' or PPP. Based on research as to how much it takes to buy the same basket of goods in different countries, PPP brings monetary income into alignment with what it will buy in a country rather than what it will do in terms of foreign exchange. When PPP is applied the value of the incomes in poor countries increases, and the increase in global economic inequality found using exchange rates disappears in the recent period (Firebaugh 1999; Wade 2004).

The second contested assumption concerns the significance of population size. If this is taken into account, instead of treating each country as equally significant, then the picture shifts because of China and India. The economies of these two countries are growing very quickly and they have very large populations, jointly making up 38 per cent of the world's people. When the analysis takes population size into account, people in the poorer parts of the world are catching up just a little with those in rich countries. However, if just China (let alone China plus India) were excluded, then there is a widening of the economic inequalities between people in the developed and developing parts of the world (Firebaugh and Goesling 2004; Wade 2004; Milanovic 2005).

A different point of view starts from this concern for China and moves to a wider consideration of regional differences more broadly. Growth rates are very uneven between regions. It is not all of the poor South that is doing well, just China, India, and East Asia. Between 1980 and 2000, there has been higher economic growth with accompanying falls in the rate of poverty in China, India, and East Asia, while in Latin America economic development has stagnated and the former Soviet Union and Central and Eastern Europe together with Sub-Saharan Africa regressed with increases in poverty (Wade 2004). Incomes have grown rapidly in the 'core' countries of North America, Western Europe, and Japan, while in others they have stagnated and in some cases fallen.

Is the rapid growth of China a sign that globalization has led to more economic growth and a reduction in poverty and economic inequality as Dollar and Kraay (2001) claim? They would argue that globalization – here operationalized as increasing world trade and understood as driven by neoliberal type concerns for deregulation – has produced economic growth in such a way as to decrease global economic inequality. However, the changes in China's trajectory of development are probably more linked to changes in internal than external relations.

This analysis has so far been restricted to inequalities between households, thereby making gender inequalities invisible. The introduction of gendered economic inequalities has implications for the analysis of inequalities on a global scale.

The global distribution of wealth is more uneven than the global distribution of income (Davies et al. 2008). The percentage of global wealth held in different regions and countries is shown in Table 9.5. North America holds 34 per cent of the wealth despite having only 6 per cent of the world's population (within which the USA holds 33 per cent of global wealth despite having only 5.5 per cent of the world population), while Europe holds 30 per cent of the global wealth with 15 per cent of the global population.

It is clear that global economic inequalities have been increasing for decades and indeed centuries, but the current picture is more opaque. Whether class-based global economic inequalities are considered to be increasing or decreasing today depends on a series of issues concerning the unit of analysis and the definition of concepts. If global economic inequality is considered to be the summation of class-based inequalities in each country, then inequality is increasing. However, if the whole world is taken as the unit, then rapid economic growth among the large populations of China and India means that the inequalities between countries that make up the majority part of global inequality are reducing a little, and with them global economic inequality overall.

Beyond the household

Most of the internationally comparative data on economic inequality use the household as the unit of analysis. Changes in this measure of inequality are usually assumed to be driven by changes in the structure of employment, capital-labour relations, and welfare transfers. Comparisons and changes over time in inequalities between households are not a good guide to changes in class inequality since the household is a social entity at the intersection of class and gender inequalities. While measuring economic inequality using the household as the unit has the advantage of a robust supply of widely available comparable data over time, it has several disadvantages associated with the conflation of the divergent dynamics of change of class-based and gender-based inequalities and the obscuring of their separate trajectories of change. The class and gender changes are better if at least initially separated for analysis: this requires an analysis of the class and gender changes using the individual as the unit. There is then the option of considering them separately as well as examining their intersection at the household level.

The major changes are class-based and gender-based. A key part of the class-based changes is the change in wage dispersion, both at the top and bottom ends; a second part is the change in tax and benefit systems. There are two major ways in which changes in gender relations will have implications for changes in the inequality of income distribution between households – changes in gendered employment rates and gender pay gaps, and changes in gendered household composition and structure.

Since the 1980s there has been an increase in wage inequality along with an increase in the dispersion of wages in many countries, though this is varyingly so. This is due to processes at both the bottom and the top of the labour market. There is a relative decline in some countries among those who are already the least paid, partly as a result of the attack on and decline in trade unionism and minimum wages (DiNardo et al. 1996; Lee 1999; Card and DiNardo 2002). There has also been a relative increase in wages among those who are already better paid, in part due to changes in the skills required in the knowledge economy and also due to significant increases in executive pay (Glyn 2001; Smeeding 2002).

Gendered economic inequalities
Gendered economic inequalities are important in two ways: they are important forms of inequalities in their own right, and they contribute to inequalities between households. They include the gender gap in employment rates (an indicator for gender equality for the UN MDG and the EU); the gender gap in unemployment rates (an indicator for gender equality for the EU); the gender pay gap (an EU indicator for gender equality); women's share of earned income (a component of the UNDP gender-related development index); occupational segregation (an EU indicator for gender equality); and the proportion of women in managerial and professional jobs (a component of the UNDP Gender Empowerment Measure).

Gender employment gaps
Gender employment gaps are a component of gender economic inequality. While the division between free wage labour and domestic care-work has sometimes been treated as a matter of difference rather than inequality, here it is treated primarily as an instance of inequality whilst also recognizing that it can simultaneously be regarded as a difference. However, it is noteworthy that the inequalities are more obvious in economies that are more fully marketized, as in the North, than where the economy is less marketized and more agriculturally based, as in (though to a declining extent) some of the South. In order to take into account the different social

Table 9.7 Women as a percentage of employees (non-agricultural wage employment) 1990 and 2005, world regions

	1990	2005
Southern Asia	13	18
Northern Africa	20	20
Western Asia	16	21
Sub-Saharan Africa	28	32
Oceania	28	38
South-Eastern Asia	38	39
Eastern Asia	38	41
Latin America and the Caribbean	37	42
Developed regions	44	47
Commonwealth of Independent States	49	51
World	36	39

Source: UN (2007c: 12).

relations in agriculture, the analysis is confined to the more marketized relations in non-agricultural production. In the global data sets this requires a specific adjustment, though in the case of the OECD and EU data sets this is not so necessary since agriculture is such a small part of these economies. (See Chapter 3 for a fuller account of these arguments.)

The gender gap in employment (non-agricultural) varies significantly between world regions: the global average female percentage in the labour force was 39 per cent in 2005 and it is highest in the North (see Table 9.7). There has been an increase in women's employment between 1990 and 2005 in all world regions save for northern Africa where it has remained static.

Female employment has also been increasing overall in the OECD countries, rising from 39 per cent to 44 per cent between 1980 and 2006 (see Table 9.8). In all countries except two, there has been an increase or plateauing of female employment between 1980 and 2006. The Czech Republic had a small (2 per cent) drop following marketization in 1989, but the trend is now one of upward recuperation. Turkey has also had a decline, but this is typical of a country that has reached this stage of industrialization. There is convergence in these rich countries of the North towards a near equal presence (47 per cent) of women and men in the labour market. This is common to both social democratic and neoliberal countries with the only caveat that the Nordic social democratic countries are reaching a plateau earlier; furthermore the former communist countries have a legacy of high female employment rates that has proved largely resilient despite marketization. This increase in female employment – which narrows the gender employment gap – is a significant decline in one aspect of gendered economic inequality.

Table 9.8 Labour force, per cent female, OECD, 1980–2006

	1980	2006
Australia	37	45
Austria	38	44
Belgium	36	44
Canada	40	46
Czech Rep	47	45
Denmark	45	46
Finland	47	47
France	40	45
Germany	39	45
Greece	33	41
Hungary	43	45
Iceland	44	46
Ireland	28	43
Italy	33	40
Japan	39	41
Korea	37	41
Luxembourg	35	42
Mexico	27	35
Netherlands	37	44
New Zealand	40	46
Norway	41	47
Poland	45	46
Portugal	39	46
Slovakia	45	45
Spain	28	41
Sweden	47	47
Switzerland	37	46
Turkey	35	26
UK	41	45
USA	41	46
High income OECD average	39	44

Source: World Bank (2008).

The gender pay gap

The gender wage gap has declined very slowly in many advanced economies since the 1980s, though in several it remains substantial. The reduction in the gender pay gap in the EU between 1996 and 2006 is shown in Table 9.9.

The EU has a smaller gender pay gap than the USA, with 15 percentage points for the EU and 22 for the United States. Among the EU countries, smaller gaps are found in southern Europe as compared with northern Europe. Although the gender pay gap is a widely agreed measure of gender inequality, there are some technical weaknesses in its construction that make it open to misleading interpretations when used in cross-country comparisons (Juhn et al. 1991; Grimshaw et al. 2002). Smaller gender pay gaps are often found in countries with lower rates of female employment (as is the case in southern as compared with northern Europe). This, perhaps

Table 9.9 Gender wage gap EU, USA, 1996, 2006

Country	1996	2006
EU (27 countries)	17	15
Belgium	10	7
Denmark	15	17
Germany	21	22
Ireland	21	9
Greece	15	9
Spain	14	13
France	13	11
Italy	8	9
Luxembourg	19	14
Hungary	23	11
Netherlands	23	18
Austria	20	20
Portugal	6	9
Romania	24	10
Slovenia	15	8
Finland	17	20
Sweden	17	16
United Kingdom	24	21
USA	22	

Sources: EU: Eurostat (2008) *Gender Pay Gap*; USA: OECD (2002) *Employment Outlook 2002*, Table 2.15. For 1998.

surprising, finding is most likely a side-effect of the lower rates of female waged labour, which means that the women who would be paid least are least likely to be in employment. In economies where there is fuller female employment, the low paid as well as high paid women are compared with men (Blau and Kahn 2003).

Given the weakness of the gender pay gap as a measure of gender economic inequality because of its sensitivity to differences in female employment rates, it is appropriate to consider alternative indicators that will better measure the concept of inequalities in access to income from employment. One such measure is that of the female share of earned income, constituted by both the extent of female employment and the size of the gender wage gap. This is used by the UNDP as a component of the Gender-related Development Index. The ratio of female to male earned income for the OECD is presented in Table 9.10. There is an increase in the proportion of income earned by women in the OECD on average from 47 per cent to 59 per cent between 1995 and 2005. There are variations among the OECD countries. While the average shows an increase, there are declines in the former communist countries that are now members of the OECD (the Czech Republic, Poland, and Slovakia), with the exception of Hungary which has remained static.

A further measure of gender inequality in employment is that of occupational segregation by sex. However, in a manner parallel to

Table 9.10 Gendered economic inequality: ratio of female to male earned income, 1995, 2005; per cent managers female, OECD, medium developed countries

	Ratio of female to male earned income, c.1995	Ratio of female to male earned income, c.2005	Managers, legislators, senior officials per cent female, c.2005
Australia	.56	.70	37
Austria	.51	.46	27
Belgium	.38	.55	32
Canada	.41	.64	36
Czech Rep	.68	.51	30
Denmark	.66	.73	25
Finland	.68	.71	30
France	.56	.64	37
Germany		.58	37
Greece	.29	.55	26
Hungary	.64	.64	35
Iceland		.72	27
Ireland	.29	.53	31
Italy	.38	.47	32
Japan	.50	.45	10
Korea	.28	.40	8
Luxembourg	.30	.51	
Mexico	.29	.39	29
Netherlands	.34	.64	26
New Zealand	.45	.70	36
Norway	.61	.77	30
Poland	.65	.60	33
Portugal	.43	.59	34
Slovakia	.66	.58	31
Spain	.23	.50	32
Sweden	.71	.81	30
Switzerland	.37	.63	8
Turkey	.43	.35	7
UK	.45	.66	34
USA	.53	.63	42
Average OECD	.47	.59	29
Average medium development		.49	28

Sources: UNDP (1995: Table 3.1); (UNDP 2007a: Table 29).
1995: Year most recently available in 1995.
2005: Year most recently available in 2007/8.
Average OECD: The average is of the OECD countries listed in the table.
Average medium development: average of UNDP medium development countries (managers N = 28; income N = 79).

that of the gender pay gap, it is sensitive to variations in female employment rates, thereby producing odd outcomes in a comparative analysis. A more robust measure of comparative gender positions in employment is that of the proportion of women in top jobs, such as managerial and professional jobs. The wide variations apparent in the proportion of managers, legislators, and senior officials that are female in OECD countries are shown in Table 9.10. These are positively associated with high rates of female employment. Interestingly, this is one of the few measures of economic equality where the USA does well.

Is it the case that economic development and increased rates of female employment drive reductions in gender inequality in other aspects of employment? This can be investigated by comparing an average of the highly developed countries of the OECD and medium developed countries (UNDP definition) see Table 9.10. The average ratio of female to male earned income in the highly developed countries of the OECD at .59 is significantly higher than the ratio of .49 in countries of medium development (UNDP classification). Part of this difference is due to the higher rate of female employment in the non-agricultural sector in the more developed countries. However, a different picture emerges when the proportion of women in managerial jobs is compared. The highly developed OECD countries have an average of 29 per cent of women among managers (managers, legislators, and senior officials) as compared with 28 per cent among those countries listed by the UNDP as of medium development. This is a near identical level of gender equality in terms of presence in managerial jobs in the countries of only medium development with those in the OECD.

Table 9.11 compares the USA with the EU, and its member states of Sweden, the UK, and Ireland. The female employment rate in each is just less than 50 per cent. The USA does poorly on indicators of pay gap and income share as compared with the others, but better on the proportion of women in managerial jobs.

Table 9.11 Gendered economic inequality, USA, EU

	USA	EU	Ireland	Sweden	UK
Female per cent of workforce (1)	46	45	43	47	45
Female per cent of non-agricultural workforce (2)	48	45	48	51	49
Gender pay gap (3)	22	15	9	16	21
Ratio of female to male earned income (4)	.63		.53	.81	.66
Female per cent of legislators, senior officials and managers (5)	42		31	30	34

(1) Female per cent of the workforce, 2006. EU is EU27 (calculated from WBI). *Source*: World Bank (2008).
(2) Female share of non-agricultural workforce, 2004. EU is EMU. *Source*: World Bank (2007b).
(3) The gender pay gap is the difference between the average gross hourly earnings of male paid employees and female paid employees. The population is paid employees aged 16–64 working 15 or more hours a week. EU is EU27. *Source*: Eurostat (2008). Data for the USA are 1998, for persons aged 20–64, from OECD (2002a: Table 2.15).
(4) Data for most recent year 1996–2005. The estimates are based on the gender pay gap and gender gap in employment rates. *Source*: UNDP (2007a: Table 29).
(5) Female per cent of legislators, senior officials and managers. Data for most recent available year 1994–2005. *Source*: UNDP (2007a: Table 29).

Gender-based changes in employment show decreasing inequality: decreases in the gender employment gap and the gender pay gap, the disproportionality of share of earned income and of presence in top jobs.

The Intersection of gender and class inequality in the household
Inequalities between households are the outcome of the intersection of class and gender inequalities in the household; the conflation or reduction of these to class-based inequalities is a mistake. With the transformation of the gender regime from a domestic to a public form, there is an increase in the relative importance of the individual rather than the household as the unit of analysis because of the increased significance of the complicated changes in gender relations for overall changes in economic inequality.

The household is at the intersection of class-based and gender-based changes. Class-based changes in employment are tending to increase inequality at least in the spread of wages at both top and bottom ends of the labour market. Gender-based changes in employment are decreasing gender-based inequality: there are decreases in the gender employment gap, the gender pay gap, male disproportionality in earned income, and male over-representation in top jobs. However, increases in the overall wage spread in most countries have encompassed the narrowing of the gender gaps within this overall change.

The intersection of class and gender in households is affected by the composition and structure of the households in several ways, including two major forms: the differential distribution of female employment across the pay and household distributions, and the changing composition and structure of households.

First, in those countries where there is not yet full female employment, those women who are in employment are disproportionately at the upper end of the educational and wage distributions. Since partners and spouses tend to be from the same position in socio-economic hierarchies, this differential female employment has the consequence of boosting the household incomes of the households in the upper part of the distribution relative to those at the bottom, thereby increasing the inequality between households.

Second, there has been an increase in lone mother households, which are disproportionately poor. This aspect of the process has often been linked to a thesis of the feminization of poverty (Pearce 1978; Northrop 1990). An increase in the proportion of lone mother households is likely to lead to an increase in inequalities between households, since these are typically poor with at best one female income. This form of household has been growing in many countries in the last half century as a consequence of a series of changes in the gender regime (for example, the percentage of births out of wedlock rose from 11.5 per cent to 41.5 per cent in the UK between 1980 and 2003, as compared with a rise in Ireland from 2.4 per cent to 11.3 per cent between 1960 and 2003), though to widely varying extents, especially in countries that have a more public gender regime and a more neoliberal form (lone mother households make up 23 per cent of households with dependent children in the UK as compared with 17 per cent in Ireland and 7 per cent in Spain). The extent of the impact of the growth in lone mother households on the income distribution between households varies with the extent to which this household form is supported not only by female employment but also by state welfare transfers: they are less well supported and more in poverty in neoliberal countries (for example, over 50 per cent of lone mother households in Ireland and just over 30 per cent in the UK are in poverty as compared with just over 10 per cent in Sweden: these data are from Trifiletti 2007). The implication of these changes in household structure is that an important part of the increase in inequality between households is due to the intersection of changes in the gender regime with class relations. It is not a class issue alone.

The rise in lone motherhood is a significant contributor to both gender inequality and to inequality between households. While this has been a widespread development, especially in the North, it is highly uneven. There are several contributory factors. It might be thought that high rates of divorce and high rates of births outside of marriage would be important. However, in a comparison of the USA with Sweden, the UK and Ireland (see Table 9.12), Sweden – despite the highest rate of births outside of marriage and a moderate divorce rate – has the lowest rate of single parent households. It is Ireland that has the highest rate of single parent households, despite a very low divorce rate and the lowest rate of births outside of marriage. A key reason for the low rate of single parenthood in Sweden and its high rate in Ireland is the rate of cohabitation, which is high in Sweden and low in Ireland. In Sweden most parents live in partnerships, even though these may well not be marriages. The permeability of marriage and partnerships in Sweden is a protection against lone parenthood and not its cause. This is supported by the high level of state expenditure on children, so that a significant part of the costs of raising children is borne collectively rather than by specific parents. Perhaps the permeability of marriage and partnerships with low risks of poverty and lone motherhood might be seen as an indicator of progress. The social democratic family and household forms reduce the risk of poverty and lone parenthood as compared with practices in more neoliberal countries.

The use of the household as a unit in the analysis of inequality needs to be rethought. It is often interpreted as if it were a measure

Table 9.12 Household forms, sexual and reproductive rights, USA, Ireland, Sweden, UK

	USA	Ireland	Sweden	UK
Household form (1)				
Single parent households	8.7	11.7	5.8	6.0
Per cent births outside of marriage	33.2	31.8	55.3	39.5
Divorce rate	6.2	1.0	3.8	4.0
Co-habitation as per cent of all couples	7	4	23	11
Fertility rate (2)	2.0	2.0	1.8	1.7
Sexual and reproductive rights				
Abortion rights (3)	3	4	1	2
Restriction of contraception (4)	1	2	1	1

(1) *Source*: Martin and Kats (2003).
(2) Fertility is births per woman, 2004. EU is EMU. *Source*: World Bank (2006b).
(3) In this ranking, 1–5, a low number indicates little legal restriction on abortion, while 4 indicates great legal restriction on abortion. *Sources*: USA: Ferree et al. (2002b). USA allows abortion in the first trimester (first three months of pregnancy) with varying forms of restriction; in the USA there is variability between states; in the UK there is legal abortion for the first two trimesters dependent upon easily obtained medical judgement there is a medical or (effectively) social need, except for Northern Ireland where abortion remains illegal; in Ireland abortion has barely emerged from a constitutional ban even in cases of rape.
(4) In this ranking, 1–4, a low number indicates little legal restriction on contraception, while 4 indicates a great legal restriction on contraception. Contraception is legal in the USA, and the UK, legal but opposed by the church in Ireland.

of class-based inequality that is predominantly determined by changes in male employment patterns. Instead it is a site of the complex intersection of class-based and gender-based changes in both the employment structure and the household structure. The dynamic of the gender changes is often in contrary directions: the increase in women's employment and presence in top jobs – with a narrowing of the gender gaps in employment and shares of earned income – reduces gender-based inequalities, while the increase in the proportion of households headed by women – both as elderly single households and younger lone mothers – increases gender inequality. The intersection of these gendered changes with changes in class-based employment produces a complex outcome which is not reducible to class. The household should not be used as the sole or primary unit in analyses of economic inequality, although it remains useful and relevant. It is important to use individuals as the unit of analysis as well as the household.

Economic inequalities and flows

Not all economic inequalities are easily measured within country-based units or the whole world. Flows of people around the world have significant impacts on inequalities. Some flows are of elite groups that are able to cross frontiers with ease to conduct business and politics at a global level. Other flows concern people who are considered as not legally entitled to cross borders yet do so nonetheless, but at the expense of their loss of citizenship rights and their ensuing vulnerability to unscrupulous profit-hungry employers and people-traffickers. Many flows are in between – neither illegal nor performed with ease but generating complex patterns of advantage and disadvantage, increasing and decreasing specific inequalities. These include long-term and short-term economic migrants, receiving wages that are low relative to the host country but high relative to their country of origin, with the flows of remittances producing further complex effects on patterns of inequalities.

Economic inequalities in summary

Is the unit in which we should think of inequality that of specific countries or the whole world? The answer is both: we live neither in hermetically sealed nation-states nor in a fully globalized world. Both units of analysis are relevant, not just one or the other. The most important reference groups for most people are still country specific, though for transnational migrants and finance capital the world is a more pertinent unit. The whole world will become more relevant to more people as the unit with which to think about inequality as global flows increase. In the meantime both frames of reference are pertinent. Changes in economic inequality are due to both global and national changes, as is indicated in Chapter 3.

Global processes both increase and decrease economic inequalities in an interaction with national processes. Within country inequality has increased in some but not all countries. Global economic inequalities would have continued to increase, except that China is narrowing the gap with the North and is thereby reducing the average global inequality. Some of these changes are due to global economic processes; some are due to the spread of neoliberal forms of capitalism, a political rather than economic process; some come from country-level processes. There are some countries where economic inequality has not increased as well as those where it has. There are differences in the trajectory of class and gender inequality and other complex inequalities which are not reducible to each other. Diverse global processes – including global flows, networks, hegemons, institutions, and waves – restructure economic inequality, not as a single linear process but rather by coevolving.

Changes in gendered economic inequality do not map simply onto changes in class-led forms of economic inequality. There are reductions in gendered economic inequality in many places, consequent on the transformation of the gender regime and the increase in women's waged labour. This has often been left out of focus not only as a consequence of theoretical and conceptual priorities, but also because of the tendency to measure empirical economic inequality in terms of inequalities between households rather than inequalities between individuals. Using the household as the unit in these analyses obscures or even erases the gender dimension to inequality.

Global processes are not simply increasing or decreasing economic inequalities, but instead are restructuring them in regionally differentiated and path dependent forms.

Inequalities in non-economic domains

While the economic domain is the area to which the principle of equality is most often applied, it is not the only one. There are equality issues in all domains, including the polity, violence, and civil society. However, while equality has been applied to some aspects of the polity, its application to civil society and violence has been very restricted. Many of the issues concerning progress in relation to the intersection of civil society and the polity have been addressed through the frame of human rights and so are addressed in the next section. Issues concerning violence are addressed in a later section in which their relationship with equality and other progress framings is considered.

Are non-economic inequalities increasing or decreasing? Are these changes associated with global processes? The main issue of equality in the polity is that of equal access for all citizens to political power, as is aspired to though rarely fully achieved in democracies. In violence there are inequalities in its deployment and regulation (addressed later). In civil society there are inequalities in access to civil liberties such as free speech and association (addressed in the section on human rights).

Democracy

Is there an increase in democracy around the world? Using the definition of democracy as suffrage-democracy, there has been an increase in democratic aspects of government during and since the twentieth century. Using data from Freedom House on civil liberties and political rights, Rummel (2008) finds a steady increase in democracy during the twentieth century. Similar findings of an increase in democracy are located using slightly different data and concepts from the Polity IV

Figure 9.3 Increase in democracy and decline of autocracy, 1946–2006

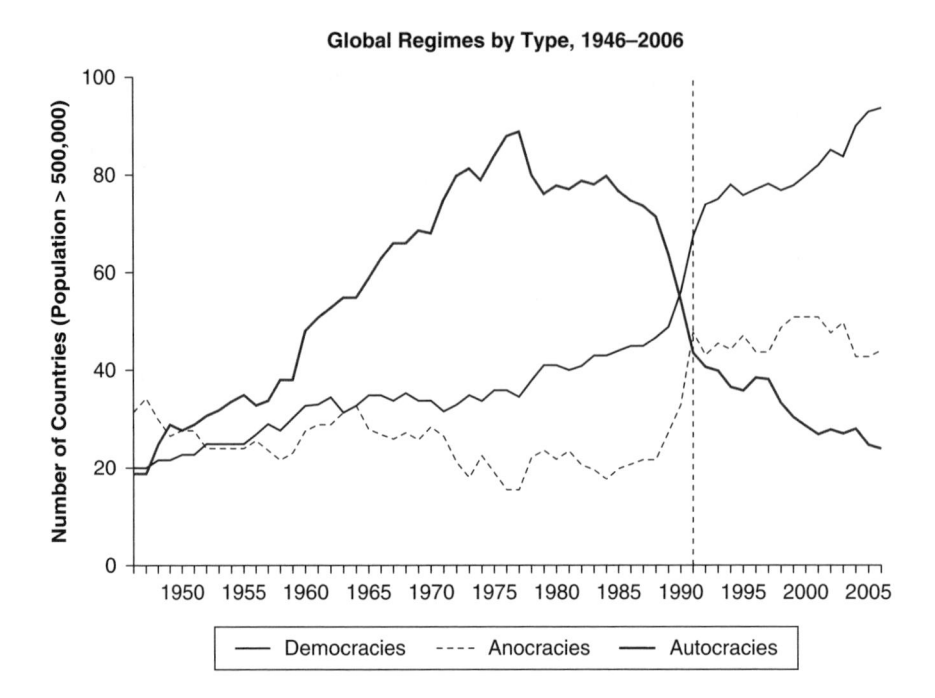

Source: Polity IV Project (2008) http://www.systemicpeace.org/polity/polity4.htm

Global Regimes by Type, 1946–2006

Project, as shown in Figure 9.3. Substantial evidence exists that there has been an increase in suffrage-democracy over the last century.

However, the definitions of democracy used in these analyses are fairly minimal – they focus on universal suffrage, free elections, free speech and association, and an absence of hereditary power. They do not include deeper aspects of democracy, such as the presence in parliament or the breadth of application of the democratic principle. Three main levels of democracy using ten aspects were identified in Chapter 4 on polities: suffrage-democracy (1–5), presence-democracy (in addition 6–9) and deep-democracy (in addition 10).

A key aspect of presence-democracy is the election of members of parliament that are proportionate to their presence in the population. In the case of gender there has been a slow and uneven increase since women were first entitled to vote. The proportion of women elected to the lower house of parliaments around the world was 12 per cent in 1997 and rose to 18 per cent in 2008 (Inter-Parliamentary Union 2008).

Using these criteria of the deepening of democracy, the comparative trajectory of the USA, the UK, Ireland, and Sweden, together with the EU institutions, is summarized in Table 9.13 (for sources here see Chapter 4 on polities), which shows the uneven development of democracy in these countries, with the deepest being in Sweden.

Table 9.13 Depth of Democracy: USA, Ireland, Sweden, UK, EU

	USA	Ireland	Sweden	UK	EU
No hereditaries or unelecteds	Yes	11/60 appointed to 2nd chamber; Republic 1937	Monarch, no powers since 1975; very few since 1907/9	Monarch, few powers; hereditary and appointed 2nd chamber	Yes
No colonies	Yes (but territories: American Samoa, Guam, Marianas Islands, Puerto Rico, US Virgin Islands); Guantanamo Bay	Yes	Yes	Since 1970s	Yes
No religious governance	Yes, but some fundamentalism	Catholic Church	Yes	Yes	Yes
Suffrage	Majority ethnic men 1776 Majority ethnic women 1920; African-American 1968	Men 1884/1918/1922 Women 1922	Men 1909/1918 Women 1918/1920	Men 1884/1918 Women 1918/1928	Men, women 1979
Free elections	Yes	Yes	Yes	Yes	Yes
Low-cost electioneering	High cost	Low cost, legal cap	Low cost, custom	Low cost, legal cap	Low cost, custom
Proportional representation	No	Yes	Yes	No	Yes
Quotas	No	No	Yes	No	No
Proportionate presence (a) parliamentary (b) ministerial (1)	(a) 16 per cent women 16/31 per cent ethnic (b) 14.3 per cent women	(a) 13 per cent women (b) 21.4 per cent women	(a) 47 per cent women 1994: >40 per cent (b) 52.4 per cent women	(a) 20 per cent women 2/10 per cent ethnic (b) 28.6 per cent women	(a) 30 per cent women
Range of institutions	Very narrow	Narrow	Broad	Medium	Narrow

1. No hereditary or unelected positions, including monarch and members in either chamber of Parliament.
2. No colonies; i.e. no governance of territories that do not also meet these criteria.
3. No powers of governance held by additional non-democratic polity, e.g. organized religion.
4. Universal suffrage, de facto as well as de jure.
5. Elections, especially those that are free, fair, and competitive; in a context of free speech and free association and developed civil society associations.
6. Low cost of electioneering, either by law or by custom.
7. Electoral system with proportional representation.
8. Electoral system with quotas for under-represented groups such as women.
9. Proportionate presence in parliament of women and minorities.
10. Wide range of institutions (e.g. welfare services) governed by the democratic polity.

(1) Data for 2005. *Source*: UNDP (2007a: Table 33); *original source*: Inter-Parliamentary Union.

There has been a decline in political inequalities due to the increase in suffrage democracy around the world over the last century, which is substantial despite variations and setbacks. There have also been increases in deeper forms of democracy, especially presence-democracy, in the increase in women's presence in parliaments around the world. However, the developments in presence-democracy and in the application of the democratic principle are highly uneven. They are more common in the developed world, but are not confined to there – for example, Rwanda has a higher proportion of women in its parliament than any other country. In the developed world they are more commonly to be found in more social democratic countries, such as the Nordics, than neoliberal countries, such as the USA and UK.

Human Rights

The UN Universal Declaration of Human Rights, adopted in 1948, remains the defining statement on the content of human rights, despite some additions in later years. The 30 Articles proclaim everyone's right to: dignity; life, liberty, and the security of the person; the absence of slavery; the absence of torture and cruel, inhuman or degrading treatment or punishment; to legal personhood; to equality before the law; to the absence of arbitrary arrest, detention or exile; to a fair trial; to be presumed innocent until proven guilty; to privacy; to freedom of movement and residence; to asylum; to a nationality; to own property; to freedom of thought, conscience and religion; to freedom of opinion and expression; to peaceful assembly and association; to take part in government where the will of the people expressed in free elections by universal suffrage is the basis of the government's authority; to the economic, social, and cultural rights needed for dignity and the free development of one's personality; to the right to work, without discrimination, to equal pay for equal work, to just remuneration, to form and join trade unions; to rest, leisure and reasonable working hours; to a standard of living that is adequate for health and well-being, including security in the event of unemployment, sickness, disability, widowhood, old age, and other circumstances beyond control; to education; and to participate freely in the cultural life of the community.

These universal human rights have been clarified and expanded in the International Covenant on Economic Social and Cultural Rights and the International Covenant on Civil and Political Rights in 1966, nine core international human rights treaties, and many universal human rights instruments. Two key additions have been on violence: one declaring violence against women to be a violation of women's human rights in 1993, and one aiming at the abolition of the death penalty in 2007. There is significant variation in the extent to which states have signed up to these conventions – sometimes signing without ratifying, sometimes signing only with reservations.

The extent to which civil liberties and political rights are realized in practice has been assessed by Freedom House (2008) using indicators that are based on an interpretation of the Universal Declaration of Human Rights (UN 1948) by Gastil (1982). There are two scales, one for political rights and the second for civil liberties, each with an index from 1–7, based on specific questions about their practical existence. According to the Freedom House approach, between 1972 and 2007 a substantial number of countries around the world improved their rankings on these indicators. Most developed countries (including the USA, the UK, Sweden, and Ireland) have achieved the highest levels of civil and political liberties – one on both counts. However, there are several areas where the Freedom House interpretation of political rights and civil liberties might underestimate the current breadth of the human rights covered by the UN instruments. For example, they do not include recent additions such as the abolition of the death penalty or violence against women. Nor do they include recent expansive interpretations such as those on sexual and reproductive rights.

Many countries have given up the use of the death penalty in law or practice during the last half century. In 1948 only eight countries had abolished the death penalty; in 1977 this had risen to 16; in 2006 to 87; and in 2007 to 133 when non-use is included. No country can join the EU without renouncing this punishment (Amnesty International 2006; Council of Europe 2006). In 1976, and against the global trend, the USA reintroduced the death penalty (Clark County Prosecuting Attorney 2007). In 2006 only 25 countries carried out the death penalty, with 91 per cent of these 1,591 executions in China, Iran, Iraq, Pakistan, Sudan, and the USA (Amnesty International 2006).

A further area of contestation over the interpretation of human rights concerns the sexual and reproductive rights of women. These have been repeatedly raised in the UN Conferences on women, including the major conference in 1995 in Beijing which produced the Platform for Action (UN 1995). There is wide variation in the extent of legal restriction on abortion. The United States allows abortion in the first trimester (the first three months of pregnancy) with varying forms of restriction, and there is variability between states; in the UK there is legal abortion available for the first two trimesters, dependent upon an easily obtained medical judgement that there is a medical or (effectively) social need, except for

Northern Ireland where abortion remains illegal; in Ireland abortion has barely emerged from a constitutional ban even in cases of rape. Sweden has the least restrictions on abortion (Ferree et al. 2002b; Center for Reproductive Rights 2007) (see Table 9.12).

While marriage and divorce are available in most countries, there are severe limitations on divorce in some. While divorce is readily available in the USA, Sweden, and the UK, it has only recently been legalized in Ireland and the conditions attached to this preclude clean breaks. The right to freely express one's sexuality is restricted in those countries that limit or make illegal gay and lesbian sexuality. There are variations between the four countries above in the extent to which same sex partnerships are recognized in institutional settings.

While there have been many instances of increases in the practical availability of human rights since the 1948 UN Declaration, these have been and remain uneven both between countries and over time. In some countries there have been reductions in specific human rights during this period (for instance, coercive interrogation techniques utilized by the USA in Guantanamo Bay and various outsourced locations, which many consider extend to torture, is one example of regress).

Human Development, Well-Being, and Capabilities

The fourth framing of progress is the newest: human development, well-being, and capabilities are its various names. It includes a range of issues beyond economic development yet more economically oriented than human rights; it is concerned with excessive inequalities, not equality in general. The human development approach, sometimes referred to as well-being or capabilities, is a major challenge to a singular focus on economic development and growth – there is more to the quality of life than having more money. This approach does not intrinsically reject economic development, rather it subordinates economic development to being one of the means by which these wider goals are to be reached. It is no longer an end in itself.

Analytic work on this vision of progress has taken disparate forms, in particular there is a division between the development of its operationalization in quantitative indicators of outcomes by the UNDP (1990) and the UN Millennium Development Goals projects (2007c) and their analysts (Bardhan and Klasen 1999; Abu-Ghaida and Klasen 2004), and the development of nuanced distinctions between various capabilities and functionings in the more philosophical literature. The theoretical work most often seen to underpin this approach to progress is led by Sen (1997, 1999) and developed by others (Nussbaum 2000; Robeyns 2003). Sen, however, has hesitated to endorse any given list of capabilities, at least partly because of the priority that he gives to the processes of democratic deliberation in their determination. Nussbaum by contrast has offered a list of ten central human capabilities derived from the philosophical literature: life and not dying prematurely; bodily health, including good health, reproductive health, and shelter; bodily integrity, including the freedom to be mobile, to be secure from violent assault including domestic violence, and opportunities for sexual satisfaction; being able to use the senses, imagination, and thought in a way that is informed and cultivated by education, as well as freedom of expression and religion; being able to have emotional attachments; being able to engage in practical reason and reflection; being able to affiliate with others and to receive social respect, whatever one's race or sex; being able to live with other species successfully; being able to play; being able to participate politically, to hold property, and to enter decent employment.

The distinction between capability and functioning derives from Sen. Capabilities are what we could do or 'substantive freedoms'; functionings are what we actually do. This distinction embeds choice between a diverse range of possible goals into the heart of the framework. Such diversity among possible preferred goals or outcomes is hard to reconcile with the notion of a single standard against which an outcome can be assessed. Choices are also notoriously open to influence from the powerful: indeed Sen himself notes that people often adapt their preferences to the current balance of power, which means that subjective preferences are not the best way to set standards against which to measure progress. Further, is there any practical way of measuring a capability except as an outcome, that is, by taking functioning as an indicator of capability? The answer here must be no, or at least that one has not yet been developed (Equalities Review 2007). Hence the UNDP and MDG approaches to the operationalization of the concepts of human development and well-being as outcomes are the ones utilized here.

One key indicator of human well-being is that of longevity or how long people live. More complex hybrid indicators have been proposed by the United Nations Development Programme (UNDP 2007b), and within the United Nations Millennium Development Goals (UN 2007a). The EU has an Employment Strategy that incorporates social cohesion alongside economic growth (European Commission 2007f). The UK Equalities Review (2007) drew on a capabilities framing for developing indicators.

Life-expectancy is the simplest, most meaningful, and most robust indicator of human well-being. It commands much consensus as a value which is perhaps closer to a universal agreement across cultures than any other. It is also methodologically robust, being well-recorded and hence easier to measure than many of the other concepts associated with human well-being, lending itself to reliable comparisons over time and between countries. However, one limitation is that it is not always equally recorded for different equality groups.

Life-expectancy has increased over time around the world, but remains highly uneven between global regions (see Table 9.14). Among the world's regions, the high income OECD countries have the longest life expectancy in the world.

There are significant differences between OECD countries. Americans live on average two years less than people in the EU (77.7 years as compared with 79.7); and as compared with the UK and Ireland, people in Sweden live the longest (80.6 years on average) (see Table 9.14).

Longevity is perhaps the most important form of inequality. Being on the wrong side of class and ethnic inequalities shortens your life. Men in the lowest social class in the UK live seven years less than men in the highest social class (78.5 years for Class I professionals and 71.1 years for Class V unskilled). In the UK, men from social class, I, professionals, have a life-expectancy of 78.5 years, while men from the social class, V, unskilled workers, live on average 7.4 years less, at 71.1 years. This is based on life-expectancy at birth, (1997–1999: ONS 2002). African-Americans live five years less than white people in the USA (72.3 years for African-Americans and 77.7 years for white people). This is based on estimates of life-expectancy at birth in turn based on estimates of the postcensal US resident population and data from death certificates (*Health, United States* 2004).

Are countries becoming less or more unequal? In the USA the White-Black gap in life-expectancy, while substantial, is narrower than it was. A hundred years ago the US White-Black gap in life-expectancy was 15 years – nine years more than it is today. In 1900 the gap between White and Black life-expectancy was 14.6 years instead of 5.4 years in 2002 – 47.6 years for whites and 33.0 for Black or African-Americans in 1900 (*Health, United States* 2004b). However, the class gap in longevity for British men has widened by nearly a year in the last 30 years. In 1999 the class gap in longevity for UK men was 0.7 years larger than it was in 1972 (Office for National Statistics 2002). The dynamics of class and ethnic forms of inequalities are not the same.

While length of life is usually measured as the entire length of the life-span, there are significant variations in mortality in infancy and for mothers during childbirth (see Table 9.15). Rates of infant,

Table 9.14 Life-expectancy, global regions, USA, EU, Ireland, Sweden, UK

World	High income OECD	East Asia & Pacific	Europe & Central Asia	Latin America & Caribbean	Middle East & North Africa	South Asia	Sub-Saharan Africa	USA	EU	Ireland	Sweden	UK
67.6	79.3	70.7	69.2	72.5	69.6	63.5	46.7	77.7	79.7	79.4	80.6	79.0

Life-expectancy at birth in 2005. *Source*: World Bank (2007b).

Table 9.15 Child and maternal mortality, obesity, world, USA, EU, Ireland, Sweden, UK

	World	USA	EU	Ireland	Sweden	UK
Infant mortality (1)	51	7	4	5	3	5
Child (under 5) mortality (2)	75	8	5	6	4	6
Maternal mortality (3)	410	17		5	2	13
Per cent obese (4)		39		10	11	23

(1) Infant mortality rate, per 1,000 births. 2004. EU is EMU. *Source*: World Bank (2006c).
(2) Child (under five years) mortality rate, per 1,000 births. 2004. EU is EMU. *Source*: World Bank (2006c).
(3) Maternal mortality, per 100,000 live births. 2000. *Source*: World Bank (2006b).
(4) Per cent of population over 15 years is obese, BMI >30. 2005. *Source*: World Health Organization (2007).

child, and especially maternal mortality (MDG indicators 4.2, 4.1 and 5.1) are much higher in the world as a whole than those in the USA and EU. The USA has nearly double the rate of infant and child (under five years) mortality of the EU. It also has rates of maternal mortality that are eight times those in Sweden, three times those in Ireland, and somewhat more than rates in the UK.

An emerging health problem in the developed world is that of over-weight, which is linked to a series of health problems including premature death. Americans are much more likely to be obese than Europeans. In the USA 39 per cent of people are obese as compared with 11 per cent in Sweden, 10 per cent in Ireland, and 23 per cent in the UK (World Health Organization 2007; see Table 9.15). The USA, the most neoliberal country with perhaps the least regulation of food production and marketing, has the highest rate of obesity.

Living longer is only one part of human capabilities. The UNDP Human Development Indicator (HDI) is made up of three parts: longevity, income per capita, and education (both achieved literacy and the current educational enrolment). The annual HDR report has expanded to include detailed alternative performance indicators and statistics on many diverse aspects of human well-being.

The UN Millennium Development Goals (UN 2007a) introduced in 2000 are oriented towards human development, while also including economic development and a commitment to reduce excessive inequality. This range of eight goals, 18 targets and 48 indicators significantly extended the range of issues that were to have policy priority. The eight goals are to: eradicate extreme poverty and hunger; achieve universal primary education; promote gender equality and empower women; reduce child mortality; improve maternal health; combat HIV/AIDS, malaria and

Table 9.16 Primary education completion rates (%), by sex, 1999, 2005, world, developing, and developed regions

	1999	1999	2005	2005
	Boys	Girls	Boys	Girls
World	86	80	90	85
Developing regions	84	77	89	83
Developed regions	98	99	99	97

Source: UN (2007a). Indicator 2.2.

Table 9.17 Tertiary education, USA, EU, Ireland, Sweden, UK

	USA	EU	Ireland	Sweden	UK
Tertiary education enrolment (1)	83	62	59	84	60
Ratio of female to male tertiary education (2)	1.4	1.3	1.3	1.6	1.4

(1) Gross enrolment in tertiary education, as a percentage of potential enrolment. 2004. *Source*: World Bank (2006c).
(2) Ratio of female to male tertiary education enrolment, 2004. EU is EMU. *Source*: World Bank (2006c).

other diseases; ensure environmental stability; and develop a global partnership for development.

Developing education is a key component in most accounts of human development, well-being, and capabilities. It is part of the original UNDP Human Development Indicator and one of the Millennium Development Goals. The targets for developing countries are focused on primary education and on literacy. Primary education completion rates have increased between 1999 and 2005, though considerable variations remain between global regions and in some countries girls are less likely to go to school than boys (UN MDG 2007a) (see Table 9.16).

In developed countries the focus is more on tertiary education. While the USA has higher enrolments in tertiary education than the EU, this level is matched by Sweden. The ratio of women to men in tertiary education is similar in the USA and the EU, though higher in Sweden (in all these countries more women are enrolled than men) (see Table 9.17).

While the full operationalization of the framing of progress as human development, well-being, or capabilities is not yet complete, the key indicator of longevity provides a robust challenge to a simple approach to economic development. While people do tend to live longer in richer countries, the association between income and longevity is loose rather than tight. People in the EU live longer and on less income than those in the USA. The social as well as economic system matters for human well-being.

Key Indicator Sets: What Indicators? What Underlying Concepts of Progress?

There are sets of indicators of progress that are intended to have global relevance. The point of departure for most of these is economic development and growth. This has been the premier goal for many national and international governmental bodies such as the International Monetary Fund and World Bank, and for many this is still the case. However, there have been several attempts to move beyond this rather narrow concept of economic development towards the broader concept of human development. These moves have taken place in particular on a global level in UN bodies, such as can be found in the United Nations Development Project, though there are in addition some significant developments in the EU. An alternative approach is one based on human rights which is focused on civil liberties, excessive violence, and suffrage-democracy, rather than on the economic domain.

From its first Human Development report in 1990 and every year since, the UNDP has sought to broaden the goal of development from a narrow economic focus to a broader human development. The annual report presented by the United Nations Development Project constitutes an alternative assessment of global economic progress to that of the global financial institutions, drawing on the intellectual work of Amartya Sen. Its first indicator – the Human Development Indicator – combined income per person with longevity and education (literacy as well as educational enrolment). In 1995, this was gendered in the Gender-related Development Index, with the female share of earned income, gendered longevity, and gendered education, and the Gender Empowerment Measure, with the proportionate female presence in top jobs (managers and professionals) and parliamentary seats (UNDP 1995). One disadvantage of the GDI is that it conflates the absolute level of development with a gender relationship in a single index (Dijkstra 2002; Dijkstra and Hanmer 2002). Second, for technical reasons, differences in the level of countries' GDI is overwhelmingly driven by one component – income share – which is itself predominantly driven by the employment rate (Bardhan and Klasen 1999). It is preferable to analyse the components of the indices separately, as is done here. Recent reports include key statistics on a range of aspects of the human condition, including environmental sustainability. They are predominantly outcome indicators: just a few are policy focused, such as governmental expenditures on education and the military. The UNDP indicator analysis is supported by a global social science epistemic community around development, which provides analytic expertise and policy support. This is fed by the more radical social movements that are pro global justice and anti-capitalist, especially when they have taken the form of global waves, challenging if not overcoming the distinction between the field of 'development' and that of 'globalization'.

The UN Millennium Development Goals launched in 2000 were the next stage of development for global indicators of human development. These contained more goals than HDI, and a more complexly defined relationship between goals, indicators, and targets. Most important was the wider buy-in into this set of goals, which extended beyond the development community that supported the UNDP indicators and also included the global financial institutions of the IMF and World Bank and the rich countries club of the OECD (Millennium Development Goals 2004). The Millennium Development Goals represent a compromise between the focus on economic growth and that on human well-being. Economic development is included, but is also centred on human development. Poverty is a more important concept than inequality in this indicator set, although one measure of inequality exists as an indicator of poverty and the gender goal is defined in terms of equality. Again the focus is led by the economic domain though this is inclusive of its welfare aspects. The goals are outcome and well-being focused, with a concern for poverty, education, and health that is consistent with a capabilities approach. There is some limited concern with equality, including gender equality in education, employment, and parliamentary representation, and also with the extent of poverty. One other goal concerns environmental sustainability. Gaps however remain in the areas covered by the MDG. There is little on human rights, especially sexual and reproductive rights, and nothing on violence. Several of the goals and almost all of the targets are primarily concerned with developing countries. Nevertheless, comparable data exist on the issues raised by the MDG at levels that are relevant to developed countries. These include: education (tertiary); child and maternal mortality; disease/health (obesity); and environmental sustainability (emission of carbon dioxide).

A contrasting indicator set is that of the Freedom House Index of Civil Liberties and Political Rights, published since 1972. This is based on Gastil's interpretation of UN Universal Human Rights and as a result is centred on a free civil society, suffrage-democracy, and the avoidance of excessive violence. As such it is often considered to be part of the Western liberal individualist tradition. But while the Universal Declaration of Human Rights makes a small reference to economic issues, this is omitted from the Freedom House index.

Neither does it include the issues of excessive violence included in the Human Rights declaration, nor the 1993 UN extension of the concept of human rights to violence against women.

The OECD produces indicators based on syntheses of research and data (e.g. protective legislation: OECD 2002a), against which evaluations can be made, however, it does not have its own preferred indicator list.

The EU has generated several sets of indicators, including: Indicators of Social Inclusion (European Commission 2006); Indicators for the European Employment Strategy (European Commission 2007f); and Indicators of Equality between Women and Men (European Commission 2008). The focus for the indicators of social inclusion is poverty rather than inequality; poverty is seen as an excessive inequality that is a major factor in social exclusion. The employment guidelines contain minor components concerning gender and age components that are simultaneously about equality, inclusion, and the increased productivity of the economy. However, the indicators on equality between women and men are led by the concept of equality. The EU institution of Eurostat ensures harmonization in data collection and the production of indicators, though the prioritization of indicators is highly political.

Development of the transnational indicator sets draws simultaneously on contesting visions of progress and detailed technical work. The early focus of indicators on economic growth and development was challenged and replaced by a broader set of concerns including human development and justice, though important omissions still remain.

Extending the Frameworks and Indicators of Progress: Where do Environmental Sustainability and Violence Fit?

Two major issues that are not well articulated within the major framings of progress are environmental sustainability and violence. It is possible to squeeze them in, but they cannot be comfortably located. In the case of environmental sustainability this is partly due to its relatively recent arrival on the political and hence social theory landscape, but the same cannot be said of violence which has long been a political issue but yet remains marginal in social theory. How might they each be conceptualized within different framings of progress?

Environmental sustainability

Environmental sustainability concerns the present and the future, both immediate and in the longer term. Certain forms of economic development are not sustainable, including in particular those that increase the gases that create the greenhouse effect, heating up the world and leading to extreme weather conditions and regionally specific drought and flooding, with adverse outcomes for food production, health, and survival (Intergovernmental Panel on Climate Change 2007). Environmental sustainability fits best within the frame of (in)equality (though this is only rarely recognized) and could be fitted into the outcome-oriented version of human development and well-being, though less so into the capabilities version. While it impacts on economic development it is marginal to its definition; it is hard to fit into human rights.

Economic development will be brought to a halt unless it takes a form that is environmentally sustainable. Environmental catastrophes, such as global heating, would bring an end to economic growth and would replace it with economic decline. However, while environmental sustainability constitutes an important limit to economic development it is not part of its usual operationalization, which is limited to current levels of economic development and rates of growth.

A decline in global environmental sustainability is a matter of equality because it is the poor and future generations who will suffer most from environmental degradation (Roberts and Parks 2007). The people who are most subject to the worst effects of a decline in environmental quality are those in the global South, those who are already poor, and future generations. Those who have the least resources are most vulnerable to the consequences of the rise in sea level that follows global warming, to shortages of food, and other aspects of environmental degradation. There is also inequality between generations, as those in the future will run out of fossil fuels (peak oil production is about now) and will suffer the long-term consequences of irreversible global changes (IPCC 2007; Roberts and Parks 2007; Stern 2007; UNDP 2007a).

It is hard to fit environmental sustainability into the frame of human rights, except in the abstract and general way as compromising the right to life.

The human development and well-being approach is perhaps the most flexible way of framing progress in encompassing new challenges, of which environmental sustainability is a key example. The degradation of the quality of life and the limits to human development consequent on the loss of environmental quality can be conceptualized as a loss in human capabilities. This is better approached as an outcome, rather than as an opportunity.

The importance of avoiding global warming (or heating) is recognized at a global level as a consequence of pressure from a wave of environmental activism combined with rigorous scientific evidence, and a change in some governmental policies, leading to the Framework Convention on Climate Change in 1992. In the Kyoto Protocol in 1997 (Kyoto Protocol 1997), produced under the auspices of the United Nations, developed countries agreed to reduce their emission of greenhouse gases by at least 5 per cent below 1990 levels during the period 2008 to 2012 if enough countries signed on. Today most countries – with the current notable exception of the USA – have signed the Protocol and it came into force in 2005 (United Nations FCCC 2007). A new round of negotiations took place in Bali in 2007, following the report of the Intergovernmental Panel on Climate Change (2007).

Table 9.18 Carbon dioxide emissions, world, developing and developed regions

	1990	2004
World	4.3	4.5
Developed regions	10.3	12.4
Developing regions	1.7	2.4

Per capita emissions (metric tons)
Source: United Nations (2008) Indicator 7.2.

Table 9.19 Carbon dioxide emissions, USA, EU, Sweden, UK, Ireland

	USA	EU	Sweden	UK	Ireland
Carbon dioxide emissions, metric tons per person (1)	19.9	8.2	5.9	9.4	10.4
Carbon dioxide emissions, Kg per $ of GDP (2)	0.56	0.32	0.22	0.34	0.30

(1) Carbon dioxide emissions as a result of burning fossil fuels and the manufacture of cement, per capita. Data for 2003. EU is EMU. *Source*: World Bank (2007b).
(2) Carbon dioxide emissions as a result of burning fossil fuels and the manufacture of cement, per international dollar of GDP, adjusted for PPP. Data for 2003. EU is EMU. *Source*: World Bank (2007b).

The emission of carbon dioxide, the most important of the greenhouse gases, is varied between different countries, as is shown in Table 9.18 and Table 9.19. The developed world produces around three times as many CO_2 emissions per person as the developing world. The USA produces more than double the amount of carbon dioxide per inhabitant than the EU. This is only partly as a result of a higher level of economic development and standard of living; per dollar's worth of goods and services produced, the USA produces nearly twice as much CO_2 than the EU and two and a half times that of Sweden. Social democratic countries have lower emissions of carbon dioxide not only per person, but also for the production of a standardized amount of goods and services.

Violence

While violence has many implications for economic development, human well-being, equality and human rights, it is rarely integrated into any of these framings of progress in a systematic way. Violence by the state, groups, or by individuals has not been included within conventional indicators of well-being, equality, or human rights constructed by the UN in the HDI, GDI, or MDG projects. Violence is most relevant to the visions of progress as equality and human well-being. Violence is not part of the definition of economic development: within the human rights framework only 'excessive' violence is included.

Violence is relevant for economic development and growth, since it has significant detriment for these processes. However, it is not part of the core definition.

Violence is rarely conceptualized as central to the frame of equality. Even though violence is recognized as a form of power, which is central to the frame of equality, it is rarely translated into an issue of equality. One of the reasons for this is that the framing of equality as part of progress is often part of a socialist heritage which prioritized economic issues and treated violence merely as an instrument of power rather than as important in its own right. Further, in a criminological understanding of violence it is treated primarily as a response by the most disadvantaged to social inequality rather than as something visited by the powerful on the powerless. This book has challenged this exclusion of violence from social theory and the neglect in criminological analyses of the violence of the powerful towards the vulnerable. Instead violence is a central dimension of social inequality and intricately interrelated with inequality in other domains.

Violence is conceptualized within the human rights tradition, but only when it takes the form of 'excessive' rather than routine violence. 'Excessive' forms of violence are seen as a violation of human rights, especially when carried out by states against vulnerable individuals and involving torture and excessive forms of punishment and limits to freedom. More recently this tradition has been expanded to encompass violence against women as a violation of women's human rights. In these ways excessive violence – but not all violence – is included within the human rights tradition.

Writers in the human development, well-being, and capabilities approach rarely refer to violence, except to include it occasionally in their abstract lists. It is not included in any of the human development influenced indicator sets such as the UNDP HDI and MDG, or those produced by the EU. However, potentially this framework is flexible enough to include violence even while it has not yet been operationalized within it.

How might the concept of violence be operationalized in indicators that can be used to make comparisons between countries? Since the range of phenomena that can be included within the concept of violence can vary significantly according to both theoretical interpretation and social context, it is important to select as indicators only those measurements where the agreement on definitions is clear. The most straightforward indicator of individual violence in a country is homicide, since the data are robustly and routinely collected because it is more usually reported to the police than most other violent crimes, and is available for international comparisons (Krug et al. 2002; Barclay and Tavares 2003). While there is considerable developmental work on indicators and statistics on violence against women, there is as yet very little data to support the indicators that are internationally comparable (Walby 2005, 2007). However, one indication of the extent of state regulation of violence against women is the timing of the criminalization of rape in marriage (Russell 1990) (see Table 9.20). The extent to which the criminal justice system is coercive can be indicated by whether or not the death penalty is used and the relative size of the prison population. The death penalty is decreasingly used in the world, and has been rejected on human rights grounds by the European Union and the UN (Amnesty International 2006). The extent of government expenditure on law and order as a percentage of GDP is a measure of the priority given to this policy area over other uses of resources, though it is not strictly a measure of the coerciveness of the criminal justice system. The level of militarization is indicated by the extent of government expenditure on the military as a percentage of either government expenditure or GDP.

The level of violence is in general less in the developed world than the developing world (see Table 9.20). Aspects of modernity, such as democracy, appear to reduce violence. However, there are very wide variations in the rates of violence among developed countries. The USA has a homicide rate over three times that of the EU and an imprisonment rate nearly eight times as high as the EU's (see Table 9.20). The USA is one of only 25 countries in the world that still use the death penalty. Among the three EU countries Sweden has the lowest homicide and imprisonment rates. The USA spends over four times as much of its central government budget

Table 9.20 Violence, USA, EU, Ireland, Sweden, UK, world

	USA	EU	Ireland	Sweden	UK	World
Homicide rate per 100,000 (1)	5.56	1.59	1.42	1.11	1.61	
Death penalty (2)	Yes	No	No	No	No	25 countries
Prison population per 100,000 (3)	689	87	79	69	129	
Law and order expenditure as per cent of GDP (4)	2.7		1.5	1.8	2.2	
Military as per cent of central government expenditure (5)	19.3	4.6	1.9	4.3	6.3	11.1
Military expenditure as per cent of GDP (6)	4.1	1.7	0.6	1.6	2.6	2.5
Year rape in marriage illegal (7)	Late 1970s varies by state		1990	1965	1994	

(1) Homicides (intentional killing of a person excluding attempts: murder, manslaughter, euthanasia, and infanticide) per 100,000 population, average per year 1999–2001, as recorded by the police. UK is England and Wales (Northern Ireland is 2.65 and Scotland is 2.16). EU is EU15. *Source*: Barclay and Tavares (2003).
(2) *Source*: Amnesty International (2006).
(3) Rate per 100,000 population in 2001. UK is England and Wales (Northern Ireland is 59 and Scotland is 120). EU is EU15. *Source*: Barclay and Tavares (2003).
(4) Data for 2003. *Source*: OECD (2006).
(5) Data for 2005. EU is EMU. *Source*: World Bank (2007b).
(6) Data for 2005. EU is EMU. *Source*: World Bank (2007b).
(7) USA: National Center for Victims of Crime (2007); Sweden: Diana Russell (1990); UK: Criminal Justice and Public Order Act 1994: Nicole Westmarland (2004) *Rape Law Reform in England and Wales*. Working Paper 7 (Bristol: School of Policy Studies); Ireland: Galligan 1998.

on the military as compared with countries in the EU: this is almost one fifth (19.3 per cent) of government expenditure and amounts to more than twice as much of its GDP as compared with countries in the EU. Among the three EU countries, the UK spends most. Countries in the EU spend below, and the USA spends above, the global average on the military.

The Achievement of Visions of Progress: Comparing Neoliberalism and Social Democracy

What is the relationship between the four major visions of progress – economic development, equality, human rights, and human well-being/capabilities – and the projects of neoliberalism and social democracy?

Economic development: neoliberalism vs. social democracy

Economic development and economic growth are central to the neoliberal project. The achievement of economic development is used as the justification of other less popular aspects of neoliberalism such as inequality. If neoliberalism does not achieve economic development, then the legitimation of its more pernicious aspects unravels. Economic development is also part of the social democratic project; but this is conditional on the form of economic development, the nature of its production, and the distribution of its rewards. The achievement (or not) of economic development is part of the contestation between the neoliberal and social democratic projects. Neoliberals accuse social democrats of putting restrictions on the nature of this development which will stifle or slow it down. Social democrats insist not only on the democratic regulation of economic development in order that all may benefit, but also that these regulations do not impede economic growth. Hence one of the empirical tests of the relative success of neoliberalism or social democracy is whether or not neoliberalism is able to generate faster economic growth.

The evidence presented in this chapter shows that neoliberalism does not generate faster rates of economic growth than social democracy. The USA is not experiencing faster growth than the EU, rather the rates of growth in per capita income have been very similar. The only way in which the USA appears to have had faster economic growth is if the measure is that of the economy as a whole rather than per person, because population growth due to in-migration increases the overall size of the economy without increasing the income per person and the standard of living. Neoliberalism does not deliver higher rates of economic growth.

Economic growth can be assisted by appropriate state actions, by appropriate levels of regulation. But at least as important in determining levels of economic development historically have been two further phenomena: positive engagement with the increase in female employment and avoiding the destruction of war. First, under some circumstances an increase in female employment that is consequent on the transformation of the gender regime from domestic to public form can generate an economic growth spurt as there can be a spiralling of changes in the gender regime with economic development. This occurred most dramatically in Sweden in the 1970s, but can also be seen in the USA in the 1960s and in Ireland around the 1990s. Second, since war is highly destructive of economic infrastructures as well as human beings, avoiding war is important for sustained economic development. The nationalist militarism that led to so many wars in Europe during the nineteenth and especially the first half of the twentieth centuries was highly destructive of their economy as well as their lives; during this time economic growth in the USA surpassed that of Europe. Without these disparities in warfare between the USA and Europe in the twentieth century the USA would not have a level of economic development that is so much higher than that of Europe today.

Equality: neoliberalism vs. social democracy

Within the neoliberal project, equality is most often treated as either irrelevant or as a limit on the project of economic growth, except for the specific and limited issues of human rights and suffrage-democracy. These narrowly defined forms of equality – more often conceptualized as freedom, as process more than outcome – are attributed to the success of the neoliberal project of economic growth.

By contrast, equality is central to the social democratic project. However, even here there are debates and nuances as to the extent of its application and it is rarely applied to all domains and practices, even in the socialist tradition. The balance between equality as process and outcome is more weighted towards outcome than in the neoliberal project, but not exclusively so. While the principle of equality is more often centred on economic issues, it is applied elsewhere. In the polity, social democracy advocates a deeper form of democracy than neoliberalism, including not only practices to ensure the representation of women and minoritized groups, but also the extension of the democratic principle to the governance of a wider range of institutions. Social democracy could potentially include environmental sustainability and violence within its concerns for equality, although these are often under-developed.

In the European Union Treaty of Lisbon equality is named as a fundamental value of the European Union in Article 2, alongside human dignity, freedom, democracy, the rule of law, and respect for human rights including those of minorities; in addition there is the specific naming of equality between women and men (European Council

2007). In practice, however, much of the emphasis is on the process of equal treatment rather than on equal outcome.

Human rights: neoliberalism vs. social democracy

Human rights are routinely championed by both neoliberalism and social democracy. Human rights contain a component of equality but one that is minimalist, often but not always understood to be limited to civil liberties and suffrage democracy. For neoliberalism the minimal version is enough, but this is not so for social democracy.

Human development, well-being, and capabilities: neoliberalism vs. social democracy

The claim of the neoliberal project is that its core component of economic growth does deliver human development, well-being, and capabilities: without economic development these will be at a much lower level. The claim of the social democratic project is that it more effectively and directly delivers human development, well-being, and capabilities because it has a democratically-assisted capacity to create these directly and not merely indirectly.

If longevity and the mortality rates of infants, children, and birthing mothers are taken as a key indicator of human development and well-being, then the neoliberal USA is much less successful than the more social democratic EU. Americans live shorter lives than EU citizens, and their rates of infant, child, and maternal mortality are higher, as was shown earlier in this chapter.

Trade-offs or complementary?

Do all the good things go together – are they alternatives, or are there trade-offs? Is economic development a means to the achievement of well-being, equality, and human rights, or is it in tension with these goals – or is it just different?

The prioritization of the goal of economic growth is usually justified on the grounds that it increases human well-being by raising the standard of living. The main reason most people want to increase their incomes is to improve the quality of their lives. Does

Table 9.21 Life-expectancy and income over time, world, USA, EU, Ireland, Sweden, UK

	World	USA	EU	Ireland	Sweden	UK
Life-expectancy (1)						
1975 (2)	61.7	72.6	72.3	71.7	75.0	72.7
2005	67.6	77.7	79.7	79.4	80.6	79.0
Increase in years of life, 1975–2005	5.9	5.1	7.4	7.7	5.6	6.3
Per cent increase in years of life, 1975–2005	9.6	7.0	10.2	10.7	7.5	8.7
Income per person $ (3)						
1975	4867	19830	14359	8544	16993	15506
2005	8477	37436	26037	35685	27783	28628
Increase in income, 1975–2005	3610	17606	11678	27141	10790	13122
Per cent increase in income, 1975–2005	74	89	81	318	63	85

(1) Life-expectancy at birth. EU is EMU. *Source*: World Bank (2004, 2006c).
(2) Date for world is 1977 not 1975.
(3) Income per person is GDP per capita, PPP based on constant 2000 international dollars. EU is EMU. *Source*: *World Bank* (2006c), except world which is World Bank (2007b).
Other figures are calculated from those in the table.

economic development deliver this? Comparing the USA and the EU, it might appear not. In the USA people have higher incomes than in the EU, but they live shorter lives: in the EU there are fewer economic resources than in the USA, longer lives.

However, this does not mean that there is no association between income and longevity. Within any given country people will live longer as the country gets richer, and richer people will live longer. Across the world as a whole over time, people have become richer and lived longer, with life-expectancy rising by six years from 62 to 67 between 1977 and 2005, while income has risen by 74 per cent.

In the USA and the EU both income and average life-span have been rising. In the USA average income in the 30 years between 1975 and 2005 increased by 88 per cent, compared with a similar but very slightly lower 81 per cent in the EU. The gap in personal incomes between the USA and EU was established before 1975, and this widened only by a very small amount in the following 30 years to 2005. By contrast, the increase in average life-expectancy between 1975 and 2005 was 5.1 years in the USA and 7.4 years in the EU. While in 1975 there was little difference between the EU and the USA in life-expectancy, by 2004 a gap had emerged (see Table 9.21).

How can it be true both that people in some of the richer countries live shorter lives than in some less rich countries and also that there is an association between income and life-expectancy within countries? The reason for this apparent paradox is that different social systems have different levels of success in converting economic resources into human well-being. The European social system is more effective in doing this than that of the USA. It is the differences in social systems that are crucial to understanding the implications for individuals. Some of the components for the differences in life-expectancy can be seen in the data on health and violence. Americans have higher rates of infant and maternal mortality than the EU as well as higher rates of obesity. Americans are more violent than Europeans, both interpersonally and collectively. The European and US social systems also link economic resources to human well-being in quite different ways. This is as a result of the different paths of development taken by these different countries and regions – one more neoliberal and the other more social democratic.

Are economic development and equality alternative and competing frames and forms of progress? Equality is often treated as an alternative framing of progress from that of economic development. However, this is not supported by the evidence. Equality does not necessarily limit economic development. The more developed or modernized countries are not necessarily more unequal. This can be seen in the similar levels of economic growth rates in neoliberal and social democratic countries, and that the level of economic development is only partly related to differential stable growth rates but is also related to growth spurts and the destruction of human and fixed capital in times of war.

Does economic development deliver less violence? The previous chapter, by using data sets with many countries, showed that there tends to be less violence in those countries that are more economically developed and more violence in those countries that are more unequal; and that there was some path dependency in evidence.

This chapter has also shown that the USA is substantially more violent than the EU on each of the indicators of violence: homicide, use of the death penalty, imprisonment, and spending on the military as a proportion of central government expenditure and of GDP. The USA is thus an exception to the general finding that modernity is associated with reduced violence, but is consistent with the finding that inequality leads to greater violence. The particularities of its path dependent development are discussed in the next chapter.

Does economic development lead to secularization and the decline of religious polities that exclude women from governing positions? In much of Europe, economic development has been associated with a decline in religiosity and the authority of organized religion to govern intimacy. However, the USA has been an exception to that trend of secularization.

Does economic development lead to more human rights? In the EU economic development has been associated with the increasing institutionalization of human rights in legal codes, enforcement institutions, and civil societal practice; this includes human rights that are relevant to women and to minorities. However, there are exceptions, as in the lack of rights shown in women's access to abortion in Ireland. In the USA the development of human rights has been more uneven in matters such as the reintroduction of the death penalty and the uneven access to sexual and reproductive rights.

Conclusions

Is there progress? For each of the four major visions or framings of progress there are some positive advancements with the development of modernity, though unevenly so and with some backward moves. In several instances the answer to this question depends upon the definitions of the concepts and indicators and the units within which they are assessed.

Increasing sophistication in both theories and indicators is needed, each to interrogate the other. The development of indicators and the data to support them constitute a critical link between social theory and the empirical world. Robust, valid, and reliable indicators of changes over time and between countries are needed for the assessment of social theories.

The unequal and more violent conditions of life in neoliberal modernity are not compensated for by more rapid economic growth. The income per person is not growing more quickly in the USA than in the EU. There is a historic difference in the levels of economic development between these two hegemons as a consequence of growth spurts in the past in the USA, but there is not currently faster economic growth per person in the USA than the EU. It is the case that the US economy as a whole is growing more quickly than most of the economies of the EU, but this is because of greater immigration and not greater increases in the economic resources available for each person. The justification of greater inequalities in the economy on the grounds that it leads to more rapid economic growth is unfounded. The USA may be richer than the rest of the world today, including the EU, but its rate of economic growth has been little different over the last 30 years. If the goal here is economic growth, emulating its practices is unlikely to achieve this. If the goal however is human well-being, then the USA is less successful in deploying its economic resources to ensure human well-being (as measured by life-expectancy) than the EU. Additionally, if the goal is equality and human rights then the USA delivers less than the EU.

Are inequalities increasing or decreasing? Class-based economic inequalities within countries are increasing in many countries, while gender-based economic inequalities within countries are often declining. When the whole world is taken as the unit within which to analyse inequality rather than individual countries, then the centuries-long increase in global economic inequalities has stopped as a result of the surging economic growth in China and to a lesser extent India. There has been an increase in the democratic access to power, not only an increase in a narrowly defined suffrage-democracy but also the increased presence of women in parliaments (though this is not so everywhere). There has been some reduction in the use of violence as a form of power against women and minoritized groups in some locations, as a result of the increased criminalization of such violence, but the neoliberal wave has tended to increase state coercion in those countries where it has been significant. There has been some increase in some civil liberties, but unevenly so.

10 Comparative Paths Through Modernity: Neoliberalism and Social Democracy

Introduction

Path dependency entails a distinctive chain of inter-connected events over time in a social system in which an event at one point in time has implications for later events. The implication of path dependency is that there is neither a single route to modernity, nor so many that distinct patterns cannot be identified. It is a concept that is situated in the tension between general social theory and the analysis of particularism. This chapter compares path dependent trajectories in order to develop theoretical aspects of path dependency and to investigate the explanation of specific trajectories.

The thesis of path dependency depends upon the divergence of the paths being sustained over time; if this divergence is only of a short and temporary duration, then the significance of the path dependency thesis is diminished. The path dependency thesis also postulates that the sequencing of events over time makes a difference to their degree of influence over the path, with events early on more significant than those that happen later. This is investigated in two ways – the implications of the sequencing of economic growth and war for the global power of hegemons; and the implications of the sequencing and gaps between the development of free wage labour and democracy for pathways taken by different regimes of inequality in a country.

The concept of critical turning point is crucial to this analysis, since it is at these events that pathways start, diverge, or turn. This concept is further developed here by making a distinction between critical turning point and tipping point: the former may be sudden, while the latter depends upon a slow build up. A further conceptual addition is that of catalysts and dampeners: catalysts speed the iterations of change in a system, while dampeners slow them.

Much of the analysis of path dependency that has invoked inequalities has been restricted to the implications of class. A major challenge to this position is that forces associated with complex inequalities in addition to those of class make a significant difference to the path dependent trajectories of countries. The extent to which complex inequalities other than class are not merely the outcome of these events but part of the causal processes is investigated.

Global processes potentially erode path dependent developments in different countries, so one question here is whether the social democratic path of development is sustained despite global flows of capital, trade, and people, a neoliberal global hegemon and a global neoliberal wave. Non-economic global processes are also investigated, in particular the implications of global civil societal waves for national trajectories of development.

The main path dependent forms of modernity in the global North are neoliberalism and social democracy (see Chapter 8 on varieties of modernity). These can vary between different institutional domains (see Chapters 3–6 on economies, polities, violence, and civil society) and regimes of inequality (see Chapter 7) even in the same country. The main loci of these path dependent forms of modernity are political economy and violence (see Chapter 8). Of further interest is the path dependent development of neoliberal and social democratic forms of gender regimes. Entwined throughout are issues of democracy and inequality, which are key to the distinction between neoliberalism and social democracy.

Four countries (the USA, Sweden, the UK, and Ireland) are selected for their contrasting development, together with relevant aspects of the European Union. Sweden is the most social democratic of the four and the USA the least, with Ireland and the UK in between as regards the regulation of employment, the state provision of welfare, and the regulation and deployment of violence. While the USA has one major polity in its state, in Sweden, the UK, and Ireland there is a second polity in the EU, and in Ireland a third in the Roman Catholic Church. They contrast in their economic and human development, democracy, violence, equality, and human rights. There is also a comparison between the USA and the EU (Sweden, the UK, and Ireland being members of the EU), global hegemons that have considerable power to shape the global fitness landscape. They contrast in their degree of modernity, in their positioning on a continuum between neoliberal and social democratic varieties of modernity, and in their welfare provision, employment regulation, violence, and regimes of inequality. Contrasting polities are involved – hegemon, former empire, states, EU, organized religions, and nations – with contrasting histories of societalization and of the relations between nations and states. The countries have contrasting positionings in relation to global flows of capital, trade and people, global waves, networks, institutions, and hegemons, as makers and takers of the global fitness landscape.

These countries are neither 'societies' nor 'nation-states'. They are empirically and territorially defined units as they exist in the early twenty-first century, each with a leading state. There is no presumption that these countries are societies or nation-states, rather there are competing societalization projects in each country that are far from complete. The extent to which processes of societalization have produced consistency between the institutional domains and regimes of inequality in these countries is varied. Each country has a history in which the territorial boundaries have changed significantly. The main focus of the analysis is that of the last century, though some longer time-frames include processes of polity formation.

This chapter compares the path dependent trajectories of the USA, the UK, Ireland, and Sweden, together with relevant aspects of the EU, with a focus on the loci at political economy, and violence and comparative gender transformations, and then considers the implications of this comparison for the theorization of path dependency.

Political Economy

Introduction

While the level of economic development makes a significant difference to the social relations involved in political economy, it is far from sufficient. There are important differences in the regulation of employment and the state provision of welfare, further differentiated by class, gender, and other inequalities, which are key to the distinction between the neoliberal and social democratic forms of political economy. Divergences in the depth of democracy and the degree of various inequalities make significant differences to these paths of development. Established ways of explaining the differences between neoliberal and social democratic (or similar) forms of political economy have focused on the power of organized labour and socialist movements, with some further interest in the organization of employers and the form of institutionalization of the state (Korpi 1983; Evans et al. 1985; Lash and Urry 1987; Esping-Andersen 1990; Lipset and Marks 2000; Hall and Soskice 2001) and key political struggles.

These are indeed important sources of difference but they are not sufficient. It is important to consider a wider range of social forces and not to restrict these to class. Other complex inequalities, including gender, ethnicity, nation, and religion, can make significant differences. Taking these complex inequalities into account provides a further challenge to the notion of a single historical moment being key, since transformation of diverse regimes of inequality do not usually occur at the same time. It is important also to consider the depth of democracy, especially but not only for regimes of inequality other than class, by not treating the formal attainment of suffrage as a sufficient marker.

Global processes are a potential challenge to the continuation of diverse paths of development. It is often argued that globalization erodes such differences, in particular social democratic forms of employment protection and state welfare provision. But the process of globalization needs to be treated in a more differentiated way, distinguishing between global flows of capital, trade, and people, global and regional hegemons and empires, and global civil societal waves. Different global processes have potentially different implications for the erosion or continuation or restructuring of established paths.

The depth of democracy is a key aspect of the variations in the form of political economy, for the development of either neoliberal or social democratic pathways. Differences in the development of democracy are themselves linked to different patterns in the development of free wage labour, the organizational capacity of the working class, minoritized ethnic groups and employed women, the strength of anti-democratic forces, the forms of polity restructuring especially during war and conquest, and global civil societal waves such as those of women's suffrage. These processes involve critical turning points, some of which are tipping points, as well as catalysts and dampeners of the relationship of democracy with other practices.

The four countries vary significantly in their political economies: the USA is the most neoliberal with Sweden the least; the UK and Ireland, both members of the EU, are in between. They also vary in their depth of democracy: while all have achieved suffrage-democracy, the USA is limited to this, Sweden alone has achieved presence-democracy and a broad range of institutions subject to democratic governance, while Ireland and the UK have uneven combinations of elements. A brief summary of some of the differences, which will be referred to in the following text, is shown in Tables 10.1 to 10.4. In the following analysis of the trajectory to diverse forms of political economy, each country is considered in turn.

The USA

The US political economy is the paradigmatic example of neoliberalism. There is limited employment regulation and state welfare

Table 10.1 Economic inequality: Gini coefficients, mid-1980s to c.2000: USA, Sweden, UK, Ireland

	Mid-1980s	2000
USA	33.8	35.7
Sweden	19.9	24.3
UK	28.6	32.6
Ireland	33.1	30.4
OECD average	29.3	31.0

Distribution of household disposal income: 0–100, the higher the more unequal.
Source: OECD (2006: 219).

Table: 10.2 Public social expenditure as per cent of GDP, 1990, 2003: USA, EU, Sweden, UK, Ireland

	1990	2003
USA	13.4	16.2
EU average	21.9	23.9
Sweden	30.5	31.3
UK	17.2	20.1
Ireland	15.5	15.9
OECD average	17.9	20.7

Source: OECD (2007b: 193).

Table 10.3 Comparative trade union density 1970–2003, USA, EU, Sweden, UK, Ireland

	1970	1980	1990	2000	2003
USA	23.5	19.5	15.5	12.8	12.4
EU15	37.8	39.7	33.1	27.3	26.3
Sweden	67.7	78.0	80.8	79.1	78.0
UK	44.8	50.7	39.3	29.7	29.3
Ireland	53.2	57.1	51.1	36.6	35.3

Source: Visser (2006: 45).

Table 10.4 Trade union membership patterns, 2004, USA, Sweden, UK, Ireland

	USA	Sweden	UK	Ireland
Public	36.4	93.0	58.8	68.0
Private	7.9	77.0	17.2	30.4
Manufacturing	12.9	95.0	24.6	40.0
Density	12.5	82.2	28.8	37.7
Coverage	13.8	92.0	35.0	

Source: Visser (2006: 46).

provision extends across all regimes of inequality – class, gender, and ethnicity. The USA has the most developed economy with the least remaining premodern elements, although religion still remains strong.

Neoliberalism in the USA is often explained as due to the weakness of labour and socialist movements as a result of internal disagreements and organizational failures (Lipset and Marks 2000), especially racialized divisions and white racism in the context of post-slavery ethnic inequality (Quadagno 1994; Manza 2000). An additional component is that of the strength of employers and their organizational capacity and sophistication, the opposition of various stakeholders (Quadagno 2006), and the mobility of capital and its ingenuity in finding new and more successful forms (Lash and Urry 1987). A further element is that of the nature of the state and political organization (Evans et al. 1985; Weir et al. 1988).

A curiously neglected aspect in the explanation of the variety of political economy is that of democracy. The USA has a shallow suffrage-democracy; this has not extended to presence-democracy, nor is there a wide range of institutions subject to democratic governance. Suffrage-democracy has not significantly deepened beyond suffrage-democracy into presence-democracy, although there have been some small increases in the proportion of women and minoritized ethnic groups in the legislature and executive in recent years. Without depth to democracy, it is hard for sections of labour marked by gender and 'race' to access the political power necessary to win the state regulation of employment and state welfare provision. A further neglected element is that of violence, which was important in the breaking up of early trade unions in the nineteenth century (Smith 2003).

While suffrage-democracy was achieved very early on for men of the majority ethnic groups, it occurred much later for women of the majority ethnic groups, indeed at the same time as in the other three countries, and very much later for African-Americans. This wide temporal disjuncture has had significant effects. There were several critical turning points: the War of Independence and the creation of the constitution; the civil war and the end of slavery; the transnational feminist wave of the late nineteenth and early twentieth century; and the civil rights movement of the 1950s and 1960s.

The USA broke free from most forms of hereditary governance and formally excluded religious organizations from government when it won independence from Britain through the War of Independence. Its new Constitution of 1776 provided the basics of suffrage-democracy, but only for the men of the dominant ethnic groups. It left outside of democracy women, African slaves, and those groups including the Native American Indians who had been subject to conquest. Indeed, as far as the slaves were concerned, the hereditary principle in governance was very much still present until they were freed in 1865 after the civil war. The early history of the USA is one of conquest of most of the North American continent, albeit none of this today has the status of colonies, though there remain some small 'territories' (with voting rights) outside the main landmass – American Samoa, Guam, the Marianas Islands, the US Virgin Islands, and Guantanamo Bay.

The extension of suffrage-democracy to all US inhabitants took centuries. In 1920 women from the majority ethnic groups gained suffrage, at the same time as many other countries in Northern Europe after a transnational feminist movement, and 144 years after US men of the same ethnicity. Although African-Americans were formally granted the right to vote after the ending of slavery in 1865, in the southern states of the USA they were de facto excluded from voting until the civil rights movement in the 1960s, thus winning their suffrage around 190 years after white men. The USA has few of the electoral mechanisms that other countries have introduced to move beyond suffrage-democracy to presence-democracy. Elections are highly expensive; the voting system is first past the post; there are no quotas. The presence of women in parliament and the executive is low despite the high rates of female employment, as is also the presence of minoritized ethnic groups. The range of institutions which are governed democratically is narrower than in other countries. In particular, there is limited democratic regulation of the economy, of finance capital, and of employment, and limited state welfare.

The modern form of free wage labour arrived at different times for different ethnicities and genders. While the north of the USA was industrializing in the nineteenth century, producing free wage labour for men and a few women, African-Americans in the southern states were still subject to slavery. Even when slavery was abolished in 1865, at the end of the civil war, the replacement form of labour relations (share-cropping) did not deliver much freedom in practice. Only later was there mass male free wage labour for African-Americans in the southern states. It was not until the 1970s that more than 40 per cent of employees were women.

Although the USA appears as the quintessential neoliberal political economy in the early twenty-first century, there were at least four moments when social democratic projects were mobilized. The first was the feminist movement from the middle of the nineteenth to the early twentieth century. This was not a purely US moment but part of a wider international wave, more regional than global, that was focused on Europe, North America, and Australasia, with a special strength in the UK. Often remembered only in terms of its suffrage victory in 1920, it was in fact a much broader project, although it declined steeply at the point of winning the vote, divided between different strategies. Second, was the New Deal response to the Depression of the 1930s, in which state welfare and job schemes were offered to the workless: this social democratic moment did not survive the strident and well-orchestrated post-war attacks on social democracy as if it were communism and alien. Third, was the movement from the 1960s, originating in the Civil Rights movement against racism in the US south, the anti-war movement opposed to the US military engagement in Vietnam, a resurgent feminism, and a student and libertarian movement. This won the right to vote for African-Americans, equal treatment employment legislation on grounds of 'race' and gender, and affirmative action programmes. Fourth, is the emergence of a social democratic project rooted in the constituency of employed women, noticeable in the gender gap in voting in which employed women voted more left than men – a key set of supporters not only for Hilary Clinton in her attempt on the US Presidency in 2008, but also for Obama's election, when he won the support of 56 per cent of women voters as compared with 43 per cent for McCain.

The neoliberal wave rose in the 1970s, partly in response to the successes of the movements of the 1960s. During the Reagan presidency (1981–1989) affirmative action for women and minorities was challenged, the move for the Equal Rights Amendment was defeated, monetarist financial policies challenged Keynesianism and squeezed the poor, and the trade union movement was successfully attacked. Reagan sacked the striking air traffic controllers in 1981 at the start of a series of attacks on trade unions, changing the climate for industrial relations and the trade unions (Nordlund 1998): aggressive and anti-union campaigns by employers have since had significant impact (Logan 2006). The weak social democratic forces in the barely institutionalized 1960s movement, a poorly unionized workforce, and only a shallow institutionalization of democracy in the legislature and executive, have proved unable to resist successfully despite the Democratic Clinton presidency and the emergence of new social democratic forces in employed women, but who found insufficient allies and too many enemies to institutionalize their project in government. The Bush presidency in the early twenty-first century saw the return of an aggressive neoliberal agenda on all fronts.

Promoted by the world's most powerful hegemon, neoliberalism developed into a global wave with various consequences for global financial policy as well for countries around the world, increasing economic inequality and attacking the institutional bases of social democratic forces. The USA is a major locus of global flows of capital, trade, and people, which feed both income growth at the top and increase those (especially undocumented in-migrants with few rights and income) at the bottom. The United States, despite some moments when social democratic projects began to mobilize, has a pathway to neoliberalism in political economy.

Sweden

Sweden is the classic example of a social democratic political economy. It had a strong labour movement quite early on in its industrialization, a broad alliance involving first agricultural workers and later employed women, organized employers who were not hostile to state welfare development, and a rapidly deepening democracy. Global pressures led to a reduction in the generosity of state welfare provision but not at a greater rate than elsewhere, partly because of the emergence of employed women as the new champions of social democracy and partly because of the depth of democracy.

Sweden has developed the deepest democracy of the four – suffrage-democracy and presence-democracy, as well as a broad range of institutions governed by democratic means. Critical turning points in the development of Swedish democracy included the thorough going Reformation of the sixteenth century; suffrage-democracy for both men and women by 1918; and a tipping point of presence-democracy for women around 1994; increased depth in the 1930s and 1980s; and decreased depth in the 1990s rounds of political economy restructuring. The 1970s and 1980s were a time that saw a rapid spiralling of gendered presence-democracy and economic growth.

The powers of the Swedish monarchy were largely removed in 1907–1909, with the final elements in 1975, even though it formally remains. During the seventeenth and eighteenth centuries Sweden, like its European neighbours, was involved in attempts for the dominance and colonization of adjacent territories but no colonies remain from that time. Sweden experienced the thorough Lutheran version of the reformation of Christianity that swept across Europe, undergoing between 1527 and 1544 a reconstruction of Christianity and a restructuring of the relationship between Church and State. Organized religion is not a significant polity in Sweden today as a consequence. Suffrage-democracy came for men in stages – 1866, 1896, 1907–1909, and 1918 – and for women a little later in 1918–1920. This is the shortest temporal gap in gendered suffrage-democracy among the four countries, though it was still of a significant duration. The procedures for presence-democracy for women, low-cost electioneering, proportional representation, and quotas for women, developed in the years from 1975 during the time of women's rapidly increasing employment. From 1994 women have constituted over 40 per cent of members of parliament, rising to 47 per cent by 2008, and 52 per cent of government ministers. Sweden has a significant breadth of democracy in that a wide range of institutions are subject to democratic control. This developed from the political restructuring and re-settlements in the 1930s (class-led) as well as in the 1970s (gender and class-based) and reduced a little during the neoliberal wave that reached Sweden in the 1990s.

The first critical turning point that is key to Swedish distinctiveness was the class compromise between workers of both industrial and agrarian bases and employers in the 1930s. The maturation of Swedish capitalism enabled the working class to develop the resources to gain political power, but only in alliance with agricultural workers. The agrarian workers in Sweden and other Nordic countries were already somewhat distinctive in their level of education resulting from a network of schools established during the first half of the nineteenth century. It is this three-fold set of class relations, employers, industrial proletarians and agrarian workers, which underpins the specificity of early Nordic social democracy (Sandberg 1979; Korpi 1983; Lash and Urry 1987; Esping-Andersen 1990; Rojas 1991).

There were two main events in the historic compromises of the 1930s. The first established a long-standing cooperation between the Social Democratic Party and the Peasant Party. This was initiated in 1933 when the Social Democrats supported better prices for the peasants and the peasants supported public relief works. (Similar compromises occurred in Denmark in 1933, Norway in 1935, and Finland in 1937.) The second social compromise was between the Swedish Labour movement – as represented in the Swedish confederation of trade unions, the LO – and the Swedish employers – as represented in the Swedish Employers Federation, the SAF – and was first established in 1938, when industrial peace was granted in exchange for reforms (Korpi 1983; Esping-Andersen 1990; Rojas 1991; Therborn 1992). This historic class compromise had implications for the development of the Swedish economy and polity, facilitating Swedish economic growth by reducing the conflict between capital and labour while requiring high levels of productivity to maintain the bargain and facilitating the development of Swedish welfare.

These developments in political economy were locked in through a series of institutional developments. The density of membership of trade unions, their coverage, bargaining power and coordination, were very high by international standards and have remained high. This was aided by particular institutional devices, such as the Ghent system, by which trade unions had responsibility for the administration of social insurance. It was supported and taken forward by a political party organized around the social democratic project. It was further supported by the development of state welfare, by the consequent vested interests of the workers in these services and by a high level of popular support (Huber and Stephens 2001; Visser 2006).

While this conventional account of the critical turning point in class relations in the Nordic countries is authoritative, the additional attempt to subsume changes in other complex inequalities such as gender to this dynamic is highly problematic. It has been suggested that the distinctive gender relations in Sweden (and other Nordic countries) countries are a consequence of this development of social democracy (Ruggie 1984; Esping-Andersen 1990, 1999). Esping-Andersen (1990) suggests that social democracy is key to gender equality because of its universalist inclusionary character while Ruggie (1984) considers women to be policy takers rather than policy makers and argues that the difference in gender relations in the UK and Sweden can be explained as a result of the social democratic nature of the Swedish state as compared with the liberal state in the UK. However, such an approach underestimates the significance of tipping points in which gender relations are central.

The critical turning point associated with the development of women's free wage labour and their effective political citizenship was different from and later than the critical turning point led by changes in class relations. Women were not initially welcomed into the process of establishing social democracy and instead were excluded. Later on they fought their own way into the political establishment by utilizing their own resources drawn from their own emerging free wage labour. Ultimately, employed women became an important political force which turned a labourist project (for the sectional interests of male workers) into the universalist inclusionary project for which Sweden is renowned. Gender politics, especially employed women's political voices, became an important input into the making and defence of Swedish social democracy, but not at its start in the 1930s moment of historic class compromise (Qvist 1980; Dahlerup and Gulli 1985; Dahlerup and Haavio-Manila 1985; Haavio-Manila 1985; Ravn 1995; Skard and Haavio-Manilla 1985; Dahlerup 1986, 1988, 1993; Eduards 1992, 1997a, 1997b; Lundgren 1992; Ohlander 1992; Wikander 1992; Tyyska 1994; Karvonen and Selle 1995; Gustafsson 1997; Gustafsson et al. 1997; Hedlund 1998; Karlsson 1998).

377

The transition in the labour movement from labourism to a social democracy that was inclusive of employed women only took place several decades after the class compromise of the 1930s. During the late nineteenth and early twentieth century the male-led labour movement was not receptive to feminist demands. The early leadership of the Social Democratic Party and LO chose, as with the labour movements in the UK and elsewhere, to prioritize the interests of working-class men, and so during the 1920s the women of the proletarian women's movement – despite wanting a more equal distribution of labour, equal pay, a general workers' protection law, and just representation within trade union bodies, and despite protests – saw collective agreements which preserved the division of labour and the wages gap, witnessed their male party comrades supporting the prohibition of night work for women, were passed over in elections and their idea of a women's section received little support. Indeed at this time trade union benefits such as strike pay and for sickness and unemployment were paid women at half the rate for men. Women's efforts at creating policies which recognized women's position as both mothers and workers were hard to develop (Qvist 1980; Ohlander 1992). So the male working-class movement was not (at least in the period through the 1920s), supportive of the inclusionary demands of women. At this point there was little to distinguish Sweden's gender politics from that of other European countries. Thus doubt must be cast on the significance of suggestions that we should look back a long way in time for either a long continuous Swedish tradition of egalitarian gender relations or for a gender-equal labour tradition.

The extent of family-friendly policies in the mid-twentieth century Sweden should not be exaggerated. During the 1940s and 1950s, the labour needed for the rapid growth of the economy was not met by the employment of women, but rather by immigration from the other Nordic countries and from southern Europe. In Sweden in 1960, women's proportion of the labour force was close to the OECD average as well as to that of the USA and UK. While the principle of equal pay was finally adopted by the Social Democrats in 1944 and the LO in 1946, policies to implement this were diffuse and weak with little more than recommendations to constituent unions, with the consequence that the wages gap among workers covered by bargaining between the LO and the Swedish employers federation was greater in 1960 than in 1950 (Qvist 1980; Ohlander 1992).

While today Sweden has one of the highest rates of female employment in the developed world, this has only been the case since the 1970s – before then, the Swedish pattern was similar to that in the rest of the OECD. It was not until the 1960s and 1970s that there was a critical turning point for gender relations in Sweden. There were a series of interacting changes in the gendered economy and polity that fuelled a positive feedback loop, or spiral, that drove these changes forward at an accelerating pace. These were: rapid economic growth; an increase in women's employment; an increase in women's parliamentary representation; the impact of a global feminist wave; an increase in publicly funded childcare; and an increase in gendered regulation of the employment regime. During these few years a series of changes in each of these interacting domains took place that projected Sweden (and its Nordic neighbours) onto a path of development that has marked them out as singular and distinctive. This spiralling transformed the gender regime from a domestic to a public form, establishing what has become the global economic model for combining fairness and efficiency with a gender equal (or less unequal) society.

This surge in employment was matched by a surge in women's presence in formal and informal politics. During the 1960s there was a large increase in the proportion of women as members of trade unions (to 29 per cent in the LO and 43 per cent in the TCO by 1970), thereby encouraging the leaders to concern themselves with women's issues (Qvist 1980). The trade unions, especially the LO, revised their policy to one of solidarity to ensure that their high wage strategy was not undercut by pockets of low pay, such as that among women workers. Although this was part of an overall economic strategy that aimed to remove pockets of low productivity and pay from the economy (Qvist, 1980), women's voices were part of this process of change. Women's presence in the Swedish parliament doubled between 1970 and 1980 from 14 per cent to 28 per cent of elected representatives, with the 1973 election being especially important (Inter-Parliamentary Union 1995). This sudden change drew Sweden away from other countries. In 1918–1920 women had won the vote in Sweden at the same time as most other countries in north-west Europe. Yet by 2002 they had 45 per cent of the seats, higher than any other country, with only other Nordic countries coming near. This greater representation of women in the Swedish parliament than other countries was a sudden development between 1970 and 1990 and not a long-standing Swedish particularity. In Sweden the proportion of women in parliament rose at the same time as the proportion of women in the workforce. In most non-Nordic countries there is a significant temporal gap between the two.

The political environment in the 1960s and 1970s was affected not only by developments in Sweden but also by an emerging global feminist wave, originating predominantly in the internal gender politics of the USA, but picking up power, energy, and breadth as it swept around the globe. For Swedish feminists this provided the additional boost of legitimation, ideas, and practices, via books, media, visits, and conferences. This wave of energy, consistent with some of the ideas and practices of Swedish feminism while differing in other respects, such as its evaluation of the potential of the state, made a contribution to the development of Swedish gender politics (Qvist 1980; Dahlerup 1986; Hernes 1987; Hirdmann 1994; Karvonen and Selle 1995; Von der Fehr et al. 1998). Within this global feminist wave ideas and practices spread rapidly between different countries, taking advantage of developing global communications both in the distribution of books and pamphlets and in the television reporting of movement activities. The development of Swedish gender politics was part of this wider international movement, contributing to and drawing from its innovations and expertise; both part of a global development and part particular.

Feminists in Sweden and other Nordic countries were distinctive in the extent to which they were already engaged with and to some extent were already inside the state by the 1970s (Dahlerup 1983; Tyyska 1994). In many countries the boundary between civil society and the state was hard for women to cross, but in Sweden women did cross this line, and relatively high proportions, by international standards, of feminist organizations saw themselves as having a positive relationship with the state (Tyyska 1994). This was at least partly a result of the earlier entry of women into parliamentary representation in Sweden and other Nordic countries than elsewhere, which meant that there were women inside the system with whom alliances could be made and who would be more responsive to political pressure from women. In contrast, in some other countries such as the UK the feminist wave from the 1970s developed a strong separatist element that ignored an unresponsive state where there were few women insiders. Thus this global feminist wave had different implications in different countries, at least partly affected by whether or not women had already gained an effective presence within a state at that time.

These interacting developments further catalysed the spiralling social change. There were changes in state policy that further facilitated the employment of women, especially mothers, by reducing discrimination against women (in 1960 employers and unions agreed to abolish separate wage rates for women and men and in 1969 schools were encouraged to adopt equal opportunity); by facilitating the combination of parenthood and employment by legislating for various kinds of leaves from employment for childcare (in 1979 the right to a six hour day was granted to parents of small children, in 1980 a law was introduced that made sex discrimination in employment illegal, and in 1995 the parental leave policy changed so that men would have to take some or lose the benefit to the household); by changing the tax-benefit system so as to increase the incentives for wives to work (in 1971 separate taxation was introduced for husbands and wives); and finally by a significant increase in publicly-funded childcare (although this was not until the 1970s) (Statistics Sweden 1995). The extent of public provision and the funding of childcare, now much emulated, was once one of the distinctive features of the Swedish gender regime, but it only dates from the 1970s.

The effects of these changes in employment, the state, and other institutions were an increase in the wages for women and an increased willingness by women to enter the labour market. The Swedish gender wage gap narrowed earlier than that in many other countries, though today it is still not completely eradicated. In particular, during 1960–1990, there was an impressive reduction in the wages gap between women and men wage earners in the manufacturing sector that resulted in women in this sector earning 91 per cent of men's wages. This is sometimes attributed to the trade union solidarity policy, but the timing of the increase – starting before the solidarity policy – and the extension of the wages gap closure to white collar workers – who were not subject to the LO policy – means that the solidarity policy cannot be the total explanation (Svensson 1995). Instead the increase in wages is better understood as part of a wider change in the gender system transforming from a domestic to a public and more equal form.

In the 1980s, Sweden was subject to the same global economic pressures as other European countries. At this time there were changes in the state provision of welfare and in the political system. Is globalization causing the demise of the distinctive social democratic path and state welfare provision in Sweden (Lindblom 2001)? The Swedish economy has a high dependence on international trade and its leading industries trade globally, so global economic conditions are felt directly. Global pressures on Swedish social democracy include: global economic competitive pressures that encourage politicians to seek to reduce state welfare expenditures and reduce the strictness of employment protection laws in order to keep footloose capital within their countries; a neoliberal wave that provides discursive support for the reduction of state welfare and services; and entry into the European Union in response to global pressures with a consequent pressure on the Swedish fiscal regime to reduce its taxation and spending. There were domestic pressures also, including a decline of those industries that traditionally generate labour movements and a shift away from the local democratic governance of services where women are strongly involved in decision making to privatized services run by corporations that have few women in senior positions (Hedlund 1993, 1998). There were global flows of people, including levels of in-migration that were highest just at the moment of a highest level of unemployment (Palme et al. 2002), breaking the traditional ethnic homogeneity and thereby potentially contributing to a decline in solidarism and a rise in racism (Pred 2000), though this was largely absorbed (Palme et al. 2002).

However, despite the pressures from global and domestic processes, reductions in social well-being in the period associated with globalization were relatively small. There have been cuts in the level of payments for those workers who become sick or unemployed and reductions in the funds given by central government to local government to support the high quality of services, so in childcare services the worker–child ratios have worsened. The party named after social democracy no longer has an unbroken electoral record (44 years of continuous rule were interrupted in 1976: *Swedish History* 1999). Public social expenditure in 2001 at 30 per cent of GDP is lower than the 37 per cent present in 1993. But the historically high rate of social expenditure and state welfare provision remains high. Sweden spent 30 per cent of its GDP on public social expenditure in 2001, almost 50 per cent higher than the OECD average of 21 per cent, more than any other country in the OECD, and little different from the 31 per cent spent in 1990. The OECD average in 2001 is 21 per cent, also peaking in 1993 at 22 per cent. Sweden actually added new benefits to its portfolio (for example, paternity and parental leave) and childcare provision was protected (Palme et al. 2002; OECD 2006; Rauch 2006).

Social democracy remains strong in Sweden, albeit in a restructured form, for two main reasons. First, there is lock-in from trade unions, welfare institutions, and the social democratic party. Second, there are new champions of social democracy in employed women. This new political constituency is key to the continuity in social democracy. They more than replace the men lost to this project as the economy restructured away from those industries where traditional men's support was centred. They develop and extend the social democratic project of developing state public services and regulating the labour market so as to ensure simultaneously equality and efficiency. In this way the employed women of Sweden have come to the rescue of the welfare state, otherwise potentially eroded by the changing balance of class and global forces. They enter and re-develop the organizations and institutions first established around men's labourist interests, such as the trade unions and their national confederations, and the political party initially established to extend the labourist influence throughout state policy. It is not merely an alliance of separate feminist and labourist projects, but more than this. The Swedish social democratic project today depends upon this new synthesis of feminist and labourist agendas and institutions.

The public and less unequal gender regime in Sweden is not merely an outcome but is also a cause of social democracy. There is coevolution rather than one-way impact. The development of social democracy as a universalist inclusionary project rather than as mere labourism depended on the active participation of and pressure from employed women. While class and gender are always entwined, there are two temporally distinct critical turning points in the development of free wage labour and effective political citizenship – one led by class, the other by gender.

The UK

The UK, while often considered neoliberal in the early twenty-first century, is a more complex case than the USA, with some parts of its political economy somewhat social democratic. This is partly because there are two major polities governing the economy, not just one – the EU as well as the British state, in which the EU governs, most aspects of employment regulation, and the British state which governs most aspects of state welfare provision. There is a divergence between class and gender regimes of inequality in some domains: the different timing of the transition to modernity of the class and gender regimes of inequality, the gender transformation being much later and not yet complete. The UK is currently pulled in two directions by the greater neoliberalism of the British state and the greater social democracy of the EU polity.

In the days of the British Empire Britain was once a global hegemon setting the rules of world trade and finance largely to suit itself. The development of the British hegemon was an early example of the extension of global capital roaming the world in search of sites for profitable activities (Marx 1954; Wallerstein 1974). Economic power was both part cause and part consequence of empire, associated with the development of institutions that set the global rules that further supported the development of British capital (Hirst and Thompson 1996). Although those days have been over since the middle of the twentieth century, they have left a legacy in British institutions as well as in those of the former colonies. As a result of this history London is a centre of global finance capital, with consequences for economic inequality in the UK as well as the rest of the world. It is this history of industrializing before the first vestiges of democracy that is at least partly responsible for the neoliberal path taken in political economy.

From the eighteenth century the British hegemon promoted and structured global free trade. The rise of the British hegemon involved not only capitalism and class relations, but also particular constitutions of ethnic and gender relations. The trade was sometimes in luxuries, such as coffee, spices, and silk; other times it was in British manufactures, such as textiles. Sometimes it was in slaves, and the commodities produced by slaves, such as cotton, sugar, and tobacco. Such trades and economies produced super-profits, thereby fuelling the British Industrial Revolution. This trade in slaves and the goods they produced, food (cheap sugar) and the raw materials for the Industrial Revolution (cotton), was a critical component in the development of British power (Walvin 1992). There were legitimating ideologies in which British civil societal practices were valued more highly than those of the conquered peoples: extending civilization and Christianity was presented as a reason to support the enterprise while liberalism was represented as progress (Ferguson 2004). The empire depended upon a construction of ethnicity in which the domination of other peoples was considered legitimate, requiring their treatment as 'other' than the inhabitants of the imperial power (Said 1978). This in turn was entwined with conceptions of gender relations that bolstered the European view of themselves as morally superior (Enloe 1989; McClintock 1995).

The UK has a suffrage-democracy, though with some small aspects of hereditary power still remaining. It has not achieved presence-democracy though some small procedural steps have been taken since 1997, such as some all-women short lists in national elections. The EU is also an important polity. The range of institutions governed by democracy is moderate and this changes over time. Several of what might have been critical turning points are better described as being constituted by a sequence of events – such as the decline in the power of the hereditary monarch and aristocracy and the development of full male suffrage – rather than a single moment in time. The Second World War was a critical turning point in the process of decolonization and the development of democratic control over a wider range of institutions. Joining the EU in 1973 was also an important moment. The UK is now governed through more than one polity: the EU is important, especially for the governance of the economy, and is of increasing significance over a range of policy areas. The EU itself has a complex form of governance that includes a directly elected parliament, which has proportional representation and has nearly achieved presence-democracy for women, but also institutions of indirect representation for the Member States, including the European Council (of Ministers) and the European Commission.

In the UK there has been a slow decline in the power of the hereditary monarchy and aristocracy for several centuries, reducing in steps at crisis points, but the monarchy still has a minor constitutional place and significant symbolic pull. In 2008 the House of Lords still had 92 hereditary peers and several bishops. The centuries-old British Empire was reduced in stages by the decolonization of the settler societies in the eighteenth and nineteenth centuries, the independence of Ireland in 1922, and following the Second World War, of India and then of most of Africa by the late 1970s. This was a consequence of both vigorous, sometimes armed, nationalist movements in the colonies and the coincidence of the decline in British military power as a consequence of the Second World War, as well as domestic democratic developments. There are some small remaining territories (with voting rights) such as the Falklands/Malvinas. There is a small religious (Protestant) presence within the institutions of governance, maintained since the Reformation that was part of the European wave of reformation. Male suffrage was won in steps that widened the limitations of the franchise on property grounds over many decades if not centuries, building on the tradition of parliamentary representation of the powerful. Important reform acts came in 1832, 1867, and 1884, and were consolidated in a final act in 1918. Women over 30 with some small property gained the vote in 1918, and all women thereafter in 1928. The gap between the dates on which women and men gained full suffrage is shorter than in the USA, from 10 to 44 years, depending on whether male suffrage is dated as 1884 or 1918 and presuming that female suffrage is dated at 1928. Both male and female suffrage were won as a result of increasingly well organized mass civil societal movements, with each involving some violence on both sides. Each had transnational components, most especially for female suffrage. By the time that suffrage was universal in 1928, the full range of practices for free and fair elections had been established. Only in 1900 was the Labour Party formed to represent class interests, forming minority governments in 1924 and 1929 before the landslide victory of 1945 secured their effective power for the first time (Labour Party 2006), followed by further Labour governments in 1964, and from 1997 to 2008 and beyond.

The development of a class-led social democratic tendency in British welfare and employment regulation was associated with the rise of the labour and trade union movement from the late nineteenth century, long after industrialization. The development of state welfare started during the early twentieth century, influenced by pressure from organized labour, the new Labour Party formed in 1900, the German Bismarckian model, and practical pressures from a modernizing economy. Social insurance was introduced in 1911, rent control in 1915, council housing in 1919, state secondary schooling in 1944. The 1945 Labour government introduced the National Health Service, proudly free at the point of use, and further developed the welfare state. The post-war period saw the development of the regulation of the labour market, partially protecting employees from risks such as illness and redundancy. These benefits were differentiated by gender. The model of welfare treated married women as dependents of their husbands and denied them benefits in their own right. Those women who worked part-time were excluded from the new employment protections.

This social democratic trajectory for class-based issues was interrupted by the sudden rise of neoliberalism in the late 1970s. The development of neoliberalism in the UK is partly attributable to a response to pressures from globalization and partly due to domestic conflicts, especially those involving industrial disputes and pressures on state welfare expenditures. This challenge to the post-war settlement, initially led by Thatcher, reduced certain forms of welfare provision, denationalized state-owned industries, privatized public services and utilities, introduced market principles within public services, diminished certain employment protections, and reduced trade union organizational power, not least through an attack on the miners (Walby and Greenwell et al. 1994; Newman and Clarke 1997; Pierson 2001). The regulation of the environment in which trade unions work was also tilted away from unions, for example the outlawing of 'closed-shop' agreements and secondary picketing (Ebbinghaus and Visser 1999). Dex and McCulloch (1997: 187–188), argued that as a consequence Britain was 'sliding into being a low wage, low skill economy in which the quality of jobs is declining'. These changes have had long-lasting effects on British political economy, even though there has been a Labour government in power since 1997. The New Labour project has sought to find a new balance, or 'third way', between earlier conceptions of social democracy and the neoliberal wave (Giddens 1994, 1998). Most importantly, the trade union base for social democracy has been diminished in strength. Through privatization, neoliberal policies have reduced the range of institutions over which there was once direct democratic control. Economic inequality has risen.

There are few practices to promote presence-democracy in the UK. Before the New Labour victory in 1997, Labour used a device in which competition for the parliamentary candidacy in particular seats was restricted to women only; this was temporarily defeated by legal challenge by male would-be candidates but was then restored by legislation. The new Parliament in Scotland and the General Assembly in

Wales set up following the 1997 election successfully used electoral devices to ensure the greater presence of women. The presence of women in the UK Parliament remains low, though not as low as in the USA. The minority ethnic presence in the UK parliament also remains low. The range of institutions that are subject to democratic control has varied. During most of the twentieth century up until 1979 there was an expansion in such institutions associated with the development of the welfare state and employment regulation, with a key moment being the post-Second World War 1945 Labour government that established the National Health Service and nationalized key utilities and industries. The neoliberal wave initiated in the USA and in the UK with the election of Thatcher in 1979 led to a steady decline in the range of institutions subject to democratic control, being replaced by the market and capital.

There have been some changes in gender relations that are contrary to those for class: gendered developments in employment regulation and welfare provision are not aligned with changes in class relations. This is a consequence of the increase in employed women as a political constituency and the increased power of the European Union. The increase in women's employment alongside other changes in the gender regime have created a new political constituency with a distinctive interest in social democratic politics, for the increased provision of public services including not only childcare but also education and health. There is an increased representation of this political voice with an increased presence of women in parliament, in the governmental machinery, and in civil society organizations such as trade unions, where women are now just as likely to be members as are men (see Table 10.6). Most importantly, the legislation and policy from an increasingly powerful European Union requires equal treatment in employment on the grounds of gender, ethnicity, disability, religion/belief, age, and sexual orientation. This has very significantly increased the regulation of gender relations and other complex inequalities in employment, even at a time of the declining regulation of class-based issues. These policy changes led by the EU did not go unchallenged by the UK, which attempted to resist the full transposition of the Directive on equal pay for work of equal value into UK law, failing however in the European Court of Justice and thus being obliged to introduce the domestic legislation that would bring it into line with EU law (Walby 1999b). The EU was a catalyst for change in the UK gendered political economy.

The late 1970s saw two contrasting critical turning points in the development of employment regulation and welfare provision in the UK. The class-based trajectory towards social democracy was challenged and sent in a neoliberal direction. The transformation of the gender regime from a domestic to a public form continued, with an increased turn in a social democratic direction. The outcome for the UK is an uneven oscillation between neoliberal and social democratic pathways of development, varying over time, between regimes of inequality and between employment regulated by the EU and welfare provided by the UK state, though currently with tendency towards neoliberalism.

Ireland

Contemporary Irish political economy is often summarized as neoliberal though it is more complicated than this, not least due to the relevance of several polities and not the Irish state alone. Ireland has one of the lowest levels of government social expenditure in the OECD. It is also one of the few OECD countries to have experienced a decline in economic inequality between households (as measured by Gini) between the mid-1980s (33.1) and 2000 (30.4) (OECD 2006). The labour movement has historically been weak: late industrialization due to its history as a British colony, plus a rapid move to service employment, meant that the typical base of trade unionism and socialism in heavy manufacturing was never significantly developed and the trade unions have historically been fragmented and poorly organized. Capital is strong as a result of its internationalism and US connections, and hence so is its potential mobility. The Catholic Church has trenchantly opposed the provision of welfare by the state rather than the family. In the Irish state, the political party system has been organized more around nationalist issues than those of class divisions. However, the European Union has been a major force for the modernization of the gender regime and for the regulation of employment for gender equality.

During the period of British colonial rule the Irish economy, trade, and the public sphere were regulated by the British state. British rule involved the regulation of the Irish economy in British interests, such as by tariff restrictions and forcing all Irish trade through British rather than Irish ports. These policies curtailed Irish industrial development (Crotty 1986; Coulter 1990; Munck 1993; O'Hearn 1994).

Ireland has a suffrage-democracy that is devoid of hereditary and colonial elements, however, there is a strong religious polity that governs intimacy for many. While it has proportional representation, this has not led to the achievement of a presence-democracy. The EU is also an important polity. The range of institutions subject to democratic control is the narrowest of the four countries. Critical turning points in Irish democracy are: its colonization by Britain; the creation of a national project entwined with a Catholic project; the success of a national project in securing de-colonization and a state of its own; and joining the EU. A potential tipping point in the future might follow the slow development of presence-democracy for women. The Catholic Church has acted as a dampener in the development of presence-democracy, while the EU has been a catalyst for the employment that promotes women's presence in parliament.

Most of Ireland won independence from Britain in 1922, following the long build up of a national project and a short period of militarized contestation. Ireland was never part of the European reformation of Christianity. The transnational Catholic Church retains considerable powers of direct governance of intimacy, including divorce and abortion, for the many Irish people who follow their teachings, as well as a significant influence over the state and civil society. The achievement of democratic self-rule depended upon the building and success of an Irish national project. The Irish national project became closely entwined with Catholicism during this period of nation formation (Larkin 1975, 1978, 1987, 1990), with considerable power granted to the Catholic Church which has had enduring consequences.

On independence, full suffrage was granted to both men and women in 1922. This might be considered as simultaneous suffrage, however, men had been granted the right to vote for MPs sent to the Westminster parliament in the same stages as men in Britain, so it was not quite a simultaneous suffrage-democracy for both sexes. Nevertheless the gap is slightly shorter than in the UK, since all women gained suffrage in 1922, none having to wait until 1928. After 1920, it became usual for newly de-colonized countries to grant suffrage to both men and women simultaneously on independence day. The removal of the hereditary British monarch as head of state took place with the adoption of the new Constitution in 1937 (Bromage and Bromage 1940). Ireland has almost all the procedures for suffrage-democracy (except that not all members of the *Senead* or upper parliamentary chamber are directly elected). It has some but not all of the procedures for presence democracy, with low cost electioneering and proportional representation but no quotas. Ireland does not have presence-democracy for women: very few women have ever been elected to the Irish parliament, but their numbers have been slowly rising since the 1990s (8 per cent in 1990, 12 per cent in 2000) following the increase in women's employment, itself at least partly consequent on joining the EU in 1973. The position of the Catholic Church in Irish governance has come under challenge since the 1980s. Critical moments in this have included sexual scandals, in particular the protection of a paedophile priest from prosecution by the church and state which led to a civil societal protest that challenged this closeness of church and state, in particular the protection of the church by the state. This erodes the authority of the governance of intimacy by the Catholic Church, but does not stop it. There have been repeated contestations over the constitutional legality of abortion and whether there are any exceptions to its illegality, but the Catholic Church's preferences on abortion have prevailed thus far.

After decolonization, the Irish government sought to develop its economic independence from Britain and an Irish national identity. Developing the Irish national project entailed a domestic gender regime: the model of womanhood inscribed in the national project was that of wife and mother, not of worker and political citizen. This was a consequence of the entwining of the national project with Catholicism. The strategy of economic independence meant autarky. De Valera, the Irish First Minister, yearned for a self-sufficient utopia free from 'contaminating' contact with Britain (Lee 1989: 17). By 1932 *Fianna Fail*, the governing party, was ideologically committed to self-sufficiency, involving a policy of a shift from livestock to tillage agriculture to increase agricultural employment, as well as a protectionist tariff barrier behind which indigenous industry could develop (Lee 1989: 193). The outcome was little economic growth (O'Malley 1992).

A new constitution in 1937 enshrined the position of the Catholic Church as a key political force in Ireland: indeed Article 44 explicitly recognized the 'special position of the Catholic Church' (Durphy 1995) by institutionalizing and codifying Catholic doctrine, especially its teaching on the family, women, and education (Beale 1986; Farrell 1988; Scannell 1988). Article 41 stated that the state recognized the family as the natural primary and fundamental group in society, that women should not have to work outside the home, and that marriage was indissoluble (Beale 1986; Jackson 1993). A marriage bar came into operation in some areas of paid work so that women were sacked on their marriage (Beale 1986; Curtin 1989). Even in the post-war period, the economic development agency refused to assist international firms to locate in Ireland if they intended to employ women (Pyle 1990).

The Catholic Church insisted on its own control over welfare and education services and opposed the state financing of medical assistance for mothers and their children, on the grounds that this was the responsibility of the family and not the state. By the 1920s all Catholic women primary teachers were being trained in teacher training colleges run by nuns, and secondary schooling for girls up until the 1960s was provided almost exclusively by convent schools run by nuns. Nuns ran the largest Irish hospitals and most nurses were trained in nursing schools attached to these hospitals. Growth in the female religious orders continued unabated: from 1,500 in 1851, to

9,000 in 1911, and peaking at 16,000 in the mid-1960s (Clear 1987; Fahey 1992; Luddy 1995a, 1995b). The Catholic Church resisted the development of welfare services by the state. A key example of this was the resistance of the church to the state financing medical services for mothers and their children (Whyte 1971; Inglis 1987). In most European countries the provision of health care for vulnerable citizens is seen as appropriate to the remit of the state. However, in Ireland this extension, in the Mother and Child Scheme of 1951 under the auspices of the 1947 Health Act, for free medical services for pregnant women and children, was fiercely opposed. While there was opposition from the medical profession, which feared their loss of control over fee-paying work, the strongest opposition came from the Catholic Church on grounds of subsidiarity. The head of the Catholic hierarchy in Ireland wrote to the head of the Irish state, the *Taoiseach,* on 5 April 1951 thus: 'To claim such powers for the public authority, without qualification, is entirely and directly contrary to Catholic teaching on the rights of the family, the rights of the Church in education, the rights of the medical profession and of voluntary institutions' (Whyte 1971: 460; Fahey 1995).

Much of the time between the founding of the Irish state and 1970, the Catholic Church and Irish state practised an uncontested division of respective arenas of authority. They divided institutions within the borders of Ireland into those to be governed by either the Church or the state. The Church in Ireland governed a wider range of institutions than is typical in many other advanced industrial countries, including most of those concerned with the provision of welfare, as well as dominating policy on the family. In those instances where the state attempted to expand its area of activities, the Catholic Church strongly, and largely successfully, resisted. In the immediate post-war period there was a social democratic wave across Britain and many other countries in Northern Europe, for example the UK building its National Health Service. The Irish did not share in this social democratic impulse. Today its state welfare expenditures are not only less than those of the UK, but also less than those in the USA.

After several decades of economic stagnation came a radical change of policy to engage internationally and to join the EU. As part of this process Ireland applied to become a member of the then European Economic Community in 1961, finally joining in 1973 (Commins 1995). This was indeed a critical turning point. Economic growth took off, the gender regime began a sudden transformation, relations between church and state fractured. The Irish state opened up its economy to the world economy, moving from protection to free trade, from the discouragement to the encouragement of foreign investment in Ireland.

Ending this strategy of economic autarky was partly due to a perception that this was desirable for growth in the Irish economy, and that it would provide an escape route from being locked into an unequal and asymmetrical relationship with Britain, and partly due to international pressure. Lee (1989: 341) locates the origin of the changed orientation to the domestic/international issue by government and ministers as taking place in 1957/8, seeing the policy documents *Economic Development* and *The First Programme* by the new Finance Secretary Whitaker as the instruments of these historic shifts. This is a view shared by Breen et al. (1990: 31), who refer to 'The turning point of 1958, when the State seized the initiative as the main force in Irish society'. It was also partly due to outside pressures. Once Ireland accepted Marshall Aid, which was offered as a US contribution to the rebuilding of post-war Europe, it was pressurized by the USA into dismantling its industrial protection and into acting to attract export-oriented foreign firms (O'Hearn 1995).

However, in relation to the gender regime the Irish state attempted, but ultimately failed, to resist the modernizing impulse of the EU. The Irish state was legally compelled by the EU to change its policy in the regulation of gender relations in the labour market. On joining the EU in 1973, the Irish were obliged to abandon the ostensibly core values of the Irish nation and the Catholic Church as to the domestic location of women. The EU had a different set of policies on gender from that of Ireland (Whyte 1988; Curtin 1989; Walby 1997, 1999b) requiring equal treatment for women and men in employment by all new Member States. The Irish state was obliged to remove the marriage bar which had prevented married women from working in certain occupations and to introduce legislation outlawing discrimination against women in employment (Whyte 1988; Curtin 1989). This was an unintended gendered consequence of joining the EU. While the change in gendered employment policy was determined by the EU, there was also an active local voice pressing for these changes. A feminist movement pushed for the implementation of equal pay legislation, for instance, in the 1977 Equal Pay Campaign, where 36,000 signatures for an equal pay petition were collected in ten days, contributing to the passing of the legislation (Smyth 1988). Nevertheless, without the EU it is unlikely that the grass-roots movement would have won equal pay at that time (Robinson 1988).

The labour movement in Ireland has historically been weak. This is despite the lack of ethnic divisions that in other countries, such as the USA, have hindered solidarity. Here the labour movement has been fragmented and poorly organized at the national level, although a moderate number of workers have been members of trade unions. There were many (more than 80) small unions, which tended to compete for members rather than focus on alliances. Progress on the several attempts at amalgamation into larger industrial unions has been slow though ongoing. United action at a national level was further made difficult by the existence of significant numbers of unions outside the Irish congress of Trade Unions (Breen et al. 1990). One reason for the weakness of the labour movement was the absence of the kinds of manufacturing that had elsewhere generated strong trade unions, such as iron and steel making and car plants. This was at least partly due to late industrialization that in turn was due to the restriction of Ireland's economic development when it was in a dependency relationship with Britain.

There were further comparative weaknesses in the development of labour and socialist politics. The employers did not form an effective national body of the kind necessary to take forward a centralized national level of collective bargaining. The three such bodies (of which the most important was the Federated Union of Employers) had insufficient authority over diverse members to make national agreements (Breen et al. 1990). Party politics were not crystallized along class lines; nationalist politics took precedence leaving less space for the articulation of working-class interests. The Catholic Church actively opposed the development of the state welfare that elsewhere was a significant part of the social democratic project, as described above. The development of employed women as a constituency to support the social democratic project came very late as compared with the other countries: in 1980 women were only 29 per cent of the workforce rising to just 35 per cent only in 1990, though since then it has risen rapidly to 43 per cent in 2005.

Unlike many other countries such as the UK and Sweden, which have seen a decline in corporatist-type arrangements during the globalizing decades since the 1980s, Ireland has had a very unusual and very late developing form of corporatism from 1987. This has been referred to as 'competitive corporatism' rather than 'social corporatism' (Rhodes 1998, 2001) and as 'neo-liberal corporatism' (Boucher and Collins 2003). The 1987 form was the culmination of a slow development of corporatist forms from the 1940s in the form of social partnerships (Boucher and Collins 2003). The early bargain was for income tax cuts, even though this entailed curtailing some public services. It is more voluntarist than most corporatism since parties can drop out and it is not legally binding until it is passed as legislation by parliament – a usual but not inevitable following step. The first bargain was struck around the agenda of economic growth and lowering unemployment and is credited with making a significant contribution to these achievements by producing stability (Baccaro and Simoni 2007). A particularly distinctive feature of the bargain is the agreement to cut taxes and social expenditure. The deal was struck at a time of perceived crisis, but has since been replicated several times even when the economy was the fastest growing in the EU. While overall state social expenditure as a percentage of GDP has not fallen between 1990 (15.5 per cent) and 2003 (15.9 per cent), it has remained low by OECD standards where the levels have risen slightly between 1990 (17.9 per cent) and 2003 (20.7 per cent) (OECD 2007b).

Globalization has affected Ireland in complex ways. The inflow of global, especially US, capital has been a factor in its rapid economic growth since the 1980s. The OECD estimates that trade accounts for 76 per cent of its GDP, so Ireland is a site of flows. The capital built branch plants, especially for manufacturing computer components for international markets, exporting high levels of profits out of Ireland. Ireland is one of the few countries where there is a significant difference between the Gross Domestic Product per person ($40,942) and the Gross National Income per person ($40,942), with the gap being largely made up of expatriated profits (World Bank 2006c). The benefit here has been high rates of economic growth and, despite the expatriated profits, a rapidly rising standard of living until the crash of 2008.

Ireland initially successfully navigated the increase in global capital flows. The rapid growth of the Irish economy earned it the name of Celtic Tiger (O'Hearn 1998), though it might be more appropriate to say Celtic Tigress in recognition of the rapid increase in female employment. While the Irish political economy may be summarized as neoliberal, it is important to make distinctions between the dynamics of change for gender and class relations and in different policy areas. The regulation of employment by the EU has meant that there has been an increase in equality regulations which are part of a social democratic project. However, state social expenditure remains low. There has been a rapid transformation of the gender regime from domestic towards public, led by the changes in employment, but this is far from complete in most domains. Relative to the other countries compared here Ireland has the most domestic gender regime.

The critical turning points are the absence of a Reformation; the colonization of Ireland by Britain; the growth of a nation project entwined with Catholicism; decolonization and suffrage-democracy; joining the EU and internationalizing the economy; and the development of neoliberal corporatism. The rapid increase in economic growth spirals with the rapid increase in female employment, with each catalysing the other. The Catholic Church acted as a dampener to change, especially through its opposition to the modernization of the gender regime. The EU was a catalyst for change, removing the restrictions on women's employment whose increase was necessary for rapid economic growth. However, openness to global flows contributed to the crash of 2008.

Conclusions

The rise of social democracy in political economy during the twentieth century was uneven and its fall is more uneven still, being resilient and even renewed in some places and dimensions but not in others. Many claims that globalization must undermine social democracy have been shown to be exaggerated. In response some have suggested that this is a simple case of path dependency, with social democracy locked into institutions in some countries. But this underestimates the significance of the rise of a new social democratic project which is supported by the new constituency of employed women.

Much work on divergent paths of social development has focused on the balance of class forces. The distinctiveness of the approach here is to consider the implications of complex inequalities in addition to class; a wider range of polities, not only states but also organized religions and the EU; not only national but also global processes. It also differentiates between the welfare and employment aspects of political economy, not least because they are governed by different polities in the Member States of the European Union. A longer and different list of critical turning points emerges when these additional inequalities, domains, and spatialities are taken into account.

While the four countries have different depths of democracy, they share several critical turning points. These include: Reformation or not of the Christian church in the sixteenth century – a regional European wave; male suffrage-democracy in the late nineteenth century – a regional European wave; female suffrage-democracy around 1920 (1918–1928) – a regional north European and North American wave; and a slight decline in depth in the 1990s as a result of a global neoliberal wave. In addition, there are some that are specific, including a decolonization of the USA from Britain and a new constitution in 1776, and a decolonization of Ireland from Britain in 1922 with a new constitution in 1937. There are significant differences in the length of the temporal gap between the achievement of suffrage-democracy on the basis of class, gender, and ethnicity. The longest temporal gap in suffrage-democracy between different groups is in the USA, which had the earliest majority male suffrage, and the shortest is in Sweden.

Violence

There is a tendency for violence to decline with modernity, with a link through increases in democracy rather than increases in economic development. There is also a countervailing tendency for violence to increase with inequality. Most important are significant variations in the level of violence between varieties of modernity: it is much higher in neoliberal than social democratic forms. This contradicts the popular thesis that neoliberal states are smaller than social democratic ones – neoliberal states spend more on the military and on law and order, including prisons. There are additional institutional components to the path dependency of violence including, especially, the history of warfare.

The four countries vary in the path of development of the violence nexus. In general, neoliberal countries with high levels of inequality and shallow forms of democracy have higher levels of violence than social democratic countries where inequality is less extreme and democracy is deeper. The neoliberal USA contrasts sharply with the more social democratic EU and especially Sweden across the range of forms of violence, including homicide, use of the death penalty, the coerciveness of the criminal justice system, and the degree of militarization. The UK and Ireland are in between, with Ireland less violent than the UK (see Table 10.5).

The USA has a homicide rate (5.56) over three times that of the EU (1.59) and an imprisonment rate nearly eight times as high (689) as that of the EU (87). The USA is one of only 25 countries in the world that still use the death penalty. Among the three EU countries, Sweden has the lowest homicide (1.11) and imprisonment rates (69). The USA spends over four times as much of its central government budget on the military as compared with countries in the EU; this is almost one fifth (19.3 per cent) of government expenditure and amounts to more than twice as much of its GDP as countries in the EU (4.6 per cent). Among the three EU countries, the UK spends the most (6.3 per cent). The USA (2.7 per cent) spends more than the three European countries on law and order with the UK (2.2 per cent) closer to the USA than Sweden (1.8 per cent) and Ireland (1.5 per cent).

Table 10.5 Violence: USA, EU, Sweden, UK, Ireland

	USA	EU	Sweden	UK	Ireland
Homicide rate per 100,000 (1)	5.56	1.59	1.11	1.61	1.42
Prison population per 100,000 (2)	689	87	69	129	79
Increase in prison population 1990–2001 as per cent (3)	61	26	17	45	43
Military as per cent of central government expenditure (4)	19.3	4.6	4.3	6.3	1.9
Military expenditure as per cent of GDP (5)	4.1	1.7	1.6	2.6	0.6
Law and order expenditure as per cent of GDP (6)	2.7		1.8	2.2	1.5
Year death sentence abolished (7)	Still legal		1921	1973	1990
Year rape in marriage became illegal (8)	Late 1970s		1965	1994	1990

(1) Homicides (intentional killing of a person excluding attempts: murder, manslaughter, euthanasia and infanticide) per 100,000 population, average per year 1999–2001, as recorded by the police. UK is England and Wales (Northern Ireland is 2.65 and Scotland is 2.16). EU is EU15. *Source*: Barclay and Tavares (2003).

(2) Rate per 100,000 population in 2001. UK is England and Wales (Northern Ireland is 59 and Scotland is 120). EU is EU15. *Source*: Barclay and Tavares (2003).

(3) UK is England and Wales. EU is EU15. *Source*: Barclay and Tavares (2003).

(4) Data for 2005. EU is EMU. *Source*: World Bank (2007b).

(5) Data for 2005. EU is EMU. *Source*: World Bank (2007b).

(6) Data for 2003. *Source*: OECD (2006).

(7) *Source*: HighBeam Research (2007).

(8) USA: State by state reform, starting in the late 1970s, *source*: National Center for Victims of Crime (2007); Sweden: *source*: Russell (1990); UK: Criminal Justice and Public Order Act 1994; *source*: Westmarland (2004); Ireland Criminal Law (Rape) Act 1990, *source*: Galligan (1998).

The USA

Despite being the most economically developed country, the USA has the highest rate of violence on all indicators. Why is the USA so violent? It has been a violent country since its origins in conquest. Many European countries, once also very violent, experienced either a critical turning point during state reconstruction or the end of a war or else slow processes of modernization leading to tipping points in the reduction of violence. The high rates of deployment of violence and its low level of regulation by democratic polities is linked to its military history, slavery, culture, and criminal justice system.

The legacy of violence in the USA starts with the conquests by the various groups of European settlers who sought land to settle and exploit, their expansion across the North American continent, and their destruction of the peoples who opposed this. For several centuries from 1620, there was armed struggle between the colonizers and the original nations of Native Americans, during which the majority of natives lost their lives (they are now less than 1 per cent of the population: see CDC 2006). This was a long process of full-scale war, attrition, and disease, in which treaties were signed and abandoned, and alliances were made and betrayed, resulting in the defeat of the native peoples of the USA by European settlers (Graymont 1972). US military history continued with the successful war of independence from the British Empire conducted in 1773–1776. This was followed by the violent subduing of French settler groups who had colonized the middle of the continent along waterways such as the St Lawrence and the Mississippi. There were also border disputes with Mexico over which tracts of land were within the USA and which were within Mexico in which the Mexicans were militarily defeated and vast tracts of land in the south and west were added to the USA. This included the US–Mexican war in 1846–1848, which led to the US annexation of Texas, California, and New Mexico from Mexico. Next was the military crushing of the attempt at independence by the southern confederacy in the civil war of 1861–1865. The military history of the USA continues, with engagements in the European Second World War followed by wars in Korea, Vietnam, Kuwait, and most recently Iraq and Afghanistan (Murphy 1967; van Alstyne 1974; Beringer et al. 1986; Reid 1996).

Slavery was an inherently violent institution that used force to capture and move millions of people from Africa to subdue them and to coerce them to work for no wages. Rebellions were few and harshly put down (Mullin 1992). Slavery was not only an economic institution, but also depended upon the use of violence, polities that legalized the practice, and legitimating ideologies. There was military violence in Africa at the point of the extraction of slaves, the violence of the transportation of the slaves during which many died, and the use and threat of violence in the everyday maintenance of labour relations. Slavery depended upon racialized discursive constructions of the other that rendered black people as 'other' than the slave-owning population (Walvin 1992). During the civil war the Confederacy in the south fought to gain their independence from the rest of the USA in order to sustain their own way of life, especially its racialized practice of slavery based on a supposed constitutional claim to the primacy of states' rights over national or federal rights, which had been fudged in the early wording of the Constitution. But there were continuing attempts to continue the subordination of African-Americans, including through lynching, in which the state provided little protection for the victims (Shapiro 1988).

This legacy of violence has had implications for its use in a series of related institutions. The lethal arming of individual citizens in the USA follows unbroken from the tradition of violence by settlers against the former inhabitants and has its consequences in the high rate of homicide. This violent history contributes to a legacy in which the widespread possession of guns is constitutionally as well as practically embedded and a cultural history of glorification of the individual and collective armed struggle (for example, in the Hollywood genre of 'cowboys and Indians'). Violence is also part of the history of industrial relations: in the late nineteenth century there were brutal violent attempts at breaking strikes and unions, with employer's own forces or with the assistance of local police and national guards (Smith 2003). The USA is almost unique among developed nations in allowing and using the death penalty (Amnesty International 2006). Corporal punishment of children is still allowed in the home, schools (though exceptions in some states), and as a form of discipline in around half the states in the penal system, though not as a sentence for a crime (End All Corporal Punishment of Children 2006).

There had been a major attempt to reduce violence by the radical social movements of the 1960s, which have continued in some restricted areas including in relation to gender-based violence. The 1960s saw considerable grass-roots protest against and in opposition to the US military engagement in Vietnam and adjacent countries, which slowly contributed to US withdrawal. This same period also saw the emergence of a feminist movement and groups committed to action to end violence against women. These were the pioneers of the rape crisis phone lines, the refuges and shelters for the survivors of domestic violence, support for the survivors of child sex abuse, legal strategies to tackle sexual harassment in the workplace, and the naming and challenging of a multiplicity of forms of violence against women. This movement took a dual form in the development of both autonomous feminist institutions and challenges to the laws and practices of the criminal justice system and other agencies of the state. The law on rape was changed, state by state, and starting in the 1970s, so that it was no longer legal to rape a woman in marriage. The movement continued even as the political climate changed, for example, gaining exceptions for battered women from the curtailing of benefit payments to only three years (Martin 1987; Russell 1990; National Center for Victims of Crime 2007). This US movement launched a global feminist wave against violence against women which reverberated around the world and found new forms in various locations (Bunch 1995; Peters and Wolper 1995; Keck and Sikkink 1998).

However, this social democratic moment was short-lived and little institutionalized at the level of the state. By the 1970s a counter wave was up and running – neoliberalism. This has a significant component that addresses issues of violence and crime. Rather than the social democratic forms of penal welfare there was a turn to more punitive and violent forms of criminal justice system (Garland

2001). In 1976, and against the global trend, the USA having previously suspended use of the death penalty reintroduced it. The number of executions per year rose from one to five during 1977–1983, to 98 in 1999, and then fell back down to 53 in 2006 (Clark County Prosecuting Attorney 2007). Between 1991 and 2001 the rate of imprisonment in the USA rose by 61 per cent as compared with 26 per cent in the EU, reaching levels ten times of that in Sweden (Barclay and Tavares 2002, 2003).

In the context of war in Iraq and the growth of terror attacks by jihadists around the world, including those on 9/11 in New York and elsewhere, there was a general increase in securitization. War and the fear of terror fed a perception that it was appropriate to increase surveillance, especially over those people who travel by air, to justify the use of coercive interrogation techniques on suspects, and to hold enemy combatants in legal limbo in Guantanamo Bay. This erosion of human rights and freedoms was a consequence of militarization and the fear of terrorism (Gregory 2004).

The USA is unique among the four countries examined here in its trajectory of violence in that there have been no significant turning points away from this pathway of violence. There is one regime of inequality where opposition has gathered, concerning gender-based violence, which is ongoing and has translated into a global wave. But the turn to neoliberalism exacerbated the violence spiral.

Sweden

Sweden has a low level of violence relative to other countries. Of the four being compared it has the lowest homicide and imprisonment rates and the earliest abolition of the death penalty and illegality of rape in marriage. However, it does have a history of militarist nationalism, though this stopped very early, which has left a legacy of average EU expenditure on military (though this has been put to uses other than war). A less coercive criminal justice system and depth of regulation of gender-based violence is associated with the depth of its democratization.

Sweden once had repeated militarized conflicts with its European, especially Nordic, neighbours. The turning point came two centuries ago in 1814, when Sweden fought its last war. Sweden has had a history of alternate warring and alliance with its Nordic neighbours and during this period there was established a strong Swedish state as well as strong Nordic alliances. Between 1397 and 1521 there was a union of Norway, Denmark, and Sweden – the Kalmar Union. In 1523 the Nordic region split into one alliance of Sweden and Finland

and another of Denmark, Norway, Iceland, Greenland, and the Faroe Islands. This started a series of conflicts and the seventeenth century saw near continuous war. In 1809 Russia attacked and occupied Finland thereby ending Swedish domination. In one last war Sweden attacked and defeated Norway, creating a union between the two in 1814. This ending of war was associated with a change in Sweden's internal politics, not least the development of greater powers for parliament at the expense of the monarch. Greater cooperation between the Nordic countries was secured with the founding of the Nordic Council in 1952, between Sweden, Denmark, and Norway, with Finland joining in 1956. Sweden was neutral in both of the twentieth century's World Wars and afterward joined NATO when it was founded in 1947. Neutrality was one of the reasons for not joining the EU at its foundation (*Swedish History* 1999; Nordic Council 2006).

Swedish legislation saw early limits to the use of official violence against its citizens. It abolished the death penalty in 1921 (HighBeam Research 2007), much earlier than many other countries, and 1950 saw the start of process by which corporal punishment was forbidden by law (*Swedish History* 1999), which was completed in the 1979 amendment to the Parenthood and Guardianship Code (End All Corporal Punishment of Children 2006).

Sweden made rape in marriage illegal in 1965 long before many other countries (Russell 1990). The country has repeatedly upgraded its legal interventions on male violence against women, for instance, in 1982 by passing a law to ensure that all assault and battery against women is subject to public prosecution and is not merely a civil matter (Statistics Sweden 1995), and this was slightly ahead of many other Western countries. While there is some controversy as to whether Sweden has lower rates of violence against women than similar countries (Lundgren et al. 2001), it has one of the most developed legal systems to address the issue. As in the other countries examined here, these reforms were the consequence of feminist pressure focused on the issue of violence against women; unlike the other countries women were present in the state to facilitate the revision of state policy and law.

Sweden did catch some of the neoliberal wave, but this had less effect than in many other countries. The rate of imprisonment did rise by 17 per cent between 1990 and 2001 (Barclay and Tavares 2003), but this was much less than the other three countries and the EU as a whole.

Sweden has a social democratic version of the violence nexus, with lower rates of the range of forms of violence. This pathway started with the ending of the last war fought by Sweden in 1814, much earlier than the other countries. The regulation of violence towards women did increase at the same time as the global feminist wave on these issues. The neoliberal global wave was merely a ripple in relation to violence in Sweden, consequently increasing the differences between path dependent trajectories of violence in Sweden as compared with the USA and UK.

The UK

The UK has undergone several turning points rather than following a single simple path of violence. Violence was used routinely in the acquisition and maintenance of empire. It decreased after decolonization, the pacification of Europe by EU, the ending of terrorism over the disputed partition of Ireland, and the feminist wave from the 1970s that led to increased regulation of gender-based violence and thereby its reduction. However, this was followed in the 1980s by the turn to neoliberalism, with wars in the Falklands/Malvinas, Kuwait, Iraq, and Afghanistan, the rise of jihadist terrorism, the resecuritization of civil society, and the increased coerciveness of the criminal justice system.

The legacy of the military in the UK centres on empire – the conquest and defence of territory and slave trading – and the end of empire removed many of the reasons for war. From the sixteenth century onward, the UK conquered and ran, through military force, a large empire covering nearly a quarter of the world at its height in the late nineteenth century. The military conflict that is associated with empire continued until its end during the late twentieth century, when former colonies became independent states.

The European continent was marked for many centuries by wars between states and other entities, in which Britain played a major role. From the eighteenth century, these wars became increasingly saturated with nationalist ideologies which purported to be seeking to bring into alignment national and state boundaries. National projects were frequently partially mapped onto religious, ethnic, and linguistic groups, which provided added meaning to these projects (Smith 1986). However, since ethno-national and religious groupings have been thoroughly mixed during the course of European history (Therborn 1995), purity-seeking projects, such as nations seeking a state of their own, would inevitably fail. This did not prevent war and irregular collective violence, including pogroms (Walby 2003).

Britain became a global hegemon during the seventeenth century and relinquished this position by the mid-twentieth century. The

British state subordinated many different countries containing many diverse nations, religions, and ethnicities, altering their economies, polities, and cultures so as to benefit Britain, or at least those who were dominant in the UK. The British Empire ruled through formal political hierarchies supported by military force based on economic power and supported by legitimating ideologies. British state power was visibly underpinned by military force – without navies and armies there would have been no Empire. These were used both in initial conquest and to put down rebellions. The profits of the resulting trade returned to the British imperial elite contributed to their interest in expanding and maintaining the British Empire. However, the cost of maintaining the military forces needed to support these specific enterprises were met by a wider section of the British population than were in receipt of the resulting profits (Davis and Huttenback 1986).

The British Empire came to an end in the latter half of the twentieth century as a result of changes across the range of domains. Its economy was overtaken by the USA in the early years of the twentieth century and by 1910 the average American was richer than the average Brit. The two World Wars (1914–1918 and 1939–1945) drained Britain's resources and potential for economic development relative to the USA. The ideological legitimacy of the Empire was undermined by a near global wave of nationalism, drawing on emerging views of democratic entitlements from the nineteenth century onwards (Kedourie 1966; Smith 1986). The whites-run settler societies gained their independence by 1910, while during the 1950s and 1960s most of the colonies in Africa, Asia, and the Caribbean and beyond were able to establish their independent statehood.

The struggle for Ireland's independence from Britain and the location of the border was a source of sporadic collective violence and terrorism. The settlement of Catholic Ireland by the Protestant British was contentious and violent rebellion was followed by violent repression, with a key moment being during the time of Cromwell in the seventeenth century. The independence granted to Ireland in 1922 did not include the six counties in the north which had an overall Protestant majority: these remained as part of the UK to the present day. This has been disputed ever since, both politically and by force of arms, with consequent terrorism in the north of Ireland and the mainland UK. The 1960s and 1970s saw the height of these 'Troubles'. From time to time the global media chose to elevate the issue of Northern Ireland to the global political stage. The difficulty in resolving the non-congruity of nation and state in Northern Ireland is to the detriment of many aspects of life there, including a lack of economic development and higher rates of violence – for example, the homicide rate in Northern Ireland (2.65) in 1999–2001, was 65 per cent higher than that in England and Wales (1.61). There are ongoing attempts to consolidate the peace agreement (Whyte 1971; Anderson and O'Dowd 1999a, 1999b; Barclay and Tavares 2003). Of these various attempts at peaceful settlements, the Good Friday Agreement of 1998 was the most important, initiating a peace process that is still active. This violent conflict is thus an example of both the legacy of empire and the legacy of the impure and contested boundaries of nation and state in Europe. This is despite countless attempts at sophisticated political solutions with a plethora of innovative interpretations of the concept of sovereignty (Kearney 1997).

During the 1970s, the UK like the USA developed a feminist movement, one part of which addressed violence against women (Hague and Malos 1993). The first shelter for battered women was established in London in 1973 (Pizzey 1974), followed by the development of a national network of such refuges – Women's Aid. A rape crisis phone line was established shortly after, followed again by a network of regional centres. The movement drew inspiration from developments in the USA as well as parallel developments occurring nearly simultaneously in other European countries. In the early years the orientation was one of building new separate institutions to help women, in the absence of any expectation that the state would be responsive to these feminist demands. Later, demands were placed upon the state to provide funding and to revise the relevant legislation (Taylor-Browne 2001); rape in marriage was made illegal in 1994 (Westmarland 2004). The most important revisions of the law took place in the decade following the election of the new Labour government in 1997, concerning domestic violence, sexual assault, female genital mutilation, and forced marriage (Hester and Westmarland 2005). From the 1980s onwards there were initiatives to get the criminal justice system to address violence against other minoritized groups, including African-Caribbeans and gays and lesbians, in response to demands from those communities.

From the 1980s the turn to neoliberalism, following the election of Thatcher in 1979, was associated with an increased coerciveness of the criminal justice system and an increased propensity to go to war. The orientation of the criminal justice system was changed from a penal–welfare focus on reform to a more punitive approach (Garland 2001): the rate of imprisonment soared, rising 45 per cent during 1990–2001 alone (Barclay and Tavares 2003). The UK went to war with Argentina over the Falklands/Malvinas – small islands off the coast of Argentina that were still a British colony – with a significant loss of life. The UK also joined the war against Iraq over Kuwait and then went to war in Iraq as an ally of the USA, followed by Afghanistan, again.

The UK became a target for jihadism, radical Islamic terrorist actions sometimes but not always linked to Al Qaeda. There was a major suicide bombing in London on 7 July 2006 and attempted bombings on 21 July 2006, as well as other events. These jihadists were second generation British-born Muslims of Pakistani descent, Pakistan having once been part of the British Empire colony (3 per cent of the population were Muslim in 2001). Britain's involvement in the US-led war in Iraq, a history of other disputes with Islamic entities such as the Palestine/Israel conflict, and wider fears have all contributed to the development of this new form of terrorism. There are now significant numbers of convicted jihadists in British jails. The non-congruence of religion, nation, and state for the Islamic diaspora in Britain had led to a complex cross-cutting of understandings of citizenship (Hussain and Bagguley 2005) and conflicts (Bagguley and Hussain 2008).

In the neoliberal climate, fears regarding the new terrorism have led to new and more intense forms of securitization which involve various erosions of civil liberties. In 2008 the number of days that a terrorist suspect could be held without charge was extended to 28 days (the longest time-span in the West). There is a proposal to introduce ID cards, not merely with a name, number, and photo, but with considerable additional items of information. Travel, especially air travel, is subject to increased security checks and surveillance. This deepening of securitization in this period is in contrast to the more low-key response to the earlier terrorism from the IRA, when neoliberalism was less entrenched.

The UK has undergone more than one critical turning point in its trajectory of violence. The development of Empire was associated with an increase in violence. Most of the twentieth century was marked by a decline in violence, with decolonization, the political settlement represented by the European Union, and the rise of social movements winning an increased regulation of violence against women and minorities. Towards the end of that century the rise of neoliberalism was associated with an increased propensity to go to war, an increased coerciveness of the criminal justice system, and an increased securitization of civil society, with the exception of the continuing increase in the regulation of violence against women and other minorities.

Ireland

Ireland has a low level of violence. It has no history of military conquest of its own, only irregular militarized resistance to colonization by Britain. It uses fewer resources for the criminal justice system and the military than many countries. As with the other countries being compared here there has been an increase in the regulation of gender-based violence. So despite its neoliberal political economy, Ireland does not have a conventional neoliberal violence nexus.

Ireland was effectively a colony of the British state, part of the British Empire, from the seventeenth century until its independence in 1922. English attempts at colonization began around 1169 and involved the establishment of plantations of settlers, with the most serious of these conquests coming during the middle of the seventeenth century. After the rebellion of 1641, Cromwell's conquest during 1649–1653 led to a confiscation of lands belonging to native Catholic landowners and their handing over to British settlers. A second rebellion (1689–1691) led to further bloodshed and subordination. Britain had had a Protestant reformation by this time, so the struggles in Ireland mapped nationality onto religion. As a British colony Ireland had no significant serious legacy of an army of its own and only occasional militias to fight (or help) the British.

The movement for Irish independence or 'Home Rule for Ireland' was pushed forward by both political and violent means, with the period 1916–1921 especially marked by politically-inspired violence. The British state conceded Home Rule for Ireland, passing the Government of Ireland Act, in 1914, under which the whole of Ireland would have elected a devolved parliament. However, the two Irish sides – nationalist and unionist – could not agree as to whether the predominantly Protestant counties of Ulster in the north of Ireland were to be included, so it was not implemented. The Easter Uprising in 1916 was a failed insurrection in Dublin but the brutality used by the British in its suppression increased support for the nationalist project. In the 1918 election, held under the old rules, the nationalist party, *Sinn Féin*, won most of the seats. Its MPs assembled not in London but in Dublin, and unilaterally declared the independence of the whole island from Britain. The new regime's armed forces, the Irish Republican Army, waged war with Britain from 1919 to 1921, until a truce in that year agreed a highly controversial settlement in which the north was allowed to opt out, which it did. In 1922 the Irish Free State was founded while the six counties in the north stayed as part of the UK. This militarized conflict over the north of Ireland, perhaps surprisingly, did not militarize the state in the Republic of Ireland. Though the location of the boundary remains contested because of the mixing of ethno-religious-national groups in the north of Ireland, generating a militarized conflict and terrorist violence until the peace settlement of the 1990s, this was fought in Northern Ireland and Great Britain and not in the Republic (Kearney 1997).

Ireland has not had any significant engagement in any war since its independence. It remained neutral throughout the Second World War, and has not joined in since with any other war. The institutional development of the military remains small and its expenditures are low by international standards.

During the 1970s in Ireland, as with the other countries, there developed a feminist movement one part of which addressed violence against women. As elsewhere there were two wings to this movement – one autonomous, building new organizations to support women who had experienced male violence, and the other oriented towards the state and the revision of the legal system. In 1978 a campaign started around rape, involving the establishment of a rape crisis centre in Dublin and leading to two revisions to the law, the first in 1981, and the second in the 1990 Criminal Law (Rape) Act, which made rape in marriage illegal for the first time. From 1969 there were campaigns around domestic violence, establishing refuges to assist women to escape violent homes and introducing new legal instruments in the Family Law (Protection of Spouses and Children) Act in 1981. The reduction in civil society tolerance to sexual abuse had implications for both church and state. One government lost office over the issue of whether they were right to protect a paedophile priest from justice at the hands of the secular courts, as Irish public opinion moved more quickly than the government with its new demands for the subordination of the church to secular law (Prendiville 1988; Smyth 1988, 1992; Reid 1992; Byrne and Leonard 1997; Kenny 1997; Galligan 1998; O'Connor 1998).

The neoliberal turn affected Ireland as well as the UK and the USA in leading to a more coercive criminal justice system in its imprisonment practices. Between 1990 and 2001 the rate of imprisonment increased by 43 per cent, which was more than the EU average of 26 per cent but less than that of the USA at 61 per cent. However, Ireland did abolish the death penalty in 1990 as EU law requires this (Barclay and Tavares 2003; HighBeam Research 2007).

Ireland's low rate of violence is at least partly due to its absence of history as either a colonial power or as a player in European nationalist militarism. The other changes are consequent on global and EU developments. The increased regulation of gender-based violence is part of a transnational feminist wave starting in the 1970s.

The ending of the death penalty was linked to its membership of the EU. Its increased imprisonment is part of the neoliberal turn.

Conclusion

There are identifiable trajectories in the nexus of violence. Differences present between the countries mentioned here are at least partly due to path-dependent processes: polity formation and restructuring; colonization and slavery; war; the mapping (or not) of nation and state; inequality; democratization; and global waves of feminism and neoliberalism.

In the eighteenth century three of the four countries had militarized states engaged in colonizing, conquest, and militarized nationalism: the USA, the UK, and Sweden. Only Ireland was absent from this because it was itself a colony of Britain, so it did not have a military of its own and nor did it ever develop a significant one. The critical turning points that differentiate the paths of violence are predominantly turning points that lead to decreases in violence. Sweden was the first, with its last war in 1814 that was associated with internal political changes and a political settlement with its Nordic neighbours: never again would it return to its high levels of militarization and violence. The UK was next, with decolonization especially during the twentieth century and the ending of nationalist-militarism in much of Europe with the establishment of the European Union following the nationalist militarism and Holocaust of the Second World War. The USA has never had a critical turning point out of its violence nexus; it remains the most violent country.

From the 1970s all four countries experienced the global feminist wave that sought to reduce and end violence against women, including both the provision of services and revisions to the law. This was seen first in the USA, but it then spread rapidly to the other three countries. It had the deepest implications in Sweden where women had established presence-democracy and not only suffrage-democracy, and hence were part of the state's democratic institutions.

All four countries from the 1980s experienced the global neoliberal wave, which increased the harshness of the criminal justice system alongside thinning civil society and increasing inequalities. In all four countries the use of imprisonment increased during the 1990s, but this increased most in the USA, which already had the highest rate, and least in Sweden which had the lowest. Thus the neoliberal wave, although global, did not erode the differences between the path-dependent trajectories of the violence nexus, but instead exacerbated their differences.

Gender Transformations: The Emergence of Employed Women as the New Champions of Social Democracy

Most accounts of the rise, fall, and resilience of social democracy are too narrowly focused on class, inappropriately marginalizing the implications of gender and other complex inequalities. There are at least four aspects to this: first, the definition and achievement of social democracy; second, the contribution of the modernization of the gender regime to the resilience and future of social democracy; third, the variations in the entwining of class and gender projects; and fourth, the significance of gender in the constitution of violence.

The conventional definition of social democracy is often ambiguous as to whether the full employment of women is a necessary component, or can be restricted to the class-based issues of welfare and employment only. The definition of social democracy used in this book (see Chapter 8) incorporates gender and other complex inequalities as well as domains beyond economies and polities. Early steps towards social democracy were often of a narrow labourist proto-social democracy type, with a focus on employment, state welfare, and suffrage-democracy. In some countries, there have also been fuller developments in the project of social democracy, incorporating the perceived interests of employed women into the projects of full employment, state provision of welfare, and employment regulations for equity, and extending the projects to deeper forms of democracy and the reduction of violence. Only if the project encompasses gender and other inequalities can it be considered fully social democratic. Fully developed social democracy is still largely an aspirational project, though it can be found to some extent in the Nordic countries.

There are several inter-related changes in gender relations: an increase in women's paid employment; a shift in women's average political preference towards social democracy as a result of this change; an increase in the number of women in trade unions; an increase in the number of women in parliament and government; an increased capacity of state welfare in gendered areas; an increased

Table 10.6 Female share of employment, trade union membership, and parliamentary seats, 1960–2005

	1960	1970	1980	1990	2000	2005
Sweden						
Labour force per cent female	30	36	47	48	47	47
Trade unions per cent female		32		50		52
Parliament per cent female	14	14	28	38	43	45
USA						
Labour force per cent female	32	36	41	44	46	46
Trade unions per cent female		24		36		45
Parliament per cent female	4	2	4	6	13	15
UK						
Labour force per cent female	32	37	39	43	46	46
Trade unions per cent female		25		38		51
Parliament per cent female	4	4	3	6	18	20
Ireland						
Labour force per cent female	26	26	29	35	41	43
Trade unions per cent female		28		32		50
Parliament per cent female	2	2	4	8	12	13
European Union						
Labour force per cent female	31	33	36	40	41	44
Parliament per cent female						30

(1) Female percentage of the labour force. *Source* for 1960, 1970: World Bank (2005) for 1980–2000: World Bank (2006c), 2005 (World Bank 2007b).
(2) *Sources*: OECD (2004:116); Visser (2006: 46).
(3) Percentage of those in Parliament (lower house if two) who are women. *Source*: 1960–1990, Inter-Parliamentary Union (1995), thereafter Inter-Parliamentary Union (2007).
(4) EU is EMU.
(5) Percentage of those in European Parliament who are women. *Source*: Inter-Parliamentary Union (2007).

regulation of employment in relation to equality issues; and increased regulation of men's violence towards women (see Chapters 3–6). These changes are inter-related aspects of the modernization of the gender regime (see Chapter 7 on regimes of inequality). There is a tendency for these to occur in both neoliberal and social democratic countries, but they have much greater consequences in those countries that already have more social democratic institutions. In some countries these changes can contribute to the completion of the project of social democracy: in others, where there are fewer allies and more enemies, contrary trends can open up in the development of gender and class regimes.

In all four countries here there has been an increase in the proportion taken by women of employment, trade union membership and parliamentary seats, and the regulation of men's violence against women (see Table 10.5 and Table 10.6). The changes in the four are all in the same direction, but these have taken place at different rates. In 1960 there was little difference between women's employment in the USA, Sweden, and the UK, nor in their very low rates of parliamentary representation (apart from a very slightly higher rate of women in parliament in Sweden): by 1970 the USA, Sweden, and the UK had all increased their female employment, but evenly so. There was nothing distinctive about Swedish women's employment in 1970. However, by 1980 in Sweden there had been a large increase in women's employment and parliamentary representation. The USA and UK increased their female employment more slowly, but by 2000 had caught up with Sweden. However, the parliamentary representation of women in the USA and the UK increased much more slowly and by 2005 the rates are barely higher than the Swedish rate in 1970 before the growth spurt. Change in the Irish gender regime occurred later: female employment grew after 1980, almost drawing level with the others in 2005, but women's parliamentary representation remains at no more than the Swedish level in 1970. The female share of trade union membership was similar in all countries in 1970: by 1990 it was equal to men's in Sweden and by 2005 this was the case in the other countries. An indicator of the increased regulation of men's violence against women is the year in which rape in marriage was made illegal: in Sweden in 1965; in the USA from the late 1970s, varying by state; in Ireland in 1990; and in the UK in 1994.

This pattern of change contains both changes in the same direction in all four countries in employment and parliamentary and trade union representation, and also significant differences in trajectories. In 1970 and 2005 each of the four had similar female shares in employment, rising from low (average 30 per cent) to high (average 46 per cent), but Sweden got there much more rapidly. In 1970 and 2005 the four had similar female shares of trade union membership (rising from an average of 27 per cent to 50 per cent), but again, Sweden got there much more quickly. In parliamentary representation, unlike these other areas, very great differences remain: while in Sweden women make up nearly half (45 per cent) of all members of parliament, in the other countries the rate is much lower – with the USA at 15 per cent, the UK at 20 per cent, and Ireland at 13 per cent.

An increase in female employment is part of the modernization of the gender regime in its transition from a domestic to a public form: it is not a marker of the distinction between different varieties of modernity – it is high in the public forms of both neoliberal and social democratic regimes (the USA, Sweden, the UK, and Ireland). While the depth of gendered democracy has increased in all four countries, there are very significant differences between the neoliberal and social democratic forms: it is much deeper in social democratic Sweden, where women make up 45 per cent of MPs, than the neoliberal USA (15 per cent of MPs are women) and Ireland (13 per cent), with the UK in between (20 per cent). The proportion of female trade unionists has risen in all four countries to around 50 per cent but this has very different consequences in different countries because of the variation in the density and coverage of trade unions in these countries (OECD 2004; Visser 2006). This transformation of the gendering of trade unions is important in Sweden where trade union density is 82 per cent and coverage is 92 per cent, of moderate significance in the UK (trade union density 30 per cent, coverage 35 per cent) and Ireland (density 38 per cent), and of little significance in the USA (density 13 per cent, coverage 14 per cent) (Visser 2006).

In social democratic Sweden, the rapid increase in female employment was linked to a rapid increase in women's representation in both formal politics (parliament and cabinet) and in civil society (such as trade unions). This was aided by the introduction of new electoral and democratic devices such as party quotas for women that moved Sweden from suffrage-democracy to presence-democracy. These changes facilitated the increase in gendered state welfare provision, such as publicly financed childcare and equality measures in employment regulation. Together they constituted a rapid spiralling of economic and political changes that not only modernized the gender regime but also developed its social democratic form. These processes were aided by the allies that employed women had in the trade unions and social democratic movement, albeit after some struggles (see earlier in this chapter for details).

In the more neoliberal countries, increases in female employment were not linked to the deepening of gendered democracy in the same way. There were small and slow increases in women's presence in parliament which were linked to moderate changes in gendered state welfare provision and the regulation of employment for equality. In the USA in the 1960s and 1970s there was the introduction of basic elements of equality regulation in employment as a consequence of an alliance of feminism with anti-racist forces, which succeeded in getting such provisions on racial equality through the US political system on the back of a strongly mobilized civil rights campaign. When this movement faded there was no significant institutionalized basis of feminist interests in the formal political system to replace it. In the UK and Ireland equality regulation in employment was linked to their entry into the European Union in 1973, aided by some feminist mobilization. In the UK, and only after 1997 with the introduction of some small electoral devices to move towards gendered presence democracy and an alliance between feminism and the labour movement, was a strategy to develop publicly funded childcare adopted. In Ireland women's presence in formal politics remains small, while the Catholic Church mobilizes strongly in favour of a domestic rather than a public gender regime.

Employed women as the new champions of social democracy

There has been concern that social democratic politics and polities are in widespread decline (Callaghan 2000), at least partly because of a decline in traditional male trade unionism. Yet the data on union membership do not show the predicted decline in all countries (see Table 10.3). This is because of the increasing unionization of women (see Table 10.6).

Because of the traditional association of trade unions with social democracy (Korpi 1983), a drop in trade union membership has been linked to this suggested decline in social democracy. There are two major reasons that have been put forward for this decline – the changing structure of the economy and changes in political approaches to unions.

The first reason for the purported decline is that those industries in which traditional trade unions developed and forged their experiences of class struggle are in decline. In the countries of the North heavy manufacturing industries, such as steel, shipbuilding, and car manufacturing, together with mining, have been in serious decline, though unevenly so, from the 1950s onwards. A decline in industries where trade unions had traditionally been strong is thus seen to lead to a fall in trade union membership and strength and hence to a decline in social democracy (Przeworski and Sprague 1986). However, despite the change in industrial structure away from heavy industry being common to most of Europe and North America, this decline in trade union power is not uniform partly because the public sector is now the most unionized area (Visser 2006). For example, in Sweden the unions have increased their membership and strength (Visser 2006); and in Ireland, despite some decline in trade union membership, there has been the development of corporatist-type institutions with government, employers, and civil societal organizations (Rhodes 1998, 2001; Boucher and Collins 2003; Baccaro and Simoni 2007). It is in the USA and the UK that trade union membership and power have fallen most (Ebbinghaus and Visser 1999; Visser 2006).

A second major reason for decline is that of strong attacks on trade unions associated with the neoliberal wave. In those countries that have been the most susceptible to the neoliberal wave, there have been attacks on trade unions both by government and employers (Nordlund 1998; Ebbinghaus and Visser 1999; Logan 2006).

Yet despite a decline in the industrial base of the traditional male trade unionist and attacks on trade unions as the neoliberal wave has entrenched itself in governments, the oft-predicted decline in trade unionism and social democracy has been greatly exaggerated. A key reason for the resilience of trade unionism and social democracy has been the influx of new participants in these projects – employed women. Female employees have been joining trade unions, compensating to some extent for falling numbers of men, and in so doing are radically changing the gender composition of these trade unions, which in several countries have now become populated by women and men equally. Politically, employed women support public services more than other social groups. This means that employed women prefer social democratic policies and are more likely to vote left than are non-employed women and men. The ongoing increase in the numbers of employed women therefore increases the amount of support for such policies and parties.

This growth in women's employment is strongly correlated with changes in state gender policy (Ferree 1980; Manza and Brooks 1999; Huber and Stephens 2000). In the USA, Manza and Brooks (1999) found that there was a gender gap in voting in the USA that is associated with the increase in women's employment in that employed women are more likely to vote in a leftwards (non-Republican) direction than other women or the average man. In the UK, the gender gap has emerged as a generational divide – it is younger women, who are most likely to be employed, who are more left voting, while older women, who are less likely to be employed, are not, producing a small gender gap in Labour's favour (Norris 1996b; Inglehart and Norris 2000). The gender gap in Sweden is compounded further by the greater presence of women in the more heavily unionized public sector. Similar patterns are emerging in most other Western countries. The effect is further increased when increased women's employment is combined with social democratic government (Huber and Stephens 2000). The increase in women's employment is also strongly correlated with changes in state gender policy (Manza and Brooks 1999; Huber and Stephens 2000). This process is also mediated by the presence of women politicians (Thomas 1991) and the extent and organization of feminist allies in adjacent institutions forming a 'velvet triangle' (Vargas and Wieringa 1998; Woodward 2004). Whether this emergent social democratic constituency makes a difference depends on the circumstances, in particular on the presence and power of different types of allies. One set of potential allies is that of sympathetic civil society organizations, including feminist organizations and feminists in universities, trade unions, and the legal profession, as well as the development of state machineries and institutions to promote gender equality (Woodward 2004; Lovenduski 2005; Verloo 2005, 2006).

Employed women are emerging as the new champions of social democracy. Their effect on politics depends on specific circumstances, but they are growing in numbers and organizational strength. Employed women are the growing present and future base for social democracy. In Sweden, where they are most established as a political constituency, they have been key to the resilience of state welfare provision despite the pressure of global flows of capital and the neoliberal political wave. The old forms of social democracy and their associated constituencies are not so resilient: only with the additional constituency of employed women is the political support sufficient to maintain, renew, and further develop the social democratic project.

Dampeners and Catalysts of Economic Growth: War and Gender Regime Transformations

Americans are richer than Europeans, with the current US income per person at around 40 per cent higher than that in Sweden, the UK, Ireland, and the rest of the EU. This gap is sometimes used as evidence that the US economy is better organized than those in Europe and in particular that neoliberalism delivers on economic growth and that social democracy does not. However, the gap in current income is not the result of post-war rates of economic growth, which have been about the same at around 2 per cent each year in the USA and the EU (see Chapter 9), until the financial crash of 2008.

The difference in income between the USA and Europe is a result of economic growth spurts in the past and not current practices. The historic growth rates of the USA, UK, Sweden, and Ireland since the middle of the nineteenth century are shown in Table 10.7. In the nineteenth century people in the UK had the highest average incomes in the world, as a consequence of the UK leading the Industrial Revolution in the previous century. During the last part of the nineteenth century the average income level in the USA caught up with that of the UK.

There are many complex reasons for changes in the rate of economic growth. Two are singled out for attention here which seem unduly neglected in the orthodox literature: war as a dampener of economic growth, and the transition in the gender regime as a catalyst of economic growth.

Average income in the USA leapt ahead of that in the UK while the latter was fighting in the 1914–1918 war (the Great War, or First World War) that was to devastate so much of Europe. Between 1910 and 1920 US GDPpc grew from $4964 to $5552, while that of the UK dropped from $4611 to $4548. A further surge in US economic growth rates as compared with those in the UK and Europe took place during the 1939–1945 war (the Second World War), which again was to devastate much of Europe. Between 1940 and 1950 US GDPpc grew from $7010 to $9561 while that of the UK changed little, being $6856 in 1940 and $6939 in 1950. By 1950 the US average income was 38 per cent greater than that of the UK. The scale of the gap in incomes changed little in the next 50 years, even though incomes in both countries nearly tripled in size during this period. In 2001 the US average income was 39 per cent greater than that of the UK – the gap in income levels is little more in 2001 than it was in 1950. The USA surged ahead of the UK while Europe destroyed itself by war, but not during the next 50 years nor during the height of neoliberalism. Within Europe, the average income level in Sweden (which avoided the 1939–1945 war) surged during the 1940s, almost closing the gap with the UK by 1950. Those countries which had been involved in the European wars of 1914–1918 and 1939–1945 rarely grew economically during the decade of the war, while other countries in North America and Europe continued to grow While US soldiers were involved, their homeland was not. Thus the destruction of war acts as a significant dampener for economic growth.

Why had there been so much war in Europe before 1945 and why has there been so little since?

Sweden and Ireland have had surges of economic growth that coincided with a rapid modernization of the gender regime and

Table 10.7 Economic growth, 1840–2005: USA, UK, Sweden, Ireland

	1840	1850	1860	1870	1880	1890	1900	1910	1920	1930	1940	1950	1960	1970	1980	1990	2000	2005
USA																		
GDP pc	1588	1806	2178	2445	2880	3392	4091	4964	5552	6213	7010	9561	11328	15030	18577	23201	28129	
Agri	67	64	59	53	50	43	38	32	27	22	18	12	6	4	4	3	3	1
wempl											24	27	32	37	42	45	45	46
wParl												2	4	2	4	6	14	15
UK																		
GDP pc	1990	2330	2830	3190	3477	4009	4492	4611	4548	5441	6856	6939	8645	10767	12931	16430	19817	
Agri	22	22	21	15	13	11	9	9	7	6		5	4	3	3	2	2	1
wempl	26	30	31	31	30	31	29	30	29	30		31	32	37	39	43	45	45
wParl									0	2	2	3	4	4	3	6	18	20
Sweden																		
GDP pc	1231	1289	1488	1662	1846	2086	2561	2980	2802	3937	4857	6739	8688	12716	14937	17695	20321	
Agri			64	61	59	59	53	46	41	36	25	20	14	8	6	3	2	2
wempl			24	32	30	30	30	28	30	31	25	26	30	35	45	48	46	47
wParl												10	14	14	28	38	43	45
Ireland																		
GDP pc				1775				2736	2533	2897	3052	3453	4282	6199	8541	11818	22015	

(Continued)

Table 10.7 (Continued)

	1840	1850	1860	1870	1880	1890	1900	1910	1920	1930	1940	1950	1960	1970	1980	1990	2000	2005
Agri	51	48	44	42	42			43	51	48	46	40	35	25	18	15	8	6
wempl	32	30	30	32	32			27	26	26	26	26	26	26	29	35	40	43
wParl												3	2	2	4	8	12	13

(1) Data nearest to this date; may vary, especially around 1940.
(2) GDP per capita, 1990 International Geary-Khamis dollars. *Source*: Angus Maddison (2003).
(3) Agri: Percent of employment in agriculture. *Sources* for agricultural and female employment: data from 1840 to 1971 is calculated (for Europe) from Mitchell (1981), (for USA, Australia) from Mitchell (1983). Data from 1980 to 2000 is from, or calculated from: OECD (1968, 1974, 1997b, 2000a, 2000b). Employment statistics up to and including 1970 are largely based on census data, while the later figures are drawn primarily from labour force surveys. The data for Ireland have a break between 1911 and 1926: the early period includes the whole of the island (though this was part of the UK at the time). The later period is for the Republic of Ireland (which excludes Northern Ireland). Data for 2000 and 2005 from World Bank (2008), so break in series.
(4) wempl: Percentage of employment that is female. Sources as for agriculture.
(5) wParl: Percentage of parliamentary seats held by women. *Source*: pre-1995, Inter-Parliamentary Union (1997); post-1995 Inter-Parliamentary Union (2007).
(6) Data for 2005. *Source*: UNDP (2007a) Table 33. Original *source*: Inter-Parliamentary Union.

increased female employment – during the 1970s and 1980s for Sweden and since the 1980s for Ireland. In Sweden during the 1970s and 1980s the rates of economic growth, female employment, and use of childcare had surged upward. In Ireland, before entry to the European Union and the removal of the barriers to married women's employment, its economic growth rate was low: however, since the 1980s Ireland has had higher economic growth rates than the USA, Sweden, and the UK, and since 2000 it had a higher income per person than Sweden or the UK. Economic growth can be catalysed by the transition of the gender regime from domestic to public.

Why have there been such gendered economic growth spirals in Sweden? Why did female employment in Sweden suddenly increase in the 1970s, overtaking that of more economically developed countries including both the USA and the UK? In 1960 Swedish women had the lowest proportion of employment of the four countries: they made up 30 per cent of the workforce as compared with 32 per cent in the USA and 37 per cent in the UK. If female employment patterns are determined by generic economic development, then the highest employment rates should be in the USA and not Sweden. In Sweden in the 1970s there was a rapid spiralling of economic growth and female employment, each feeding an increase in the other and catalysing both economic development and the modernization of the gender regime. Why did a similar (in the UK) or greater (in the USA) level of economic development not lead to a similar modernization of the gender regime in the UK and USA? A key difference here is that the rise of female employment in Sweden led to an increased political participation by women in formal politics – they entered parliament, with numbers rising rapidly to 38 per cent of members by 1990. This did not occur in the other three countries (the USA, UK, and Ireland). While in general, and as shown in Chapter 8, there is an association between increased female employment and female political representation there was divergence in the paths taken by these countries. Before 1970 Swedish gender relations were not distinctive; but the new path of development that began in the 1970s is now deeply institutionalized.

Conclusions

The two main paths through modernity (neoliberal and social democratic) do not necessarily affect the whole of a country; they may differ by nexus and by regime of inequality. The main nexi identified here are political economy, differentiated by employment relations and welfare provision, and violence. Each of these is linked with different depths of democracy in the relevant polities which affect the processes of lock-in. There can be differences between regimes of inequality in the pathway followed as well as in the extent to which it is modern or not.

These paths differ from those conventionally identified. The nexus of path dependency does not only rest on a singular conception of political economy, political economy is also divided into at least two major nexi – employment regulation and welfare provision. There is a further nexus in violence at the intersection of violence, polity, and civil society. Much of what has been previously considered 'conservative' is understood here not as a form of modernity but as premodern, especially in relation to the gender regime. A further key difference from preceding accounts is the differentiation of pathways according to the regime of inequality; this means that there can be more than one level of modernity, more than one pathway, coexisting within the same country. This also means that it is not necessarily the whole of a country that has a path dependency, though of course averaging across the regimes is possible: this theoretical move is essential if complex inequalities are to be identified at the heart of theories of social change.

One of the main challenges to the significance of the concept of path dependency has been whether the paths are significant enough to merit such an identification, whether they can last long enough before they either rejoin the mainstream/average (Kiser and Hechter 1991; Liebowitz and Margolis 1995) or become something new (Crouch 2001). Are there too few paths of significant duration, or too many? The analysis in Chapter 8 showed that while there are many minor nuances these do not detract from the finding of major paths. The analysis of paths in this chapter provides evidential support for the claim that paths are significant: they make a difference for significant periods of time, typically lasting for decades, before being restructured into something new, rarely returning to the mainstream or average.

There are two major potential challenges to the maintenance of contemporary forms of path dependency and the consequent pressures for convergence: first, global processes, and second, general processes towards the completion of modernity. The question as to whether globalization is eroding the distinctiveness of different countries – by undermining their distinctive forms of political economy in employment regulation and welfare provision – can be answered in the negative. While there has been some increase in economic inequalities, this has not occurred disproportionately in the more social democratic countries (although it has happened in these as well) but instead has happened to a greater extent in the more neoliberal countries. This means that global processes have interacted with the divergent paths in a way that does not erode their differences, rather it exacerbates them. This applies to the nexus of path dependency in violence as well. The evidence is that there is increased divergence between the paths of the four countries rather than convergence: as the USA becomes more heavily militarized the EU, since its foundation and since decolonization, becomes much less so, and while the neoliberal countries of the USA and UK are increasing the harshness of their criminal justice systems social democratic Sweden does not.

A second potential pressure for convergence arises from the modernization of the gender regime from a domestic to a public form. This process is common to all countries and generates the emergence of a new constituency of employed women which tends to support social democratic rather than neoliberal projects. However, while this is a common process it does not generate convergence, since its effects depend upon its interaction with pre-existing path dependent nexi. In particular, these effects are much greater where an established social democratic pathway already exists, generating new and deeper forms of social democracy and an increased resilience against its erosion by global processes.

A critical turning point is an event that changes the trajectory of development onto a new path. It is an event at a point in time that has effects upon the balance within a system, resulting in its internal reconfiguration so as to establish a new path or direction of development. The event results in a change in institutionalized forms of social practice. It is this new institutionalized configuration that 'locks-in' the new trajectory of development.

Several critical turning points have been identified. These include: the Reformation; the rise and fall of Empire, colonies, and slavery; state and other polity formation, especially in relation to adjacent entities of nation and organized religion; the development of free wage labour within each regime of inequality; the development of democracy within each regime of inequality; war; and economic growth spirals.

There are two important related concepts to that of the critical turning point. First is that of the 'tipping point' – a special case of a critical turning point in which it becomes clear that there has been a slow build up of changes that have eventually reached a point at which the system as a whole has tipped into a new form, a new path of development. A tipping point has a distinctive temporality in that, while a point of change can be identified, so also can the slow build up of forces within the system that mean that it is ready and available for tipping. A second related concept is that of a polity as a 'catalyst' or 'dampener' of a path of development. Here the notion is not that of an event of short duration, but rather an institutional form that either speeds up or slows down development along a particular path. By catalysing (speeding) or dampening (slowing) the rate of development, attaining a tipping point may be sooner or later. So the main concept of interest is that of a critical turning point, of which a tipping point is a special case where the implication is that there is a change in the path of development. The concepts of catalyst and dampener are slightly different and predominantly concern the rate of change rather than its direction.

The concept of a critical turning point is important in facilitating the analysis of multiple forms of modernity while retaining the concept of system. The concept is needed to identify and define the event at which new paths of development start. Critical turning points interrupt paths of development and the tendency towards societalization. The concept of a critical turning point derives from complexity theory and draws many of its connotations from these theoretical developments, as is outlined in Chapter 2. At its heart lies the notion of non-linearity, that a small cause can have large consequences. However, this is non-linearity in the context of a specific analysis of a system which is already finely balanced on the edge of chaos or criticality, a system that is already far from equilibrium. It is important not to over-state, or take out of context, the notion of the lack of proportion between a small cause and large consequences. A 'small' 'cause' is only important in the context of a large system that is already on the edge of criticality.

A critical turning point may derive from processes within a system, for example, as in the slow build up of pressures that leads to a tipping point, or they may derive from outside a system, for example, as in the case of a global wave.

One of the distinctive claims made for the concept of path dependency is that the sequencing of events through time makes a difference to social development. The order of events makes a difference to the path dependent outcome; in addition, the earlier in the path dependent trajectory that an event takes place, the more important it is in determining the nature of that path. The sequencing issues drawn together here include the relationship between economic growth and war for a global hegemonic position, and the relationships between the development of democracy and free wage labour in the range of forms of regimes of inequality.

Does it make a difference if democracy or free wage labour occurs first, if they are simultaneous or if there is a short or long gap between them? Does it make a difference if their achievement for diverse regimes of inequality is simultaneous or if there is a short or long gap? For dominant ethnic men there is a well established correlation between suffrage-democracy and economic development with free wage labour usually coming earlier, though the USA is a special case with settler male suffrage on the establishment of their new state. Does this link apply to women? Suffrage-democracy for women largely arrived in three main waves – 1920, 1945, and decolonization – which do not link to the development of free wage labour for either women or for men. And does it apply to minoritized ethnic groups? Most minority ethnic groups access suffrage-democracy alongside the dominant ethnic group (divided by gender), with the major exception of enslaved African-Americans who, in the southern states of the USA, even after formal emancipation, did not access de facto suffrage-democracy until the rise of the civil rights movement of the 1960s. However, when the operationalization of democracy is shifted to take into account the dimensions of deep democracy a different picture emerges. For women, there is then an association between the dimensions of deep democracy, especially represented by presence in parliament, and the development of women's free wage labour. This produces a complex pattern of sequencing of the development of democracy (both narrow suffrage-democracy and deeper democracy) and free wage labour among the various regimes of inequality.

There is no single point in the development of democracy and thus in the nexus of political economy or that of violence, but potentially several. The USA has had the longest gaps in suffrage-democracy between different social groups – early for white men, average for majority ethnic women, very late for African-Americans in the southern states. For the UK the gap in suffrage-democracy is long because of late de-colonization, but this is not as long as in the USA. Sweden has the shortest gaps between groups. Ireland is in between Sweden and the UK. For women the relationship between democracy and free wage labour is particularly seriously affected by the depth of democracy: suffrage-democracy often occurs much earlier than presence-democracy; the regulation of intimacy by organized religion or by a democratic state affects the extent of democracy. For women, the Swedish case of a near simultaneous gender presence-democracy and free wage labour catalysed the rapid modernization of the gender regime thus producing rapid spirals of change. This is in contrast to the later increase in gender presence-democracy in the USA, UK, and Ireland, despite the early development of free wage labour for women in the USA and UK. In these three countries, the modernization of the gender regime has been slower and more uneven.

The sequencing of economic growth and war has made a significant difference to which polity emerges as global hegemon. For a couple of centuries the combination of economic and military power made Britain the global hegemon. The violence of the two 'World' Wars in Europe in the twentieth century that so damaged the British economy made a significant contribution to the USA taking over this position from 1945, since that economy grew more rapidly than those in Europe during these destructive periods of war. Today, it is often wrongly assumed that the US economy is growing more quickly than those in Europe. Instead the level of economic development is higher in the USA as a result of differential growth rates in earlier years, especially when Europe was destroying itself in repeated bouts of nationalist militarist violence. So while the USA is not more economically efficient than Europe it is still the leading global hegemon, with a disproportionate influence over the global rules for economic and military conduct as a consequence of those earlier violent events when its economy surged ahead.

The development of the concept of path dependency has significant implications for social theory. It means that there is neither a single modernity nor an infinite number of different and unique instances. This is one example where complexity theory enables a synthesis that goes beyond the old polarities of modernism and postmodernism.

11 Contested Futures

Introduction

There are contested futures, contested forms of modernity. The financial crisis of 2007–2009 and the ensuing recession/depression in the real economy create the potential for a global tipping point away from neoliberalism. There may be an alternative form of global modernity that is either social democratic or one that is nationalist, protectionist, authoritarian, and xenophobic. Whether the future is neoliberal, social democratic or something else depends in part on whether the USA or the EU leads in the creation of the new financial architecture that is constructed to replace the old. While the global South has been increasing its influence in global governance, at this moment the key contesting forces are still the hegemons of the USA and EU, although these hegemons have varying levels of internal cohesion. A tipping point in the balance of power of the USA and EU had been on the horizon before the development of the 2007–2009 financial crisis, but has not yet occurred. This potential tipping point from a more neoliberal USA to a more social democratic EU is key to the wider global futures. This pathway has implications for the extent and nature of inequalities and globalization.

Financial and Economic Crisis 2007–2009

The crisis of 2007–2009 is the latest and largest of a series of financial crises. Its current impact on the 'real' economy and social relations is already enormous and its potential impact is cataclysmic. A range of policy and political responses have been developed, drawing from different projects and visions of society including neoliberal, social democratic, and premodern. These have different implications for (de)-globalization and inequalities.

The significance of the crisis of 2007–2009 depends upon whether this becomes a tipping point in the global financial and economic system, or whether it is just the bursting of yet another bubble, though with wider effects than previously because of the extent of global processes. Bursting financial and asset bubbles are not uncommon in the history of capitalism. Since the Dutch tulip bulb mania in seventeenth-century Holland and the South Sea Bubble in England in 1720, there have been a long series of bubbles (Morris 2008). During the 1990s, financial crises laid low the economies of East Asia and Latin America, followed by the bursting of the dot.com bubble (Stiglitz 2002; Krugman 2008).

The most important financial crisis in the twentieth century was the bursting of the stock market bubble in 1929, which led to deep depression in the USA and Europe (Galbraith 1975; Krugman 2008). This produced a critical turning point in which the countries of Europe diverged: the Nordic countries produced a social democratic settlement while much of central Europe descended into fascism. While social democracy in the Nordic countries has been locked-in through the development of a wide range of supporting institutional formations, fascism in central Europe was defeated by war. There is thus a historic precedent for financial crises and their consequent depressions to produce new alternative pathways of development.

The 2007–2009 financial crisis is larger and deeper than previous crises (except 1929), with the simultaneous global bursting of bubbles in housing and the stock market and consequently larger effects on the real economy (Fleckenstein and Sheehan 2008), together with effects that are spread further and faster as a consequence of globalization and electronic communications. The depth of this latest financial crisis is exacerbated by the effects of deregulation and the emergence of a non-regulated shadow banking system (Stiglitz 2006; Haseler 2008; Krugman 2008). The relative absence of regulations on the financial sector was part of the neoliberal orthodoxy (Greenspan 2008).

There are several features of the 2007–2009 financial crisis that are relatively new, consequent upon developments in a much less regulated financial environment.

Controls upon the conduct of banks were lightened with consequences in the extension of credit to ever riskier projects. One key example of this was the growth of the 'sub-prime' housing market in the USA, in which people with low and precarious incomes were granted mortgages to buy homes, which were only repayable if housing values were to continue to escalate (Fleckenstein and Scheehan 2008; Krugman 2008; Shiller 2008). The bubble in housing values affects more people than the bubble in stock markets in those countries where the level of home ownership has increased to very high levels and where equity withdrawal became commonplace, such as in the USA and UK.

The most important of the changes has been the growth of a shadow banking system that is not subject to regulation, which rivalled the regulated banks in size. Hedge funds operate largely outside the regulatory framework set up for banks. Private equity operates largely outside the regulatory framework set up for limited liability companies publicly quoted on the stock exchange. In 2007, while the total assets of the top five US banks was around $6 trillion, that of the five major 'investment' banks was around $4 trillion and the hedge funds just under $2 trillion (Krugman 2008). The new financial derivatives included synthetic securitizations or collateralized debt obligations and credit default swaps. Since the 1990s, until the crash of 2007–2009, there was a rapid increase in the scale of this market. In 1990 the size of the collateralized debt obligation market was estimated at $2.2bn, rising to $250bn in 2002, of which 75% is estimated to be the new synthetic CDOs (Tavakoli 2003), further rising to $600bn in 2007 (Treanor 2008). The collateralized debt obligations (CDOs) use a special purpose company or vehicle, with assets, liabilities, and a manager, to transfer risk between financial institutions such as banks (Picone 2002), ostensibly tiering the level of risk so that it could be separately costed. The risks in this system were compounded by poor assessment of the risk by the ostensibly specialized risk-rating agencies (Fleckenstein and Sheehan 2008; Morris 2008). By 2007 the combined size of asset-backed commercial paper conduits in structured investment vehicles, auction-rate preferred securities, tender option bonds, and variable rate demand notes in the USA was around $2.2 trillion (Krugman 2008). The period of light financial regulation also saw the increased use of tax havens and banking regimes that permitted secrecy and hence the possibility of tax avoidance and evasion, which permitted corporations and wealthy individuals to avoid tax obligations in the countries where they had earned or created their wealth (Murphy 2007). There has been some variation between countries and regions in the extent of regulation of the financial sector, but the global system is now highly inter-connected. For example, the financial packages that contained poor quality US mortgage debt were sold to banks around the world. Hence the financial crisis is global in reach.

The financial crisis of 2007–2009 was precipitated by the collapse of the sub-prime mortgages in the US housing market, triggering a general collapse in that market. This was followed by a collapse in the value of the financial derivatives that contained US sub-prime debt and, when it became clear that no one really knew which financial packages contained this poor debt, a collapse in confidence and value of a range of financial derivatives. This in turn provoked a collapse in the bubble in the stock market. Each of these has global consequences because of the extent of global interconnections.

The collapse in this series of interrelated bubbles in the valuation of financial assets caused the collapse of a series of financial institutions, including banks. Some of these financial institutions went bankrupt, such as Lehman Brother. In the UK there was a run on Northern Rock (a housing bank) before it collapsed. Mergers were arranged for weaker institutions, such as Lloyds and HBOS in the UK. Vast quantities of public funds were used to support financial institutions, including banks and insurance companies linked to the housing market (such as Fannie Mae, Freddie Mac, and AIG in the US), often resulting in part or occasionally full public ownership (Fleckenstein and Sheehan 2008; Morris 2008; Shiller 2008).

The crisis in the financial sector caused a crisis in the 'real' economy in several ways. The rapid depreciation of assets reduces the income people have available to spend, as dividends and pensions linked to the stock market decline and falls in housing equity limit withdrawals. The collapse in confidence in the financial sector led to a credit crunch, with the resulting lack of access to credit, meaning that some businesses went bankrupt, with knock-on effects on people's income. There is a rapid downward spiralling of the real economy leading to recession and maybe to depression. While the financial crisis started in the USA, and despite the significant variations between countries in the regulation of finance, the effects on the real economy are spreading around the world. Table 11.1 shows the declines in the USA, EU, Ireland, Sweden, and the UK in GDP, stock market and rise in unemployment in 2008. The downturn in the real economy created unemployment and poverty, thereby deepening inequalities (because of the gaps between employed and unemployed) unless radical policy interventions were made.

Pathways out of the crisis

There were a range of policy responses to the crisis, which depended on political responses which varied over time and between countries. There are three main areas of policy development: the financial architecture; the rescue of financial institutions; and the response to the emerging recession. First, the overall structure of the global financial architecture has been challenged by the crisis and critics have found it to be wanting. Several bodies set up processes to review the global financial architecture and make proposals for reform,

Table 11.1 Economic recession 2008–2009: USA, EU, Eurozone, Sweden, UK, Ireland

	GDP Q2 2008 change on previous quarter	GDP Q4 2008 change on previous quarter	Unemployment per cent June 2008	Unemployment per cent Dec 2008	Share price change on previous year Feb 2009, per cent	House price change during 2008, per cent
USA	0.70	−1.60	5.6	7.2	−44	−18
EU			6.9	7.4		
Eurozone	−0.25	−1.50				
Ireland	−0.61		6.0	8.2	−66	−10
Sweden	−0.46	−2.40	5.8	6.9	−36	−13
UK	−0.02	−1.53	5.5	6.1 (Oct)	−31	−18

Data for GDP, unemployment and share prices: OECD (2009) *OECD. StatExtracts* http://stats.oecd.org/wbos/Index.aspx?QueryName=251&QueryType=View&Lang=en (accessed 6 March 2009). Data for house prices: Ireland (Finfacts Ireland 2009); Sweden (Sweden Price History 2008); UK (BBC 2009); USA (Hopkins 2009).

including the UN's Commission (Stiglitz 2009) and the G20 summits (G20 2008). Issues concern the functioning of the World Bank and the International Monetary Fund and whether a new institution to promote financial stability is needed; transparency and governance; as well as tax havens and secret banking regimes. Second, there is the immediate response to the collapse of financial institutions, especially by states. A range of instruments has been tried including: funds to bank in trouble supplied variously as loans, equity, and insurance, and recapitalization and liquidity schemes. The implications have included full or partial nationalization of threatened institutions. There are issues as to the implications of the forms of the funds, the nature of the conditionalities attached such as in relation to lending criteria and revision of the remuneration of bankers so as to reduce short-term incentives. Third, there are policy responses to the recession and threatened depression in the real economy. Some of these are explicitly stimulus packages to increase the flow of funds through the economy, though not all countries accept such a Keynesian approach. The funds have taken a variety of forms including: tax cuts, increases in public works expenditure, and loans to big companies. The implications of these stimulus packages for different social groups and inequality are potentially highly varied depending on who receives the funds. There is also a significant issue in the extent to which the conditionalities are protectionist, explicitly prioritizing the country's own citizens or not.

Within each of these three areas of policy response, there are significant variations. They vary significantly in relation to: governance, distribution and scape-goating. The reforms to institutions entail a position on governance, as to whether they are going to be made more transparent, accountable, and democratic. The changes might be minimal, such as increased transparency, or more substantial, such as ensuring a significant presence of women on decision-making boards. The stimulus packages vary as to their distributional consequences: whether the beneficiaries are richer or poorer, men or women, majorities or minorities. The use of tax cuts tends to favour the better off and men who pay more tax, and disadvantage the poor and women who benefit significantly from state expenditures on welfare, health and education. Spending on public works and bail outs to companies will benefit those who are employed in these, for instance, more often men if these are construction jobs. The conditions applied vary in the extent to which they identify groups to blame or to protect: bankers, foreign workers, the unemployed, or the poor. If bankers' bonuses are targeted then this is a class and gender redistribution taking money away from rich men; if foreign workers, then it is often the poor from minority nationalities and ethnicities who will suffer.

There are three potential pathways out of the crisis: neoliberalism with minor reforms; social democracy and global justice; or nationalist protectionism.

Neoliberal. The neoliberal response to the financial crisis has usually been one of minor reforms in order to stabilize the financial system within the context of a restatement of the principles of a free and open global market economy (see G20 2008). In this perspective, there is a need for slight adjustments rather than major changes. The policy responses are thus a small increase in the regulation of and degree of multilateralism in the global financial institutions; temporary bail outs of banks that retain their autonomous decision making; and modest if any stimulus packages. Financial institutions are considered so important to the economy that they need to be rescued at almost any price, including significant transfers of taxpayer funds to banks. The freezing of the credit markets due to the existence of bad debts is also to be remedied by the provision of taxpayers' money. The transfer from citizens to financiers at times of financial crisis is a common feature of neoliberal financial systems (Stiglitz 2002). Any transfer of ownership of banks to the public is to be regretted and rectified as soon as circumstances allow (for example, in the USA in 2008). Financialization is not seen as a problem in principle; indeed its further development is to be applauded (G20 2008; Greenspan 2008; Shiller 2008.) This approach involves reforms to governance that concern greater transparency rather than more substantial aspects of democracy. There is little concern with distributional inequalities and the bank bail outs often involve significant transfers from the majority of the population to financiers.

Social democracy. The social democratic response to the financial crisis has usually been one of a call for substantial change in the financial architecture; to substantially increase public democratic control over banks in exchange for state funds; and to put substantial funds into stimulus packages so as to prevent the recession turning into a global depression. The rescue of banks in times of financial crisis in social democratic systems, such as in Sweden in the early 1990s, involved the banks taking responsibility for their bad debts, not citizens (Aslund 2009). Proposed reforms and regulations of the financial architecture include: the abolition of the shadow banking system, so that no financial transactions are outside of public scrutiny and regulation; the abolition of tax havens and secret banking regimes by which corporations and rich individuals avoid and evade taxation; the severe regulation if not abolition of financial derivatives and the practice of financialization of the economy; the separation and support of utility banking but not speculation; changing the governance of financial institutions, making them and their transactions transparent, ensuring that boards of companies, banks and regulators include a wide range of people, including a proper proportion of women (e.g. quotas for women on Boards as in Norway); the reform of the global financial architecture including the World Bank, International Monetary Fund so that their aims include global justice; fair trade; the introduction of the Tobin tax on currency transactions to slow down speculation in currencies; promote public and mutual forms of ownership rather than privatization; take governmental control over part-nationalized banks in order to secure more appropriate forms of remuneration to bankers to reduce the incentive for short-term risk-taking and develop appropriate policies for access to credit; reduce the propensity for housing bubbles by increasing the proportion of homes for social renting; ensure that the stimulus packages focus on productive and sustainable investment rather than tax cuts and that they disproportionately benefit the poor who are most vulnerable in the downturn rather than the rich; expand alternatives to unemployment including education and jobs; provide a floor to the real economy through facilitating access to essentials and reduce financialization and bubbles, such as social rented housing, allotments and free school meals (George 2004; Stiglitz 2006; Murphy 2007; Attac 2008; Krugman 2008; World Social Forum 2008).

Nationalist authoritarian protectionism. This focuses the blame for the scarcity of resources in the recession following the financial crisis on foreigners or ethnic minorities. Various components of this approach have emerged, especially populist blaming of foreign workers for taking jobs (e.g. UK 2009), the insertion of protectionist clauses into stimulus packages (e.g. USA 2009), and the national limitations to the bail outs for banks and companies (Europe and US 2008). Responses to the recession/depression can be led by states for the protection of their own populations at the expense of citizens of other countries, pulling away from the principles and practices of more open global processes. Historically, this response has appeared in some countries to some economic recessions, most notoriously in Germany in the 1930s. The approach to governance is a demand for control to be re-centred in the country rather than internationally, though with no necessary implications for transparency and democracy. The implication for inequalities is to privilege the national population to the detriment of those defined as 'other', especially foreigners whether in that country or abroad.

The three projects have implications for different forms of inequalities and for global processes. The neoliberal approach is likely to increase inequalities, as it moves resources from taxpaying citizens to banks and financial institutions, away from the less developed to the more developed countries of the world. The nationalist protectionist approach is likely to increase inequalities based on citizenship, nationality, and ethnicity. Only the social democratic approach is likely to resist increasing inequalities, though whether this applies to all inequalities depends upon the specific policies introduced. States remain an important node in democratic as well as authoritarian responses to economic events, a focal point for attempts to change the financial architecture and the structure of the economy. This is especially the case in the nationalist-xenophobic responses, but is sometimes an element in social democratic programmes to regulate finance capital. However, de-globalization is not the only route to financial regulation; indeed some forms of regulation of finance require global cooperation.

The relative importance of these three potential pathways is subject to change. The outcome depends on struggle, resources and the wider environment: who participates in the political discussions and struggles; what alliances are built; how the issues get to be framed; what resources are mobilized behind each position; and how events intervene. They are embedded in projects, programmes and social formations at national, regional and global levels with different resources for their promotion. There are planned for 2009 a series of global meetings at which there will be competition for the hegemony of one or other view, including those of the G20 and the UN's Stiglitz Commission. The G20 includes Argentina, Australia, Brazil, Canada, China, France, Germany, India, Indonesia, Italy, Japan, Mexico, Russia, Saudi Arabia, South Africa, South

Korea, Turkey, the UK, The USA, and the EU (G20 2009). The Commission established by the UN is intended to represent all the countries of the world (Stiglitz 2009). The EU is striving to achieve an internal cohesion over these issues, with the UK and some of the new Member States in the east taking more neoliberal positions than the old core of Germany and France (Traynor and Gow 2009). Key to the outcome of these meetings will be the positions adopted by the USA and the EU and the strength with which they are promoted, though many other countries and global organizations are making representations. The relative balance of power between these two hegemons is key to whether the global pathway out of the crisis takes a neoliberal or social democratic form.

Contesting Hegemons and the Future of the World

The USA and the EU are contesting global hegemons with competing societalization projects. Rather than a unitary West or North there are significant differences in the projects of these hegemons, with the USA leading a neoliberal project and the EU adopting a more social democratic one. The outcome of this contestation is having important implications for all people in the world because of their power in structuring the rules by which the world is governed. The balance of power is currently in the favour of the USA, but a tipping point is coming that will change this to the EU.

Which are the current and future global hegemons?

Global hegemons are polities that have extended their dominance beyond their territorial borders to affect the whole world (as is discussed in Chapter 4 on polities). Hegemony is established through a mixture of coercion and consent, using multiple forms of power drawn from the economy, polity, violence, and civil society.

The EU and the United States are the current contesting global hegemons. There are further potential or would-be global hegemonic projects that have not currently achieved such hegemonic power, including Islamic jihadism (not Islam as a whole), China, Japan, and the G77. Global hegemons are not new, nor ever permanent: the British Empire once ruled over one quarter of the world.

The USA and EU have different powers and potentials. In 2005 the EU was larger in population size than the USA: the EU27 at 486,616,440 is more than one and a half times larger than the USA with 296,410,404 people. The EU has a slightly larger economy than the USA: the GDP of the EU27 is $12,886,810m as compared with $12,416,505m for the USA. The USA owns slightly more of the world's wealth than the EU: 33 per cent in the USA, 30 per cent in Europe. Both the USA and the EU are influential in determining the policies and personnel of the institutions of global financial governance, including the WTO, the IMF, and the World Bank, but the USA is more powerful. It also has a larger military than the EU. It spends 4.1 per cent of its GDP on the military as compared with 1.7 per cent by the EU (EMU), indeed spending more than twice as much overall at $509,077m as compared with $219,076m for the EU (Data for 2005; World Bank 2007b; Davies et al. 2008). European countries and the USA are represented on the UN Security Council and NATO, but the USA is more powerful.

China has the potential to become a global hegemon, but not yet. It has the largest population in the world (1,304 million) making up 20 per cent of the world's population. It also has the largest military in the world, with 3.755 million people, though with a smaller budget (2 per cent of its GDP, costing $174,534m) than that of the USA (World Bank 2007b). Its market economy of $8,914,960m is smaller than that of the EU or USA however, if it continues to grow at 8 per cent a year (since 1975) as compared with 2 per cent of the USA and EU, it might eventually have a larger GDP, though this date may be significantly deferred as the USA is likely to continue to grow through immigration and the EU through the accession of more countries. China has 3 per cent of the world's wealth, significantly less than that of the USA or Europe. Historically, China has been a relatively self-contained country politically, perhaps near to a nation-state, with international engagements that are more regional (for example with Korea and Iran) than global. However, this may be changing, for example, in 2008 China hosted the Olympic Games. But at the moment China is not a global hegemon, despite the size of its population and army. If and when China seeks to restructure the global fitness landscape to suit itself remains a question for the future, especially for when the Chinese economy becomes more fully developed and its GDP becomes the world's largest.

Islam is being increasingly confidently articulated, but with internal differences. There is economic power from oil, political power through its states, and violence by its states and jihadists. It is a religion that is practised by many people in the world and it also acts as a frame of reference for many. However, Islam is not politically cohesive and has many divisions and different forms. Its relationship with states is highly varied and the use of religious Shari'a law to govern intimacy is highly varied. There are also severe divisions between jihadists and less theologically-minded leaders which are especially acute in those Islamic countries with Western links, such as Pakistan and Saudi Arabia. Huntington (1998) is wrong to suggest that there is a civilizational divide between the West and Islam; Islam has its own internal divisions as great as those in the West. This does not mean that Islam does not act as a frame of reference to many, but it does mean that it is not an effective global hegemon.

There are various further entities and alliances that operate at a global level. One of these is the Catholic Church. As with Islam, this organized religion has power through the countries in which it is embedded, variously governs intimacy through its religious rulings, and acts as a frame of reference to many. Historically it once acted as a major division that drove group and state killings, from the burning of heretics at the stake to the crusades, but this is not so today. It has a presence at the UN not least because it has its own state, the Vatican, through which it coordinates opposition to sexual and reproductive freedoms for women. During the 1970s Japan was looked upon as an emergent hegemon, but with the slowing of its rate of economic growth since the bursting of its financial bubble, it is now better thought of as a major regional leader and no longer a global model for economic growth let alone a global hegemon. At the UN there are various alliances between states: the largest here is the G77 alliance of 130 developing countries that is active in protecting their interests in global trade negotiations, but none of these are hegemonic.

Differences between the EU and the USA

Globalization should not be equated with Westernization because there is no single coherent practice of being Western. The USA and the EU have significantly contrasting models despite sharing some similarities: the USA is more neoliberal while the EU is more social democratic. These differences between the two matter. There is a tipping point coming between these two hegemons, with major consequences for the nature of the global fitness landscape. The USA and EU differ on each of the main framings of progress: economic development; well-being; equality; and human rights. An explanation of their differences requires bringing their divergent trajectories of democratization and violence and the transformation of complex inequalities into focus.

The conventional view has been that the USA has higher economic growth leading to higher income per capita (GDPpc) than in the EU as a result of a neoliberal form of capitalism that frees the economy from regulations and costs that might hinder growth. However, while it does have higher income per person, it does not currently have a faster rate of economic growth per person than the EU. The source of these greater levels of income lies in the past at a time when the USA did grow its economy more quickly than Europe's. In particular, the US economy grew while Europeans destroyed their own economies through war, especially in 1914–1918 and 1939–1945. Different histories of violence are key to explaining varying levels of economic development.

When other framings of progress are considered, the United States does less well than the EU. Americans live slightly shorter lives than citizens of the EU – around two years less on average despite their higher income. The USA is more violent than the EU: it has higher murder rates, locks up more criminals in prison, spends more resources on law and order and the military, and goes to war more frequently. It also has a narrower range of human rights than the EU: it still uses the death penalty and sexual and reproductive rights are less widespread. In addition, the USA has more class and ethnic inequality than the EU.

Comparative trajectories of development of the EU and the USA

The USA has fewer areas of premodern relations than the EU and this is marked in gender relations, especially in the economy. However, the significance of religion in the USA is an exception to this. The transition of the gender regime from the domestic to the public is further developed in the USA than the EU. There are significant variations in the EU, with Sweden and the Nordic countries at least matching the USA in the public nature of the gender regime. The USA is more neoliberal and the EU more social democratic. The USA has few regulations on employment and smaller state welfare provision than the EU, in both class and gender relations.

The USA and EU, despite similar levels of economic development, are very different. The EU has seen the development of social democracy and its deepening by employed women, and changes in the institutionalization of ethno-nation relations so as to prevent state violence. The development of social democracy in Europe was associated with the mass organization of labour in trade unions that was much less common in the USA. Its maintenance and transformation in the context of a decline in the industries where this unionization was most dense is due to the emergence and mobilization of employed women as the new champions of social democracy, in the context of polities that allow for the emergence of women as a political force in democracy. The emergence of employed women as a political constituency maintains and transforms the project of social democracy in the EU. In the USA, despite similar levels of female employment, the political system is less democratically open to their participation, precluding a similar outcome to the EU. A critical turning point away from violence took place in the mid-twentieth century in Europe but not the USA. In a Europe devastated by the Holocaust and wars of nationalist militarism, the formation of the European Union with the aim of preventing ever again a holocaust against a minority and war between European states, constituted a critical turning point in the violence nexus in Europe. A reduction in the significance of ethno-national boundaries with the emergence of a new transnational polity has led to the cessation of war between those countries that are members of the European Union. The association between militarism and other forms of violence means that there is less violence in the EU than the USA.

Tipping point

While currently the USA wins almost all of the contests with the EU on the global stage, this will not last. A tipping point will come when the EU overtakes the USA in power and global influence. The EU is increasing in power relative to the USA. At some point, as the EU grows in terms of its size, economy, and internal governmental coherence, the EU will overtake the USA as the pre-eminent global hegemon.

The EU is getting bigger as a consequence of enlargement through the accession of countries from ever further east in Europe. The EU started in 1957 with only six Member States (Belgium, France, Germany, Italy, Luxembourg, and the Netherlands), and in 1973 this grew to nine (with the accession of Denmark, Ireland, and the UK). In 1981 this became ten (Greece), in 1986 this grew to 12 (Spain and Portugal), in 1995 to 15 (Austria, Finland, Sweden), in 2004 to 25 (Cyprus, the Czech Republic, Estonia, Hungary, Latvia, Lithuania, Malta, Poland, Slovakia, and Slovenia) and in 2007 to 27 (Bulgaria and Romania). It will grow further with the accession of more countries in Eastern Europe: three are already formal candidates (Croatia, Macedonia, and Turkey), with several more

(Albania, Bosnia, and Herzegovina, Kosovo, Montenegro and Serbia) in discussions over membership. There are additional countries that are members of the Council of Europe, some of which might be expected to seek membership at some point: these are Andorra, Armenia, Azerbaijan, Georgia, Iceland, Liechtenstein, Moldova, Norway, the Russian Federation, San Marino, Switzerland, and the Ukraine.

The EU has invited all associated countries in Central and Eastern Europe to join if and when they meet the conditions laid down. Countries that join the EU are obliged to change their internal governance so that they reach EU standards. Known as the Copenhagen criteria and adopted in 1993, these require that in order to join the EU a country must have achieved: a stability of institutions guaranteeing democracy, the rule of law, human rights, and respect for and protection of minorities; the existence of a functioning market economy as well as the capacity to cope with competitive pressure and market forces within the Union; and the ability to take on the obligations of membership, including adherence to the aims of political, economic, and monetary union. In 1995 an additional criterion was added at the Madrid European Council – that a country must have created the conditions for its integration through the adjustment of its administrative and judicial structures, as well as the transposition of all European Community legislation into national legislation. These conditions mean that not only do candidates to being Members of the EU have to adopt the entire legal corpus of the EU (or 'acquis'), but they must also have in place the democratic and institutional mechanisms to effectively implement these laws and their principles. For example, they must not merely adopt the laws on equal treatment on grounds of gender, ethnicity, disability, religion/faith, sexuality, and age, but must also create institutions to ensure their implementation. During the history of the EU there has been a stream of countries eager to join and willing to accept the conditions. During the long process by which countries seek to become candidates they must steadily bring their domestic laws into alignment with the EU.

The EU has long been larger in its population size than the USA. In 2007 the EU population was 487 million as compared with 296 million in the USA, more than one and a half times as big. If the three candidate countries (Croatia, Macedonia, and Turkey) with a combined population of 74,543,410 and the potential candidate countries (Albania, Bosnia and Herzegovina, Kosovo, Serbia, and Montenegro) with a combined population of 15,101,000 were to join, then the EU population would increase to 576,260,850, nearly double the size of the USA.

The economy of the EU became larger than that of the USA in 2004, with the accession of ten more states. The EU27 GDP is $12,886,810m, the USA's stood at $12,416,505m in 2005. If the candidate countries (GDP $678,469m) and the potential candidate countries (GDP $52,800m) were to join, the size of the EU economy would grow to $13,618,079m. At the moment not all members of the EU are members of the Eurozone, but many are expected to join as their economies develop and stabilize. At some point this change in the relative size of the US and EU economies will contribute to this tipping of the balance of power between the two economies and their currencies of the dollar and the Euro. This will have implications for the power balance within the bodies of global financial governance, including the World Bank, the IMF, the WTO, and G8.

The economy of the USA has been more badly affected than most of the EU by the 2008 crisis in the financial system. Although this financial crisis has global repercussions, it is centred in the USA and created by the development of financial instruments and institutions that operate outside of an effective regulatory framework, now expressed in bad debts and collapsing financial bubbles for instance in the housing market. In September 2008, the USA planned to spend an estimated trillion dollars of tax proceeds from its workers to pay off the bad debts accrued by its financial institutions in order to avoid an even worse financial crisis. This crisis in the financial sector will have an effect on the 'real' economy, draining resources and creating recession. Most European economies, with some exceptions, are less exposed to this financial crisis and its repercussions on the 'real' economy because of different policies for the financial sector and the smaller development of financial bubbles. The draining of real US resources to support a failing finance system may further tilt the balance away from the USA towards the EU.

The EU is less politically centralized and cohesive than the USA, but this is changing as powers continue to stream from the Member States to the EU. The process of integration and the centralization of powers slowed for a short period after the over-reach on the proposed Constitution, but it has not stopped and will not stop. Most of the changes proposed for the Constitution were agreed via the Treaty of Lisbon in 2007, including a Foreign Minister (High Representative of the Union for Foreign Affairs and Security Policy), a less temporary President, and streamlined majority voting (Council of Europe 2007a). The logic for further powers to move to the EU level of political institutions is as strong now as it ever has been. In particular, outward facing policy areas such as trade and foreign policy are very likely to become more cohesive, generating a significantly greater capacity to act as a global hegemon.

The importance of the EU as a significant player on the global stage in matters of economic policy is increasing. It is a major trading bloc which gives it a presence in the context of geo-politics (such as collective membership as the EU of the World Trade Organization) and is able to command deference from other polities for its actions (such as representing the interests of all Member States of the EU in world trade discussions) (Leibfried and Pierson 1995; Bornschier 1999; Held et al. 1999; Hettne 1999). The EU and the USA are both influential in determining the policies and personnel of the WTO, the IMF, and World Bank. As the size of the EU economy continues to grow even larger than that of the USA, it will become more significant relative to the USA. When the Euro becomes larger than the dollar, further changes are to be expected.

The military is one area where the USA holds considerably more power than the EU, both in the size and cohesion of the forces. The EU does not yet have its own standing army, however there are plans to develop the EU's military and policing capacity, coherence, and engagement. The EU increasingly articulates a common position during international crises and has had a sustained foreign policy on certain issues, for example, it financially supports the Palestinian Authority. In 2003 the European Council adopted a European Security Strategy, identifying key threats, terrorism, a proliferation of weapons of mass destruction, regional conflicts, state failure, and organized crime (but not large-scale aggression) and agreeing how to address them: a European Union that was more active, more capable, and more coherent. The policies were to intervene in regional conflicts and failed states, including the Balkans, especially in the neighbourhood, including the resolution of the Arab/Israeli conflict, and strong support for a multilateral international order led by the UN. In 2004 there was the first deployment of the European Union Force (EUFOR) in Bosnia, followed by the Congo and Chad. In 2007 this move to greater coherence was considerably enhanced by the Lisbon Treaty which created an EU Foreign Minister (High Representative of the Union for Foreign Affairs and Security Policy) for the first time (Council of the European Union 2007a). There must be doubts as to whether the UK would have followed the USA into the war in Iraq if the EU foreign policy capacity had been more developed at that time. Further, as the EU grows in size and resources, its participation in decision making within NATO and the UN is likely to grow. The USA is currently overstretched militarily and faces a failure to achieve its goals. This is likely to diminish its capacity and willingness to enter into new armed conflicts, perhaps enhanced by democratic pressures. Thus, the greater power of the USA in the domain of the military may become less overwhelming. Further, it is unlikely that it would use direct force against the EU, although this does not rule out disputes by proxy. This lesser deployment of violence by the EU than the USA means that it wastes fewer human and economic resources in death and destruction, both in its external relations and the associated interpersonal, group, and criminal justice system violence at home.

Once, the USA held the moral high ground on issues of freedom and democracy, human rights, and equality. From its inception the Constitution of the USA claimed that it championed democracy, freedom of speech and religion, democracy, and equality before the law; and from 1968, laws to rule out various forms of inequality in employment; (despite many practical exceptions, such as slavery). At one time, Europe was the home of hereditary monarchs, religious persecution, and the Holocaust. But today the USA has squandered its leading position as a defender of freedom and human rights. With its military action without UN endorsement, its retention of the death penalty, its extreme inequalities in ethnicity and class, its opposition to the extension of sexual and reproductive rights to women, its denial of human rights and the due process of law in Guantanamo Bay and Abu Ghraib, and its opposition to effective action on global climate change in the UN conferences in Kyoto and Bali, the USA no longer has the basis to effectively claim the moral high ground on human rights. Its power in the world has become based more on coercion than consent. However, it is possible that the election of Obama in 2008 might lead to a change in some of these policies. The EU has a significant and effective presence at the UN on the promotion of a human rights regime (even though it is not a legal entity within the UN's processes). For example, during the UN conferences on women in Beijing in 1995 and the follow-up in 2005, the Member States of the EU developed and presented a common position in favour of the extension of women's human rights, including their sexual and reproductive rights, in opposition to an alliance of the USA, the Vatican, and some Islamic countries (Moghadam 1996). The EU has emerged as the champion of the extension of human rights and their effective institutionalization and the leader on global action against the catastrophic over-heating of the planet.

Both the EU and the USA hold significant sway outside of those territories over which they have direct rule. This influence rests on a mix of powers – economic, military, political, and civil societal. There is both influence over specific countries and influence over the governance of the global environment. In the case of the EU, several neighbouring European countries have adopted many EU practices, especially but not only those countries that have ambitions to become members of the EU. In the case of the USA several countries have been coerced by military force, actual or threatened, into changing their policies to suit the USA. In addition, both the USA and EU have tremendous influence over the policies of bodies of global governance, including those governing the economic fitness landscape, which polities are accepted as sovereign, the legality of specific forms of coercion and the human rights regime.

The tipping point in the balance of power between the EU and USA on the world stage will happen. But it is not clear when. This depends on changes in the EU – how quickly new states will join the EU, how quickly new Member States convert their currencies into the Euro, how rapidly the next steps on cohesion of internal governance can be taken. It also depends on changes in the USA – whether it will continue with its high violence route and military actions and how quickly its military over-extension bites into its economic performance. In addition it depends on the global environment – the actions of emerging powers such as China, the re-emergence of Russia on the global stage, the actions of jihadists, the extent and response to the crisis in the global financial system, and the sustainability of the environment undergoing global heating. It depends on the consequences of the financial crisis, but these are caveats over timing; not over whether the tipping point in the balance of power between the USA and EU will happen.

So what might be different? The neoliberal dominance of the global financial institutions would be softened and reduced, with consequences for developing countries as well as the developed world. The liberalization of world trade in the WTO in the interests of the USA would be slowed; the neoliberal conditions attached to loans would be softened; safety would be given greater priority in the development of risky science such as genetically modified crops. On human rights, the EU would face less opposition in the deepening of the human rights regime and its institutionalization in the UN and other international bodies, from the International War Crimes Tribunal to women's rights to sexual and reproductive freedoms. On the environment, the USA would lose some of its power to obstruct the environmental agenda to prevent catastrophic climate change as a result of the emission of greenhouse gases from the burning of fossil fuels, and UN treaties would be more likely to be effective. The likelihood of wars led by the USA would reduce. The EU could restrain its Member States from military adventures in support of the USA and could strengthen the UN machinery of committees and inspectors in support of the peaceful resolution of conflicts. This would be a different global path.

12 Conclusions

Introduction

Complex inequalities and global processes are a challenge to social theory. In order to insert them into the heart of social theory a series of changes is needed; in consequence new processes become visible and alternative futures thinkable.

The purpose of this analysis is to understand the implications of alternative forms of social change for progress. Rather than rejecting the notion of progress, it is better treated as a contested concept. Four main progress projects were identified and investigated: economic growth and development, equality, human rights, and human development and well-being.

Neoliberalism is not inevitable. There are two main forms of modernity in the global North – social democracy as well as neoliberalism. A key difference between them is the depth of democracy: neoliberalism does not go beyond suffrage-democracy, while social democracy has presence-democracy and a breadth of democracy. A further difference in the varieties of modernity is in the extent of inequality.

Each complex inequality is constituted by a regime of inequality with ontological depth in each institutional domain of economy, polity, violence, and civil society. For example, the gender regime is not reducible to family or culture, but is constituted in all of these domains. Within each domain no one regime of inequality saturates its institutions, rather multiple inequalities coexist and intersect in the same domain.

The conventional trilogy of economy, polity, and civil society is extended with a fourth domain of violence. Violence is an institutional domain, a set of coherently inter-related social practices. It is essential to include violence as an institutional domain alongside the others if complex inequalities other than class are to be understood, since violence by the majority on minoritized groups is part of the constitution of these social relations.

The notion of a modern society as being constituted by a nation-state is rejected. The domains of economy, polity, violence, and civil society have different temporal and spatial reach; they do not simply map onto each other in the way required by the conventional concept of society. There are non-saturating and overlapping regimes of inequality and institutional domains. There are processes of societalization, but these will rarely reach completion in a 'society' before another project intervenes.

Even the global North is no yet fully modern. Social relations are not yet modern where there is no free wage labour; where the state does not have a monopoly of legitimate violence in its territory; and where there is not democracy. The modernization of the gender regime is ongoing but this is rarely fully completed. During this gender transformation there is the emergence of employed women as a new political constituency, as the new champions of social democracy. However, only where there are allies does this lead to the practice of social democracy.

Globalization is not a unified force, rather it is constituted by diverse global processes that include global flows of capital, trade, and people, global financial and governance institutions, global hegemons, and global civil societal waves. The concept of the global wave is an important addition to the range of global processes. However, rather than eroding national path dependent trajectories, global processes restructure social processes.

Complexity theory is used in order to make the theoretical innovations needed to address these challenges and to undertake the necessary revisions to social theory. This involves rethinking and reworking rather than rejecting the concept of a social system. This book is a rare example of the application of complexity theory to empirical social scientific analysis that is larger than specific organizations.

The Challenge of Complex Inequalities and Globalization to Social Theory

Progress

It is better to think of progress as a contested concept, rather than to reject it because it does not have a universal meaning. Different projects vigorously contest the shape of the social world informed by their own understanding of progress. It is possible to discern four major framings of progress that are important at a global level: economic growth and development, equality, human rights, and human development and well-being.

These goals were operationalized into quantitative indicators in Chapter 9 and the performance of different countries was compared and assessed.

The common assumption that neoliberalism is linked to faster economic growth is wrong. The USA achieved its higher level of individual income in the past when many European countries were destroying each other in war, as was shown in Chapter 10. In the current era, the rate of economic growth is almost exactly the same in the neoliberal USA and the more social democratic EU. On other indicators of progress (such as living a long life, human rights, and equality) citizens of the EU do better than those in the USA. Social democracy is a more effective path of development in delivering equality, human rights, and human well-being than neoliberalism, while there is no significant difference between them on the rate of economic growth.

Modernity and its varieties

Modernity does not take a single form, instead there are path-dependent varieties of modernity. Some of the social arrangements that are called a different modernity may be more properly understood as premodern. This is especially the case in relation to gender relations.

Modernity in the economy entails free wage labour for all and no forced or domestic labour. Free waged labour often occurs among men of the dominant ethnic group before it does so for women or less powerful ethnic groups. While women's main livelihood is based on domestic labour the economy is not yet modern. Likewise, while there is slavery or feudalism among any minority ethnic or other group, there is not yet modernity.

Modernity in the polity involves not only rationalization but also democracy. Rationalization involves the replacement of governance by superstition, religion, and by persons with ascribed characteristics with that by secular and bureaucratic institutions. Contemporary conceptions of modern governance not only involve the bureaucratic application of rules and procedures but also democratic procedures. If a polity restricts membership of governing bodies to those with ascribed characteristics, such as 'sex' or 'race', it is not democratic and thus not modern.

Modernity requires a free civil society. This includes not only the traditional notion of the practice of free association, but also personal autonomy and bodily integrity. This includes, for instance, the ability to individually control fertility through contraception and abortion and to have the expectation of the absence of physical or sexual harassment or violation on the basis of 'race' or 'sex'.

Modernity in the domain of violence was rarely commented upon by the classical social theorists. The existence of widespread interpersonal violence against women and minority ethnic and religious groups in civil society that is not effectively criminalized means that a state has not yet modernized so as to actually achieve a monopoly of legitimate violence in a given territory. Weber defined the state as a body with a monopoly over legitimate violence over a given territory, yet men's violence against women is but little regulated by the state, nor that by the dominant against minority ethnic groups.

The practice of describing a country as modern if it is modern for men of the dominant ethnicity should be rejected. Some regimes of inequality may be modern while others are not. When gender is brought into focus, we are not yet modern.

The (potentially) many varieties of modernity cluster into two major forms in the global North: neoliberalism and social democracy (as shown in Chapter 8). The key areas in which they differ are democracy and inequality. While both have democracy, since these forms are limited to modernity, it is much shallower in neoliberalism and much deeper in social democracy. Neoliberalism is marked by high levels of inequality, social democracy with lower levels of inequality.

In the economy, the distinction can be identified in the level of regulation of employment and finance and the extent of state provision of welfare: neoliberalism has little regulation and little state provision, while social democracy has more regulation and more state provision. This can be further differentiated by regime of inequality: gender equality forms are not reducible to those of class in either regulation or state welfare provision.

In the polity, democracy is deeper in the social democratic than neoliberal forms. In neoliberalism, democracy is little more than suffrage-democracy; in social democracy, it extends to the presence of women and minoritized groups in parliament and a wider range of institutions to which it is applied as a form of governance.

The rate of violence is higher in neoliberal rather than social democratic countries, whether this is interpersonal, group, or state violence. The state apparatus to deploy violence is larger in a neoliberal than a social democratic state, contradicting claims that neoliberalism is linked to a smaller state. The more democratic the polity, the more likely there are to be laws and practices to de-legitimate and regulate violence from dominant to weaker social groups.

Civil societies are formally free in both neoliberal and social democratic forms: in neoliberalism personal and intimate relations are more likely to be commercialized and unequal, while in social democracy they are more likely to be mutual and equal.

Complex inequalities

Theorizing the simultaneity of multiple complex inequalities has challenged social theory. A tendency to prioritize one main axis of inequality around class was confronted by the significance of multiple inequalities. Postmodernism challenged modernist social theory, offering a move from an assumed universalism to the prioritization of difference. This unfortunate polarization can be transcended using complexity theory.

Rather than dichotomizing equality and difference, these are better recognized as usually entwined. The concept of complex inequalities makes explicit the simultaneity of both inequality and difference in social relations. Even class relations, which are usually presented as if they are about inequalities of income, wealth, and power, can also incorporate positively valued differences such as solidarity. This simultaneity is more obvious with gender and ethnic relations, where there are often overt discussions as to the relationship between the components of inequality and difference. In the case of gender relations there is contestation as to whether the gender division of labour in which women more frequently perform unpaid domestic care-work than men constitutes a negatively valued inequality or a positively valued difference. The concept of 'complex inequalities' does not resolve this issue a priori, but keeps open the simultaneity of difference and inequality and the often contested balance between them.

Multiple complex inequalities beyond class need to be mainstreamed into the centre of social theory, to move beyond their development in relatively separate, segregated, specialist sub-fields. Instead what is required is that the centre of social theory changes, not merely that concepts of complex inequality are adjusted so that they fit into an unchanged theoretical agenda. This is as much adjustment by the mainstream as it is the renewal of the conceptualization of complex inequalities – a two-way movement of mutual adaptation, of the coevolution of complex systems of thought, and not a one-way impact.

This requires the rethinking of core concepts and analytic strategies. The definition of each of the institutional domains of economy, polity, and civil society needs reconsideration so as to include more adequately those aspects of concern to the wider range of complex inequalities; and violence needs to be included as a fourth institutional domain. The economy includes unpaid domestic care-work as well as the market economy; the polity includes organized religions and the EU as well as states; civil society includes intimacy as well as other forms of association. This analysis goes beyond humanism to include bodies and technology in causal chains, not only human agency. Each complex inequality needs to be theorized as a system with ontological depth in economy, polity, violence, and civil society, and at macro, meso, and micro levels: this is achieved in the analyses of regimes of inequality. For example, gender may be perceived as performance or experienced as identity but it is socially constituted with ontological depth. Each institutional domain contains multiple intersecting regimes of inequality. In order to theorize the relationship between these systems the concept of social system is rethought using the insights of complexity theory.

The inclusion of complex inequalities in addition to class makes a difference to the explanation of social development, including the critical turning points and tipping points that create divergent path dependent trajectories of development. The balance of class forces and alliances between them are not the only forces that are relevant, also important are gender, ethnic, religious, and national projects. In particular, and first, the transformation of the gender regime from a domestic to a public form is creating a new constituency in employed women who support and restructure the social democratic project. Second, the non-alignment of nation and state in the context of the search for the mythical nation-state, especially if compounded by ethnicity and religious divides, is a major cause of organized violence. Third, some economic growth spurts have been associated with the transformation of the gender regime and the employment of women previously engaged in unpaid domestic care-work.

Regimes of inequality

Complex inequalities are systems of social relations and here are named regimes of inequality. There are multiple coexisting and intersecting regimes of inequality, including (but not only) those of gender, class, and ethnicity. Each regime of inequality is non-reducible to other regimes. At the points of intersection, there is a mutual adaptation of these complex systems.

Too often the ontological depth of inequalities has been narrowed: to identity, to performance, or to the economic. It may be expressed as performance, and experienced as identity, or be constituted within the economy, but it is more than that. Each regime has ontological depth, including the domains of economy, polity, violence, and civil society, as well as micro, meso, and macro levels. Unless all domains are included in a theorization of the constitution of each inequality, the theoretical understanding of the inter-relationship between the domains will fail. The theorization of an inequality as primarily constituted in only one social domain leads to the failure to theorize it elsewhere in the social, either to the neglect of gender, or to an overly simplistic base-superstructure theorization that cannot grasp the complexity and ubiquity of these relations.

The separate identification of both institutional and relational forms of social relations is essential. Only when the distinction is made is it possible to theorize adequately the simultaneity of multiple complex inequalities with full ontological depth.

Institutional domains: the addition of violence

The mainstreaming of complex inequalities in addition to class requires the reconfiguration of the concepts of economy, polity, and civil society, and the addition of violence as a fourth institutional domain.

A traditional definition of the economy is the system of relations, institutions, and processes concerned with the production, consumption, distribution, and circulation of goods and services to support human life. However, in practice much work on the economy has narrowed the definition to the marketized or monetized section of the economy. This narrowing is reversed here and the concept of economy is developed and clarified so as to include unpaid domestic work as well. This reconceptualization of the economy allows for the inclusion of gendered divisions of labour and the significance of the transformation of the gender regime in which household production is replaced by paid employment within the market or the state. This shift repositions those forms of welfare that are care-work (such as childcare) as production, rather than as luxuries or forms of redistribution.

The concept of the state is replaced by the broader concept of polity so as to include not only states, but also nations, the EU, organized religions, empires, and hegemons. In addition, there is a need to disaggregate the concept of the 'nation-state' into nations and states, which overlap but are rarely co-terminus. This is not an argument that states are not important – they are, but they are not the only form of polity. Each polity carries different ethnic, religious, and gender projects. Using the broader concept of polity allows for a better analysis of the implications of religion, nation, and gender within global processes. Polities overlap and contest each other's domains, so that any given territory is likely to be subject to several competing and accommodating polities.

The concept of civil society is deployed to encompass phenomena that are variously categorized as culture, discourse, and identity. It is preferred because it highlights the contestation over the construction of meaning rather than consensus, and links to other social domains. It includes all forms of association, including intimate ones. The concept is developed beyond its Gramscian origins in order to capture social practices associated with a wider range of complex inequalities rather than class.

Violence is added to the traditional trilogy of economy, polity, and civil society as a fourth institutional domain. Violence is especially important in the constitution of non-class relations of inequality, including gender, nation, and ethnicity. Violence takes interpersonal, group, and state forms; it is deployed and regulated in different ways with different outcomes. Violence constitutes a social system, an institutional domain, rather than being merely a set of individual behaviours or a tool used as an instrument by states.

Societalization rather than societies: non-saturation of territory

There are neither fully globalized nor fully separate societies. Societies as they have been traditionally understood in Sociology and the other social sciences do not exist. Conventional conceptions of society involve the coincidence of economy, polity, and culture in the same territory, indeed that a modern society is a nation-state (Giddens 1984). However, ethos and polis, culture and polity, rarely map onto each other completely, notwithstanding nationalist aspirations in this regard or sociological conceptions of 'society' and the 'nation-state'. The notion that a single culture, state, and economy map onto each other in a one-to-one way in modern nation-states is a myth (Walby 2003).

Specific institutional domains and regimes of inequality do not saturate their territory. Rather they overlap and are non-nested. Multiple regimes of inequality coexist within each institutional domain.

There are different spatial and temporal reaches to the various systems of economy, polity, violence, and civil society. This means that systems may be bounded at a variety of spatial levels, including the local (e.g. local labour markets or travel to work areas), country (e.g. welfare state), regional (e.g. EU regulation of the Single European Market), or global (e.g. global financial governance by a complex of bodies such as the IMF). For example, in the European Union the legal regime regulating the market economy is predominantly constituted at the level of the EU, while the welfare regime is predominantly at the Member State level.

Rather than societies there are processes of societalization. This process, often attempted, is rarely if ever completed. There are attempts at homogenization, of making consistent the mapping of culture, religion, state, and economy, as in the idealized image of the nation-state, but this is rarely achieved. There are many potential bases or principles underpinning projects of societalization. These projects of societalization take time. They are usually stopped by the development of competing alternative projects of societalization before they achieve completion. As a consequence there are few if any examples of a fully completed society, with a full and exclusive mapping of economy, nation, state, violence, and civil society. Attempts to create a society around a consistent set of principles with sets of relations that are consistent with each other and mutually reinforcing are not usually completed. The social processes swirl too fast; they are not stabilized.

While some societalization projects have been focused on the development of a homogeneous system in one country, others have had a much larger intent. In a global era, these include societalization projects that include the whole globe as their aspiration. There are competing projects of globalization, seeking to create and fill institutions with their own preferred forms of social relations. These include the contesting projects of the USA and EU hegemons, as well as those centred on specific religious, ethnic, and national projects, such as Catholicism and certain forms of Islam. Globalization is a developing process that has not yet formed a single system of economy, polity, violence, and civil society.

The concept of 'society' should be replaced by a focus on the process of 'societalization', a process often begun but rarely fully completed. This requires abandoning assumptions that polities saturate a given territory. Rather they coexist and cross-cut each other, in competition and cooperation, as they coevolve. The concept of the nation-state should be abandoned except as a powerful myth and replaced by separate concepts of nations and states. There are degrees of societalization, not fully formed societies.

Global processes, including waves

There are many diverse global processes, not just one globalization. These include: global flows of capital, trade, and people; global financial and governance institutions; global hegemons; and global waves. These flows and institutional developments are uneven: there is no single uniform process of globalization. Global processes are not only economic and political but also involve violence and civil societies. There are emergent forms of global civil societal practices, but not the homogenization of culture.

Understanding global processes demands new ways of thinking about space that avoid both the excesses of the de-territorialization thesis and the denial of globalization, instead developing new concepts to capture the nuanced ways in which space is implicated in new forms of economies, polities, violence, and civil societies. There is a restructuring rather than an annihilation of space.

The changes are not simple one-way impacts, which may be successfully or unsuccessfully resisted, but rather involve the coevolution of economies, polities, violence, and civil societies in an uneven global fitness landscape.

There are no neatly bounded, hermetically sealed 'societies', instead many inter-connections across national boundaries, at regional and global levels, are usual rather than exceptional. This is not as new as has been sometimes assumed, but nonetheless it is taking new forms and gaining increased significance. Globalization highlights the importance of challenging the conventional equation of a 'society' with a 'nation-state'.

Globalization should not be equated with the spread of neo-liberal capitalism, nor modernity, nor Westernization. There are competing projects of globalization, not least between the hegemons of the USA and the EU. Global processes are complex, cross-cutting and sometimes contradictory, not only at an economic level but also involving polities, violence, and civil society. It is not enough to consider whether global processes have a tendency to erode polities since there is a more diverse range of relationships between globalization and political entities, including resistance to globalization, the creation of new polities, and most importantly the development of contesting global hegemons.

Global processes are implicated in the restructuring of complex inequalities: some increase while others decrease; all are restructured. Class relations have frequently become more unequal, while complex gender transitions and interconnections lead to new opportunities for some but not for others. Changes in ethnicities are altogether more varied.

The distinctive nature of social connections in a global era requires the development of new concepts. The concept of wave is developed to address the simultaneous and unique temporal and spatial dimensions of the spread of civil societal and political ideas and practice around the globe. The notion of wave captures the way that this occurs as a movement of social energy that only lightly touches institutions, parallel to the way that light moves as a wave rather than as a particle. It also captures the sudden non-linear escalation of energy within a wave through endogenous processes. Global civil societal waves – including neoliberalism, human rights, fundamentalisms and feminism – cross-cut national trajectories of development.

Comparative paths of development: employed women as the new champions of social democracy

The differences between varieties of modernity are the consequence of divergent paths of development into neoliberalism and social democracy. Political economy is not the only nexus in which these are locked-in, there is another in violence also. Violence, especially but not only wars, is important in shaping paths of development, not least for its much neglected implications for economic growth and development.

Complex inequalities, not only class, are important in these trajectories. The emergence of employed women as the new champions of social democracy has implications not only for gender relations but also for class and other complex inequalities as well. The critical turning points into different forms of modernity occur at different times in different regimes of inequality; there is no single moment. The temporality and sequencing of these events matter: a longer rather than a shorter gap between groups in their access to democracy has implications for the development of a country as a whole.

Global processes are potentially a challenge to path dependent trajectories embedded in particular countries. However, the distinctions between varieties of modernity are not being eroded even though they are being restructured. This is especially because of a rapid spiralling of the effects of the emergence of employed women as champions of social democracy where emergent forms of social democracy are already established. The catalysing rather than dampening of the coevolution of the modernization of these systems makes a difference to their form.

The concepts of path dependency and critical turning points derived from complexity theory are important in enabling an appropriate balance to be struck between general social theory and an analysis of the particular.

Tipping points

There are tipping points between different paths of development. These critical turning points have immense implications for patterns of subsequent development of social relations. The struggles that take place at these moments are constituted not only by class forces, but also by those aligned with gender, ethnicity, and religion.

The financial and economic crisis of 2007–2009 may be a tipping point away from neoliberalism, perhaps to social democracy and global justice, but perhaps towards a more nationalist and protectionist future. The contestation between the hegemons of the USA and the EU is a key part of this moment, together with a wide range of global actors. These hegemons carry different projects, programmes, and social formations: the USA more neoliberal, and the EU, though less cohesively so, more social democratic. A tip in the balance of power between these two hegemons would have immense implications for the world.

Complexity theory

Complexity theory is used to solve difficulties in social theory so as to address multiple complex inequalities and globalization; it provides a toolbox for innovation. Theorizing multiple complex systems of inequality requires new ways of thinking about social systems in order to be able to conceptualize the relationship between regimes of inequality and institutional domains. While Sociology has had something of a hiatus in the use and development of the concept of system, this has proceeded apace in other disciplines. The concept of a social system should not be abandoned but instead re-worked using the insights of complexity theory. Complexity theory enables the development of a more flexible and nuanced conception of systems that do not need to be presumed to return to equilibrium in order to be theorized. Complex social systems do not have only negative feedback loops but also positive ones that can send systems accelerating and spiralling forward. The system/environment distinction allows for the insight that regimes of inequality are overlapping and do not saturate the territory that they are in. There is neither a single universal form of modernity nor an infinite number of forms, but rather clusters of path dependent developments. Globalization has not eroded the differences between social forms to create a single social system, but is implicated in their restructuring. They are connected not only by their processes of coevolution in a changing fitness landscape, but also by global civil societal waves. Complexity theory is needed to address change in a global era, to conceptualize the critical turning points, tipping points, into path dependent and not universal paths of development. There are non-linear global waves, polities that catalyse or dampen, positive as well as negative feedback.

It is important to re-work rather than reject the concept of system; while it is important to utilize the concept of non-linearity, this does not mean abandoning systematic explanatory analysis; only some phenomena are non-linear. Social theory is situated in the tension between universalism and particularism, foundationalism and relativism, and none of these extreme poles are sustainable. Complexity theory allows us to transcend the dichotomy between modernism and postmodernism in social theory.

Bibliography

Abbott, Andrew (2001) *Time Matters*. Chicago: Chicago University.
Abu-Ghaida, Dina and Klasen, Stephan (2004) 'The costs of missing the Millennium Development Goal on gender equity', *World Development*, 32, 7, 1075–107.
Acker, Joan (1989) *Doing Comparable Worth*. Philadelphia: Temple University.
Acker, Joan (2000) 'Revisiting class', *Social Politics*, 7, 2, 192–214.
Adams, Julia and Padamsee, Tasleem (2001) 'Signs and regimes', *Social Politics*, 8, 1, 1–23.
Adkins, Lisa and Lury, Celia (1999) 'The labour of identity', *Economy and Society*, 28, 4, 598–614.
Adkins, Lisa and Skeggs, Beverley (eds) (2004) *Feminism After Bourdieu*. Oxford: Blackwell.
Afshar, Haleh (1998) *Islam and Feminisms*. Basingstoke: Macmillan.
Alderson, Arthur and Nielson, François (2002) 'Globalization and the great U-turn: Income inequality trends in 16 OECD countries', *American Journal of Sociology*, 107, 5, 1244–99.
Alexander, Jeffrey (1982) *Theoretical Logic in Sociology: Volume 1*. London: Routledge and Kegan Paul.
Alexander, Jeffrey (1984) *Theoretical Logic in Sociology: Volume 4*. London: Routledge and Kegan Paul.
Alexander, Jeffrey (1998) *Neofunctionalism and After*. Malden, MA: Blackwell.
Alexander, Jeffrey (2006) *The Civil Sphere*. Oxford: Oxford University Press.
Aliaga, Christel (2006) *How is the Time of Women and Men Distributed in Europe?* Available at http://epp.eurostat.cec.eu.int/cache/ITY_OFFPUB/KS-NK-06-004/EN/KS-NK-06-004-EN.PDF
Althusser, Louis (1971) *Lenin and Philosophy and Other Essays*. London: New Left Books.
Álvarez-Rivera, Manuel (2007) 'Election resources on the internet: Parliamentary elections in Ireland'. Available at http://electionresources.org/ie/ (accessed 8 January 2008).
Amer, Mildred (2005) *Black Members of the United States Congress, 1870–2005*. Washington, DC: Library of Congress.
Amnesty International (2006) *The Death Penalty*. Available at http://web.amnesty.org/pages/deathpenalty-countries-eng (accessed 2 October 2006).
Anderson, Benedict (1983) *Imagined Communities*. London: Verso.
Anderson, James (1995) 'The exaggerated death of the nation-state', in James Anderson, Chris Brook and Allan Cochrane (eds), *A Global World?*, Oxford: Oxford University Press.

Anderson, James and Goodman, James (1994) 'European and Irish integration', *European Journal of Urban and Regional Studies*, 1, 1, 49–62.
Anderson, James and O'Dowd, Liam (1999a) 'Borders, border regions and territoriality', *Regional Studies*, 33, 7, 592–604.
Anderson, James and O'Dowd, Liam (1999b) 'Contested borders', *Regional Studies*, 33, 7, 681–96.
Anderson, Kristi (1975) 'Working women and political participation, 1952–1972', *American Journal of Political Science*, 19, 3, 439–53.
Anderson, Michael, Gillig, Paulette, Sitaker, Marilyn et al. (2003) '"Why doesn't she just leave?"', *Journal of Family Violence*, 18, 3, 151–5.
Anderson, Perry (1974) *Lineages of the Absolutist State*. London: New Left Books.
Anderson, Perry (1976/7) 'The antinomies of Antonio Gramsci' *New Left Review*, 100, 5–78.
Anheier, Helmut, Glasius, Marlies and Kaldo, Mary (eds) (2005) *Global Civil Society 2004/5*. London: Sage. pp. 26–39.
Anker, Richard (1998) *Gender and Jobs: Sex Segregation of Occupations in the World*. Geneva: International Labour Office.
Annan, Kofi (1999) 'Secretary-General says "Global People-Power" best thing for United Nations in long time'. Available at http://www.unis.unvienna.org/unis/pressrels/1999/sg2465.html
Anthias, Floya and Yuval-Davis, Nira (1992) *Racialized Boundaries*. London: Routledge.
Appadurai, Arjun (1996) *Modernity at Large*. Minneapolis: University of Minnesota.
Arber, Sara, Davidson, Kate and Ginn, Jay (2007) *Gender and Ageing*. Buckingham: Open University Press.
Archer, Margaret (1995) *Realist Social Theory*. Cambridge: Cambridge University Press.
Arestis, Philip and Sawyer, Malcolm (2005) 'Neoliberalism and the Third Way', in Alfredo Saad-Filho and Deborah Johnston (eds), *Neoliberalism*. London: Pluto. pp. 177–83.
Arrighi, Giovanni (1994) *The Long Twentieth Century*. London: Verso.
Arthur, Brian (1989) 'Competing technologies, increasing returns, and lock-in by historical events', *The Economic Journal*, 99, 116–31.
Arthur, Brian (1994) *Increasing Returns and Path Dependence in the Economy*. University of Michigan.
Arts, Wil and Gelissen, John (2002) 'Three worlds of welfare capitalism or more?', *Journal of European Social Policy*, 12, 2, 137–58.
Ash, Amin (ed.) *Post-Fordism*. Oxford: Blackwell. pp. 1–39.
Aslund, Anders (2009) 'Lessons for the US from the Swedish banking crisis', *Real Time Economic Issues Watch*, 24 February 2009.
Atkinson, Anthony (1999) 'Is rising income inequality inevitable?' *WIDER Angle*, 2, 3–4.
Attac (Association for the Taxation of Financial Transactions to Aid Citizens) (2008). Available at http:www.attac.org/
Baccaro, Lucio and Simoni, Marco (2007) 'Centralized wage bargaining and the "Celtic Tiger" pheonomenon', *Industrial Relations*, 46, 3, 426–55.
Bagguley, Paul (2002) 'Contemporary British feminism', *Social Movement Studies*, 1, 2, 169–85.
Bagguley, Paul and Hussain, Yasmin (2008) *Riotous Citizens: Ethnic Conflict in Multiculturaal Britain*. Aldershot: Ashgate.
Bagguley, Paul, Shapiro, Dan, Urry, John, Walby, Sylvia and Alan Warde with Jane Mark-Lawson (1990) *Restructuring: Place, Class and Gender*. London: Sage.
Bakker, Isabella (1998) *Unpaid Work and Macroeconomics*. Ottawa, Canada: Status of Women in Canada.
Ball, Philip (2004) *Critical Mass*. London: Heinemann.
Banks, Arthur and Muller, Thomas (eds) (1998) *Political Handbook of the World: 1998*. Binghampton, NY: CSA Publications.
Banks, Olive (1981) *Faces of Feminism*. Oxford: Martin Robertson.

Barclay, Gordon and Tavares, Cynthia (2002) 'International comparisons of criminal justice statistics 2000'. Accessed 2 March 2005 at http://www.homeoffice.gov.uk/rds/pdfs2/hosb502.pdf

Barclay, Gordon and Tavares, Cynthia (2003) 'International comparisons of criminal justice statistics 2001'. Accessed 13 May 2006 at http://www.homeoffice.gov.uk/rds/pdfs2/hosb1203.pdf

Bardhan, K. and Klasen, Stephan (1999) 'UNDP's Gender-related indices', *World Development*, 2, 6, 985–1010.

Barnes, Colin, Mercer, Geof and Shakespeare, Tom (1999) *Exploring Disability*. Cambridge: Polity.

Barr, Michael (2002) *Cultural Politics and Asian Values*. London: Routledge.

Barrett, Michèle and Phillips, Anne (eds) (1992) *Destabilizing Theory*. Cambridge: Polity.

Barro, Robert (1998) *Determinants of Economic Growth*. Cambridge, MA: MIT Press.

Bartolini, Stefano (2000) *The Political Mobilization of the European Left, 1860–1980*. Cambridge: Cambridge University Press.

Bauman, Zygmunt (1989) *Modernity and the Holocaust*. Cambridge: Polity.

Bauman, Zygmunt (1991) *Modernity and Ambivalence*. Cambridge: Polity.

Bauman, Zygmunt (1993) *Postmodern Ethics*. Oxford: Blackwell.

Bauman, Zygmunt (2000) *Liquid Modernity*. Cambridge: Polity.

BBC (2009) 'House prices' BBC News, 5 March 2009.

Beale, Jenny (1986) *Women in Ireland*. Dublin: Gill and Macmillan.

Beck, Ulrich (1992) *Risk Society*. London: Sage.

Beck, Ulrich (2002) *Individualization*. London: Sage.

Beck, Ulrich (2006) *The Cosmopolitan Vision*. Cambridge: Polity.

Beck, Ulrich and Beck-Gernsheim, Elisabeth (1994) *The Normal Chaos of Love*. Cambridge: Polity.

Beck, Ulrich, Giddens, Anthony and Lash, Scott (1994) *Reflexive Modernization*. Cambridge: Polity.

Becker, Gary (1965) 'A theory of the allocation of time', *Economic Journal*, 75, 493–517.

Becker, Gary (1981) *A Treatise on the Family*. Cambridge, MA: Harvard University Press.

Becker, Gary (1993) *Human Capital* (3rd edition). Chicago: Chicago University Press.

Beetham, David, Weir, Stuart and Ngan, Pauline (eds) (2002) *Democracy Under Blair: A Democratic Audit of the United Kingdom*. London: Politico's.

Benhabib, Seyla (1992) *Situating the Self*. Cambridge: Polity.

Benhabib, Seyla (1999) 'Sexual difference and collective identities: The new global constellation', *Signs*, 24, 2, 335–61.

Benton, Ted (1993) *Natural Relations*. London: Verso.

Berger-Schmitt, R. and Jankowitsch, B. (1999) *Systems of Social Indicators and Social Reporting*. EUReporting WP1. Mannheim: Centre for Survey Research and Methodology.

Bergmann, Barbara (1986) *The Economic Emergence of Women*. New York: Basic.

Beringer, Richard, Hattaway, Herman, Jones, Archer and Still, William (1986) *Why the South Lost the Civil War*. Athens, GA: University of Georgia.

Berkovitch, Nitza (1999) *From Motherhood to Citizenship*. Baltimore, MA: Johns Hopkins University Press.

Bertalanffy, Ludwig von (1968) *General Systems Theory*. New York: George Braziller.

Bertilsson, Margareta (1999) 'The Balkan tragedy', in Thomas P. Boje, Bart van Steenbergen and Sylvia Walby (eds), *European Societies: Fusion or Fission?* London: Routledge.

Beveridge, William Henry (1942) *The Beveridge Report* (CMND 6404). London: HMSO.

Beyer, Peter (1994) *Religion and Globalization*. London: Sage.

Bhambra, Gurminder (2007) 'Multiple modernities or global interconnections', in Nathalie Kargiannis and Peter Wagner (eds), *Varieties of World-Making: Beyond Globalization*. Liverpool: Liverpool University Press. pp. 59–73.

Bhaskar, Roy (1979) *The Possibility of Naturalism*. London: Harvester.

Bhaskar, Roy (1997) *A Realist Theory of Science*. London: Verso.
Bhopal, Kalwant (1997) *Gender, 'Race' and Patriarchy*. Aldershot: Ashgate.
Biggs, Michael (2001) 'Fractal Waves', Working Paper Series. Oxford: Department of Sociology, University of Oxford.
Björnberg, Ulla (2002) 'Ideology and choice between work and care: Swedish family policy for working parents', *Critical Social Policy*, 22, 1, 33–52.
Blackwell, Louisa (2001) 'Occupational sex segregation and part-time work in modern Britain', *Gender, Work and Organization*, 8, 2, 146–63.
Bland, Nick, Miller, Joel and Quinton, Paul (2000) *Upping the PACE? An Evaluation of the Recommendations of the Stephen Lawrence Inquiry on Stops and Searches* (Police Research Series Paper 128). London: The Home Office.
Blau, Francine and Kahn, Lawrence (2003) 'Understanding international differences in the gender pay gap', *Journal of Labor Economics*, 21, 1, 106–44.
Bobbio, Norberto (1997) *Left and Right*. Chicago: University of Chicago.
Bockman, Johanna and Eyal, Gil (2002) 'Eastern Europe as a laboratory for economic knowledge', *American Journal of Sociology*, 108, 2, 310–52.
Bogg, Jan and Geyer, Robert (eds) (2007) *Complexity, Science and Society*. Oxford: Radcliff.
Boje, Thomas, van Steenbergen, Bart and Walby, Sylvia (eds) (1999) *European Societies: Fusion or Fission?* London: Routledge.
Boli, John and Thomas, George (1997) 'World culture in the world polity: A century of international nongovernmental organization', *American Sociological Review*, 62, 171–90.
Bollen, Kenneth and Jackson, Robert (1995) 'Income inequality and democratization revisited', *American Sociological Review*, 60, 983–9.
Bordo, Susan (1993) *Unbearable Weight*. Berkeley: University of California.
Bornschier, Volker and Chase-Dunn, Christopher (eds) (1999) *The Future of Global Conflict*. London: Sage.
Bornschier, Volker and Ziltener, Patrick (1999) 'The revitalization of Western Europe and the politics of the "social dimension"', in Thomas Boje, Bart van Steenbergen and Sylvia Walby (eds), *European Societies: Fusion or Fission?* London: Routledge.
Bose, Catherine (1979) 'Technology and changes in the division of labour in the American home', *Women's Studies International Quarterly*, 2, 295–304.
Boserup, Ester (1970) *Women's Role in Economic Development*. New York: St Martin's.
Boswell, Terry and Chase-Dunn, Christopher (2000) *The Spiral of Capitalism and Socialism*. Boulder, Co: Lynne Rienner.
Boucher, Gerry and Collins, Grainne (2003) 'Irish neo-liberal corporatism', *Review of Social Economy*, 61, 3, 295–316.
Bourdieu, Pierre (1984) *Distinction*. London: Routledge and Kegan Paul.
Bourke, Joanna (1993) *Husbandry to Housewifery*. Oxford: Clarendon.
Boyer, Robert and Durand, Jean-Pierre (1997) *After Fordism*. Basingstoke: Macmillan.
Bradshaw, Jonathan, Kennedy, Steven and Kilkey, Majella (1996) *The Employment of Lone Parents*. London: Family Policy Studies Centre.
Brah, Avtar and Phoenix, Ann (2004) 'Ain't I a woman? Revisiting intersectionality', *Journal of International Women's Studies*, 5, 3, 75–86.
Braidotti, Rosi (1994) *Nomadic Subjects*. Columbia: Columbia University.
Braverman, Harry (1974) *Labor and Monopoly Capital*. New York: Monthly Review.
Breen, Richard, Hannan, Damian, Rottman, David and Whelan, Christopher (1990) *Understanding Contemporary Ireland*. Dublin: Gill and Macmillan.
Brenner, Neil (1999) 'Beyond state-centrism?', *Theory and Society*, 28, 39–78.
Brenner, Neil and Theodore, Nick (eds) (2002) *Spaces of Neoliberalism*. Oxford: Blackwell. pp. 2–32.
Breslau, Naomi, Kessler, Ronald, Chilcoat, Howard, et al. (1998) 'Trauma and posttraumatic stress disorder in the community', *Archives of General Psychiatry*, 55, 7, 626–32.
Bretherton, Charlotte and Vogler, John (2006) *The European Union as a Global Actor* (2nd edition). London: Routledge.

Brewer, Mike, Goodman, Alissa, Shaw, Jonathan and Sibeieta, Luke (2006) *Poverty and Inequality in Britain: 2006*. (IFS Commentary No. 101). London: Institute for Fiscal Studies.

Brine, Jacky (2006) 'Lifelong learning and the knowledge economy', *British Educational Research Journal*, 32, 5, 649–65.

Briskin, Linda and Eliasson, Mona (eds) (1999) *Women's Organizing and Public Policy in Canada and Sweden*. Montreal: McGill-Queen's University Press.

Bromage, Arthur and Bromage, Mary (1940) 'Foreign government and politics: The vocational Senate in Ireland', *The American Political Science Review*, 34, 3, 519–38.

Brooks, Clem and Manza, Jeff (2006) 'Why do welfare states persist?', *Journal of Politics*, 68, 4, 816–27.

Brown, Gordon (2009) Speech to Congress on 4 March 2009. London: Office of the Prime Minister.

Brownmiller, Susan (1976) *Against Our Will*. London: Penguin.

Brubaker, Rogers (1996) *Nationalism Reframed*. Cambridge: Cambridge University Press.

Brubaker, Rogers and Cooper, Frederick (2000) 'Beyond "identity"', *Theory and Society*, 29, 1–47.

Bruce, Steve (1996) *Religion in the Modern World*. Oxford: Blackwell.

Bruce, Steve (2002) *God is Dead: Secularization in the West*. Oxford: Blackwell.

Bruce, Steve and Voas, David (2004) 'The resilience of the nation–state: Religion and polities in the modern era', *Sociology*, 38, 5, 1019–28.

Brush, Lisa (2002) 'Changing the subject: Gender and welfare regime studies', *Social Politics*, 9, 161–86.

Bryant, Christopher (2006) *The Nations of Britain*. Oxford: Oxford University.

Budig, Michelle and England, Paula (2001) 'The wage penalty for motherhood', *American Sociological Review*, 66, 2, 204–25.

Buergenthal, Thomas, Shelton, Dinal and Steward, David (2002) *International Human Rights in a Nutshell* (3rd edition). St. Paul, MN: West Group.

Bull, Hedley (1977) *The Anarchical Society*. London: Macmillan.

Bunagan, Katrine, Reyes, Melanie and Yancha, Dashell (2000) 'The quota system: Women's boon or bane?', *Women Around the World*, 1, 3. Available at http://www.cld.org/waw5.htm accessed 17 May 2005.

Bunch, Charlotte (1995) 'Transforming human rights from a feminist perspective', in Julie Peters and Andrea Wolper (eds), *Women's Rights, Human Rights*. London: Routledge.

Bunge, M. (2001) 'Systems and emergence, rationality and imprecision, free-wheeling and evidence, science and ideology', *Philosophy of the Social Sciences*, 31, 3, 404–23.

Burawoy, Michael (2005) 'For Public Sociology', *American Sociological Review*, 70, 1, 4–28.

Burstein, Paul, Bricher, Marie, R. and Einwohner, Rachel L. (1995) 'Policy alternatives and political change: Work, family and gender on the congressional agenda, 1945–1990', *American Sociological Review*, 60, 67–83.

Butler, Judith (1990) *Gender Trouble*. New York: Routledge.

Butler, Judith (2004) *Undoing Gender*. New York: Routledge.

Byrne, Anne and Leonard, Madeleine (eds) (1997) *Women and Irish Society*. Belfast: Beyond the Pale.

Byrne, David (1998) *Complexity Theory and the Social Sciences*. London: Routledge.

Byrne, David (2002) *Interpreting Quantitative Data*. London: Sage.

Cabinet Office (1998) *Policy Appraisal for Equal Treatment*. Available at http://www.womens-unit.gov.uk/1999/equal.htm

Çagatay, Nilüfer and Özler, Sule (1995) 'Feminization of the labor force: The effects of long-term development and structural adjustment', *World Development*, 23, 11, 1883–94.

Calhoun, Craig (1995) *Critical Social Theory*. Oxford: Blackwell.

Calhoun, Craig (1998) 'Explanation in historical sociology', *American Journal of Sociology*, 104, 3, 846–71.

Callaghan, John (2000) *The Retreat of Social Democracy*. Manchester: Manchester University Press.
Callon, Michel (1991) 'Techno-economic networks and irreversibility', in John Law (ed.), *A Sociology of Monsters: Essays on Power, Technology and Domination*. London: Routledge.
Callon, Michel, Law, John and Rip, Arie (eds) (1986) *Mapping the Dynamics of Science and Technology*. Basingstoke: Macmillan.
Cameron, Euan (1991) *The European Reformation*. Oxford: Oxford University.
Capra, Fritjof (1997) *The Web of Life*. London: Flamingo.
Card, David and DiNardo, John E. (2002) 'Skill-based technological change and rising wage inequality', *Journal of Labor Economics*, 20, 4, 733–83.
Casey, Bernard, Metcalf, Hilary and Millward, Neil (1997) *Employers Use of Flexible Labour*. London: Policy Studies Institute.
Castells, Manuel (1996) *The Information Age; Volume 1: The Rise of the Network Society*. Oxford: Blackwell.
Castells, Manuel (1997) *The Information Age; Volume II: The Power of Identity*. Oxford: Blackwell.
Castells, Manuel (1998) *The Information Age; Volume III: The End of Millennium*. Oxford: Blackwell.
Castles, Francis (2003) 'The world turned upside down: Below replacement fertility, changing preferences and family-friendly public policy in 21 OECD countries', *Journal of European Social Policy*, 13, 3, 209–27.
Castles, Francis and Mitchell, Brian (1993) 'Worlds of welfare and families of nations' in Francis Castles (ed.), *Families of Nations*. Aldershot: Dartmouth.
Castles, Stephen and Miller, Mark (2003) *The Age of Migration* (3rd edition). Basingstoke: Palgrave Macmillan.
Center for Reproductive Rights (2007) *The World's Abortion Laws*. Available at http://www.crlp.org/pub_fac_abortion_laws.html
Centers for Disease Control and Protection Office of Minority Health (CDC) (2006) *Racial and Ethnic Populations*. Available at http://www.cdc.gov/omh/Populations/populations.htm
Cerny, Philip (1990) *The Changing Architecture of Politics*. London: Sage.
Cerny, Philip (1995) 'Globalization and the changing logic of collective action', *International Organization*, 49, 4, 595–625.
Cerny, Philip (1996) 'International finance and the erosion of state policy capacity', in Philip Gummett (ed.), *Globalization and Public Policy*. Cheltenham: Edward Elgar.
Chabot, Sean and Duyvendak, Jan (2002) 'Globalization and transnational diffusion between social movements', *Theory and Society*, 31, 697–740.
Chafetz, Janet Saltzman and Dworkin, Anthony (1986) *Female Revolt: Women's Movements in World and Historical Perspective*. Totowa, NJ: Rowman and Allanheld.
Chase-Dunn, Christopher (1998) *Global Formation* (2nd edition). Oxford: Blackwell.
Chase-Dunn, Christopher, Kawano, Yukio and Brewer, Benjamin (2000) 'Trade globalization since 1795: Waves of integration in the world-system', *American Sociological Review*, 65, 77–95.
Chesters, Graeme and Welsh, Ian (2006) *Complexity and Social Movements*. London: Routledge.
Chu, Dominique, Strand, Roger and Fjelland, Ragnar (2003) 'Theories of complexity', *Complexity*, 8, 3, 19–30.
Cilliers, Paul (1998) *Complexity and Postmodernism*. London: Routledge.
Clark County Prosecuting Attorney (2007) *US Executions since 1976*. Available at http://www.clarkprosecutor.org/html/death/usexecute.htm
Clear, Caitriona (1987) *Nuns in Nineteenth Century Ireland*. Dublin: Gill and Macmillan.
Cockburn, Cynthia and Omrod, Susan (1993) *Gender and Technology in the Making*. London: Sage.

Cohen, Jean and Arato, Andrew (1992) *Civil Society and Political Theory*. Cambridge, MA: MIT.

Cohen, Robin (1997) *Global Diasporas*. London: UCL.

Coleman, Diane and Straus, Murray (1986) 'Marital power, conflict, and violence in a nationally representative sample of American couples', *Violence and Victims*, 1, 2, 141–57.

Coleman, James (1990) *Foundations of Social Theory*. Cambridge, MA: Belknap, Harvard University.

Collins, Patricia Hill (1998) 'It's all in the family: Intersections of gender, race, and nation', *Hypatia*, 13, 3, 62–82.

Commins, Patrick (1995) 'The European Community and the Irish rural economy', in Patrick Clancy, Sheelagh Drudy, Kathleen Lynch and Liam O'Dowd (eds), *Irish Society: Sociological Perspectives*. Dublin: Institute of Public Administration. pp. 178–204.

Connell, Robert (1987) *Gender and Power*. Cambridge: Polity.

Connell, Robert (1990) 'The state, gender, and sexual politics', *Theory and Society*, 19, 507–44.

Connell, Robert (1995) *Masculinities*. Cambridge: Polity.

Connell, Robert (2002) *Gender*. Cambridge: Polity.

Conte, Rosaria and Gilbert, Nigel (1995) 'Introduction: Computer simulation for social theory', in Nigel Gilbert and Rosaria Conte (eds), *Artificial Societies*. London: UCL. pp. 1–15.

Cotter, David, Defiore, JoAnn, Hermsen, Joan, Kowaleski, Brenda and Vanneman, Reeve (1997) 'All women benefit: The macro-level effect of occupational integration on gender earnings inequality', *American Sociological Review*, 62, 714–34.

Coulter, Carol (1990) *Ireland: Between the First and the Third Worlds*. Dublin: Attic.

Council of Europe (1998) Recommendation *R(98) 14 on Gender Mainstreaming*. Strasbourg: Council of Europe.

Council of Europe (2006a) *Human Rights Conventions and Protocols*. Available at http://conventions.coe.int/Treaty/Commun/ListeTraites.asp?MA=3&CM=7&CL=ENG (accessed 17 May 2006).

Council of Europe (2006b) *About Council of Europe*. Available at http:www.coe.int/T/e/Com/about_coe/

Council of the European Union (2003) *European Security Strategy*. Available at http://www.consilium.europa.eu/cms3_fo/showPage.ASP?id=266&lang=EN&mode=g

Council of the European Union (2007a) *Treaty of Lisbon*. Available at http://www.consilium.europa.eu/cms3_fo/showPage.asp?id=1296&lang=EN&mode=g

Council of the European Union (2007b) *European Security and Defence Policy*. Available at http://www.consilium.europa.eu/cms3_fo/showpage.asp?id=268&lang=en&mode=g

Counts, Dorothy Ayers, Brown, Judith K. and Campbell, Jacquelyn (eds) (1992) *Sanctions and Sanctuary – Cultural Perspectives on the Beating of Wives*. Boulder, CO: Westview.

Cox, Robert W. (1999) 'Civil society at the turn of the millenium', *Review of International Studies*, 25, 3–28.

Crenshaw, Kimberlé Williams (1991) 'Mapping the margins: Intersectionality, identity politics, and violence against women of color', *Stanford Law Review*, 43, 6, 1241–99.

Crewe, Ivor, Sarlvik, Bo and Alt (1977) 'Partisan dealignment in Britain 1964–1974', *British Journal of Political Science*, 7, 129–50.

Criminal Statistics, England and Wales (1997) London: Stationery Office.

Crompton, Rosemary (1986) 'Credentials and careers: some implications of the increase in professional qualifications among women', *Sociology*, 20, 1, 25–42.

Crompton, Rosemary and Mann, Michael (eds) (1986) *Gender and Stratification*. Cambridge: Polity.

Crossley, Nick and Roberts, John (eds) (2004) *After Habermas: New Perspectives on the Public Sphere*. Oxford: Blackwell.

Crotty, Raymond (1986) *Ireland in Crisis: A Study of Capitalist Colonial Underdevelopment*. Dingle, Ireland: Brandon.

Crouch, Colin (1993) *Industrial Relations and European State Traditions*. Oxford: Clarendon.
Crouch, Colin (1999) 'Employment, industrial relations and social policy', *Social Policy and Administration*, 33, 4, 437–57.
Crouch, Colin (2001) 'Welfare state regimes and industrial relations systems: The questionable role of path dependency', in Bernhard Ebbinghaus and Philip Manow (eds), *Comparing Welfare Capitalism: Social Policy and Political Economy in Europe, Japan and the USA*. London: Routledge. pp. 105–24.
Crouch, Colin and Streeck, Wolfgang (eds) (1997) *Political Economy of Modern Capitalism: Mapping Convergence and Diversity*. London: Sage.
Cudworth, Erika (2003) *Environment and Society*. London: Routledge.
Cudworth, Erika (2005) *Developing Ecofeminist Theory: The Complexity of Difference*. Basingstoke: Palgrave Macmillan.
Curtin, Deidre (1989) *Irish Employment Equality Law*. Dublin: Round Hall.
Dahl, Robert (1971) *Polyarchy*. New Haven: Yale University.
Dahlerup, Drude (ed.) (1986) *The New Women's Movement*. London: Sage.
Dahlerup, Drude (1988) 'From a small to a large minority: Women in Scandinavian politics', *Scandinavian Political Studies*, 11, 4, 275–98.
Dahlerup, Drude (1993) 'From movement protest to state feminism: The Women's Liberation Movement and unemployment policy in Denmark' *NORA*, 1, 1, 4–20.
Dahlerup, Drude (1998) 'Using quotas to increase women's political representation', in Azza Karam (ed.) *Women in Parliament: Beyond Numbers*. Sweden: International IDEA. Also available at http://archive.idea.int/women/parl/ (accessed 17 May 2005).
Dahlerup, Drude and Freidenvall, Lenita (2005) 'Quotas as a "fast track" to equal representation of women', *International Feminist Journal of Politics*, 7, 1, 26–48.
Dahlerup, Drude and Gulli, Brita (1985) 'Women's organisations in the Nordic countries' in Elina Haavio-Manila (ed.), *Unfinished Democracy: Women in Nordic Politics*. Oxford: Pergamon.
Dahlerup, Drude and Haavio-Manila, Elina (1985) 'Summary', in Elina Haavio-Manila (ed.), *Unfinished Democracy: Women in Nordic Politics*. Oxford: Pergamon.
Daly, Mary (1978) *Gyn/Ecology: The Metaethics of Radical Feminism*. London: Women's Press.
Daly, Mary and Rake, Katherine (2003) *Gender and the Welfare State*. Cambridge: Polity.
Danieli, Ardha (2006) 'Gender: The missing link in industrial relations research', *Industrial Relations Journal*, 37, 4, 290–425.
Darcy, R., Welch, Susan and Clark, Janet (1994) *Women, Elections, and Representation* (2nd edition). Lincoln, Nebraska: Nebraska University.
David, Paul (1985) 'Clio and the economics of QWERTY', *American Economic Review*, 75, 2, 332–7.
Davies, James, Sandstrom, Susanna, Shorrocks, Anthony and Wolff, Edward (2008) *The World Distribution of Household Wealth* (UNU-WIDER Discussion Paper No. 2008/03). Available at http://www.wider.unu.edu/publications/working-papers/discussion-papers/2008/en_GB/dp2008-03/_files/78918010772127840/default/dp2008-03.pdf
Davies, M. (ed.) (1993) *Women and Violence: Realities and Responses Worldwide*. London: Zed.
Davis, Angela (1981) *Women, Race and Class*. London: The Women's Press.
Davis, Lance and Huttenback, Robert (1986) *Mammon and the Pursuit of Empire: The Political Economy of British Imperialism 1860–1912*. Cambridge: Cambridge University Press.
Deininger, Klaus and Squire, Lyn (1996) 'A new data set measuring income inequality', *The World Bank Economic Review*, 10, 1, 565–91.
De Landa, Manuel (2000) *A Thousand Years of Nonlinear History*. New York: Swerve.
Deleuze, Giles and Guattari, Félix (1987) *A Thousand Plateaus: Capitalism and Schizophrenia*. London: Continuum.

Delphy, Christine (1984) *Close to Home*. London: Hutchinson.
Della Porta, Donatella and Diani, Mario (1999) *Social Movements*. Oxford: Blackwell.
Dennis, Suzanna and Zuckerman, Elaine (2006) *Gender Guide to World Bank and IMF Policy-Based Lending*. Washington, DC: Gender Action.
Derrida, Jacques (1976) *Of Grammatology*. Baltimore, MA: Johns Hopkins University.
Dex, Shirley and McCulloch, Andrew (1997) *Flexible Employment: The Future of Britain's Jobs*. Basingstoke: Macmillan.
Diamond, Larry (1992) 'Economic development and democracy reconsidered', in Gary Marks and Larry Diamond (eds). *Reexamining Democracy*. Newbury Park, CA: Sage.
Diani, Mario (1996) 'Linking mobilization frames and political opportunities: Insights from regional populism in Italy', *American Sociological Review*, 61, 1053–69.
Dijkstra, A. G. (2002) 'Revisiting UNDP's GDI and GEM: Towards an alternative', *Social Indicators Research*, 57, 301–38.
Dijkstra, A. G. and Hanmer L. C. (2000) 'Measuring socio-economic gender inequality: Toward an alternative to the UNDP Gender-related development index', *Feminist Economics*, 6, 2, 41–75.
DiNardo, John, Fortin, Nicole and Lemieux, Thomas (1996) 'Labor market institutions and the distribution of wages, 1973–1992', *Econometrica*, 64, 5, 1001–44.
Dobash, Rebecca and Dobash, Russell (1980) *Violence Against Wives: The Case Against the Patriarchy*. Shepton Mallet: Open Books.
Dobbin, Frank, Simmons, Beth and Garrett, Geoffrey (2007) 'The global diffusion of public policies: Social construction, coercion, competition, or learning?', *Annual Review of Sociology*, 33, 449–72.
Dollar, David and Kraay, Aart (2001) *Trade, Growth, and Poverty* (World Bank Policy Research Working Paper No. 2615). Washington, DC: World Bank.
Donnelly, Jack (2003) *Universal Human Rights in Theory and Practice*. (2nd edition). Ithaca, NY: Cornell University.
Drucker, P (1993) *Post-Capitalist Society*. Oxford: Butterworth Heinemann.
Du Gay, Paul (1996) *Consumption and Identity at Work*. London: Sage.
Duncan, Simon and Edwards, Rosalind (1999) *Lone Mothers, Paid Work and Gendered Moralities*. Basingstoke: Macmillan.
Durbin, Susan (2004) *Is the Knowledge Economy Gendered?* Unpublished PhD, School of Sociology and Social Policy, University of Leeds.
Durbin, Susan (2007) 'Who gets to be a knowledge worker? The case of UK call centres', in Sylvia Walby, Heidi Gottfried, Karin Gottschall and Mari Osawa (eds), *Gendering the Knowledge Economy: Comparative Perspectives*. London: Palgrave. pp. 228–47.
Durkheim, Emile (1952) *Suicide*. London: Routledge.
Durkheim, Emile (1966) *The Rules of Sociological Method*. New York: Free.
Durkheim, Emile (1984) *The Division of Labour in Society*. Basingstoke: Macmillan.
Durphy, Richard (1995) *The Making of Fianna Fail Power in Ireland, 1923–1948*. Oxford: Clarendon.
Ebbinghaus, Bernhard and Hassel, Anke (2000) 'Striking deals: Concertation in the reform of continental welfare states', *Journal of European Public Policy*, 7, 1, 44–62.
Ebbinghaus, Bernhard and Manow, Philip (eds) (2001) *Comparing Welfare Capitalism: Social Policy and Political Economy in Europe, Japan and the USA*. London: Routledge.
Ebbinghaus, Bernhard and Visser, Jelle (1999) 'When institutions matter: Union growth and decline in Western Europe, 1950–1995', *European Sociological Review*, 15, 2, 135–58.
Economist (2001) 'Islamic banking: forced devolution', 17 February, pp. 112–15.
Economist (2007) 'Minorities and legislatures: Must the rainbow turn monochrome in parliament?' 25 October.
Eduards, Maud (1992) 'Against the rules of the game: On the importance of women's collective actions' in Maud Eduards, Inga Elgquist-Saltzman, Eva Lundren, Christina

Sjoblad, Elisabeth Sundin and Ulla Wikander (eds), *Rethinking Change: Current Swedish Feminist Research*. Stockholm: HSFR.

Eduards, Maud (1997a) 'Introduction', in Gunnel Gustafsson, Maud Eduards and Malin Ronnblom (eds), *Towards a New Democratic Order? Women's Organising in Sweden in the 1990s*. Stockholm: Publica Norstedts Juridik.

Eduards, Maud (1997b) 'The women's shelter movement', in Gunnel Gustafsson, Maud Eduards and Malin Ronnblom (eds), *Towards a New Democratic Order? Women's Organising in Sweden in the 1990s*. Stockholm: Publica Norstedts Juridik.

Edwards, Susan (1989) *Policing 'Domestic' Violence*. London: Sage.

Eisenstadt, Schmuel (ed.) (2002) 'Multiple modernities' in Schmuel Eisenstadt (ed.), *Multiple Modernities*. New Brunswick: Transaction. pp. 1–30.

Eisner, Manuel (2001) 'Modernization, self-control and lethal violence: The long-term dynamics of European homicide rates in theoretical perspective', *British Journal of Criminology*, 41, 618–38.

Elder-Vaas, Dave (2007) 'For emergence', *Journal for the Theory of Social Behaviour*, 37, 1, 25–44.

Eldredge, Niles (1985) *Unfinished Synthesis: Biological Hierarchies and Modern Evolutionary Thought*. Oxford: Oxford University Press.

Eldredge, Niles (1986) *Time Frames: The Rethinking of Darwinian Evolution and the Theory of Punctuated Equilibria*. London: Heinemann.

Electoral Reform Society (2007) *A Brief History of Electoral Reform*. Available at http://www.electoral-reform.org.uk/diary/historylesson.htm (accessed 4 January 2007).

Elias, Norbert (1994) *The Civilizing Process*. Oxford: Blackwell. (Originally published in 1939 as *The History of Manners* and *State Formation and Civilisation*.)

Ellis, Valerie and Ferns, Sue (2000) 'Equality bargaining', in Suzanne Gagnon and Sue Ledwith (eds), *Women, Diversity and Democracy in Trade Unions*. Oxford: Oxford Brookes.

Elson, Diane (ed.) (1991) *Male Bias in the Development Process*. Manchester: Manchester University Press.

Elson, Diane (1995) 'Gender awareness in modeling structural adjustment', *World Development*, 23, 11, 1851–1995.

Emirbayer, Mustafa (1997) 'Manifesto for a relational sociology', *American Journal of Sociology*, 103, 2, 281–317.

Emirbayer, Mustafa and Sheller, Mimi (1998) 'Publics in history', *Theory and Society*, 27, 6, 727–79.

End All Corporal Punishment of Children (2006) *Legality of Corporal Punishment Worldwide*. Available at http://www.endcorporalpunishment.org/pages/frame.html (accessed 10 November 2006).

Engels, Friedrich (1940) *The Origin of the Family, Private Property and the State*. London: Lawrence and Wishart.

England, Kim and Ward, Kevin (eds) (2007) 'Introduction: Reading neoliberalizations', in Kim England and Kevin Ward (eds), *Neoliberalization: States, Networks, Peoples*. Oxford: Blackwell. pp. 1–22.

England, Paula, Farkas, George, Stanek-Kilbourne, Barbara and Dou, Thomas (1988) 'Explaining occupational sex segregation and wages', *American Sociological Review*, 53, 544–58.

Enloe, Cynthia (1983) *Does Khaki Become You? The Militarisation of Women's Lives*. London: Pluto.

Enloe, Cynthia (1989) *Bananas, Beaches and Bases: Making Feminist Sense of International Relations*. London: Pandora.

Epstein, Joshua M. (1999) 'Agent-based computational models and generative social science', *Complexity*, 4, 5, 41–60.

Equalities Review (2007) *Fairness and Freedom: The Final Report of the Equalities Review*. London: The Cabinet Office.

Ersson, Svante and Lane, Jan-Erik (1996) 'Democracy and development: A statistical exploration', in Adrian Leftwich (ed.), *Democracy and Development*. Cambridge: Polity.

Esping-Andersen, Gøsta (1990) *The Three Worlds of Welfare Capitalism*. Cambridge: Polity.

Esping-Andersen, Gøsta (1997) 'Hybrid or unique? The Japanese welfare state between Europe and America', *Journal of European Social Policy*, 7, 3, 179–89.

Esping-Andersen, Gøsta (1999) *Social Foundations of Postindustrial Economies*. Oxford: Oxford University Press.

Esping-Andersen, Gøsta (2002) *Why We Need a New Welfare State*. Oxford: Oxford University Press.

Estevez-Abe, Margarita (2005) 'Gender bias in skills and social policies: The varieties of capitalism perspective on sex segregation', *Social Politics*, 12, 2, 189–215.

Estevez-Abe, Margarita, Iversen, Torben and Soskice, David (2001) 'Social protection and the formation of skills', in Peter Hall and David Soskice (eds), *Varieties of Capitalism*. Oxford: Oxford University Press. pp. 145–83.

Europa (2006) *The History of the European Union*. Available at http://europa.eu/abc/history/index_en.htm (accessed 3 January 2007).

European Commission (1994a) *Sex Equality Legislation in the Member States of the European Community* (by Barry Fitzpatrick, Jeanne Gregory and Erika Szysczak). Brussels: DGV, European Commission.

European Commission (1994b) *Equal Treatment After Maastricht* (by Sacha Prechal and Linda Senden). Brussels: DGV, European Commission.

European Commission (1999) 'Gender Mainstreaming in the European Employment Strategy' (Doc EQOP 61–99 DG EMPL/D/5, 1 October 1999). Brussels: European Commission.

European Commission (2000) *Towards a Community Framework Strategy on Gender Equality (2001–2005)* (Brussels, 7.6.2000, COM (2000) 335 final, 2000/0143 (CNS)).

European Commission (2001) *Employment in Europe 2001: Recent Trends and Prospects*. Brussels: European Commission.

European Commission (2002) *Employment in Europe 2002: Recent Trends and Prospects*. Luxembourg: European Commission.

European Commission (2003) *Council Decision of 22 July 2003 (2003/578/EC) on guidelines for the employment policies of the Member States* (*Official Journal of the European Union* L 197/13, 05.08.2003).

European Commission (2004) Report to the Spring European Council. (Brussels 20.2.2004 COM).

European Commission (2006) *Gender Equality Legislation*. Available at http://ec.europa.eu/employment_social/gender_equality/legislation/index_en.html (accessed 11 June 2006).

European Commission (2007a) *Gender Equality: Legal Acts on Equal Treatment*. Available at http://ec.europa.eu/employment_social/gender_equality/legislation/legalacts_en.html

European Commission (2007b) *Gender Equality: Gender Mainstreaming*. Available at http://ec.europa.eu/employment_social/gender_equality/gender_mainstreaming/general_overview_en.html

European Commission (2007c) *Daphne II Programme to Combat Violence against Children, Young People and Women*. Available at http://ec.europa.eu/justice_home/funding/2004_2007/daphne/funding_daphne_en.htm

European Commission (2007d) *Action Against Discrimination*. Available at http://ec.europa.eu/employment_social/fundamental_rights/legis/legln_en.htm

European Commission (2007e) *Women and Men in Decision Making*. Available at http://ec.europa.eu/employment_social/women_men_stats/out/measures_out438_en.htm (accessed 10 December 2007).

European Commission (2007f) *European Employment Strategy*. Available at http://ec.europa.eu/employment_social/employment_strategy/index_en.htm

European Commission (2008) *Report on Equality Between Women and Men*. Available at http://ec.europa.eu/employment_social/publications/2008/keaj08001_en.pdf

European Industrial Relations Observatory On-Line (2004) *Trade Union Membership 1999–2003*. EIRO. Available at http://www.eiro.eurofound.eu.int/2004/03/update/tn0403105u.html (accessed 27 September 2006).

European Parliament, Directorate General for Research (1994) *Measures to Combat Sexual Harassment at the Workplace: Action taken in the Member States of the European Community* (Working Paper in the Women's Rights Series). Strasbourg: European Parliament.

Eurostat (1997) *Structure of Earnings Survey 1995*. Luxembourg: Eurostat.

Eurostat (2005a) *Technology and Knowledge Intensive Sectors*. Available at http://europa.eu.int/estatref/info/sdds/en/hrst/hrst_sectors.pdf

Eurostat (2005b) *Eurostat Science and Technology Statistics*. Available at http://epp.eurostat.cec.eu.int/portal/page?_pageid=1996,45323734&_dad=portal&_schema=PORTAL&screen=welcomeref&close=/I/I5&language=en&product=Yearlies_new_science_technology&root=Yearlies_new_science_technology&scrollto=295

Eurostat (2008) *Structural Indicators*. Available at http://epp.eurostat.ec.europa.eu/portal/page?_pageid=1133,47800773,1133_47802558&_dad=portal&_schema=PORTAL

Evans, Peter (1995) *Embedded Autonomy: States and Industrial Transformation*. Princeton: Princeton University.

Evans, Peter, Rueschemeyer, Dietrich and Skocpol, Theda (eds) (1985) *Bringing the State Back In*. New York: Cambridge University Press.

Evans, Richard (1977) *The Feminists: Women's Emancipation Movements in Europe, America and Australasia 1840–1920*. London: Croom Helm.

Eve, Raymond, Horsfall, Sara and Lee, Mary (eds) (1997) *Chaos, Complexity and Sociology*. Thousand Oaks, CA: Sage. pp. 79–90.

Eyerman, Ron and Jamieson, Andrew (1991) *Social Movements*. Cambridge: Polity.

Eyerman, Ron and Jamieson, Andrew (1998) *Music and Social Movements*. Cambridge: Cambridge University Press.

Fagan, Colette (2001) 'Time, money and the gender order', *Gender, Work and Organization*, 8, 3, 239–66.

Fahey, Tony (1992) 'Catholicism and industrial society in Ireland', in John Goldthorpe and Christopher Whelan (eds), *The Development of Industrial Society in Ireland*. Oxford: Oxford University/British Academy. pp. 241–63.

Fahey, Tony (1995) 'Privacy and the family', *Sociology*, 29, 4, 687–702.

Fajnzylber, Pablo, Lederman, Daniel and Loayza, Norman (1998) *Determinants of Crime Rates in Latin America and the World*. Washington, DC: World Bank. Available at http://www.worldbank.org/research/conflict/papers/fajnzy.pdf (accessed 16 May).

Farmer, A. and J. Tiefenthaler (1997) 'An economic analysis of domestic violence', *Review of Social Economy*, LV, 3, 337–58.

Farrell, Brian (ed.) (1988) *De Valera's Constitution and Ours*. Dublin: Gill and Macmillan.

Fausto-Sterling, Anne (1985) *Myths of Gender: Biological Theories About Women and Men*. New York: Basic.

von der Fehr, Drude, Jónasdóttir, Anna and Rosenbeck, Bente (eds) (1998) *Is There a Nordic Feminism?* London: UCL.

Felski, Rita (1995) *The Gender of Modernity*. Cambridge, MA: Harvard University.

Felski, Rita (1997) 'The doxa of difference', *Signs*, 23, 1, 1–22.

Ferguson, Niall (2004) *Empire: How Britain Made the Modern World*. London: Penguin.

Ferree, Myra Marx (1980) 'Working class feminism', *Sociological Quarterly*, 21, 173–84.

Ferree, Myra Marx (2000) 'Patriarchies and feminisms: The two women's movements of post-unification Germany', in Barbara Hobson (ed.), *Gender and Citizenship in Transition*. London: Macmillan. pp. 156–72.

Ferree, Myra Marx and Gamson, William (2003) 'The gendering of governance and the governance of gender', in Barbara Hobson (ed.) (2003) *Recognition Struggles and Social Movements*. Cambridge: Cambridge University Press.

Ferree, Myra Marx and Hall, Elaine (1996) 'Rethinking stratification from a feminist perspective: Gender, race and class in mainstream textbooks', *American Sociological Review*, 61, 6, 1–22.

Ferree, Myra Marx and Hess, Beth (1995) *Controversy and Coalition: The New Feminist Movement across Three Decades of Change* (2nd edition). New York: Simon and Schuster/Macmillan.

Ferree, Myra Marx, Gamson, William, Gerhards, Jürgen and Rucht, Dieter (2002a) 'Four models of the public sphere in modern democracies', *Theory and Society*, 31, 289–324.

Ferree, Myra Marx, Gamson, William, Gerhards, Jürgen and Rucht, Dieter (2002b) *Shaping Abortion Discourse: Democracy and the Public Sphere in Germany and the United States*. Cambridge: Cambridge University Press.

Ferreira, Maurizio (1996) 'The "Southern" model of welfare in Social Europe', *Journal of European Social Policy*, 6, 1, 17–37.

Fine, Ben (2001) *Social Capital Versus Social Theory: Political Economy and Social Science at the Turn of the Millennium*. London: Routledge.

Finfacts Ireland (2009) 'Irish house prices to January 2009', *Finfacts Ireland*, January 2009.

Finke, Roger (1992) 'An unsecular America', in Steve Bruce (ed.), *Religion and Modernization*. Oxford: Clarendon Press.

Firebaugh, Glenn (1999) 'Empirics of world income inequality', *American Journal of Sociology*, 104, 6, 1597–630.

Firebaugh, Glenn and Goesling, Brian (2004) 'Accounting for the recent decline in global income inequality', *American Journal of Sociology*, 110, 2, 283–312.

Firestone, Shulamith (1974) *The Dialectic of Sex: The Case for Feminist Revolution*. New York: Morrow.

Fleckenstein, William and Sheelan, Frederick (2008) *Greenspan's Bubbles*. New York: McGraw Hill.

Fleming, P., Harley, B. and Sewell, G. (2004) 'A little knowledge is a dangerous thing: Getting below the surface of the growth of "knowledge work" in Australia', *Work, Employment and Society*, 18, 4, 725–47.

Fligstein, Neil (2001) *The Architecture of Markets*. Princeton, NJ: Princeton University.

Fligstein, Neil and Sweet, Alex (2002) 'Constructing polities and markets: An institutionalist account of European integration', *American Journal of Sociology*, 107, 5, 1206–43.

Flora, Peter and Alber, Jens (1981) 'Modernization, democratization and the development of welfare states in Western Europe', in Peter Flora and Arnold Heidenheimer (eds), *The Development of Welfare States in Europe and America*. London: Transaction.

Flores, Fernando and Gray, John (2000) *Entrepreneurship and the Wired Life : Work in the Wake of Careers*. London: Demos.

Folbre, Nancy (1994) *Who Pays for the Kids? Gender and the Structures of Constraint*. London: Routledge.

Ford, Reuben and Millar, Jane (eds) (1998) *Private Lives and Public Responses: Lone Parenthood and Future Policy in the UK*. London: Policy Studies Institute.

Forsythe, Nancy, Korzeniewicz, Roberto and Durrant, Valerie (2000) 'Gender inequalities and economic growth', *Economic Development and Cultural Change*, 573–617.

Foucault, Michel (1979) *The History of Sexuality: Volume 1*. London: Allen Lane.

Foucault, Michel (1991) 'Governmentality', in Graham Burchell, Colin Gordon and Peter Miller (eds), *The Foucault Effect: Studies in Governmentality*. Chicago: Chicago University. pp. 87–105.

Foucault, Michel (1997) *Discipline and Punish*. London: Penguin.

Fourcade-Gourinchas, Marion and Babb, Sarah (2002) 'The rebirth of the liberal creed', *American Journal of Sociology*, 108, 3, 533–79.

Frank, André Gunder (1975) *On Capitalist Underdevelopment*. New York: Oxford University Press.
Fraser, Nancy (1989) *Unruly Practices*. Cambridge: Polity.
Fraser, Nancy (1997) *Justice Interruptus*. London: Routledge.
Freedom House (2008) *Freedom in the World Country Ratings from 1972 to 2007.* Available at http://www.freedomhouse.org/uploads/FIWAllScores.xls
Freeman, Jo (1975) *The Politics of Women's Liberation*. New York: Longman.
Freeman, Jo and Johnson, Victoria (eds) (1999) *Waves of Protest: Social Movements Since the Sixties*. Lantham, MA: Rowman and Littlefield.
Friedman, Milton (1962) *Capitalism and Freedom*. Chicago: Chicago University.
Fukuyama, Francis (1992) *The End of History and the Last Man*. London: Penguin.
Fung, Archon and Wright, Erik Olin (2001) 'Deepening democracy', *Politics & Society*, 29, 1, 5–41.
Fuss, Diana (1989) *Essentially Speaking*. New York: Routledge.
G20 (2008) *Declaration: Summit on Financial Markets and the World Economy*. Available at http://www.g20.org/Documents/g20_summit_declaration.pdf
Gagnon, Suzanne and Ledwith, Sue (eds) (2000) *Women, Diversity and Democracy in Trade Unions*. Oxford: Oxford Brookes University.
Galbraith, John Kenneth (1975) [1954] *The Great Crash of 1929*. London: Penguin.
Gallie, Duncan (1998) *Restructuring the Employment Relationship*. Oxford: Clarendon.
Galligan, Yvonne (1998) *Women and Politics in Contemporary Ireland: From the Margins to the Mainstream*. London: Pinter.
Gardiner, Jean (1997) *Gender, Care and Economics*. Basingstoke: Macmillan.
Garland, David (2001) *The Culture of Control*. Oxford: Oxford University Press.
Gastil, Raymond (1982) *Freedom in the World*. Westport, CN: Greenwood.
Gatrell, Caroline (2004) *Hard Labour: The Sociology of Parenthood*. Maidenhead: Open University.
Gellner, Ernest (1983) *Nations and Nationalism*. Oxford: Blackwell.
Geneva Centre for the Democratic Control of Armed Forces (2008) *About DCAF*. Available at http://www.dcaf.ch/about/index.cfm?nav1=1
George, Susan (2004) *Another World is Possible If …* London: Verso.
George, Vic (1998) 'Political ideology, globalisation and welfare futures in Europe', *Journal of Social Policy*, 27, 17–36.
Gereffi, Gary and Korzeniewicz, Miquel (1993) *Commodity Chains and Global Capitalism*. Westport, CT: Greenwood.
Gershuny, Jay (2000) *Changing Times*. Oxford: Oxford University Press.
Giddens, Anthony (1984) *The Constitution of Society*. Cambridge: Polity.
Giddens, Anthony (1985) *The Nation-State and Violence*. Cambridge: Polity.
Giddens, Anthony (1990) *The Consequences of Modernity*. Cambridge: Polity.
Giddens, Anthony (1991) *Modernity and Self-Identity*. Cambridge: Polity.
Giddens, Anthony (1992) *The Transformation of Intimacy*. Cambridge: Polity.
Giddens, Anthony (1994) *Beyond Left and Right*. Cambridge: Polity.
Giddens, Anthony (1998) *The Third Way: The Renewal of Social Democracy*. Cambridge: Polity.
Giddens, Anthony (ed.) (2001) *The Global Third Way Debate*. Cambridge: Polity.
Gilbert, Nigel (1995) 'Emergence in social simulation' in Nigel Gilbert and Rosaria Conte (eds), *Artificial Societies*. London: UCL. pp. 144–56.
Gilman, Charlotte Perkins (1966 [1898]) *Women and Economics*. New York: Harper Torchbooks.
Gilroy, Paul (1993) *The Black Atlantic*. London: Verso.
Gladwell, Malcolm (2000) *The Tipping Point*. London: Little, Brown.
Gleick, James (1988) *Chaos: Making a New Science*. London: Heinemann.
Glyn, Andrew (2001) 'Inequalities of employment and wages in OECD countries', *Oxford Bulletin of Economics and Statistics*, 63, special issue, 697–713.

Goffman, Erving (1969) *The Presentation of the Self in Everyday Life*. London: Allen Lane.

Golding, Jacqueline (1999) 'Intimate partner violence as a risk factor for mental disorders: A meta-analysis', *Journal of Family Violence*, 14, 2, 99–132.

Goldstone, Jack (1998) 'Initial conditions, general laws, path dependence, and explanations in historical sociology', *American Journal of Sociology*, 104, 3, 829–45.

Goldthorpe, John (2000) *On Sociology*. Oxford: Oxford University Press.

Goodman, Alissa and Shephard, Andrew (2002) *Inequality and Living Standards in Great Britain* (IFS Briefing Note No. 19). London: Institute for Fiscal Studies.

Gorski, Philip (2000) 'Historicizing the secularization debate', *American Sociological Review*, 65, 138–67.

Gottfried, Heidi (2000) 'Compromising positions: Emergent neo-Fordism and embedded gender contracts', *British Journal of Sociology*, 51, 2, 235–59.

Gottfried, Heidi (2003) 'Temp(t)ing bodies: Shaping gender at work in Japan', *Sociology*, 37, 2, 257–76.

Gottschall, Karin and Kroos, Daniela (2007) 'Self-employment in comparative perspective: General trends and the case of new media', in Sylvia Walby, Heidi Gottfried, Karin Gottschall and Mari Osawa (eds), *Gendering the Knowledge Economy*. London: Palgrave. pp. 163–87.

Gramsci, Antonio (1971) *Selections from the Prison Notebooks of Antonio Gramsci*. London: Lawrence and Wishart.

Graymont, Barbara (1972) *The Iroquois in the American Revolution*. Syracuse, NY: Syracuse University.

Greenspan, Alan (2008) *The Age of Turbulence*. London: Penguin.

Gregory, Derek (2004) *The Colonial Present: Afghanistan, Palestine, Iraq*. Oxford: Blackwell.

Griffin, Larry (1993) 'Narrative, event-structure analysis, and casual interpretation in historical sociology', *American Journal of Sociology*, 98, 5, 1094–133.

Grimshaw, Damian and Rubery, Jill (2002) 'The adjusted gender pay gap: a critical appraisal of standard decomposition techniques' (Group of Experts on Gender and Employment, Equal Opportunities Unit, European Commission). Available at http://www2.umist.ac.uk/management/ewerc/

Grossberg, Lawrence (1996) 'Identity and cultural studies', in Stuart Hall and Paul du Gay (eds), *Questions of Cultural Identity*. London: Sage. pp. 87–107.

Grove, Richard (1996) *Green Imperialism*. Cambridge: Cambridge University Press.

Group of 77 (2007) *About the Group of 77*. Available at http://www.g77.org/doc/

Grown, Caren, Elson, Diane and Çagatay, Nilüfer (2000) 'Introduction', *World Development*, 28, 7, 1145–56.

Guibernau, Montserrat (1999) *Nations Without States*. Cambridge: Polity.

Guibernau, Montserrat (2004) 'Anthony D. Smith on nations and national identity', *Nations and Nationalism*, 10, 1–2, 125–41.

Gurr, T. R. (1981) 'Historical trends in violent crime', *Crime and Justice: An Annual Review of Research*, 3, 295–350.

Gustafsson, Gunnel (1997) 'A cultural perspective on women, politics and democracy', in Gunnel Gustafsson, Maud Eduards and Malin Ronnblom (eds), *Towards a New Democratic Order? Women's Organising in Sweden in the 1990s*. Stockholm: Publica Norstedts Juridik.

Gustafsson, Gunnel, Eduards, Maud and Rönnblom, Malin (eds) (1997) *Towards a New Democratic Order? Women's Organising in Sweden in the 1990s*. Stockholm: Publica Norstedts Juridik.

Haas, Ernst (1958) *The Uniting of Europe: Political, Social, and Economic Forces, 1950–1957*. Stanford: Stanford University.

Haas, Ernst (1964) *Beyond the Nation-State: Functionalism and International Organization*. Stanford: Stanford University.

Haas, Peter (1992) 'Introduction: Epistemic communities and international policy coordination', *International Organization*, 46, 1, 1–35.

Haavio-Manila, Elina (ed.) (1985) *Unfinished Democracy: Women in Nordic Politics*. Oxford: Pergamon.
Habermas, Jürgen (1987 [1981]) *The Theory of Communicative Action: Volume Two: The Critique of Functionalist Reason*. Cambridge: Polity.
Habermas, Jürgen (1989) *The Structural Transformation of the Public Sphere*. Cambridge: Polity.
Habermas, Jürgen (1991 [1981]) *The Theory of Communicative Action: Volume One: Reason and the Rationalization of Society*. Cambridge: Polity.
Habermas, Jürgen (1996) *Between Facts and Norms*. (translated by William Rehg). Cambridge, MA: MIT.
Habermas, Jürgen (2001) *The Postnational Constellation*. Cambridge: Polity.
Hague, Gill and Malos, Ellen (1993) *Domestic Violence: Action for Change*. London: New Clarion.
Haintrais, Linda (1995) *Social Policy in the European Union*. Basingstoke: Macmillan.
Hakim, Catherine (1991) 'Grateful slaves and self-made women', *European Sociological Review*, 7, 2, 101–21.
Hall, Peter and Soskice, David (eds) (2001) *Varieties of Capitalism: The Institutional Foundations of Comparative Advantage*. Oxford: Oxford University Press.
Hall, Stuart (1996) 'Introduction: Who needs identity?', in Stuart Hall and Paul du Gay (eds), *Questions of Cultural Identity*. London: Sage.
Hallstein, Walter (1973 [1969]) *Europe in the Making*. New York: Norton.
Halpern, David (2001) 'Moral values, social trust and inequality: Can values explain crime?', *Journal of British Criminology*, 41, 236–51.
Handy, Charles (1994) *The Empty Raincoat*. London: Hutchinson.
Hancké, Bob and Rhodes, Martin (2005) 'EMU and labor market institutions in Europe: The rise and fall of national social pacts', *Work and Occupations*, 32, 2, 196–228.
Hanmer, Jalna and Griffiths, Sue (1998) *Domestic Violence and Repeat Victimisation* (Police Research Group Briefing Note No. 1/98). London: The Home Office.
Hanmer, Jalna, Radford, Jill and Stanko, Elizabeth (eds) (1989) *Women, Policing and Male Violence*. London: Routledge.
Haraway, Donna (1988) 'Situated knowledges', *Feminist Studies*, 14, 3, 575–99.
Haraway, Donna (1989) *Primate Visions*. London: Routledge.
Haraway, Donna (1990) 'A manifesto for cyborgs', in Linda Nicholson (ed.), *Feminism/Postmodernism*. London: Routledge. pp. 190–233.
Haraway, Donna (1997) *Modest_Witness@Second_Millennium.FemaleMan_MeetsOncomouse*. New York: Routledge.
Hardacre, Helen (1993) 'The impact of fundamentalism on women, the family, and interpersonal relations', in Martin Marty and Appleby Scott (eds), *Fundamentalisms and Society*. Chicago: Chicago University.
Harding, Sandra (1986) *The Science Question in Feminism*. Ithaca, NY: Cornell University.
Hardt, Michael and Negri, Antonio (2000) *Empire*. Cambridge, MA: Harvard University.
Hardt, Michael and Negri, Antonio (2006) *Multitude: War and Democracy in the Age of Empire*. London: Penguin.
Harris, Jerry (2002) 'The US military in the era of globalisation', *Race and Class*, 44, 2, 1–22.
Harris, Jerry (2005) 'The military-industrial complex in transnational class theory', in Richard Appelbaum and William Robinson (eds), *Critical Globalization Studies*. New York: Routledge.
Harris, Jessica and Grace, Sharon (1999) *A Question of Evidence? Investigating and Prosecuting Rape in the 1990s* (HORS 196). London: The Home Office.
Hartmann, Heidi (1976) 'Capitalism, patriarchy and job segregation by sex', *Signs*, 1, 137–70.
Harvey, David (1989) *The Condition of Postmodernity*. Oxford: Blackwell.
Harvey, David (2003) *The New Imperialism*. Oxford: Oxford University Press.

Harvey, David (2005) *A Brief History of Neoliberalism*. Oxford: Oxford University Press.
Haseler, Stephen (2008) *Meltdown*. London: Forumpress.
Hawkesworth, Mary (1997) 'Confounding gender', *Signs*, 22, 3, 649–85.
Haxton, Eva and Olsson, Claes (eds) (1999) *Gender Focus on the WTO*. Uppsala, Sweden: Global Publications Foundation.
Haydu, Jeffrey (1998) 'Making use of the past', *American Journal of Sociology*, 104, 2, 339–71.
Hayek, Friedrich von (1960) *The Constitution of Liberty*. London: Routledge and Kegan Paul.
Health, United States (2004) Available at http://www.cdc.gov/nchs/data/hus/hus04 trend.pdf#027 (accessed 9 February 2005).
Hearn, Jeff (1998) *The Violences of Men*. London: Sage.
Hedlund, Gun (1998) 'Women's interests in local politics', in Kathleen Jones and Anna Jónasdóttir (eds), *The Political Interests of Gender*. London: Sage.
Heelas, Paul and Woodhead, Linda (with Benjamin Seel, Karin Tusting and Bron Szerszynski) (2004) *The Spiritual Revolution*. Oxford: Blackwell.
Heise, Lori (1996) 'Violence against women', in Jeffrey Edleson and Zvi Eisikovits (eds), *Future Interventions with Battered Women and their Families*. London: Sage.
Heiskanen, Markku and Piispa, Minna (1998) *Faith, Hope, Battering – A Survey of Men's Violence against Women in Finland*. Yliopistopaino, Helsinki: Statistics Finland.
Held, David (1995) *Democracy and the Global Order*. Cambridge: Polity.
Held, David (2004) *Global Covenant: The Social Democratic Alternative to the Washington Consensus*. Cambridge: Polity.
Held, David and McGrew, Anthony (2002) *Globalization/Anti-Globalization*. Cambridge: Polity.
Held, David, McGrew, Anthony, Goldblatt, David and Perraton, Jonathan (1999) *Global Transformations*. Cambridge: Polity.
Helie-Lucas, Anne-Aimee (1994) 'The preferential symbol for Islamic identity: Women in Muslim personal laws', in Valentine Moghadam (ed.), *Identity Politics and Women*. Boulder, CO: Westview.
Hernes, Holga (1987) *Welfare State and Women Power*. Oslo: Norwegian University.
Herrigel, Gary (2005) 'Institutionalists at the limits of institutionalism', *Socio-Economic Review*, 3, 559–67.
Hester, Marianne and Westmarland, Nicole (2005) *Tackling Domestic Violence* (HORS 290). London: The Home Office.
Hettne, Bjorn, Inotai, Andras and Sunkel, Osvaldo (eds) (1999) *Globalism and the New Regionalism. Volume I*. Basingstoke: Macmillan.
Hicks, Alexander and Kenworthy, Lane (2003) 'Varieties of welfare capitalism', *Socio-Economic Review*, 1, 27–61.
Hicks, Stephen and Palmer, Tom (2004) 'Trade union membership: estimates from the autumn 2003 Labour Force Survey', *Labour Market Trends*, March, 99–101.
HighBeam Research (2007) *The Death Penalty Worldwide*. Available at http://www.infoplease.com/ipa/A0777460.html (accessed 20 March 2008).
Himmelweit, Susan (1999) 'Caring labour', *Annals of the American Academy of Political Science*, 561, 1, 27–38.
Himmelweit, Susan (2002) 'Making visible the hidden economy: the case for gender impact assessment of economic policy', *Feminist Economics*, 8, 1, 49–70.
Hirdmann, Yvonne (1994) *Women – From Possibility to Problem? Gender Conflict in the Welfare State – The Swedish Model* (Research Report No. 3). Stockholm, Sweden: Arbetslivcentrum.
Hirst, Paul and Thompson, Grahame (1996) *Globalization in Question*. Cambridge: Polity.
Hirst, Paul and Zeitlin, Jonathan (1997) 'Flexible specialization', in J. Rogers Hollingsworth and Robert Boyer (eds), *Contemporary Capitalism*. Cambridge: Cambridge University Press. pp. 220–39.

Hobcraft, John (1987) 'The proximate determinants of fertility', in John Cleland and Chris Scott (eds), *The World Fertility Survey*. Oxford: Oxford University Press, pp. 796–837.

Hobsbawm, Eric and Ranger, Terence (eds) (1983) *The Invention of Tradition*. Cambridge: Cambridge University Press.

Hobson, Barbara (1994) 'Solo mothers, social policy regimes, and the logics of gender', in Diane Sainsbury (ed.), *Gendering Welfare States*. London: Sage.

Hobson, Barbara (ed.) (2000) *Gender and Citizenship in Transition*. London: Macmillan.

Hobson, Barbara (ed.) (2003) *Recognition Struggles and Social Movements*. Cambridge: Cambridge University Press.

Hochschild, Arlie (1997) *The Time-Bind*. New York: Henry Holt.

Hochschild, Arlie (2000) 'The nanny chain', *The American Prospect*, 11, 4, (available at http://www.prospect.org/print/V11/4/hochschild-a.html and accessed 26 May 2006).

Holland, Janet, Weeks, Jeffrey and Gillies, Val (2003) 'Families, intimacy and social capital', *Social Policy and Society*, 2, 4, 339–48.

Holland, John (1995) *Hidden Order: How Adaptation Builds Complexity*. Reading, MA: Addison-Wesley.

Holland, John (2000) *Emergence: From Chaos to Order*. Oxford: Oxford University Press.

Holli, Anne Maria (1997) 'On equality and Trojan horses', *European Journal of Women's Studies*, 4, 2, 133–64.

Hollingsworth, J. Rogers (1997) 'Continuities and change in social systems of production: The cases of Japan, Germany, and the United States', in J. Rogers Hollingsworth and Robert Boyer (eds), *Contemporary Capitalism*. Cambridge: Cambridge University Press. pp. 265–310.

Holmwood, John (2001) 'Gender and critical realism', *Sociology*, 35, 4, 947–65.

Honneth, Axel (1996) *The Struggle for Recognition*. Cambridge: Polity.

Hopkins, Kathryn (2009) 'US house prices continue to plunge', *Guardian*, 27 January 2009.

Horton, Susan (ed.) (1996) *Women and Industrialization in Asia*. London: Routledge.

Hoskyns, Catherine (1996) *Integrating Gender: Women, Law and Politics in the European Union*. London: Verso.

Hoyle, Carolyn and Sanders, Andrew (2000) 'Police response to domestic violence', *British Journal of Criminology*, 40, 14–36.

Huber, Evelyne and Stephens, John D. (2000) 'Partisan governance, women's employment, and the social democratic service state', *American Sociological Review*, 65, 323–42.

Huber, Evelyne and Stephens, John D. (2001) *Development and Crisis of the Welfare State: Parties and Policies in Global Markets*. Chicago: Chicago University.

Huda, Sigma (2006) *Report of the Special Rapporteur on the Human Rights Aspects of the Trafficking in Persons, Especially Women and Children*. (United Nations Commission on Human Rights. E/CN.4/2006/62). Available at http://daccessdds.un.org/doc/UNDOC/GEN/G06/109/64/PDF/G0610964.pdf?OpenElement (accessed 9 June 2006).

Human Rights Watch (2006) *Women's Rights: Sexual Autonomy*. Available at http://hrw.org/women/autonomy.html (accessed 3 July 2006).

Humphries, Jane (1998) 'Towards a family-friendly economics', *New Political Economy*, 3, 2, 223–40.

Huntington, Samuel (1998) *The Clash of Civilizations and the Remaking of the World Order*. London: Touchstone.

Hussain, Yasmin and Bagguley, Paul (2005) 'Citizenship, ethnicity and identity: British Pakistanis after the 2001 "Riots"', *Sociology*, 39, 3, 407–25.

Hutchings, Kimberly (1997) 'Moral deliberation and political judgement', *Theory, Culture and Society*, 14, 1, 131–42.

Hutton, Will (2003) *The World We're In*. London: Abacus.

Huws, Ursula, Jager, Nick and O'Regan, Siobhan (1999) *Teleworking and Globalisation*. (Institute of Employment Studies Report 358). London: IES.

Ibrahim, Saad Eddin (1980) 'Anatomy of Egypt's militant Islamic groups', *International Journal of Middle East Studies*, 12, 4, 423–53.

IDEA (2005) *Global Database of Quotas for Women*. International IDEA (Institute for Democracy and Electoral Assistance) and Stockholm University. Available at http://www.quotaproject.org/country.cfm (accessed 17 May 2005).

Illner, Michal (1999) 'Second thoughts on the transformation in Eastern and Central Europe', in Thomas Boye, Bart van Steenbergen and Sylvia Walby (eds), *European Societies: Fusion or Fission?* London: Routledge. pp. 234–45.

Inglehart, Ronald (1997) *Modernization and Postmodernization*. Princeton: Princeton University.

Inglehart, Ronald and Norris, Pippa (2000) 'The developmental theory of the gender gap', *International Political Science Review*, 21, 4, 441–63.

Inglehart, Ronald and Norris, Pippa (2003) *Rising Tide: Gender Equality and Cultural Change around the World*. Cambridge: Cambridge University Press.

Inglis, Tom (1987) *Moral Monopoly: The Catholic Church in Modern Irish Society*. Dublin: Mill and Macmillan.

Institute for National Strategic Studies (2008) *INSS Research and Analysis*. Available at http://www.ndu.edu/inss/research/inss_research.htm

Intergovernmental Panel on Climate Change (IPCC) (2007) *Climate Change 2007*. Available at http://www.ipcc.ch/

International Labour Office (ILO) (2005) *A Global Alliance Against Forced Labour*. Geneva: ILO.

International Monetary Fund (2007) 'What the IMF does'. Available at http://www.imf.org/external/work.htm

Inter-Parliamentary Union (1995) *Women in Parliaments: 1945–1995*. Geneva: Inter-Parliamentary Union.

Inter-Parliamentary Union (1997) *Men and Women in Politics: Democracy Still in the Making: A World Comparative Survey*. Geneva: Inter-Parliamentary Union.

Inter-Parliamentary Union (2003) *Women in Regional Parliamentary Assemblies*. Available at http://www.ipu.org/wmn-e/regions.htm

Inter-Parliamentary Union (2008) *Women in National Parliaments*. Available at http://www.ipu.org/wmn-e/classif.htm

Irish Family Planning Association (2007) *Abortion Law in Ireland*. Available at http://www.ifpa.ie/abortion/hist.html

Ironmonger, Duncan (2001) *Household Production and the Household Economy* (Research Paper). Melbourne: University of Melbourne, Department of Economics.

Irwin, Sarah (2005) *Reshaping Social Life*. London: Routledge.

Iversen, Torben (2001) 'Dynamics of welfare state expansion', in Paul Pierson (ed.), *The New Politics of the Welfare State*. Oxford: Oxford University. pp. 45–79.

Jackson, Pauline (1993) 'Managing the mothers: the case of Ireland', in Jane Lewis (ed.), *Women and Social Policies in Europe*. Aldershot: Edward Elgar.

Jackson, Stevi (1999) *Heterosexuality in Question*. London: Sage.

Jacobs, Sheila (1995) 'Changing patterns of sex segregated occupations throughout the life-course', *European Sociological Review*, 11, 2, 157–71.

Jacobs, Susie, Jacobson, Ruth and Marchbank, Jennifer (eds) (2000) *States of Conflict: Gender, Violence and Resistance*. London: Zed.

Jacobson, Gary (1978) 'The effects of campaign spending', *American Political Science Review*, 72, 2, 469–91.

Jacobus, Mary, Keller, Evelyn Fox and Shuttleworth, Sally (eds) (1990) *Body/Politics: Women and the Discourses of Science*. New York: Routledge.

Jakobsen, Janet (1998) *Working Alliances and the Politics of Difference*. Bloomington: Indiana University.

Jamieson, Lynn (1998) *Intimacy: Personal Relationships in Modern Societies*. Cambridge: Polity.

Jayawardena, Kumari (ed.) (1986) *Feminism and Nationalism in the Third World*. London: Zed.

Jenson, Jane (1997) 'Who cares? Gender and welfare regimes', *Social Politics*, 4, 2, 182–7.
Jervis, Robert (1997) *System Effects: Complexity in Political and Social Life*. Princeton: Princeton University.
Jessop, Bob (1999) 'The changing governance of welfare', *Social Policy and Administration*, 33, 4, 348–59.
Jessop, Bob (2002) *The Future of the Capitalist State*. Cambridge: Polity.
Jessop, Bob and Sum, Ngai-Ling (2006) *Beyond the Regulation Approach*. Cheltenham: Edward Elgar.
Johnson, Chalmers (2000) *Blowback: The Costs and Consequences of American Empire*. London: Little, Brown.
Johnson, Holly (1996) *Dangerous Domains – Violence Against Women in Canada*. Canada: Nelson Canada.
Johnson, Michael (1995) 'Patriarchal terrorism and common couple violence', *Journal of Marriage and the Family*, 57, 283–94.
Johnson, Michael and Leone, Janel (2005) 'The differential effects of intimate terrorism and situational couple violence', *Journal of Family Issues*, 26, 3, 322–49.
Jónasdóttir, Anna (1991) *Love, Power and Political Interests*. Örebro: University of Örebro, Sweden.
Jones, Kathleen and Jónasdóttir, Anna (eds) (1988) *The Political Interests of Gender*. London: Sage.
Joshi, Heather and Paci, Periella (1998) *Unequal Pay for Women and Men*. Cambridge, MA: MIT Press.
Juhn, Chinhui, Murphy, Kevin and Pierce, Brooks (1991) 'Accounting for the slow-down in Black-White wage convergence', in M. Kosters (ed.), *Workers and Their Wages*. Washington, DC: AEI.
Kaldor, Mary (2006) *New and Old Wars* (2nd edition). Cambridge: Polity.
Kalmuss, Debra and Straus, Murray (1982) 'Wife's marital dependency and wife abuse', *Journal of Marriage and the Family*, 44, 2, 277–86.
Kandiyoti, Deniz (ed.) (1991) *Women, Islam and the State*. Basingstoke: Macmillan.
Kanter, Rosabeth Moss (1977) 'Some effects of proportions of group life: skewed sex ratios and response to token women', *American Journal of Sociology*, 82, 965–90.
Kapteyn, Paul (1996) *The Stateless Market*. London: Routledge.
Karam, Azza (ed.) (1998) *Women in Parliament: Beyond Numbers*. Sweden: International IDEA. Available at http://archive.idea.int/women/parl/ (accessed 17 May 2005).
Karlsson, Gunnel (1998) 'Social democratic women's coup in the Swedish parliament', in Drude von der Fehr, Anna Jónasdóttir and Bente Rosenbeck (eds), *Is There a Nordic Feminism?* London: UCL.
Karvonen, Lauri and Selle, Per (eds) (1995) *Women in Nordic Politics*. Aldershot: Dartmouth.
Kauffman, Stuart (1993) *The Origins of Order: Self-Organization and Selection in Evolution*. Oxford: Oxford University.
Kauffman, Stuart (1995) *At Home in the Universe: The Search for Laws of Self-Organization and Complexity*. London: Viking.
Keane, John (2003) *Global Civil Society?* Cambridge: Cambridge University Press.
Kearney, Richard (1997) *Postnationalist Ireland*. London: Routledge.
Keating, Michael (2002) *Plurinational Democracy: Stateless Nations in a Post-Sovereignty Era*. Oxford: Oxford University.
Keck, Margaret and Sikkink, Kathryn (1998) *Activists Beyond Borders: Advocacy Networks in International Politics*. Ithaca: Cornell University.
Kedourie, Elie (1966) *Nationalism* (3rd edition). London: Hutchinson.
Keller, Evelyn Fox (1985) *Reflections on Gender and Science*. New Haven: Yale University.
Kelly, John and Kaplan, Martha (2007) 'Nation and decolonization: Toward a new anthropology of nationalism', *Anthropological Theory*, 1, 4, 419–37.
Kelly, Liz (1997) *Final Report of the Activities of EG-S-VL Including a Plan of Action for Combating Violence Against Women*. Strasbourg: Council of Europe.

Kelly, Liz, Bindel, Julie, Burton, Sheila, et al. (1999) *Domestic Violence Matters: An Evaluation of a Development Project*. London: Home Office.

Kelly, Liz, Lovett, Jo and Regan, Linda (2005) *A Gap or a Chasm? Attrition in Reported Rape Cases* (HORS 293). London: Home Office.

Kenny, Mary (1997) *Goodbye to Catholic Ireland*. London: Sinclair-Stevenson.

Kenworthy, Lane (2004) *Egalitarian Capitalism*. New York: Russell Sage.

Kenworthy, Lane and Malami, Melissa (1999) 'Gender inequality in political representation: A worldwide comparative analysis', *Social Forces*, 78, 1, 235–69. (Data set at http://www.u.arizona.edu/~lkenwor/sf99-gender.htm)

Keohane, Robert (1989) *International Institutions and State Power*. Boulder, Co: Westview.

Kerr, Clark, Dunlop, John T., Harbison, Frederick H. and Myers, Charles A. (1960) *Industrialism and Industrial Man*. Cambridge, MA: Harvard University.

Kiely, Ray (2005) *The Clash of Globalisations*. Lieden: Brill.

Kilbourne, Barbara Stanek, England, Paula, Farkas, George et al. (1994) 'Returns to skill, compensating differentials, and gender bias', *American Journal of Sociology*, 100, 3, 689–719.

Kirby, Peadar (2006) *Vulnerability and Violence: The Impact of Globalization*. London: Pluto.

Kiser, Edgar (1996) 'The revival of narrative in historical sociology', *Politics and Society*, 24, 3, 249–71.

Kiser, Edgar and Hechter, Michael (1991) 'The role of general theory in comparative-historical sociology', *American Journal of Sociology*, 97, 1, 1–30.

Kitschelt, Herbert (1986) 'Political opportunity structures and political protest', *British Journal of Political Science*, 16, 1, 57–85.

Kitschelt, Herbert (1994) *The Transformation of European Social Democracy*. Cambridge: Cambridge University Press.

Kitschelt, Herbert, Lange, Peter, Marks, Gary and Stephens, John (eds) (1999) *Continuity and Change in Contemporary Capitalism*. Cambridge: Cambridge University Press.

Klasen, Stephan (2002) 'Low schooling for girls, slower growth for all? Cross-country evidence on the effect of gender inequality in education on economic development', *The World Bank Economic Review*, 16, 3, 345–73.

Klein, Naomi (1999) *No Logo*. New York: Picador.

Klein, Naomi (2007) *The Shock Doctrine: The Rise of Disaster Capitalism*. London: Allen Lane.

Knodt, Eva (1995) 'Foreword' to Niklas Luhmann, *Social Systems*. Stanford: Stanford University.

Knutsen, Oddbjørn (2001) 'Social class, sector employment, and gender as party cleavages in the Scandinavian countries', *Scandinavian Political Studies*, 24, 4, 311–50.

Koonz, Claudia (1988) *Mothers in the Fatherland*. London: Methuen.

Korpi, Walter (1983) *The Democratic Class Struggle*. London: Routledge and Kegan Paul.

Korpi, Walter (2000) 'Faces of inequality: Gender, class, and patterns of inequalities in different types of welfare states', *Social Politics: International Studies in Gender, State, and Society*, 7, 2, 127–91.

Korpi, Walter (2002) 'The great trough in unemployment', *Politics and Society*, 30, 365–426.

Korpi, Walter (2003) 'Welfare-state regress in Western Europe', *Annual Review of Sociology*, 29, 589–609.

Korzeniewicz, Roberto and Moran, Timothy (1997) 'World-economic trends in the distribution of income, 1965–1992', *American Journal of Sociology*, 102, 4, 1000–39.

Koza, Mitchell and Lewin, Arie (1998) 'The co-evolution of strategic alliances', *Organization Science*, 9, 3, 255–64.

Krasner, Stephen (ed.) (1983) *International Regimes*. Ithaca: Cornell University.

Krasner, Stephen (1995) 'Compromising Westphalia', *International Security*, 20, 3, 115–51.

Krug, Etienne, Dahlberg, Linda, Mercy, James, Zwi, Anthony and Lozano, Rafael (2002) *World Report on Violence and Health*. Geneva: World Health Organization.
Krugman, Paul (2008) *The Return of Depression Economics and the Crisis of 2008*. London: Penguin.
Kuhn, Thomas (1979) *The Structure of Scientific Revolutions*. Chicago: Chicago University.
Kumar, Krishan (2000) 'Nation and empire', *Theory and Society*, 29, 575–608.
Kumar, Krishan (2005) *From Post-Industrial to Post-Modern Society*. Oxford: Blackwell.
Kurzer, Paulette (1997) 'Decline or preservation of executive capacity?' *Journal of Common Market Studies*, 35, 1, 31–56.
Kuznets, Simon (1955) 'Economic growth and income inequality', *American Economic Review*, 45, 1, 1–28.
Kymlicka, Will (1991) *Liberalism, Community and Culture*. Oxford: Clarendon.
Kymlicka, Will (1995) *Multicultural Citizenship: A Liberal Theory of Minority Rights*. Oxford: Clarendon.
Kyoto Protocol (1997) *Kyoto Protocol to the United Nations Framework Convention on Climate Change*. Available at http://unfccc.int/resource/docs/convkp/kpeng.html
Labour Party (2006) *History of the Labour Party*. Available at http://www.labour.org.uk/labourhistory (accessed 4 January 2007).
Laclau, Ernesto and Mouffe, Chantal (1985) *Hegemony and Socialist Strategy*. London: Verso.
Lakatos, Imre and Musgrave, Alan (1970) *Criticism and the Growth of Knowledge*. Cambridge: Cambridge University Press.
Lam, Alice (2002) 'Alternative societal models of learning and innovation in the knowledge economy', *International Social Science Journal*, 54, 171, 67–82.
Landes, Joan (1998) *Women and the Public Sphere in the Age of the French Revolution*. Ithaca: Cornell University.
Larkin, Emmet (1975) *The Roman Catholic Church and the Creation of the Modern Irish State 1878–1886*. Dublin: Gill and Macmillan.
Larkin, Emmet (1978) *The Roman Catholic Church and the Plan of Campaign in Ireland, 1886–1888*. Cork: Cork University.
Larkin, Emmet (1987) *The Consolidation of the Roman Catholic Church in Ireland, 1860–1870*. Dublin: Gill and Macmillan.
Larkin, Emmet (1990) *The Roman Catholic Church and the Home Rule Movement in Ireland 1870–1874*. Dublin: Gill and Macmillan.
Lash, Scott and Urry, John (1987) *The End of Organized Capitalism*. Cambridge: Polity.
Lash, Scott and Urry, John (1994) *Economies of Signs and Space*. London: Sage.
Lash, Scott, Wynne, Brian and Szerszynki, Bronislav (eds) (1995) *Risk, Environment and Modernity: Towards a New Ecology*. London: Sage.
Latour, Bruno (1987) *Science in Action: How to Follow Scientists and Engineers Through Society*. Milton Keynes: Open University Press.
Latour, Bruno (1988) *The Pasteurization of France*. Cambridge, MA: Harvard University.
Latour, Bruno (1991) 'Technology is society made durable', in John Law (ed.), *A Sociology of Monsters: Essays on Power, Technology and Domination*. London: Routledge.
Latour, Bruno (1993) *We Have Never Been Modern*. Cambridge, MA: Harvard University.
Latour, Bruno and Woolgar, Steve (1979) *Laboratory Life: The Social Construction of Scientific Facts*. London: Sage.
Law, John (ed.) (1991) *A Sociology of Monsters*. London: Routledge.
Layard, Richard (2005) *Happiness: Lessons from a New Science*. London: Allen Lane.
Lea, John and Young, Jock (1984) *What is to be Done about Law and Order?* Harmondsworth: Penguin.
Lechner, Frank and Boli, John (2005) *World Culture: Origins and Consequences*. Malden, MA: Blackwell.
Ledwith, Sue and Colgan, Fiona (2000) 'Women, democracy and diversity and the new trade unionism', in Suzanne Gagnon and Sue Ledwith (eds), *Women, Diversity and Democracy in Trade Unions*. Oxford: Oxford Brookes.

Lee, David (1999) 'Wage inequality in the United States during the 1980s', *The Quarterly Journal of Economics*, 114, 3, 977–1023.
Lee, J.J. (1989) *Ireland 1912–1985*. Cambridge: Cambridge University Press.
Lees, Sue (1996) *Carnal Knowledge: Rape on Trial*. London: Hamish Hamilton.
Leftwich, Adrian (ed.) (1996) *Democracy and Development Theory*. Cambridge: Polity.
Leftwich, Adrian (2000) *States of Development: On the Primacy of Politics in Development*. Cambridge: Polity.
Leibfried, Stephan (1993) 'Towards a European welfare state?', in Catherine Jones (ed.), *New Perspectives on the Welfare State in Europe*. London: Routledge.
Leibfried, Stephan and Pierson, Paul (eds) (1995) *European Social Policy*. Washington, DC: Brookings.
Leitner, Sigrid (2003) 'Varieties of familialism', *European Societies*, 5, 4, 353–75.
Lenton, Rhonda (1995) 'Power versus feminist theories of wife abuse', *Canadian Journal of Criminology*, July, 305–30.
Lewis, Jane (1992) 'Gender and the development of welfare regimes', *Journal of European Social Policy*, 3, 159–73.
Lewis, Jane (ed.) (1993) *Women and Social Policies in Europe: Work, Family and the State*. Aldershot: Edward Elgar.
Lewis, Jane (2002) 'Gender and welfare state change', *European Societies*, 4, 4, 331–57.
Lewis, Ruth (2004) 'Making justice work: Effective legal interventions for domestic violence', *British Journal of Criminology*, 44, 204–24.
Liddington, Jill and Norris, Jill (1978) *One Hand Tied Behind Us: The Rise of the Women's Suffrage Movement*. London: Virago.
Liebowitz, S.J. and Stephen Margolis (1995) 'Path dependence, lock-in, and history', *The Journal of Law, Economics, and Organization*, 11, 1, 205–26.
Lindblom, Anders (2001) 'Dismantling the social democratic welfare model?', *Scandinavian Political Studies*, 24, 3, 171–93.
Lipset, Seymour Martin (1959) 'Some requisites of democracy: Economic development and political legitimacy', *American Sociological Review*, 53, 69–105.
Lipset, Seymour Martin (1960) *Political Man*. New York: Doubleday.
Lipset, Seymour Martin and Marks, Gary (2000) *It Didn't Happen Here: Why Socialism Failed in the United States*. New York: Norton.
Lister, Ruth (1997) *Citizenship: Feminist Perspectives*. Basingstoke: Macmillan.
Lister, Ruth (1998) 'From equality to social inclusion: New Labour and the welfare state', *Critical Social Policy*, 18, 215–25.
Lloyd, S. (1997) 'The effects of domestic violence on women's employment', *Law and Policy*, 19, 2, 139–67.
Lockwood, David (1992) *Solidarity and Schism: "The Problem of Disorder" in Durkheimian and Marxist Sociology*. Oxford: Clarendon.
Logan, John (2006) 'The union avoidance industry in the United States', *British Journal of Industrial Relations*, 44, 4, 651–75.
López, José and Scott, John (2000) *Social Structure*. Buckingham: Open University.
Lorber, Judith (2000) 'Using gender to undo gender: a feminist degendering movement', *Feminist Theory*, 1, 1, 79–95.
Lorber, Judith (2005) *Breaking the Bowls: Degendering and Feminist Change*. New York: Norton.
Lorgelly, Paula and Owen, P. Dorian (1999) 'The effect of female and male schooling on economic growth in the Barro-Lee model', *Empirical Economics*, 24, 537–57.
Lovenduski, Joni (ed.) (2005) *State Feminism and Political Representation*. Cambridge: Cambridge University Press.
Luddy, Maria (1995a) *Women and Philanthropy in Nineteenth Century Ireland*. Cambridge: Cambridge University Press.

Luddy, Maria (1995b) *Women in Ireland 1800–1918*. Cork: Cork University.
Luhmann, Niklas (1985) *A Sociological Theory of Law*. London: Routledge and Kegan Paul.
Luhmann, Niklas (1990) 'The autopoiesis of social systems', in Niklas Luhmann (ed.), *Essays on Self-Reference*. New York: Columbia University.
Luhmann, Niklas (1995) *Social Systems*. Stanford: Stanford University.
Luhmann, Niklas (2000) *Art as a Social System*. Stanford: Stanford University.
Lundgren, Eva (1992) 'The hand that strikes and comforts', in Maud Eduards, Inga Elgquist-Saltzman, Eva Lundren, Christina Sjoblad, Elisabeth Sundin and Ulla Wikander (eds), *Rethinking Change: Current Swedish Feminist Research*. Stockholm: HSFR.
Lundgren, Eva, Heimer, Gun, Westerstrand, Jenny and Kalliokoski, Anne-Marie (2001) *Slagen Dam: Mäns Våmot Kvinnor I Jämställda Sverige – en Omfåsngsundersökning*. Stockholm: Fritzes Offenentliga Publikationer.
Lykke, Nina (2004) 'Between particularism, universalism and transversalism', *NORA: Nordic Journal of Women's Studies*, 12, 2, 72–82.
Lyotard, Jean-Francois (1978) *The Postmodern Condition*. Minneapolis: University of Minneapolis.
MacKinnon, Catharine (1989) *Toward a Feminist Theory of the State*. Cambridge, MA: Harvard University.
Macnaghten, Philip and Urry, John (1998) *Contested Natures*. London: Sage.
Macpherson, William (1999) *The Stephen Lawrence Inquiry* (Cmnd 4262–1). London: HMSO.
Maddison, Angus (2003) *The World Economy: Historical Statistics*. Paris: OECD.
Mahon, Rianne (1997) 'Child care in Canada and Sweden', *Social Politics*, 4, 3, 382–418.
Mahon, Rianne (2002) 'Child care: Toward what kind of "Social Europe"?', *Social Politics*, 9, 3, 343–79.
Mahoney, James (2000) 'Path dependency in historical sociology', *Theory and Society*, 29, 507–48.
Malos, Ellen (ed.) (1980) *The Politics of Housework*. London: Allison and Busby.
Maidment, Richard (1997) 'Democracy in the USA since 1945' in David Potter, David Goldblatt, Margaret Kiloh and Paul Lewis (eds), *Democratization*. Cambridge: Polity. pp. 118–38.
Majone, Giandomenico (1996) *Regulating Europe*. London: Routledge.
Majone, Giandomenico (1998) 'Europe's "democratic deficit": The question of standards', *European Law Journal*, 4, 1, 5–28.
Mandelbrot, Benoit (1982) *The Fractal Geometry of Nature*. San Francisco, CA: W.H. Freeman.
Mann, Michael (1986) *The Sources of Social Power: Volume 1: A History of Power from the Beginning to A.D. 1760*. Cambridge: Cambridge University Press.
Mann, Michael (1993a) *The Sources of Social Power: Volume II: The Rise of Classes and Nation-states, 1760–1914*. Cambridge: Cambridge University Press.
Mann, Michael (1993b) 'Nation-states in Europe and other continents: diversifying, developing, not dying', *Daedalus: Journal of the American Academy of Arts and Sciences*, 122, 3, 115–40.
Mann, Michael (1997) 'Has globalization ended the rise and rise of the nation-state?', *Review of International Political Economy*, 4, 3, 472–96.
Mann, Michael (2003) *Incoherent Empire*. London: Verso.
Mann, Michael (2004) *Fascists*. Cambridge: Cambridge University Press.
Mann, Michael (2005) *The Dark Side of Democracy: Explaining Ethnic Cleansing*. Cambridge: Cambridge University Press.
Mann, Michael and Riley, Dylan (2006) 'Explaining macro-regional trends in global income inequalities, 1950–2000', *Socio-Economic Review*, 5, 1, 81–115.
Mansfield, Edward and Snyder, Jack (1995) 'Democratization and war', *Foreign Affairs*, 74, 3, 79–97.
Manza, Jeff (2000) 'Race and the underdevelopment of the American welfare state', *Theory and Society*, 29, 819–32.

Manza, Jeff and Brooks, Clem (1998) 'The gender gap in US Presidential elections', *American Journal of Sociology*, 103, 5, 1235–66.
Manza, Jeff and Brooks, Clem (1999) *Social Cleavages and Political Change*. Oxford: Oxford University Press.
Markoff, John (1996) *Waves of Democracy*. Pine Forge.
Marshall, T. H. (1950) *Citizenship and Social Class*. Cambridge: Cambridge University Press.
Martin, Emily (1987) *The Woman in the Body*. Boston, MA: Beacon.
Martin, Gary and Kats, Vladimir (2003) 'Families and work in transition in 12 countries, 1980–2001', *Monthly Labor Review*, September, 3–31.
Martin, Hans-Peter and Schumann, Harald (1997) *The Global Trap: Globalization and the Assault on Democracy and Prosperity*. London: Zed.
Martin, Patricia Yancey (2005) *Rape Work*. New York: Routledge.
Marty, Martin and Appleby, Scott (eds) (1993) *Fundamentalisms and Society*. Chicago: Chicago University Press.
Marx, Karl (1954) *Capital* (Volumes, 1, 2, 3). London: Lawrence and Wishart.
Marx, Karl (1963) *The Eighteenth Brumaire of Louis Bonaparte*. New York: International Publishers.
Marx, Karl and Engels, Friedrich (1967) *The Communist Manifesto*. London: Penguin.
Mason, Gail and Tomsen, Stephen (eds) (1997) *Homophobic Violence*. Sydney: Hawkins.
Massey, Doreen and Meegan, Richard (1982) *The Anatomy of Job Loss*. London: Methuen.
Matland, Richard (1998) 'Women's representation in national legislatures', *Legislative Studies Quarterly*, 23, 109–25.
Maturana, Humberto and Varela, Francisco (1980) *Autopoeisis and Cognition*. Dordrecht: Reidel.
Mazur, Amy (2002) *Theorizing Feminist Policy*. Oxford: Oxford University Press.
Mazur, Jay (2000) 'Labor's new internationalism', *Foreign Affairs*, 79, January–February, 79–93.
McAdam, Doug (1999) *Political Process and the Development of Black Insurgency, 1930–1970* (2nd edition). Chicago: Chicago University.
McBride, Dorothy and Mazur, Amy (eds) (1995) *Comparative State Feminism*. London: Sage.
McCall, Leslie (2001) *Complex Inequality: Gender, Class, and Race in the New Economy*. New York: Routledge.
McCall, Leslie (2005) 'The complexity of intersectionality', *Signs*, 30, 3, 1771–1800.
McCarthy, John and Zald, Mayer (1977) 'Resource mobilization and social movements: a partial theory', *American Journal of Sociology*, 82, 1212–41.
McClintock, Anne (1995) *Imperial Leather: Race, Gender and Sexuality in the Colonial Contest*. New York: Routledge.
McCrone, David (1992) *Understanding Scotland: The Sociology of a Stateless Nation*. London: Routledge.
McKenzie, Jane (2000) 'Review paper of "Emergence" John Holland'. Available at http://www.psych.lse.ac.uk/complexity/PDFiles/publication/MacKenzie_REVIEW_1.pdf (accessed 24 July 2004).
McLaughlin, Eugene, Muncie, John and Hughes, Gordon (eds) (2003) *Criminological Perspectives* (2nd edition). London: Sage.
McLennan, Gregor (2006) *Sociological Cultural Studies*. London: Palgrave Macmillan.
McMorran, Chris (2003) 'International War Crimes Tribunals', in Guy Burgess and Heidi Burgess (eds), *Beyond Intractability*. Conflict Research Consortium, University of Colorado, Boulder. Available at http://www.beyondintractability.org/essay/int_war_crime_tribunals/ (accessed 17 May 2006).
McNeill, William (1963) *The Rise of the West*. Chicago: Chicago University.
Mead, George Herbert (1934) *Mind, Self and Society*. Chicago: Chicago University.
Medaglia, Azadeh (2000) *Patriarchal Structures and Ethnicity*. Avebury: Ashgate.
Medd, Will and Haynes, Paul (1998) 'Complexity and the social'. Available at http://www.keele.ac.uk/depts/stt/cstt2/comp/medd.htm
Melucci, Alberto (1989) *Nomads of the Present*. London: Hutchinson.

Merry, Sally Engle (2001) 'Spatial governmentality and the new urban social order: Controlling gender violence through law', *American Anthropologist*, 103, 1, 16–29.
Merton, Robert (1968) *Social Theory and Social Structure*. New York: Free.
Meyer, John and Hannan, Michael (eds) (1979) *National Development and the World System: Educational, Economic and Political Change, 1950–1970*. Chicago: Chicago University.
Meyer, John, Boli, John, Thomas, George and Ramirez, Francisco (1997) 'World society and the nation-state', *American Journal of Sociology*, 103, 1, 144–81.
Meyer, Mary and Prügl, Elisabeth (eds) (1999) *Gender Politics in Global Governance*. Lanham, MD: Rowman and Littlefield.
Mies, Maria (1986) *Patriarchy and Accumulation on a World Scale: Women in the International Division of Labour*. London: Zed.
Mies, Maria and Shiva, Vandana (1993) *Ecofeminism*. London: Zed Books.
Milanovic, Branko (2005) *Worlds Apart: Measuring International and Global Inequality*. Princeton: Princeton University.
Miles, Robert (1989) *Racism*. London: Routledge.
Miller, David (1973) *Church, State and Nation in Ireland 1898–1921*. Dublin: Gill and Macmillan.
Mills, Charles Wright (1956) *The Power Elite*. New York: Oxford University Press.
Milward, A.S. (1992) *The European Rescue of the Nation-State*. New York: Routledge.
Minahan, James (2002) *Encyclopedia of the Stateless Nations*. Westport, CT: Greenwood.
Mincer, Jacob (1962) 'Labor force participation of married women', in National Bureau of Economic Research's *Aspects of Labor Economics*. Princeton: Princeton University.
Mincer, Jacob and Polachek, Solomon (1974) 'Family investments in human capital: earnings of women', *Journal of Political Economy*, 82, 2, S76–S108.
Mirza, Heidi Safia (ed.) (1997) *Black British Feminism*. London: Routledge.
Mitchell, Brian (1981) *European Historical Statistics 1750–1975*. London: Macmillan.
Mitchell, Brian (1983) *International Historical Statistics: The Americas and Australasia*. London: Macmillan.
Mitchell, Brian (1995) *International Historical Statistics: Africa, Asia and Oceania 1750–1988*. (2nd edition). London: Macmillan.
Mitleton-Kelly, Eve (2001) *Ten Principles of Complexity and Enabling Infrastructures*. Available at http://www.psych.lse.ac.uk./complexity/Papers/CH2final.pdf (last accessed 19.05.2009)
Moghadam, Valentine (1993) *Modernizing Women*. Boulder, CO: Lynne Riener.
Moghadam, Valentine (ed.) (1994) *Identity Politics and Women*. Boulder, CO: Westview.
Moghadam, Valentine (1996) 'The fourth world conference on women: Dissension and consensus', *Indian Journal of Gender Studies*, 3, 1, 93–102.
Moghadam, Valentine (2005) *Globalizing Women: International Transnational Feminist Networks*. Baltimore: Johns Hopkins University.
Mohanty, Chandra Talpade (1991) 'Under Western eyes', in Chandra Talpade Mohanty, Ann Russo and Lourdes Torres (eds), *Third World Women and the Politics of Feminism*. Bloomington: Indiana University.
Mol, Arthur (2001) *Globalization and Environmental Reform*. Cambridge, MA: MIT Press.
Mol, Arthur and Sonnefield, David (2000) 'Ecological modernization around the world', *Environmental Politics*, 9, 1, 3–16.
Montanari, Ingalill (2001) 'Modernization, globalization and the welfare state', *British Journal of Sociology*, 2, 3, 469–94.
Mooney, Jayne (2000) *Gender, Violence and the Social Order*. London: Macmillan.
Moore, Barrington (1966) *Social Origins of Dictatorship and Democracy*. Harmondsworth: Penguin.
Moore, Henrietta (1994) *A Passion for Difference*. Cambridge: Polity.

Moravcsik, A. (1993) 'Preferences and power in the European Community: A liberal intergovernmentalist approach', *Journal of Common Market Studies*, 31, 473–526.

Morgan, Bryn and Connelly, Joseph (2001) *UK Election Statistics: 1945–2000*. London: House of Commons Library.

Morgan, Glenn and Kubo, Izumi (2005) 'Beyond path dependency?', *Socio-Economic Review*, 3, 1, 55–8.

Morris, Charles (2008) *The Two Trillion Dollar Meltdown*. New York: Public Affairs.

Moser, Caroline (1993) *Gender Planning and Development*. London: Routledge.

Mósesdóttir, Lilja (2001) *The Interplay between Gender, Markets and the State in Sweden, Germany and the United States*. Aldershot: Ashgate.

Mósesdóttir, Lilja, Serrano Pascual, Amparo and Remery, Chantal (eds) (2006) *Moving Europe Towards the Knowledge-Based Society and Gender Equality*. Brussels: ETUI-REHS.

Mouzelis, Nicos (1993) *Back to Sociological Theory*. London: Macmillan.

Mouzelis, Nicos (1995) *Sociological Theory: What Went Wrong? Diagnosis and Remedies*. London: Routledge.

Muller, Edward (1995a) 'Economic determinants of democracy', *American Sociological Review*, 60, 966–82.

Muller, Edward (1995b) 'Income inequality and democratization', *American Sociological Review*, 60, 990–6.

Mullin, Michael (1992) *Africa in America*. Illinois: University of Illinois.

Munck, Ronnie (1993) *The Irish Economy: Results and Prospects*. London: Pluto.

Murphy, Josette (1995) *Gender Issues in World Bank Lending*. Washington, DC: World Bank.

Murphy, Richard (2007) 'Written submission of evidence on private equity to the Treasury Select Committee by the Tax Justice Network UK and Tax Research LLP'. Treasury Select Committee July 2007. Available at http://www.taxresearch.org.uk/Documents/TJNPrivateEquityJuly2007.pdf

Murphy, William (1967) *The Triumph of Nationalism*. Chicago, IL: Quadrangle.

Nairn, Tom (1977) *The Break-Up of Britain*. London: New Left.

National Center for Victims of Crime (2007) *Spousal Rape Laws*. Available at http://www.ncvc.org/ncvc/main.aspx?dbName=DocumentViewer&DocumentID=32701

National Defense University (2008) *National Defense University*. Available at http://www.ndu.edu/

National Statistics (2003) *Census 2001: Religion and Ethnicity in England and Wales*. Available at http://www.statistics.gov.uk/pdfdir/ethnicity0203.pdf (accessed 2 November 2006).

Nederveen Pieterse, Jan (2001) 'Hybridity, so what? ', *Theory, Culture and Society*, 18, 2–3, 219–45.

Nee, Victor and Cao, Yang (1999) 'Path dependent societal transformation', *Theory and Society*, 28, 799–834.

Nelson, Barbara and Chowdhury, Nalma (eds) (1994) *Women and Politics Worldwide*. New Haven: Yale University.

Newman, Janet and Clarke, John (1997) *The Managerial State*. London: Sage.

Nicolis, Gregoire and Prigogine, Ilya (1989) *Exploring Complexity*. New York: W.H. Freeman.

Nishikawa, Makiko and Tanaka, Kazuko (2007) 'Are care workers knowledge workers?', in Sylvia Walby, Heidi Gottfried, Karin Gottschall and Mari Osawa (eds), *Gendering the Knowledge Economy*. London: Palgrave.

Noll, Heinz-Herbert (2002) 'Towards a European System of Social Indicators', *Social Indicators Research*, 58, 1–3, 47–87.

Nonaka, Ikujiro and Nishiguchi, Toshihiro (eds) (2001) *Knowledge Emergence*. New York: Oxford University Press.

Nonaka, Ikujiro and Takeuchi, Hirotaka (1995) *The Knowledge-Creating Company*. Oxford: Oxford University.

Nordic Council (2006) *History of Nordic Co-operation*. Available at http://www.norden.org/web/1-1-fakta/uk/1-1-4-nordens_hist.asp?lang=6 (accessed 31 December 2006).

Nordlund, Willis (1998) *Silent Skies: The Air Traffic Controllers' Strike*. Westport, CT: Greenwood.
Norris, Pippa (1985) 'Women's legislative participation in Western Europe', *West European Politics*, 8, 90–101.
Norris, Pippa (1996a) 'Women politicians: Transforming Westminster?', *Parliamentary Affairs*, 49, 1, 89–102.
Norris, Pippa (1996b) 'Mobilising the "Women's Vote": The gender-generation gap in voting behaviour', *Parliamentary Affairs*, 49, 2, 333–42.
Norris, Pippa and Inglehart, Ronald (2004) *Sacred and Secular: Religion and Politics Worldwide*. Cambridge: Cambridge University Press.
Norris, Pippa and Lovenduski, Joni (1995) *Political Recruitment: Gender, Race and Class in the British Parliament*. Cambridge: Cambridge University Press.
North, Douglass (1990) *Institutions, Institutional Change and Economic Performance*. Cambridge: Cambridge University Press.
Northrop, Emily (1990) 'The feminization of poverty', *Journal of Economic Issues*, 24, 1, 145–60.
Nussbaum, Martha (2000) *Women and Human Development: The Capabilities Approach*. Cambridge: Cambridge University Press.
Oakley, Ann (1974) *The Sociology of Housework*. Oxford: Martin Robertson.
Oakley, Ann (2005) *The Ann Oakley Reader*. Bristol: Policy.
O'Connor, Julia, Orloff, Ann Shola and Shaver, Sheila (1999) *States, Markets, Families*. Cambridge: Cambridge University Press.
O'Connor, Pat (1998) *Emerging Voices: Women in Contemporary Irish Society*. Dublin: Institute of Public Administration.
OECD (Organisation for Economic Co-operation and Development) (1968) *Labour Force Statistics: 1956–1966*. Paris: OECD.
OECD (1974) *Labour Force Statistics 1961–1972*. Paris: OECD.
OECD (1990) *OECD Employment Outlook*. Paris: OECD.
OECD (1993) *OECD Employment Outlook*. Paris: OECD.
OECD (1994) *OECD Employment Outlook*. Paris: OECD.
OECD (1996) *OECD Employment Outlook*. Paris: OECD.
OECD (1997a) *OECD Employment Outlook*. Paris: OECD.
OECD (1997b) *Labour Force Statistics 1976–1996*. Paris: OECD.
OECD (2000a) *Labour Force Statistics 1979–1999*. Paris: OECD.
OECD (2000b) *Quarterly Labour Force Statistics* (No.3 2000). Paris: OECD.
OECD (2002a) *OECD Employment Outlook*. Paris: OECD.
OECD (2002b) *Measuring the Information Economy*. Paris: OECD.
OECD (2003) *OECD Employment Outlook*. Paris: OECD.
OECD (2004) *OECD Employment Outlook*. Paris: OECD.
OECD (2005) *Guide to Measuring the Information Society* (JT00193469.DSTI/ICCP/IIS (2005)6/FINAL). Paris: OECD. Available at http://www.oecd.org/dataoecd/41/12/35654126.pdf (accessed 30 November 2005).
OECD (2006) *OECD Factbook 2006*. Paris: OECD.
OECD (2007a) *OECD Family Data Base*. Available at http://www.oecd.org/document/4/0,3343,en_2649_34819_37836996_1_1_1_1,00.html
OECD (2007b) *OECD Factbook 2007*. Paris: OECD.
Office for National Statistics (2002) *Trends in Life Expectancy by Social Class 1972–1999*. Available at http://www.statistics.gov.uk/downloads/theme_population/Life_Expect_Social_class_1972-99/Life_Expect_Social_class_1972-99.pdf (accessed 9 February).
Office of the United Nations Commissioner for Human Rights (2006) *Convention on the Rights of the Child*. Available at http://www.ohchr.org/english/law/crc.htm (accessed 10 November 2006).
O'Hearn, Denis (1994) 'Innovation and the world-system hierarchy: British subjugation of the Irish cotton industry, 1780–1830', *American Journal of Sociology*, 100, 3, 587–621.
O'Hearn, Denis (1998) *Inside the Celtic Tiger*. London: Pluto.

Ohlander, Ann-Sofie (1992) 'The invisible child? The struggle over Social Democratic Family Policy', in Klaus Misgeld, Karl Molin and Klas Amark (eds), *Creating Social Democracy: A Century of the Social Democratic Labor Party in Sweden*. University Park: Pennsylvania University.

Ohmae, Kenichi (1990) *The Borderless World*. London: Collins.

Ohmae, Kenichi (1995) *The End of the Nation State*. London: Harper Collins.

Oldfield, Sybil (1989) *Women Against the Iron Fist*. Oxford: Blackwell.

Oliver, Melvin and Shapiro, Thomas (1997) *Black Wealth/White Wealth* (2nd edition). New York: Routledge.

Olsen, Wendy and Walby, Sylvia (2004) *Modelling Gender Pay Gaps*. Manchester: Equal Opportunities Commission.

Olson, Mancur (1982) *The Rise and Decline of Nations*. New Haven: Yale University.

O'Malley, Eoin (1992) 'Problems of industrialisation in Ireland', in John Goldthorpe and Christopher Whelan (eds), *The Development of Industrial Society in Ireland*. Oxford: Oxford University Press. pp. 31–52.

Omi, Michael and Winant, Howard (1994) *Racial Formation in the United States* (2nd edition). New York: Routledge.

Orloff, Ann Shola (1993) 'Gender and the social rights of citizenship', *American Sociological Review*, 58, 3, 303–28.

Ostner, Ilona and Lewis, Jane (1995) 'Gender and the evolution of European social policies', in Stephan Leibfried and Paul Pierson (eds), *European Social Policy*. Washington, DC: Brookings. pp. 159–93.

Oswald, Andrew (1997) 'Happiness and economic performance', *Economic Journal*, 107, 445, 1815–31.

Palme, Joakim, Bergmark, Åke, Bäckman, Olof et al. (2002) 'Welfare trends in Sweden: Balancing the books for the 1990s', *Journal of European Social Policy*, 12, 4, 329–46.

Paine, Thomas (1984 [1791]) *The Rights of Man*. Harmondsworth: Penguin.

Pampel, Fred and Tanaka, Kazuko (1986) 'Economic development and female labor force participation', *Social Forces*, 64, 3, 599–619.

Pape, Robert (2003) 'The strategic logic of suicide terrorism', *American Political Science Review*, 97, 3, 343–61.

Park, Robert and Burgess, Ernest (1925) *The City*. Chicago: Chicago University.

Parreñas, Rhacel Salazar (2001) *Servants of Globalization*. Stanford: Stanford University.

Parsons, Talcott (1949) *The Structure of Social Action* (2nd edition). Glencoe, IL: Free.

Parsons, Talcott (1951) *The Social System*. New York: Free.

Parsons, Talcott (with Robert Bales, James Olds, Morris Zelditch and Philip Slater) (1955) *Family Socialization and Interaction Process*. Glencoe. IL: Free.

Pascual, Amparo Serrano and Behning, Ute (eds) (2001) *Gender Mainstreaming in the European Employment Strategy*. Brussels: European Trade Union Institute.

Paxton, Pamela (2000) 'Women's suffrage in the measurement of democracy', *Studies in Comparative International Development*, 35, 3, 92–111.

Paxton, Pamela and Kunovitch, Sheri (2003) 'Women's political representation', *Social Forces*, 82, 1, 87–113.

Paxton, Pamela, Bollen, Kenneth, Lee, Deborah and Kim, HyoJoung (2003) 'A half-century of suffrage', *Studies in Comparative International Development*, 38, 1, 93–122.

Pearce, Diane (1978) ' The feminization of poverty', *Urban and Social Change Review*, 11, 28–36.

Pearse, Emma (2005) 'Germany in angst over low birthrate', *Women's E-News*, 4 November. Available at http://www.womensenews.org/article.cfm/dyn/aid/2253

Perez, Carlota (2002) *Technological Revolutions and Financial Capital: The Dynamics of Bubbles and Golden Ages*. Cheltenham: Edward Elgar.

Perrons, Diane (2007) 'Living and working patterns in the new knowledge economy', in Sylvia Walby, Heidi Gottfried, Karin Gottschall and Mari Osawa (eds), *Gendering the Knowledge Economy*. London: Palgrave. pp. 188–206.

Perry, Barbara (ed.) (2003) *Hate and Bias Crime*. New York: Routledge.
Peters, Julie and Wolper, Andrea (eds) (1995) *Women's Rights, Human Rights*. London: Routledge.
Peterson, V. Spike and Sisson Runyan, Anne (1999) *Global Gender Issues*. Boulder, CO: Westview.
Phillips, Anne (1995) *The Politics of Presence*. Oxford: Clarendon.
Phillips, Anne (1999) *Which Equalities Matter?* Cambridge: Polity.
Phizacklea, Annie (1990) *Unpacking the Fashion Industry*. London: Routledge.
Phoenix, Ann and Pattynama, Pamela (2006) 'Editorial: Intersectionality', *European Journal of Women's Studies*, 13, 3, 187–92.
Pickering, Andrew (1995) *The Mangle of Practice*. Chicago: Chicago University.
Picone, Domenico (2002) *Collateralised Debt Obligations*. Available at http://avikram.freeshell.org/uploads/50.pdf (accessed 16 March 2008).
Pierson, Paul (2000) 'Increasing returns, path dependence, and the study of politics', *American Political Science Review*, 94, 2, 251–68.
Pierson, Paul (ed.) (2001) *The New Politics of the Welfare State*. Oxford: Oxford University Press.
Pillinger, Jane (1992) *Feminising the Market*. Basingstoke: Macmillan.
Piore, Michael and Sabel, Charles (1984) *The Second Industrial Divide*. New York: Basic.
Pitkin, Hannah (1967) *The Concept of Representation*. Berkeley: University of California.
Pitkin, Hannah (2004) 'Representation and democracy', *Scandinavian Political Studies*, 27, 3, 335–42.
Pizzey, Erin (1974) *Scream Quietly or the Neighbours Will Hear*. London: Penguin.
Plummer, Kenneth (1975) *Sexual Stigma*. London: Routledge.
Polity IV Project (2008) Available at http://www.systemicpeace.org/polity/polity4.htm
Pollert, Anna (1996) 'Gender and class revisited', *Sociology*, 30, 4, 639–59.
Potter, David, Goldblatt, David, Kiloh, Margaret and Lewis, Paul (eds) (1997) *Democratization*. Cambridge: Polity.
Poulantzas, Nicos (1973) *Political Power and Social Classes*. London: Verso.
Pred, Allan (2000) *Even in Sweden: Racisms, Racialized Spaces, and the Popular Geographical Imagination*. Berkeley: University of California.
Prendiville, Patricia (1988) 'Divorce in Ireland', *Women's Studies International Forum*, 11, 4, 355–63.
Prigogine, Ilya (1997) *The End of Certainty*. New York: Free.
Prigogine, Ilya and Stengers, Isabelle (1984) *Order Out of Chaos*. London: Heinemann.
Przeworski, Adam and Sprague, John (1986) *Paper Stones*. Chicago: Chicago University.
Purvis, June and Joannou, Maroula (eds) (1998) *The Women's Suffrage Movement*. Manchester: Manchester University.
Putnam, Robert (2000) *Bowling Alone*. New York: Simon and Schuster.
Pyle, Jean (1990) *The State and Women in the Economy*. New York: State University of New York.
Quadagno, Jill (1994) *The Color of Welfare*. Oxford: Oxford University Press.
Quadagno, Jill (1999) 'Creating a capital investment welfare state', *American Sociological Review*, 1, 1–11.
Quadagno, Jill (2006) *One Nation, Uninsured*. New York: Oxford University.
Qvist, Gunnar (1980) 'Policy towards women and the women's struggle in Sweden' *Scandinavian Journal of History*, 5, 51–74.
Ramazanoglu, Caroline (ed.) (1993) *Up Against Foucault*. London: Routledge.
Ramirez, Francisco, Soysal, Yasemin and Shanahan, Suzanne (1997) 'The changing logic of political citizenship', *American Sociological Review*, 62, 735–45.
Rankin, Katharine (2001) 'Governing development: Neoliberalism, microcredit, and rational economic woman', *Economy and Society*, 30, 1, 18–37.
Raper, Arthur (1933) *The Tragedy of Lynching*. Chapel Hill: University of North Carolina.

Raphael, J. and Toman, R. M. (1997) 'Welfare reform: Prescription for abuse?', *Law and Policy*, 19, 2, 123–37.
Rauch, Dietmar (2006) 'Institutional fragmentation, institutional engineering and the development of elderly care and childcare in Sweden', *Scandinavian Political Studies*, 29, 4, 285–307.
Ravn, Anna-Birte (1995) 'Equality versus difference and gender versus class in Danish women's history'. *NORA*, 3, 1, 45–54.
Rawls, John (1999) *A Theory of Justice* (2nd edition). Oxford: Oxford University Press.
Raymond, Janice, D'Cunha, Jean, Dzuhaytain, Siti Ruhaini, Hynes, H. Patricia, Rodriguez, Zoraida Ramirez and Santos, Aida (2002) *A Comparative Study of Women Trafficked in the Migration Process*. Available at http://action.web.ca/home/catw/attach/CATW%20Comparative%20Study%202002.pdf (accessed 6 June 2006).
Reed, Michael and Harvey, David (1992) 'The new science and the old', *Journal for the Theory of Social Behaviour*, 22, 4, 353–80.
Rees, Teresa (1998) *Mainstreaming Equality in the European Union*. London: Routledge.
Reich, Robert (1993) *The Work of Nations*. London: Simon and Schuster.
Reid, Brian Holden (1996) *The Origins of the American Civil War*. London: Longman.
Reid, Madeleine (1992) 'Abortion law in Ireland after the Maastricht Referendum', in Ailbhe Smyth (ed.), *The Abortion Papers: Ireland*. Dublin: Attic. pp. 25–39.
Reid, Margaret (1934) *The Economics of Household Production*. New York: Wiley.
Rex, John (1973) *Race, Colonialism and the City*. London: Routledge and Kegan Paul.
Rhodes, Martin (1998) 'Globalisation, labour markets and welfare states: A future of "competitive corporatism"?', in Martin Rhodes and Yves Mény (eds), *The Future of European Welfare*. London: Macmillan. pp. 178–203.
Rhodes, Martin (2001) 'The political economy of social pacts: "Competitive corporatism" and European welfare reform', in Paul Pierson (ed.), *The New Politics of the Welfare State*. Oxford: Oxford University Press. pp. 165–94.
Richardson, Diane (2000) *Rethinking Sexuality*. London: Sage.
Risman, Barbara (2004) 'Gender as a social structure', *Gender & Society*, 18, 4, 429–50.
Risse, Thomas (1999) 'International norms and domestic change', *Politics and Society*, 27, 4, 529–59.
Ritzer, George (1993) *The McDonaldization of Society*. Newbury Park, CA: Sage.
Roberts, J. Timmons and Parks, Bradley (2007) *A Climate of Injustice*. Cambridge MA: MIT Press.
Robertson, Roland (1992) *Globalization*. London: Sage.
Robeyns, Ingrid (2003) 'Sen's capability approach and gender equality', *Feminist Economics*, 9, 2.3, 61–92.
Robinson, Mary (1988) 'Foreword', in Gerry Whyte (ed.), *Sex Equality, Community Rights and Irish Social Welfare Law*. Dublin: Irish Centre for European Law, Trinity College. pp. (i)–(ii).
Robinson, William (2001) 'Social theory and globalization: The rise of a transnational state', *Theory and Society*, 30, 157–200.
Roche, William (2007) 'Social partnership in Ireland and new social pacts', *Industrial Relations*, 46, 3, 395–425.
Rodrigues, Maria (2003) *European Policies for a Knowledge Economy*. Cheltenham: Edward Elgar.
Rojas, Maurico (1991) 'The "Swedish model" in historical perspective', *Scandinavian Economic History Review*, XXXIX, 2, 64–74.
Rooney, Andy (2007) *Presidential Price Tag*. Available at http://www.cbsnews.com/stories/2007/03/30/60minutes/rooney/printable2629080.shtml
Rosaldo, Michelle (ed.) (1974) *Woman, Culture and Society*. Stanford: Stanford University.
Rose, Nikolas (1996) *Inventing Ourselves*. Cambridge: Cambridge University Press.

Rose, Nikolas (2000) 'Government and control', *British Journal of Criminology*, 40, 321–39.
Rose, Steven (1997) *Lifelines*. London: Allen Lane.
Rothstein, Bo (1992) 'Explaining Swedish corporatism', *Scandinavian Political Studies*, 15, 3, 173–91.
Rowbotham, Sheila and Linkogle, Stephanie (eds) (2000) *Women Resist Globalization*. London: Zed.
Rueschemeyer, Dietrich, Huber Stephens, Evelyne and Stephens, John (1992) *Capitalist Development and Democracy*. Cambridge: Polity.
Ruggie, John (1996) *Winning the Peace*. New York: Columbia University.
Ruggie, John (1998) *Constructing the World Polity*. London: Routledge.
Ruggie, Mary (1984) *The State and Working Women*. Princeton: Princeton University.
Rule, Wilma (1981) 'Why women don't run', *Western Political Quarterly*, 34, 60–77.
Rule, Wilma (1987) 'Electoral systems, contextual factors, and women's opportunity for election to parliament in twenty-three democracies', *Western Political Quarterly*, 40, 477–98.
Rule, Wilma (1994) 'Parliaments of, by, and for the people: Except for women?', in Wilma Rule and Joseph Zimmerman (eds), *Electoral Systems in Comparative Perspective*. Westport, CT: Greenwood.
Rummel, R.J. (1995) 'Democracies are less warlike than other regimes', *European Journal of International Relations*, 1, 457–79.
Rummel, R.J. (1997) *Power Kills*. New Brunswick: Transaction.
Rummel, R.J. (2008) *Democratic Peace Clock*. Available at http://www.hawaii.edu/powerkills/DP.CLOCK.HTM
Russell, Diane (1990) *Rape in Marriage* (2nd edition). Bloomington: Indiana University.
Russell, Meg (1999) 'Second chambers overseas', *The Political Quarterly*, 70, 4, 411–17.
Russell, Meg (2000) *Reforming the House of Lords*. Oxford: Oxford University Press.
Rycroft, Robert and Kash, Don (1999) *The Complexity Challenge*. London: Pinter.
Saad-Filho and Johnston, Deborah (eds) (2005) *Neoliberalism*. London: Pluto.
Said, Edward (1978) *Orientalism*. London: Routledge and Kegan Paul.
Said, Muhammad Ikmal (1996) 'Malay nationalism and national identity', in Muhammad Ikmal Said and Zahid Emby (eds), *Malaysia: Critical Perspectives*. Kuala Lumpur: Persatuan Sains Sosial Malaysia.
Sainsbury, Diane (ed.) (1994) *Gendering Welfare States*. London: Sage.
Sainsbury, Diane (1996) *Gender, Equality and Welfare States*. Cambridge: Cambridge University Press.
Sandberg, L.G. (1979) 'The case of the impoverished sophisticate', *Journal of Economic History*, 1, 225–41.
Sandel, Michael (1998) *Liberalism and the Limits of Justice* (2nd edition). Cambridge: Cambridge University Press.
Sassen, Saskia (2001) *The Global City* (2nd edition). Princeton: Princeton University.
Sassen, Saskia (2008) *Territory. Authority. Rights. From Medieval to Global Assemblages*. Princeton: Princeton University.
Sawyer, R. Keith (2005) *Social Emergence*. Cambridge: Cambridge University.
Sayer, Andrew (1997) 'Essentialism, social constructionism and beyond', *Sociological Review*, 45, 3, 453–87.
Sayer, Andrew (2000a) 'System, life-world and gender: Associational versus counter-factual thinking', *Sociology*, 34, 707–25.
Sayer, Andrew (2000b) *Realism and Social Science*. London: Sage.
Sbw01f (2008a) *GDP nominal per capita world map IMF 2008.png* http://commons.wikimedia.org/wiki/Image:GDP_nominal_per_capita_world_map_IMF_2008.png
Sbw01f (2008b) *Gini Coefficient World Human Development Report 2007–2008.png* http://commons.wikimedia.org/wiki/Image:Gini_Coefficient_World_Human_Development_Report_2007–2008.png

Scannell, Y. (1988) 'The constitution and the role of women', in Brian Farrell (ed.), *De Valera's Constitution and Ours*. Dublin: Gill and Macmillan. pp. 123–36.

Schmal, John (2005) *Latino Congressional Representation, 1960–2005*. Available at http://www.hispanicvista.com/HVC/Columnist/jschmal/080805jpschmal.htm

Schmidt, Volker (2006) 'Multiple modernities or varieties of modernity?', *Current Sociology*, 54, 1, 77–97.

Schmidt, Volker (ed.) (2007) *Modernity at the Beginning of the 21st Century*. Cambridge: Cambridge Scholars Publishing.

Schmitter, Philippe (1974) 'Still the century of corporatism?', *The Review of Politics*, 36, 1, 85–131.

Scholte, Jan (2000) *Globalisation*. Basingstoke: Macmillan.

Schreiner, Olive (1911) *Woman and Labour*. London: Unwin.

Scott, Jacqueline (1998) 'Changing attitudes to sexual morality', *Sociology*, 32, 4, 815–45.

Scott, Joan (1988) 'Deconstructing equality-versus-difference', *Feminist Studies*, 14, 1, 33–49.

Scott, John (2000) *Social Network Analysis*. London: Sage.

Seccombe, Wally (1974) 'The housewife and her labour under capitalism', *New Left Review*, 83, 3–24.

Segal, Lynne (1987) *Is the Future Female?* London: Virago.

Seidman, Steven (ed.) (1996) *Queer Theory/Sociology*. Oxford: Blackwell.

Seltzer, Kimberley and Bentley, Tom (1999) *The Creative Age*. London: Demos.

Sen, Amartya (1997) *Human Rights and Asian Values*. New York: Carnegie Council.

Sen, Amartya (1999) *Development as Freedom*. Oxford: Oxford University Press.

Serrano-Pascual, Amparo and Mósesdóttir, Lilja (eds) (2003) *The Implications of the KBS for Employment and Gender Relations* (WELLKNOW HPSE –CT 2002–00119).

Sennett, Richard (1998) *The Corrosion of Character*. New York: Norton

Shaffer, Gregory (2000) 'Globalization and social protection', *Yale Journal of International Law*, 25, 1–88.

Shamsul, A.B. (1996) 'The construction and transformation of a social identity: Malayness and Bumiputeraness re-examined', *Journal of Asian and African Studies*, 52, 15–33.

Shapiro, Herbert (1988) *White Violence and Black Response*. Amherst: University of Massachusetts.

Shaw, Jenny and Perrons, Diane (eds) (1995) *Making Gender Work*. Buckingham: Open University.

Shaw, Martin (2005) *The New Western Way of War*. Cambridge: Polity.

Shiller, Robert (2008) *The Subprime Solution*. Princeton: Princeton University Press.

Shilling, Chris (1993) *The Body and Social Theory*. London: Sage.

Shire, Karen (2007) 'Gender and the conceptualization of the knowledge economy in comparison', in Sylvia Walby, Heidi Gottfried, Karin Gottschall and Mari Osawa (eds), *Gendering the Knowledge Economy*. London: Palgrave. pp. 51–77.

Silva, Elizabeth (2000) 'The cook, the cooker and the gendering of the kitchen', *Sociological Review*, 48, 4, 612, 628.

Simmel, Georg (1955) *Conflict; The Web of Group Affiliations*. Glencoe, IL: Free.

Simmel, Georg (1984) *Georg Simmel on Women, Sexuality and Love*. New Haven: Yale University.

Sisters in Islam (1991) *Are Women and Men Equal Before Allah?* Kuala Lumpur: Sisters in Islam.

Skard, Torild and Haavio-Manila, Elina (1985) 'Mobilization of women at elections', in Elina Haavio-Manila (ed.), *Unfinished Democracy: Women in Nordic Politics*. Oxford: Pergamon.

Skeggs, Beverely (1997) *Formations of Class and Gender*. London: Sage.

Skocpol, Theda (1979) *States and Social Revolutions*. Cambridge: Cambridge University Press.

Skocpol, Theda (1992) *Protecting Soldiers and Mothers*. Cambridge, MA: Belknap, Harvard University.

Smeeding, Timothy (2002) *Globalization, Inequality and the Rich Countries of the G-20* (Luxembourg Income Study Working Paper No. 320).

Smelser, Neil (1959) *Social Change in the Industrial Revolution*. London: Routledge and Kegan Paul.
Smith, Anthony D. (1986) *The Ethnic Origins of Nations*. Oxford: Blackwell.
Smith, Dorothy (1987) *The Everyday World as Problematic*. Boston: Northeastern University.
Smith, Karen (2003) *European Union Policy in a Changing World*. Cambridge: Polity.
Smith, Michael E. (2004) *Europe's Foreign and Security Policy*. Cambridge: Cambridge University Press.
Smith, Robert Michael (2003) *From Blackjacks to Briefcases: A History of Commercialized Strikebreaking and Unionbusting in the United States*. Athens: Ohio State University.
Smyth, Ailbhe (1988) 'The contemporary women's movement in the Republic of Ireland', *Women's Studies International Forum*, 11, 4, 331–41.
Smyth, Ailbhe (ed.) (1992) *The Abortion Papers: Ireland*. Dublin: Attic.
Snow, David, Rochford, E. Burke, Worden, Steven and Benford, Robert (1986) 'Frame alignment processes, micromobilization, and movement participation', *American Sociological Review*, 51, 464–81.
Snyder, Paula (1992) *The European Women's Almanac*. London: Scarlet.
Somers, Margaret (1998) '"We're no angels": Realism, rational choice, and relationality in social science', *American Journal of Sociology*, 104, 3, 722–84.
Soothill, Keith and Walby, Sylvia (1991) *Sex Crime in the News*. London: Routledge.
Soros, George (2008) *The New Paradigm for Financial Markets*. London: Public Affairs.
Soysal, Yasemin (1994) *The Limits of Citizenship: Migrants and Postnational Membership in Europe*. Chicago: University of Chicago.
Sparr, Pamela (ed.) (1994) *Mortgaging Women's Lives*. London: Zed.
Spellman, Elizabeth (1988) *Inessential Woman*. Boston, MA: Beacon.
Spender, Dale (1983) *Women of Ideas*. London: Ark.
Squires, Judith (1999) *Gender in Political Theory*. Cambridge: Polity.
Squires, Judith (2005) 'Is mainstreaming transformative?', *Social Politics*, 12, 3, 366–88.
Stamatov, Peter (2000) 'The making of a "bad" public', *Theory and Society*, 29, 549–72.
Standing, Guy (1999) *Global Labour Flexibility*. Basingstoke: Macmillan.
Stanko, Elizabeth (1990) *Everyday Violence*. London: Pandora.
Stanworth, Michelle (1984) 'Women and class analysis', *Sociology*, 18, 2, 159–70.
Stanworth, Michelle (1987) *Reproductive Technologies*. Cambridge: Polity.
Statistics Sweden (1995) *Women and Men in Sweden*. Stockholm: Sweden.
Stern, Nicholas (2007) *The Economics of Climate Change: The Stern Review*. Cambridge: Cambridge University Press.
Stiglitz, Joseph (2002) *Globalization and its Discontents*. London: Allen Lane.
Stiglitz, Joseph (2006) *Making Globalization Work*. London: Penguin.
Stiglitz, Joseph (2009) 'Principles for a New Financial Architecture'. The Commission of Experts of the President of the UN General Assembly on Reforms of the International Monetary and Financial System. Available at http://www.un.org/ga/president/63/commission/newfinancialarchitecture.pdf
Stompka, Piotr (1999) 'The cultural core of post-communist transformations', in Thomas Boye, Bart van Steenbergen and Sylvia Walby (eds), *European Societies: Fusion or Fission?* London: Routledge. pp. 205–14.
Strange, Susan (1986) *Casino Capitalism*. Oxford: Blackwell.
Strange, Susan (1996) *The Retreat of the State*. Cambridge: Cambridge University Press.
Strathern, Marylin (1992) *After Nature: English Kinship in the Late Twentieth Century*. Cambridge: Cambridge University Press.
Straus, Murray and Gelles, Richard (eds) (1990) *Physical Violence in American Families*. New Brunswick: Transaction.
Streeck, Wolfgang (1992) *Social Institutions and Economic Performance*. London: Sage.

Streeck, Wolfgang (2005) 'Rejoinder: on terminology, functionalism, (historical) institutionalism and liberalization', *Socio-Economic Review*, 3, 3, 577–87.

Streeck, Wolfgang and Yamamura, Kozo (eds) (2002) *The Origins of Nonliberal Capitalism*. Ithaca: Cornell University.

Suchman, Lucy (2001) 'Human/machine reconsidered'. Lancaster: Department of Sociology, Lancaster University. Available at http://www.comp.lancs.ac.uk/sociology/soc040ls.html

Svensson, Lars (1995) *Closing the Gender Gap*. Lund University, Sweden: Lund Ekonomisk-historiska foren.

Swain, John, Sally, French, Colin, Barnes and Carol, Thomas (eds) (2004) *Disabling Barriers: Enabling Environments*. London: Sage.

Swank, Duane (2002) *Global Capital, Political Institutions, and Policy Change in Developed Welfare States*. Cambridge: Cambridge University Press.

Sweden Price History (2008) 'Credit crunch grounds Sweden's housing market', *Sweden Price History*, 27 August 2008.

Swedish History (1999) Available at http://www.utb.boras.se/uk/se/projekt/HISTORY/ie5.htm (accessed 10 November 2006).

Swenson, Peter (2002) *Capitalists Against Markets*. Oxford: Oxford University Press.

Szalai, Julia (1999) 'Women and democratization', in Thomas Boye, Bart van Steenbergen and Sylvia Walby (eds), *European Societies: Fusion or Fission?* London: Routledge. pp. 118–31.

Tam, Tony (1997) 'Sex segregation and occupational gender inequality in the United States: Devaluation or specialized training?', *American Journal of Sociology*, 102, 6, 1652–92.

Tarrow, Sydney (1998) *Power in Movement* (2nd edition). Cambridge: Cambridge University Press.

Tarrow, Sidney (2005) *The New Transnational Activism*. Cambridge: Cambridge University Press.

Tavakoli, Janet (2003) *Collateralized Debt Obligations and Structured Finance: New Developments in Cash and Synthetic Securitization*. Indianapolis: John Wiley.

Tax Justice Network (2007) *Tax Havens Cause Poverty*. Available at http://www.taxjustice.net/cms/front_content.php?idcat=2

Taylor, Charles et al. (1994) *Multiculturalism: Examining the Politics of Recognition*. Princeton: Princeton University.

Taylor, Verta (1989) 'Social movement continuity: The women's movement in abeyance', *American Sociological Review*, 54, 755–61.

Taylor-Browne, Julie (ed.) (2001) *What Works in Reducing Domestic Violence?* London: Whiting and Birch.

Taylor-Gooby, Peter (1997) 'In defence of second-best theory: State, class and capital in social policy', *Journal of Social Policy*, 26, 2, 171–92.

Teubner, Gunther (ed.) (1997) *Global Law Without a State*. Aldershot: Dartmouth.

Therborn, Göran (1977) 'The rule of capital and the rise of democracy', *New Left Review*, 103, 3–41.

Therborn, Göran (1992) 'A unique chapter in the history of democracy: The social democrats in Sweden', in Klaus Misgeld, Karl Molin and Klas Amark (eds), *Creating Social Democracy*. Pennsylvania: Pennsylvania University.

Therborn, Göran (1995) *European Modernity and Beyond*. London: Sage.

Therborn, Göran (2004) *Between Sex and Power*. London: Routledge.

Thomas, Albert (1996) 'The International Labour Organization: Its origins, development and future', *International Labour Review*, 135, 3–4, 261–76.

Thomas, Sue (1991) 'The impact of women on state legislative policies', *Journal of Politics*, 53, 4, 958–76.

Thompson, Edward Palmer (1963) *The Making of the English Working Class*. London: Gollancz.

Thompson, John B. (1995) *The Media and Modernity*. Cambridge: Polity.

Thompson, Mark (2000) 'The survival of "Asian values" as *"Zivilisationskritik"'*, *Theory and Society*, 29, 651–86.
Thrift, Nigel (1999) 'The place of complexity', *Theory, Culture and Society*, 16, 3, 31–69.
Tilly, Charles (1978) *From Mobilization to Revolution*. Reading, MA: Addison–Wesley.
Tilly, Charles (1990) *Coercion, Capital and European States*. Oxford: Blackwell.
Tilly, Charles (2003) *The Politics of Collective Violence*. Cambridge: Cambridge University Press.
Timms, Jill (2005) 'Chronology of global civil society events', in Helmut Anheier, Marlies Glasius and Mary Kaldo (eds), *Global Civil Society 2004/5*. London: Sage. pp. 350–60.
Tjaden, Patricia and Thoennes, Nancy (2000a) *Full Report of the Prevalence, Incidence, and Consequences of Violence Against Women*. Washington, DC: US National Institute of Justice.
Tjaden, Patricia and Thoennes, Nancy (2000b) 'Prevalence and consequences of male-to-female and female-to-male intimate partner violence as measured by the National Violence Against Women Survey', *Violence Against Women*, 6, 2, 142–61.
Tjaden, Patricia and Thoennes, Nancy (2000c) *Extent, Nature and Consequences of Intimate Partner Violence: Findings From the National Violence Against Women Survey*. (NCJ 181867). Washington, DC: US Department of Justice, National Institute of Justice.
Tomaskovic-Devey, Don and Skaggs, Sheryl (2002) 'Sex segregation, labor process organization, and gender earnings inequality', *American Journal of Sociology*, 108, 1, 102–28.
Traxler, Franz and Woitech, Birgit (2000) 'Transnational investment and national labour market regimes: A case of "regime shopping"?', *European Journal of Industrial Relations*, 6, 2, 141–59.
Traynor, Ian and Gow, David (2009) 'Summit fails to heal EU's divisions over recession', *Guardian*, 2 March 2009.
Treanor, Jill (2008) 'Toxic shock: How the banking industry created a global crisis', *Guardian*, 8 April. Available at http://www.guardian.co.uk/business/2008/apr/08/creditcrunch.banking
Trifiletti, Rosanna (2007) *Study on Poverty and Social Exclusion among Lone-Parent Households*. Brussels: European Commission.
Tronto, Joan (1993) *Moral Boundaries*. New York: Routledge.
Turner, Bryan (1987) *Medical Power and Social Knowledge*. London: Sage.
Turner, Bryan (1992) *Regulating Bodies*. London: Routledge.
Turner, Bryan (1996) *The Body and Society*. (2nd edition). Cambridge: Polity.
Turner, Bryan (1999) *Classical Sociology*. London: Sage.
Tyyska, Vappu (1994) 'Women facing the state', *NORA*, 2, 2, 95–106.
UN (United Nations) (1945) *United Nations Charter*. Available at http://www.un.org/aboutun/charter/ (accessed 16 May 2006).
UN (1948) *Universal Declaration of Human Rights*. Available at http://www.un.org/Overview/rights.html (accessed 16 May 2006).
UN (1993) *World Conference on Human Rights*, (Vienna). Available at http://www.unhchr.ch/huridocda/huridoca.nsf/(Symbol)/A.CONF.157.23.En
UN (2002) *The International Criminal Court*. Available at http://www.un.org/News/facts/iccfact.htm
UN (2007a) *The Millennium Development Goals*. Available at http://mdgs.un.org/unsd/mdg/Host.aspx?Content=Indicators/OfficialList.htm
UN (2007b) *Feeling the Heat*. Available at http://unfccc.int/essential_background/feeling_the_heat/items/2917.php
UN (2007c) *The Millennium Development Goals Report 2007*. Available at http://mdgs.un.org/unsd/mdg/Resources/Static/Data/Stat%20Annex.pdf

UNDP (1990) *Human Development Report*. New York: Oxford University Press.
UNDP (1995) *Human Development Report 1995*. New York: Oxford University Press.
UNDP (2005) *Human Development Report 2005: International Cooperation at a Crossroads*. New York: Oxford University Press.
UNDP (2006) *Human Development Report 2006: Beyond Scarcity*. New York: Oxford University Press.
UNDP (2007a) *Human Development Report 2007/8: Fighting Climate Change*. New York: Oxford University Press.
UNDP (2007b) *Measuring Human Development: A Primer: Guidelines and tools for statistical research, analysis and advocacy*. Available at http://hdr.undp.org/en/media/Primer_ch2.pdf
UN Division for the Advancement of Women (1995) *The United Nations Fourth World Conference on Women, Beijing, Platform for Action*. Available at http://www.un.org/womenwatch/daw/beijing/platform/plat1.htm
UN Framework Convention on Climate Change (2007) *Negotiating the Kyoto Protocol*. Available at http://unfccc.int/kyoto_protocol/items/2830.php
UN General Assemby (2007) *United Nations General Assembly Adopts Landmark Text Calling for A Moratorium on Death Penalty*. Available at http://www.un.org/News/Press/docs//2007/ga10678.doc.htm
UNIFEM (2000a) *Progress of the World's Women*. Available at www.undp.org/unifem/progressww/
UNIFEM (2000b) *Promoting Women's Human Rights*. Available at http://www.undp.org/unifem/hrights.htm
UNIFEM (2000c) *Women @ Work to End Violence: Voices in Cyberspace*. Available at http://www.undp.org/unifem/w@work/w@work11.htm
UNIFEM (2000d) *Bringing Equality Home: Implementing the Convention on the Elimination of All Forms of Discrimination Against Women, CEDAW*. Available at http://www.undp.org/unifem/cedaw/cedawen5.htm
UN Statistics Division (2005a) *Information Sector*. Available at http://unstats.un.org/unsd/cr/registry/docs/i31_information.pdf (accessed 13 December 2005).
UN Statistics Division (2005b) *Information and Communication Technology (ICT)* Available at http://unstats.un.org/unsd/cr/registry/docs/i31_ict.pdf (accessed on 13 December 2005).
UN Statistics Division (2006) *Demographic Yearbook 2003*. Available at http://unstats.un.org/unsd/demographic/products/dyb/DYB2002/Table25.xls
Urry, John (2000) *Sociology Beyond Societies*. London: Routledge.
Urry, John (2003) *Global Complexity*. Cambridge: Polity.
Urry, John (2004) 'The "system" of automobility', *Theory, Culture and Society*, 21, 4/5, 25–39.
Urry, John (2007) *Mobilities*. Cambridge: Polity.
Valiulis, Maryann and O'Dowd, Mary (eds) (1997) *Women and Irish History*. Dublin: Wolfhound.
Valticos, Nicolas (1969) 'Fifty years of standard-setting activities by the International Labour Organisation', *International Labour Review*, 100, 3.
Van Alstyne, Richard (1974) *The Rising American Empire*. New York: Oxford University.
Van Wilsem, Johan (2004) 'Criminal victimization in cross-national perspective', *European Journal of Criminology*, 1, 1, 89–109.
Vargas, Virginia and Wieringa, Saskia (1998), 'The triangles of empowerment', in Geertje Lycklama à Nijeholt, Virginia Vargas and Saskia Wieringa (eds), *Women's Movements and Public Policy in Europe, Latin America and the Caribbean*. New York: Garland.
Verloo, Mieke (2001) *Another Velvet Revolution*. Working Paper No. 5/2001. Vienna: IWM.
Verloo, Mieke (2005) 'Mainstreaming gender equality in Europe', *The Greek Review of Social Research*, 117, B, 11–34.

Verloo, Mieke (2006) 'Multiple inequalities, intersectionality and the European Union', *European Journal of Women's Studies*, 13, 3, 211–28.

Victim Support (1992) *Domestic Violence – Report of a National Inter-Agency Working Party*. London: Victim Support.

Visser, Jelle (2006) 'Union membership statistics in 24 countries', *Monthly Labor Review*, January, 38–49.

Wade, Robert (2002) 'US hegemony and the World Bank', *Review of International Political Economy*, 9, 2, 215–43.

Wade, Robert (2004) 'Is globalization reducing poverty and inequality', *World Development*, 32, 4, 567–89.

Wagner, Peter (1994) *A Sociology of Modernity*. London: Routledge.

Wahl, Angelika von (2005) 'Liberal, conservative, social democratic, or … European? The European Union as equal employment regime', *Social Politics*, 12, 1, 67–95.

Wajcman, Judy (1991) *Feminism Confronts Technology*. Cambridge: Polity Press.

Wajcman, Judy and MacKenzie, Donald (eds) (1999) *The Social Shaping of Technology*. Buckingham: Open University Press.

Walby, Sylvia (1986) *Patriarchy at Work*. Cambridge: Polity.

Walby, Sylvia (1990) *Theorizing Patriarchy*. Oxford: Blackwell.

Walby, Sylvia (1992) 'Post-post-modernism? Theorizing social complexity', in Michèle Barrett and Anne Phillips (eds), *Destabilizing Theory: Contemporary Feminist Debates*. Cambridge: Polity.

Walby, Sylvia (1994a) 'Is citizenship gendered?', *Sociology*, 28, 2, 379–95.

Walby, Sylvia (1994b) 'Methodological and theoretical issues in the comparative analysis of gender relations in Western Europe', *Environment and Planning A*, 26, 1339–54.

Walby, Sylvia (1997) *Gender Transformations*. London: Routledge.

Walby, Sylvia (1999a) 'The new regulatory state: the social powers of the European Union', *British Journal of Sociology*, 50, 1, 118–40.

Walby, Sylvia (1999b) 'The European Union and equal opportunities policies', *European Societies*, 1, 1, 59–80.

Walby, Sylvia (2000a) 'Gender, nations and states in a global era', *Nations and Nationalism*, 6, 4, 523–40.

Walby, Sylvia (2000b) 'Gender, globalization and democracy', *Gender and Development*, 8, 1, 20–8.

Walby, Sylvia (2001a) 'Against epistemological chasms: the science question in feminism revisited' *Signs: A Journal of Women in Culture and Society*, 26, 2, 485–509.

Walby, Sylvia (2001b) 'From community to coalition: the politics of recognition as the handmaiden of the politics of redistribution', *Theory, Culture and Society*, 18, 2–3, 113–35.

Walby, Sylvia (2001c) 'Gender mainstreaming in the European employment strategy: the British case', in Ute Behning and Amparo Serrano Pascual (eds), *Gender Mainstreaming in the European Employment Strategy*. Brussels: European Trade Union Institute.

Walby, Sylvia (2002) 'Feminism in a global age', *Economy and Society*, 31, 4, 533–57.

Walby, Sylvia (2003) 'The myth of the nation-state', *Sociology*, 37, 3, 531–48.

Walby, Sylvia (2004a) 'The European Union and gender equality: Emergent varieties of gender regime', *Social Politics*, 11, 1, 4–29.

Walby, Sylvia (2004b) *The Cost of Domestic Violence*. London: Department of Trade and Industry.

Walby, Sylvia (2005) 'Gender mainstreaming: Productive tensions in theory and practice', *Social Politics*, 12, 3, 1–25.

Walby, Sylvia (2006) *The Gendered Knowledge Economy in the UK*. Report for University of Tokyo Institute of Social Science. Tokyo: Tokyo University.

Walby, Sylvia (2007a) 'Complexity theory, systems theory, and multiple intersecting social inequalities', *Philosophy of the Social Sciences*, 37, 4, 449–70.

Walby, Sylvia (2007b) 'Introduction: Theorizing the gendering of the knowledge economy: Comparative approaches', in Sylvia Walby, Heidi Gottfried, Karin Gottschall and Mari Osawa (eds), *Gendering the Knowledge Economy*. London: Palgrave. pp. 3–50.

Walby, Sylvia and Allen, Jonathan (2004) *Domestic Violence, Sexual Assault and Stalking: Findings from the British Crime Survey* (HORS 276). London: The Home Office.

Walby, Sylvia and Myhill, Andrew (2001a) 'New survey methodologies in researching violence against women', *British Journal of Criminology*, 41, 3, 502–22.

Walby, Sylvia and Myhill, Andrew (2001b) 'Assessing and managing the risk of domestic violence', in Julie Taylor-Browne (ed.), *What Works in Reducing Domestic Violence?* London: Whiting and Birch. pp. 309–35.

Walby, Sylvia and Olsen, Wendy (2002) *The Impact of Women's Position in the Labour Market on Pay and Implications for Productivity*. London: Department of Trade and Industry Women and Equality Unit.

Walby, Sylvia, Gottfried, Heidi, Gottschall, Karin and Osawa, Mari (eds), (2007) *Gendering the Knowledge Economy: Comparative Perspectives*. London: Palgrave.

Waldrop, Mitchell, M. (1992) *Complexity*. London: Penguin.

Walecki, Marcin (2007) *Spending Limits as a Policy Option* (IFES Political Finance White Paper). Washington, DC: IFES.

Wallace, W. (1994) 'Rescue or retreat? The nation-state in Western Europe, 1945–93', *Political Studies*, 42, 52–76.

Wallerstein, Immanuel (1974) *The Modern World-System*. New York: Academic.

Wallerstein, Immanuel (1980) *The Modern World-System II*. New York: Academic.

Wallerstein, Immanuel (1989) *The Modern World-System III*. New York: Academic.

Wallerstein, Immanuel (1996) *Open the Social Sciences: Report of the Gulbenian Commission on the Restructuring of the Social Sciences*. Stanford: Stanford University.

Walt, Stephen (1999) 'Never say never: Wishful thinking on democracy and war', *Foreign Affairs*, 78. 1. 146–51.

Waltz, Kenneth (1979) *Theory of International Politics*. Reading, MA: Addison-Wesley.

Walvin, James (1992) *Black Ivory: Slavery in the British Empire*. Oxford: Blackwell.

Wängnerud, Lena (2000) 'Testing the politics of presence', *Scandinavian Political Studies*, 23, 1, 67–91.

Ward, Kathryn (1984) *Women in the World-System*. New York: Praeger.

Waterman, Peter and Timms, Jill (2005) 'Trade union internationalism and a global civil society in the making', in Helmut Anheier, Marlies Glasius and Mary Kaldo (eds), *Global Civil Society 2004/5*. London: Sage. pp. 178–202.

Waters, Malcolm (1995) *Globalization*. London: Routledge.

Waylen, Georgina (1996) *Gender in Third World Politics*. Buckingham: Open University.

Weart, Spencer (1998) *Never at War: Why Democracies Will Not Fight One Another*. New Haven: Yale University.

Weber, Max (1947) *The Theory of Economic and Social Organization*. New York: Free.

Weber, Max (1948) *From Max Weber* (translated and edited by H.H. Gerth and C.W. Mills). London: Routledge and Kegan Paul.

Weber, Max (1949) *The Methodology of the Social Sciences*. Glencoe, IL: Free.

Weber, Max (1952) *Ancient Judaism*. Glencoe, IL: Free.

Weber, Max (1958) *The Religion of India*. Glencoe, IL: Free.

Weber, Max (1968) *Economy and Society* (Volumes 1, 2, 3). Edited by Guenther Roth and Claus Wittich. New York: Bedminster.

Weber, Max (1994) *The Protestant Ethic and the Spirit of Capitalism*. London: Routledge.

Weeks, Jeffrey (1995) *Invented Moralities*. Cambridge: Polity.

Weeks, Jeffrey (2007) *The World We Have Won*. London: Routledge.

Weeks, Jeffrey, Donovan, Catherine and Heaphy, Brian (2001) *Same Sex Intimacies: Families of Choice and other Life Experiments*. London: Routledge.

Weeks, John (2005) *Inequality Trends in Some Developed OECD Countries* (United Nations Department of Economic and Social Affairs Working Paper 6). New York: United Nations.

Weiler, J.H.H. (1997) 'The reformation of European Constitutionalism', *Journal of Common Market Studies*, 35, 1, 97–129.
Weir, Margaret, Shola Orloff, Ann and Skocpol, Theda (eds) (1988) *The Politics of Social Policy in the United States*. Princeton: Princeton University.
Weitzman, Leonore (1985) *The Divorce Revolution*. New York: Free.
Wendt, Alexander (1987) 'The agent-structure problem in international relations theory', *International Organization*, 4, 3, 335–50.
Western, Bruce (1999) *Between Class and Market: Postwar Unionization in the Capitalist Democracies*. Princeton: Princeton University.
Westmarland, Nicole (2004) *Rape Law Reform in England and Wales* (Working Paper 7). Bristol: School of Policy Studies.
Westwood, Sallie (1984) *All Day, Every Day*. London: Pluto.
Whitley, Richard (2000) *Divergent Capitalisms*. Oxford: Oxford University Press.
Whyte, Gerry (ed.) (1988) *Sex Equality, Community Rights and Irish Social Welfare Law*. Dublin: The Irish Centre for European Law, Trinity College.
Whyte J. H. (1971) *Church and State in Modern Ireland, 1923–1970*. Dublin: Gill and Macmillan.
Wieviorka, Michel (1995) *The Arena of Racism*. London: Sage.
Wikander, Ulla (1992) 'International Women's Congresses, 1878–1914', in Maud Eduards, Inga Elgquist-Saltzman, Eva Lundren, Christina Sjoblad, Elisabeth Sundin and Ulla Wikander (eds), *Rethinking Change*. Stockholm: HSFR.
Wikipedia (2006) *List of Countries by Date of Independence*. Available at http://en.wikipedia.org/wiki/List_of_countries_by_date_of_independence (accessed 10 November 2006).
Wilensky, Harold (2002) *Rich Democracies*. Berkeley: University of California.
Wilke, Helmut (1997) 'Autopoeisis and organised complexity'. Available at http://bprc.warwick.ac.uk/lseeg3.html
Wilkinson, Richard (2005) *The Impact of Inequality*. London: Routledge.
Willborn, Steven (1989) *A Secretary and a Cook*. Ithaca, NY: ILR Press, Cornell University.
Williams, Fiona (1995) 'Race/ethnicity, gender and class in welfare states', *Social Politics*, 2, 127–59.
Williams, Simon (1998) 'Modernity and the emotions', *Sociology*, 32, 4, 747–69.
Wilson, William (1987) *The Truly Disadvantaged*. Chicago: Chicago University.
Wiltshire, Anne (1985) *Most Dangerous Women*. London: Pandora.
Wincott, Daniel (2006) 'Paradoxes of New Labour social policy', *Social Politics*, Summer, 286–312.
Winickoff, David, Jasanoff, Sheila, Busch, Lawrence, Grove-White, Robin and Wynne, Brian (2005) 'Adjudicating the GM food wars', *Yale Journal of International Law*, 30, 81–121.
Witz, Anne (1992) *Professions and Patriarchy*. London: Routledge.
Witz, Anne (2000) 'Whose body matters?', *Body & Society*, 6, 2, 1–24.
Wolfgang, Marvin and Ferracuti, Franco (1967) *The Subculture of Violence*. London: Tavistock.
Wollstonecraft, Mary (1992 [1790]) *A Vindication of the Rights of Women*. London: Penguin.
Women's Unit (1999) *Voices*. London: The Cabinet Office Women's Unit.
Women's Unit (2000) *Women's Incomes Over the Lifetime*. London: HMSO.
Wood, Adrian (1994) *North–South Trade, Employment and Inequality*. Oxford: Oxford University.
Woodhead, Linda (2007) 'Gender differences in religious practice and significance', in James Beckford and Jay Demerath III (eds), *The Sage Handbook of the Sociology of Religion*. London: Sage. pp. 550–70.
Woodiwiss, Anthony (1998) *Globalisation, Human Rights and Labour Law in Pacific Asia*. Cambridge: Cambridge University Press.
Woodward, Alison (2003) 'European gender mainstreaming', *Review of Policy Research*, 20, 1, 65–88.

Woodward, Alison (2004) 'Building velvet triangles', in Thomas Christiansen and Simona Piattoni (eds), *Informal Governance in the European Union*. Cheltenham: Edward Elgar.
Woolf, Virginia (1938) *Three Guineas*. London: Harcourt, Brace and Ward.
World Bank (1992) *Governance and Development*. Washington, DC: World Bank.
World Bank (2001) *Engendering Development*. Washington, DC: World Bank.
World Bank (2004) *World Development Indicators 2004*. Washington, DC: World Bank.
World Bank (2005) *World Development Indicators 2005*. Accessed at ESDS International (Mimas), University of Manchester.
World Bank (2006a) *The Economics of Civil Wars, Crime and Violence*. Available at http://www.worldbank.org/research/conflict/overview/intro.htm (accessed 16 May 2006).
World Bank (2006b) *World Development Indicators*. (April 2006 edition). Washington, DC: World Bank.
World Bank (2006c) *World Development Indicators* (September 2006 edition). Accessed at ESDS International (Mimas), University of Manchester.
World Bank (2007a) 'About us'. Available at http://web.worldbank.org/WBSITE/EXTERNAL/EXTABOUTUS/0,,pagePK:50004410~piPK:36602~theSitePK:29708,00.html
World Bank (2007b) *World Development Indicators* (April 2007 edition). Accessed at ESDS International (Mimas), University of Manchester.
World Bank (2008) *World Development Indicators* (April 2008 edition). Accessed at ESDS International (Mimas), University of Manchester.
World Health Organisation (2007) *What is the Scale of the Obesity Problem in your Country?* Available at http://www.who.int/ncd_surveillance/infobase/web/InfoBase-PolicyMaker/reports/Reporter.aspx?id=1
World Social Forum (2007) *World Social Forum Nairobi 2007*. Available at http://wsf2007.org/
World Social Forum (2008) 'Another world is possible'. Available at http://www.wsf2008.net/eng/about
World Trade Organization (2007) 'What is the World Trade Organization?' Available at http://www.wto.org/english/thewto_e/whatis_e/tif_e/fact1_e.htm
Wright, R.E. and Ermisch, J. (1991) 'Gender discrimination in the British labour market', *The Economic Journal*, 101, 508–22.
Wynne, Brian (1996) 'May the sheep safely graze?', in Bron Szerszynski, Scott Lash and Brian Wynne (eds), *Risk, Environment And Modernity*. London: Sage. pp. 44–83.
Yamamura, Kozo and Streeck, Wolfgang (eds) (2003) *The End of Diversity?* Ithaca: Cornell University.
Yearley, Steven (1996) *Sociology, Environmentalism, Globalization*. London: Sage.
Yeates, Nicola (2005) *Global Care Chains* (Global Migration Perspectives No. 44, Global Commission on International Migration). Available at http://www.gcim.org/attachements/GMP%20No%2044.pdf (accessed 26 May 2006).
Yllo, Kirsti and Straus, Murray (1990) 'Patriarchy and violence against wives', in Murray Straus and Richard Gelles (eds), *Physical Violence In American Families*. New Brunswick: Transaction. pp. 383–99.
Yoko, Nuita, Mitsuko, Yamaguchi and Kimiko, Kubo (1994) 'The UN Convention on Eliminating Discrimination Against Women and the Status of Women in Japan', in Barbara Nelson and Nalma Chowdhury (eds), *Women and Politics Worldwide*. New Haven: Yale University. pp. 398–414.
Young, Brigitte (2000) 'Disciplinary neoliberalism in the European Union and gender politics', *New Political Economy*, 5, 1, 77–98.
Young, Iris (1981) 'Beyond the unhappy marriage', in Lydia Sargent (ed.), *The Unhappy Marriage of Marxism and Feminism*. London: Pluto. pp. 43–69.
Young, Iris (1990) *Justice and the Politics of Difference*. Princeton: Princeton University.
Young, Iris (1997) *Intersecting Voices*. Princeton: Princeton University.

Young, Iris (2000) *Inclusion and Democracy*. Oxford: Oxford University Press.

Young, Kate (1988) 'Introduction', in Kate Young (ed.), *Women and Economic Development*. Oxford: Berg/UNESCO.

Yuval-Davis, Nira (1997) *Gender and Nation*. London: Sage.

Yuval-Davis, Nira and Anthias, Floya (eds) (1989) *Woman-Nation-State*. London: Macmillan.

Yuval-Davis, Nira (2006) 'Intersectionality and feminist politics', *European Journal of Women's Studies*, 13, 3, 193–209.

Zabalza, A. and Tzannatos, Z. (1985) *Women and Equal Pay*. Cambridge: Cambridge University Press.

Zakaria, Fareed (2008) *The Post-American World*. New York: Norton.

Zippel, Kathrin (2004) 'Transnational advocacy networks and policy cycles in the European Union', Social Politics, 11, 1, 57–85.

Index

Please note that page references to non-textual information such as Tables will be in *italics*

abortion 345–6
accumulation 38, 70
actants 59, 78, 79
actor-network theory (ANT) 79
affiliations 33
Africa, colonial rule of 165
  see also South Africa; Sub-Saharan Africa, poverty in
African Americans
  free wage labour 373
  lynching of 197, 201, 202
  right to vote 373, 374
age, and inequality 19
agency
  humanistic conception of, rejection 79
  or structure 71–3
  and performance 62, 255
  and systems 49
  voluntarism inherent in 248
Al Qaeda 245, 405
Althusser, Louis 67, 252
America *see* United States
Amsterdam Treaty 173
anti-globalization movement 10
anti-neoliberalism 45
Arthur, Brian 86
Asian values, and democracy 178
Austria, corporatism in 134
authority, organized religions 163
automobility system 54
autopoiesis 45, 51, 90

Bali agreement (2007) 244
banks, rescue of 431
base-superstructure model 67, 77, 252
  gender regimes 255, 258
Basque nation 160, 197
Bauman, Zygmunt 15, 26
Beck, Ulrich 26, 34, 223
Beijing conference on women (1995) 226, 243, 345, 441
Benhabib, Seyla 15
Bergmann, Barbara 223
Berkovitch, Nitza 223

Bertalanffy, Ludwig von 51, 53
Biggs, Michael 97
biology 74
Black Atlantic culture 269
bodies
  in social theory 59, 75–7, 79
  and violence 198
Bourdieu, Pierre 73, 218, 219–20
Braidotti, Rosi 23, 62
breadwinner models 145–6, 147, 257
Breen, Richard 392
Bretton Woods monetary agreement (1944–1971) 121, 170
  demise of 122
Britain *see* United Kingdom
British Empire 164–5
  and political economy 383, 385
  slavery 116
  termination of 403
  and United States 398
  and violence 405
broad-democracy 178, 180, 342
  and social democracy 190
Brooks, Clem 414
bubbles, financial 119, 132, 426
  collapse of 428
Burawoy, Michael 15–16
bureaucracy 25, 69–70
Butler, Judith 62, 71–2
Byrne, David 52

call centres 78
Callon, Michel 77
Canada, aboriginal Indians in 8
capabilities approach 9–10, 16, 108
capital
  cultural 219
  finance 40–1, 119
  flows of, global processes 118–20
  forms of 116–17
  industrial 40, 119
capitalism
  and domestic labour 104

capitalism *cont.*
  and gender regime 273
  and globalization 35–6, 39–40, 116
  and nationalism 241
  and neoliberalism 245–6
  and social democracy 452
  and societalization 70
  varieties of 81, 135–6, 137
carbon dioxide, emission of 356
Card, David 131
care-work, domestic 112, 146, 331, 448
  see also domestic labour
Castells, Manuel 37, 41
catalysts 59, 416–17
  and path dependency 80, 83
categories, rejection of use 61–2
Catholic Church 94, 164, 239, 435
  in Ireland 173, 388, 389, 390–1, 393
causation 77, 84
chain,
  care chain 112, 121, 268
  commodity chain 40, 112
  concept 40
chaos theory 97
Chase-Dunn, Christopher 36, 40, 44
Chicago School 268
childbirth, death in 348, 350, 364
childcare 112–13, 307
  welfare provision 286–7, 288–90
childcare, state support for, and neoliberalism 113
children, corporal punishment of 399
China
  and global economic inequality 329, 330
  as hegemon 169, 434
choice 9–10, 26
Christian fundamentalism, and neoliberalism 10
Christianity
  see also Catholic Church
  and decline of religion 226–7

Christianity *cont.*
　fundamentalism 10, 32
　in Sweden 375
Cilliers, Paul 52
civil rights/civil rights movement 7, 242–3
civil societies 21, 36, 65, 188, 218–49, 271
concept 450
　global, and waves 233–8
　and modernity 221–8, 248, 445–6
　neoliberalism and social democracy 279
　projects 228–35, 238
　theorizing 218–21
civilizing process theory 31, 203
class *see* social class
classical social theory 71
climate change 108
Clinton, Hilary 374
coalitions, and political institutions 131
coercion 158, 166
coevolution of complex adaptive systems 43, 59, 91, 94
　in changing fitness landscapes 90–5
　and complexity theory 49, 50, 52
Cohen, Robin 161
collateralised debt obligations (CDOs) 427
colonies, absence of in democracies 180
Commission on Human Rights, on death penalty 215
commodification 145
commodity chain analysis 40, 112
communicative action 73
communitarianism 14, 15
competitive corporatism 134, 393
complex adaptive systems/ complex evolutionary systems 90
　coevolution *see* coevolution of complex adaptive systems
complex inequalities 1, 2, 22, 155, 186, 222, 311, 443, 447–8
　and employment relations 137–40
　and equality approach 320
　examples 60
　multiple 18–21
　political economy, varieties of 132
　and segregation 137–8
　terminology 21
　and violence 31, 191
complex inequality regimes 250–76
　class 251–2, 253
　disability 270–1
　ethnic 264–9
　gender *see* gender regimes
　intersecting of 272–5
　sexual orientation 271–2
complex realism 17
complexity theory 3, 47–56, 99, 444, 454–5
　and coevolution 43, 90

complexity theory *cont.*
　and non-linearity 50, 52, 84
　and path dependency 81
　and realism 74
　and social theory 49, 55
Connell, Robert (Raewyn) 257–8
consciousness 220
consent, manufactured 166
conservative corporatism 113, 143, 144, 151
contested futures 1
　European Union and United States 435–6
　comparative trajectories 436–7
　financial and economic crisis (2007–2009) 425–33
　hegemons *see* hegemons
　tipping points 437–42
contingencies 82, 83
coordinated market economies (CMEs) 135, 136
Copenhagen criteria 438
corporal punishment 399
corporatism 134–5, 393
　conservative 113, 143, 144, 151
cosmopolitan universalists 10
cosmopolitanism 7, 8, 269
Council of Europe 215
country processes, economies
　changing balance of economic sectors within country 124–5
　domestic economy, decline of 128–9
　economically-based constituencies, decline in? 129
　fiscal crisis of welfare state considerations 129–30
　knowledge economy 125–8
　political institutions and coalitions 130–1
coupling 90, 94
Crenshaw, Kimberlé 61
criminal justice systems 194, 201, 209, 404
Criminal Law (Rape) Act (1990), Ireland 407
critical junctures 83
critical realism 17
critical sociology 15
critical turning points 59, 80, 83–4
　claims for 422
　complex inequality regimes 252
　and complexity theory 51, 52
　and crises 150–1
　definitions 82, 421, 454
　in Ireland 388–9, 394–5
　and political economy 149–52
　in Sweden 375, 376, 377
　and tipping points 367
　in United Kingdom 384
Cromwell, Oliver 406
Crouch, Colin 118
cultural difference 22
cultural forms 23
cultural reductionism 61
cultural turn, social theory 252
culture 41, 44
Czech Republic, female employment rates 332

Daly, Mary 76
dampeners 59, 80, 83
Darwinian theory 51
De Landa, Manuel 52
De Valera, E. 390
death penalty 209, 401
　as contrary to human rights 215, 345, 358
　in United States 209, 358, 398, 400
decolonization, waves 241–2
de-commodification 145
deconstruction 62
defamilialisation/de-familialism 63, 146
de-gendering 22
Deleuze, Giles 62
democracy
　see also broad-democracy; presence-democracy; suffrage-democracy
　concept 20, 22
　conventional definition 34, 156–7, 178, 342
　revision required 184
　depth of
　　indicators 179–80
　　and inequality 308
　　measurement of progress 342, 343
　　modernity varieties 279
　　and political economy 370
　　significance 184
　　and violence 207, 208
　development of 156, 185–8, 190, 204
　and economic development 88–9, 185–6
　hereditary principle, absence of 80
　and human rights 34–5
　and inequality 308–9, 312
　measurement of progress 341–4
　and modernity 178–9
　and neoliberalism 184
　redefining 179–84, 189–90
　social *see* neoliberalism and social democracy
　and war, likelihood of 206–7, 208
dependency theory 40
Derrida, Jacques 62, 265
descriptive representation 183
determinism 252
de-territorialization 43, 68, 175
differences
　ethnic regimes 265
　gender regimes 256, 257
　and inequality 7, 9–10, 22, 62
　recognition of 23
　regional 117
　varieties of capitalism approach 29
DiNardo, John E. 131
disability
　and bodies 76
　and inequality 19, 270–1, 272
discourse 49, 62, 77, 265
divorce, limitations on 346
Dollar, David 329

domains 64–6, 68
  gender relations 259–60
  institutional *see* institutional domains
domestic appliances, increased purchase of 111, 112
domestic economy, decline of 128–9
domestic gender regimes
  and gender inequality 305–7
  position of women 260
  and public gender regimes 304, 309
    transition to 146–7, 261, 262, 301, 302, 421
domestic labour
  and capitalism 104
  care-work 112, 146, 331, 448
  complex inequalities 22
  as part of economy 103–5
  premodern forms of welfare as 144–7
  redistribution within household 112
domestic violence 195, 201, 209
domestic welfare 287–90
dot.com bubble, bursting of 426
dual systems theory 60
duality 72–3
Durkheim, Emile 2, 24, 27, 28
  complexity theory 47, 49, 54
  humanism 75
  social theory of 55, 71

East Asia
  financial crisis 426
  inequality in 323
Easter Uprising (1916), Ireland 406
Eastern and Central Europe, post-1989 developments 87
economic determinism 252
economic development 5–6
  and democracy 88–9, 185–6
  and global processes 154
  measurement of progress 315–19
  neoliberalism versus social democracy 360–1
  path dependent forms 153
  and public gender regimes 304–5
  and violence 206, 298
economic growth
  and capabilities 16
  dampeners and catalysts 415–17
  and gender 416–17
  measurement of 316
  in Sweden and Ireland 416–17, 418–19
  war as dampener of 416–17
  and World Bank 9, 123, 316
economic inequalities 101, 107–9, 321–6
  choice of unit 107
  class-led forms 153
  within countries 326
  and domestic violence 209
  and flows 339–40
  gendered 331
  Gini statistic, as indicator of 297, 306

economic inequalities *cont.*
  and global processes 115–17, 340
  poverty 322
  and violence 298–9, 300–1
  worldwide 322–30
economic power, polities 158
economic/polity nexus, modernity 280–1
economies 101–55
  concept of economy 19
  country processes 124–31
  divergence in analysis 152
  domain of economy 65
  domestic economy, decline of 128–9
  domestic labour *see* domestic labour
  economic inequalities 107–9
  economy/non-economy, distinguished 102
  employment relations, varieties 133–42
  political economy, varieties of 132–3
  premodern, transition to modern 109–15, 154–5
  redefining 102
  welfare *see* state welfare; welfare provision
education
  human capital produced through 106
  human development, well-being and capabilities approach 351
  and knowledge economy 126
  and rationalisation 32
Eisenstadt, Schmuel 27
Eldredge, Niles 92
elections, in democracy 181–2
Elias, Norbert 31, 203
emergence
  and complexity theory 50, 51–2
  concept 59
  and ontological depth 74
  and projects 73–5
empires 159, 161, 164–6
  British *see* British Empire
employment of women *see* women: employment of
employment protection 135, 136
employment regulation
  care and employment 139
  class-oriented 279
  distinctions between forms 148
  equal treatment 22, 138
  gender 291–3
  inequality 295
  mode of implementation 139
  modernity 290–5
  neoliberal and social democratic forms 140, 279
  non-standard employment 136
  operationalization of forms 135
  path dependencies 291
  political economy 295
  types of regulations 140
  in United Kingdom 387
  welfare and employment 293–5
  and welfare provision 147–9, 293–5

employment relations
  and complex inequalities 137–40
  corporatism 134–5
  gender regimes 263
  market-based production, associated institutions 133
  varieties 133–42
Engels, Friedrich 76, 104
Enlightenment 14
environmental sustainability 108
  progress, measurement of 354, 355–6
environmentalism, waves 45, 244–5
epistemic communities 15, 95
equal opportunities legislation 243
Equal Pay Campaign (1977), Ireland 392
equal treatment 22, 138
equality
  and economics 108
  in employment 139, 141
    see also employment protection; employment regulation; women: employment of
  and human rights 8
  and measuring progress 319–21
  neoliberalism versus social democracy 361–2
  as outcome 320
  progress as 6–7
  sameness and difference approaches to 23
  single standard of, in economic inequality 22
  and social inclusion 13
  and transformation 23
equilibrium 50, 54, 85, 86
Esping-Andersen, Gøsta
  conservative corporatism 143, 144
  gender 63–4, 145, 147
  modernity 29
  path dependency 89
  social democracy 377
essentialism 23, 62
Estevez-Abe, Margarita 135
ethnic cleansing 196, 197, 200
ethnicity
  see also racial violence
  and inequality 19, 264–9
  projects 229
  regimes 264–9
EUFOR (European Union Force) 168, 440
European Charter of Fundamental Rights 270
European Defence Community 168
European Security Strategy 440
European Union (EU)
  and changing fitness landscape 93
  Charter of Fundamental Rights 270
  and economy 316, 439
  education development 351
  employment regulation 139
  Employment Strategy 347
  enlargement 437–8
  and environmental sustainability 108

European Union (EU) *cont.*
  Equal Treatment Directive (1975) 243
  equality strategy 22
  formation, reasons for 267
  and gender 149, 333
  as hegemon 45, 123, 167, 169–70, 433
  indicators of 354
  Irish membership 391
  and knowledge economy 126
  life-expectancy 363
  as 'merely' an inter-governmental body 168
  and militarism 211
  money versus longevity 3
  neoliberalism and social democracy 13–14
  and political institutions/ coalitions 131
  as polity 167
  and religion 33
  and scientific knowledge 227
  Security Strategy 214
  social system 4
  as state? 167–8
  UK membership 384
  United States contrasted
    comparative trajectories 436–7
    differences 435–6
    economic growth, measurement of 316
    environmental sustainability 108
    gender pay gap 333
    hegemons 167
    income differences 416
    military strategy 213–14
    powers and potentials 434
    religion 33
    size 438
    violence 364
  violence 364
  and Western civilization 39
evolution 92

fascism, waves 241
familialism 63
family 26, 33, 63, 104
Family Law (Protection of Spouses and Children) Act (1981), Ireland 407
Fawcett Society 241
Federated Union of Employers, Ireland 393
feedback/feedback loops
  concept of feedback 85
  negative *see* negative feedback/ negative feedback loops
  positive *see* positive feedback/positive feedback loops
feminism 243–4
  see also gender
  early theory 254–5
  first wave 240–1
  and globalization 45
  organizations 188, 231
  projects 233
  radical 76–7
  in United Kingdom 404

feminism *cont.*
  in United States 399
  and universal human rights 243–4
  and wave concept 96
Fianna Fail (Irish Party) 390
finance capital 40–1, 119
financial bubbles 119, 132, 426
  collapse of 428
financial crises 122, 426
  of 2007–9 123, 425–33, 453–4
  pathways out of 428–33
financial derivatives 427, 428
financial markets, volatility 119
Firestone, Shulamith 76
first wave feminism, waves 240–1
fitness landscape
  changing 43, 46, 47, 177
  coevolution of complex adaptive systems in 90–5
  concept 46, 55, 91
  and hegemons 167
  and social systems 59
fixed capital 119
force, by state 31
Fordism 133
Foucault, Michel
  civil society 218, 219
  critique of 205–6
  discipline, in modern world 31, 203, 204, 209
  discourse 62, 77, 265
  governmentality 204–5
  sexuality 224
  social order 192
Framework Convention on Climate Change (1992) 356
framings, global 236–7
Fraser, Nancy 231
free trade 120
free wage labour 107, 331
  and modernity 30–1, 445
  transition to 109–10, 114
  for women 112
  in United States 373
Freedom House Index of Civil Liberties and Political Rights 353
freedom of speech, in democracy 181
Friedman, Milton 11, 245
functionalism, and complexity theory 47, 52–3
functionings, and capabilities 9, 347
fundamentalism 10, 32, 245

G8 121
G20 432–3
G77 435
Gastil, Raymond 345, 353
GDI (Gender-related Development Index) 334, 351
GDP (Gross Domestic Product) 104, 316, *317*, 319
gender
  see also feminism; women
  as catalyst of economic growth 416–17
  economic inequalities 331
  employment regulation 291–3

gender *cont.*
  and equal rights 8
  gendered state social expenditure 285–7
  and inequality 19, 305–7
    complex inequality regimes *see* gender regimes
    economic 331
  in employment 333–6
  multiple inequalities 63–4
  occupational segregation 334–5
  projects 229
  regimes *see* gender regimes
  and social democratic projects 12
  and violence 195, 261, 299
    see also domestic violence
  welfare, public or domestic 287–90
gender gaps
  education 32
  employment 331–2
  pay 333–6
  in Sweden 414
gender regimes 254–64, 273, 301–3
  base-superstructure model 255
  breadwinner models 257
  and class regimes 302
  definitions 301
  differences 256, 257
  domestic *see* domestic gender regimes
  female membership, increases in 412
  groups 256
  indicators *303*
  inequalities 259, 302
  institutional domains 259–60
  meso and micro levels 260
  neoliberalism and social democracy 263
  public *see* public gender regimes
  state welfare 263
  varieties of 259
Gender-related Development Index (GDI) 334, 351
General Assembly, UN 215–16
genes 92
genocide 200
Germany
  breadwinner models 257
  corporatism in 134
  female employment rates 141
  and social democracy 136
  two states in 160
Giddens, Anthony 26, 34, 72–3, 85, 223
Gilman, Charlotte Perkins 104
Gilroy, Paul 269
Gini statistic, as indicator of
  economic inequality 297, 322
  and gender inequality 306
global care chains 40, 112, 121
global framings 236–7
global justice movement, as global wave 246
global processes 1, 101–2, 451–3
  see also globalization
  and changing fitness landscape 93

global processes *cont.*
  complex inequality regimes 252
  components 42
  and development/development paths 41–6, 154, 370
  and economic inequalities 115–17, 340
  ethnic inequality 268
  and measuring progress 321
  and neoliberalism 42
  types 117–24
  violence 192–3, 212–16
global warming/heating 108, 356
global wave, neoliberalism as 123, 245–6
globalization 1, 165
  see also global processes
  approaches to 36–7
  definitions 35, 36
  of economy 153–4
  as erosion of distinctive and separate societies 37–8
  and impact 93
  origins 37
  and progress 16
  resistance to 38–9, 45
  waves of 44, 116
    see also waves
  world as already global 39–41
glocalization 44
GNI (Gross National Income) 316
GNPpc (Gross National Product per capita) 328
Gottfried, Heidi 274
governance
  democratic 178
  and financial crises 429, 430
  internal, collapse of institutions 159
  polities 158
'governing the soul', notion of 204
Government of Ireland Act (1914) 406
governmental programmes, projects in 10
governmentality 204
Gramsci, Antonio 54, 166
  civil society 65, 218, 220–1, 248
Great Depression (1930s) 119, 426
Gross Domestic Product (GDP) 104, 316, *317*, 319
Gross National Income (GNI) 316
Gross National Product per capita (GNPpc) 328
Group of 77 122, 177
groups
  affiliations 33
  gender regimes 256
  versus individuals 22
  rights 8
  violence 193
Guattari, Félix 62

Haas, Ernst 15
habeas corpus 20
Habermas, Jürgen 15, 73, 177
  on civil society 218, 219, 223
habitus 73, 219, 220
  stasis inherent in 248
Hall, Peter 29, 135
harassment 196, 200

Haraway, Donna 78
Hardt, Michael 165, 166
Harvey, David 38
Hayek, Friedrich von 11, 245
HDI (Human Development Indicator) 350, 351, 352
Health Act (1947), Ireland 391
hedge funds 427
hegemons 159, 166–70
  contesting, and world future 433
  current and future 433–5
  EU as 45, 123, 167, 169–70
  global 40, 43, 123, 213, 226
  current and future 433–5
  military violence by 213–14, 217
  potential 169
  and societalization 46, 166
  United Kingdom as 123, 384, 402
  United States as 46, 123, 167, 168–9, 170, 212
hegemony 54, 220–1
Held, David 36
hereditary principle, absence of in democracies 180
Hicks, Alexander 144
hierarchies, nested 174
high modernity 25
Hinduism, fundamentalism within 32, 245
Hollywood 43
Holocaust 296
Home Rule, for Ireland 406
homicide
  see also violence
  and economic development 206, 298
  and economic inequality 298–9
  and gender 299
  indicators of violence 297
  United States 396
House of Lords 385
household
  intersection of gender and class inequality in 336–9
  single-parent 112, 337–8
  as unit of analysis 330, 338
housework *see* domestic labour
housing markets 426–7
Human Development Indicator (HDI) 350, 351, 352
human development, well-being and capabilities approach 9, 347, 351, 355
  life-expectancy 348, *349*, 350
  measurement of progress 346–51
  Millennium Development Goals 346, 350–1, 353
  neoliberalism versus social democracy 362
human rights 7–8
  breaches of codes 215
  Conventions and Covenants 237, 247, 344–5
  and democracy 34–5
  and economics 108
  and globalization 8, 45
  measurement of progress 344–6
  neoliberalism versus social democracy 362
  and social democracy 10
  and United States 441

human rights *cont.*
  universal *see* universal human rights
  UN-recognized, list of 16
  and violence 215–16, 357
humanism 75
Huntington, Samuel 27, 38–9, 169, 435
hybridity/hybridization 44, 269
hypothetical line of perfect equality 322

'I' and 'me' analysis, social theory 72
identity analysis 61, 62, 265–6
IMF *see* International Monetary Fund (IMF)
impact, concept 92, 93
imprisonment rates 209–10
income inequalities 19–20, 131, 322
India, and global economic inequality 329, 330
individuals
  and agency concept 72
  versus groups 22
  human rights of 7
    see also human rights; universal human rights
individuation 33–4, 222–3, 223
industrial capital 40, 119
industrialization
  early 117
  and employment of women 110, 114
  transition to 28, 29
inequalities
  between-country 117, 120, 152
  complex *see* complex inequalities
  and democracy 308–9, 312
  and differences 7, 9–10
  economic *see* economic inequalities
  gender *see* gender: and inequality
  income 19–20, 131, 322
  non-economic domains 341
  political, decline in 344
  regimes 448–9
  regulations eroding 138
  restructuring of patterns 121
  sexuality 224
  structural generation of 138–9
information sector 127
information society 37
institutional domain
  economy, polity and civil society 58–9, 65–6, 68–9
  gender regimes 259–60
  violence 443–4, 449–50
International Labour Organization 239
International Monetary Fund (IMF) 5, 121, 154, 170, 236, 429, 431
  and capabilities 16
  conditions on loans from 11, 122
  and economic growth approach 9, 123, 352
International War Crimes Tribunal 170

inter-personal violence
	see also violence
	bodies and technologies 75–6
	criminalization 193, 194, 203
	increased regulation of 216
	and inequality 217
	and modernity 298
	quality of life, effect on 196
	and state monopoly on legitimate coercion 200
intersectionality
	and gender 255
	gender and class inequality in household 336–9
	intracategorical 61
	and multiple inequalities 60–4
intimacy
	and modernity 224
	and organized religions 163, 164
	and social change 26
intracategorical intersectionality 61
Ireland
	Catholic Church in 173, 388, 389, 390–1, 393
	as Celtic Tiger 394
	competitive corporatism 134
	conflict with Britain 160
	democracy 388–95
	economic growth 416–17, 418–19
	equal opportunities legislation 243
	founding of Irish Free State 406
	and gender regimes 392
	and globalization 394
	independence from Britain (1922) 389, 403, 406
	labour movement 392–3
	nation of 160
	and neoliberalism 407
	political economy 388–95
	single-parent households 338
	violence 197, 403, 405–8
Irish Republican Army (IRA) 406
Islam
	fundamentalism within 32, 245
	as hegemonic 169, 434–5
	as polity 164
	relations with states 172–3
	and universal human rights 44
	and West 39

Japan
	as hegemon 169, 435
	welfare provision 143
Jessop, Bob 54, 55, 70
Jihadists 164, 169, 198, 245, 433
	and United Kingdom 405
'Jim Crow' laws, United States 181, 186, 202
job evaluation schemes 138
Judaism, fundamentalism within 32, 245
justice
	and equality 6
	groups versus individuals 22
	rights-based tradition of 7–8
	social, securing 13
	social contract approach to 8

Kaldor, Mary 212
Kalmar Union 400

Kanter, Rosabeth Moss 182–3
Kash, Don 87
Kauffman, Stuart 43, 46, 51–2, 91, 167
Kenworthy, Lane 144
Kerr, C. 88
Keynesian macro economic management 12, 374
knowledge
	development 78–9
	neoliberalism 227
	scientific forms 227
	and technology 78
knowledge economy 125–8
knowledge intensive services 126–7
Koran 172
Korpi, Walter 89
Korzeniewicz, Roberto 328
Kraay, Aart 329
Kuhn, Thomas 55
Kuznets, Simon 125
Kuznets curve 117, 125
Kymlicka, Will 8
Kyoto Protocol (1997) 244, 356

labour markets, conservative coordinated 140, 154
Labour Party, UK 385, 386
labour power, commodification 30
Lakatos, Imre 55
late modernity 24, 25
Latin America
	financial crisis 426
	inequality in 322, 323
	and Western civilization 39
Latour, Bruno 77, 78
Law, John 77
Lawrence, Steven 202
League of Nations 239, 242
Lee, David 131
Lee, J. J. 392
legal power, polities 158
Lewis, Jane 29, 145, 257
liberal market economies (LMEs) 135
liberalisation, world trade 15
Liebowitz, S. J. 81
life-expectancy 348, 349, 363
lifeworld 104, 219, 223
light 96
linearity 84, 97
	see also non-linearity
Lipset, Seymour Martin 88
liquid modernity 24, 26
Lisbon Treaty (2007) 439, 440
lock-in of development paths 86, 87, 151, 252
	Nordic countries, social democracy in 426
longevity
	and equality 6
	and income 363
	as key indicator of well-being 347
	versus money 3–4
López, José 64
Lorber, Judith 22
Lorenz curve 322
Luhmann, Niklas 47, 52–3, 54
Luther, Martin 239
Luther King, Martin 202
lynching 197, 200, 201, 202

MacKinnon, Catharine 76
Madrid European Council 438
Mahoney, James 82, 87
Malaysia, Islam in 172–3
male-breadwinner-female housewife model, typology 145–6, 147, 257
Mann, Michael 161, 165, 323
manufacturing, high technology 126, 127, 128
Manza, Jeff 414
Margolis, Stephen 81
market economies, liberal and coordinated 135, 136
market effectiveness, neoliberalism 11
marriage
	rape in 201, 358, 401
	and sexuality 226
Marshall Aid 392
Martin, Hans-Peter 118
Marx, Karl 2, 24, 27, 28
	capitalism 30–1, 53–4
	complexity theory 47
	forces of production 76
	global expansion of capital 39
	social theory of 55
Marxism
	complexity theory 47, 53
	segregationary reductionist approach 63
	social theory 71
	systems 66
Maturana, Humberto 51, 90
McCall, Leslie 61
McClintock, Anne 256
McDonalds 38, 43
Mead, George Herbert 72
Medaglia, Azadeh 274
Merton, Robert 49
meta-narratives 61, 66
micro-macro relation 73
micro-reductionism 61
migration 160, 266–7
militarism/military force
	and neoliberalism 210–11
	and polities 162, 164, 166, 167
	in United Kingdom 402, 403
	in United States 213–14, 440–1
	and violence 193–4, 210
	and war 207
Millennium Development Goals 9, 16, 123, 236
	education development 351
	human development, well-being and capabilities approach 346, 350–1, 353
	poverty eradication 322, 323
Minahan, James 161
modernisation, dualisms of before and after 27–8
modernity 1, 2, 25, 206, 278
	and civil society 221–8, 248
	defining 30–5
	and democracy 178–9
	and employment regulation 290–5
	Foucault on 203, 204
	and gender regime 301–3
	high or late 24, 25
	indicators 297–8
	and intimacy 224

modernity *cont.*
  liquid 24, 26
  multiple modernities 26–7
  neoliberalism and social
    democracy 278–9, 446
  or postmodernity 14, 24–5
  path dependencies 28–9, 277,
    280–1, 296–7
  as progress 4, 25
  reflexive or second 24, 25–6
  religion, decline of 32–3, 226–7
  varieties of 28–30, 277–312,
    445–7
    neoliberal and social
      democratic 278–9
  and violence 199–208, 446
Moghadam, Valentine 223
money, versus longevity 3–4
Moore, Barrington 29, 89
Moran, Timothy 328
Mósesdóttir, Lilja 128
Mother and Child Scheme (1951),
  Ireland 391
multiple complex inequalities
  18–21, 99
multiple inequalities, and
  intersectionality 60–4
multiple modernities 26–7
  modernity and pre-modernity,
    boundary between 221
  not yet modern 27–8
multiple social systems 58–100
  bodies and technologies 75–9
  complex adaptive systems,
    coevolution 90–5
  emergence and projects 73–5
  path dependencies 79–89
  regimes and domains 64–6
  wave concept 95–9

NAFTA (North America Free
  Trade Agreement) 168
National Health Service, UK
  386, 387
nationalism, waves 241–2
nationalist protectionism 430, 431–2
nations 159–60
  conflicts over borders 160, 211
  cross-cutting of 160, 161
  desire for own state 162–3
  origins 241
nation-states 41, 47, 159, 241
  myth of 160–3, 170
  sovereignty of 44, 404
NATO (North Atlantic Treaty
  Organization) 170
negative feedback/negative feedback loops 80, 84, 85, 86
Negri, Antonio 165, 166
neo-liberal corporatism 393
neoliberalism
  and capitalism 245–6
  and childcare, state support
    for 113
  and Christian fundamentalism 10
  and democracy 184
  and financial crises 430, 432
  and global processes/
    globalization 37–8,
    42, 45, 154
  as global wave 123, 245–6
  and Ireland 407

neoliberalism *cont.*
  and knowledge 227
  and market effectiveness 11
  and militarism 210–11
  as not inevitable process 102,
    118, 443
  projects 10–11, 13–14
  and social democracy *see*
    neoliberalism and social
    democracy
  and state interventions 12
  and suffrage-democracy 190
  in United Kingdom 386,
    404, 405
  in United States 12, 372, 373,
    374, 399
  and violence 210
neoliberalism and social
  democracy 367–424
  see also neoliberalism;
    neoliberalism versus
    social democracy
  class regimes 253
  employment relations 140
  ethnic regimes 268
  gender regimes 263
  modernity 278–9, 446
  political economy 151, 369–70
  public gender regimes 307
  violence 210, 396–7
  welfare provision 143–4
neoliberalism versus social
  democracy
  economic development 360–1
  equality 361–2
  human development, well-being
    and capabilities 362
  human rights 362
nested hierarchies 174
Netherlands, competitive
  corporatism 134
network 49, 78, 98
New Labour (UK) 13, 386
Newtonian conceptions,
  causation 84
9–11 terrorist attacks 197
1960s movement, waves 242–3
nomadic subject, metaphor of 23,
  62, 257
non-humans, in social theory 59,
  108
non-linearity 59, 97
  and complexity theory 50, 52, 84
Nordic Council 401
Nordic countries
  see also Sweden
  class relations 377
  corporatism 134
  female employment rates 332
  feminism in 380
  gendered state social
    expenditure 286
  inequality in 325
  social democracy, lock-in 426
  state supported
    childcare 113
normalization 204
Norris, Pippa 182
North, Douglass 87
North America, distribution of
  wealth in 330
nuclear weapons 213

Oakley, Ann 103
Obama, Barack 374
obesity, in developed world
  350, 364
objects, within social theory 77–8
OECD (Organization for
  Economic Cooperation and
  Development)
  countries
    employment regulation 291
    female employment rates 332
    indicators of 354
    inequality in 324–5
    life-expectancy 348
    modernity, varieties of 278,
      283, 291
    path dependency of violence
      nexus in 299–300, 301
    public social expenditure 130
    state welfare 283
ontological depth, and
  emergence 74
opportunities 6, 9, 10
Ostner, Ilona 145
outcomes 6, 9, 10, 320
over-generalisations, false 61

Parenthood and Guardianship
  Code, Sweden 401
Parsons, Talcott
  complexity theory 47, 49, 54
  feedback loops 85
  segregationary reductionist
    approach 63
  social theory of 55
  sub-systems of 67
particularism, and universalism
  8, 14
part-time employment 136, 138
part-whole analysis 58, 67
path dependencies
  challenges to significance of
    concept 420
  complex inequality regimes
    252–3
  and complexity theory
    49, 51, 55
  concept 59, 424, 454
  economic development 153
  within economics 81
  at economy/polity nexus 280–1
  employment regulation 291
  gender regime 290–4
  lock-in of development paths
    86, 87, 151
  modernity 28–9, 277, 296–7
  multiple social systems 79–89
  political economy 149–150
  transitions/transformations 87–8
  violence 192, 208–12, 296–8
    OECD countries 299–300, 301
path dependency, violence 208–12
pay gaps, gender 333–6
penal welfare 209, 210
people, flows of 121
performance 62, 255
phenomenology, and complexity
  theory 52–3
Pierson, Paul 81–2, 87
Platform for Action, Beijing
  conference 226, 243,
    345, 441

pogroms 196–7
policy sociology 15
political consciousness 30
political democracy, and
   economic development 88–9
political economy
   causes 132
   differences among countries 371
   employment regulation 295
   indicators 282
   Ireland 388–95
   neoliberalism and social
      democracy 151, 369–70
   Sweden 375–83
   United Kingdom 383–8
   United States 370, 372–5
   varieties of 132–3
      and critical turning points
         149–52
political institutions 130–1
   and coalitions 131
   complex inequality regimes 252
   global 170–1
   polities 158
polities 156–90
   concept of polity 20
   domain of 65
   empires 159, 164–6
   and ethnic relations 267
   fluidity of 175–6
   global political institutions 170–1
   hegemons 159, 166–70
   membership 158
   minimal definition of a
      polity 158
   nations 159–60
   nation-states see nation-states
   non-saturation of territory by
      any one 156, 171–8
   overlapping of 156, 171–8
   polity/economy nexus 300–1
   power, types of 158
   reconceptualizing types of 156,
      157–60
   regional 159
   religions, organized 159, 163–4
   and states 159, 449
pornography 225
positive feedback/positive
   feedback loops
   and complexity theory 49
   employment of women 114
   and path dependency 83, 84, 86
   trajectories of development 59
   wave theory 97
postmodernity 2, 62
   or modernity 14, 24–5
poststructuralism, and
   differences 62
Poulantzas, Nicos 54, 252
poverty 322, 323
   feminisation of 337
PPP (Purchasing Power Parity)
   316, 329
precautionary principle 227
presence-democracy 178, 180,
   184, 185–6, 342
   in Ireland 389
   and social democracy 190
   in Sweden 375
   in United Kingdom 386
   for women 187–8

Prigogine, Ilya 84
Prigogine school 52
privatization, and neoliberalism 184
production 76, 102, 133
professional sociology 15
progress 3–18
   alternative goals 4
   as contested concept/project
      1–2, 4–5, 25, 314, 444
   contesting conceptions 14–17
   defined 3–4
   economic development see
      economic development
   measurement of see progress,
      measurement of
   as modernity 4, 25
   money versus longevity 3–4
   social theory, challenge to 444–5
   visions of, achievement 359–65
progress, measurement of 314–66
   economic development 315–19
   economic inequalities 321–6
   global 326–30
   environmental sustainability
      and violence 354–9
   equality 319–21
   gendered economic
      inequalities 331
   household as unit of analysis 330
   intersection of gender and
      class inequality in
      household 336–9
   key indicator sets 352–4
   neoliberalism versus social
      democracy
      economic development
         360–1
      equality 361–2
      human development,
         well-being and capabil-
         ities 362
      human rights 362
      trade offs 362–5
      visions of progress,
         achievement 359–65
progressive liberalism 144
projects
   civil society 228–33
   and waves 234–5, 238
   concept of project 75
   and emergence 73–5
   feminist 233
   ideas 232
   neoliberalism 10–11, 13–14
   societalization 451
projects, competing 10–14
proportional representation 183
proportionality 84
public execution 203
public gender regimes
   see also gender regimes
   and civil societies 225
   and development 304–5
   and domestic regimes 304, 309
      transition to public regimes
         146–7, 261, 262, 301,
         302, 421
   forms of 261–2
   and gender inequality 305–7
   position of women 260
   varieties of 307–8
public sociology 15–16

public sphere 219
punctuated equilibria 50, 92
punishment, and discipline 204
Purchasing Power Parity (PPP)
   316, 329

Quebecois, Canada 160
QWERTY keyboard, and path
   dependency 80

racial violence 196–7
   African Americans, lynching of
      197, 201, 202
   in United Kingdom 202–3
radical feminism 76–7
Ramirez, Francisco 187, 240
rape, in marriage 201, 358
   illegal in Sweden 401
rationalisation, and modernity 32–3
rationality 25
Rawls, John 7–8
Reagan, Ronald 11, 245
realism 17, 52, 74
recession, economic 428–9
recognition 15, 23
redistribution 106
reductionism 49, 61, 71, 73
   economic 220
   gender regimes 256
   segregationary 62–3
reflexive modernity 24, 25–6, 32
reflexivity 72, 73
Reformation, waves 239
regime influence 44
regime shopping 37, 118
regimes
   complex inequality see
      complex inequality regimes
   concepts 49
   and domains 64
   ethnic 264–9
   gender see domestic gender
      regimes; gender regimes;
      public gender regimes
relative autonomy 67, 252
religion
   Christianity see Catholic
      Church; Christianity
   and civil societies 226
   and inequality 19
   Islam see Islam
   organized religions 159, 163–4,
      180–1
   decline of 32–3, 226–7
   in United States 32, 33, 227
religious bodies, non-elected 180
representation 183
restructuring, rounds of 95–6
rights
   human see human rights; uni-
      versal human rights
   notion of 7
Riley, Dylan 323
Rio conference (1992) 244
Risse, Thomas 177
Robinson, William 40
Ruggie, John 177
Ruggie, Mary 377
rule of law, and democratic
   governance 178
Rummel, R. J. 341
Rycroft, Robert 87

saltation 52
sameness, equality through 23
Santa Fe school 52
saturate, concept 171
Scandinavia, and Reformation 239
'scapes', cultural 68
Schreiner, Olive 104
Schumann, Harald 118
science
  and path dependency 80
  and rationalisation 32
  and reductionism 71
Scotland, nation of 160
Scott, John 64
Seattle riots 15
second modernity 24, 25–6
secularism/secularization 32, 33, 163, 204, 226
segregation, and complex inequalities 137–8
segregationary reductionist approach 62–3
selection 91, 92
self-equilibration, and complexity theory 49
self-organization 51, 52
Sen, Amartya 9, 347, 352
Sennett, Richard 118
Serrano-Pascual, Amparo 127–8
services, knowledge intensive 126–7
sex crimes 225
sexual orientation and inequality 19
  complex inequality regimes 271–2
sexuality
  and civil societies 224, 225
  and marriage 226
shadow banking system, growth 427
Simmel, Georg 2, 24, 25, 27, 28
  complexity theory 47
  individuation 33, 34
  modernity 223
  relational approach of 64
Single European Market 173
single-parent households 112, 337–8
Sinn Féin 406
Skeggs, Beverley 256
Skocpol, Theda 89
slavery 116, 266
  in United States 181, 186, 373, 398
Smelser, Neil 49
Smith, Anthony D. 241
social class
  and civil societies 220
  employment regulation 279
  and inequality 19, 22, 153
    complex inequality regimes 251–2, 253, 302
  confined to class 198
  economic 331
  privilege 219–20
  projects, civil society 229
  welfare provision 279
  working class, restructuring of 230–1
social contract approach, justice 8
social democracy
  conventional definition 409
  and decline in economically-based constituencies 129

social democracy cont.
  and democracy 184
  and employed women 12, 114, 409–15, 453
  and financial crises 430, 431, 432
  and human rights 10
  lock-in, in Nordic countries 426
  and neoliberalism see neoliberalism and social democracy; neoliberalism versus social democracy
  and presence-democracy/broad democracy 190
  progress as equality 6
  projects 10, 11–14
  in Sweden 12, 378, 382–3, 401–2
  and trade unions 413, 414
  and violence 210
social fact, concept 75
social formations, projects in 10
social inclusion, and equality 13
social movement theory, and wave concept 96
social partnerships, Ireland 393
social relations, concept 49
social structure 64–5, 75
social systems
  concept, re-working of 58, 99
  European Union 4
  multiple see multiple social systems
  overlapping of 59
  traditional theory 71
  United States 4
  waves as connections between 98
social theory 1
  challenge of complex inequalities and globalization to 444–51
  classical 71
  and complexity theory 49, 55
  and globalization 2, 46–7
  macro level 19, 60
  objects within 77–8
  and violence 191, 193
socialism 6, 23, 239–40
socialization, and women's activities 104
societalization 42, 45, 69–70
  and complexity theory 55
  and coupling 94
  and hegemons 46, 166
  ongoing processes 59
  processes of 451
  projects 451
  and societies 450–1
societies 47, 450–1
sociology
  and complexity theory 47, 49, 53
  public 15–16
  system, concept of 66
Soskice, David 29, 135
South Africa
  inequality in 322
  opposition to apartheid 243
South America, colonial rule of 165
South Asia, inequality in 323
sovereignty of nation-states 44, 404

space 43, 68, 174–5
Spain, single-parent households 338
species 92
state
  conventional concept 20, 168
    limitations of 156, 157, 189, 449
  interventions by 11–12
  modern, defined 31
  nation distinguished 159–60
  as polity 159, 170
  self-interest 176
  social justice, role in securing 13
  violence by 12, 194
    legitimate, monopoly of 31, 199–200
  Westphalian 175
state interventions, neoliberalism 12
state welfare 283, 284, 285
  see also welfare provision
  class-oriented 279
  concept of welfare 106
  gender regimes 263
  neoliberal and social democratic varieties of modernity 279
  as part of economy 105–7
statistical analysis 84
statute law, and violence 200
Stiglitz Commission, USA 432
stock market collapse (1929) 426
Streeck, Wolfgang 118
structural adjustment 11
structural-functionalism 66
structuration theory 73
structure, or agency 71–3
sub-cultures, and crime 195
sub-prime housing market, USA 426, 427
Sub-Saharan Africa, poverty in 323
substantive representation 183
suffrage-democracy 157, 178, 180, 184, 342
  in Ireland 388, 389
  neoliberalism 190
  and neoliberalism 190
  in Sweden 375
  in United Kingdom 384, 423
  in United States 372, 373, 395–6
  for women 187
Suicide (Durheim) 75
suicide bombing 198, 232, 245, 405
Swank, Duane 82
Sweden
  and childcare, state support for 113
  death penalty, abolition 401
  democracy 375–383
  economic growth 416–17, 418–19
  education development 351
  female employment in 412
  feminism in 379, 380
  gender relations 377
  neutrality in war 401
  political economy 375–83
  political parties 376, 378
  presence-democracy in 375
  single-parent households 338
  social democracy in 12, 378, 382–3, 401–2
  suffrage-democracy in 375
  violence 400–2
  women, employment of 411
  women in politics 182

symbolic power, polities 158
systems
  complex adaptive see coevolution of complex adaptive systems
  concept of system 47, 66
    re-worked 49–50, 55
  and environments 67–9, 91
    system/environment distinction 50, 58, 67
    overlapping of 68, 69
    social see multiple social systems; social systems
  and structures 65
systems theory 66, 85

tax avoidance 427
tax havens 119, 427
technologies
  high technology manufacturing 126, 127, 128
  multiple social systems 77–9
  and social theory 59
temporality 91
temporary employment 136, 138
terrorism 197–8, 232
Thatcher, Margaret 11, 245, 387
thermodynamics, second law of 51
thermostats, and feedback loops 85
Thomas, Sue 182
tipping points 80, 82, 437–42, 453–4
  definitions 421
  and Ireland 389
Tobin tax 431
trade flows, global processes 120–1
trade offs, measurement of progress 362–5
trade unions
  and civil society projects 230–1
  drive to reduce power of 136
  female membership 231, 411
  in Ireland 393
  political institutions and coalitions 131
  and social democracy 413, 414
  in Sweden 377, 379
  in United Kingdom 385
  women in 114
transformation
  and equality 23
  and global processes 44
  path dependencies 87–8
  transitions
    from domestic to public gender regimes 146–7, 261, 262, 301, 302, 421
    see also domestic labour; gender regimes; women: employment of
    Eastern and Central Europe, post-1989 developments 87
    to free wage labour 109–10, 112, 114
    to industrialization 28, 29
    path dependencies 87–8
    from pre-modern to modern economies 109–15, 154–5
truth 14, 15
Turkey, female employment rates 332

UK see United Kingdom
UN see United Nations
UNDP (United Nations Development Project) 9, 10, 347
  Human Development Indicator 350, 351
United Kingdom
  black people, treatment of 202
  British Empire see British Empire
  conflict with Ireland 160
  democracy 383–8
  economic growth 417, 418–19
  employment protection 136
  equal opportunities legislation 243
  Equalities Review 347
  feminism in 404
  financial market 119
  gender regime 411
  as hegemon 123, 384, 402
  neoliberalism in 386, 404, 405
    neoliberalism/social democracy boundary 13
  political economy 383–8
  single-parent households 338
  suffrage-democracy in 384, 423
  violence 402–5
  women, employment of 411
  women in politics 182
United Nations
  on death penalty 215–16
  Development Project see UNDP (United Nations Development Project)
  founding of 242
  Group of 77 122, 177
  human rights Conventions and Covenants 237, 247, 344–5
  Millennium Declaration 16
  Millennium Development Goals see Millennium Development Goals
  Security Council 170, 213
  Universal Declaration of Human Rights see Universal Declaration of Human Rights
United States
  see also Latin America; South America, colonial rule of
  abortion in 345–6
  civil war 398
  Constitution 372
  death penalty 209, 358, 398, 400
  democracy 370–5
  distribution of wealth in 330
  economy 316, 417, 418–19, 439
  education development 351
  as empire? 165
  employment regulation 139
  and environmental sustainability 108
  European Union
    contrasted comparative trajectories 436–7
    differences 435–6
    economic growth, measurement of 316
    environmental sustainability 108
    gender pay gap 333

United States: European Union cont.
  hegemons 167
  income differences 416
  military strategy 213–14
  powers and potentials 434
  religion 33
  size 438
  violence 364
  and feminism 243
  financial market 119
  gender pay gap 333
  gender regime 411
  as hegemon 46, 123, 167, 168–9, 170, 212, 433
  and human rights 441
  increasing economic inequality in 131
  life-expectancy in 348, 363
  Mexico, war with 398
  military force by 213–14, 440–1
  money versus longevity 3
  neoliberalism in 12, 372, 373, 374, 399
  political economy 370, 372–5
  and religion 32, 33, 227
  and scientific knowledge 227
  single-parent households 338
  slavery in 181, 186, 373, 398
  social system 4
  'sub-prime' housing market 426, 427
  suffrage-democracy in 372, 373, 395–6
  Vietnam war 242, 399
  violence 364, 396, 397–400
  War of Independence 372, 398
  and Western civilization 39
  women, employment of 411
  women in politics 182
Universal Declaration of Human Rights 8, 21, 35, 237, 247, 345, 353
universal human rights
  see also human rights
  and equality 320
  and feminism 243–4
  and global civil society 238
  as global wave 246–7
  and glocalization 44
  and progress 16
universal suffrage 181
universalism 15
  and particularism 8, 14
Urry, John 54, 55
USA see United States
utilitarian theory 7–8

Varela, Francisco 51, 90
varieties of capitalism approach 29
VHS, and path dependency 80
Vietnam war 242, 399
violence 191–217, 356–9
  and British Empire 405
  and civil society projects 231–2
  and complex inequalities 31, 191
  domain of 65
  domestic 195, 201, 209
  and economic development 206

violence cont.
  and economic inequalities 300–1
  and ethnic relations 267
  excessive forms 357
  and gender 195, 261, 299
    see also domestic violence
  global processes 192–3, 212–16
  and globalization 36, 215
  and governmentality 203
  group 193
  and human rights 215–16, 357
  as institutional domain 443–4, 449–50
  inter-personal see inter-personal violence
  Ireland 405–8
  legitimate, state monopoly of 31, 199–200
  and militarism/military force 193–4, 210
  and modernity 199–208, 446
  and multiple inequalities 20–1
  neoliberalism and social democracy 210, 279, 396–7, 446
  nexus of, path dependency at 296–8
  OECD countries 299–300, 301
  ontology of, developing 191, 193–9
  path dependencies 192, 208–12, 296–8
    OECD countries 299–300, 301
  progress, measurement of 354–9
  racial 196–7
  sex crimes 225
  and social theory 191, 193
  state 12, 194
  Sweden 400–2
  United Kingdom 402–5
  United States 396, 397–400
  women, against 195, 196, 201, 407
    see also domestic violence
    as human rights violation 16, 216

Wallerstein, Immanuel 39–40, 41
Wängnerud, Lena 182
war
  as dampener of economic growth 416–17
  nations and states, cross-cutting 160
  new forms of 212

wars of position/wars of manoeuvre 166
'Washington consensus', economic policy 5, 11, 122
waves 451–3
  and civil society projects 234–5
  and complexity theory 55
  concept 59, 95–9, 100, 234, 452–3
  as energy 96
  examples 238–47
  global 44, 45, 98–9, 123–4
    civil societies 233–8, 249
    feminist 114, 379
    neoliberalism 374
  and networks 98
weapons of mass destruction 213
Weber, Max 2, 24, 27, 45
  complexity theory 47
  definition of modern state 31
  rationalisation 32
  social theory of 55
  on societalization and bureaucracy 69–70
  on states 168, 175, 192, 199
welfare provision 281–90
  see also state welfare
  and employment regulation 147–9, 293–5
  extent of 142–3
  gender and class regime 147–9
  gender and public or domestic welfare 287–90
  gendered state social expenditure 285–7
  neoliberal and social democratic varieties of 143–4
  premodern forms of welfare, as domestic labour 144–7
  public social expenditure 285
  in United Kingdom 387
  varieties 142–9
welfare state
  fiscal crisis considerations 129–30
  forms 29
  and multiple inequalities 63
  and path dependency 81
well-being
  see also human development, well-being and capabilities approach
  longevity as key indicator of 347
  and violence 191, 196
Westphalia, Treaty of (1648) 161
Westphalian states 175

women
  Beijing conference (1995) 226, 243, 345, 441
  childcare 112–13
  and democracy 187–8
  elected 182
  employment of 64, 109, 110, 137, 153, 414
    see also domestic labour
    effects 111–12
    in OECD countries 332
    and social democracy 12, 114, 409–15, 453
    in Sweden 378–9
  individuation for 223
  refuges for 243, 404
  sexual and reproductive rights of 345
  suffrage, winning of 186–7, 240
  trade union membership 231
  unpaid domestic work 22
  violence against 195, 196, 201, 407
    see also domestic violence
    as human rights violation 16, 216
World Bank 154, 170, 236
  and capabilities 16
  conditions on loans from 122
  and economic growth 9, 123, 316, 352
  and global processes 121–2
  policy revisions by 246
  and recession 429
  reform 431
world culture 44
World Social Forum 235, 246
world society thesis 39, 41, 187
World Trade Organization see WTO (World Trade Organization)
world-systems theory 39, 40, 41
WTO (World Trade Organization) 154, 170, 236
  and global processes 120, 121, 122
  liberalization of public services, directive 184
  liberalization of world trade 442
  setting of global rules for trade by 91, 167

Young, Iris 22
Yuval-Davis, Nira 62, 255

zero-sum approach 166, 173